PROSPEROUS BRITISH INDIA

Owing to the antiquity and rarity of this book, certain pages are regrettably absent, and readability is compromised due to the blurring of the original text. If you possess any insights regarding the availability of these missing sections, kindly inform us. Your assistance is crucial in ensuring the completion of this significant work for the benefit of future generations.

PROSPEROUS BRITISH INDIA

A REVELATION FROM OFFICIAL RECORDS

BY

WILLIAM DIGBY C.I.E.

GYAN

Published by

Gyan Publishing House
5, Ansari Road
Daryaganj, New Delhi-110002
Phone: 011-47034999, 9811692060
E-mail: books@gyanbooks.com

Distribution Network
gyanbooks.com
India, USA, Canada, UK, Australia

ISBN: 978-93-6208-095-0 (PB)
First Published, 1901

2nd Impression 2024

Printed at: Gyan Press, Delhi.

PROSPEROUS BRITISH INDIA
Author: WILLIAM DIGBY

ADMISSION BY THE RT. HON. LORD GEORGE HAMILTON, M.P., SECRETARY OF STATE FOR INDIA, IN THE HOUSE OF COMMONS, AUGUST 16, 1901:

'I admit at once that if it could be shown that India has retrograded in material prosperity under our rule we stand self-condemned, and we ought no longer to be trusted with the control of that country.'

[An analysis shows that during his period of service at the India Office the present Secretary of State for India has drawn as salary a sum which represents one year's average income of ninety-thousand Indian people !]

The DIMINISHING INCOME of The Indian People.

NON-OFFICIAL ESTIMATED INCOME IN **1850:**

2D. per head per day.

OFFICIALLY ESTIMATED INCOME IN **1882:**

1 1/2D. per head per day.

ANALYTICAL EXAMINATION OF ALL SOURCES OF INCOME IN **1900**, LESS THAN

3/4D. per head per day.

'PROSPEROUS' BRITISH INDIA

'PROSPEROUS' BRITISH INDIA

A REVELATION FROM OFFICIAL RECORDS

> 'The question I wish to consider is, whether that Government, with all its machinery, as now existing in India, has, or has not, promoted the general prosperity of the people of India, and whether India is better or worse off by being a Province of the British Crown: THAT IS THE TEST?'—Sir H. H. FOWLER.

BY

WILLIAM DIGBY C.I.E.

AUTHOR OF

'THE FAMINE CAMPAIGN IN SOUTHERN INDIA, 1877–1879'; 'THE NEWSPAPER PRESS OF INDIA AND THE FAR EAST'; 'FORTY YEARS' OFFICIAL AND NON-OFFICIAL LIFE IN A CROWN COLONY'; 'INDIA FOR THE INDIANS—AND FOR ENGLAND'; 'INDIAN PROBLEMS FOR ENGLISH CONSIDERATION'; 'INDIA AND THE BRITISH BALLOT-BOX'; 'THE DARK SIDE OF BRITISH RULE IN INDIA'; 'OPEN LETTERS TO LORD CURZON'; ETC. ETC.

LONDON: T. FISHER UNWIN
PATERNOSTER SQUARE 1901

'Only for myself I speak.
Nowise have I right to play the spokesman for my brothers.'

Earth is sick and Heaven is weary
Of the hollow words that States and Kingdoms utter
When they talk of truth and justice.'

THIS BOOK IS DEDICATED

(WITHOUT PERMISSION)

TO

THE RIGHT HONOURABLE LORD GEORGE HAMILTON,
P.C., M.P.,

His Majesty's Secretary of State for India,

Who has said:

'You speak of the increasing impoverishment of India, and he annual drain upon her as steadily and continuously exhausting her resources. I assert you are under a delusion';

TO

HIS EXCELLENCY LORD CURZON OF KEDLESTON,
G.M.S.I., G.M.I.E.,

Viceroy and Governor-General of India,

Who is endeavouring, though in a too-facile way (avoiding searching inquiry), to ascertain why the country he rules is in such sore distress;

TO

THE RIGHT HONOURABLE SIR HENRY H. FOWLER,
G.C.S.I., P.C., M.P.,

Ex-Secretary of State for India,

Who does 'not think that history has ever known so fair, so just, so equitable, so peaceful, so successful, a government as the government by Great Britain of the Empire of India';

AND TO

EVERY MAN OR WOMAN OF BRITISH BIRTH

Who is desirous that our rule should become a Blessing to the People of India;

WITH THE HOPE

That the Facts herein recorded may lead to the amelioration of the condition of Many Millions of British Subjects who, on every New Year's Day, enter upon a period which is certain, for their country as a whole, to be worse than the years already past.

Dorset House,
Dorset Square,
London, N.W.;
Nov. 15, 1901.

The Right Hon'ble
Lord George Hamilton, P.C., M.P.,
Secretary of State for India,
India Office, London.

My Lord,

It was my privilege, from a gallery seat in the House of Commons, to listen to your speech when you introduced, on the 16th of August last, the annual financial statement concerning India.

In that speech, according to the report in The Times, you said:—

> There is a small school in this country as well as in India who are perpetually asserting that our rule is bleeding India to death. Since I have been Secretary of State I have taken great pains to collect and investigate any information or evidence I could obtain, no matter from what quarter it came, which by facts, figures, or other reliable information tended to support this allegation. I admit at once that if it could be shown that India has retrograded in material prosperity under our rule we stand self-condemned, and we ought no longer to be entrusted with the control of that country. But no such facts, figures, or evidence have I ever been able to obtain. That a section of the public both here and in India believe this allegation is clear from their constant and unwearied repetition of the charge. But this belief is founded not on figures, or facts, or economic *data*, but on a plausible syllogistic formula that they are never tired of repeating.

These remarks call for some reply.

2

1 The most distinguished, as well as one of the earliest, Masters in the 'small school' to which you refer was the Most Noble the Marquis of Salisbury, K. G., now Prime Minister in the United Kingdom. In 1875, when he was Secretary of State for India, he urged that 'as India must be bled,' the bleeding should be done judiciously. He also lamented that 'much of the revenue' of India 'is exported without a direct equivalent.' None of us who write concerning India's impoverishment have yet bettered the phrases of our great Master, your political chief. So far as I know he was the first to speak of the 'bleeding' of India.

2. Probably you will agree that the second sentence quoted above, and some of the passages which follow, must have been uttered by you in a moment of forgetfulness, was, in fact, one of those 'oratorical necessities' which become sad indiscretions. A little later in your speech you repeated certain statements made by Lord Curzon in his Budget speech, disproof of which, based wholly on statements in the most recently-published official records, had been in your

possession exactly four months before you said over again what the Viceroy had incorrectly said. I know that you received the evidence of disproof, for the receipt of the document in which this disproof appeared was acknowledged on your instructions about the middle of April last. You have done a great wrong to India in repeating and emphasizing statements of which you possessed proof that they had no foundation in fact

3. You assert that if it could be proved India had retrograded in material prosperity under our rule we stand self-condemned; and 'we ought,' you go on to say, 'no longer to be trusted with the control of that country.' I ask your kind acceptance of the accompanying work in which, without going outside the covers of your own Office productions, I establish, as I think, beyond all peradventure, the great, the dismal, the awful, retrogression, not only in material prosperity but also in other important respects, of the country you govern. That is to say, I establish all this if

your own facts and figures are to be depended upon. You put them forward year by year for the information and guidance of the public, and must be content to be judged by them. Unhappily, they appear only too closely to approximate to absolute accuracy.

4. You say that you have 'never been able to obtain' 'facts, figures, or evidence' to prove 'material prosperity has retrograded.' You admit that belief in this retrogression exists, but, you assert, it is not founded 'on figures, or facts, or economic data.' You need not remain in the unhappy condition of wanting data any longer. In what I send you there is abundance of figures, of facts, of economic data. I have nothing to do with 'syllogistic formula,' whether 'plausible' or otherwise. I deal with economic data concerning the people of India; in doing so I simply employ your figures, your evidence, your facts. In this connection, I venture especially to ask your attention to Chapters VI. to XII.; particularly the twelfth chapter.

5

I go farther, and express the hope that you will not overlook the Introductory Chapter and Chapters I to V. Everywhere I depend upon the facts which the India Office furnishes—upon them and upon none other. My fount of knowledge flows from Whitehall; its source is the lofty chamber you have occupied for many years.

I ask your lordship's careful perusal of the pages of my work. I do not ask this as a mere 'man in the street,' though such men have been held by one of your colleagues to know enough to put them on a level with Cabinet Ministers. In such a matter as this I have a right to some consideration at your hands. Twenty-three years ago, during your novitiate at the India Office, there passed through your hands at least one dispatch from the Government of India in which that Government was pleased to express its indebtedness to my humble self for the manner in which, the Viceroy and his Councillors said. I had kept them informed week by week concerning the voluntary Relief efforts throughout India. The Viceroy thought so well of what I was able to do in 1877, and of the way I did it, that he informed me of his intention to nominate me for a seat on the Famine Commission which was appointed in the following year. From that distant period until the hour in 1901 in which I am writing this letter, I have not, for one moment, faltered in the interest then aroused in me respecting the condition of our Indian fellow-subjects, nor have I neglected any opportunity of making myself acquainted with their needs. If, in some of my chapters, I write impassionately from a full heart, as I confess I do, in them as in all the other chapters I write from an equally full mind.

Because of the facts I marshal, and because my many years' study of the question call for a consideration of the evidence I submit and the conclusions drawn therefrom,

7

I ask, in the public interest, that my assertions and conclusions may be submitted to searching examination by some of the very many able gentlemen who, at Whitehall, assist you to govern India. If I am proved to be wrong in what I state I will as publicly withdraw my statements as I now publicly make them. On the other hand, if it be admitted that I am correct in what I assert, your lordship, I feel certain, will at once accept the fact of India's retrogression in material prosperity and will consider in what way an effectual remedy shall be applied. That way should be one which shall render unnecessary that heroic measure of retirement from India which you declare will be our duty.

The statements in my book, I respectfully submit, may not be ignored. The challenge contained in your speech is specifically met. You can only desire that the truth should be known. In that we are at one. The writer of the book is naught: leave him, if you will, out of consideration first, last, and all the time. But, as the allegations made are declared to be wholly yours in essentials and often yours in actual words, I implore you, for India's sake, to show that what I state is untrue; or, if that be not possible, to entirely change your policy so that it may be brought into line with the facts. I repeat, nowhere is the evidence the author's evidence. Always is it yours. It must be accepted or it must be disproved. Of my own poor volition, possessing no power or influence save such as is contained in the truth and justice of the cause I advocate, moved wholly by feelings of our common humanity on behalf of a silent, helpless, too-patient, always long-suffering people,

I challenge your Lordship to the disproof.

I have the honour to remain,

Yours most truly,

Wm Digby.

PREFACE

THIS work, unintentionally, has grown into a big book. That would be regretable if it were not that India is a big country and space commensurate with its extent and with the variety and complexity of the problems affecting it must necessarily be given. As it is I have not dealt with one tithe of the questions demanding attention, even though I have referred to many topics. To readers of different proclivities certain sections of the book may specially appeal; therefore, to one who does not care for all of it, selection of topic has been made easy.

The object with which the book has been written is, if it be feasible, to bring to a definite issue two contrary views regarding India. Two schools exist. One is always referring to the increasing prosperity of the country and people, and claiming unstinted praise for England as the creator of this prosperity; the other is incessantly dilating upon the rapidly-growing and now alarming impoverishment of both country and people. The latter declare that, by the principles of our rule, deliberately adopted, the impoverishment is made inevitable. Both cannot be right. Nor is there, to my seeming, any middle course which would reconcile the views held by both protagonists, and provide a working arrangement including both views. One is right; the other is wrong.

Which of them is right? I, unhesitatingly, say, 'That

school which declares the country is in a bad way and the people in a worse way.' I endeavour to prove, and think I succeed in proving, the correctness of this statement. I do so from evidence furnished to me—sometimes gratuitously, oftener on payment—by the authorities themselves in India and in England. It is they who tell the story I try to unravel from the complexities in which it is concealed; that story I endeavour to make plain for my countrymen's information. May I ask, kindly interested reader or keen critic, or both of you, that one circumstance be always borne in mind as the various facts herein discussed are produced and considered? It is that I am not responsible for the facts I cite. All that I do is to use the material which the Government of India and the Secretary of State supply. If what I put forward seems, as it well may, far too terrible to be true, let me beg that it be always borne in mind, and let me say it again, that I do no more than put before the reader the evidence, impartially dealt with, scheduled by the authorities themselves. If I be right in my deductions, nothing is to be gained by denouncing me for drawing those deductions. The facts on which they are based are there, whether attention be drawn to them or not. To describe an evil does not make the describer the author of that evil. If a true statement be given concerning an existing disaster, and accurate signs of a coming catastrophe are announced, he who makes the statement and utters the announcement does not cause the disaster or create the catastrophe. It is a satire on present-day controversy that it should be necessary to say this: unhappily it *is* necessary. Always, in this book, the evidence is given, given in too much detail may be, and the reader is put in a position to judge for himself or herself whether any given deduction is fair or unfair.

To write such a book as this which I have written is for a man to take his (literary and public) life in his hands. No treatment, some people think and say, can be too bad for him who dares to declare that everything in

India is not perfect; who desires to procure adequate reforms and solid benefits for Indians. This has long been a characteristic of the British people in regard to India. Lord Ripon, to his cost, found that this was the case. One of the greatest of the Governors-General before Lord Ripon had drunk from the same cup. 'A part of Lord Wellesley's just policy towards India in 1800 was an endeavour to obtain the admission of Indian ships and their cargoes into the ports of England on terms approaching in some degree to reciprocity; but his Lordship's humane efforts on this point caused him great opposition at home, embarrassed considerably his Government, and was the cause of the treatment which he received in England in 1806–7.' So wrote Mr. Montgomery Martin, nearly seventy years ago, and, in this respect, the average Briton of to-day, who is in any way connected with India, or fancies that his craft may be in danger if justice be done to India, is precisely as were his fathers before him.

All my sources of information, I repeat, are to be found in the scores of Indian Blue Books—of most of which I have been a diligent student—issued year by year from the Government Press at Calcutta or Simla, and from the presses of His Majesty's Printers in London. There is one exception. The more important details relating to the condition of the people in all parts of India, but especially in Northern India and Bombay, are abstracted from a series of volumes which were printed in the printing offices of the various Local Governments. They are all marked 'Confidential,' and their publication has more than once been refused in the House of Commons. This is not the place in which to argue whether evidence taken in an official inquiry conducted by public servants, in the public time, at the public cost, respecting the condition of the people may, rightly, be withheld from publication, and a more or less accurate summary suffice for the information of those deeply interested in what has been stated. I assume (as I assert) that it is a great wrong to the community to keep the evidence of such an inquiry in pigeon-holes over the entrance to which, maybe, spiders spin their webs, since it is anxiously desired that no one shall see the contents of those pigeon-holes. All I am concerned with in this place is to account for my possession of the set of volumes, the substance of which, in the words of the witnesses themselves, I put before my readers. The volumes I have used were received from the Parliamentary representative of the India Office by the late Mr. Bradlaugh, M.P., early in 1891, on a request made by him and at first refused; they were handed to me by the honourable member for Northampton himself. Indeed, I have reason to believe that he told the official from whom he received them that they were coming into my hands and would be used by me, that it was, indeed, at my suggestion and for my use that he required them. With this clear understanding, as I was informed, they were given to that great champion of Indian rights, and were by him passed to me absolutely without any conditions which could in the slightest degree fetter my discretion in using them.

Other points, which would have been appropriately referred to in the preface of such a work as I herein venture to put forward, will be found in a letter to Lord George Hamilton, a copy of which forms a part of this volume.

I have simply to add that, in the invidious and most disagreeable and painful duty which the writing of a book of such conclusions must, necessarily, be to one whose faith in England's good work, in England's destiny, has been passionately cherished,[1] I have striven to hold

[1] 'I that shall stand for England till I die.'

England? Yes,—

'. . . The England that rejoiced to see
Hellas unbound, Italy one and free;
The England that had tears for Poland's doom,
And in her heart for all the world made room;

. . . .

Accounting her all living lands above,
In justice, and in mercy, and in love.'

the scales fairly. I have not, consciously, strained any argument to enforce a foregone opinion, nor have I refrained from stating aught, germane to the discussion, that, in the course of the statements I was dealing with, would tell against the conclusions which I drew; those conclusions were drawn because the facts left me no other course but to draw them. I was not a free agent. The reader must judge as to that. I express only that which I was compelled to express. All I ask is that the evidence be carefully considered, especially that portion which is recorded in the first chapter where foundation-principles are dealt with, and the still greater part appearing in chapters six to twelve. In the latter, particularly, are to be found the facts which make the optimism of the Secretary of State for India, as expressed in his latest (and twelfth) Budget speech, a mockery, a frivolity: this optimism and this frivolity, exhibited, as they were, in connection with sorely-suffering men, women, and children, in multitude such as no man has ever before numbered, were worse than a blunder: they were a cruel wrong.

My first request to such readers as I may be honoured with is also my last request. It is that my statements be tested by the evidence I furnish. Only as those statements are adequately supported by the evidence—all, be it never overlooked, obtained from Government sources; in economic matters my sole reliance is on the official evidence—do I ask for their acceptance. Having said this I am, I think, entitled to go farther, and to say that, if the case I put forward be proved, no man or woman who becomes acquainted with it may, henceforth, refrain from doing something to remedy so gross and so grievous a wrong as is embodied in the material impoverishment and the political degradation of two hundred and thirty millions of British subjects. The times of past ignorance may be pardoned: with knowledge comes responsibility. In my own imperfect way I endeavour to supply a portion of the needed knowledge. Others will come and examine deeply and more searchingly where I, a pioneer, have been able to do little more than indicate the tracts along which trained bands of experts may pass to fully explore the distressful region of which I treat. I am not—

> The first who ever burst
> Into this troubled sea.

Mr. Dadabhai Naoroji has circumnavigated its shores, and Mr. Romesh Dutt and Mr. Hyndman have indicated many of the perils of the way, while Mr. A. J. Wilson, of the *Investors' Review*, never wearies in well-doing where India is concerned, nor does Sir William Wedderburn ever falter in his endeavours to ascertain what really is wrong, with a view to providing a remedy. But, like Columbus, in discovering America, the Parsee patriot and these others only point the way to research and investigation which statesmen like Lord Rosebery, Mr. John Morley, Mr. Asquith, Sir Robert Reid, Mr. C. P. Scott, Sir Edward Clarke, Mr. W. S. Caine, Mr. C. E. Schwann, and many others are, in honour, bound to undertake. Will they do their duty? Possibly, the continuance of British empire in the East depends upon the answer they and those like-minded with them give to this question.

My acknowledgments are due, and are hereby cordially expressed, to friends who have aided me in my task. Amongst them must be mentioned Miss Annie A. Smith, of Hampstead, whose admirable work in preparing the Index all who need to refer to it will appreciate; Mr. Hedley V. Storey, who prepared the diagrammatic sketches which so vividly illustrate statements in the text that might otherwise be imperfectly apprehended, and whose experience in the villages and towns of India has been of some service to me in connection with the proof-reading of this work; and my son, Everard Tuxford Digby.

Finally, I must be permitted to say that the writing of this book has been the hatefullest and most painful duty I have ever performed. I have put to myself, a score of times, Lord Melbourne's question, 'Can't you let it alone?' and always I have had to answer, 'No, I can't.' And it's as well I can't. For, if I could I should be a contemptible creature. To me, things in India are as I describe them to be, and I have no choice but to so describe them.

DORSET HOUSE, DORSET SQUARE,
LONDON, N.W.
November, 1901.

SOME OF THE AUTHORITIES CONSULTED

OFFICIAL.

The Dufferin Inquiry in 1887–88 as to the Steadily Underfed Population of India:

'Confidential' Volumes:

a. **An Inquiry into the Economic Condition of the Agricultural and Labouring Classes in the North-Western Provinces and Oudh.**

b. **Similar Inquiries for Bombay, Madras, Bengal, Panjab, Central Provinces, Assam, the Berars, and Ajmere-Merwara.**

[These volumes constitute the nearest approach to an economic inquiry into Indian conditions yet undertaken.]

Statistical Abstracts of British India, Nos. 1 to 35.

Statement Exhibiting the Moral and Material Progress and Condition of India, Nos. 16 to 36.

Famine Commission Inquiries and Reports:

The Orissa Famine of 1866.

The Famine of 1877–78;—

Especially

a. **Miscellaneous Papers bearing on the Condition of the Country and People;**

b. **Appendix—Vol. III., Chapter I.—Condition of the Country and the People; and**

c. **Information Furnished by the Madras Board of Revenue to the Famine Commission of 1878–9.**

The Famine of 1897–98;—

Report and Evidence. Several volumes.

Area and Yield of Crops. Third Issue, 1901.

Parliamentary Inquiries into the East India Company's Administration prior to Renewal of the Charter—

1813, 1833, | 1853.

About thirty volumes in all.

Reports of Select Committees of Parliament on the Affairs of the East India Company during the Last Half of the Eighteenth Century. Ten volumes.

Administration Reports for

Bengal,	The Panjab,
Madras,	Central Provinces,
Bombay,	Burma,
North-Western Provinces	Assam,
and Oudh,	Ajmere, The Berars,

for past Twenty Years. Over two hundred volumes.

Tables of Trade of British India.

Inquiry into Panjab Indebtedness, by S. S. Thorburn.

Agricultural Statistics of British India. Tenth to Fifteenth Issues.

Financial and Commercial Statistics of British India. Several Issues.

Report on the Revised Settlement of the Gurgaon District, 1872–88.

Census of India—

a. General Report, 1881. Three volumes.

b. „ „ 1891. One volume.

Several District Manuals of Madras and Bombay.

And Numerous other Official Publications, including the *Gazette of India* and Provincial *Gazettes*;

Also, the Several Official Commission Inquiries of the past Twenty Years.

NON-OFFICIAL.

'India,' by Sir John Strachey, G.C.S.I.

'England's Work in India,' by Sir W. W. Hunter, and other works by the same author.

'The Dictionary of Statistics,' by Mulhall.

'The Law of Civilisation and Decay,' by Brooks Adams.

'The Science of Civilisation.' by C. B. Phipson.

'The Poverty of India,' by Dadabhai Naoroji.

'Famines in India,' by Romesh C. Dutt, C.I.E.

'The Great Famine,' by Vaughan Nash.

'The Indian Tribute,' by Thos. Inwood Pollard.

'Asia and Europe,' by Meredith Townsend.

'Life of Major-General Sir Thomas Munro, K.C.B.,' by the Rev. G. R. Gleig. Two volumes.

'Eastern India,' vol. i., 'Behar and Shahabad.' Montgomery Martin.

Max Müller's Works.

'The Indian Problem Solved.'

'Mussulmans and the Moneylenders in the Panjab,' by S. S. Thorburn.

'Improvement of Indian Agriculture,' by J. A. Voelcker.

'The Economic Revolution of India,' by A. K. Connell, and more than Two Hundred Other Volumes, such as the Rulers of India Series, Biographies, *e.g.*, Marquis of Wellesley, Lord Hastings, and others,

With Several Files of Indian Newspapers, and Volumes of the Sarvajanik Sabha Journal.

TABLE OF CONTENTS

CHAPTER III.

WHOSE IS THE AGRICULTURAL AND INDUSTRIAL WEALTH OF INDIA?

CHAPTER IV.

FAMINES: THEIR PRESENT FREQUENCY AND THE CAUSE OF THAT FREQUENCY.

Famine Losses in Ten Years; War Losses in One Hundred and Ten Years.

Two Famine Maps: First Famine and Last Famine of the Nineteenth Century.

CHAPTER V.

'THE EXTRAORDINARY AMOUNT OF PRECIOUS METALS THAT IS ABSORBED BY THE PEOPLE.'

Absentee Landlordism ;—Absorption of All Land Revenue by England.

CHAPTER VI.

THE 'TRIBUTE': WHAT IT IS, HOW IT WORKS.

Average Length of Life in India and in England.

CHAPTER VII.

THE 'DRAIN': ITS EXTENT; ITS CONSEQUENCES.

Consumption of Salt—as Required and as Possible.

CHAPTER IX.

'IS INDIA DISTRESSED? WE SEE NO DISTRESS.' 'IF INDIA BE DISTRESSED AND NON-PROSPEROUS, WHY DO WE NOT SEE THE DISTRESS?'

CHAPTER X.

THE CONDITION OF THE PEOPLE OF THE NORTH-WESTERN PROVINCES AND OUDH.

CHAPTER XI.

THE ALLEGED INCREASED AGRICULTURAL AND NON-AGRICULTURAL INCOME.

AN EXPLANATORY STATEMENT.

PAGE

CHAPTER XII.

THE PRESENT ECONOMIC CONDITION OF INDIA: THE REAL INCOME OF THE PEOPLE.

The Declining Income—A Typographical Sketch.

FORMER WORKS ON INDIA BY THE AUTHOR.

DIAGRAMS

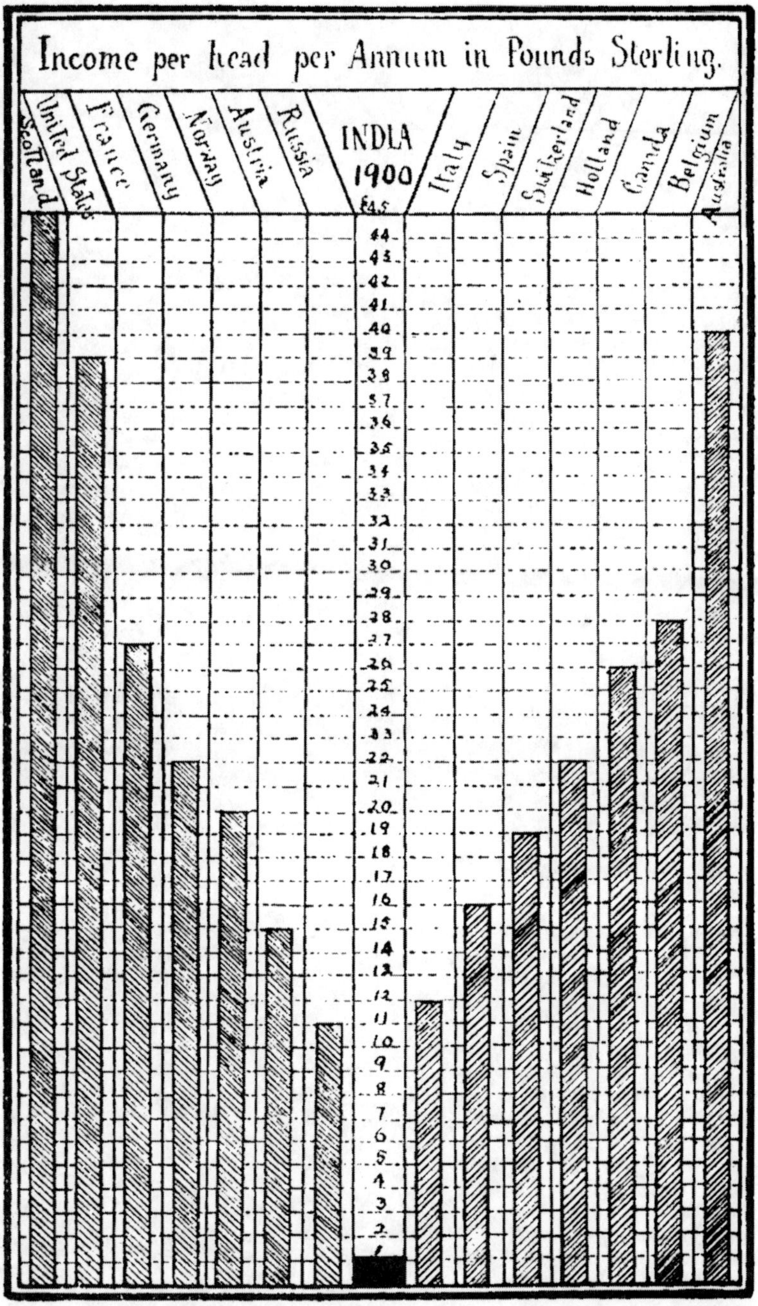
Income per head per Annum in Pounds Sterling.
Scotland
United States
France
Germany
Norway
Austria
Russia
INDIA
1900
Italy
Spain
Switzerland
Holland
Canada
Belgium
Australia

PROEM

National Incomes—A Comparison.

Alleged Lightness of Taxation in India (Sir J. Strachey's Inaccurate Statement).
English and Indian Taxation Compared.
England's Beneficent Work in India: a Notable Instance.
Obsolete Indian Customs.
Unwillingness in England and in India to discern Ill-Consequences of Present Rule.
A Famine Comparison between the Beginning and End of the Century.
Some personal considerations, chiefly affecting the Author and this Book.

'THERE is no country possessing a civilised administration where taxation is so light' as in India.

'Mr. J. S. Mill declared his belief that the British Government in India was "not only one of the purest in intention, but one of the most beneficent in act, ever known among mankind."

'I do not doubt that this is still truer now.'

Thus writes Sir John Strachey, G.C.S.I., who, towards the close of a long official career in India, was Finance Minister. The passages are to be found on page 395 of 'India,'[1] new and revised edition.

[1] Kegan Paul, Trench, Trubner, and Company, Limited, London, 1894. When one reads Sir John Strachey's book in the light of the facts recorded in these pages, the wonder arises whether anything more misleading than that book has appeared since William Caxton first made movable type by which to record Anglo-Saxon utterances of voice and pen, and printed his first pages at Westminster. Sir John Strachey possesses a very acute intellect;

If they were true in form and essence I should have been spared the writing of this book.

The Census Commissioner for India, in 1881 (App. p. lxv) before 'India' was written, had put on record an opinion concerning the Panjabis which gave no warrant for Sir John Strachey's remark. 'There can be little doubt,' it was said, 'that the Panjab population is less long-lived than that of England. It would indeed be strange if it were not so. The peasant of our villages leads a life of unceasing labour, even if that labour be not so severe as that of the English workman. He inhabits a mud hovel in the middle of a crowded village surrounded by festering dunghills and stagnant pools, the water of

it is harder to believe that he could not see the other side (of the shield which he has adorned so skilfully) than that he deliberately shut his eyes to the widespread poverty and growing destitution of which the 'drain' from India to England is alike the sign and the cause. There is the dilemma, and there is no way out of that dilemma which can be complimentary to the intelligence of the veteran civilian. Only on the ground of the Divine Right of British Civilisation is praise of the results of the British rule in India possible without the qualifications the present work attempts to supply. In reading such books as that by Sir John Strachey it should never be forgotten that they necessarily partake of the nature of Newman's *Apologia pro vita sua*. The writers are face to face with the work of their own hands, and, unless they are to write themselves down as having failed in promoting the happiness and ensuring the prosperity of the Indian people, they must either drop the pen or indulge in glowing eulogy. 'Nevertheless,' he remarks, 'I cannot say that our Government is loved; it is too good for that.' Lord Lawrence's dictum, in 1867, when he was Viceroy, is quoted: 'The masses of the people are incontestably more prosperous and—*sua si bona nórint*—far more happy in British territory than they are under native rulers.' A few years later, and instructed India, led by British civilians, was crying out against the rack-renting which especially marked that part of Northern India which John Lawrence had 'settled.' The state of things which, in the Panjab, has led to the necessity for passing the Act to stop land alienation in that Province, is the direct offspring of the Laurentian over-assessment of newly-acquired territories. If an absolutely impartial judge, with a full knowledge of all the circumstances in each instance, were to place side by side the wrong and human suffering caused by Timour the Tartar, or Genghis Khan, with the mental, moral, and physical, misery endured in India during the past fifty years, the ill consequences properly debitable against Christian Englishmen, who have a high place in the national Valhalla, would be as great as those for which the ruthless brutes of ancient days have had to answer to history, and maybe to God. Our power of self-deception as to the consequences which follow from British acts is truly marvellous.

which latter is not seldom his only drink. His food is poor, and he has to make up by quantity what he lacks in quality. His life is monotonous almost beyond conception. He is born, sickens, and dies, almost like a beast of the field, with only such rude care as his neighbour's ignorance can afford.'

'*Almost like a beast of the field.*'

The reader will judge whether, tested by the results recorded in the present volume, however pure the intention of the rulers may have been and may still be, their rule has not been one of the least beneficent, if not, actually, the least, ever known among mankind.

Meanwhile, be it remarked here:

Taxation in India, declares Sir John Strachey, is the lightest in the world. By what principle is the lightness or heaviness of taxation to be reckoned? Sir John Strachey does not condescend to particulars. The lightness, or otherwise, of national burdens, is not to be reckoned by the sum total obtained from each person taxed, irrespective of the means or income of such person. Yet, apparently, this is Sir John Strachey's contention. There is the less excuse for the remark seeing that Sir William Hunter, several years before 'India' was published, had put the facts clearly forward in the following passage:—

> 'It may seem a contradiction in terms to say that the English who pay at the rate of forty shillings per head to the Imperial Exchequer, besides many local burdens, are more lightly taxed than the Indians who pay only at the rate of three shillings and eightpence to the Imperial Exchequer, with scarcely any local burdens. But the sum of forty shillings per head bears a much smaller proportion to the margin between the national earnings and the national requirements for subsistence in England than the sum of three shillings and eightpence bears to that margin in India. In estimating the revenue-yielding powers of India, we must get rid of the delusive influence which hundreds of millions of taxpayers exercise upon the imagination. We must think less of the numbers and more of the poverty of the Indian people.'

As to the pressure of taxation, Mr. Samuel Smith, M.P.,

in a speech in the House of Commons in August, 1894, remarked: 'Only one man in seven hundred in India comes within the category of £50 a year. I will make a further statement. The right hon. gentleman is well aware that in this country one penny in the income-tax yields £2,000,000 sterling. In India it yields considerably less than £200,000. India contains 220,000,000 of people under British rule. These people yield on the income-tax less than one-tenth of what 38,000,000 yield in the United Kingdom. The meaning of that is that every million of the people in India yield just one-sixtieth of what a similar number yield in this country. If this is not conclusive of the poverty of the people, nothing will satisfy the most exacting mind. It is indeed difficult to realise the small amount of wealth that there is in India.' Not only is the small sum assessed a matter for indignation, but the Government, 'the most beneficent in act ever known among mankind,' is responsible for such incidents in the collection of this tax as the following:—

'One Damodar Kohli was informed last year that he would have to pay Rs.28 (37s.) income-tax. He was thunderstruck; the amount was absolutely beyond his means to raise. He informed the authorities accordingly, but the only result of his appeal was that a fine of Rs.7 (9s. 4d.) was imposed on him for delaying to pay the tax. He was unable to pay the impost as well as the penalty, so his dwelling was searched. But nothing worth taking away was found in it. Next his shop was ransacked, and everything found in it attached and sold. The sum of *about* Rs.2 (2s. 8d.) was realised by the sale. Then the "house" of the man was attached and put to auction. It fetched the sum of Rs.65 (£4 6s. 8d.). Out of this the Sirkar's dues—Rs.28 (£1 17s. 4d.) tax and Rs.7 (8s. 8d.) for delay—were realised. The balance is under attachment for the present year's demand! Imagine a man whose stock-in-trade was worth only a couple of rupees, and the hovel in which he lived was sold for not more than Rs.65, required to pay Rs.28, or nearly half the value of his whole worldly possessions, as income-tax! Damodar Kohli is a native of Donlat Nagar in Gujrat Tahsil, Panjab.'[1]

---

[1] The *Tribune* newspaper, Lahore, July 23, 1901. The *Tribune*, in a later part of the same article, says:—

'The *final* income-tax demand in the year before Captain Elliott

The taxation per head in India is stated to be 3s. 3d.[1] It is really more than that amount, as all the items of taxation are not included. But it may be taken at this sum:—

Average income, £1 2s. 4d. | Average taxation, 3s. 3d.
Proportion: *One-seventh*,

if an equal division be made amongst all the people. But 230,000,000 out of 231,085,132 people in British India have an income, before any taxation is imposed, of only about 12s. per head per annum, or *less than one halfpenny per head per day*.

Out of that 12s. *at least 2s. 6d. are taken by way of taxation*, or twenty per cent. of the total income.

To account for the whole £1 2s. 4d., it may be supposed that the balance of 10s. 4d. goes in larger or smaller aggregates to princes, officials, zemindars, professional men, merchants, and others—that is to say, to 1,085,132 people.[2] This one million persons probably pay the ninepence balance, a too great estimate in favour of the few rich perhaps.

The average income in Scotland is put at £45. If taxation in the United Kingdom—apart from Post Office

came was below Rs.20,000, almost equal to that of Montgomery, Jhang, Jhelum, and Gurgaon. Considering what a poor, tradeless, district Gujrat is, even Rs.20,000 was regarded as too heavy. And in consequence of two successive bad years, during which the trading classes suffered no less severely than the agriculturists, a deduction in the assessment was eagerly looked forward to, and regarded as almost certain. But thanks to Captain Elliott the initial demand this year has already come up to Rs.50,000 in round numbers, and the work of assessment is still going on. Has ever such a leap from *twenty* to *fifty* thousand been heard of? We have a statement before us showing the initial as well as the final demands of all the districts in the Province for the last five years. The usual difference between year and year is seldom more than of two or three thousand rupees. But in Gujrat in the famine year the moneylenders so prospered that there is already an increase of Rs.30,000 in the assessment proposed!'

1 'Explanatory Memorandum of the Accounts of India,' 1901, p. 29.

2 See particulars in last chapter of this volume.

and other receipts which are not taxation, and which in the Indian estimate have been eliminated—be taken at £107,000,000,[1] that may be regarded as the average impost, even in the present days of increased expenditure on army and navy and in other directions. This instructive parallel results:—

PROPORTION OF TAXATION TO INCOME.

Scotland, with £45 per head as average, One-seventeenth.	*India* (outside 1,000,000 well-to-do people), with 12s. per head as average, nearly One-fourth

Therefore, proportionately to income, the Indian subject of the British Crown is

Taxed more than four times higher

than is his Scottish fellow-subject, and three times higher than his English compeer. Further, it is one thing to take 2s. 6d. out of 12s. and quite another thing to take £2 13s. 8d. out of £45, especially when the latter income is spendable in a land where foodstuffs are ever growing cheaper, and the former in a country where food is ever becoming dearer and dearer, and life in every direction increasingly hard.

Yet Sir John Strachey, to whom these respective facts are available, who has been Finance Minister of one of the largest empires in the world, who should know these things as he knew the Settlement rules when he was a district officer, puts before the British public, necessarily ignorant of such details, the statement that 'there is no country possessing a civilised administration where taxation is so light' as in India.

Alas! there is no Court of Justice in which a man may be arraigned who has misstated facts to the detriment of his fellow-creatures, no Court where, if one be found guilty of having made a misstatement which has resulted

[1] The amount was actually £106,970,000 for 1900–1.—'Statesman's Year Book,' p. 45.

in human suffering and death, any punishment may be meted out. In the Court of Public Opinion, to which alone there is appeal, the judges never take sufficient notice of what is brought to their attention to be aware whether they should or should not turn down their thumbs.

Sir John Strachey has eaten India's salt since 1842. He has filled every office of importance in India save the highest. There were times when it seemed as if he might become even Viceroy and Governor-General, as had John Lawrence before him. His faulty arithmetic in one of our Afghan wars made this impossible. His emoluments, from 1842 until the day in 1901 on which this sentence is written, have been on a princely scale; —the pension he still draws is equal to the yearly incomes of twelve hundred agriculturists in Madras. In retirement he consumes resources drawn from a land for which, by way of return, he can do nothing better than to convey an altogether inaccurate description of its condition. And in doing this he makes the poverty he is unable to recognise deeper and deeper. Sir John's book is regarded as an authority. So far as it tells the number of miles of railway constructed and of the other public works undertaken, or describes the abolition of the great Salt Customs line extending for thousands of miles, the work is all that could be desired. But when it comes to the condition of country and people, apart from Anglo-Indian interests, it partakes of that 'make-believe' concerning India which is a greater source of injury to country and people than were the exactions of any of the ancient conquerors or any Feudatory Prince.

With Sir John Strachey in any other capacity than that of apologist for the form and consequences of British rule in India I have naught to do. An able official, an estimable man, I mention his name simply because of his book and because of the esteem, as a guide and counsellor concerning India, which it has brought him. I mention his name and his book because if India is ever to be brought under beneficent governance, it can only be so brought as the 'make-believe' concerning our rule, of which his work, in its larger senses, in its deeper suggestions, is crammed full, is blown away, as—miasmatic fog that it is—it needs to be blown away; then a clear conception of the position as it really is in India can be obtained.

I may not go on with the task before me until I have said again what the preceding pages record.

India is not lightly taxed. In proportion to its income it is so heavily taxed that a like weight of taxation in this country would procure no mercy and short shrift for the administrators who were responsible for its imposition. More than that, any attempt to maintain it would lead to a complete change of governmental institutions. That is, assuming taxation were ever allowed to become anywhere near so burdensome. Such a contingency is not possible in England. It would involve the yearly abstraction of from one-seventh to one-fourth of the whole incomes of rich and poor alike, with an absolute certainty each year of the proportion growing higher.[1] That may do for India; it would not be suffered in England—no, not for one hour. A like policy in the Britains oversea would have led to the Colonists 'cutting the painter' long, long, ago.

Has, then, England done naught that is good for India? Aye, even in material things, some Indians have benefited directly by British administration. There are, of course, many good results following a definite policy,

[1] 'The Budget for 1901-2 shows a deterioration of £1,949,973 as compared with the account for 1898-99. The net revenue is increased by £443,083, chiefly the result of an improvement under opium. The net expenditure, however, is increased by £2,393,056, the charges in India being heavier by £738,634, while in England they are enhanced by £1,654,192.'—'Exp. Mem. Accounts, India,' 1901. Here is where the certainty of India's condition growing worse is to be found, 'while in England they are enhanced.' Will that leak never be stopped? Or will it go on enlarging until the ship can no longer make any headway, and becomes a derelict on the ocean of history?

whatever that policy may be. So far as they exist, they have served to mitigate consequences which, ere now, would have become insupportable. For example, were it not for the vastly increased quantity and certainty of produce which canal and well irrigation ensure, year in and year out, the economic crisis, involving a general non-payment of rent which, in regard to dry land cultivation, cannot now be far off, would have already come, and our lips would still be bitter with the distaste caused in India and in England, and our hearts sore at the discredit which would have accrued to the British name throughout the world.

I take the irrigated districts of Madras because I happen to know a good deal concerning them. The same thing, doubtless, can be said of the Panjab works, the area of the North-Western Provinces, and the deserts in Sind which have been made to blossom as the rose, of which I know less. But for the irrigation works in Madras—partly improvements of ancient works dating back to the beginning of the Christian era, as in Tanjore, or, wholly new, the creation of British energy, as in the Godavari and Kistna districts—a complete breakdown would have overtaken us years ago.

In a recent work,[1] the money and the material value to India of the work of the greatest of irrigation engineers, the late Sir Arthur Cotton, have been estimated, and the following gains recorded :—

THE MONEY RETURN.

(a) *To Government (after Interest on Capital Expenditure has been reckoned).*

	Rs.
Godavari Delta System	3,70,98,763
Kistna Delta System	2,02,11,515
Cauveri Delta System	2,35,38,320
Lower Coleroon	94,10,951
Total, Direct	Rs. 9,02,59,549[2]

[1] 'The Life of General Sir Arthur Cotton, R.E., K.C.S.I.,' by his daughter, Lady Hope. I have the permission (for which I tender my thanks) of Lady Hope and of the publishers, Messrs. Hodder and Stoughton, for the citations I make in the text here and once elsewhere in this book.

[2] 'Madras Administration Report,' 1898-99; section 'Irrigation.'

	Rs.
Of remainder, one-half may be reckoned, as it is certain but for the earlier successes so much irrigation would not have been undertaken ...	58,74,758
Total in Madras, Direct and Indirect ...	Rs. 9,61,84,307
Much of this was earned at the old rate of currency (Rs.10 = £1), and might, half of it, be represented at this = £9,508,430. The present rate, however, may be taken, Rs.15 = £1	£6,408,954

(b) *To the Districts Affected, and the People thereof.*

Some difference of opinion exists as to the increase in produce which comes from irrigated land: certain authorities give Rs.10 per acre in Northern India, Sir Arthur Cotton says Rs.15,[1] and as he appears to have had good ground for his estimate, it is only fair to him to calculate on his basis. There are 5,875,874 acres under irrigation in Madras. Sir Arthur Cotton, who designed and executed, or (as in Kistna) was the originator and partial designer of the great works, may be credited with this increased produce. The annual increased value thus given to the land, the extra money coming into the hands of the people, is Rs. 8,81,30,610; or, at Rs. 15 to £1 sterling	£5,875,874
Sixty years have passed since one of the greatest of Sir Arthur Cotton's works was completed—the Cauveri delta—and nearly fifty since the Godavari began to yield large returns. It would not be unfair to reckon for such an estimate as this, thirty years of the above figures. Such an estimate shows that Sir Arthur Cotton has been the means of adding to the income of the inhabitants of certain districts in Madras only, £5,875,874 × 30 =	£176,261,220

[1] I should like to put the Government estimate, but it varies so much that I cannot strike a fair average. Generally, the rate for wet cultivation is four times that for dry cultivation. The Hon. R. A. Dalyell, of the Madras Board of Revenue, gives statistics for 1856 and 1866, which would justify a much higher calculation than is given here, but, all through, I have been desirous to give estimates below the actuals (p. 399, 'Administrative Experience Recorded in Former Famines,' 1874).

Summarised, we have this :—

(*a*) **Money return to the Government, wholly profit, as interest has been already reckoned, £800,644 per annum, also multiplied by 30**	**= £24,019,320**
(*b*) **Money return to the people ... ...**	**176,261,220**
Total	**£200,280,540**

No public works undertaken in India, or, probably, anywhere else in the world, have been so bountiful in results, even to the bringing in of net revenue to the Government in addition to ordinary land revenue, as has irrigation. The latest results are thus described :—

IRRIGATION WORKS.

Financial Result.	Account, 1899–1900.	Revised Estimate, 1900–1901.
Major Works :	£	£
Direct receipts	1,578,529	1,717,200
Portion of Land Revenue due to Irrigation	670,174	730,600
Total Revenue	2,248,703	2,447,800
Working Expenses	664,753	695,200
Net Revenue	1,583,950	1,752,600
Interest on Debt	896,749	921,800
Net Receipts	687,201	830,800
Minor Works and Navigation: net Charge	550,814	522,900
Total net Receipts	£136,387	£307,900

Yet money upon so beneficial an object is doled out with

a niggardly hand, and the progress year by year is as that of the snail or of the tortoise.

Every work published on India is full of the benefits alleged to have accrued to country and to people by the consolidation, under such wise and kindly conquerors as the British, of all races from Persia to China, from the borders of Kashgar to Komorin. The India Office itself annually trumpets forth pæans of praise of the work of its own hands, of the achievements of its own servants. Few of the trumpeters, however, recognise that whatever may have been done has been paid for by the Indian people. The editor of an Indian journal once remarked: 'We may not have done for the people all we might have done, but *we* have educated them.' The emphasis on the 'we' led to the question, 'Whom do you mean by "we"? All "we" have done is to use the people's money with which to educate them, and even then we have not regarded the matter from their point of view.' The insistence of this view was regarded as very bad taste. 'We' had done it all. It would be wasted space for me to tell once again, even briefly, what a thousand voices have trumpeted, what a hundred new voices today are trumpeting. Nevertheless I have never written a treatise on India without bearing my testimony to certain good things, the consequences of British rule, which, indeed, are writ so large as to be seen of all. I never deny them. I have no desire to deny them. Why should I? I, too, am a Briton. So far as they go I am proud of them. In these respects British administrators have, in words familiar enough to all English people, 'done the things which they ought to have done,' but, at the same time, they 'have left undone the things they ought to have done,' and, because of this, in the eye of Justice, 'There is no health in us.'

So unmistakable is the change for the better which, in some directions, has followed British rule, that Mr.

Balfour's man in the street, who knew as much about the South African war as did the Government responsible for its conduct, if India be mentioned, is able to dilate upon what has been accomplished. 'Why, before we went there,' any Englishman will tell you, 'the natives used to burn their widows! We soon stopped that.' Having said this much he considers he has said enough, and sniffs at the remark that it was, perhaps, good to stop suttee, but in only certain parts of India was suttee practised, and, it may be, certain evils have been developed as the result of our rule which kill more people in a week than suttee was responsible for in fifty years. However, be that as it may, I am anxious to put in the forefront the beneficent results of British rule. The more they are recorded the better for the argument of this book. For the incidents related show that the power to ensure beneficence exists as well as the desire to do well by India. And while these are in existence, awaiting appropriate circumstances for manifestation, there is hope for India's recovery. Without them only hopelessness and despair could exist.

For a record of 'some of the beneficent effects of British rule in India during the past, on the social life of the people' I will go to one of the staunchest of the supporters of the Indian Government.[1] I quote as follows :—

'OBSOLETE INDIAN CUSTOMS.

'[SPECIAL FOR THE "ENGLISHMAN."]

'At the beginning of a new century it may not be out of place to note some of the beneficent effects of British rule in India during the past on the social life of the people. This is strikingly shown by the following list of the manners and customs (compiled by an Indian missionary) which have been made illegal by the British Government :—

I. *Murder of Parents.*

(*a*) By suttee.
(*b*) By exposure on the banks of rivers.
(*c*) By burial alive. Case in Jodhpur territory, 1860.

---

[1] The *Englishman* newspaper, Calcutta.

II. *Murder of Children.*

(*a*) By dedication to the Ganges, to be devoured by crocodiles.
(*b*) By Rajput infanticide. West of India, Panjab, East of India.

III. *Human Sacrifices.*

(*a*) Temple Sacrifices.
(*b*) By wild tribes—Meriahs of the Khonds.

IV. *Suicide.*

(*a*) Crushing by idol cars.
(*b*) Devotees drowning themselves in rivers.
(*c*) Devotees casting themselves from precipices.
(*d*) Leaping into wells—widows.
(*e*) By Traga.

V. *Voluntary Torment.*

(*a*) By hook-swinging.
(*b*) By thigh-piercing.
(*c*) By tongue extraction.
(*d*) By falling on knives.

VI. *Involuntary Torment.*

(*a*) Barbarous executions.
(*b*) Mutilation of criminals.
(*c*) Extraction of evidence by torment.
(*d*) Bloody and injurious ordeals.
(*e*) Cutting off the noses of women.

VII. *Slavery.*

(*a*) Hereditary predial slavery.
(*b*) Domestic slavery.
(*c*) Importation of slaves from Africa.

VIII. *Extortion.*

(*a*) By Dharma.
(*b*) By Traga.

IX. *Support of Caste by Law.*

(*a*) Exclusion of low castes from offices.
(*b*) Exemption of high castes from appearing to give evidence.
(*c*) Disparagement of low castes.
(*d*) Exclusion of widows from legal marriage.

'It must be conceded that the above is no mean record, and that it shows in a convincing manner that British rule has created an atmosphere throughout the length and breadth of India unfavourable to the continuance of social and religious customs and practices, however ancient, which are injurious to the well-being of the people.

'Many of the customs referred to have not been put down by the strong force of law against obstinate resistance; they have simply melted away, in the fulness of time, under the silent but irresistible influence of the ameliorating principles with which Christian civilisation has been permeating society in India. Much remains yet to be done, but the leaven is still working, and the spirit of fair play towards all classes alike, which lies at the heart of British government in this great empire, will ensure greater progress in the social, commercial, and religious, condition of the people during the early years of this twentieth century than has been possible during the past generation.'

In this book there is no denial either of the beneficent reforms which have been already brought about or of the desire of the rulers themselves to do good to India—that is to say, to do good according to their preconceived ideas of what is fitting for India. On the contrary there is full recognition of this; nowhere (consciously) is there aspersion of individuals or imputation of motives. Everywhere a man's own words are fully quoted. Nowhere is there a quotation which, by the selection of certain passages, and quoting only them, gives a different impression from that which the writer or speaker intended. What I am trying to deal with is the terrible condition of the people, the backward state of the country, and how it is the things I comment upon and explain have been brought about. This is done in no spirit of fault-finding, or in inappreciation of what my countrymen have done. But I see that the evil daily wrought, though it may be unintentionally wrought, is causing unspeakable and unbearable misery to many, many, millions of our fellow-subjects. I am satisfied the wrong may be righted—if only the facts be realised. I see my official and non-official countrymen in India unable or unwilling to discern significance in such a fact as this:

1800 to 1825, FOUR Famines.	1875 to 1900, TWENTY-TWO Famines.

To me it appears that the twenty-two as contrasted with the four are the product of our system of rule, of what we have done, of what we have not done. And, without malice towards any, with a heart very full of sympathy and very sore for those who have become so degraded and so full of suffering and who are wholly blameless (save that they are too 'patient in suffering'), I tell the tale of India as I know it;—I cannot, if I am to retain any sense of duty, refrain from so telling it. I foresee my effort may be all in vain, my pains expended to no purpose. Nevertheless, the effort is made, the pains are expended.

Finally, before entering upon my criticism, I beg forgiveness in that I purpose intruding a few autobiographical remarks which have a bearing upon the publication of this book. I do not like the mode I must needs adopt in setting forth the views I here put on record. My objection arises from the circumstance that I am unable to compel attention on the part of the Secretary of State for India, the Viceroy, any Governor or Councillor, to whatsoever I may say. My points may be unassailable; I cannot ensure they will be heeded. In 1885 I wrote a small work on India. Soon after it was published, the late John Slagg, M.P., saw the Parliamentary Under-Secretary of the day, J. Kynaston Cross. Asked if he had read the book, Mr. Cross said, Yes, he had. 'What are you going to do about it?' 'Oh,' he replied, 'nothing.' 'But,' it was urged, 'see what is said, and official authority is quoted.' 'Yes,' was Mr. Cross's reply, 'Mr. Digby has obtained his facts from our books, but we shall ignore what he has said.' And, as I am a person of no importance, and as I, that year, failed in my attempt to enter the House of Commons, the book was ignored.[1] One might have thought the thing said was that which was of value; who

[1] But not utterly lost. There are men in public life in India who tell me the book I refer to was a primer which led them to the study of Indian questions.

said it surely mattered little—in that instance, particularly, this should have been the case.

I have always felt, since India took possession of me, that under our system of ruling India, only the fully-informed critic in Parliament, or one associated with the administration of India, could ensure attention being given to what he might say. So long ago as 1878 I thought my chance in this respect had come. Having, in appreciation of such work as I had been able to do in 1877 in the relief of the famine-stricken, recommended my name to the late Empress for recognition (which came on January 1, 1879), Lord Lytton (the then Viceroy) greatly surprised and gratified me, early in 1878, by forwarding to me an intimation that he proposed to nominate me as a member of the Famine Commission, the early appointment of which had been announced from London. Here, I thought, is the very chance I want. I shall be able to get at facts first-hand. I can, as Commissioner, probe certain phases of India's troubles to the bottom; I can form conclusions which, laid before my colleagues, may secure their adhesion; or, if they be not accepted by them, I can prepare a Minority Report, of which some notice will be taken. Unfortunately, as I think, the appointment was not made. Sir Steuart Colvin Bayley, Acting Private Secretary to the Viceroy and Governor-General of India, in a letter to me, dated Simla, April 17, 1878, said:—

'His Excellency the Viceroy desires me to tell you that personally he was much inclined to place you on the Famine Commission, and that for some time he had the matter under his careful consideration, but, after consulting with General Strachey, and referring to the despatch about the constitution of the Commission, he is of opinion that he is precluded from availing himself of your services. You can certainly not be said to have taken no part in the labours or controversies of the past year, and apart from your prominent position in regard to the Famine Committee, your position as a journalist must of necessity have committed you to decided opinions on many of the points which will come before the Commission for discussion; so that, in Lord Lytton's opinion he could not, without infringing the spirit as well as the letter of the restriction (placed deliberately on his choice by the Secretary of State) appoint you to be a member of the Commission.'

The real objection to my appointment, General Strachey himself subsequently told me, was that I was a non-official residing in India, and that my appointment would have led to a cry for mercantile and other representatives being nominated to seats on the Commission. *That* had to be prevented at any cost.

Twenty-two years later the famine of 1900–1 rendered another Commission necessary. In the interval I had maintained my interest in Indian affairs and I had come to see many things in Indian administration requiring reform the existence of which were not apparent to me in 1878. I wanted to have a free run of official documents so as to ascertain whether I was right or wrong in the conclusions to which I had come. So, putting my pride into my pocket, I wrote to Lord George Hamilton, Secretary of State for India, proffering my services, and frankly stating my object in doing so, namely, that I might have an opportunity, by diligent research as a Famine Commissioner, not only to do that for which a Commissioner would, specifically, be appointed, but also to see whether a more thorough study of Indian conditions would leave me where I now am. Lord George received my offer with courtesy, but he was unable, he said, to avail himself of it. I was known, he said, to hold strong views on certain features of Indian administration, and so I was ruled out from even the possibility of appointment. Apparently, admitted knowledge on a very complex and highly important subject concerning India disqualifies a man and renders him unfit to inquire concerning that very subject. One might have supposed that exactly the opposite would have been the case, as indeed it is everywhere save in Government offices.

I accepted the hand of fate. But I did not remain wholly quiescent. Lord Curzon called this famine 'the most terrible famine of the century.' In one of his speeches he made observations upon the condition of the country which led me to address to him an Open Letter, and, subsequently, a Postscript thereto, in the course of which I showed that his statements involved certain conclusions which indicated India to be on a steep declivity; and that in respect to many parts of the country, a continuance of present methods could end only in total impoverishment. When the Financial Statement was under consideration in the Viceregal Council at Calcutta towards the end of March, 1901, His Excellency the President, in the course of his remarks, replied, in some measure, to my communications. What was said by him was so incorrect in its details and so unsatisfactory in its deductions that I addressed Lord Curzon in another Open Letter, a copy of which I forwarded to the India Office for the information of the Secretary of State.

Out of that Open Letter has come this book. As I have said, any book in itself alone affords but a sorry means of putting forward my views. But it is all that I can do. As in 1885 so in 1901, it may, privately, be acknowledged that my statistics cannot be overthrown because they are the statistics of the India Office. My deductions? 'Oh! we have nothing to do with the deductions a man may choose to draw from the facts before him.' Again, I may be ignored (officially). Whether I have so poorly dealt with the facts I have handled, whether I have used the information, as open to others as to me, in such a way that my countrymen and countrywomen generally, and my Indian fellow-subjects as a whole, find in them no call to action, I know not. I have done my best during the spare hours (of a specially hard-worked year), which alone I am able to give to public duties. There I leave my humble part, which, with myself, may be ignored and forgotten, if but the facts recorded lead to the amelioration of the condition of a lovable and worthy people—a condition the like of which no country but 'God's England,' in the administration of a subject land, can show.

CHAPTER I

INDIA RULED BY PRECONCEIVED IDEAS, NOT IN ACCORDANCE WITH FACTS

British Delusions regarding India.
Principles of Government during Early Period of British Rule.
Foreign Rule Always a Scourge—now Greater than Before.

I.—*Conquest by Trade.*

Britain's Industrial Supremacy due to Indian Wealth being 'Appropriated' in the Eighteenth Century.
Amount of Wealth Transferred from India to the United Kingdom.

II.—*Conquest by Deliberate Subjection.*

Lord William Bentinck and Mr. W. Thackeray on what 'Ought to be Suppressed' in the Indian Character; Subsequent Adoption of the 'Suppression' Suggestion
Indian Lack of Ambition and other qualities—according to James Mill.
Sir Thomas Munro and Bishop Heber to the Contrary.
Thackeray and James Mill against Munro and Heber.
The Big Words of the Charter Act of 1833.
Mr. Robert Rickards on the Policy which should be Adopted towards Indians and India.
A New Era Inaugurated—in Words.

III.—*Conquest by 'Pousta.'*

Macaulay's Disclaimer of the 'Pousta' as a British Governing Instrument.
The 'Pousta's' Effect on the British Mind.
For Bread a Stone—for Daily Food Powdered Rocks.

A Choice between Prohibition and Cheating; Cheating Adopted
What We Choose to Believe concerning India is Alone Fact

***Appendices*:**
I. 'Durbar Charges Unjustly Made.'
II. Early Tributes to Indian Fitness for Official Positions:
(*a*) By John Sullivan, Collector of Coimbatore.
(*b*) By W. Chaplin, Commissioner of Deccan.
(*c*) By Major-General Sir L. Smith, K.C.B.

THE British world is under a delusion in regard to India. No greater delusion ever possessed a people as no delusion before it—though many disastrous delusions are writ large and graven deep on the page of history—has ever wrought so much moral, mental, and physical, ill to those who were its subjects.

If the delusion should remain after the chapters of this book have been written, then—so far as the knowledge of one man is concerned, albeit that knowledge is but small—there is no value in evidence. Fact and circumstance, in such case, cease to be verities, while Preconceived Ideas and the Seeing of that which the Eye Wishes to See become Unassailable Truth.

What were the principles on which our rule in India began? There were, at first, no principles whatsoever. We were too much occupied in establishing a footing to trouble ourselves concerning the people and their interests present and future. From 1740 to nearly the end of the eighteenth century our controlling action was a scramble for wealth. The manner in which that wealth was obtained was a secondary matter, or, indeed, of no matter. We were in India to make money, and all shadow of pretence at even making money honestly, was cast aside. Burke, in the Ninth Report from the Select Committee on the Administration of Justice in India, has told the story in full. Macaulay, in certain of his Essays, has summarised the facts in a narrative which should induce great consideration towards India by all English folk. Burke, nowadays, is seldom read; Macaulay has become a classic, and what he wrote is not held to have any particular connection with events of to-day. The classics are for culture, not for common, workaday, righteousness. We read what he writes as we read Gibbon: the events described are entertaining, but we do not recognise their relation to the happenings under our own eyes from year to year, even from day to day. Nevertheless, what was done in Bengal, Madras, and Bombay during the eighteenth century and in the early years of the nineteenth century, is of supreme importance to us.

> For what was done then, on the one hand, provided the capital by which Britain's industrial supremacy was established, and on the other hand laid the foundations of a system of alien rule which, in essentials, is the same to-day as it was one hundred years ago. Superficially there have been changes; fundamentally there has been no change.

The present can only be understood as the facts and circumstances of the past are clearly apprehended. Whatever of deficiency exists in our mode of administration of India in 1901, so far as the Indian people are concerned, and whatever of unusual poverty is to be found on the Indian Continent, are as they are because of the system of rule which, with every good intention but mistakenly, was then begun and was finally adopted. Those principles of rule were threefold.

1. CONQUEST BY TRADE. Exploitation of India undisguisedly—'naked and not ashamed'—1700–1783.
2. CONQUEST BY DELIBERATE SUBJECTION. India for England first and last—1783–1833.
3. CONQUEST BY 'POUSTA.' A show of Fair Dealing accompanied with the maintenance, rigidly and uncompromisingly, of Indian National Inferiority—1833–1901.

To understand the India of to-day each of the above-mentioned aspects must be examined, and evidence adduced in support of the conclusions they compel. This evidence shall be as brief as may be, but the facts represented must be stated even if the reader has to suffer what, otherwise, might be deemed an over-weighting of official statement.

England did not enter into relations with India with empire in view. For a long time after the opportunity of seizing power was ours, we were not anxious to lay hold of it. In agonising tones, repeated again and again, the Committee of Merchants in London commanded their servants not to acquire additional territory. One of the greatest of the Governors-General listened,—Hazael-like, with protest, and denial that we could do such things—to the prophecy of an Ambassador from Nepaul, who, early in the nineteenth century, declared British supremacy in India would not stay in its course until it reached the Indus.

Until 1774, when Warren Hastings was made the first Governor-General, little of blame, maybe, attached to the British in India, judged from the point of view of a State responsible for the good government of subordinate peoples. Till then, disguised as the position may have been by the presence of the French in Southern India and the frequent conflicts which took place with the Country Powers, as the phrase quaintly puts it, the British were adventurers, with so much to be said in their favour as may rightly be said of adventurers, and no more. If they possessed power it was mainly by deputy. The position then occupied was like unto that of the British people towards India before the Crown—that is, the nation—became directly responsible for Indian rule.

As adventurers nearly two centuries ago the early Britons in Bengal and the sister Presidencies regarded the land and the people as fair game for plunder. Under King Edward VII., Emperor of India, and under the later Britons, as administrators, disguised with all the speciousness which Western civilisation abundantly supplies for such purposes, and glossed over with words of forceful sound but scant meaning, such as Secretaries of State delude themselves and the House of Commons with once at least in every year—the day on which the Indian idol is brought out for British worship—India is still fair game for plunder, and is plundered. Hard as the saying may sound in the ears of the ordinary Englishman, the plunder is proceeding far more outrageously to-day than at any preceding period. The thin whips of the early days of our rule have become bundles of wire thongs; the exactions of Clive and Hastings fall into insignificance by the side of the drain which, in ever-augmenting volume, is over-enriching one country at the cost of the life-blood of another. Behind the fairest product which any administration in the world's history has ever put in the window-front to challenge admiration, there lurks a degree of daily-increasing misery—not intended truly, and, therefore, its very existence denied even when it is exposed to view—which few Britons dream of, and which far fewer realise. We did not *mean* to cause misery, we do not *desire* there should be misery, and, therefore, what is exhibited as such cannot be human misery. To believe it to be so is maya, illusion. There *is* illusion, but it is more correctly spelt delusion.

I. Conquest by Trade.

'We are,' say the Court of Directors, in their General Letter to Bengal, April 26, 1765, 'extremely anxious for the arrival of Lord Clive, and the gentlemen who accompanied him; as they have been so lately in England, they are the best judges of the opinion the Government and the nation entertain of the conduct of the English in Bengal for these last four years; which we are sorry to say is, in general, that they have been guilty of violating treaties, of great oppression, and a combination to enrich themselves.

'We do not here mean to enter into a discussion respecting the political conduct of our late Governor and Council; but must say that an unbounded thirst after riches seems to have possessed the whole body of our servants to a degree that they have lost all sight of justice to the Country Government and of their duty to the Committee.'

Burke tells the story with more of detail. He says:—

'This new system of trade, carried on through the medium of power and public revenue, very soon produced its natural effects. The loudest complaints arose among the natives, and among all the foreigners who traded in Bengal. It must have unquestionably thrown the whole mercantile system of the country into the greatest confusion. With regard to the natives, no expedient was proposed for their relief. The case was serious with respect to European powers. The Presidency plainly represented to the Directors that some agreement should be made with foreign nations for providing their investment to a certain amount, or that the deficiencies then subsisting must terminate in an open rupture with France.'[1]

'Notwithstanding the famine in 1770, which wasted Bengal in a manner dreadful beyond all example, the investment, by a variety of successive expedients, many of them of the most dangerous nature and tendency, was forcibly kept up; and even in that forced and unnatural state it gathered strength almost every year. The debts contracted in the infancy of the system were gradually reduced, and the advances to contractors and manufacturers were regularly made; so that the goods from Bengal, purchased from the territorial revenues, from the sale of European goods, and from the produce of the monopolies, for the four years which ended with 1780, when the investment from the surplus revenues finally closed, were never less than a million sterling, and commonly nearer twelve hundred thousand pounds. This million is the lowest value of the goods sent to Europe for which no satisfaction is made.'[2] [The sale, to the amount of one hundred thousand pounds annually, of the export from Great Britain ought to be deducted from this million.]

'In all other countries, the revenue, following the natural course and order of things, arises out of their commerce. Here, by a mischievous inversion of that order, the whole foreign maritime trade, whether English, French, Dutch, or Danish, arises from the revenues; these are carried out of the country without producing anything to compensate so heavy a loss.'

'But that the greatness of all these drains, and their effects, may be rendered more visible, your Committee have turned their consideration to the employment of those parts of the Bengal revenue which are not employed in the Company's own investments for China and for Europe. What is taken over and above the investment

---

[1] Ninth Report, p. 47; Burke, Collected Works, vol. iii.
[2] *Ibid.* pp. 47–48. [3] *Ibid.* p. 50.

(when any investment can be made) from the gross revenue, either for the charge of collection or for the civil and military establishments, is in time of peace two millions at least. From the portion of that sum which goes to the support of civil government the natives are almost wholly excluded, as they are from the principal collections of revenue. With very few exceptions they are only employed as servants and agents to Europeans, or in the inferior departments of collection, when it is absolutely impossible to proceed a step without their assistance. Some time after the acquisition of the territorial revenue, the sum of £420,000 a year was paid, according to the stipulation of a treaty to the Nabob of Bengal, for the support of his government. This sum, however inconsiderable, compared to the revenues of the Province, yet, distributed through the various departments of civil administration, served in some degree to preserve the natives of the better sort, particularly those of the Mahomedan profession, from being utterly ruined. The people of that persuasion, not being so generally engaged in trade, and not having on their conquest of Bengal divested the ancient Gentu proprietors of their lands of inheritance, had for their chief, if not their sole, support the share of a moderate conqueror in all offices, civil and military. But your Committee find that this arrangement was of short duration. Without the least regard to the subsistence of this innocent people, or to the faith of the agreement on which they were brought under the British Government, this sum was reduced by a new treaty to £320,000, and soon after (upon a pretence of the present Nabob's minority, and a temporary sequestration for the discharge of his debts) to £160,000; but when he arrived at his majority, and when the debts were paid (if ever they were paid) the sequestration continued; and so far as the late advices may be understood, the allowance to the Nabob appears still to stand at the reduced sum of £160,000.

'The other resource of the Mahomedans, and of the Gentus of certain of the higher castes, was the army. In this army nine-tenths of which consists of natives, no native, of whatever description, holds any rank higher than that of a Subahdar Commandant, that is, of an officer below the rank of an English subaltern, who is appointed to each company of the native soldiery.

'Your Committee would here be understood to state the ordinary establishment; for the war may have made some alteration. All the honourable, all the lucrative, situations of the army, all the supplies and the contracts of whatever species that belong to it, are solely in the hands of the English; so that whatever is beyond the mere subsistence of a common soldier and some officers of a lower rank, together with the immediate expenses of the English officers at their table, is sooner or later, in one shape or another, sent out of the country.' [1]

[1] Ninth Report, pp. 51–53.

Governor Verelst, with great particularity, himself an observer of the events he describes, confirms all that Burke states.

Much of modern European national prosperity is based upon the plunder of nations representing ancient civilisations. Spain robbed South America; England—from Drake under Elizabeth to Blake under Cromwell—seized as many of the Lusitanian treasure ships on their way to Spain as she could, and appropriated what they carried. Later, in the development of the land and its dependencies even these additional riches were not enough; more money was needed by the country, and none was locally forthcoming.[1] England was vigorously asserting herself on the Continent of Europe and elsewhere. For a time an issue of bank-notes helped the situation. But coin was needed, a metallic foundation for the paper issued, and at last coin was obtained—from India. How it was obtained Macaulay has told in his Essays on Clive and Hastings. The historian's works are in the hands of, or are available to, every reader; I may, therefore, be pardoned if I simply call upon the memory of my reader and forbear quotation, especially as I have much, not within reach of the ordinary student, with which I must deal.

England's industrial supremacy owes its origin to the vast hoards of Bengal and the Karnatik being made available for her use. Had this happened honourably and in the ordinary course of trade it would have been matter for satisfaction. Before Plassey was fought and won, and before the stream of treasure began to flow to England, the industries of our country were at a very low ebb. Lancashire spinning and weaving were on a par with the corresponding industry in India so far as machinery was

[1] 'No foreigner was robbed, and the stock of domestic silver dwindled from year to year, until at the Revolution the golden guinea, which from its first issue in 1662 down to the accession of William and Mary had been nominally current for twenty shillings, actually sold in the market for thirty shillings of the money in use.'—'The Law of Civilisation and Decay,' by Brooks Adams, p. 249; Swan Sonnenschein and Co., Ltd., London, 1900.

concerned, but the skill which made Indian cottons a marvel of manufacture was wholly wanting in any of the Western nations. As with cotton so with iron; industry in Britain was at a very low ebb, alike in mining and in manufacture.

The connection between the beginning of the drain of Indian wealth to England and the swift uprising of British industries was not casual: it was causal. Mr. Brooks Adams[1] says:—

'In discussing the phenomena of the highly centralised society in which he lived, Mill defined capital "as the accumulated stock of human labour." In other words, capital may be considered as stored energy; but most of this energy flows in fixed channels; money alone is capable of being transmuted immediately into any form of activity. Therefore the influx of the Indian treasure, by adding considerably to the nation's cash capital, not only increased its stock of energy, but added much to its flexibility and the rapidity of its movement.

'Very soon after Plassey, the Bengal plunder began to arrive in London, and the effect appears to have been instantaneous, for all authorities agree that the "industrial revolution," the event which has divided the nineteenth century from all antecedent time, began with the year 1760. Prior to 1760, according to Baines, the machinery used for spinning cotton in Lancashire was almost as simple as in India; while about 1750 the English iron industry was in full decline because of the destruction of the forests for fuel. At that time four-fifths of the iron used in the kingdom came from Sweden.

'Plassey was fought in 1757, and probably nothing has ever equalled the rapidity of the change which followed. In 1760 the flying-shuttle appeared, and coal began to replace wood in smelting. In 1764 Hargreaves invented the spinning-jenny, in 1779 Crompton contrived the mule, in 1785 Cartwright patented the power-loom, and, chief of all, in 1768 Watt matured the steam-engine, the most perfect of all vents of centralising energy. But, though these machines served as outlets for the accelerating movement of the time, they did not cause that acceleration. In themselves inventions are passive, many of the most important having lain dormant for centuries, waiting for a sufficient store of force to have accumulated to set them working. That store must always take the shape of money, and money not hoarded, but in motion.

'Thus printing had been known for ages in China before it came to

[1] 'Law of Civilisation and Decay,' Brooks Adams, pp. 259–260; Swan Sonnenschein and Co., Ltd.

Europe; the Romans probably were acquainted with gunpowder; revolvers and breech-loading cannon existed in the fifteenth and sixteenth centuries, and steam had been experimented upon long before the birth of Watt. The least part of Watt's labour lay in conceiving his idea; he consumed his life marketing it. Before the influx of the Indian treasure, and the expansion of credit which followed, no force sufficient for this purpose existed; and had Watt lived fifty years earlier, he and his invention must have perished together. Considering the difficulties under which Matthew Boulton, the ablest and most energetic manufacturer of his time, nearly succumbed, no one can doubt that without Boulton's works at Birmingham the engine could not have been produced, and yet before 1760 such works could not have been organised. The factory system was the child of the "industrial revolution," and until capital had accumulated in masses capable of giving solidity to large bodies of labour, manufactures were necessarily carried on by scattered individuals, who combined a handicraft with agriculture.'[1]

'Possibly since the world began no investment has ever yielded the profit reaped from the Indian plunder, because for nearly fifty years Great Britain stood without a competitor. That she should have so long enjoyed a monopoly seems at first mysterious, but perhaps the condition of the Continent may suggest an explanation. Since Italy had been ruined by the loss of the Eastern trade, she had ceased to breed the economic mind; consequently no class of her population could suddenly and violently accelerate their movements. In Spain, the priest and soldier had so thoroughly exterminated the sceptic, that far from centralising during the seventeenth century, as England and France had done, her empire was in full decline at the revolution of 1688. In France something similar had happened, though in a much less degree. After a struggle of a century and a half, the Church so far prevailed in 1685 as to secure the revocation of the Edict of Nantes. At the revocation many Huguenots went into exile, and thus no small proportion of the economic class, who should have pressed England hardest, were driven across the Channel to add their energy to the energy of the natives. Germany lacked capital. Hemmed in by enemies, and without a sea-coast, she had been at a disadvantage in predatory warfare; accordingly she did not accumulate money, and failed to consolidate until, in 1870, she extorted a treasure from France. Thus, in 1760, Holland alone remained as a competitor, rich, maritime, and peopled by Protestants. But Holland lacked the mass possessed by the great antagonist, besides being without minerals; and accordingly, far from accelerating her progress, she proved unable to maintain her relative rate of advance.

'Thus isolated, and favoured by mines of coal and iron, England not only commanded the European and American markets, at a time

---

[1] 'The Law of Civilisation and Decay,' ch. xi. p. 263.

when production was strained to the utmost by war, but even undersold Hindoo labour at Calcutta. In some imperfect way her gains may be estimated by the growth of her debt, which must represent savings. In 1756, when Clive went to India, the nation owed £74,575,000, on which it paid an interest of £2,753,000. In 1815 this debt had swelled to £861,000,000, with an annual interest charge of £32,645,000. In 1761 the Duke of Bridgewater finished the first of the canals which were afterwards to form an inland waterway, costing £50,000,000, or more than two-thirds of the amount of the public debt at the outbreak of the seven years' war. Meanwhile, also, steam had been introduced, factories built, turnpikes improved, and bridges erected, and all this had been done through a system of credit extending throughout the land. Credit is the chosen vehicle of energy in centralised societies, and no sooner had treasure enough accumulated in London to offer it a foundation, than it shot up with marvellous rapidity.

'From 1694 to Plassey, the growth had been relatively slow. For more than sixty years after the foundation of the Bank of England, its smallest note had been for £20, a note too large to circulate freely, and which rarely travelled far from Lombard Street. Writing in 1790, Burke mentioned that when he came to England in 1750 there were not "twelve bankers' shops" in the provinces, though then, he said, they were in every market town. Thus the arrival of the Bengal silver not only increased the mass of money, but stimulated its movement; for at once, in 1759, the bank issued £10 and £15 notes, and in the country private firms poured forth a flood of paper.' [1]

Thus England's unbounded prosperity owes its origin to her connection with India, whilst it has, largely, been maintained—disguisedly—from the same source, from the middle of the eighteenth century to the present time. 'Possibly, since the world began, no investment has ever yielded the profit reaped from the Indian plunder.' [2]

What was the extent of the wealth thus wrung from the East Indies? No one has been able to reckon adequately, as no one has been in a position to make a correct 'tally' of the treasure exported from India. Estimates have been made which vary from £500,000,000 to nearly £1,000,000,000. Probably between Plassey and Waterloo the last-mentioned sum was transferred from Indian hoards to English banks. In an appendix to

[1] 'Law of Civilisation and Decay,' pp. 263, 264. [2] *Ibid.*, p. 263.

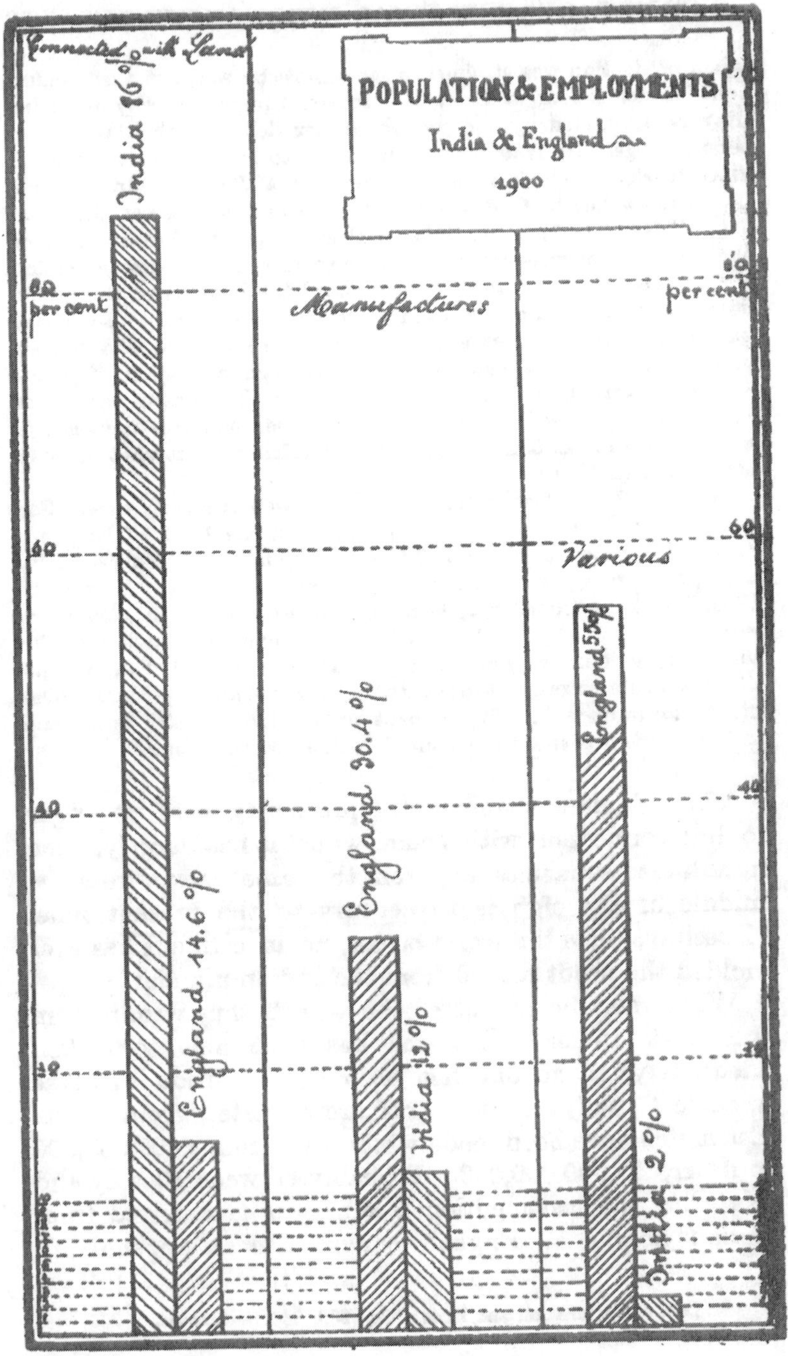
POPULATION & EMPLOYMENTS
India & England
1900
Connected with Land
India 86 %
England 14.6 %
Manufactures
England 30.4 %
India 12 %
Various
England 55 %
India 2 %
80
per cent
60
40
20

this chapter will be found some details of individual 'embezzlements,' as the phrase of that day expressed it. These will indicate the scale on which nearly every Briton in India enriched himself. Modern England has been made great by Indian wealth, wealth never proffered by its possessor, but always taken by the might and skill of the stronger. The difference between the eighteenth and the twentieth centuries is simply that the amount received now is immensely larger, is obtained 'according to law'; British money is seen to be invested, British goods are purchased—and payment must be made for whatever one buys. Further, 'services are rendered': these must be paid for.

'Could you not find the service in India itself, from among the Indian people?'
'We have never really tried, and do not intend to try.'

Apparently, everything is straightforward. But India has never said she wants these things. Indeed, her opinion on the matter, even though she pays, is the last consideration to be regarded, and no one troubles to regard it.

> Here and here has India helped us,
> What have we for India done?

Later pages will show how much of good has come to India from the British connection; likewise, how much of evil. But, once for all, with the result writ so large and writ so indelibly before our eyes, let us cast away the now out-of-date morality which taught that ill-gotten wealth cannot bring blessing or prosperity with it. Considering what England, owing to her appropriation of Indian moneys, counted for amongst the nations of the world during the whole of the nineteenth century, there can no longer be any doubt that 'out of evil good cometh,' nor, perhaps, of the sequel, 'Do ill that good may come.' With some of the money thus obtained England struck down the ancient industries of India, and, during a whole century, has done naught that is worthy to constitute India a land of varied industries.

These be hard and cruel words for an Englishman to write. Written, however, they must be so as to help to an understanding of the wrong which has thus been done to India—and, in a deeper sense, to England. With understanding *may* come a redeeming of the wrong;—may, more likely, may *not*.

England's conquest by trade being complete, India lying at the feet of her conqueror, the time had come for a further step. How was this new (yet ancient) country, its brow wrinkled with the learning of the ages, its people steeped in spirituality, its morals equal, if not superior, to those of the West, to be ruled? Were its peoples to become British citizens or British helots? There was not much delay in coming to a conclusion. Peoples who had allowed themselves so easily to be robbed, who, in the astute intellect of a Nuncomar could be outwitted by the subtler mind of a Hastings—what was there for such a people but subjection?

II. Conquest by Deliberate Subjection:

India—not for India first, and then for England, but India—for England, first and last.

1783—1833.

With the advent of Lord Cornwallis as Governor-General of India in 1786, were exhibited the first real glimmerings of a conscience as to the principles on which the newly-acquired territories were to be ruled. Philip Francis, it is true, had revealed some facts, but he was unpopular, and therefore his views were ignored. It was open to us to associate the people of India with us in the administration of Indian affairs. Recognising how much they knew and how little we knew of the complexities of rule in their own land, such a course seemed the commonest of common sense. Time has proved that the adoption of such a course would have been the noblest, as it would have been the most profitable, line of policy which could have been adopted. Through some strange psychological change in the mind of the inhabitants of India, or by the working out of some spiritual force,[1] the time had arrived when a foreigner's domination became acceptable, nay, more, seemed as if it were desired in fact if not in words. Strange to relate, this was as true of the martial races as of the peaceful peoples. Hindu and Muslim, Bengali, Madrassi, Maratha, Sikh—they all for a time resisted the foreign domination, they fought fiercely, but, having been beaten, they all accepted defeat, and contentedly acquiesced in the rule of the alien overlord. History records in its annals no greater marvel of one race overmastering another in all matters alike of mind and body. The leaders of British thought in those distant days may be partly forgiven in that they did not discern the possibilities of the future. 'Put the people of India in a position of equality with us?' they asked; 'that would never do. If we let them co-operate with us, if we give them the same facilities to acquire knowledge and experience as we possess, as they gain such knowledge and experience they will use it to get rid of us.'

So it has not been. Never has there been a national revolt in India against British rule. Never, I think, will there be. There was, in 1857, a mutiny of mercenaries. Never has there been an uprising of the people. Nor, had another course been adopted than that which unhappily was taken with the soldiers, and had not our

[1] Mr. Meredith Townsend ('Asia and Europe,' Archibald Constable), in his chapter, 'Will England Retain India?' calls it a lack of the power 'of accumulating thought.' He claims that the French ethnologist, the Count de Gobineau, has explained and justified this view in detail. The subject merits separate treatment, but I may say here the phrase does not seem to me to adequately describe, or even approximately, that 'something' which, in this age, has made ten thousand Indians quietly accept the domination of one Englishman.

'bad faith' with the Feudatory States been so manifest, would there have been even a revolt of the troops. England, when she obtained supremacy in India, had a golden opportunity to enrich India whilst bringing prosperity to herself. She threw it away. Deliberately, she threw it away. There were not wanting, even then, wise men in plenty to show the truer way. Nevertheless, the wrong course was taken. Not colleagues, but subordinates; not, in their own land, rulers and chiefs, with reasonable ambition satisfied and a scope for natural and national energies provided—not these things for Indians. For them, of every caste and creed, the doom was fixed; they at home, among their fellows, were to become 'hewers of wood and drawers of water,' with such employment in governmental service as would not be worth the acceptance of any Englishman, however poor. The decision was fateful, alike for India and for England. It was consciously taken. It has been accepted by the under dog in the struggle; it has only been varied infinitesimally by the dog on top, accordingly as to whether he found himself in a good humour or not.

Nowhere, perhaps, has the policy of keeping the Indians under found such plain-spoken and emphatic demonstration as in an official document written by a favoured Madras civilian, Mr. William Thackeray. At the time when Lord William Bentinck was Governor of Madras—August, 1803, to September, 1807—Mr. Thackeray was a member of the Board of Revenue in that Presidency: that Board is a survival, an atrophied survival, to the present day. The great fight as to whether peasant farmers, with the Government revenue periodically fixed, should be settled on the land, or whether landed proprietors and the permanent settlement, such as Lord Cornwallis had established in Bengal, should be adopted, was the subject of consideration. The Governor was a strong advocate for the peasant farmer; the Revenue Board member was even stronger on the same side. In the course of many inquiries, and in the voluminous discussions carried on in the favourite Indian form of elaborate Minutes, each enough to fill a 200-page octavo volume, the foundation principles of Indian subordination and British supremacy were laid down most absolutely. Never, perhaps, has the arrogance and cruelty of alien rulers towards their subjects been more nakedly and cynically announced. That which was essential for English greatness in its home land, and for every other people in their respective home lands, was to be withheld, deliberately withheld, from the Indian people in their own country. Without circumlocution and with a cynicism which belies the profession expressed at the same time that the happiness of the people was the sole object of the new conquerors,[1] the subjection of many scores of millions of people for at least a century and may be for ever—(this world is to the strong and not to the amiable, to the brutal and not to the saintly)—was unconcernedly set forth in clear terms. The paragraphs in Mr. Thackeray's report which are the very negation of the charters in which nearly every civilised people find their rights enshrined, the paragraphs which have rendered futile Acts of Parliament subsequently passed, and even have made of none effect the Queen-Empress's Proclamation of 1858, deserve quotation in full. The argument is too interesting to be summarised, has been too fruitful in its baneful consequences not to be recalled and enshrined in twentieth-century literature, *verbatim et literatim*.

After arguing in vigorous terms against a landlord settlement—'one fat rajah supposes fifty-two ryots'[2] (peasant farmers)—Mr. Thackeray remarks:—

[1] Mr. Thackeray, although knowing the principle of land taxation depended wholly upon produce being actually forthcoming, did not hesitate to put the following cynical—and in practice cruelly harsh—dictum on record:—'It may be said the revenue will not be secure under a ryotwar settlement; however, if *the ryots are put on such a footing that their lands are saleable, and that they ought to pay whether they cultivate or no, the revenue will be secure.*'

[2] Later in these pages it will be seen what one Secretary of State, one Councillor, one Civilian or Military Pensioner, presupposes in the way of ryots' revenues.

'This quality of condition, in respect to wealth in land; this general distribution of the soil among a yeomanry, therefore, if it be not most adapted to agricultural improvement, is best adapted to attain improvement, in the state of property, manners, and institutions, which prevail in India; and it will be found still more adapted to the situation of the country, governed by a few strangers, where pride, high ideas, and ambitious thoughts must be stifled. It is very proper that in England, a good share of the produce of the earth should be appropriated to support certain families in affluence, to produce senators, sages, and heroes for the service and defence of the state, or, in other words, that great part of the rent should go to an opulent nobility and gentry, who are to serve their country in Parliament, in the army and navy, in the departments of science and liberal professions. The leisure, independence, and high ideas, which the enjoyment of this rent affords, has enabled them to raise Britain to the pinnacle of glory. Long may they enjoy it;—but in India, that haughty spirit, independence, and deep thought, which the possession of great wealth sometimes gives, ought to be suppressed. They are directly adverse to our power and interest. The nature of things, the past experience of all governments, renders it unnecessary to enlarge on this subject. We do not want generals, statesmen, and legislators; we want industrious husbandmen. If we wanted rank, restless, and ambitious spirits, there are enough of them in Malabar to supply the whole peninsula; but these people are at least an encumbrance, if nothing worse; they can never do good, and, at all events, consume a good deal without rendering any equivalent service to the public. We must, therefore, avoid the creation of more; though we submit to the necessity of supporting those who now are.

'Considered politically, therefore, the general distribution of land, among a number of small proprietors, who cannot easily combine against Government, is an object of importance. The power and patronage, and receipt of the sircar rent, will always render zemindars formidable, but more or less so, according to the military strength and reputation of the Government. It is difficult to foresee what may happen in the course of a few years; and it is our interest to retain in our own hands as much power and influence as is consistent with the preservation of the rights of the people. By retaining the administration of the revenues in our own hands, we maintain our communication and immediate connection with the people at large. We keep in our own hands the means of obtaining information, the knowledge on which alone the resources of the country can be drawn out; the policy administered with effect; and perhaps the body of the proprietors secured in their possessions.

'Our first object is to govern India; and then to govern it well; and in these provinces it would seem that both these objects, a strong government and the security of private rights, would be attained by such a settlement as I have proposed.'[1]

[1] Pp. 990-991, Appdx., Fifth Report, Sel. Com. E. I. Co., 1812.

'It is very proper that, in England, a good share of the produce of the earth should be appropriated to support certain families in affluence, to produce senators, sages, and heroes for the service and defence of the State.'

And, in India? Are not Indians human beings? It may be, in the opinion of some, a contemptible few, that they are human beings; according to Mr. Thackeray if they are human beings they are of quite another order than ourselves, ranking distinctly below that order of human beings of which British folk are members.

'. . . ;—but, in India, that haughty spirit, independence, and deep thought, which the possession of great wealth sometimes gives,

'OUGHT TO BE SUPPRESSED.'

'We do not want generals, statesmen, and legislators; we want industrious husbandmen.'

Clearly, an Indian hath not eyes, hath not hands, organs, dimensions, senses, affections, passions, is not fed with the same food, hurt with the same weapons, subject to the same diseases, healed by the same means, warmed and cooled by the same summer and winter, as hath and as is an Englishman. If we prick Indians they do not bleed—at least, they do not bleed as do Europeans; their suffering from famine, fever, and pestilence is not like the suffering of others: they are occupants of a 'human cattle farm,' placed in that position after careful thought and consideration, and—kept there.

Mr. Thackeray was without excuse. Lord William Bentinck, who of set purpose selected Mr. Thackeray as his mouthpiece, they holding ideas in common, is even more without excuse. 'Tis not as if they considered the people of India were incapable of reaching great intellectual heights, of developing and exhibiting noble character. In this same report Mr. Thackeray says:—'It would be impertinent to show that the people of hot countries have been conquerors, sages, and statesmen.'[1] If it be impertinent to remark upon so self-evident a fact, what word is adequate with which to describe the carefully arranged shutting of the door leading to advancement upon an admittedly capable people? Once it was closed it was securely locked and barred. A small postern gate has been constructed through which a few Indians have been permitted to pass to certain positions of honour and emolument. But the great door is still closed—an impassable barrier. 'No Indians need apply.'

What Mr. Thackeray urged, nearly every Viceroy, every Governor, every Lieutenant-Governor, every Chief-Com-

[1] Further observations in the same paper show that Mr. Thackeray could discern good characteristics in the Indian people. He wrote:—'The general distribution of land among a great number of small proprietors will also contribute to the general happiness of the people. I say happiness, because it is our duty to consider the happiness of the mild, industrious, race, which Providence has placed under the British Government, before revenue or any other objects. The domestic happiness, independence, and pleasure of a country life, which the distribution of landed property alone can confer on the multitude, makes this far superior to any system. It may be considered an Utopia by some; however, I think that Government can, and ought, to extend this happy system to the provinces. The people of this country are peculiarly adapted to thrive as small proprietors. All their customs, opinions, and virtues are suited to this sort of life, and adapted to make them succeed in it. No people are fonder of a house, ground, and place of their own, of their families, of fame among their equals, of their hereditary occupations, and of the profession of agriculture, than the Hindus. Had they a field for the display of the industry which these feelings would excite, this great country would have a different appearance. The ryots are laborious, and, in some respects, parsimonious, inherit their skill and attachment to husbandry. We sometimes, especially those among us who know least of them, affect a contempt for the natives; they are indeed objects of pity, if our contempt for their character suggests ideas of arbitrary government: but, considered as husbandmen, who have understood and carried to perfection that primeval business of man (the cultivation of the earth) for thousands of years, they are very respectable. A few centuries ago the peasantry of England, and even now, the peasantry in many parts of Europe, are considered as inferior beings by their proud masters the great landholders the (zemindars), who urged their idleness, ignorance, and brutality, as a reason for keeping them in vassalage. Some great philosophers have affected to attribute to them indolence, not to be excited by any inducement; want of mental and bodily strength, which fitted them only for slavery to the people of hot climes.'—P. 991. Appdx. Fifth Rept. Sel. Com. E. I. Co., 1812.

missioner, aided by their respective subordinates, has consolidated into concrete facts. In so doing they have brought India to its present condition—so far as its native inhabitants are concerned—of national, mental, and social, degradation. An Act of Parliament with sonorous words as to equal treatment, words of Magna Charta strength, are so much waste paper in the presence of the gospel which Thackeray preached in 1807, and which James Mill, unashamedly, reiterated in 1831. It almost passes credence that one with the intellectual and political advantages possessed by James Mill should, apparently after due consideration, have urged the keeping of the Indian people in a condition of subjection, and even to argue that they would be the better for such subjection. He did this, however, and did it, too, with an effrontery which, in these days of smooth phrases and periphrastic disguises, appears brutal. The majority of Anglo-Indians and Britons, who take any interest in India, still think as James Mill thought and spoke. The difference is that Mill was frank; the others are disingenuous. He said exactly what he meant; they are past masters in the use of language which deceives. On the 25th of August, 1831, this happened before a House of Commons Committee [1]—James Mill, of the India House, under examination:—

'4193. Would not a considerable advantage accrue to the natives of India by the introduction of a system whereby natives and not Europeans might be largely employed in the collection of revenue? —The great advantage I should contemplate would be the cheapness. If the payments of the ryots were accurately defined, and there were an administration of justice sufficiently perfect to afford redress to the ryot for every grievance, you might then employ, without danger, the greatest rogues in the world in collecting the revenue.

'4194. Would not the people of India derive very considerable benefit from the natives being employed in the collection of revenue,

---

[1] The Houses of Parliament seventy years ago were not so much afraid of work in the months of August and September as they now appear to be. This important inquiry into Indian affairs was carried on through those months.

where Europeans are at present employed?—An opinion is very generally entertained, but which I confess I do not participate, that it would be good for the natives of India to be more largely employed in the business of government than they are now. It appears to me that the great concern of the people of India is, that the business of government should be well and cheaply performed, but that it is of little or no consequence to them who are the people who perform it. The idea generally entertained is that you would elevate the people of India by giving them a greater share in their own government; but I think that to encourage any people in a train of believing that the grand source of elevation is in being an *employé* of Government is anything but desirable. The right thing, in my opinion, is to teach people to look for their elevation to their own resources, their industry, and economy. Let the means of accumulation be afforded to our Indian subjects; let them grow rich as cultivators, merchants, manufacturers, and not accustom themselves to look for wealth and dignity to successful intriguing for places under Government; the benefit from which, whatever it may be, can never extend beyond a very insignificant portion of the whole population.

'4195. Do you not conceive that the exclusion of the natives from the higher branches of the revenue employment is looked upon by them, and is, in point of fact, a stigma upon them?—I do not believe that they look upon it in that light.

'4196. Do you know any country in which it would not be so considered?—I should point to India as a country in which it is not so considered.'

'4197. Supposing, for example, Englishmen alone were employed in the higher branches of employment in Ireland, do you not conceive that the Irish would consider it a stigma upon them?—I consider that the feeling of degradation, from being governed by foreigners, is a feeling altogether European. I believe it has little or no existence in any part of Asia.

'4198. Do you not think that by the greater employment of the natives of India in the higher branches of employment the character of the natives would be ameliorated?—I should think that such employment would have little effect in that way. The thing of importance in order to elevate the character of any people is to protect them. Elevation is the natural state of a man who has nothing to fear, and the best riches are the effects of a man's own industry: effects which never fail when the protection is good.

'4199. Have you ever been in India?—I have not.

'4200. And you can only speak from what you have read and heard?—Yes.

'4201. Are you aware that petitions have been sent home by the natives of India, most numerously and respectably signed, complaining in the strongest terms of their exclusion from the civil, judicial, and financial, departments of government?—I am perfectly aware of such petitions having been sent home, but I am far from supposing that these petitions speak the general language of the country.

'4202. What reason have you to think so?—I can only speak generally, because my reason is an inference from all I know, from all I have heard, and from all I have read, about the people.

'4203. Is the correspondence you have read native correspondence?—Not native correspondence.

'4204. Do you allude to the correspondence of the Company's servants in India exclusively?—Not exclusively.

'4205. You have not seen anything stated by the natives themselves upon that subject?—Not anything written by themselves upon that subject.

'4206. Are the petitions that have been referred to from the Presidencies or from the provinces?—From the Presidencies, I believe, exclusively.

'4207. Do you conceive that it is possible for any person to form an adequate judgment of the character of a people without being personally acquainted with them?—If the question refers to myself, I am far from pretending to a perfect knowledge of the character of the Indian people.'

It remains to the credit of the British race that, even during the days of darkness in India when such views were promulgated, men of light and leading protested against the iniquitousness as well as the folly and short-sightedness of such a mode of ruling India. Two witnesses may suffice—a Madras civilian [at the time Mr. Thackeray wrote what, for the credit of the British name had better never have been written, and which every one has striven to ignore so far as the words themselves are concerned], afterwards Governor of the Presidency, Sir Thomas Munro; and the second Protestant Bishop of India, Reginald Heber. Several citations from the former's writings are necessary: what he wrote early in the last century is in this century fulfilled prophecy. I have taken much; I have left untouched ten times as much, equally good. All of ill that he predicted has come to pass, while the burning injustice of it all thrills one now as it must have thrilled the noble-minded writer twice forty years ago.

'When we have determined the principles, the next question is, by what agency it is to be managed? There can be no doubt that it ought, as far as practicable, to be native. Juster views have of late years been taken of this subject, and the employment of the natives on higher salaries and in more important offices have been authorised. There is true economy in this course, for by it they will have better servants and their affairs will be better conducted. It is strange to observe how many men of very respectable talents have seriously recommended the abolition of native and the substitution of European agency to the greatest possible extent. I am persuaded that every advance made in such a plan would not only render the character of the people worse and worse, but our Government more and more inefficient. The preservation of our dominion in this country requires that all the higher offices, civil and military, should be filled with Europeans; but all offices that can be left in the hands of natives without danger to our power might with advantage be left to them. We are arrogant enough to suppose that we can with our imited numbers do the work of a nation. Had we ten times more, we should only do it so much worse. We already occupy every office of importance. Were we to descend to those which are more humble and now filled by natives, we should lower our character and not perform the duties so well. The natives possess, in as high a degree at least as Europeans, all those qualifications which are requisite for the discharge of the inferior duties in which they are employed. They are in general better accountants, more patient and laborious, more intimately acquainted with the state of the country and the manners and customs of the inhabitants, and are altogether more efficient men of business.

'Unless we suppose that they are inferior to us in natural talent, which there is no reason to believe, it is much more likely that they will be duly qualified for their employments than Europeans for theirs, because the field of selection is so much greater in the one than in the other. We have a whole nation from which to make our choice of natives, but in order to make a choice of Europeans we have only the small body of covenanted servants.

'If it be admitted that the natives often act wrong, it is no reason for not employing them; we shall be oftener wrong ourselves. What we do wrong is not noticed, or but seldom or slightly; what they do wrong meets with no indulgence! We can dismiss them and take better men in their place; we must keep the European because we have no other, or perhaps none better, and because he must be kept at an expense to the public and be employed some way or other, whatever his capacity may be, unless he has been guilty of some gross offence. But it is said that all these advantages in favour of the employment of the natives are counterbalanced by their corruption, and that the only remedy is more Europeans with European integrity. The remedy would certainly be a very expensive one, and would as certainly fail of success were we weak enough to try it. We have had instances of corruption among Europeans, notwithstanding their liberal allowances; but were the numbers of Europeans to be considerably augmented, and their allowances, as a necessary consequence, somewhat reduced, it would be contrary to all experience to believe that this corruption would not greatly increase, more particularly as Government could not possibly exercise any efficient control over the misconduct of so many European functionaries in different provinces, where there is no public to restrain it. If we are to have corruption, it is better that it should be among the natives than among ourselves, because the natives will throw the blame of the evil upon their countrymen; they will still retain their high opinion of our superior integrity; and our character, which is one of the strongest supports of our power, will be maintained. No nation ever existed in which corruption was not practised to a certain extent by the subordinate officers of the Government: we cannot expect that India is in this point to form an exception. But though we cannot eradicate corruption, we may so far restrain it as to prevent it from causing any serious injury to the public interest. We must for this purpose adopt the same means as are usually found most efficacious in other countries; we must treat the natives with courtesy, we must place confidence in them, we must render their official situations respectable, and raise them in some degree beyond temptation, by making their official allowances adequate to the support of their station in society.

'With what grace can we talk of our paternal Government if we exclude these from every important office, and say, as we did till very lately, that in a country containing fifteen millions of inhabitants, no man but a European shall be entrusted with so much authority as to order the punishment of a single stroke of a rattan? Such an interdiction is to pass a sentence of degradation on a whole people, for which no benefit can ever compensate. There is no instance in the world of so humiliating a sentence having ever been passed upon any nation. The weak and mistaken humanity which is the motive of it can never be viewed by the natives as any just excuse for the disgrace inflicted on them by being pronounced to be unworthy of trust in deciding on the petty offences of their countrymen. We profess to seek their improvement, but propose means the most adverse to success. The advocates of improvement do not seem to have perceived the great springs on which it depends; they propose to place no confidence in the natives, to give them no authority, and to exclude them from office as much as possible; but they are ardent in their zeal for enlightening them by the general diffusion of knowledge.

'No conceit more wild and absurd than this was ever engendered in the darkest ages; for what is in every age and every country the great stimulus to the pursuit of knowledge, but the prospect of fame, or wealth, or power? or what is even the use of great attainments if they are not to be devoted to their noblest purpose—the service of the community, by employing those who possess them, according to their respective qualifications, in the various degrees of the public administration of the country? How can we expect that the Hindoos will be eager in the pursuit of science unless they have the same inducements as in other countries? If superior acquirements do not open the road to distinction, it is idle to suppose that the Hindoo would lose his time in seeking them; and even if he did so, his proficiency, under the doctrine of exclusion from office, would serve no other purpose than to show him more clearly the fallen state of himself and his countrymen. He would not study what he knew could be of no ultimate benefit to himself; he would learn only those things which were in demand, and which were likely to be useful to him, namely, writing and accounts. There might be some exceptions, but they would be few; some few natives living at the principal settlements, and passing much of their time among Europeans, might either from a real love of literature, from vanity, or some other cause, study their books, and if they made some progress, it would be greatly exaggerated, and would be hailed as the dawn of the great day of light and science about to be spread all over India. But there always has been, and always will be, a few such men among the natives, without making any change in the body of the people. Our books alone will do little or nothing; dry simple literature will never improve the character of a nation. To produce this effect, it must open the road to wealth and honour and public employment. Without the prospect of such reward, no attainments in science will ever raise the character of a people.

'This is true of every nation as well as of India; it is true of our own. Let Britain be subjected by a foreign power to-morrow; let the people be excluded from all share in the government, from public honours, from every office of high trust or emolument, and let them in every situation be considered as unworthy of trust, and all their knowledge and all their literature, sacred and profane, would not save them from becoming, in another generation or two, a low-minded, deceitful, and dishonest, race.

'Even if we could suppose that it were practicable, without the aid of a single native, to conduct the whole affairs of the country, both in the higher and in all the subordinate offices, by means of Europeans, it ought not to be done, because it would be both politically and morally wrong. The great number of public offices in which the natives are employed is one of the strongest causes of their attachment to our Government. In proportion as we exclude them from those, we lose our hold upon them; and were the exclusion entire, we should have their hatred in place of their attachment; their feeling would be communicated to the whole population, and to the native troops, and would excite a spirit of discontent too powerful for us to subdue or resist. But were it possible that they could submit silently and without opposition, the case would be worse; they would sink in character, they would lose with the hope of public office and distinction all laudable ambition, and would degenerate into an indolent and abject race, incapable of any higher pursuit than the mere gratification of their appetites. It would certainly be more desirable that we should be expelled from the country altogether than that the result of our system of government should be such a debasement of a whole people. This is, to be sure, supposing an extreme case, because nobody has ever proposed to exclude the natives from the numerous petty offices, but only from the more important offices now filled by them. But the principle is the same, the difference is only in degree; for in proportion as we exclude them from the higher offices, and a share in the management of public affairs, we lessen their interest in the concerns of the community, and degrade their character.

'It was from a conviction of the policy of extending native agency that the establishment of the revenue board cutcherry was recommended in 1822. The right of the people to be taxed only by their own consent, has always, in every free country, been esteemed amongst the most important of all privileges; it is that which has most exercised the minds of men, and which has oftenest been asserted by the defenders of liberty. Even in countries in which there is no freedom, taxation is the most important function of government, because it is that which most universally affects the comfort and happiness of the people, and that which has oftenest excited them to resistance; and hence both its utility and its danger have, under the most despotic governments, taught the necessity of employing in its administration the ablest men of the country.

'In this point, at least, we ought to be guided by the example of those governments, and employ intelligent and experienced natives at the head of the revenue to assist the revenue board. If in other departments we have experienced natives to assist the European officers, shall we not have them in this, whose duties are the most difficult and most important? We cannot exclude them from it without injury to ourselves as well as to them; we cannot conduct the department efficiently without them. But even if we could, policy requires that we should let them have a share in the business of taxing their own country.'

The above wise and weighty observations, a parallel to which is not to be found in present-day Anglo-Indian writings, are, as I have said, but a few sentences out of a hundred pages of equally luminous, high-minded, and statesmanlike utterances. Exigencies of space, however, forbid further citations.

Rightly is Sir Thomas Munro's fame maintained in Madras by one of Chantrey's finest equestrian statues. Had his spirit been permitted to pervade the purlieus of Indian administration as Chantrey's representation of the man dominates 'the Island' in the Chinnapatnam of olden days, such a work as this of mine would have been unnecessary—would never have been written. So wise and perspicuous were his teachings that it is difficult for one who knows what he counselled to pass that statue without raising his hat as to a living personage. As for Bishop Heber, writing to the Right Honourable Charles Williams Wynn, in England, in a letter dated Karnatik, March, 1826, he says :—

'But there is one point which, the more I have seen of India, since I left Bengal for the first time, has more and more impressed itself on my mind. Neither native nor European agriculturist, I think, can thrive at the present rate of taxation. Half the gross produce of the soil is demanded by Government, and this, which is nearly the average rate wherever there is not a permanent settlement, is sadly too much to leave an adequate provision for the peasant, even with the usual frugal habits of Indians, and the very inartificial and cheap manner in which they cultivate the land. Still more is it an effectual bar to everything like improvement; it keeps the people, even in favourable years, in a state of abject penury; and when the crop fails, in even a slight degree, it involves a necessity on the part of Government of enormous outlays, in the way of remission and distribution, which, after all, do not prevent men, women, and children dying in the streets in droves, and the roads being strewed with carcasses. In Bengal, where, independent of its exuberant fertility, there is a permanent assessment, famine is unknown. In Hindustan, on the other hand, I found a general feeling among the King's officers, and I myself was led, from some circumstances, to agree with them, that the peasantry in the Company's provinces are, on the whole, worse off, poorer, and more dispirited, than the subjects of the native Princes; and here, in Madras, where the soil is, generally speaking, poor, the difference is said to be still more marked. The fact is, no native Prince demands the rent which we do; and making every allowance for the superior regularity of our system, etc., I met with very few public men who will not, in confidence, own their belief that the people are overtaxed, and that the country is in a gradual state of impoverishment. The Collectors do not like to make this avowal officially. Indeed, now and then, a very able Collector succeeds in lowering the rate to the people, while by diligence, he increases it to the State. But, in general, all gloomy pictures are avoided by them as reflecting on themselves, and drawing on them censure from the secretaries at Madras or Calcutta; while these, in their turn, plead the earnestness with which the Directors at home press for more money.

'I am convinced that it is only necessary to draw less money from the peasants, and to spend more of what is drawn within the country, to open some door to Indian industry in Europe, and to admit the natives of India to some greater share in the magistracy of their own people, to make this Empire as durable as it would be happy. But as things now go on, though I do not detract any part of the praise which I have, on other occasions, bestowed on the general conduct of the Company's servants, their modesty, their diligence, and integrity, I do not think the present Empire can be durable.

'I have sometimes wished that its immediate management were transferred to the Crown. But what I saw in Ceylon makes me think this a doubtful remedy, unless the Government, and, above all, the *people* of England were convinced that no country can bear to pay so large a revenue to foreigners, as to those who spend their wealth within their own borders; and that most of the causes which once made these countries wealthy have ceased to exist in proportion as the industry and ingenuity of England have rivalled and excelled them. Even Bengal is taxed highly, not indeed directly on its land, but in salt and other duties. But Bengal is naturally of such exuberant fertility, that whoever has seen it alone will form a too flattering estimate of these vast countries.'[1]

Why have I disinterred from ancient volumes the foregoing unwise and supremely wise observations? Because the conflict represented by such protagonists—

THACKERAY and JAMES MILL *against* MUNRO and HEBER

is proceeding now as it proceeded in the second and third decennial periods of the nineteenth century. The wrong step was then taken. The right step has yet to be taken. The mischief is that not a single high official connected with India at the beginning of the twentieth century considers any forward step is required. They all think of Indian Administration as the Great Duke thought of the British Constitution prior to 1832. It was from heaven. It is sacro-sanct. It may be that in the fortuitous (or other) concourse of circumstances

[1] Bishop Heber's Memoirs and Correspondence, by his Widow, vol. ii. pp. 413, 414. John Murray, 1830.

which we call national development, there is still room for the right step to be taken in India. It is to help in that being done, if haply it may be done, that the quoted passages, in such fulness, have been placed before the reader.

That sentiment in our national character which is proclaimed *ore rotundo* as 'British justice,' revolted at the condition of things Thackerayan. In the inquiry which preceded the renewal of the Charter in 1833 many questions were asked concerning the capacity of the Indian subjects of the King and the development of India's resources from within and through her own people. The evidence of Mr. Robert Rickards, who served for many years in Madras and Bombay, is wise far beyond the average of the evidence that has, from time to time, been given before British Committees on Indian subjects. Probably it is due more to what Mr. Rickards said than to anything else that the Act of Parliament of 1833, by which the Charter was renewed, contained so emphatic a declaration in favour of the employment of Indians in their own land, irrespective of caste, colour, or creed, as is to be found in the clause which runs:

> 'That no Native of the said territories, nor any natural-born subject of His Majesty resident therein, shall, by reason only of his religion, place of birth, descent, colour, or any of these, be disqualified from holding any place, office, or employment under the said Company.'

Used in the sense intended by their framers those words are among the most noble and most worthy ever legislatively recorded by a conquering Power. Had they been acted upon, the condition of the great country for which we are responsible and the welfare of the vast multitude of its inhabitants, for which we do not have to account, as there is now no one to call us to account, would have been far better than can now be recorded.[1]

Mr. Rickards was asked whether India did not require capital to bring forth her resources. 'She certainly does,' he replied. 'But the best and the fittest capital for this purpose would, in my opinion, be one of native growth. And such a capital would certainly be created among the natives themselves if our institutions did not obstruct it, by curbing the energies and confirming as they now do, the poverty of the great mass of the inhabitants.'[2]

It was pressed upon the witness that India would 'derive great advantages from men of talent and science and art' proceeding to settle in India. 'Yes, undoubtedly,' replied Mr. Rickards. 'But the presence of such men,' he went on to say, 'is not enough. A people in a state of confirmed and degraded poverty cannot, I apprehend, be roused to energetic habits by the mere stimulus of foreign example. On this account I think that our first attention should, as well in common justice as in policy, be directed to the improvement of the state and condition of the natives of that country.'[3]

In a fashion known so well in the last days of the nineteenth century, the question was asked: 'Have not many branches of commerce and manufacture been commenced and carried on by British capital and British settlers,

[1] This remark is true in the human sense as well as in the Divine sense in which it is used in the text. I myself heard Lord George Hamilton, during the early evening of August 16, 1901, taunt the friends of India in the House of Commons with the observation that in 1877 and 1878, when he was Under-Secretary of State for India, he had much more to do in the House than he had had since, in 1895, he became Secretary of State. If Indians want to know one reason why a back-wave has overthrown liberties they once possessed, they may see it in this observation. Such activity in the House of Commons as marked the years 1889, 1890, and 1891, when Charles Bradlaugh was 'Member for India,' would have prevented the falling back which all educated Indians mourn, while it would have ensured a great advance.

[2] East India Company's Affairs, 1831. Reports from Committees, vol. v. Q. 2795.

[3] *Ibid.* Qns. 2796, 2797.

and is not this enough?' No doubt, it was answered, there has been much of what you mention—indigo cultivation, for example, 'but'—and here I ask the reader's most careful attention, for in the sentence which follows is indicated, as though with the pen of Inspiration, the course which England would have adopted had she, in her intercourse with India, been really solicitous first of the interests of the Indian people :—

> 'But I still maintain that any improvement which may have arisen in consequence of the introduction of British capital and British enterprise into India, *is nothing in comparison with what would be the case if the natives of India were sufficiently encouraged, and proper attention paid to their cultivation and improvement.*'

In this sentence, for the advice it contains has been wholly ignored, lies the greatest condemnation imaginable of present Indian poverty and present Indian suffering. The path to prosperity was the path of honour and chivalry : it was clearly indicated ; it was, in 1833, it is, in 1901, wilfully ignored. The Secretary of State will not acknowledge the existence of such a contingency. Not India, but England, is the first consideration always held in view in connection with Indian matters. Viscount Cross, when Secretary of State for India, furnished evidence thereof, without being aware that he was doing a gross wrong to the Indian people in the course he took. Each of his successors has taken special care to make their predecessor's sentiments their own. Whatever else concerning India may have been overlooked, that which was calculated to make English influence more and more dominant has never been forgotten.

I have linked the two preceding questions, asked in 1831, with the views held and announced at the present time. Two other questions asked at the inquiry seventy years ago—2807 and 2808—may similarly be specially regarded as indicating that there is no real difference in the manner in which India is viewed now and at that distant period. It was a Lieutenant-Governor of Bengal, still living and engaged in strenuous work in London, who, a few years ago, remarked, in response to a suggestion that closer co-operation in the higher spheres of rule between Europeans and Indians would give the latter an opportunity of teaching us many things we did not know:—

'The Indians teach us! Absurd! Why, they know nothing we have not taught them! The natives teach us!'

In exactly the same spirit Mr. Rickards, in 1831, was asked:—

'Can you name any one improvement which has been made by the natives in your time that cannot fairly be traced to the example, or influence, of Europeans?'

The answer was as emphatic as it was lucid and undeniable:—

'I have already observed,' he said, 'that the improvements introduced by Europeans are limited in comparison with what might be the case if the natives of India were sufficiently encouraged; but in their present state of extreme poverty and almost slavery, it is not reasonable to expect that any great improvements can flow from them. One of the greatest improvements, however, of which the mind of man is susceptible, has been made by natives from their own exclusive exertions. Their acquirement of knowledge, and particularly of the English language and English literature, of which there are many examples in Bengal, Madras, and Bombay at the present moment, is quite astonishing. It may even be questioned whether so great a progress in the attainment of knowledge has ever been made under like circumstances in any of the countries of Europe.'

'Is not that,' it was asked, 'limited to those who have had particular intercourse with Europeans?'

Mr. Rickards, with observations which might with conspicuous benefit be reprinted and placed in a prominent position in every room of the India Office, and in all official rooms in India, particularly in the working rooms of the Viceroy, Governors, Lieutenant-Governors, and of Members of Council, Commissioners, and Residents at Feudatory Courts, replied as follows:—

'The examples to which I allude are among natives that have kept up an uninterrupted intercourse, certainly with Europeans, from residing at the different presidencies of India: but the exertions of those with whom I am acquainted have been altogether independent of European assistance; the natives to whom I allude being perfectly self-taught. I would beg leave here to add that if it be meant to imply, as some of the most distinguished literary authorities in this country have asserted, that the natives of India are incapable of improvement, I must protest against the doctrine, as being, in my humble opinion, an unjust and libellous judgment passed on the whole community. We have at this moment an illustrious example [1] in this country of what native Indians can attain by their own unaided exertions. Let it also be recollected that in many branches of art their skill is absolutely unrivalled. Several of their fabrics, such as muslins, shawls, embroidered silks, handkerchiefs, etc., together with pieces of workmanship in gold, silver, and ivory, have never yet been equalled by British artists. Their architecture, though peculiar, is of a superior order, and in the construction of great public buildings they have exerted powers of moving and elevating large masses which are unknown to European architects. Agriculture also made its first progress, and attained considerable perfection in the East, which in this respect set the example to Europe. In these, and many other arts connected with the comforts and conveniences of life, the natives of India have made great progress in some, and attained perfection in others, without being in the smallest degree indebted to the European patterns or example. I do not mean to say that their progress or advancement has been a hundredth part so great or so rapid as that of Europeans in the arts of life generally, but I do not think it fair to compare their present backward state with the advancement made by Europeans, considering the very different circumstances in which both are respectively placed. . . . Many persons, I apprehend, who now contend for the freest introduction of Europeans into India, to operate as a stimulus to native improvement, seem to forget the vast difference of character existing in the two parties; that consequently, to overrun India with Europeans before a better system of protection shall have been provided, would be to mingle a race of overbearing conquerors with submissive slaves, and that oppression and injustice

---

[1] The great religious reformer, Ram Mohun Roy, doubtless, is here referred to. About this time he visited England, and wrote several valuable Memoranda for the Parliamentary Committee.

would be the inevitable result. Until the natives of India are raised (and I am sure they can be so raised with great advantage) to participate largely and actively in the government of themselves, I feel persuaded that India never will be justly or securely ruled under any European sovereignty.'

The reader must suffer some further citations in the text (and not be referred to a footnote or to an appendix) from Mr. Rickards' evidence. I wish to draw special attention to his remarks because, in every particular, they are applicable to the conditions of India to-day. Perchance where they failed to convince in the nineteenth century they may persuade in the twentieth century. Even now they contain such statesmanlike wisdom as to constitute them 'a counsel of perfection' quite within the realisable possibilities of the time—if the spirit to do justice to India were commensurate with the 'talk' on the same topic. I quote questions 2815 to 2820 (Question 2824 relates to a work in two volumes written by Mr. Rickards) and from 2825 to 2829; and also 2840–2842.

'2815. Are you aware that the natives of Bengal, in Oude, at present imitating European indigo settlers, prepare a considerable portion of that article now exported?—The natives of Oude have got lately into a better mode of preparing indigo for this market. This may be occasioned partly, no doubt, by the influence and example of Europeans, but in a great measure also, as I conceive, by the unsaleable state of the article in this country, from the badness of its quality, and which rendered it indispensably necessary that some improvement should take place before it could be brought into general consumption and use by manufacturers.

'2816. Did the natives ever manufacture any indigo for export twenty-five or thirty years ago, or was it not entirely begun by Europeans?—Certainly not begun entirely by Europeans; for indigo as a colour was known and used in the East from earliest times, and therefore manufactured as well as exported by natives alone. The great extension of the manufacture of indigo in Bengal of late years is no doubt to be ascribed to British enterprise and capital, but of the present produce of the Bengal provinces (exclusive of what is produced in Oude) at least about 20,000 chests are actually grown and manufactured by natives alone, and consigned by them to other natives in Calcutta. Some of the specimens manufactured by natives are to the full as fine as the most beautiful products of European factories; but this is not generally the case; a few of the native merchants only export this article direct to Europe, from not having correspondents in this country to whom to send it; the greater part, therefore, passes always through the hands of Europeans, as the exporting merchants.

'2817. Are the inhabitants of Calcutta, Madras, and Bombay living under the protection of the King's Courts, and in daily intercourse with Europeans, equal or superior in education and intelligence to the mass of British native subjects living in the provinces under the exclusive Government of the East India Company?—They are, generally speaking, a better educated race than the inhabitants of the interior, but this I ascribe to their living in much more comfortable circumstances than the inhabitants of the interior, and coming more habitually into contact with European refinement. Although the poverty of the interior habitually consigns its inhabitants to a state of confirmed degradation, in which improvement, either of their circumstances or moral habits, seems equally hopeless, there are still to be found in every part of India numerous individuals whose natural talents and capacity are fully equal to the inhabitants of the Presidencies.

'2818. Had the commerce of Calcutta and Bombay been left as formerly, exclusively to the East India Company and the natives, what in your opinion would at this day have been the condition of the natives of those places?—They would have remained, I conceive, as stationary, or perhaps declining, as all countries invariably do which are subject to arbitrary governments and monopolies.

'2819. Then the present improved state you attribute principally to the opening of the trade with that country?—I do.

'2820. Have such of the natives of Bombay as came under your observation any repugnance to commercial pursuits, or any indisposition to engage in external and internal trade, other than what may arise from the want of their having sufficient means?—Certainly no repugnance; they are on the contrary like all the natives of India I am acquainted with, very much given to commercial and industrial pursuits, and exceedingly well qualified to succeed in them.'

'2825. Are you not able to point out a few of those taxes which principally restrict and affect the commerce of the country to which the allusion principally was?—Where the revenue is collected as it is in India, on the principle of the Government being entitled to one-half of the gross produce of the soil, and vast numbers of officers, whose acts it is impossible to control, are also employed in the realisation of this revenue, it is a moral impossibility for any people whatever to live, or prosper, so as to admit of a very extensive commercial intercourse being carried on with them.

'2826. Are those observations which you have made the result of your own personal experience, or do you state them as acquired from others ?—The result of my own personal experience in the provinces in which I have served in India, coupled with official information as regards the other districts of India, taken from a very valuable collection of papers printed by the Court of Directors in four folio volumes and other official and authentic sources.

'2827. Is the revenue levied on fruit trees, betel, pepper, sugarcane, indigo, and other similar productions a fixed and moderate land tax, or in the nature of an excise in those parts of the territories of Bombay and Madras with which you are acquainted ?—It is anything but a moderate tax; for, as I have shown in the above-mentioned work, it is in all cases exorbitant; and strange to say, in some instances even exceeds the gross produce of the lands or plantations on which it is levied.

'2828. Do you consider it practicable, under such a system as you have stated, to manufacture those articles for foreign exportation, and competition with other countries ?—It may be done in lands not subject to the afore-mentioned exorbitant tax. It may also be the case in Bengal, where the permanent settlement has been enforced for many years, and where its original ruinous pressure is no longer so severely felt; but it would be quite impossible in lands, for example, subject to the ryotwar tax, or from lands where from 45 per cent. to 50 per cent. of the gross produce is actually levied as revenue.

'2829. You have stated that the tax is equal in some cases to the produce of the land; has land then a saleable value in any part of India where the taxes take away the whole of this produce ?—I am personally acquainted with instances where the revenue assessed upon certain lands has actually exceeded the gross produce. I have also known other lands in India where a revenue has been assessed as being specifically derivable from rice lands, plantations of fruit trees, pepper, vines, and other articles, and each portion particularly described; but on comparing the assessment with the lands in question those very lands have been found to have been nothing but jungle within the memory of man. Land, however, has a saleable value in those parts of India where our revenue systems admit of some rent being derived from the land by the land-holder or proprietor; but when the whole rent is absorbed by the Government tax or revenue, as under ryotwar or Aumaunee management, the land is of course, destitute of saleable value.'

'2840. Under such a system of judicature, police, and taxation as you have described, what prospect do you think there is of the inhabitants of British India becoming either a wealthy, a prosperous, or a commercial, people, and of their conducting a trade with this country commensurate with their numbers, and the extent and fertility of the country they occupy ?—None whatever; the people of India are sufficiently commercial to answer the highest expectations that can be formed, or desired, in respect to trade between the two countries; but our local institutions, including the revenue system, must be greatly altered or modified before the natives can become wealthy or prosperous; if the condition of the natives, their habits, their wants, their rights and their interests were properly attended to, all the rest would follow as a matter of course.

'2841. Does the answer you have now given apply to the Bombay, Madras, and Bengal Presidencies, where the nature of settlement varies?—To all.

'2842. Would you make any exception with regard to those parts of India where the permanent settlement has been established?—As regards the judicial system I think no difference exists; it appears to me to have been a failure everywhere, and to be ill-suited to the habits and wants of the natives of India; the revenue system has gradually grown into improvement in Bengal, owing in a great measure to the effect produced by the opening of trade, in occasioning increased demand for the productions of lands on which an unalterable tax has been fixed; in this way I conceive that the opening of trade to India has greatly conduced to give additional value to the lands of Bengal, and to enable those who now possess estates in that quarter to obtain a rent for them, and sometimes a high rent, where in the first instance there was none at all, or scarcely a sufficiency for a scanty subsistence.'

From the foregoing and from the evidence generally some good results followed. The tone of the debates in the House of Lords and in the House of Commons was eminently reasonable, while the Act that was passed inaugurated a new era—IN WORDS.

Apparently, if one might judge from the anticipations expressed, a really new era had dawned, New Heavens and a New Earth in which alone *Right*eousness should prevail were to mark the future of Indian and English relations. Perhaps, if steam communications and the application of steam power to manufactures had not then begun to change the face of the whole world industrially, the halcyon time indicated in the Act of 1833 might have come to distressed (and, therefore, oppressed) India. Unhappily for India, once more a market was wanted, and, under the mistaken idea that the great Eastern Empire of Britain would provide more customers, and more profitable customers, by the people being kept in subjection and poor, compelled to take such exports as we chose to consider they needed, instead of enabling them to grow rich, and, themselves, of their own volition to buy of us, we entered upon the third stage of Conquest—a stage which continues to this day. It is a stage out of which thousands of millions of pounds have been made for and by England. Where that policy has secured thousands of millions sterling against the will of the people, the other policy would, probably, have brought us tens of thousands of millions from buyers who purchased out of their superfluity, and not, as now, who buy from us simply that which will only half cover their bodies against the cold o' nights at the expense of food which those bodies need for ordinary health.

III. Conquest by 'Pousta':

A Show of Fair Dealing accompanied with the Continuance of Indian National Inferiority—

1833 to ——?

Amid the glow of self-satisfaction which came to every British heart from the freeing of negro slaves, and with the anticipations which were then widely prevalent concerning the improvement of the human race by political enfranchisement and general reform, the East India Company's Charter was renewed in 1833. Something of that glow irradiates the pages of this work on which certain passages from speeches then made are printed. The climax is reached by Thomas Babington Macaulay, then Member for Leeds, who was in himself—as Law Minister in India, as Member of Parliament afterwards—to show that much of what he said was of the tongue merely and not of the heart. Contemplating the Government of India of that day, he remarked, truly enough · 'I see a Government anxiously bent on the public good. Even in its errors I recognise a paternal feeling towards the great people committed to its charge. I see toleration strictly maintained; yet I see bloody and degrading superstitions gradually losing their power. I see the morality, the philosophy, the taste, of Europe, beginning to produce a salutary effect on the hearts and understandings of our subjects. I see the public mind of India, that public mind which we found debased and contracted by the worst forms of political and religious tyranny, expanding itself to noble and just views of the ends of government and of the social duties of man.'

This was not all. He proceeded, with vivid illustration and in eloquent phrases, to indicate what India should gain from England. He said :—

'There is, however, one part of the Bill on which, after what has recently passed elsewhere, I feel myself irresistibly impelled to say a few words. I allude to that wise, that benevolent, that noble clause, which enacts that no native of our Indian Empire shall, by reason of his colour, his descent, or his religion, be incapable of holding office. At the risk of being called by that nickname which is regarded as the most opprobrious of all nicknames by men of selfish hearts and contracted minds, at the risk of being called a philosopher, I must say that to the last day of my life I shall be proud of having been one of those who assisted in the framing of the Bill which contains that clause . . . It would be, on the most selfish view of the case, far better for us that the people of India were well governed and independent of us, than ill-governed and subject to us; that they were ruled by their own kings, but wearing our broadcloth and working with our cutlery, than that they were performing their salaams to English collectors and English magistrates, but were too ignorant to value, or too poor to buy, English manufactures. To trade with civilised men is infinitely more profitable than to govern savages. That would, indeed, be a doting wisdom which, in order that India might remain a dependency, would make it a useless and costly dependency, which would keep a hundred millions of men from being our customers in order that they might continue to be our slaves.[1]

'It was, as Bernier tells us, the practice of the miserable tyrants

[1] 'Doting wisdom' prevailed then, prevails now, nearly seventy years later. Exactly what Macaulay then denounced is what is true of our administration to-day. Proof of this is given in Chapter VIII.

whom he found in India, when they dreaded the capacity and spirit of some distinguished subject, and yet could not venture to murder him, to administer to him a daily dose of the pousta, a preparation of opium, the effect of which was in a few months to destroy all the bodily and mental powers of the wretch who was drugged with it, and to turn him into a helpless idiot. The detestable artifice, more horrible than assassination itself, was worthy of those who employed it. It is no model for the English nation. We shall never consent to administer the pousta to a whole community, to stupefy and paralyse a great people whom God has committed to our charge, for the wretched purpose of rendering them more amenable to our control. What is power worth if it is founded on vice, on ignorance, on misery; if we can hold it only by violating the most sacred duties which, as governors, we owe to the governed, and which, as a people blessed with far more than ordinary measure of political liberty and of intellectual light, we owe to a race debased by three thousand years of despotism and priestcraft? We are free, we are civilised to little purpose, if we grudge to any portion of the human race an equal measure of freedom and civilisation.

'Are we to keep the people of India ignorant in order that we may keep them submissive? Or do we think that we can give them knowledge without awakening ambition? Or do we mean to awaken ambition and to provide it with no legitimate vent? Who will answer any of these questions in the affirmative? Yet one of them must be answered in the affirmative by every person who maintains that we ought permanently to exclude the natives from high office. I have no fears. The path of duty is plain before us: and it is also the path of wisdom, of national prosperity, of national honour.

'The destinies of our Indian Empire are covered with thick darkness. It is difficult to form any conjecture as to the fate reserved for a state which resembles no other in history, and which forms by itself a separate class of political phenomena. The laws which regulate its growth and its decay are still unknown to us. It may be that the public mind of India may expand under our system till it has outgrown our system; that by good government we may educate our subjects into a capacity for better government; that, having become instructed in European knowledge, they may, in some future age, demand European institutions. Whether such a day will ever come, I know not. But never will I attempt to avert or retard it. Whenever it comes, it will be the proudest day in England's history. To have found a great people sunk in the lowest depths of slavery and superstition, to have so ruled them as to have made them desirous and capable of all the privileges of citizens, would indeed be a title to glory all our own. The sceptre may pass away from us.

Unforeseen accidents may derange our most profound schemes of policy. Victory may be inconstant to our arms. But there are triumphs which are followed by no reverse. There is an empire exempt from all natural causes of decay. Those triumphs are the pacific triumphs of reason over barbarism; that empire is the imperishable empire of our arts and our morals, our literature, and our laws.'[1]

And yet, seventy years later, we have advanced but a few short and mincing steps on the road so wisely and so daringly depicted. India's peoples are now much poorer than they were then. In one district in 1900 85 per cent. of the land revenue was directly paid to the Government officials by moneylenders, the cultivators being wholly without means to fulfil their obligations, while the leading medical journal in the world,[2] through its correspondent in Bombay, estimates that nineteen millions of British Indian subjects have, during the last decennium of the nineteenth century, died of starvation, and one million from plague. So far have we fallen from the noble and generous position of seventy years ago, when Macaulay, amid all men's applause, unfolded so glowing a scheme of administration and upliftment, that such a statement as the one quoted above arouses no interest of any kind amongst the members of so humane a profession as the *Lancet* represents. Even the editor of the journal himself did not consider his correspondent's remarks called for any comments from him. The doctors, in common with nearly all other Englishmen, seem to think that may be suffered by Indians, the twentieth part of which in this country would cause a revolution, with these now quiescent and

[1] Macaulay, Speeches, p. 78. Longmans, Green, and Co., Ltd.

[2] The *Lancet*, June, 1901. The estimate alluded to above will be found recorded in its appropriate Famine place, and thus appears twice in this work, for which I make no apology:—

'Once printing may not suffice,
Though printing be not in vain;
And the mem'ry failing once or twice,
May learn, if we print again.'

thoroughly satisfied professional gentlemen amongst the leaders of the revolt. These many millions of deaths in India have become a commonplace in English current thought of so slight a character that two millions of Indian people may, on an average, die year by year in India for ten years on end, and when this fact is stated in a great medical journal, no single word of surprise or sorrow shall be expressed concerning so portentous a statement! While suffering almost beyond matching elsewhere in the world is going on, Lord George Hamilton, as Secretary of State for India, in the House of Commons, in the present writer's hearing, and Lord Curzon of Kedleston, as Viceroy and Governor-General of the Empire, take the spirit of the words of Macaulay as applicable to themselves. They are, they say, a Government anxiously bent on the public good of India. They are sensible, in their own bosoms, of 'a paternal feeling towards the great people committed to their charge.' Nevertheless, what was an impossible antithesis eighteen centuries ago, and was used by the Saviour of Mankind because of its impossibleness in practice, is not merely possible, it is actual fact to-day:

> Of Lord George Hamilton and of Lord Curzon, the Indian people ask for bread and receive a stone;[1] they beg for an egg and are given a scorpion.

Yet, while this is distinctly the fact, each of these estimable noblemen will feel as if, in my stating the above fact, which remains a fact whether I tell it or whether

[1] Actually, a stone. In the *Times of India* a British colonel, who had been engaged in famine relief service, tells of people within his cognisance who ground certain rocks to powder to mix with the scanty portion of food they were able to obtain. This substance caused grave internal injury and frequently death, which was a pity, of course, but there was nutritious food in the country—if only the people had had the means to obtain it, if only the perennial needs of the India Office were not so great. The means which would have given them food was needed to swell the £860,000,000 of pensions, interest, etc., which the India House and the India Office have expended in England since 1835.

I do not, a gross libel were uttered concerning him. As against facts, undeniable and patent facts, intentions may be Heavenly, but they should not avail as a plea in mitigation of responsibility for the consequences of what this man or that man does or leaves undone. Nor do they in the captain of a ship, be that ship a billyboy or a first-class battleship, nor in an engine-driver. But the plea is all-sufficient when the captain or driver is called an Administrator and the people affected are dark-skinned. That the dark-skinned people are British subjects makes no difference.

How has all this come about? Why is it that to-day we regard with complacency horrors which, a generation ago, moved us to our inmost depths? Why do British hearts no longer beat responsively to, or appreciate, such noble and humane sentiments regarding India as those to which Macaulay gave expression? Why is it that now there are no Munros and Elphinstones among the Governors sent to India from England, few Rickards's or John Sullivans among Indian civilians, no Sir Lionel Smith among military men? Among thousands of civilian and military officials, in office and retired, who may be named in the same breath with these? There were none on the last Public Committee on Indian Affairs—that which inquired into Expenditure in India—save Sir William Wedderburn, and the only help he had from English sources came from Mr. W. S. Caine. It was a Native of India on the Commission, Mr. Dadabhai Naoroji, and Natives of India among the witnesses, Surendra Nath Banerjee, Dinshaw E. Wacha, G. V. Gokhale, G. Subramania Aiyar, who chiefly voiced the sentiments of Rickards and of Sullivan.

Why is it?

Because, shorn of the fatal consequences which accompanied the 'pousta' of which Bernier tells, the British 'pousta' has affected our moral and mental powers as well as those of the Indian people more immediately subject to it, but at the same time has left us active in all other respects. Only our sympathy, self-respect, and righteousness have been numbed; our baser qualities have been quickened into greater activity. The need for markets for our products, combined with the fear, unacknowledged and carefully concealed but always with us, that if the Indians are permitted to occupy seats in the Executive Councils—Viceregal, Presidency, and Provincial, and in the Secretary of State's Council—it will not be possible, logically, for us to prevent a large measure of self-government being soon after accorded to India;—these things account for our utter indifference and neglect. Therefore it is that we make brave promises and break them; this is why we pretend to clear the way for Indians of capacity to rise high in the service of their country, and then 'cheat' them out of the offices we declared should be theirs—if they proved themselves to be capable of occupying them.[1] We have become so accustomed to regarding India as a milch-cow, though we never shock the facts or our sensibilities by using such an inelegant and indelicate expression, that anything which in the slightest degree appears to interfere with the continuance of this state of things seems to us to be contrary to what Divine Providence has designed on our behalf, the British nation, as every one knows, being God's own, incapable of wrong-doing. India is our wash-pot, and over the islands of the sea have we cast our shoe.

'WHATEVER IS, IS BEST.'

So I heard it stated in the House of Commons by the Secretary of State for India. Therefore, of course, it

[1] Lord Lytton, in a despatch addressed to the Secretary of State, said: 'No sooner was the Act (1833) passed than the Government began to devise means for practically evading the fulfilment of it. . . . We have had to choose between prohibiting them and cheating them, and we have chosen the least straightforward course . . . are all so many deliberate and transparent subterfuges for stultifying the Act and reducing it to a dead letter. . . . I do not hesitate to say that both the Government of England and of India appear to me up to the present moment unable to answer satisfactorily the charge of having taken every means in their power of breaking to the heart the words of promise they had uttered to the ear.'

must be so. And there is an end to all argument and to all patience with such misguided persons as those who, with irrefragible testimony in their hands, which they produce, would urge the contrary. What we choose to believe concerning India is alone that which is true. If there be evidence to the contrary, so much the worse for the evidence. We *know* we are doing well in India for India, and that knowledge suffices us. Any other opinion is condemnable, if not criminal.

APPENDICES

I[1]

EXTRACT OF REVENUE CONSULTATIONS, FORT WILLIAM, MARCH 17, 1775.

THE HONOURABLE MR. MONSON,—From the proceedings of the last consultation it appears that Bridjoo Kishore, during his short stay at Calcutta in 1174, acknowledges to have dissipated the sum of 84,500 Sicca rupees in nuzzars (presents) to the gentlemen of the Council, in a present to Mr. Coxe, and in his own expenses; that he procured for himself the office of Dewan to the Rajah, contrary to the intentions of the Ranny. In his Accounts considerable charges are made to several persons: one of the enormous sum of 2,02,485 Rupees to Mr. John Graham; another of 30,425 Rupees to Bobanny Churn Metre, Bayan to Mr. Graham; 5,500 to Cantoo Baboo, Bayan to Mr. Hastings; and 500 to Kishen Churn Chatterjea, Cantoo Baboo's servant. From this conduct it appears that Bridjoo Kishore has been an unworthy and unthrifty servant to the Rajah, disrespectful to the Ranny, and a calumniator of the servants of the Company. Unless it should hereafter be shown that the sums debited the Gentlemen should have been received by them, I think him an improper person to be employed by the Company, or to hold any office of confidence or trust near the Rajah's person, or in his household.

I therefore move, That Bridjoo Kishore be entirely dismissed from the Rajah's service; and that the Ranny be permitted to appoint such persons as she shall think proper for the education of the Rajah, her son, and for the management of his household.

The Board agree to the motion.

---

[1] From the Eleventh Report from the Select Committee on the Administration of Justice in India, pp. 759, 762–764.

Extract of Proceedings of the Committee of Revenue, Fort William, May 12, 1775.

Read the following Petition and Enclosures, from the Vackeel of the Rajah of Burdwan:—

To the Honourable Warren Hastings, Esquire, President and Governor, etc., Council of Revenue.

Honourable Sir and Sirs,—I beg leave to enclose the following papers, which are all the accounts of embezzlements which the Paishcar Roopnarain Chowdry, has been hitherto able to make out from Bridjoo Kishore's books, or rather leaves. In order to bring the Burdwan transactions under one point of view, I have brought into these Accounts what I formerly delivered into consultation on the 10th of March last.

Durbar Expenses Unjustly Made by Bridjoo Kishore Roy, out of the Consummany, etc.

Cash paid to the following persons, from Bengal Year 1174 to the month of Poos, Bengal Year 1181, as follows:—

		Rs.
Mr. John Graham, as per Account No. 1, delivered in Council on the 10th March, 1775 ...	Rs.2,02,485	
Ditto, No. 2 do. do. ...	86,065	
		2,88,550
The Honourable Mr. Stuart, as per Account enclosed, No. 3		2,17,684
Mr. Becher, ditto No. 4		2,100
Mr. James Alexander, ditto No. 5		81,000
Mr. Hastings, as per Account No. 8, delivered in Council on the 10th March, 1775		15,000
Mr. George Vansittart, as per particular Account enclosed, No. 6		35,400
Mr. Mackdonald, in Bengal Year 1179, in the 30th Assin, through the hands of Rammoo Podar, Provincial Cash-keeper		500
Mr. Fleetwood, as per particular Account enclosed, No. 7...		23,450
Mr. Shott, in Bengal Year 1181, in the Month of Augum, through the hands of Rammoo Podar, but wrote in Kazedaun Account, in the month of Poos		4,000
Mr. Swain, in Bengal Year 1179, in the 20th Assar Ackeray, through the hands of Rammoo Podar, by Callypersaud Bose		6,000
Colonel Sample, as per Account enclosed No. 8		3,000

		Rs.
Mr. Samuel Lewis, in Bengal Year 1181, in 27 Srabon, through the hands of Rammoo Podar, Provincial Cash-keeper, by Ramlocceon Mitre		2,000
Mr. Goodlad, as per particular Account enclosed, No. 9 ...		10,000
Bobanny Churn Metre, as per Account No. 5, delivered in Council on the 10th March, 1775	Rs.30,425	
Ditto, No. 10, enclosed this day	50,500	
		80,925
Callypersaud Bose, as per Account enclosed, No. 11 ...		1,01,675
And smaller sums, the whole amounting to Sicca Rupees		12,05,054 11a. 6p.

(*Signed by*) ROOPNARAIN CHOWDRY.

Calcutta, 9th May, 1775.

II

TRIBUTES, AT THE INQUIRY OF 1831, TO INDIAN FITNESS FOR OFFICIAL POSITIONS IN INDIA.

Evidence of JOHN SULLIVAN, ESQ., *Collector of Coimbatore.*

Mr. John Sullivan, of the Madras service, testified as follows :—

4769. You have stated your opinion of the native character, as far as you have had an opportunity of observing it, to be generally very favourable; do you confine that opinion to the natives of the district of Coimbatore, or to the Peninsula generally, as far as your knowledge extends?—It is a general opinion, as far as I have had an opportunity of observing it.

4770. You have visited Calcutta and Bombay?—Yes, I have.

4771. Consequently you can speak from your own personal experience?—Yes; my opinion was very favourable, particularly of the Parsees of Bombay.

4772. Would you not be disposed to place as much confidence in the natives of India as you would in your own countrymen?—Yes, if equally well treated.

4773. Are they not extremely anxious to be raised in the scale of society?—I consider them most anxious to be raised, and to feel acutely the depressed state in which they are kept.

4774. Have you not found that feeling to be general throughout India, as far as you have had an opportunity of observing?—Yes, universal, as far as my observation has gone.

4775. Are they not more anxious, in your opinion, upon that score, than even for the improvement of their worldly circumstance? —Yes, I think that the feeling dearest to their hearts, to be trusted with that degree of power and official emoluments they invariably enjoyed previously to our obtaining possession of India.

4776. Have you not found, where you have placed confidence in natives, it has generally or always been rewarded by a faithful discharge of their duties?—It has been very frequently so. I have had cause to complain, like others whose confidence has been abused.

4777. Are you not of the opinion, that the more they are encouraged, and the more they are admitted into the employment of the government of the country, the more they will improve themselves?—I am decidedly of that opinion; and I should think that the best system that could be established at this moment, would be to entrust all the details of the revenue, and all the original suits in judicature, to natives, leaving the business of control to Europeans; the natives would do the details much more effectually than Europeans.

4778. Would not the situation of European servants in India be most completely helpless without the natives?—Yes, entirely so.

4779. So that they may be said to be mainly dependent upon the natives for carrying on the affairs of the country?—I consider the most efficient officers of the Government quite helpless without the assistance of the natives.

4780. Do you consider the natives of India a very sensitive race of people, and alive to kindness?—Yes.

4781. And grateful for it?—I think so, certainly.

4782. And anxious to make suitable returns?—Yes, I think so, certainly. I speak under qualification here, but fully as much so as any other people with whom I am acquainted.

. . . .

5080. You were understood to say, that supposing the natives to be more generally employed in the different departments of Government, the expenditure of Government might be considerably diminished, do you conceive that the present Government of India is an expensive Government?—A most enormously expensive one, in the civil administration of the country.

5081. In what branches do you think a saving could be effected? —In every civil department, revenue and judicial.

5082. Do you mean by the employment of natives?—By the employment of natives, and by simplifying the machinery of government.

5089. When you say that you think the expenses of the Government might be reduced by simplifying the machinery, and calling more natives into employ, do you contemplate any reduction of the number of Europeans?—A very considerable reduction.

5090. Out of the five in Coimbatore, how many do you think might be dispensed with?—Four.

5091. Do you think that one European superintendent, with natives under him, could manage the revenue and civil concerns?—I think that he could. When I speak of the machinery of the Government, I allude to the presidency. The present mode of carrying on the Government is by a system of boards which are as complicated as anything can be. There is the revenue board, the military board, and the board of trade, so that the Government, in fact, have no direct communication with their executive officers, everything passes through these boards, and that leads to an enormous multiplication of records, and of course to great delays and expense.

5092. Would you propose that the one superintendent in the district should exercise the functions of superior judge of the district, and also of magistrate and collector of revenue?—My own idea is that the European should be confined to superintendence and control. I should conceive that both the revenue and civil and magisterial functions might be managed by the natives, with a strict European control. The greatest abuses of authority always arise out of the fiscal jurisdiction, not out of the ordinary magisterial or judicial functions.

5093. Do you conceive that the natives that would be called into action would be the persons who now act under the European officers, or that a new class of persons would be brought into operation?—Undoubtedly, those who have been regularly brought up; none but those duly qualified by previous education in the inferior offices of the civil administration should be permitted to occupy the higher grades.

5094. Are they not now found to be generally very corrupt?—If they are found to be so, it is in consequence, I conceive, entirely of our treatment of them; they have no interest in working for us, and therefore they invariably work against us when they can.

5095. And you conceive, that if they had better salaries and better prospects their corruption would be materially diminished?—I think that they would be nearly, I will not say altogether, as honest as Europeans, if we held out the same motives to them.

5096. Would not a larger extension of confidence to them produce a better state of feeling among them?—Unquestionably, that would be the result.

5097. Do you conceive that the experiment of the employment of native agency might be tried with advantage, in a particular district?—I am satisfied it might be, with great advantage—that is to say, if the experiment was made by a person favourable to its introduction, but not otherwise.

5098. Do you apprehend, that under the Madras presidency there are many persons of sufficient rank who concur with you in opinion?—I should suppose there are a considerable number; it is a growing opinion; I think it is an opinion amongst all those persons who are most conversant with the natives. Those in the trammels of a judicial office have but little to say to the natives; this is not a matter of choice but of necessity. The Collector, on the contrary, has constant intercourse with all classes of the people; he has a deep personal interest in the prosperity of the country, and his object is to consult the wishes and inclinations of the people on all subjects. On the other hand, people who pass their time at Madras know very little of the natives; but amongst that class who have free intercourse with the natives, a considerable number, I imagine, concur in opinion with me.

Evidence of W. CHAPLIN, ESQ., *Collector in Madras, and Commissioner in the Deccan.*

5296. You have stated that you conceive the reduction of the land revenue would be the best mode of improving the character and condition of the lower orders; have the goodness to state what occurs to you with a view to the amelioration of the character and condition of the superior orders.—I conceive the best way of improving the character and condition of the superior orders would be to leave open to their ambition some of the higher and more lucrative offices of the Government, and to allow them to participate as much as possible in the administration of their own country; it may not be politic to allow them to hold the highest departments, which, I conceive, should always be filled by Europeans.

5297. To what departments do you allude?—The judicial and revenue; from the chief political offices I should always exclude them.

5298. Did you say the higher or the highest?—In the highest I would not recommend their employment; those, I think, must always be in the possession of Europeans. By permitting the natives to fill a few of the high situations, we shall gradually raise a native aristocracy of our own, who, being indebted to our Government, will feel an interest in maintaining it, being sensible that they would be the first to suffer by any revolution; they would then consider the security of their own fortunes identified with the safety of the Government.

5299. How do they stand affected to our Government now?—The exclusion of natives from all offices and places of trust, except the subordinate ones, has a tendency to produce a deterioration of character. In this respect they sensibly feel the consequences of foreign rule, all the paths of honourable ambition being shut against them, and it may be feared that discontent will increase so that we may eventually become extremely unpopular. Indeed, I conceive that a general disaffection might be expected to take place, were it not for the sense generally entertained of the good faith of the Company's government, its regard for the rights of persons and property, and its strict attention to the religious customs and prejudices of its subjects. Hence, though there is little attachment to our rule, and no great interest in its stability, there is a general feeling of respect, and a thorough confidence in the integrity of the English character, which, supported by the fidelity of our native troops, forms the chief support of our tenure in India.

5300. You consider that their feelings are at present those of a conquered and degraded people ?—I conceive very much so.

5301. Are you of opinion that any improvement in the circumstances of the people has yet been effected by our government ?—I am afraid that the nature of our government is not calculated for much improvement. The natives enjoy under our sway more security of property and person, and they suffer less oppression and less exaction than under the native rule. They have generally, also, an incorrupt and impartial administration of justice, though, I am sorry to say, a very tardy and expensive one; but I conceive the degradation already adverted to tends very much to check improvement. The nature of our government is, in fact, adverse to improvement. Its officers from the Court of Directors here, and from the Governor and Council in India, downwards, are constantly fluctuating. Partial and limited experience is no sooner acquired than a change takes place before it can be brought into effectual operation. Plans of improvement are followed for a time, and then relinquished under a new Chairman of the Court of Directors, a new Governor-General, or a new administrator of the revenue; these frequent revolutions, by flood and field, occasion, in my opinion, a vacillation in the administration of affairs extremely injurious to the interests of the community in India.

5442. The Committee have no further question to put to you, but would be glad to know whether there are any suggestions you would make on any topics which have or have not been touched upon ?—I am not prepared to offer to the Committee any suggestions further than to recommend, as far as I am able to do, the expediency of making throughout our territories the land assessment as light as the finances of government will admit, but above all to fix the limit of the field assessment, as the only sure means of affording protection to the ryot and providing against mal-administration. This I presume to be the grand secret for the good government and the maintenance of tranquillity in India.

5443. Upon the whole the Committee are to understand that the more you have seen of the natives, the better your opinion of them ?—I have always formed a good opinion of the native character generally; I think they will bear an advantageous comparison with the natives of any country in the world.

INDIAN CHARACTER AND SUPERIOR ATTAINMENTS.

Evidence of Major-General SIR L. SMITH, K.C.B.

5481. You have had a great deal of experience, enabling you to know the character of native officers?—I have.

5482. You have had also great means of knowing what European officers have done?—I have.

5483. Speaking of the conduct of both deliberately, what is your opinion of the comparison?—I think, generally speaking, native officers are on all questions of evidence, and certainly in reference to their own customs and laws, infinitely more to be depended upon than European officers.

5600. What is your opinion of the moral character of the natives of India generally?—I think, considering the disadvantages they have been under many years—not those of Bombay, but those above the Ghauts, where they have had formerly a very vicious government—they are a very good people, and in my opinion they have been greatly belied by all those who have written about them.

5601. Are they a cruel people?—By no means; all their chiefs were of rude military habits, which made the body of the people what they were, rude and violent, but they are essentially a good people; and where they have taken to cultivation, they are one of the most quiet, orderly, people I have ever lived amongst. In my own cantonment I had generally before the war upwards of 80,000 followers, and for four years we had only four capital crimes; what the punishments were I do not know, for we sent them to the Peishwa, we had not then any criminal law of our own; I do not believe there are many parts of Europe which could boast of such absence of crime.

5616. What do you think would be the effect on public feeling of giving the natives a power of deciding on the crimes committed by Christians?—I think the Europeans in general at first would be displeased at it. There is a tone, of course in proportion as they are ignorant of the natives, of superior feelings—a superiority which perhaps would make them shrink from coming into close contact with them in the exercise of such duties, but that ought to be done away; and it is to give them a beginning, and make the Europeans come in contact more with the people of the country, that I think the greatest good may be done to the country. They would resist a little, I think, at first; some of them are very haughty, some of them dislike natives, but do that away by bringing them together by law, and one party will feel himself more respectable, and both in the end be satisfied.

5618. Would there be any feeling on the part of Europeans in acting with natives on this service?—Perhaps at first they would object, in proportion as some men find it very difficult to conquer old tastes and prejudices; the greatest fault of Europeans in India is that they are a little too aristocratical or distant, and keep aloof from the natives, not mixing half enough with them.

5619. Would you have any objection to be tried by a jury of natives?—No, I should not, myself, but I think I am, perhaps, an exception to most.

5624. You have said that the people generally have advanced in knowledge and intelligence during the last few years?—Yes, to a great degree.

5625. Are you speaking of the whole population of the country? —Yes; a school was established in the Deccan before I came away, and I had an immense number of applications to get poor boys in from my native friends,[1] and in Bombay it has been going on for many years, and is on a most beautiful footing on the Lancasterian system.

5626. Do you consider that the people consider themselves degraded by not being admitted into the superior offices?—I think they must feel it.

5627. Is that not likely to increase with their increasing intelligence?—Most decidedly, it must increase.

5628. How is it to be met, if that is so?—Let them participate in the administration of the country, I should say.

5629. Should you say it would be safer for the government of this country to allow that intelligence to increase under that feeling of separation from the English, or to attempt to identify the natives and the English?—I think the first effect of it will certainly be, that it will tend to identify and make the people happy; I think that the ultimate end, when you have succeeded in educating the large proportion of the people, will be that they must find by every amelioration that you can give them, that they are still a distinct and degraded people, and if they can find the means of driving you out of the country they will do it.

5630. Can you prevent their finding out their strength?—I think the circumstance is so unprecedented in the history of man, that a handful of foreigners should continue to govern a country of sixty millions, which is fashionably called the empire of opinion, that the moment you have educated them they must feel that the effect of education will be to do away with all the prejudices of sects and religions by which we have hitherto kept the country—the Mussalmans against Hindoos, and so on; the effect of education will be to expand their minds, and show them their vast power.

5631. Would not the abolition of the existing disqualifications of natives, which they feel to be a degradation, and their participation with Europeans in all the advantages of our civil institutions in India, be a material corrective of such a tendency arising out of education? —For a time, as I have said before, no doubt it will.

[1] A poor Deccani boy from this very region, helped by Mr. J. N. Tata to continue his education at an English university, was bracketed senior wrangler at Cambridge in 1899.

5632. Would it not identify them with British dominion, and give them a common interest in preserving it, which they do not now feel? —To a certain extent it might do so.

5633. Do you not consider that such securities for the attachments of the inhabitants of India would be both more honourable to the country, and more to be permanently depended upon than any other attempts to govern India by keeping its natives in darkness and ignorance?—I would decidedly enlighten them as much as possible; but then you lose the country.

5634. Supposing any rival European Power were to find its way into India, would it not, by holding out the abolition of the existing disqualifications of natives, find the certain means of seducing them from their allegiance to us?—If they can once establish themselves, of course it would depend vastly on the Power; they know there is no European Power like ours likely to conquer the country.

5636. Supposing those disqualifications were removed in time by ourselves, would any inducement remain to the people of India to prefer the dominion of any other European Power?—No, I do not think any European Power could have any influence with them, if we use our power properly, by giving them a participation in the government of the country, and promoting education and civilisation.

5639. If in the progress of time India were to become sufficiently instructed to understand the principles of the Christian religion, and to comprehend the nature of government, such as that which belongs to the British Constitution, is it your opinion that in that state of civilisation India would permit itself for any length of time to be governed by the authority of England?—No, I should say not; taking the history of nations, that they would feel the value of governing themselves; it is human nature, I think, that they should.

5640. Is it not the case that in that state of civilisation which you contemplate as of advantage, the British dominion in India must also be contemplated by you as to cease?—I have expressly said, that I feel the effect of imparting education will be to turn us out of the country.

5641. If that should take place, are you prepared to say that India may not be of more value to us than it now is?—By no means; America has been of more value to us separate than as a colony.

5642. What portion of the population of India is most attached to the British rule, whether the most ignorant or the most intelligent; or, in a word, is there any part of India with which you are acquainted where the attachment to the British Government is so strong as at Bombay?—I should say the most intelligent; I look upon it the people of Bombay, who are intelligent and well educated, have higher expectations from those advantages, and look up to Government with more confidence to derive those advantages; therefore that they must have stronger excitement of loyalty and affection to Government than those who are perfectly ignorant.

5643. Are the Committee to understand your opinion to be, that in proportion as India becomes civilised and instructed, there would be a desire for independence ?—I should think there naturally would.

5644. Even if that independence took place, you are not prepared to say that India might not be equally valuable to England as it now is ?—Certainly not; there would not be such an outlet for gentlemen's sons for appointments and things of that kind, but I should think the profit of the country would be as great; there would be none of the expense and all the advantages.

CHAPTER II

THE BEGINNING OF THE CENTURY: WHERE DOES INDIA STAND?

India in a Worse Position To-day than on January 1, 1801.
A Condescension to Particulars:
- **(*a*) Wealth.**
- **(*b*) The Poverty of the People.**

A Significant Contrast.

- **(*c*) National Industries.**
- **(*d*) Government Service.**
- **(*e*) Moral, Intellectual, and Spiritual, Position.**

Appendix:
How Lascars voyaging to England would suffer moral harm and India material damage.

'The arrival in the port of London of Indian produce in Indian-built ships created a sensation among the monopolists which could not have been exceeded if a hostile fleet had appeared in the Thames. The shipbuilders of the port of London took the lead in raising the cry of alarm; they declared that their business was on the point of ruin, and that the families of all the shipwrights in England were certain to be reduced to starvation.'—TAYLOR's *History of India*, p. 216.

1801.	1901.
Lord WELLESLEY,	Lord CURZON,
Governor - General.	Viceroy and Governor-General.

WITH the beginning of a new century it may not be unsuitable to ask and to answer the question contained in the heading to this chapter. So far as the present writer is concerned there can, unhappily, be no hesitation as to what must, of necessity, be the reply. The question cannot, with any approach to accuracy, be answered save in some such sentence as this:—

India stands in a terribly worse position to-day than that which it occupied when the first dawn of 1801 trembled across the bay of Bengal and flashed upon the hilltops on the north-eastern coast of Hindustan.

It matters not in what direction one looks, so far as the material prosperity of the vast mass of the population goes, the answer must be seriously adverse in comparison with the ancient time. Not now is prosperity, but once was prosperity. In all of a material character that goes to make a prosperous realm, India on January 1, 1901, was a greater number of leagues behind India on January 1, 1801, than I, for one, care to try to count. To finish assertion and to come to facts:—

Wealth.

One hundred years ago, in spite of the conveyance ('convey, the wise it call,' said Shakspeare) of vast amounts of ill-gotten wealth by civilians and military men and others to England, especially from Bengal and Madras, there was still much accumulated wealth throughout the continent. Other conquerors before us in India settled in the country; what they stole remained in India; they spent it or hoarded it in India. It might be taken from Bengal to Delhi, but much of it found its way back to Bengal, and Bengalis in high office in Delhi had their fair share of what was available. Save in a few historical instances India's treasure was not removed from India, and even what was taken was not extraordinary in amount. Nearly the whole of the wealth remaining in the country a hundred years ago has been so drained away that there is now less of popular pecuniary reserve in India than in any civilised country in the world. During the famine of 1900 so completely had the reserves been exhausted that a large number of very ancient coins found their way into circulation, and, in 1901, were offered to numismatists in London. How terrible the drain has been may be judged by various statements made at divers times. Notable amongst them Montgomery Martin's remarks of nearly seventy years ago. 'The annual drain of £3,000,000 from British India,' he said, 'has mounted in thirty years, at 12 per cent. (the usual Indian rate) compound interest, to the enormous sum of £723,900,000 sterling.' From that day to this there has been no cessation in the flow. More: with every year it has increased until the stream which in 1830 was regarded as almost beyond control, has increased tenfold, and has become altogether beyond control. It is true the area drained is larger now than then, but the proportion of wealth annually taken is far greater. During the closing ten years of the nineteenth century it became beyond control, to the extent of involving more than half the cultivators in the Empire in almost irremediable debt;[1] it has turned the moneylender into the real lord and sovereign of India, while twenty millions of patient, suffering, excellent, people have died prematurely from want of food and from the diseases occasioned by privation and from plague. During the last thirty years of the century the average drain cannot have been far short of £30,000,000 per year, or, in the thirty years, £900,000,000, not reckoning interest! Against this great and forcible withdrawal, forcible by economic law in the first instance, by British might in the second, is to be set the money loaned by England to India for warlike purposes and public works, only a small portion of which has been wealth-creating to an appreciable extent, so far as the masses of the people are concerned, and the sum total of which does not compare with the drain to England. And, further, all of it has to be repaid some day. It may, in another chapter, be possible to strike the balance, although only approximately, between the two sides of the account,

[1] In the Bombay Presidency, according to the Macdonnell Famine Commission Report, four-fifths of the cultivators are indebted.

7

but the very best that can be shown will leave an almost unthinkable deficit on India's side, a deficit only realisable as it may be brought to bear year by year on the existing population, and thus carried to the individual home. The argument applied to the individual Indian will be found developed at greater length elsewhere. Here, it can only be stated in outline. That India is not far from collapse is proved by the frequent famines now prevailing and the ominous fact that although, even in the worst of years—the years 1900 and 1901—enough food was grown to feed the people, the people had not the wherewithal to buy the food which would have kept them alive, and, obtaining which, with their own means, they would have retained their homes and not have lost their families and their few possessions. The present Secretary of State (Lord George Hamilton) has made the expression, that the recent famines are famines of money and not of food, a part of current historical phraseology. It is not, however, an accurate statement, save to a very limited extent. There would not be food enough for all the people, nor anything like food enough, were a favourable response given to the Christian's prayer: 'Give us this day our daily bread.' My information and calculations lead me to express the opinion that if provision were made for as much to be eaten as is needed for health, three-fourths of the country, for at least three months in the year, would be on short rations and many millions of people on none at all. Speaking in general terms, India, at the beginning of this century, has *no working capital*: all her working capital has, under a mistaken system of government, been drained to another country, and she is, in herself, wholly resourceless, as resources go among modern nations. She cannot recuperate herself from herself in existing conditions.

The Poverty of the People.

If the foregoing remarks be sustainable, it follows that now there is vastly much more requirement of the necessaries of life among the people than was the case a hundred years ago. Statistics for 1801, by which an exact comparison can be made, are not available. One of the witnesses at the inquiry which preceded the renewal of the Charter in 1833, said[1] :—

'It may be asked if the labourer of India is placed on a par with the labourer of Europe. In India, within our own provinces, it may be said there is no distress except in times of scarcity; and since we have ensured to the merchant the unrestricted sale of his grain, prices have adapted themselves to the productiveness of the crops, and there has been no scarcity or famine similar to what was known when the grain merchant was forced to sell his grain at whatever price the Government of the country was pleased to dictate. In India the labourer of our provinces has no difficulty in maintaining himself and his family with independence without resorting to the charity of the public, and we know the reverse to be the case in our native country.'

Here, too, are rough means by which the grave decadence of the past twenty years may be apprehended :—

In 1880: 'There remain forty millions of people who go through life on insufficient food.'—*Sir W. W. Hunter* at Birmingham.

In 1893: The *Pioneer* sums up Mr. Grierson's facts regarding the various sections of the population in Gaya, and remarks that the conclusion is by no means encouraging. 'Briefly, it is that all the persons of the labouring classes, and ten per cent. of the cultivating and artisan classes, or forty-five per cent. of the total population, are insufficiently clothed, or insufficiently fed, or both. In Gaya district this would give about a million persons without sufficient means of support. If we assume that the circumstances of Gaya are not exceptional—and there is no reason for thinking otherwise—it follows that nearly one hundred millions of people in British India

[1] Mr. Wood, p. 580, 'Affairs of the East India Company,' 1833 (445–II.).

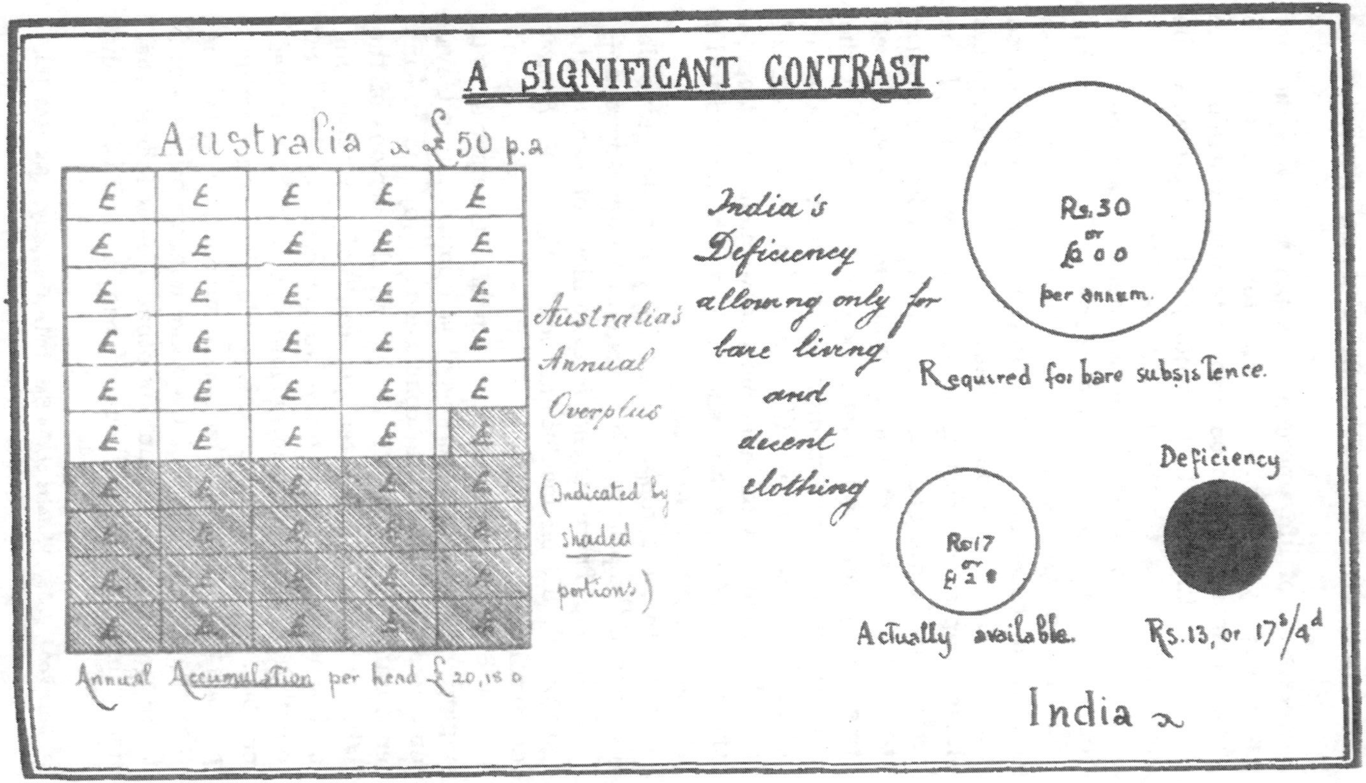
A SIGNIFICANT CONTRAST
Australia x £50 p.a
Australia's Annual Overplus
(Indicated by shaded portions)
Annual Accumulation per head £20,18 0
India's Deficiency allowing only for bare living and decent clothing
Rs.30 or £2 0 0 per annum.
Required for bare subsistence.
Rs17 or £1 2 8
Actually available.
Deficiency
Rs.13, or 17s/4d
India x

are living in extreme poverty.' The whole of the article from which this passage is taken is quoted later.

In 1901: 'The poverty and suffering of the people are such as to defy description. In fact, for nearly fifteen years there has been *a continuous famine in India* owing to high prices.' Thus, on May 16, 1901, wrote an Indian Publicist of ripe experience and wide knowledge.

Since Sir William Hunter's remarks were made the population has increased (or is alleged to have increased) by nearly thirty millions. Meanwhile the income of the Empire has greatly decreased during this period. Wherefore this follows: that if, with the same income, in 1880 forty millions were insufficiently fed, the additional millions cannot have had, cannot now have, enough to eat; this, again, ensues:—

40,000,000 *plus*, say, 30,000,000, make 70,000,000; and *there are this number of continually hungry people in British India at the beginning of the twentieth century.*

That is my own estimate, made several months ago, and, like all my estimates, is too conservative; for it will have been observed that the *Pioneer*, the ever-ready apologist for British rule in India, eight years ago put the 'British people who are living in extreme poverty' at 'one hundred millions.'

NATIONAL INDUSTRIES.

These have been ruthlessly destroyed, and, during the earlier part of the century, destroyed without any pretence at concealment of the circumstance that English industries were to be benefited by the destruction. The passage quoted at the head of this chapter furnishes a notable illustration. A hundred years ago shipbuilding was in so excellent a condition in India that ships could be (and were) built which sailed to the Thames in company with British-built ships and under the convoy of British frigates. The Governor-General in 1800, reporting to his masters in Leadenhall Street, London, said: 'The port of Calcutta contains about 10,000 tons of shipping, built in India, of a description calculated for the conveyance of cargoes to England.'[1] The teakwood vessels of Bombay were greatly superior to the 'oaken walls of old England.' Let note be taken of this testimony[2]:—

It is certain that our present policy prevents us availing ourselves of all the advantages which our Indian possessions are capable of producing. Perhaps the time is not yet arrived when this question can be calmly, impartially, and without prejudice, discussed. Nations are slower than individuals in ascertaining their real interests, and it is only lately, notwithstanding that we have acknowledged the scarcity of timber at home for shipbuilding, that we have endeavoured to avail ourselves of the valuable productions of the forests of India.

In Bombay alone, two ships of the line, or one ship and two frigates, can be produced to the British navy every eighteen months. The docks at Bombay are capable of containing ships of any force.

Situated as Bombay is, between the forests of Malabar and Gujarat, she receives supplies of timber with every wind that blows. Flax of a good quality is also the produce of our territories in India. It is calculated that every ship in the navy of Great Britain is renewed every twelve years. It is well known that teakwood-built ships last fifty years and upwards. Many ships Bombay-built, after running fourteen or fifteen years, have been bought into the navy and were considered as strong as ever. The *Sir Edward Hughes* performed, I believe, eight voyages as an Indiaman before she was purchased for the navy. No Europe-built Indiaman is capable of going more than six voyages with safety.

Ships built at Bombay also are executed by one-fourth cheaper than in the docks of England.

Let the result of these observations be reduced to calculation, and the advantages will be evident.

Every eighteen months two ships-of-the-line can be added to the British navy, four in three years, and in fifteen years twenty ships-of-the-line. Thus in fifteen years we should be in possession of a fleet

---

[1] Again: 'From the quantity of private tonnage now at command in the port of Calcutta, from the state of perfection which the art of shipbuilding has already attained in Bengal (promising a still more rapid progress, and supported by abundant and increasing supplies of timber), it is certain that this port will always be able to furnish tonnage, to whatever extent may be required, for conveying to the port of London the trade of the private British merchants of Bengal.'—*Lord Wellesley*, in 1800.

[2] 'Considerations on the Affairs of India, written in the year 1811,' by Lieutenant-Colonel A. Walker. H. L., 1853 (445–VI.), p. 316.

which would last fifty years. The English-built ships requiring to be renewed every twelve years, the expense is quadruple. Suppose, therefore, a ship built in England to cost £100, in fifty years it would cost £400, but as a ship of equal force to last the same period would cost in India only £75 of the sum, the difference in favour of India-built ships would be £325 per cent.

Say that a ship-of-the-line in its original cost is £100,000.

	£
Four times renewed	400,000
A Bombay ship...	75,000
Saving	£325,000

This calculation is excessive, but it is chosen to show how much may be saved, even although one-half may be erroneous.

Were it not for our numerous captures we should probably have had some difficulty in keeping our navy complete. Has it been found that the number of prizes brought into our ports has diminished the demand for our own ships; or has it had the effect of producing any of those consequences which jealousy imputes to our Indian-built shipping?

The docks that have recently been constructed at Bombay, under the superintendence of Major Cooper of the Engineers, are elegant specimens of architecture, and excite universal admiration. They are capable of containing vessels of any force.

In Bengal, Prince of Wales Island, and other maritime stations, excellent ships may be constructed, and the number may be increased to a much greater extent than the above estimate; but the estimate has been purposely confined to Bombay, which is furnished with docks, and the ships are there constructed with more advantage than anywhere else; and it is our grand naval arsenal in India.

Of course no heed was given to such wise counsel. Nor, were opportunity to offer for India to-day to render like service to the Empire at large, would it receive any greater favour.

To mention the above is to show, as by a lightning flash on a dark night, how far, industrially, with the sole exception of the spinning and weaving of cotton by steam machinery in Bombay, the India of Lord Curzon is behind the India of Lord Wellesley. As, again and again, I have wandered through the records of obscurant administration in India during the past century, growing more and more woeful as instance upon instance forced upon me the unteachability of the Anglo-Indian civilian, scarcely anything has struck me more forcibly than the manner in which the Mistress of the Seas in the Western World has stricken to death the Mistress of the Seas in the East. Statistics for the beginning of the century are not available—to me at least; I can only learn about India that which is permitted to appear in Blue Books and in works written about India—official generally. But from the Statistical Abstracts I gather these significant facts:—

1857.		Vessels.	Tonnage.
Indian	(entered and cleared)...	34,286	1,219,958
British and British-Indian	,, ...	59,441	2,475,472
1898–99.			
Indian	(entered and cleared)...	2,802	188,038
British and British-Indian	,, ...	6,219	7,685,009
Foreign	... ...	1,165	1,297,604

That is to say, the Indian tonnage in 1898–99, compared with British and foreign in 1857, is one-seventieth of the whole trade now against one-half then. And, from Mr. O'Conor's report on the trade of India for 1899–1900, which carries the figures a year later than the above, I take the following funereal comment on the extinction of Indian shipping:—

Native craft continues to decline:—

	No.	Tons.
1898–99	2,802	188,038
1899–1900	1,676	109,813

As for Indian manufactures generally, on the theories prevalent early in the nineteenth century, they were deliberately throttled. The circumstance that the British authorities acted in accordance with the teaching of the times is a plea which is barred by the principle on which we held the country. The story I am about to tell throws a curious light on our frequent professions that we remain in India for the good of the Indian people first, and for any benefit to ourselves next. 'No Government ever manifested, perhaps, a more constant solicitude to promote the welfare of a people; and it is with satisfaction and with pride that I can bear an almost unqualified testimony in its favour.' Thus Mr. St. George Tucker, a Director of the East India Company, who, immediately, proceeds to make his own eulogy ridiculous by substituting a statement of fact for a flight of fancy. He said:—

> On the other hand, what is the commercial policy which we have adopted in this country in relation with India? The silk manufactures, and its piece goods made of silk and cotton intermixed, have long since been excluded altogether from our markets; and, of late, partly in consequence of the operation of a duty of 67 per cent., but chiefly from the effect of superior machinery, the cotton fabrics which heretofore constituted the staple of India, have not only been displaced in this country, but we actually export our cotton manufactures to supply a part of the consumption of our Asiatic possessions.[1]

We compelled India to take our goods either with no import, or with a merely nominal import, duty. How we treated Indian articles appears from what Mr. Tucker says in the preceding paragraph, but the testimony of Mr. Rickards,[2] may be cited. He remarks:—

> The duties on many articles of East India produce are also enormously high, apparently rated on no fixed principle, and without regard to market price. For example:—

Aloes, subject to a duty of from			70	to 280	per cent.
Assafœtida	,,	,,	288	,, 622	,,
Cardamums	,,	,,	150	,, 266	,,
Coffee	,,	,,	105	,, 373	,,
Pepper	,,	,,	266	,, 400	,,
Sugar	,,	,,	94	,, 393	,,
Tea	,,	,,	6	,, 100	,,

> . . . The rates of duty imposed on Indian imports into Britain, when compared with the exemption from duty of British staples into India (cotton goods being subject to a duty of only 2½ per cent.), constitute an important feature in the present question. Indians

---

[1] From a letter to Mr. Huskisson, written in 1823. 'Memorials of Indian Government.' Richard Bentley, 1853, p. 494.

[2] Report Select Committee, East India Company, 1831. Appendix, p. 581.

within the Company's jurisdiction, like English, Scotch, or Irish, are equally subjects of the British Government. To make invidious distinctions, favouring one class but oppressing another, all being subjects of the same empire, cannot be reconciled with the principles of justice; and whilst British imports into India are thus so highly favoured, I know that Indo-British subjects feel it a great grievance that their commodities when imported into England should be so enormously taxed.

The following charges on cotton manufactures in 1813 are significant:—

	£	s.	d.
Flowered or stitched muslins of white calicoes (for every £100 of value)	32	9	2
And further ditto ... ... ditto ...	11	17	6
Calicoes and dimities ... ... ditto ...	81	2	11
And further ditto	3	19	2
Cotton, raw (per 100 lbs.)	0	16	11
Cotton, manufactured ditto...	81	2	11
Articles of manufacture of cotton, wholly or in part made up, not otherwise charged with duty (for every £100 of value)	32	9	2
Hair or goat's wool, manufactures of, per cent....	84	6	3
Lacquered ware, per cent.	81	2	11
Mats and matting, per cent.	84	6	3
Oil of Aniseed, per cent.	84	6	3
Oil of Cocoanut, per ton	84	3	3
Tea, in 1814, custom and excise	96	0	0

These burdensome charges were subsequently removed, but only after the export trade in them had, temporarily or permanently, been destroyed. The manufacturing industries which have been established during the century will be found described in some detail in the chapter on The Resources of India—Who Possess Them? When, however, all has been considered and allowed for, it remains that, practically, in the clash of machinery in the million and more of the world's workshops to-day there is no contributing sound from India, a British country. One-fifth of the people of the world, in an age of mechanical production, take no recognisable part in manufacture by machinery. Once they occupied a respectable manufacturing and exporting position; now they have no position as such save in the Western Presidency, and there side by side with the most poverty-stricken of all the agricultural regions in India.

GOVERNMENT SERVICE.

In 1801 a large part of India had not come under British domination: it was not indeed until nearly fifty years later that the Lawrences and others of their day began the 'settlement' of the region of the Five Rivers. With what disastrous result a previous 'settlement' in the North-Western Provinces was arranged the *Pioneer's* description of the settlement of Gurgaon by John Lawrence will tell.[1] A hundred years ago the many Indian Courts provided positions of influence, honour, emolument, which gave scope to the proper ambition of thousands of able men, benefited tens of thousands of families, and produced, by the lavish expenditure of the resources of the country *in the country*, a widespread prosperity and personal contentment. Wars, it is true, now and then occurred; acts of rapine and cruelty were not unknown. But for ten persons affected by such incidents ten thousand persons were unaffected, while variety of service and occupation were open in a vast number of directions; these, by the opportunities they provided, more than counter-balanced the injustice which was but occasional. In all parts of their own land, save that already under British domination, Indians of a

[1] Gurgaon was, in 1877, a district with nearly 700,000 inhabitants.

From 1837 (Lord Lawrence—then Mr. Lawrence—being Settlement Officer) the district has been steadily rack-rented.

In 1877 the rents were raised.

Rains failed, crops were ruined, the Government demand was nevertheless exacted, with these consequences, as officially admitted:—

At the end of five years it was found that 80,000 people had died; 150,000 head of cattle had perished; 2,000,000 rupees of debt, to pay the Government rents, incurred; the people were emaciated, and unable to reap a good crop when it came.

Mr. S. S. Thorburn, ex-Commissioner in the Panjab, says the first effect of the British occupation of the Panjab was over-assessment, and, referring specially to Gurgaon, remarks, 'at first ignorantly over-assessed by us.'

hundred years ago could become that for which their personal bravery and intellectual acumen fitted them. Every civilised country requires a certain number of high officials: where now Europeans occupy important positions, Indians were then at the top of the tree.[1] In a phrase,

[1] In 'Asia and Europe,' by Meredith Townsend, published by Archibald Constable and Co., Ltd., Westminster, the following observations on this point occur:—

'It is the active classes who have to be considered, and to them our rule is not, and cannot be, a rule without prodigious drawbacks. One of these, of which they are fully conscious, is the gradual decay of much of which they were proud, the slow death, which even the Europeans perceive, of Indian art, Indian culture, Indian military spirit. Architecture, engineering, literary skill, are all perishing out, so perishing that Anglo-Indians doubt whether Indians have the capacity to be architects, though they built Benares; or engineers, though they dug the artificial lakes of Tanjore; or poets, though the people sit for hours or days listening to rhapsodists as they recite poems, which move them as Tennyson certainly does not move our common people. Another is, that the price of what they think imperfect justice is that they shall never right themselves, never enjoy the luxury of vengeance, never even protect their personal dignity and honour, about which they are as sensitive as Prussian officers. They may not even kill their wives for going astray. And the last and greatest one of all is the total loss of the interestingness of life.

'It would be hard to explain to the average Englishman how interesting Indian life must have been before our advent; how completely open was every career to the bold, the enterprising, or the ambitious. The whole continent was open as a prize to the strong. Nothing was settled in fact or in opinion except that the descendants of Timour the Lame were entitled to any kind of ascendency they could get and keep. No one not of the great Tartar's blood pretended to the universal throne, but with that exception every prize was open to any man who had in himself the needful force. Scores of sub-thrones were, so to speak, in the market. A brigand, for Sivajee was no better, became a mighty sovereign. A herdsman built a monarchy in Baroda. A body-servant founded the dynasty of Scindia. A corporal cut his way to the independent crown of Mysore. The first Nizam was only an officer of the Emperor. Runjeet Singh's father was what Europeans would call a prefect. There were literally hundreds who founded principalities, thousands of their potential rivals, thousands more who succeeded a little less grandly, conquered estates, or became high officers under the new princes. Each of these men had his own character and his own renown among his countrymen, and each enjoyed a position such as is now unattainable in Europe, in which he was released from law, could indulge his own fancies, bad or good, and was fed every day and all day with the special flattery of Asia—that willing submissiveness to mere volition which is so like adoration, and which is to its recipients the most intoxicating of delights. Each, too, had his court of followers, and every courtier shared in the power, the luxury, and the adulation accruing to his

the measure of Indian degradation now, as compared with then, may be thus expressed :—

Not one Indian, during a whole century, has occupied a seat in the Supreme, or Presidency, or Provincial, Executive Councils, nor in the Secretary of State's Council in England.

It is true there has only been an average of about one hundred and fifty millions of people in British India

lord. The power was that of life and death; the luxury included possession of every woman he desired; the adulation was, as I have said, almost religious worship. Life was full of dramatic changes. The aspirant who pleased a great man rose to fortune at a bound. The adventurer whose band performed an act of daring was on his road to be a satrap. Any one who could do anything for "the State"—that is for any ruler—build a temple, or furnish an army with supplies, or dig a tank, or lend gold to the Court, became at once a great man, honoured of all classes, practically exempt from law, and able to influence the great current of affairs. Even the timid had the chance, and, as Finance Minister, farmers of taxes, controllers of religious establishments, found for themselves great places in the land. For all this which we have extinguished we offer nothing in return, nor can we offer anything. We can give place, and, for reasons stated elsewhere, it will be greedily accepted, but place is not power under our system, nor can we give what an Asiatic considers power—the right to make volition executive; the right to crush an enemy and reward a friend; the right, above all, to be free from that burden of external laws, moral duties, and responsibilities to others with which Europeans have loaded life. We cannot even let a Viceroy be the ultimate appellate court, and right any legal wrong by supreme fiat—a failure which seems to Indians, who think the Sovereign should represent God, to impair even our moral claim to rule. This interestingness of life was no doubt purchased at the price of much danger and suffering. The Sovereign, the favourite, or the noble, could cast down as easily as they raised up, and intrigue against the successful never ended. The land was full of violence. Private war was universal. The great protected themselves against assassination as vigilantly as the Russian Emperor does. The danger from invasion, insurrection, and, above all, mutiny, never ended. I question, however, if these circumstances were even considered drawbacks. They were not so considered by the upper classes of Europe in the Middle Ages, and those upper classes were not tranquilised, like their rivals in India, by a sincere belief in fate. I do not find that Texans hate the wild life of Texas, or that Spanish-speaking Americans think the personal security which the dominance of the English-speaking Americans would assure to them is any compensation for loss of independence. I firmly believe that to the immense majority of the active classes of India the old time was a happy time; that they dislike our rule as much for the leaden order it produces as for its foreign character; and they would welcome a return of the old disorders if they brought back with them the old vividness, and, so to speak, romance of life.'

throughout this period, and that number of human beings MAY never have produced one man fit for such a position anywhere in the world. Yet, in the Feudatory States—so far as Residential control would permit, which was not very far—some of the finest administrators of the century in any country have arisen, men who may be matched, so far as opportunity served, with the leading statesmen of any European country or the United States of America. The men to whom I refer, with a very few exceptions, were subordinate officers in the British service, and, but for the chance given by the Feudatory States, would never have risen higher than a Deputy Collectorship. In Sir Salar Jung, Sir Madhava Row, Sir Dinkar Row, Sir K. Seshadri Aiyar, and many other Indian administrators, were found instruments which in the old days of faith (days now, alas! destroyed for Anglo-Saxondom by Imperialism so-called) would have been regarded as Providential provisions to solve the difficulties in the way of a true and righteous government of India. Compare Sir Salar Jung's administration with that of the British Provinces. As against the interference of the Resident and the friction caused by the retention of the Berars, (although each of the articles of the treaty had been or would be complied with—powerful hindrances these to successful work—) must be placed the force of one mind continuously acting towards a given end. This gave Sir Salar Jung and all other native-Indian statesmen, in their respective spheres, a power the greatness of which may easily be overlooked. What Lord Salisbury has said of the rule of India in its higher ranks, that it was 'a government of incessant changes'—('It is,' he added, 'the despotism of a line of kings whose reigns are limited by climatic causes to five years')—may be said also of British rule in little. After making full allowance for continuity of policy, Sir Salar Jung's achievements rank before those of any administrator with like duties and opportunities which India has known. Take this series of comparisons prepared by me sixteen years ago:—

GROSS LAND REVENUE COLLECTED.

The Nizam's Dominions.		*The British Indian Empire.*	
	Rs.		£
Collected in 1853 ...	64,85,098	Collected in 1853 ...	16,190,000
" in 1881 ...	1,83,40,861	" in 1881 ...	21,860,000
Increase	Rs.1,18,55,763	Increase	£5,650,000
Percentage of increase 260 per cent.		Percentage of increase less than 25 per cent.	

INCREASE OF REVENUE.

Sir Salar Jung's last year of office compared with his first shows:—

1853.	Rs.	1881–82.	Rs.
Total revenue	68,01,130	Total revenue	3,11,40,538

Or an increase of 357·84 per cent. This was the result of unremitting care and consideration, combined with the exercise of the often disunited qualities of prudence and stonewall firmness. In this unique combination of qualities the late Sir Salar Jung stands head and shoulders above his contemporaries—Anglo-Indian and Indian.

COST OF COLLECTION OF CUSTOMS REVENUE.

The Nizam's Dominions.	Rs. a. p.	*The Berars.*[1]	Rs. a. p.
Average per cent.	6 7 3	Average per cent. ...	45 14 5

Or seven times higher!

REVENUE COMPARISONS.

The Nizam's Dominions.		*The British Indian Empire.*	
	Rs.		£
Revenue in 1853 ...	68,01,130	Revenue in 1853	28,610,000
" in 1881 ...	3,11,40,658	" in 1881	68,370,000
Increase	Rs.2,43,39,528	Increase	£39,760,000
Increase nearly 357·84 per cent.		Increase 230 per cent.	

[1] The condition in H.H.'s districts and in the Berars are exactly the same, or should be, seeing the territories join each other. The expensive administration of the Berars, and the consequent withholding of profit revenues from the Nizam, has long been known to all acquainted with Indian affairs. It is a transaction which, if it were the other way about, would draw from English public men comments concerning 'oriental perfidy' which would be unparliamentary in their vigour.

It will probably be said that Sir Salar Jung did all this so well because he followed the British plan. Granted. I am not contending for the overthrow of British rule, but for its being remodelled in such a way as may bring satisfaction to the Indian mind and prosperity to the country. What denial of service has meant in the loss to India of men who could wisely and well have administered her affairs may be judged by what Ranjitsinghi has done in cricket against the best batsmen of England and Australia; by what Paranjpe, Balak Ram, Chatterjee, and the brothers Cama have done at Cambridge University against intellectual athletes from all parts of Britain; by what Professor Bose is now doing in electrical science, and Dr. Mullick in medical practice. There may be a few Indian judges in the High Courts of India—not a dozen in all—and a couple of score great Indian pleaders, here and there an Indian Collector, and one solitary Commissioner in Bengal; but they are as naught in number compared with what their numbers should have been and would have been under a rational and fair system of government. Great work has been done by Indians; but it has been in Feudatory States and in England where a chance, denied to them in their own land, was open to them. Given fair-play, Indian administrators would, in their way, and so far as circumstances permitted, have become the equals of Bismarck, of Cavour, of Gortschakoff, of Gladstone, or of Disraeli.

Sir John Malcolm, in his day, warned the authorities of the mingled folly and injustice of the course they had then too long adopted. As usual, the words of three generations ago possess an application as great now as they ever did. 'There are reasons,' said Sir John Malcolm (or supposed reasons, let me interpolate) 'why, as foreign rulers, we cannot elevate the natives of India to a level with their conquerors. We are compelled by policy to limit their ambition, both in the civil government and in the army, to inferior grades, but this necessity constitutes, in my opinion, the strongest of reasons for granting them all that we can with safety. Their vanity and love of distinction are excessive, and a politic gratification of such feelings may be made a powerful means of creating and preserving a native aristocracy worthy of the name, and exciting to honourable action men whom a contrary system must degrade in their own estimation and in that of the community, and who, instead of being the most efficient of all ranks to preserve order, and give dignity to the society to which they belong, and strength to the Government to which they owe allegiance, are depressed by our levelling system into a useless and discontented class. Many, judging from results, ascribe it to the want of virtue and good feeling, and to rooted discontent in this class, what appears to me to be distinctly attributable to our conduct as rulers. We shape our system to suit our own ideas. The constitution of our Government requires in all its branches an efficient check and regularity; but in our attention to forms and routine we too often forget the most essential maxims of State policy, and every deviation is arraigned that disturbs the uniform usage of our affairs in courts of justice. No motives suited to their prejudices and habits are supplied to awaken the inert to action, to kindle the embers of virtue, or to excite an honourable ambition among our native subjects. Yet pursuing this system, our record teems with eulogies on the excellences of our establishments, and the degeneracy of all, and particularly the higher classes of India, whom, in the case before me, it is desired (from no cause that I can understand but rigid adherence to system) to exclude from a few unimportant privileges, which, though little more than a shadow of distinction, are sought for with an eagerness that shows singularly the character of the community, and confirms me in the belief I have long entertained, that by our neglect in conciliating and honouring the higher and more respectable class of our native subjects, we cast away the most powerful means we possess of promoting the prosperity and permanence of the Empire.'[1]

MORAL, INTELLECTUAL, AND SPIRITUAL POSITION.

In this region there cannot be any proper comparison, only a summing-up as to how India, with all her demerits, ranks among the world's peoples during this eventful century. May an Englishman, without shame, ask the question? The natural abilities of the Indian people being what they are, their inheritance of military courage, of administrative ability, of spiritual insight and saintly living, being of so varied and remarkable a character as they are, what has India to show in the array of the world's great men of the nineteenth century? This is her record:—

That is all. 'But,' asserts the reader, 'that is nothing.'

True; it is nothing. India has furnished no commanding intellect in the department of human service which may be denominated moral, intellectual, and spiritual, which may rank with those in Europe and America whose names are known the world over. The sole reason for this is that there is no scope for such development in their own country. The 'pousta' has worked too effectually. In the words of Mr. Thackeray, quoted in the preceding chapter, everything which would produce sages, statesmen, heroes, has been 'suppressed.' To-day we are shocked at such remarks as Mr. Thackeray's—and go on doing exactly what the remarks recommend. Yet India's people, as Lord George Hamilton never tires of

[1] Page 360, Appendix to Report from Select Committee, East India Company, 1853. Minute of Sir John Malcolm, November 30, 1830.

telling us, number one-fifth of the population of the globe. On an appropriate stage the late Mr. Justice Ranade would, for his goodness and his great character, have moved the admiration of all mankind. Only in spiritual things has India made any show at all. Ram Mohun Roy, Keshub Chunder Sen, Rama Krishna, Bengalis to a man, to mention spiritual workers only who have passed away, who are known everywhere and who are honoured as amongst humanity's noblest spiritual teachers. What are these amongst so many? What, especially, are they in a land which contains more real spirituality than, maybe, all the rest of the world put together? Opportunity has been denied to India to show her vast superiority in this or in any other respect. When Europe produced a Martin Luther she gave the world a religious reformer. At the same period India produced her religious hero: he was an Avatar of the Eternal, and is to-day worshipped by vast numbers of devout men and women as The Lord Gauranga. During the last century the finest fruit of British intellectual eminence was, probably, to be found in Robert Browning and John Ruskin. Yet they are mere gropers in the dark compared with the uncultured and illiterate Rama Krishna, of Bengal, who, knowing naught of what we term 'learning,' spake as no other man of his age spoke, and revealed God to weary mortals.

Why is India, spiritually, so little recognised, and the world, as a consequence, deprived of the advantage which the recognition would bring? Chiefly, I think, because of the existence of the Societies for the Conversion of the Heathen to Christianity. While Christian missions are sent by all the Churches to India it will be impossible for more than a select few to realise that Indian spirituality may as assuredly be an expression of the Divine Essence as are the faith and good works of pious men in the West who believe that the Holy Spirit of God is an abiding and helpful influence to them in all their thought and action. As a hindrance to their proper recognition as men of character and often of noble life, the Christian Missionary Societies of England interested in India have done the Indian people almost irremediable mischief.

In one respect there is much that is common to the two time periods, 1801 and 1901, offering themselves for comment. It was not merely for effect that I put at the head of this chapter in juxtaposition the names of Lord Wellesley and Lord Curzon, though a comparison of these rulers of India would not be unworthy to either. Making allowances for the different circumstances of the different periods, both noblemen go about their work in much the same spirit: each was confronted by a harder task than even whole-hearted devotion to his sense of duty and desire to serve India and England could, apparently, perform, and greater than any predecessor had to contend with. The one aimed to bring all India under British rule; the other is endeavouring to grapple with an accumulation of adverse circumstances which has grown Himalaya-high without the officials in the past, including Lord Curzon himself as Parliamentary Under-Secretary of India, recognising what was going on, and quite contrary to what they all believed would happen. Each of the statesmen grapples with the situation before him in a broad-minded spirit. If anything, the ancient ruler was the more courageous. For, so far, Lord Curzon, brave as he is, has done nothing so great as was Lord Wellesley's beginning of the education of the Indian people. The English had been in touch with India for one hundred and sixty years, and in supreme power for thirty years in Bengal, for many more years in Madras. It was high time something was done for education. Lord Wellesley, to his lasting credit, made a beginning. Yet fifty-three more years passed, and there was then only one English school in the oldest Presidency—that of Madras. As to-day an organ of Anglo-Indian opinion, generally most loyal to the Raj, blind sometimes in its devotion, does not hesitate to say of Lord Curzon that he is 'inclined to take too much upon himself,' that he 'is breaking with English traditions,' while he is derisively and sneeringly informed that 'the British have not conquered India in order that, in the fulness of time, Lord Curzon might be a Viceroy,' and further, that having two enemies in himself, he is on the way to making more enemies—so Lord Wellesley was subjected, in the Court of Directors and elsewhere, to like criticism, and was saved from penal discipline by the Board of Control as Lord Curzon may be saved by the devotion of the people whose best interests he seems desirous to appreciate and to serve.

As the round circle of the century's years comes once more to a beginning, that which hath been is now again passing before our eyes, and he who would measure its effect and forecast its consequences may learn much by looking backward over the long course of years since 1801.

APPENDIX.

In opposing the employment of Indian-built ships in the trade between England and India, the Court of Directors employed an argument which, in some of its terms, sounds very curious at the present time when so many Lascars are employed by all the great lines of steamers running to the East. After reciting other reasons against shipbuilding and ship-manning in India, the Court, writing from East India House on the 27th of January, 1801, said :—

'XVII. Besides these objections which apply to the measure generally, there is one that lies particularly against ships whose voyages commence from India, that they will usually be manned in great part with Lascars or Indian sailors. Men of that race are not by their physical frame and constitution fitted for the navigation of cold and boisterous latitudes ; their nature and habits are formed to a warm climate, and short and easy voyages performed within the sphere of the periodical winds; they have not strength enough of mind or body to encounter the hardships or perils to which ships are liable in the long and various navigation between India and Europe, especially in the winter storms of our Northern Seas; nor have they the courage which can be relied on for steady defence against an enemy. To have any considerable portion of the Property and Trade of this country, therefore, dependent on the energy of men of this stamp unless on the coasts of India, where they are less exposed to dangers, cannot be advisable: Yet on the employment of Indian sailors the chief freight of Indian ships seem naturally to turn: for if these ships, rigged and fitted out as they are with stores chiefly brought from Europe, were manned with Europeans, receiving wages far higher, and provisioned at a much greater cost than Lascars, it does not appear how they could be afforded at a lower rate of freight than British bottoms. But this is not all. The native sailors of India, who are chiefly Mahomedans, are, to the disgrace of our national morals, on their arrival here, led into scenes which soon divest them of the respect and awe they had entertained in India for the European character: they are robbed of their little property, and left to wander, ragged and destitute, in the streets; a sight that, whilst it wounds peculiarly the feelings of men connected with India and the Company, raises both the compassion and indignation of the Public; the one in favour of those miserable objects, the other against the Company, as if they had drawn the poor creatures into such a state of suffering, or neglected them in it; when in fact, though individuals bring them home, the Company are at great pains and expense to collect, maintain, and return them; but such are the bad habits they acquire, that they often escape from the houses where the Company have them lodged and provided for, and take to a mendicant state for the chance of obtaining from the pity of passengers new means of vicious indulgence. From causes of this nature, and from the severity of our winters, not a few have lost their lives or become incapable of further service. On the Continent of Europe, and even in America, where some of these Lascars are also now carried, they have no protector as here, and their case must be still more deplorable; so that, instead of a larger introduction into the Western world of this feeble race, it is very seriously to be wished, that before their numbers are thinned by fatigue, climate, or disease, some means were devised for preventing them from leaving their own seas.

'The contemptuous reports which they disseminate on their return, cannot fail to have a very unfavourable influence upon the minds of our Asiatic subjects, whose reverence for our character, which has hitherto contributed to maintain our supremacy in the East (a reverence in part inspired by what they have at a distance seen among a comparatively small society, mostly of the better ranks, in India) will be gradually changed for most degrading conceptions; and if an indignant apprehension of having hitherto rated us too highly or respected us too much, should once possess them, the effects of it may prove extremely detrimental.

'From the waste of life and other losses attending the employment of this class of sailors, perhaps it may appear at length necessary to resort to European Mariners; these, in such case, will flock in great numbers to India; and hence it may be expected that colonisation will be accelerated there. Indeed the return of peace might call for this substitution of British seamen, many of whom must have to seek employment in the Merchants' Service; and no British heart would wish that any of the brave men who had merited so much of their country, should be without bread whilst natives of the East brought ships belonging to our own subjects into our ports. Considered, therefore, in a physical, moral, commercial, and political, view, the apparent consequences of admitting these Indian sailors largely into our navigation, form a strong additional objection to the concession of the proposed privilege to any ships manned by them.'[1]

---

[1] Appendix, No. 47.—Supplement to Fourth Report, East India Company, pp. 23–24.

CHAPTER III

WHOSE IS THE AGRICULTURAL AND INDUSTRIAL WEALTH OF INDIA?

A Detailed Inquiry concerning—

1. **The Fields.**
2. **The Cattle.**
3. **The Forests.**
4. **Minerals.**
5. **Fisheries.**
6. **Manufactures.**
7. **Joint Stock Enterprises.**
8. **Railways.**
9. **Irrigation Works.**
10. **Shipping.**
11. **Civil Service.**
12. **Military.**
13. **Learned Professions.**

British Lower Middle Class Savings Contrasted with Indian Total Income.

When Lord Clive entered Murshidabad, the old capital of Bengal, in 1757, he wrote of it: 'This city is as extensive, populous, and rich as the City of London, with this difference—that there are individuals in the first possessing infinitely greater property than in the last City.'

'IF,' it has been remarked to the present writer, 'you say the Indian people are growing poorer, whose is the huge trade, whose the wealth, we see on every hand, at every port we touch at in India, in every big town through which we go?'

A very proper question, and one which, as a British patriot, jealous for the good name of Britain and for the beneficial results of British rule, I am compelled to answer, not with pride and rejoicing but with pain and sorrow.

India's wealth to-day consists of her fields, her cattle, her forests, her minerals, her fisheries, her shipping, her railways, her roads, her civil service, her learned professions, her military offices, and so on all through the various phases of human endeavour and human possession. How much of all this belongs to the people of India, by whom I mean all those who regard the land as their domicile, look upon it as their home and depend upon it for their sustenance, desiring that their children, also, shall do likewise?

A more or less detailed inquiry will show :—

1. The Fields.

They, subject to the rights of the Government, are India's in the sense I have just mentioned, with these deductions—

(*a*) The tea plantations,

(*b*) The coffee gardens,

(*c*) The jute and indigo estates,

which are mainly in alien hands, and such profits as are made in connection with them do not go to the Indians, do not stay in India, save in a slight degree. For example, one-twelfth of the tea-cultivated area is in Indian hands.

Further—

(*d*) The fields and the produce are mortgaged for such portion of the national debt of the country as is not covered by public works, a sum of over £63,000,000—the total land revenue of all India for three years and a half. The exact figures which this mortgage represents are not available, but I estimate them, at least, at one-third of the whole produce of the land in a good year. This is an under-estimate, probably, by ten crores of rupees, or £6,666,667. As the mortgagee (under civilised laws) can realise, if he will, the Indian cultivator all the Empire over, holds his fields at the mercy of the lenders, who are mainly English.[1] The village

[1] Not, however, as are Indian moneylenders, subject to the new legislation in the Panjab and the similar legislation in Bombay. It is only in regard to Indian moneylenders that legislation limiting security is contemplated. The English moneylenders to India are left untouched. Not a pleasant thing for an Englishman to record, but the fact nevertheless.

moneylender really holds only a second mortgage on the lands which are pledged to him. The extent of the moneylenders' hold on the soil and its produce may be estimated from the special legislation in the Panjab to prevent the moneylender becoming universal landowner, from the revelations made to the Deccan Riots Commission, and from the fact that in the Surat District of Bombay Presidency in 1900 eighty-five per cent. of the year's revenue was paid to the Government by the moneylenders. In respect to all these points details and comments will be found elsewhere.

2. Cattle.

These especially belong to the Indian people. Here the stranger intermeddleth not: it is not worth his while; that is why he has not meddled. For after all there are so few cattle in India, too few to attract his attention, or to make it worth his while to purchase them and to exact a tax on the produce they supply and on the fields they plough, to say nothing of the manure and fuel they furnish. In referring to the comparative fewness of the cattle I do not, for argumentative purposes, select the recent famine years in which the loss of cattle was appalling. I will take 1890, which was not a famine year—that is, not officially proclaimed as such.[1] During that year, among a population of 140,000,000 in British India (Bengal omitted, particulars not then available) there were only 90,750,065 animals (including cows, bulls, buffaloes, horses, ponies, mules, donkeys, sheep, and goats). Australia, with only four millions of population, had 113,550,831 animals. If India, an agricultural

[1] 'In my own missionary experience I once carefully investigated the earnings of a congregation of 300, and found the average amounted to less than a farthing a head per day. They did not live; they eked out an existence. I have been in huts where the people were living on carrion. I have taken photographs of famine groups which are enough for most people; *yet in all these cases there was no recognised famine.*'—Rev. J. Knowles, London Missionary Society, Southern India, in letter to the *Manchester Guardian.*

country if there be an agricultural country anywhere, had had the same proportion as Australia, she would have had 2,628,000,000 animals! This, however, would have been more than she wanted, and grazing land enough for them could not have been found. In respect to this same question of grazing land, here is an example of injustice to which the people are exposed. The Salvation Army in Gujarat wanted land for cultivation; about 560 acres were found which suited them admirably. But it was mainly grazing land, and had been under grass from time immemorial. If it were broken up or taken away from them a large village of cultivators would suffer. The cultivators protested. They might have saved their breath. The new-comers were in the land to bring the people into the way of eternal life, even though this life were ended through the combination (by the missionaries) of things seen with things unseen, things earthly with things heavenly. Only by very great exertions was a riot averted. To the man who told me this story I said, 'The people ought to have rioted.' He answered, 'Perhaps they ought. They were not very far from a riot once.'

3. The Forests.

Conserved by Government and managed for general revenual purposes, India, so far as may be, getting the whole benefit, though not, perhaps, in the way her people desire. The total revenue from this source in 1898 was £1,239,912. To obtain this amount a little over 10s. in the £ was paid for oversight and maintenance. What the people lost by deprivation of grazing grounds, dead wood for fuel, etc., is unknown. A large sum would be needed to recompense the cultivators deprived of ancient rights of grazing, fuel collection, gathering of roots, and other privileges.

4. Minerals.

(*a*) *Coal.*—Over 4,000,000 tons are raised annually, nearly all by English companies.

(*b*) *Iron Ores.*—Neglected everywhere—by Europeans because the ore-measures are too far from the seaboard, by Indians for want of capital and business connections, and often by both because of the stupid restrictions which are put upon would-be enterprise. A startling example of this occurred only a few years ago in the Central Provinces. Now the authorities would be glad to see the effort they then thwarted carried to success. With them, however, as with others:—

> 'He that will not when he may,
> When he would he shall have nay.'

(*c*) *Gold.*—Produced wholly by European exploitation.

(*d*) *Petroleum.*—Products of Assam and Burma, in whose hands does not appear from the records.

5. Fisheries.

These are almost wholly in the hands of Indians. A few years ago an attempt was made in England to form a limited liability company to exploit the Fisheries in the Hooghly, the northern part of the Bay of Bengal, and on the coast of Burma. Sufficient capital, however, was not raised to enable the project to be carried through.

6. Manufactures.

(*a*) *Cotton Mills.*—One hundred and seventy-six in 1898–99. Capital, £14,900,000. Persons employed, 156,056, Almost entirely in Indian hands, and capital largely (but not exclusively) subscribed by Indians. The proportions are said to be—two-thirds Indian investments, one-third European. The advantages derivable from the employment of native Indian capital is apparent in Bombay and Ahmedabad especially. A noble use has, from the first, been made of the wealth thus acquired. Parsee benefactors of the community have been numerous; their generosity forms an indication of what India might have done in the way of kindly and gracious acts of generousness under a judicious mode of administration.

(*b*) *Jute and Hemp Mills.*—Thirty-three in number. Capital, £4,955,000. Persons employed, 95,540. Almost wholly European.

(*c*) *General.*—Woollen and Paper Mills, Breweries, Cotton Ginning, Cleaning and Pressing Mills, Coffee Works, Flour Mills, Rice Mills, Oil Mills, Jute Presses, Indigo Factories, Timber Mills, Sugar Factories, and Silk Filatures. Three-fourths in European hands.

7. Joint Stock Enterprises.

In all India there are the following Companies :—

	No.		Capital.
Banking and Loan	405	...	£4,411,358
Insurance...	105	...	146,062
Navigation	9	...	1,287,300
Railways and Tramways	19	...	1,970,120
Other Trading Companies	252	...	8,090,885
Tea...	135	...	8,212,310
Other Planting Companies	15	...	113,186
Coal Mining	34	...	1,274,862
Gold Mining	12	...	500,842
Other Mining and Quarrying Companies	17	...	248,278
Cotton Mills	66	...	5,526,984
Jute Mills...	20	...	2,571,063
Mills for Cotton, Wool, Silk, Hemp, etc.	113	...	6,927,308
Cotton and Jute Screws and Presses ...	116	...	1,607,281
Other Companies...	99	...	2,670,665
Total ...	1,417	...	£35,506,449

Of this £36,000,000, even reckoning in all the Cotton Mills, by the utmost straining of estimates, not more than £10,000,000 can be credited to the Indian people. Note also that, for all India, Banking and Insurance, and, indeed, everything else, financial as well as industrial, the total capital invested is less than £36,000,000. How unimportant and insignificant all this is for a mighty Empire, which has been under British control for nearly one hundred and fifty years, may be judged from the fact that, in Manchester, the money extent of—

Trading operations in 1872 were	...	...	£207,000,000
Ditto " 1881 "	...	...	318,000,000

'The commercial institutions of Manchester are too numerous for detailed description. Its chamber of commerce has for more than sixty years held a position of much influence in regard to the trade of the district and of the nation. There are eleven joint-stock banks, seven of which have their head offices in the town; these banks, besides numerous branches in the surrounding district, have sixteen branches in the town; and there are several private bankers.'[1] Since then the progress of this city in the United Kingdom has been very great. Mr. Elijah Helm, secretary of the Manchester Chamber of Commerce, in answer to inquiries I made of him, courteously writes to me thus:—

'The estimates of the total value of the trading operations of this city, to which you refer, must have been conjectural, I think. I know of no method of arriving at anything like precise figures. Perhaps the most reliable way of forming an opinion as to the rate of progress is to take the yearly returns of the Manchester Bankers' Clearing-house. In 1891 the total amount of the clearings was £181,163,961, and in 1900, £248,750,600. These sums represent the value of the cheques exchanged between the various banks in Manchester, and do not of course include the cheques paid, or credited to the amounts of their customers, by the banks themselves. The increase between these two years may no doubt be, to some extent, the result of an extension of the practice of paying debts by cheque, but any allowance on this score must, I fancy, be comparatively small, and in the main the increase of clearings must be taken as indicative of increase of business.

'There can be no doubt that for many years both the industries and the commerce of Manchester have been growing—not always steadily perhaps—but still growing, both in variety and in magnitude. But I should not like to have to put the rate of progress into figures pretending to be at all authentic.

'Nor do I think one could give an entirely satisfactory account of the number and capital of the joint stock enterprises here. Some of

[1] *Encyc. Brit.*, vol. xiv., p. 464.

them are merely conversions of private concerns into limited companies, and some of these are placed under the Companies Acts for family reasons, their shares being privately held.

'I may add that the amount of the Manchester Bankers' clearings far exceeds that of any other city in the country except London, and these are swollen, as you know, by international and national settlements in London as well as by the payments of the Government.'

8. Railways.

Over 22,000 miles in length, and have cost, with land acquired, loss on interest, and other expenses, considerably more than £300,000,000. Practically, the whole of the sum invested in railways is held by Europeans, barring that which certain Feudatory States benevolently 'loaned'; in regard only to a portion of it has amortisation been provided, and that—as in the cases of the East India and Great Indian Peninsular Railways—on most costly terms to the Indian taxpayer; amortisation from the start would have made a difference of many millions of pounds sterling to the advantage of the Indian taxpayer, and, with wise provision, the earlier railways might have been largely redeemed before the great fall in the value of silver occurred. India has been very hard hit in all these transactions. The accounts show that £40,000,000 have been taken from the general revenue to make up the guaranteed interest to shareholders. That sum will never be repaid.

How the guarantee system has worked in practice may be judged from the facts narrated by Miss Ethel Faraday, M.A., in a paper on 'Indian Guaranteed Railways: An Illustration of *Laisser Faire* Theory and Practice,' read before the Economic Science and Statistics Section of the British Association in 1900. Miss Faraday says: 'The result, that *laisser faire*, like other religions, proves somewhat less beneficent in practice than in theory, might be illustrated by the later history of the Indian guaranteed railways. The guaranteed system, in origin a purely practical expedient, had outlived its utility before it was revived by the English Government of 1868–74, apparently as being preferable, from the *laisser faire* point of view, to the direct State ownership which was considered by Lord Lawrence, as by Roscher, advisable in India. In the contracts renewed with three railways—the Great Indian Peninsular, Bombay, Baroda, and Central India, and Madras lines—it was agreed that the companies should receive interest at the guaranteed rate of five per cent. and half the surplus profits, no account being taken of deficits; that remittances to England should be converted at the rate of 1s. 10d. the rupee; and that calculations should be made on a half-yearly basis. The result was that the Indian Government bore all the loss of the unprofitable half-years, and, after 1875, never received its full share of gain in the profitable ones, since, as the exchange value of the rupee fell below 1s. 10d., the shareholders received a gradually increasing proportion of the surplus profits, while the contract obligation to pay interest at five per cent. deprived the State of advantage from cheaper money and improved credit, which would lately have enabled it to raise money at two and a half or three per cent. to pay off loans advanced at a higher rate of interest. On the three lines in question, taken together, the average proportion of earnings yearly remitted to England, 1892–7, was 99·70 per cent., and the net annual loss to Government amounted to Rs.13,000,000, a tax imposed on the Indian public for the benefit of the British shareholder.'

On this same subject some other comments may be added. The late Mr. Robert Brown, of Glasgow, an earnest student of Indian conditions, in one of his pamphlets (1892) wrote: 'Government occasionally buys up a railway originally constructed by a nominally independent company, the most recent cases being the Oudh and Rohilcund in 1888, and the Southern Indian in 1890. They are fine illustrations of the way in which the guaranteed company system has "developed the resources" of India. The former line from the date of its opening had involved the Government in a total loss of Rs.2,323,287 for deficiency of guaranteed interest, and yet they bought up its share capital of £4,000,000 at a premium of £25 18s. 0¼d. per cent., being the average price at which the stock had stood in the market for the previous three years! That price, however, had no connection with the railway's traffic earnings, but depended entirely upon the Government's own guarantee. The market price would have been the same, although the traffic receipts had been *nil*. Similarly the Southern Indian ordinary stock, £3,208,508, was bought up at a premium of £989,048 11s. 2d., although till 30th June, 1888, Government had sustained a loss of £1,948,599 from deficiency of receipts to meet guaranteed interest. Some years earlier the East Indian, one of the few profitable lines, was bought up at a premium of £6,550,000.'

Finally, the Director-General of Railways, in his Report for 1900, published while these pages are in the printers' hands, remarks: 'The expenditure side of the account is further heavily weighted by the terms of the contracts of the guaranteed railways. Under these contracts payment of interest has to be made at a higher rate than is now necessary, and the calculation of the surplus profits has to be made at 22 pence to the rupee, while the current rate of exchange is nearer 16 pence. Until these contracts terminate, the State is unable to obtain any advantage from cheaper money, or from the improved credit of the country, or from a favourable exchange.'

9. Irrigation Works.

£35,000,000 capital expenditure, probably the whole of which is held in England.[1]

[1] Much boasting is indulged in concerning this expenditure by some official apologists, *e.g.*, Mr. J. D. Rees, C.I.E., paper on 'Famine Facts and Fallacies,' East India Association, p. 23. Mr. John Bright ridiculed all such pretensions effectually when, in 1878, he said:—

We hear that there has been £9,000,000 or £16,000,000 spent on such

10. Shipping.

All, except an infinitesimal portion, is of foreign construction out of foreign capital, and, save as ordinary seamen, in certain 'Lines,' such as the Lascars in the Peninsular and Oriental and British India services, no occupation in connection with shipping is found for Indians, save, of course, as clerks and coolies at the wharves and docks, and as seamen in the few craft still denominated in the returns as 'Native.'

Shipping employed in 1898–9: 9,115,646 tons, of which 133,033 tons were Indian. Forty years ago one-third of the tonnage employed in Indian waters was Indian.

11. Civil Service.

The 'salaries and expenses of Civil Departments,' which in 1886–87 amounted to Rx.11,726,148 (£7,817,432), had grown two years later to Rx.13,013,544 (£8,675,976), and in 1898–99 is returned at Rx.15,732,303 (£10,488,147). Out of this enormous sum 8,000 Europeans received Rx.8,000,000 (£5,333,334), while nearly 130,000 Indians received Rx.7,000,000 (£4,666,667), the remaining Rx.731,000 (£487,667) going to less than 6,000 Eurasians.

These figures showed average annual salaries in these proportions:—

works. What is that in India? The town of Manchester alone, with a population of 500,000 has spent £2,000,000 already, and is coming to Parliament now to ask to be allowed to spend £3,500,000 more: that will be £5,500,000 to supply the population of that town and its immediate surroundings with pure water, and a sufficient quantity of it. But in India we have 200,000,000 of population subject to the English Government, and with a vast supply of rainfall and great rivers running through it with the means—as I believe there are the means—of abundant irrigation, and still the whole expended has been only £16,000,000. We have heard some authorities say it is £20,000,000; but be it £16,000,000 or £20,000,000, what is it when we consider the vast extent of the country, and the greatness of the need?'

It is not an unfair criticism of Mr. Rees's paper to say that it is marked by an unacquaintance with the real position of non-official critics which vitiates its whole argument.

Each European received	... ...	£607
,, Eurasian ,,	... ...	81
,, Indian ,,	... ...	36

12. Military.

All the superior officers, in European and Indian forces alike, are Europeans. Lord Curzon has propounded a scheme, the announcement of which has moved the whole Empire of Britain to its depths, whereby opportunities are to be given to a score or two of Indian youths, after passing through an Indian Sandhurst, to obtain commissions in the Indian Army.

13. The Learned Professions.

Here, again, though many most capable Indian gentlemen, at great cost, and often at much sacrifice in many ways, have qualified themselves for professional positions in the law, in the educational service, and in other directions, they have done this only to discover that nearly all the best positions everywhere are occupied by Europeans.

Such, in general outline, but tolerably exact, so far as Indian official figures may be relied upon, is my answer to the question I quoted at the beginning of this chapter. I say, 'So far as the Indian figures may be relied upon,' for, when a painful proof of their own statements being hopelessly contradictory is held before their eyes, leading officials (in England) have been heard to say, 'Oh! those are only estimates! They are guesses at the facts! We don't know for certain what is the real state of things!' This is an actual confession made by a Secretary of State. But, as to the statistics given above, they may be accepted as fairly accurate on the whole.

'What then?'

That is *my* question. And I put it respectfully, but strenuously, to Lord George Hamilton, Secretary of State for India, to his Under-Secretaries, to the Members of his Council, to the Heads of Departments in the India Office, and to Lord Curzon, Viceroy and Governor-General, and each and all of His Excellency's subordinates in India. Until it be answered, I shall go on asking it:

> 'Although I be the feeblest of mankind,
> I will not cease to grasp the hope I hold,'

that some day, somewhere, somehow, the question may be answered in such a way that India shall once more become a prosperous land for its own people as it now is for the stranger encamped within its gates. I, again, ask the question of the Viceroy and of every Member of his Council, and outside the Council, especially of Mr. H. J. S. Cotton, C.S.I., Chief Commissioner of Assam, whose praise as a humane administrator is in all men's mouths, and who, in 1887, discerned so wisely and so well what the deplorable effects of the Economic Revolution, which British rule has brought about in India, has had upon the prosperity of the country.[1]

I put another question. It is this: Who will arouse England to a sense of the wrong she is doing to India in, year by year, draining large sums of money from that country without giving a direct equivalent in return? A rich nation, and that nation amongst the wealthiest in the world, is taking from the arteries and the veins of the very poor of another nation, and that nation the poorest in the whole world, their very life-blood. By the term 'rich' as applied to England I do not mean wealthy people only. Look at this fact:

The lower middle and artisan population of England—say, 6,000,000 families at the outside—have the very large sum of £322,146,422 invested as *savings* in Building Societies, Co-operative Societies, Friendly Societies,

[1] 'New India,' by H. J. S. Cotton, C.S.I., Chief Commissioner of Assam.

Trades Unions, Labour Loan Societies, Railway Savings Banks, Trustee Banks, and Post Office Savings Banks. How many people realise what these savings mean? They are *savings*—let me emphasise the fact!—and therefore PROPERTY, in addition to all that the homes of these investors contain of valuables of every kind, and after all indebtedness has been met.

In a prosperous year in India, when the rains have come in due season, when the land has been sufficiently ploughed, when the sun has been all-beneficial, when insect pests have been at a minimum, when cattle have been in plenty, and when a bountiful harvest has been gathered in, which happens hardly once in ten years, not even when the land has lain fallow in a 'jubilee' year of famine; conceive, I say, what all this would mean from Himalayan snows to Equatorial heat over so vast an area as the India of the Emperor Edward VII. covers; then bear in mind

the full value of all the produce is £150,000,000 *less than the savings—the well and safely-invested savings—of the labourer, the artisan, and the lower middle-class person, in England.*

This may be stated in another way:—

British lower middle class and artisan invested savings: £322,146,422.	Total value of all the crops raised in India in a good year: 258 crores of rupees, £172,000,000
Number affected: say, 25,000,000.	Number affected: 230,000,000.

I ask the reader to turn to the first page of this chapter, to once more go through the various matters discussed, to remember all the figures employed are Indian official figures, and then to put to himself the question, 'How *can* such a condition of things denote the prosperity of the native Indian people?' And, that they are prosperous is stoutly proclaimed by the Secretary of State of India by voice and pen on every conceivable opportunity.

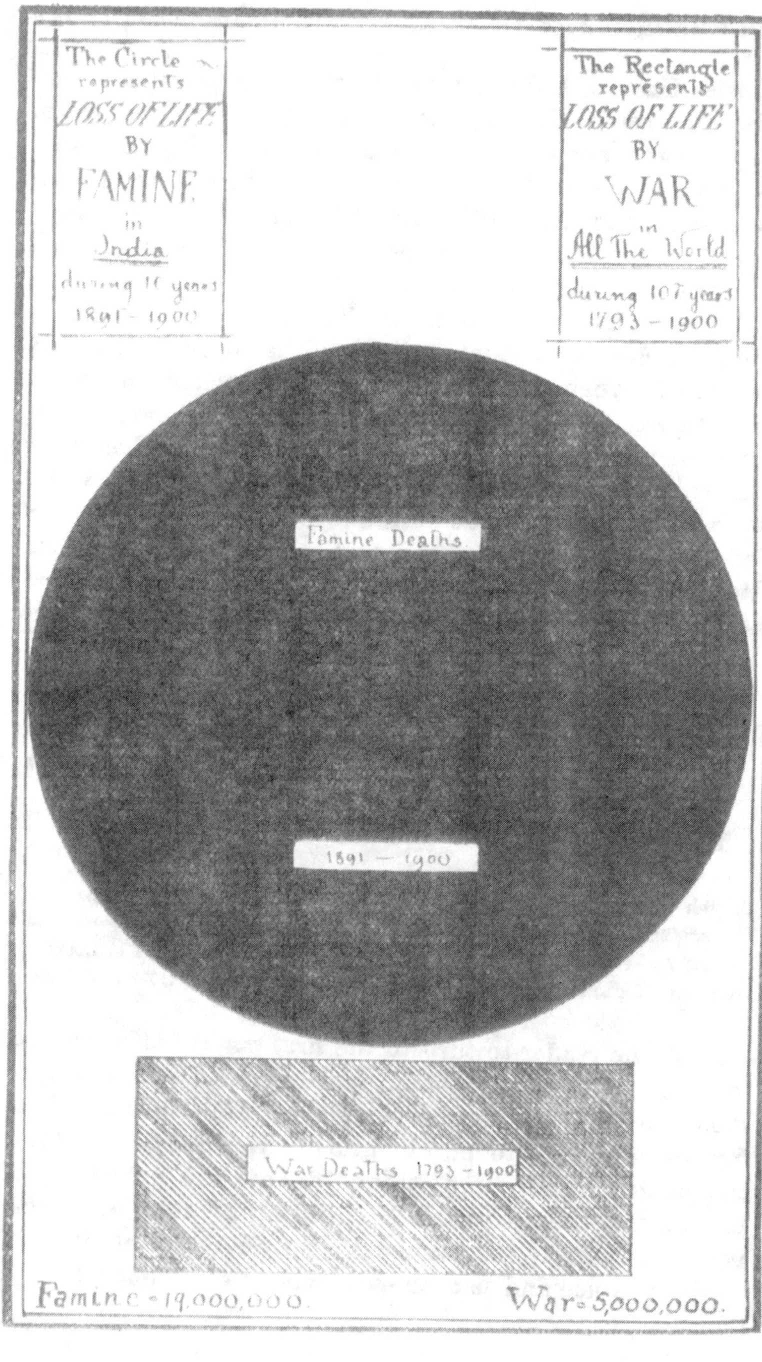
The Circle represents
LOSS OF LIFE
BY
FAMINE
in
India
during 10 years
1891 - 1900
The Rectangle represents
LOSS OF LIFE
BY
WAR
in
All The World
during 107 years
1793 - 1900
Famine Deaths
1891 — 1900
War Deaths 1793 - 1900
Famine = 19,000,000.
War = 5,000,000.

CHAPTER IV

FAMINES: THEIR PRESENT FREQUENCY AND THE CAUSE OF THAT FREQUENCY

Famine Deaths versus War Deaths.

The Exceptional Famine-Position of India: Famine Come to Stay.

Famine 'a Good Thing: There are Too Many People in India.'

Frequency Much Greater than in Past and Proceeding at Accelerated Pace.

Sympathy 'Always with an Over-ruling Consideration for the Revenue.'

Famines Prior to British Rule.

Sir George Campbell on 'Frequency.'

The Famines of the Eighteenth Century.

A Comparison between 1769—1800 and 1868-69—1900.

Famines of the First Half of the Nineteenth Century.

Famines during Second Half of the Century.

Over Twenty-six Million Famine Deaths Officially Admitted.

The Four Quarters of the Nineteenth Century compared:

First Period..................Five Famines.
Second ,, ...Two ,,
Third ,, ...Six ,,
Fourth ,, ...Eighteen ,,

Maps showing the First and the Last Famines of the Nineteenth Century.

The Economic Drain the Chief Cause of Famine.

Mr. W. L. Hare's Table of Famines since 1729.

After the Word, the Deed.

A Minus Population of 86,000,000.

Estimate by the *Lancet* and the *Friend of India* of 19,000,000 Famine Deaths in past Ten Years.

Famines More Destructive Now than in Ancient Days.

Scarcity of Means more than Absence of Food Stores.

British Supremacy founded on Belief that a Dark Skin means a Combined Evil Heart and Lack of Administrative Ability and Common Honesty.

To the Honoured Memory of the Famine-Slain, 1891–1901.

'A red-haired child
Sick in a fever, if you touch him once
Though but as little as a finger-tip,
Will set you weeping: but a million sick—
You would as soon weep for the rule of three
Or compound fraction.' BROWNING.

THE time has passed when, in beginning a chapter on Famines in India, argument was essential to indicate the present exceptional position of India in respect to the most dire scourge known to humanity. On all hands, and by every one who has made any study of the question, it is accepted that famine is now chronic in certain parts of India, including even some irrigated regions. So much has the fact of famine having come to stay grown into the warp and woof of our ordinary life in Britain, that we hear of tens of millions of our fellow-subjects actually perishing, and, literally, of nine-tenths of us, it is true that we pass by on the other side of the way as if the fact concerned us not at all. Or, we say, 'A good thing, surely. There are too many people in India.' This—will it be believed?—is said to me by two out of every four Englishmen to whom I mention the fact of India's gruesome state. Even more significant is the circumstance that, as with hospitals and other necessary alleviations of suffering, an Indian Famine Relief Fund is now looked upon as always in existence or needing to be in existence, and rich, philanthropically-minded, maiden ladies are beginning to leave legacies to such a Fund.[1] Therefore, it is not with famine as with some strange portent from the Unseen with which we have to deal, but something abiding with us;—slightly varying familiar words, famine has become

> 'No more a stranger or a guest,
> But like a child at home.'

'A child at home'—part of the imagery is exact; to be quite exact, in the portion of the home it occupies, the child has become Master.

My observations on Indian famines must be general in their character rather than exhaustive. There is no need for an exhaustive treatment in these pages. A small library of books has already been published on the subject. I shall simply show that India, under British rule, has *become* (the reader will, please, in his reading, carefully note and emphasise this word) chronically famine-stricken, and shall furnish some particulars, from official sources, which indicate that the famines of the past twenty years might have been prevented if the course which was strongly recommended to the Indian authorities by the Famine Commission in 1880, had been adopted. Following from these statements is the deduction—of the truth and accuracy of which, sorrowfully, I am fully convinced—that famines in India, under our

[1] On August 6, 1901, the provisions of the will of Miss Eliza Warrington, of the Belvidere, Malvern Wells, were published. The first provision in it read as follows: '£1,000 to the Lord Mayor of London as trustee to pay the same into the Indian Famine Fund; if there be no such Fund in existence at her decease, then on trust to be held and invested by the Lord Mayor and his successors until another Indian Famine Fund shall be opened, and thereupon such grant and its accumulations shall be paid to such Fund.'

enlightened and all-embracing rule, are the direct result of our neglect as rulers to do the right thing, at the right time, in the right way; and that, even now, their recurrence may be stopped if we will but do that which the commonest feelings of humanity, to say nothing of our plain and imperative duty, call upon us to attempt.

To what are famines in India due? That question may wait a moment or two for reply, until another question has been asked and answered: Are famines more frequent and more destructive now than in past times? Upon the answer to this inquiry depends the urgency of the task which the English people are, by every conceivable sense of duty, summoned immediately to undertake.

When the part played by the British Empire in the nineteenth century is regarded by the historian fifty years hence, by which time the true perspective of events will have been attained, the most striking and most saddening of all incidents for comment will be the steady sinking of India and its population into a state of chronic famine-strickenness. It was not until 1879, when the Famine Commission of that year reported that, in some part or other of India, famine might be expected once in four years, that famine relief and famine administration became a part of the current work of the Indian authorities. Since that time one of the most admirable of all administrative machines has evolved the Famine Code. This Code is evidence that the Government fully realised famine had come to stay. In regard to palliatives much has been done; in respect to prevention the hand has been slack, for reasons which will be obvious to the least observant reader of these chronicles.

The history of famines prior to, and during, early British rule is not exact or abundant. One thing, however, stands out most clearly. All the famines were local; not one approached in extent or intensity the three great distresses of the last quarter of the nineteenth century. The list which follows may not be exhaustive. It is put forward on investigations made independently and at different times by one English student of history and two Indians, one of the latter being an ex-Prime Minister of an important Feudatory State.

BEFORE BRITISH RULE.

In the	Eleventh Century	2	Famines,	both local.
,,	Thirteenth ,,	1	,,	around Delhi.
,,	Fourteenth ,,	3	,,	all local.
,,	Fifteenth ,,	2	,,	both local.
,,	Sixteenth ,,	3	,,	all local.
,,	Seventeenth ,,	3	,,	'General': area not defined.
,,	Eighteenth ,, (to 1745)	4	,,	North-Western Provinces; Delhi; Sind (twice); all local.

UNDER BRITISH RULE.

As to *frequency*. The late Sir George Campbell, K.C.S.I., M.P., who passed through the gamut of official experience, from a writership in Calcutta in the old days of The Company, to the Lieutenant-Governorship of Bengal, under the Crown, when, in 1866, he was deputed to inquire into previous famines in India, confined himself to the period 'since the establishment of British rule.' The Famine Commissions follow the same plan. As the Reports of those Commissions are, largely, my authorities, I must follow the example they furnish. Sir George records, for Eastern India, drought in 1769 and famine in 1770, accompanied with much suffering and great loss of life. But the harm then done could not have been of a very intense character, judging from the collections of the land revenue in 1771, which were Rs.530,000 (the rupee, then, was over 2s.—say 2s. = £53,000) higher than in 1768, before any failure of rain was recorded. 'The British authorities were early alive to the evil,' says Sir George Campbell, '*and much sympathised with it,* BUT ALWAYS *with an overruling consideration for the revenue.'* A reporter of the last famine—(that of 1900—in spite of the elaborate Famine Code—that Code being, in far-reaching detail and completeness one of the most creditable as it is one of the most remarkable achievements of British administration in India)—might have used precisely these same words of events one hundred and thirty years later. The reporter would find the British authorities in the Bombay Presidency, in their 'overruling consideration for the revenue,' acting in a manner hardly to be reconciled with common (to say nothing of Christian) humanity. As a fact both non-official critic and official historian, dealing with far-apart periods, must say the same thing—cannot, honestly, say any other. In essentials, in some parts of India, there seems little advance on 1770. Whatever the condition of the country the revenue is squeezed from the people.

In 1784 the North-Western Provinces, Oudh, and the Panjab were in distressful condition, owing to 'extraordinary drought' during two previous years. The worst recorded price of the grain most generally consumed by the people was about thirty-two pounds for a rupee. Compared with the present depleted condition of the people that does not seem very terrible, though, contrasted with the one hundred and thirty-six pounds, which was what the people then were accustomed to, it may have seemed terrible. In 1897, when the same region was but secondarily, *i.e.*, through the railways, affected by the famine of that year, only twenty-six pounds and a quarter of the same kind of grain could be bought for a rupee. While the course of events in the United Kingdom during the last half of the nineteenth century has vastly cheapened food for the poor, and the means of purchasing have increased, a consideration of these figures will show that in India the exactly opposite state of things has been brought about—'been *brought* about': the words accurately describe the situation.

In 1787 there was again distress in various parts of Bengal, owing to a cyclone and floods. Though recorded as a famine the resulting distress ought not to be so regarded, seeing that it does not even begin to compare with scarcities, such as that in the district of Ganjam, Northern Madras, in 1889, when twenty thousand people died of starvation before the Governor of Madras awoke to his duty (on pressure exerted through the House of Commons by the late Charles Bradlaugh, M.P.) and visited the district. Of such minor calamities we hardly deign to take any notice nowadays; so full have we supped of famine horrors they no longer cause repulsion.

> 'The dewfall of compassion now is o'er
> So soon. So soon is dead indifference come.'

The Presidencies of Madras and Bombay suffered from drought in 1782, but the distress did not reach famine as famine is now understood; still it may be included in the count. In 1792 Hyderabad, Southern Bombay, the Deccan, Gujarat, and Madras, suffered from 'severe famine.' No particulars are given as to the extent of the distress, which, probably, was only locally 'severe'—the severity, in many parts, arising from defective communications, which we have removed by our roads, railways, and (a few) navigable canals.

There were thus four (or, if the cyclone damage be counted, five) famines in the last third of the eighteenth century. What is the record for the similar period in the nineteenth century? For answer I abstract, from official records, the following most significant (and most fearful) comparison of famines and scarcities during the respective periods:—

1769—1800.		1868-69—1900.[1]	
Year.	Region.	Year.	Region.
1769-70	Bengal.	1868-69	Rajputana.
1783 ...	Madras and Bombay.		North-Western Provinces.
1784 ...	Upper India.		

[1] Details concerning these famines and scarcities will be found in the Reports of the Famine Commissions of 1878-80 and of 1898.

1769—1800.		1868–69—1900.[1]	
Year.	Region.	Year.	Region.
1792 ...	Madras, Hyderabad, Southern Bombay, Deccan, Gujarat, Marwar.	1868–69	Panjab.
			Central Provinces.
			Bombay.
		1873–74	Bengal and Behar.
			North - Western Provinces and Oudh.
		1874–77	Bombay.
			Hyderabad.
		1876–78	Madras.
			Mysore.
		1877–78	North - Western Provinces and Oudh.
		1884 ...	Panjab.
		1884–85	Lower Bengal.
			Madras.
		1886–87	Central Provinces.
		1888–89	Behar.
		1889 ...	Orissa (Tributary States).
		1888–89	Madras (Ganjam).
		1890 ...	Kumaun and Garwhal.
		1890–92	Ajmere Merwara.
		1892 ...	Madras.
			Bombay (Deccan).
			Bengal and Behar.
			Upper Burma.
		1897–98	Madras and Bombay.
			Central Provinces.
			North - Western Provinces.
			Central India.
		1899-1900	Bombay.
			Panjab.
			Central Provinces.
			Rajputana.
			Central India.
			Hyderabad, Deccan.
			Berar.

Stated roughly, famines and scarcities have been four times as numerous during the last thirty years of the

[1] Details concerning these famines and scarcities will be found in the Reports of the Famine Commissions of 1878–80 and of 1898.

nineteenth century as they were one hundred years earlier and four times more widespread.

To make the record complete the whole series of famines since a British Governor-General began rule as such in Bengal, may be appended. The arrangement and enumerations are those of the various Famine Commissions in their respective Reports :—

(1) *The Last Thirty Years of the Eighteenth Century.*

YEAR.	REMARKS.
1769–70...	Bengal. Drought followed by floods. In certain districts mortality very great.
1783 ...	Madras and Bombay. No mortality record.
1784 ...	Upper India. Ditto.
1792 ...	Bombay and Madras Deccan, and Southern India generally.

(2) *The First Half of the Nineteenth Century.*

1802–3 ...	Bombay. Deaths exceedingly many. Famine due to war. Plentiful supply of water and grazing for cattle.
1803–4 ...	North-Western Provinces and Rajputana. Life loss not severe.
1805–7 ...	Madras. Estimate of deaths 'very large.'
1811–14...	Madras. No serious distress.
,, ...	Bombay. Severe, but 'not much mention of mortality.'
1812–13...	Rajputana. Exceedingly bad; mortality, probably one and a half to two millions.
1823 ...	Madras. 'Deaths of frequent occurrence.'
1824–25...	Bombay. Scarcity 'nowhere amounting to famine.'
,, ...	North-Western Provinces. Ditto.
1833–34...	Northern Madras. Mortality very great. In some districts nearly 50 per cent. of the population perished.
,, ...	Bombay. Scarcity, but no famine.
1837–38...	Upper India. Mortality, probably one million.

(3) *The Second Half of the Nineteenth Century.*

		MORTALITY
1854 ...	Madras. 'Considerable check to growth of population.'	—
1860–61...	North-Western Provinces and Panjab. Estimates vary; not less than...	500,000
1865–66...	Orissa. In six districts alone	1,300,000
,, ...	Behar and Northern Bengal	135,000
,, ...	Madras	450,000

YEAR.	REMARKS.	MORTALITY.
1868–69...	Rajputana	1,250,000
,, ...	North-Western Provinces	600,000
,, ...	Panjab	600,000
,, ...	Central Provinces	250,00
,, ...	Bombay. Life-loss not stated; emigration very extensive	—
1873–74...	Bengal and Behar...	None
,, ...	North-Western Provinces and Oudh	,,
1876–77...	Bombay. Estimates vary from 1,000,000 to 800,000, say	900,000
,, ...	Hyderabad (Deccan)	70,000
1876–78...	Madras, North-Western Provinces and Oudh. Noteworthy for the imposition of the '1 lb. ration' for famine-workers, subsequently withdrawn. The most terrible famine, to that date, known in India. The mortality was estimated by the Famine Commissioners in Southern India at 5,250,000; it was, probably, much more than that. Elsewhere it was at least three millions ...	8,250,000
,, ...	Mysore (then under British administration) ...	1,100,000
1880 ...	Deccan, Southern Bombay, Central Provinces, and Nizam's Dominions. High prices, but relief measures not taken. Mortality not stated	—
,, ...	North-Western Provinces. Ditto. Ditto. ...	—
1884 ...	Scarcity in the Southern and South-Eastern Panjab. Relief measures provided, and remissions of revenue granted. Mortality not stated. Vital statistics show increased deaths over previous year of	750,000
1884–85...	Bengal, Behar, and Chota Nagpore. Also Bellary and Anantapur districts in Madras. Mortality included in foregoing	—
1886–87...	Central Provinces. Earthworks prepared, but late autumn rains secured ripening of winter crops	—
1888–89...	Behar. Works established and relief granted for several months	—
1889 ...	Tributary States of Orissa. Relief works, 'many of the people brought on relief were in bad condition, specially the children'	—
1888–89...	Ganjam, Madras. South-west Monsoon late and scanty. Relief postponed until too late, and much suffering ensued	—

YEAR.	REMARKS.	MORTALITY.
	[The vital statistics show for the above year, and for 1890, an additional mortality of 1,500,000.]	1,500,000
1890 ...	Kumaon and Garwhal. Comparatively small help sufficed	—
1892 ...	Garwhal and Almora. '150,000 persons assisted by advances of grain by Government' ...	—
1891–92...	Madras. Failure of North-east Monsoon. 'A period of severe agricultural distress prevailed for over two years throughout the Madras Presidency.' Relief works opened, and nearly £1,000,000 spent in relief ...	—
" ...	Bombay Deccan. Only slight relief granted ...	—
" ...	Bengal. Relief of all kinds provided. 'Mortality in all the affected districts above the normal'	—
" ...	Upper Burma. Relief works, gratuitous relief, and agricultural loans, amounted to Rs.20,50,000	—
" ...	Ajmere-Merwara. Relief works of various kinds, and help to weavers provided ...	—
	[The mortality, all India, for 1891 and 1892, above the normal, was:— 1891 ... ... 420,000 1892 1,200,000	1,620,000
1895–97...	An exceeding great famine. Bundelkhund, North-Western Provinces and Oudh, Bengal, Central Provinces, Madras, Bombay, Panjab, Berar, and Burma. Widely extended relief of all kinds provided. The Commissioners profess to be unable to make an estimate of mortality. The vital statistics show increase above the normal, of:— 1895 ... ... 1,200,000 1896 ... ... 1,800,000 1897 2,650,000	5,650,000
	1898, a so-called non-famine year, shows excess of	650,000
1899–1900	The most widely-extended and most 'terrible' (Lord Curzon's word) famine known in Indian history. Its area covered most of the country west of the Ganges, from the borders of Kashmir to Mysore, with 'spots'	

YEAR.	REMARKS.	MORTALITY.
	in Madras, and from Sind to the Orissa boundary. Crop and incidental losses, not less than £150,000,000. Mortality stated by Famine Commissioners at 1,250,000, but, judging from analogy, it is three or four times that figure. I carry forward only double the official estimate	2,500,000
1901	... Gujarat, Deccan, Bombay, Karnatak, Madras (part of), Southern Panjab (probably will be at least)	750,000
	Total (admitted) mortality in forty-seven years—1854 to 1901 ...	28,825,000

The foregoing official figures (official, with exceptions stated) show over one million deaths on the average per annum during the past ten years, or, *two British subjects passed away from starvation or starvation-induced diseases every minute of every day and every night from January 1, 1889, to September 30, 1901!* Nevertheless, only a few persons in the United Kingdom are doing aught to prevent a continuance of such an awful condition of things, and the Secretary of State for India stands amazed at the 'prosperity' of the regions he is governing!

A little more detail will make the GROWING impoverishment of India, as writ in famine deaths, more clear.

The nineteenth century, for comparison purposes, may be taken in four equal periods, and the immense increase in the last quarter as compared with the years, 1800 to 1825, be noted.

1800 to 1825.—FIVE famines, with SLIGHT loss of life (1802–3, 1804, 1807, 1812–13, 1823–25). Some of these 'famines' arose from wars, and none extended over a large area.

1826 to 1850.—TWO famines: 1833, 1837.
These were mainly local, and great suffering was caused in particular districts, notably in Northern Madras.

The '33 famine led to the Great Godavari Irrigation works being begun.

By this time, practically all India, as we know it, had come under our sway.

1851 to 1875.—SIX famines, with the loss of five millions of lives, spread over the whole series of calamities. The worst famine was in Orissa.

1876 to 1900.—EIGHTEEN famines, including the FOUR most terrible famines ever known in India; in the first of these four, SIX AND A QUARTER MILLIONS OF LIVES WERE LOST; in the last two, during the ten years in which they occurred, according to the correspondent in India of the *Lancet*, and the estimate of the *Statesman and Friend of India*, Calcutta, NINETEEN MILLIONS OF LIVES were lost from famine and famine diseases.

During this quarter of a century, *eighteen parts of the Empire suffered from famines of varying degrees of poignancy.* There were thus, in the official reckoning, EIGHTEEN FAMINES in the last twenty-five years of the nineteenth century.

How completely famine has gained a hold on the Empire may be judged from this summary:—

			Deaths.	
1st period, 25 years	FIVE FAMINES.		Perhaps	1,000,000
2nd ,, ,,	TWO	,,	,,	500,000
3rd ,, ,,	SIX	,,	Recorded	5,000,000
4th ,, ,,	EIGHTEEN	,,	Estimated	26,000,000

THE FIRST FAMINE OF THE NINETEENTH CENTURY

1802-3.

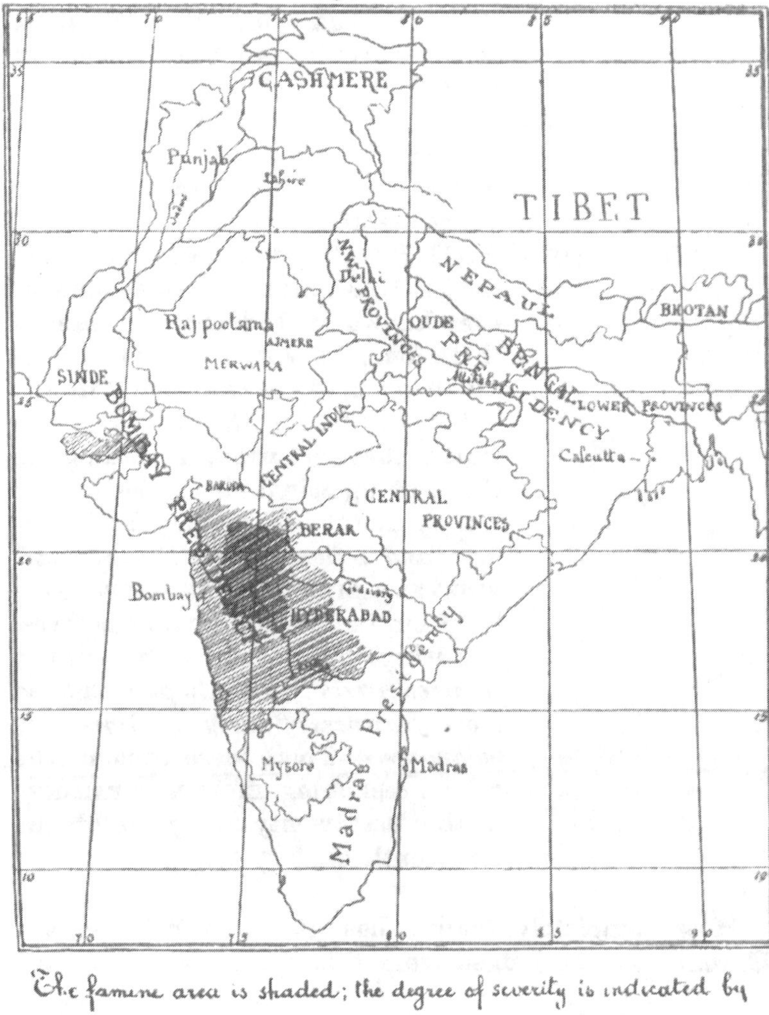

The famine area is shaded; the degree of severity is indicated by the intensity of shading.

THE LAST FAMINE OF THE NINETEENTH CENTURY

1900

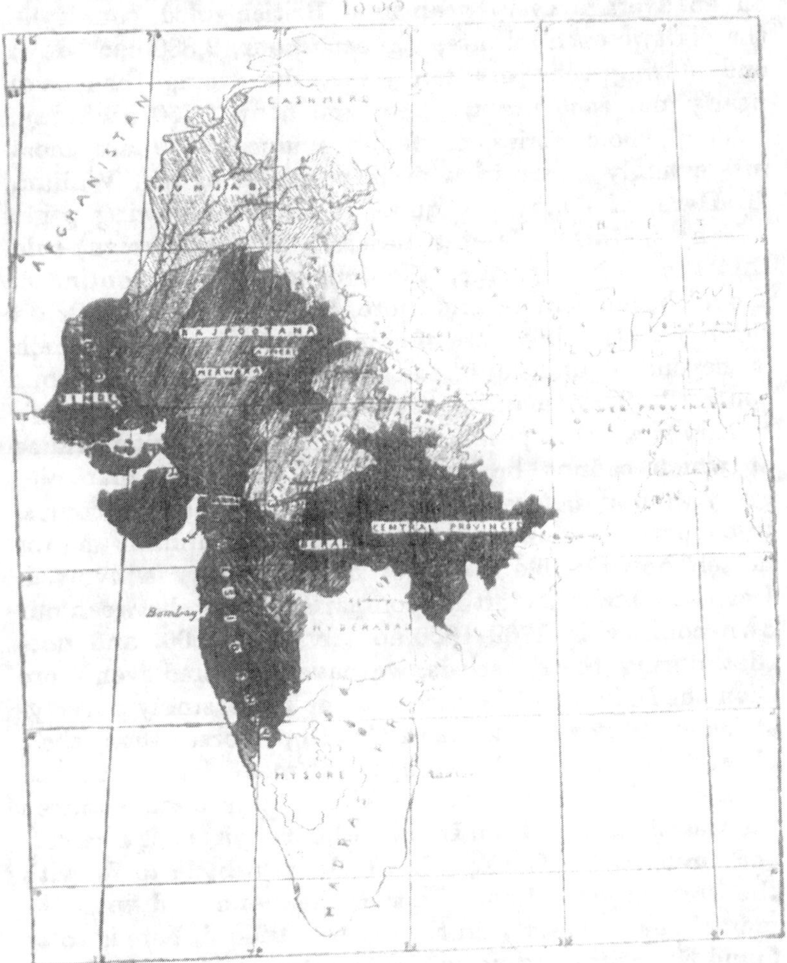

The famine areas are shaded, the degree of severity is indicated by the intensity of shading. The native States are shaded from right to left, thus ///

In the last twenty-five years of the past century more than one million of people died from famine and its effects on an average every year in a British-ruled country—that is two each minute, 120 each hour, 2,880 each day; and, during the past ten years, the average has been nearly four each minute, 240 each hour, 5,760 each day.

The whole series of famines since 1729 are most interestingly shown in a table prepared by Mr. William L. Hare, of Derby. I quote it on the following page.

Why is this? Is it a necessity of our (foreign) rule that the Indian people, the longer our rule continues, should become more and more famine-stricken? Or, is this most alarming state of things, the existence of which is beyond denial, due to causes entirely beyond our control? That matters get worse and worse with each twenty years that passes is a fact the alarming significance of which cannot be overrated. I ask every man and every woman, before whose eyes this comparison comes, to ponder its significance, to ascertain for himself and for herself how terrible a sum of human misery is involved. Let each make a further comparison—say, between our own country in 1769–1800 and in 1869–1900, and note that, during these periods, we have prospered even more than the Indian people have become increasingly poverty-stricken. 'Poverty-stricken?' No, worse than that, FAMINE-stricken. This comparison made, let it be carried a little farther and heed be paid to this circumstance: the wealth drained from India without a direct equivalent, and brought to England, has had not a little to do with the famine conditions on the one hand and with the marvellous prosperity on the other. Indeed, here is to be found the primary cause of India's deplorable condition—*the Economic Drain.* One step farther to be taken by my imagined sympathising readers of both sexes: it is that they should ask themselves the question, 'Is it possible that, recognising these facts, remembering that all the famines have passed into history without effectual measures having been taken to prevent a recurrence, is it

PROVINCE. / YEAR	1729	1770	1781	1783	1790	1791	1799	1802	1803	1805	1812	1823	1833	1837	1854	1860	1865	1868	1873	1877	1885	1889	1890	1891	1897	1900
Bengal		F															F		F		F			F	F	
Behar		F															F		F			F			F	
Orissa																	F					F				
Oudh				F																F			F		F	
N.W. Provinces				F					F		F			F		F		F	F	F			F		F	
Panjab				F														F							F	F
Central Provinces ...																		F							F	F
Central India				F														F							F	F
Rajputana...											F							F							F	F
Sind																										F
Gujarat						F		F	F																	F
Bombay						F		F			F							F		F				F	F	F
Berar																									F	F
Hyderabad						F		F					F		F					F					F	F
Madras	F		F		F		F			F		F	F		F		F			F	F	F			F	
Mysore																				F						
Burmah																								F	F	
PROVINCES AFFECTED ...	1	2	1	4	1	3	1	3	2	1	3	1	2	1	2	1	4	6	3	6	2	3	2	3	13	9

possible, I ask, for any dweller in these home realms in whom is any bowels of compassion, to sit with folded hands and do nothing? Rather, will not all, with a modern patriot poet, cry to their rulers, cry without ceasing, and follow their cries with untiring action :—

> 'O England! O Beloved! O Re-born!
> Look that thou fall not on sleep again!
>
> Thou art a star among the nations yet:
> Be thou a light of succour unto them
> That else are lost in blind and 'whelming seas.
> Around them is the tempest; over them
> Cold splendours of the inhospitable night,
> Augustly unregardful: thou alone
> Art still the North Star to the labouring ship,
> In friendless ocean the befriending orb,
> And, if thou shine not, whither is she steered?
>
> Shine in thy glory, shine on her despair,
> Shine lest she perish—lest of her no more
> Than some lone flotsam of mortality
> Remain to catch the first auroral gleam
> When, in the East, flames the reluctant dawn.'

After the word, the Deed. Who *can* refrain from an effort, however slight, to remove the awful doom which now continually impends over many millions of our fellow-subjects—not strangers, but the King's lieges—in India? Only through the enlightenment of Englishmen and Englishwomen, and through pressure exerted from England, can India be saved from even worse and worse famine conditions than those which have been already described almost times without number. Redemption will not be found *in* India. The Viceroy is too much occupied with the daily work of an Empire too vast for any man, whatever his self-confidence, to imagine he can properly rule, while every civilian is so much concerned with his section of the machinery of State as to be unable to judge of the working of the machine as a whole, or to do anything affecting the whole. If India can be redeemed—which is not at all certain—her redemption will come from the enlightened, and therefore quickened, consciences of British people.

Are Indian famines more destructive to human life now than in ancient days? Yes, and (until the 1901 Census statistics appeared I used to say) No. Yes—they were more destructive within the famine areas until '76–78: since then, the Famine Code, when acted upon as it mercifully was acted upon in the Central Provinces in 1900, checks mortality. The administration of relief, in that year, in that Province, was grappled with in a manner worthy of the best traditions of our nation. The extent may be judged when, in the district of Raipur, forty inhabitants out of each one hundred were on relief. As much time and energy given to the devising of means of prevention as have been given by numberless officials to relief measures, would, ere this, have stopped famine.

There were districts in Bombay in which, despite the Famine Code, the people 'died like flies.' So remarked Sir Antony Macdonnell, President of the latest Famine Commission. Meanwhile the Census Returns have been published :—

Population in 1891, all India ...	287,223,431
Population in 1900, as it should have been with normal increase, put forward by the Government of India as 'normal'	330,306,945
Population in 1901, as it actually was	294,000,000
Minus	36,306,945

The Indian special correspondent of the *Lancet* newspaper, to whom I have already alluded, writing to that journal on May 16, 1901, allowing for a lower rate of increase than did the Indian authorities, put the life loss from famine at nineteen millions of people, '. . . and if,' he remarks, 'we put one million deaths down to plague there remain nineteen millions which can be attributed, with some reason, either to actual starvation or to the diseases arising therefrom.'[1] This statement by the correspondent of what is, probably, the foremost medical journal in the world, means that the loss of life thus recorded represented the 'disappearance' of fully one-half of a popu-

[1] The whole paragraph from which the remark is quoted is as follows: 'During the past ten years it is estimated that the population of the whole of India has only increased by 2,800,000—a rate considerably less than that of the previous decade. There are only two factors which can have an appreciable effect on the number of the people. A diminished birth-rate may have contributed to this lessened increase, but its influence cannot have been very great. At the outside 20 per cent. may be put down to this cause. An enhanced mortality must be the chief factor. It is estimated that there were 20,000,000 more deaths than under ordinary circumstances there should have been, and if we put 1,000,000 deaths down to plague there remain 19,000,000 which can be attributed with some reason either to actual starvation or to the diseases arising therefrom. It is impossible to know how many people have suffered from the famines of the past few years. A further increase in the numbers under famine relief has recently occurred and the total now requiring help is 312,169. These facts speak for themselves.' It would be a singular coincidence if the correspondent in India of the *Lancet* and the Editor of the *Friend of India* should have come to identically the same conclusion on this subject. On May 16, 1901, the *Friend*, in a second article on the Famine Mortality, reviewing the Census results, remarked: 'Even on the violent supposition that, taking the country all round, the reduction in the birth-rate was so great during the three worst years that it no more than sufficed to counterbalance a normal death-rate, still it would account for less than one-third of the defect in the increase of population. We are driven, in short, to the conclusion that, in round numbers, 20,000,000 of the defect were due to enhanced mortality; and, making the most liberal allowance for mortality from plague, we have a balance of at least 19,000,000 deaths which can reasonably be attributed to no other cause than actual starvation, or disease arising indirectly from insufficiency of food. This is a terrible fact, however it may be regarded; and it points to one of two conclusions. Either the Government did not do enough—did not spend enough, labour enough—for the saving of life, or its methods were seriously defective. . . . The inference is that, exert itself as it may on the present lines, and spend as much money as it may, the Government cannot hope to prevent extensive failure of the harvests, even for a single year, from being attended by a mortality so appalling that in any civilised country it would be regarded as conclusive proof of inefficient administration.' Possibly, what has happened is this—the *Lancet* correspondent has borrowed the *Friend's* calculations without acknowledgment of the source of the calculation.

lation as large as that of the United Kingdom! Yet, as I have already remarked, and must again observe, it did not occur to the Editor of that journal, sitting at the very heart of the Empire in his office in the Strand, that he was called upon to make any comments on his correspondent's appalling statement, not even to suggest that the Government might take such steps as should prevent any similar suffering in the future. We have, all of us, grown callous to Indian hunger and starvation, and our medical men, whose sympathies should be the last to become atrophied, judged by this incident, are in the front rank of the heedless, and are among the most unconcerned.

Once more the question may be asked, Are Indian famines more destructive to human life than in ancient days? Again the answer: Yes, and in a more deadly fashion. 'Tis suffering everywhere in India now.

Aforetime, as a rule famine was experienced only after two years of drought or three years of deficient rainfall not amounting to drought;

Now, one year's failure of rain at the right time for agricultural operations, even though plenty of rain fall *during the year* for one harvest, produces acute famine:

Then, the grain stores which every village possessed greatly mitigated suffering. Further, as all India has never, during recorded history, suffered from drought at one and the same time, the pangs of hunger arising from this cause and not to be satisfied were felt only in particular regions—regions isolated, for want of communications, from other parts of India where there was plenty and where the people ate fully from their abundance;

Now, thanks (sour thanks!) to railways which have found their way into every part of the Empire, each year sees the surplus exported which, in other days, was stored; when the faulty rainfall gives them trouble the empty districts are supplied from whatever district has grown a decent crop, with the result that all over India prices rise and rise and never again fall to the old level. Consequently everywhere food is dear, and two hundred millions feel the pinch where, even under the pre-British conditions, a few millions only would have suffered. It is true, as Mr. Vaughan Nash shows in an interesting and well-informed chapter in his book on 'The Great Famine,' there is, even in famine years, food enough grown in India to meet the needs of each year—at a price. There would, however, be no surplus if all the people could, in any given year, eat what they need. The satisfaction of their hunger would empty every bunniah's store as well as absorb every trader's reserves. The railways, by the conveyance of grain to the affected districts, preserve the lives of millions, but they do this at the cost of making the people everywhere pay so high a price that a daily sufficiency of food becomes impossible to ever-increasing millions. The poorer classes who, at any time during the past half-century, seldom seem to have had enough to eat, as a consequence readily succumb to disease until now it is a normal condition of things in India for 'fever' to needlessly slay more Indian folk in three years than war all the world over destroys in thirty years. 'Fever,' said an Anglo-Indian medical authority nearly twenty years ago, 'is a euphemism for insufficient food, scanty clothing, and unfit dwellings.'[1]

Why is it that India is more liable to devastation by famine than are other countries?

In a phrase: Not because rains fail and moisture is denied; always, even in the worst of years, there is water enough poured from the skies on Indian soil to germinate and ripen the grain,[2] but because India is steadily and rapidly growing poorer. Time was when

[1] See the Fever statistics of the last ten years in *The Statistical Abstract of British India*.

[2] For detailed information on this point and an analysis of rain registers for nearly ninety years the reader is referred to a chapter in the *Life of Sir Arthur Cotton* (Hodder and Stoughton) entitled 'Is Famine in India due to an Insufficiency of Rain?'

the Empire was wealthy and prosperous, when, as Milton says of the East, she showered

'on her kings barbaric pearl and gold.'

Time was, not more distant than a century and a half ago, when Bengal was much more wealthy than was Britain. How is it now? Thus: there are many, many, more rich men in the little bit of England comprised between Liverpool and Barrow on the west coast and Hull and Newcastle-on-Tyne on the east coast than there are in the whole of the British Provinces of India. Why? Because, with the best of intentions in the world, or at least what we have deluded ourselves into believing were the best of intentions, we have done that which we ought not to have done and have left undone that which we ought to have done; consequently there is little 'health' in all that vast territory. In existing conditions there can be no improvement, but, contrariwise, further retrogression.

We started our supremacy in India with the fixed idea that dark skins must necessarily cover ignorant and inexperienced minds and wicked souls, especially the latter. The wickedness of an Indian was appalling to one who himself was probably a greater sinner than any Indian he had ever met. That the Founder of Christianity was an Oriental with a brown skin, as brown as that of many Indian races, did not prevent our associating such a skin with more than original sin. We did not *then* consider the Indians to be physical cowards, for it was only by the undaunted courage of Madrassi and Bengali soldiers that we attained our supremacy on the Indian continent. Because of the views we entertained respecting the people, instead of undertaking our rule with the light of local experience, by the aid of men with local knowledge and ability, and, first of all, to the advantage of the people ruled, we assumed that what we did not know, even about the government of an Asiatic kingdom—its climate, its people, its customs, its history, of all of which we were quite ignorant, was not worth knowing. There was, we reasoned, to be no gainsaying that the ideas and practices which had made certain islands in the Western Ultima Thule great and prosperous were good enough for any country anywhere: and, it went without saying, particularly for India. Our practice in this respect was always tempered with the notion that we had to get something handsome out of our connection with India. ['The labourer,' we piously observed, 'is worthy of his hire,' and our hire we put at many millions of pounds sterling every year—paid regularly on monthly or quarterly pay-days.] So we embarked on a course of government founded upon certain economic principles which, in the result, has drained India of nearly all its resources, deprived it of working capital, and in so doing have rendered it helpless to cope with the changing necessities of a scientific and mechanical age—an age in which above all the ages that have preceded it money is required to make money. Although the consequences of what we have done, of the almost insane conceit we had (and still have) that we know everything and that India can teach us nothing, particularly in the art of ruling Oriental territories[1] —though the consequences are before our eyes, we will not see that (in some cases without meaning it) we have done ill to India and not good.

A potent example of our recent mispolicy is at hand as I write. Railways proved to be essential to the successful development of the mechanical arts in the United Kingdom. Therefore India, almost entirely an agricultural country, must be gridironed with steel rails. The locomotive must be as omnipresent among the bare fields of India as it is among the tall chimneys of Lancashire and Yorkshire factories. The members of a Select Com-

[1] Even Sir Henry Maine, philosopher and jurist, could find nothing valuable in the Indian life and thought of to-day, or even in the India of the past. And yet India *was* great in both spiritual and material things; is great to-day—no country in the world so great in many respects.

mittee of the House of Commons which, in 1878, conducted an inquiry into Public Works (East India) are, primarily, the authors of the recent famines—that is to say, the Report which they agreed upon makes those Committeemen jointly responsible with the India Office and the Government of India, who accepted and carried out the recommendations, for much, if not for all, of the vast amount of human anguish and widespread loss recently experienced. My matured conviction, after an exhaustive study of the whole question, is that, had the views which the greatest of Indian irrigation engineers, Sir Arthur Cotton, put forward in 1878 been adopted, instead of having been contemned, the recent famines would not have occurred, or if there had been scarcities in some parts of India they would have borne no relation to the 'terrible' famines which have wrought so much devastation. What makes our conduct as the nation responsible for the good government of India the more blamable is that the greatest of all the Famine Commissions—that which reported in 1880—gave the same advice to the authorities in India and in England two years after the Select Committee had reported, as did the veteran irrigation engineer. The Commissioners, in their Report, said:—

'Among the means that may be adopted for giving India *direct protection from famine arising from drought, the* FIRST PLACE *must unquestionably be assigned to works of irrigation.* It has been too much the custom, in discussions as to the policy of constructing such works, to measure their value by their financial success, considered only with reference to the net return to Government on the capital invested in them. The true value of irrigation works is to be judged very differently. First must be reckoned the direct protection afforded by them in years of drought by the saving of human life, by the avoidance of loss of revenue remitted and of the outlay incurred in costly measures of relief. But it is not only in years of drought that they are of value. In seasons of average rainfall they are of great service and a great source of wealth, giving certainty to all agricultural operations, increasing the out-turn per acre of the crops, and enabling more valuable descriptions of crops to be grown. From the Panjab in the north to Tinnevelly at the southern extremity of the peninsula, wherever irrigation is practised, such results are manifest; and we may see rice, sugar cane, or wheat taking the place of millets or barley, and broad stretches of indigo growing at a season when unwatered lands must lie absolutely unproductive.'

The way in which the India Office and the Government of India acted upon the deliverance of the Commission of their own creation is this: From 1882–83 to 1897–98 they expended—

from REVENUE nearly *seven* times more on railways than on irrigation works, and

from CAPITAL more than *six* times as much.

Not only is irrigation in such a country as India quite needful if crops are to be grown every year, not only does irrigation immensely increase the productive power of the soil—four times at least—but by the supply-canals being made navigable nearly all that India wants in the way of district development and of general communication, with a few trunk lines of railway, could have been provided at a very moderate cost—a cost easily within a prosperous India's own providing. Increased production, cheaper communication, from one and the same source. Unsuited and costly locomotion with no production was the other and favoured policy. Direct water communication with every part of India could have been provided. The adoption, in 1878, of the policy which was rejected would have changed the whole face of India and have brought to England a ray of glory of a character which she may not now claim. Indeed, discredit has taken the place of what would have been a monument of unassailable praise.

In the mistaken Report of 1878, which was too readily acted upon, and in the neglect to follow the wise course recommended by the Commission of 1880, are, I repeat, to be found the chief reasons why there have been so many and such terrible famines in India during the past twenty years.

Irrigation is *a* remedy for famine: there are no famines in any fully canal-irrigated districts in India, though terrible disasters occurred in some of them in pre-irrigation days. Irrigation is more than *a* remedy; it is a *great* remedy. But if all that the venerable water prophet of Madras predicted and indicated in his plans for every part of India had been carried out, or were yet to be adopted, and a great accession came, as it would come, to the annual income of our Eastern Empire, all this would merely postpone for twenty, forty, years, maybe, that collapse which is inevitable unless the whole economic principles on which India is governed be radically amended. We are, literally, draining India dry—bleeding, was Lord Salisbury's term in 1875; it is more accurate than my own. One consequence is discernible in the increased frequency of famines, to which attention has already been drawn. Now, as in the days of old, neither more nor less, rain-failure, monsoon-disturbance, occur. Wherein the present differs from the past is in the lamentable fact that the people are now so poor that they cannot stand any strain, not even the slightest.

There are no stores of grain in the villages;

the property represented by gold and silver (and pewter) ornaments is greatly depleted, has almost disappeared;

the ancient occupations of the people on sea and land have been destroyed, and more and more of men and women are driven to the soil without capital wherewith to properly cultivate it;

the ships which now carry its coastwise trade are steamers built in Britain, the officers are Britons, the profits derivable from the trade go to Britain;

the hillsides, joyous with the richly-blossomed tea and coffee bushes, the plains radiant at harvest-time with the indigo and jute plants, are cultivated with foreign capital and the profits arising therefrom go out of India, while all the managers are foreigners;

every profession and every mercantile enterprise which

spell profit are, in their higher and more largely-paid positions, exploited by foreigners to the detriment of the natives of the country;

all this is likewise true of the *personnel* of the Administration in each of its higher branches, where, above everything else, such a state of things ought not to have been conceivable even in a modified or remote degree.

This is why famine approximates more and more towards becoming a representation of the normal condition of many parts of India. As regards the future, it is not more certain that to-morrow's sun will rise on its annual course and perform its diurnal journey than it is that the sufferings of the Indian people will—a vast change denied—year by year become greatly increased. Even now those sufferings cry to Heaven for amelioration, and cry vainly, for the Eye which erstwhile saw the sparrow fall, and the Ear which heard the faintest cry, appear to be both closed for ever. Saddest of all, in any backward glance over British-Indian history, is the thought that the very opposite to what is now experienced was, if we cared to adopt it, before us as a certain achievement. This I have shown by citations from early documents in a previous chapter. Had the wiser policy been adopted, Britain would have built, for Britons to rejoice over, an edifice of imperishable renown based on the greater prosperity of the Indian people; England's trade with India would have been vastly bigger than it now is and have become a token of imperial prosperity instead of, as now, a sign of approaching death. The two policies have always been before us. As if under an almost demoniac possession, every time the choice has been ours, we have chosen the wrong. Under the East India Company the renewal of the Charter gave us the choice once every twenty years; to-day Parliament gives us the opportunity every year, but if India be mentioned, it is true of our legislators that 'they all with one consent begin to make excuse,' they troop out of the legislative chamber, and

India remains unredeemed. That is one reason why famine is to-day chronic in India.

Do any of us, I wonder, realise what the great nations of the world are thinking and saying of our administration in connection with these many dreadful famines? Depend upon it, they see the consequences which we will not allow ourselves to see and concerning which we comfort ourselves by describing what we do see by other and inoffensive appellations. I have seldom, as a Briton, felt more humiliated than I did in January, 1900, when I happened to be in Paris. *Le Matin*, one of the most trustworthy of Parisian journals, one day contained a long article descriptive of the sufferings of the famine-stricken Indian people, and depreciatory of British rule. Knowing I had lived in India, the President of the British Chamber of Commerce in Paris came to me, as he said, so that I should supply him with material whereby he could demolish such horrible slanders on the British name as were contained in the article in question. I replied that I should only be too happy to do what he wanted. I read the article carefully. When I got to the end of it, I found I could not contradict or disprove a single statement it contained. There were some alleged incidents as to which I could say nothing, as I had no information concerning them, except that they were not improbable. The main story was unassailable, the deductions not unreasonable. The story was not complimentary, the deductions were not flattering, either to our self-esteem or to our humanity as the rulers of India.

The like thing happened in the United States. When Lord Curzon, in 1900, carried a begging bowl among the nations beseeching subscriptions for the famine-stricken, the question was asked, 'Why should America give?' It was urged that India's millions were starving because of England's neglect of duty to India.

Is it too late to bring India back to prosperity? More often than not, in pondering over the situation, I think it is too late. Only by a change in the mind and attitude of the English people, requiring a great miracle to bring it about, is it possible to cherish even a hope for better things, for a brighter outlook. In the best of circumstances, which is that the British people, on being instructed as to the real facts of the case, should put their whole heart and strength into an effort for reform—the task will be tremendously difficult. But will the instruction be given? Where are the instructors? Who amongst us have eyes to see, ears to hear? If we would but see, did we dare to let ourselves hear, what India from nearly all her hundreds of districts is showing to us, is saying to us, only one thing *could* happen; we should be so worked upon as to determine, God helping us, that this one thing we would do:

We would so change the conditions of our rule in India that the inhabitants of that distressful country should once again in their history have daily bread enough for comfortable sustenance, and that the whole realm of India once more should taste the sweets of prosperity.

Meanwhile, whether we heed them or whether we scorn them—

> 'A sorrowing people, in their mortal pain,
> Toward one far and famous ocean isle
> Stretch hands of prayer.'

Shall they—

> 'stretch those
> Hands in vain?'

VOX INDIÆ CLAMANTIS.

['"In their prosperity will be our strength, in their contentment our security, and in their gratitude our best reward." The forthcoming debate on the Indian Budget reminds us that we have still to profit by the wise words of Queen Victoria.'—*Daily Paper*.]

PROSPERITY!—when year by year
Grim poverty I see
Draw ever nearer and more near,
Devouring all my children's gear—
Why, what a mockery is here
Of Her benign decree!

What strength, O England, shall be thine
When such prosperity is mine?
Contentment!—what contentment lies
In that poor slavish heart,
That dumb despair, with sunken eyes,
That bears its ills, and rather dies
A thousand deaths than dare to rise
And play a freeman's part?

Ah, what security can be
On such contentment based by thee?
My gratitude?—ah, empty name!
Thy charitable mites
But feed to-day the feeble frame
That starves to-morrow; for the same
Old wrong grows on untouched. I claim
Not charity, but rights—
England, what gratitude have I?
Canst find reward in apathy?

—*Punch*, July 31, 1901.

TO

THE HONOURED MEMORY OF THE FAMINE-SLAIN

IN INDIA DURING THE PERIOD

1891—1901.

To you, Hira Singh Puri, your Wife and Little Ones,
,, Abe Ram, ,, ,,
,, Pershotum Cundy, ,, ,,
,, Krishna Das, ,, ,,
,, Hassan Khan, ,, ,,
,, Ram Suk, son of Luchman, ,,
and
,, Muttu Ramaswamy, ,, ,,

With all others of your respective races, there were at the least nineteen millions of you between 1891 and 1901, who

PERISHED FROM FAMINE,

I,

humbly, on behalf of myself and my fellow-Britons, men, women, and children, who, under God, are responsible for your welfare,

Pay my Sincere Homage

to

your patience, your long-suffering, your resignation, your general acquiescence in a condition of affairs which afflicted you so sorely; and, above all, for the entire absence on your part from holding us responsible for your sufferings.

For, had you been strict to mark accountability, all justification were wanting.

I CANNOT SAY, 'GOD HELPING US, WE WILL ENSURE THAT

NEVER AGAIN SHALL SUCH SUFFERINGS AFFLICT YOUR RACE-FELLOWS WHO REMAIN.'

Believe me,

this is not because we in England were deliberately heartless, cruel in our thoughts, or wilfully careless concerning your well-being.

No! that was not our position:

We were among the Kindest-Hearted and Most Sympathetic People in the World (at least, this is what we often told ourselves),

But,

We were your Rulers, whatever happens in India happens as the result of what we do, and our eyes are holden so that we cannot see, our minds are numbed so that we cannot understand, that what is happening in India may be (I, for one, say *is*)

THE NECESSARY RESULT OF OUR SYSTEM OF RULE.

If this fact were once realised
by my Countrymen and Countrywomen,
The Hunger and Thirst, the Nakedness and Poverty, of Your People would speedily come to an end.

How shall this fact be brought home to the English Mind?

I KNOW NOT. I DESPAIR OF ITS EVER BEING DONE.

There is no Hope for Your Race.

YOU HAVE DIED. YOU HAVE DIED USELESSLY.

No one learns the lesson which your dying should teach.

Those you have left behind (less happy are they than are you) cannot do anything. They are listless in their energies, they are blind to the peril in which they stand.

Why? All their energies, necessarily, are concentrated in trying to keep life in their emaciated bodies.

WHO SHALL RESCUE YOUR SUCCESSORS FROM THIS BODY OF DEATH?

Again: I KNOW NOT. No one in authority here seems to know, or even to care very much, that they need salvation. I judge from their playing with words, their refraining from taking adequate action, their intense self-satisfaction with themselves, their belief that everything they do is for the best.

Nevertheless,
we deeply sympathise with them, and, when the next Famine becomes acute,

WE WILL SUBSCRIBE FOR THEIR RELIEF,

Less than Sixpence for every Hundred Pounds we have received from India since 1700.

It is true, really true,

we are sorry for them; as for stopping Famines, we are (we say) in God's Hands, and when He sends India less rain than we should like, or fails to send it at the moment which best suits their unirrigated fields, we say we can do nothing but help them to pull through—with the money we first take from them. If your people do *not* 'pull through,' we are sorry, but the fault, as you must know, really, is not ours; it is all God Almighty's. Kismet. His will be done.

That, actually, is not the whole truth, but it is the 'truth' with which we deaden our consciences. We *could* conserve the rain which does fall, if we would, and so save many of those who remain.

There, however, I must leave this matter. As I have said: We are sorry, very, very, sorry; but, you know, God is great. His will is powerful among the nations. We are but His instruments!

To my Countrymen, however, I say:
'AWAKE! ARISE! Remain not for ever fallen!'

Britons, protect the hungry ones: their fathers' bones
Lie scattered on vast Indian plains and hills;
Protect e'en them who, loyal, serve and trust
While all around them waste and die.
Forget not; day by day note thou the groans
Of those thy subjects, in their ancient homes
Slain by the ruthless Fiend, Starvation, who
Takes Mother and her infant heedlessly. Their moans
The vales redouble to the hills, and they
To Heaven. Their martyred blood and ashes sow
O'er all the English fields, where still do sway
Those who COULD prevent; that from these may grow
A hundredfold of succour, and, having learnt the way
You will, ere long, securely end this woe.

Sunday Morning, March 10, 1901.

APPENDICES

I

Letter *extracted from a long Correspondence with* **Sir Henry H. Fowler**, G.C.S.I., P.C., M.P., *sometime Secretary of State for India.*

Valyevo, Bromley, Kent,
February 4, 1901.

The Right Honourable Sir Henry H. Fowler, G.C.S.I.,
M.P., P.C., etc., etc., Woodthorne, Wolverhampton.

Dear Sir,—I now proceed to deal with the questions contained in your letter of January 30th, acknowledgment of which I made on the 31st ultimo.

The questions you ask are two in number, namely,—

1. 'With reference to the question you put to me as to the expected recurrence of a famine in a small portion of the famine area of last year I shall be glad to know whether if this district had shared in the abundant rains in the autumn which have ensured good crops in four-fifths of that area, it would not have reaped the same harvest?'

2. 'And, in what respect you think the Government is responsible for the difference between the two portions of the same area.'

First, I must demur to the use of your expression 'small portion of the famine area,' 'good crops in four-fifths of that area.' So far as I can follow Lord Curzon's definition of areas they cover considerably more than one-fifth of last year's famine area, and, this time, a part of the Carnatic as well. In the Carnatic, let me add, it is a sin for us to permit a famine to occur for want of water, so abundant are Nature's supplies even in the worst rainfall years. In India it is the experience of administrators that their early forecasts are always exceeded. The ninety millions 'affected' last year began with about forty millions. It is not a minor disaster now facing us, but a serious one. To draw the right lesson from it is 'a man's job,' and that is one reason why I am troubling you, an experienced administrator and one of the leaders of an historic English political party, with my observations.

Next, as I read your questions once more, and especially the second one, Tennyson's lines occur to me:

'Flower in the crannied wall,
I pluck you out of the crannies;—
I hold you here, root and all, in my hand,
Little flower—but *if* I could understand
What you are, root and all, and all in all,
I should know what God and man is.'

So, in like manner, if I am to answer your second question I shall need to write a long treatise; for, to indicate in what respects the Indian Government is responsible for the frequent famines in India is to deal with every branch of Indian administration, and to go back to the roots of the evil which were planted, in some cases deliberately planted (of which I have official proof) nearly one hundred years ago. Unhappily, though I have a knowledge as to how all this should be done and have my authorities handy for reference, I am a man who is under the necessity to give all his days to the earning of his living, and have only spare hours in the evenings and on Sunday mornings and afternoons to devote to this grave matter. I can, therefore, only give you brief statements of what I regard as indisputable facts, and in respect to which, where I do not state it, you must take my word that I have adequate authority for all I state.

You ask: 'If this' (the now affected) 'district had shared in the abundant rains in the autumn which have ensured good crops in four-fifths of that area, would it not have reaped the same harvest?'

(*a*) I do not know positively whether it would or would not. The requisite information for answering the question is not available here. So much depends upon the *period* at which the rain falls. Replying (as he imagines) to my letter in last Tuesday's *Standard* Colonel Bloomfield, an official of thirty-five years' experience, says famines are due, 'simply and manifestly from the failure of the rains. . . . when one of these (monsoon currents) fails, *e.g.*, Orissa suffers.' The answer to this is that in 1865–66, the year of the Orissa famine, fully sixty inches of rain fell in the Province. It fell at wrong times and too much at one time. Sir Arthur Cotton declares that if storage lakes had been provided and other consequential arrangements made, the crops could have been saved and the famine prevented. I do not know that sufficient rain did not fall in the now affected districts to answer every purpose, if only we had preserved it in storage lakes and from them led channels to existing tanks and have built others. My belief, founded on my close study of the irrigation needs of some of these regions, is that enough rain did fall to ensure crops but that our want of prevision—(your own, Sir, in some respects, especially during the years you were Secretary of State)—in storing what God's reservoirs supplied to us, is really to blame. If I had time to take you, with adequate plans, district by district, over this whole area I am satisfied that I could demonstrate to you that it is only supineness and our determination in the past to build railways instead of navigation canals and irrigation works and our (needlessly) swollen military expenditure, which have prevented all these districts being protected—in like manner, if not to the same extent—as have the districts of Godaveri and Kistna in Madras and the Ganges Valley in Bengal and the North-Western Provinces.

For myself, I repeat that I believe enough rain lately has fallen in the particular area to which you allude, to grow crops, if only we had conserved it.

(b) You further ask whether the people in this area, given plenty of rain, would not have reaped as good crops as are being reaped in the other parts of last year's famine area. I don't know what you intend to convey by the term 'good crops.' Save, under canal irrigation chiefly, and in a few exceptional instances otherwise, no good crops, properly so called, are nowadays grown on 'dry land' in India. (The dry land area includes 166,078,159 acres against 30,414,499 in the 'wet' area.) Owing to the great 'drain' from India which has been going on for a hundred and thirty years—and more, and never to so great an extent as now, no capital remains in the country for use by the cultivator. Mill ('Political Economy,' ch. v.) says: 'Industry is limited by capital. Industry cannot be employed to any greater extent than there is capital to invest.' Once the cultivator could manure his fields—now he cannot; once he could well afford to allow land to lie fallow and also to arrange for a rotation of crops—now he cannot; consequently, the production of the fields has greatly fallen off—to the extent of thirty per cent. says one authority. In my letter of the 27th ultimo to your two Wolverhampton newspapers, I stated that since 1882—

16,000,000 additional acres have been brought under cultivation,
Rs.14,50,00,000 have been spent on irrigation (which means an increase of produce *six* times greater than dry land of the same area as the irrigation channels serve could supply, even when moderately manured), and
Rs. 60,00,00,000 have been expended on railway extension.

Nevertheless, the agricultural income of India in 1898–99 was only Rs.285,86,34,562 against Rs.350,00,00,000 in 1882, a *decrease* of Rs.64,11,65,438. That decrease, I unhesitatingly assert, is largely due to the decreasing fertility, the increasing sterility, of the soil.

That sterility arises from want of manure, which indicates the absence of any working capital. Our economic system of rule is responsible for this state of things; it is that system which has sucked the orange nearly juiceless. We have brought to England for our enrichment that which should have remained in India to fructify and increase the wealth of that land. If it had been so left, India would, probably, have been a better customer of ours than she is now—herself prosperous.

I have given such answer as my limited time permits to your first question. Now for your second inquiry.

2. 'And, in what respect you think the Government is responsible for the difference between the two portions of the same area.'

Do you know, Sir, I do not think there is very much difference 'between the two portions of the same area,' even though crops will be reaped on one portion? So far as many, many, millions of the agricultural population of India are concerned, there is not much to choose between a famine year and a non-famine year. Twenty-one years ago, in a Midland town, the smoke from the factory chimneys of which can almost be seen from the heights of Tettenhall, the late Sir William Hunter discoursed on 'England's Work in India.' He discussed normal, not abnormal, conditions—non-famine years, not famine years. He said: 'There remain forty millions of people who go through life on insufficient food.'

Since those remarks were made the population has increased (or is alleged to have increased) by nearly sixty millions. Meanwhile—Lord Curzon's latest famine speech being my authority—the income of the Empire has not increased during this period. Wherefore this follows that if, with the same income, in 1880, forty millions were insufficiently fed, the additional millions cannot have had—cannot now have—enough to eat. This, then, ensues—

40,000,000 plus, say, 50,000,000 make 90,000,000; and there are this number of continually hungry people in British India at the beginning of the twentieth century.

In addition to this dreadful conclusion, one million and a half *more* people die of 'fever' (an official medical report, published in 1886 or thereabouts, speaks of fever as a euphemism for innutrition and insufficient clothing) now than died from like causes ten years ago, and the aggregate was high then! For every person who now dies from fever twenty persons are attacked by the disease. As, in 1897, the total number of 'fever' deaths was 5,015,842, you can estimate how much of physical suffering at least fifty millions of men, women, and children whom you once ruled, and may rule again, have to endure. An appreciable portion of these five millions of deaths are, practically, famine deaths in (so-called) non-famine years. 'A great majority of the rural population pass through at least one or two attacks of fever during the year,' is stated of one region.

Then, when I find that, in response to Lord Dufferin's inquiry in 1887, such reports as I hereunder summarise are put forward as 'satisfactory,' I again say that I am not sure there is such a thing as a non-famine year at any time in any 'dry'-cultivation regions in India. Here are a few records from the North-Western Provinces, which Mr. Romesh Dutt tells us are as fairly assessed as any of the territory not under a Permanent Settlement—

Mr. Crooke, Collector of Etah, under the stimulus of the Dufferin Circular in 1887, convened a meeting 'of the most experienced cultivators . . . and asked them to make an estimate of the income and expenditure of a man—owner of a pair of oxen and a single plough, and cultivating a patch of average land irrigated from a well.' The sample holding taken represented five acres and a half. 'The crops grown, out-turn, and value of the produce of such a holding would be as follows':—

Income.	Rs.	a.	p.	*Expenditure.*	Rs.	a.	p.
Kharif harvest ...	129	8	0	Rent...	75	0	0
Rabi „ ...	84	8	0	Seed grain	13	8	0
				Other cultivating expenses	79	10	0
				Balance	45	14	0
Total ...	214	0	0	Total ...	214	0	0

That Rs.45 14a. (English money, £3 1s. 1d.) was all the family of this small farmer had to live upon for one year. Food was 17 seers a rupee—a seer is just over 2 lbs.—which required Rs.54 per annum for this necessary of life alone, leaving nothing whatever for clothing, though Rs.2 per head represent the minimum requirement. Thus, with only four reckoned to a family instead of five, as should have been, these families (for this a *typical* case) were Rs.16 short of enough money for food and decent clothing; and if five were reckoned, as ought to have been, the shortage would then have been Rs.32. Sir, I ask you, who are wont to make much of what you call the light taxation of India, to ponder these facts, especially the fact that Rs.75 out of Rs.214 produce value goes for rent, and not to overlook the other details as to the unmet needs of the family, including something for religion. There is no wonder English Christians have to pay for Christian teaching in India; with such particulars as these throwing light on the inability of the Indian people to give anything even to save their own immortal souls, it is clear they cannot hear the Gospel at their own charge. No Million Guineas New Century Fund could be suggested here by your political co-worker, Mr. R. W. Perks, although the population is six times that of our own, and a great deal more than sixty times that of the Wesleyan Methodist membership of the United Kingdom.

Kindly note that this land was irrigated (well-watered) land.

Of this same region an official reporter says: 'As to clothes, the women and children are worse off than the men. *It is unusual to find a village woman who has any wraps at all.* Most of them have to pass the night as best they can in their day clothes—a cotton petticoat, wrapper, and bodice.'

Here are some sample cases:—

Name of Cultivator.	Receipts.			Expenditure.			Rent.		
	Rs.	a.	p.	Rs.	a.	p.	Rs.	a.	p.
Rup Ram (17 acres) ...	341	9	0	350	0	0	306	0	0
Baksha, Chamar (7 acres)...	102	0	0	124	0	0[1]	40	0	0
Hira, Lodha (24 acres) ...	162	0	0	284	0	0	72	8	0

Parsi, Lodha, aged 62, labourer, earns Rs.16 per annum; his daughter for grinding grain earns Rs.11 4a. The joint income is Rs.27 4a., which is just enough to buy two seers of grain a day, and leaves nothing for any other purpose. 'No children are to be married: he had one son and four daughters, who have all been married. Through poverty, in the marriage of his daughters, he had recourse to a less formal way of marriage, viz., *dola*, *i.e.*, he went to the house of the daughter's intended husband and consummated the marriage by giving only a small sum of Rs.5 or Rs.6.'

Here are two examples from Muttra District, North-Western Provinces:—

Name.	Receipts.			Expenditure.			Rent.		
Kamle, Chamar (10 acres and 6 kinds of produce)	Rs. 91	a. 0	p. 0	Rs. 104	a. 12	p. 0	Rs. 32	a. 0	p. 0
Abe Ram (9 acres) ...	103	4	0	129	15	0	68	15	0

This man's crops, when sold, realised Rs.70 4a.; the rent he paid was Rs.68 15a. 'When he had grain the family (five) ate five seers daily; at other times and now, when grain is dear, only three seers or less.' 'He ate the bajra before it was ripe.' 'He has no blanket.' Yet he is a farmer tilling nearly nine acres![2]

Two brothers, both married, no children—household: their wives, themselves, a cousin, an aunt—six in all. 'Fields are irrigated from a first-class well.' Income and expenditure show a debit of Rs.8 2a. 6p. They 'can afford a blanket.' Fancy, dear Sir, Indian farmers who, probably, have lived and laboured under your own painstaking and benign rule, *if they have no children* can actually afford to possess a blanket—one a-piece, I imagine, though this is not stated. The nights are cold enough in all conscience in the North-Western winter to make one hope there *was* a blanket each for these Indian yeomen and their womankind.

---

[1] Out of this expenditure the shockingly extravagant sum of Rs.2 is put down as having been spent on 'Marriage and funeral expenses.'

[2] These incidents are told again in these pages, in a consideration of the economic condition of the North-Western Provinces. They cannot be told too often.

In the Etawah District, Mr. Alexander reports: In the village Marhapur 'the fifty-five cultivating householders were all in debt at the close of the year for sums varying from Rs.800 to Rs.10, and the day-labourers for sums varying from Rs.18 to Rs.2: most of the farmers were also obliged to part with jewelry or cattle.'

The above facts, I may once more state, are reported concerning what is declared to be the most fairly assessed Provinces under British rule outside the Lower Provinces of Bengal. I was going to say, God help the rest! But such people seem to be outside the help even of a Divine Ruler. If they had a hymn-book containing spiritual songs, I wonder how they would feel if they were called upon to sing such a verse as this—

> 'Thou art coming to a King:
> Large petitions with thee bring,
> For His grace and power are such
> None can ever ask too much.'

Evidently so far as India is concerned, He 'is asleep, or is on a journey.' Anyhow, whether their petition be for little or much, it is wholly unheeded. They get worse, not better.

I pause, sick at heart with what I could not help but write. Necessity is laid on me to say all this to you. If these things be typical—and in nothing I have stated have I gone elsewhere than to the reports of British officials who were put upon their defence to show that Sir W. W. Hunter's statements could not be true—how can I concern myself with the point you make in your second question?

'In what respect,' you ask, 'is the Government responsible for the difference between the two portions of the same area?' To me it seems that as between the cropped area and the partially cropped area (the non-famine and the famine districts, as they are officially called) there is very little to choose. Under the admirable Famine Code, admirable when fairly administered as it was last year in the Central Provinces—still admirable, but a cloak for great inhumanity, when administered as it was in Bombay (see Sir Antony Macdonnell's remarks on the 31st of January last) until Mr. Vaughan Nash, quoting a work on famines which I wrote in 1878, publicly demonstrated its cruelty—under the Famine Code, I say, the position of the famine-stricken farmer with his crops and the labourer will be as good as that of the farmer with his crops, as that of the prisoner in the district jail is—so far as food goes, better than either. For the revenue authorities and the moneylender between them will carry off every particle of grain beyond what is needed for daily food. Nay, worse: it is doubtful if the majority of cultivators in the well-cropped area will get as much to eat the year through as they would if they were located in famine camps—that is so long as they are not under the 'penal' control of the Bombay authorities.

The only real answer, dear Sir, which can be given to your questions is that, famine year or no (official) famine year, India is always in a state of famine and every year we are making matters worse, or if you do not like that word 'making' I will say we are permitting matters to get worse. In the end, so far as the cultivator is concerned, it comes to the same thing. I cannot, in the presence of such a state of things as now exists in India, split hairs in the way which would be necessary if I answered your second question in detail. I have not the inclination, even if I had the power attributed, by Butler in 'Hudibras,' to the controversialist—

> 'Who could a hair divide
> Betwixt the south and south-west side.'

Nor, I conceive, do you want to 'greatly quarrel with a straw.' Substantial justice, I am sure, is what you desire. If you could be convinced, as I am convinced, of the steady heaping up of wrath against the day of wrath, the weight of which England must one day bear, which is characterising our administration of India, and which, when it bursts, will be the consequence of that administration, I am sure you would not be less eager than I am that a change for the better should be at once made. If I still believed in the God, amongst whose steadfast worshippers in the Free Churches of this favoured land you rank high, I would pray to Him to touch your heart with experiences such as He granted in another famine-time to his prophet Elijah, so that you might grapple with the Indian evil and overcome it. For, with your great abilities, and occupying the high political position that you have won for yourself, if the scales could only be made to fall from your eyes and you could see things as they really are and not 'see men as trees walking,' you could not refrain from throwing all your energies into the conflict. But I cannot now appeal to you by the most sacred of all names, and, for Christ His sake, ask you to study this question for yourself, and without the help of the gentlemen of the Council of the Secretary of State for India. My study of Indian conditions has taken away from me every vestige of the trust I once had in the Redeemer, in Him of whom it was said, 'We trusted that it was He who should redeem Israel.' It is only on the grounds of a common humanity, in the light of my sense of duty as a British citizen to our Indian wards, I can now appeal to you. And, with all my heart, I do so appeal to you as man to man, as Liberal to Liberal, as Englishman to Englishman. As I have repeatedly said, the conclusions I arrive at I base entirely on official statistics and official statements. I judge the result of the rule in which you have had a great and responsible share solely by what those carrying on that rule themselves put forward. From their lips I receive the information which reduces everything I would fain write on India, let me struggle to the contrary never so strenuously, to an indictment of British rule.

In all that I have written I have only distantly alluded to the economic and political causes which have brought about the state of things in India which makes it possible such a letter as this should be addressed to an English statesman. I cannot touch upon those causes to-day. But somewhere and somehow I trust the opportunity may come to me to lay them before you and my countrymen generally. Meanwhile, enough has, I hope, been said to induce you to resume your Indian studies, this time to pursue them in official documents, and not leaning upon the arms of those who are responsible for what needs to be examined and to whose minds it doth not yet appear there is spot or blemish or any such thing on their administration of India.

I remain,

Yours most truly,

WM. DIGBY.

II

THE CAUSE OF INDIAN FAMINES.—'THE EXTREME, THE ABJECT, THE AWFUL, POVERTY OF THE INDIAN PEOPLE'

The *New England Magazine* for September, 1900 (vol. xxiii., No. 1. Boston, Massachusetts), contained a summary investigation of the causes of famine in India by the Rev. J. T. Sunderland, who is able to speak of the condition of the people from personal observation. Referring to the series of famines, he says:—

'Such a state of things naturally awakens the sympathy of the world. But it ought to do more. It ought to compel a far more careful inquiry than has yet been made as to the causes of the famines, with a view to ascertaining whether these causes can be removed or not, and thus whether such scourges as now visit India with such appalling frequency are or are not preventable.'

Mr. Sunderland commences with an examination of the two most commonly alleged causes. The first question is: 'Does the failure of the periodic rains of India necessitate famine?'

'FAILURE OF RAINS IS NOT THE CAUSE.

'The great monsoon rains which supply most of the moisture for India vary greatly from year to year. These rains of course man cannot control. If they are abundant over the whole land, the whole land has abundant crops. If they fail in parts, those parts have agricultural scarcity. Three things, however, should be remembered. One is, that there is never failure of water everywhere; when drought is severest in certain sections, other sections have plenty. The second is that India is a land where there is much irrigation, and easily might be much more; and wherever irrigation exists failure of rain does not necessarily mean failure of crops. The third thing to be remembered is that transportation is easy between all parts of the land. On two sides is the sea; navigable rivers and canals penetrate large sections; there is no extended area that does not have its railway. Thus food can readily be conveyed from areas of abundance to areas of scarcity. Under these circumstances it is easy to see that, even if we admit to the fullest extent the uncertainty of rains in many large areas of India, it does not follow that there need be famine or loss of life in those areas.

'It should not be forgotten that the aggregate of rainfall in India, taking the country as a whole, is large. The heaviest recorded precipitation in the world is found here. The only difficulty is that of distribution; and even in the matter of distribution, India's mountains and rivers furnish such facilities as are seen in few other lands of the world. . . . Thus India has two sources of water supply on a large scale: one is her rains, which fall in abundance in many parts; the other her mountains, which send down numerous and in some cases vast rivers to afford opportunities for almost limitless irrigation as they travel on their long journeys to the sea. As a result, the agricultural possibilities of India are greater than those of almost any other country in the world.

'Wherever in India water can be obtained for irrigation, crops are certain. From time immemorial there has been much irrigation. Since India came under the control of the British, the Government has interested itself to some extent in promoting irrigation works. But unfortunately it has also been guilty of much neglect. Not only have important opportunities for supplying extensive areas with water for irrigation purposes been allowed to go unimproved, but irrigation canals and storage reservoirs that were constructed in earlier times have been permitted to fall into decay. An enormous amount of water goes to waste that ought to be saved. Great numbers of new canals ought to be dug; old canals ought to be reopened; canals now in use ought to be deepened and widened. In regions where water cannot be obtained for the supply of canals, more wells ought to be sunk, and old wells in many cases ought to be deepened. New tanks and reservoirs ought to be constructed, and old reservoirs ought to be enlarged to store more adequately the surface water. In these ways the certainty of India's water supply, and therefore the certainty and abundance of her food supply, might be greatly increased.

'But even under present conditions, with irrigation as imperfectly developed as it is now, India is one of the greatest of food-producing lands. No matter how severe the drought may be in some parts, in others there is always sufficient water and are therefore abundant crops; so that there is seldom or never a time when India, as a whole, does not contain food enough for all her people. Three years ago, when the famine was most severe, there was no difficulty in getting food, if one only had money to buy it with; and the same is true in the midst of the terrible famine that is prevailing at the present time. Thus it becomes evident that, if we would discover the causes of the periodic starvation of such vast numbers of the Indian people, we must look deeper than mere failure of the rains.'

The second question is: 'Are the famines of India caused by over-population?' Mr. Sunderland says:—

'Over-Population is Not the Cause.

'A very little study of the facts shows that they are not. The population of India is not so dense as in a number of the States of Europe which are prosperous, have no difficulty in supporting their people, and in which famines are never dreamed of. Nor is the birth-rate high in India. It is less than in England, and much less than in Germany, and several other Continental countries. Indeed it is 75 per 1,000 less than the average birth-rate of all Europe. India is not over-populated. As already pointed out, even under present conditions she produces food enough for all her people. But if her agricultural possibilities were properly developed, she could easily support a greatly increased population. There are enormous areas of waste land that ought to be subdued and brought under cultivation. . . . Another, larger still, is the extension of irrigation in those regions where there is danger of lack of water. In these two ways alone all possible increase of population for a hundred years to come might easily be provided for.

'But beyond this is another resource even greater. Indian agriculture is for the most part primitive and superficial. The Indian rayat is industrious and faithful, but he tills his soil according to methods that are two or three thousand years old. The result is, he raises crops which are only a fraction of what they would be with improved methods of tillage. Sir James Caird pointed out to the Indian Government long ago that a single additional bushel an acre raised by the rayat would mean food for another 22,000,000 of people. But the addition of a bushel an acre is only the mere beginning of what might be done. Mr. A. O. Hume, long connected officially with the agriculture of India, declared that "with proper manuring and proper tillage, every acre, broadly speaking, of the land in the country can be made to yield 30, 50, or 70 per cent. more of every kind of crop than it at present produces." Here is a resource that is practically inexhaustible. Add this to the other two named, and we see at once that the suggestion that population is outstripping agricultural possibilities, and that famines are inevitable for that reason, becomes hardly better than ludicrous.'

Having cleared these untenable allegations out of the way, Mr. Sunderland asks, 'What, then, is the cause of famines in India?'

The answer, he says, 'becomes clear and unmistakable as soon as one begins really to investigate.'

'"THE REAL CAUSE IS THE EXTREME, THE ABJECT, THE AWFUL, POVERTY OF THE INDIAN PEOPLE."

'The cause of Indian famines is the extreme poverty of the Indian people—a poverty so severe that it keeps a majority of all on the very verge of suffering, even in years of plenty, and prevents them from laying up anything to tide them over years of scarcity. If their condition were such that in good years they could get a little ahead, then when the bad years came they could draw on that as a resource; this would not save them from hardship, but it would save them from starvation. But, as things go, the vast majority have no such resource. Even in the best years they have all they can do to live and support their families in the barest possible way, without laying by a rupee for a rainy day. The result is, when their crops fail they are helpless. For a while they manage to keep the wolf of famine from the door by selling their cow, if they have one, their plough bullock, such bits of simple furniture from their poor dwellings, or such cooking utensils or such articles of clothing as they can find a purchaser for at any price. Then, when the last thing is gone that can be exchanged for even an anna or a handful of millet, there is nothing left for them except to sit down in their desolate homes, or wander out into the fields and die. This is the history of hundreds of thousands and millions of the Indian people in times of drought. If the poor sufferers are so fortunate as to be received by the Government at the famine relief works, where in return for continuous hard labour they are supplied with the smallest amount of food that will sustain life, the hardiest of them survive until the rains come; then with depleted strength they go back to their stripped homes, and, barehanded, begin as best they can the task of raising a new crop and supporting such members of their families as are left alive.

'Here, then, we have the real cause of famines in India. It is simply the extreme poverty of the Indian people which keeps them living absolutely from hand to mouth, with no chance to make provision beforehand for any kind of contingency; so that, if such a disaster as the failure of a crop comes, they are at once undone. The truth is, the poverty of India is something that we can have little conception of unless we have actually seen it, as, alas! the writer of this paper has.'

To meet the not unnatural charge of exaggeration, Mr. Sunderland cites 'some facts and figures from authorities which cannot be questioned'—Sir William Hunter, Mr. A. O. Hume, Sir Auckland Colvin, Sir Charles Elliott, Lord Cromer (Major Baring). These statements would indeed 'seem incredible did they not come from men whose knowledge and character we cannot doubt, and who could have no motive for exaggeration'—'officials of the Indian Government, who are trained and careful men, and whose interest it is to understate and not to exaggerate.' 'Is it, then,' he asks, 'any wonder that the Indian peasant can lay up nothing for a rainy day, and, therefore, that he finds starvation invariably staring him in the face if any disorder overtakes that little crop which is the only thing which stands between him and death?' 'The real cause of Indian famines,' he concludes, 'is *the extreme, the abject, the awful, poverty of the Indian people.*' The italics are Mr. Sunderland's.

'And now we come to the final, the deepest, the crucial, questions of all: Why this terrible poverty? Is it necessary? Is there no remedy for it? What has produced it?'

'The Enormous Foreign Tribute.

'India is a land rich in resources beyond most other lands in the world. It would seem as if her people ought to live in plenty, comfort, and security, with ample and more than ample provision made in her many fat years against any possible lack in her few years of comparative leanness. Why does not the fatness of her fat years prevent suffering and starvation in the lean?

'Fortunately here, too, an answer is not difficult to find, when once we begin really to look for it. John Stuart Mill saw the answer plainly in his day. John Bright saw it in his. The real friends of India in England very generally see it now. The intelligent classes in India all see it. It is found in the simple fact that India is a subject land, ruled by a foreign Power, which keeps her tributary to itself, not only politically, but commercially, financially, and industrially, and drains away her wealth in a steady stream that is all the while enriching the English people, and of course correspondingly impoverishing the helpless people of India. A farm may be naturally very rich, but let its products be carried away and consumed abroad, and let nothing be put back upon the soil, and no intelligent farmer will wonder if in two or three hundred years the farm becomes impoverished. The Indian people are much in the condition of such a farm. India is an orange which England got possession of by the sword, and holds firmly in her grasp by means of a big army, and has long been industrially sucking. It is not strange if what is left after the sucking process has gone on all these years is not very life-sustaining to the Indian people.

'Again and again has attention been called to the effects of this heavy and constant drain of wealth from India to England. . . . This drain from India has been going on and steadily increasing for more than two centuries. There is no country in the world that could endure such a steady loss of wealth without becoming impoverished.'

Mr. Sunderland, like the rest of us, finds it difficult to estimate the amount of the drain, 'because the streams through which the tribute flows are many, and constant efforts are made by the British and Indian Governments to hide them out of sight.' But taking it at from twenty-five to thirty millions sterling a year, 'it is to be borne in mind,' he points out, 'that all this is *in addition* to the regular and very heavy *home* expenses of the Indian Government'—'a *foreign tribute*, paid to a nation on the other side of the globe for the privilege of being a subject people.' 'Is it,' then, 'any wonder that India is poor?'

'Where does this Enormous Tribute come from?

'Of course, from the taxpaying Indian people. Who are the taxpaying Indian people? More than ninety per cent. of them are the people who have already been described, who with their utmost endeavours are able to obtain only the barest possible subsistence, who have to support families of five on incomes not amounting all told to more than thirty or forty dollars a year. These people, many of whom often go months at a time, even in reasonably good years, with only one full meal a day, are yet compelled to pay a tax of 500 per cent. on imported salt, or 4,000 times its cost of manufacture if the salt is home-made; and of their little crops they have to pay to the Government as taxes from one-sixth to one-third of all they raise. The attention of both the Indian and the British Governments has been called again and again to this excessive and crushing taxation, and every possible means has been tried to secure some amelioration, but without result. For many years the settled policy has been not to lessen the burden of taxation upon the peasant, but constantly to seek new pretexts and opportunities for increasing it.'

Again Mr. Sunderland cites authorities, all of them well known to the readers of this journal, including Sir William Wedderburn and Mr. Romesh Dutt. He then considers the home expenses of the Indian Government.

'"The most Expensive Government in the World"—"Big Salaries and Big Pensions."

'It has often been pointed out that the British Government in India is the most expensive Government in the world. The reason is, it is a Government of foreigners. These foreigners, having it in their power to fix their own salaries, do not err on the side of making them too low. Having to exile themselves from their native land, they naturally want plenty to pay for it. Nearly all the higher officials throughout India are British. The civil service is nominally open to Indians; but it is hedged about with so many restrictions (among others Indian young men being required to make the journey from India to London to take their examinations) that as a fact only one-fiftieth of the places in the service, and these generally the lowest and poorest, are occupied by Indians; although there are thousands of well-educated and competent Indians who would be glad to get the places and who would fill them well if they were allowed. The amount of money which the Indian people are required to pay for the salaries of this great army of civil servants and appointed higher officials, and then, later, for pensions for the same after they have served a given number of years in India, is enormous. That quite as good service could be obtained for the Government at a small fraction of the present cost by employing Indians (who much better understand the needs of the country) in three-fourths, if not nine-tenths, of these positions, is no doubt true. But that would not serve the purpose of England, who wants these fat offices for her sons. Hence poor Indian rayats must sweat and bleed and go hungry and, if need be, starve, that an ever-growing number of Englishmen may have big salaries and big pensions. Of course much of the money paid for these salaries, and practically all paid for the pensions, goes permanently out of India.

'The large military establishment that England maintains in India (of course primarily for the purpose of keeping the Indian people in subjection) is very costly, and is paid for out of the Indian taxes. Nor is the Indian Army proper all the military expense that India is required to pay. During the century just closed the Indian and the Imperial Governments have carried on wars in Afghanistan and other regions beyond the North-Western frontier, involving a total expense of 500,000,000 dollars. Who has paid this vast sum? All but 50,000,000 dollars (one-tenth of the whole) has been charged to poor overtaxed India.'

Mr. Sunderland is really too liberal; he should have said one-twentieth, not one-tenth of the whole—Mr. Gladstone's contribution of £5,000,000 to the cost of the Second Afghan War. But that is a detail.

Mr. Sunderland does not omit to consider the claim that 'England has done much for India, and conferred upon her substantial advantages.'

'The Advantages of British Rule.

'This is true; but in all cases India has paid the bills, and in many cases the advantages have been small compared with the heavy cost. Much is said about education. How much does the Indian Government spend annually for education? A little less than a penny per person of the population. Compare this with the enormous sums spent for military purposes; and then remember that the whole expenditure, whether for education or the Army, comes from the pocket of the Indian taxpayer. We are pointed to the railways of India as a striking illustration of what England is doing for her dependency. Yes, whatever lack of money there may be for education, or for sanitary improvements, or for irrigation, or for other things which the people of India so earnestly desire and pray for, the Indian Government always seems to have plenty for railways. Why? Because the railways of India help the English people to wealth. It is true that the Indian people make some use of them and derive certain advantages from them; but they also suffer from them certain very serious disadvantages. The railways have broken up many of the old industries of India, and thus have brought hardships and suffering to millions of the people; but they enrich the ruling nation, and they give her a firmer military grip upon her valuable dependency, and so money can always be found for them, whatever else suffers. If half the money that has been spent on railways had been spent for irrigation, droughts would to-day have little terror for the Indian people. What a commentary it is upon British management in India that more than eight millions are spent on railways for every million spent on irrigation!'

After all, in Mr. Sunderland's judgment, the British Indian Empire is the most gigantic of the monopolies of the world—a ghastly example of 'Imperialism.'

'British Indian "Imperialism."'

'America stands appalled at the magnitude and tyranny of her Standard Oil Company. But the Standard Oil monopoly is a pigmy compared with England's monopoly in India. The world has no other such monopoly as this. England holds not only the government, but virtually the commerce, the finance, and the industries of 250,000,000 people in her hand, to shape them as she will, responsible to nobody but herself. She claims to manage Indian affairs with India's welfare in view. I believe that the Standard Oil Company makes a similar claim. The answer to make to both is, "By their fruits ye shall know them." The fact that at the end of two hundred years of commercial dominance, and of more than forty years of absolute political sway, we are confronted with such indescribable poverty of the people, and with famine after famine of such magnitude and severity as to make the world stand aghast, seems to prove beyond answer that England in all these years has not made the welfare of India her first aim, but has subordinated India's good to her own enrichment. We denounce ancient Rome for impoverishing Gaul, and Egypt, and Sicily, and Palestine, and her other conquered provinces, by draining away her wealth to enrich herself. We denounce Spain for robbing the New World in the same way. But England is doing exactly the same thing in India, and on a much larger scale; only she is doing it skilfully, adroitly, by modern and "enlightened" modes of procedure, under business and judicial forms, and with so many pretences of "governing India for her advantage, and enriching her by civilised methods" that the world has been largely blinded to what has been really going on. But probe down through the surface of fine words and legal forms to what lies below, and we have the same hideous business that Rome and Spain were engaged in so long, and for which in the end they paid so dear. Called by its right name, what is this treatment of India by England? It is national parasitism. It is the stronger nation sucking the blood of the weaker. It is "Imperialism."'—Quoted from *India*, January, 1900.

III

WHAT THE FAMINE OF 1877-78 COST

		£
1. GOVERNMENT EXPENDITURE:—		
'The direct outlay on relief reached the sum of nearly'[1]		8,000,000
2. LOSS OF LAND REVENUE:—[2]		
1876	£90,000	
1877	1,800,000	
1878	1,130,000	
		2,520,000
3. LOSS OF CROPS:—		
Assume the revenue taken by Government represents, as the Famine Commissioners, on p. 112, of Part II. of their Report say it does, one-sixteenth of the gross produce, the loss to the cultivators is £2,520,000 × 15[3]		37,800,000

---

[1] Famine Commission Report, Part I., 1880, p. 32, para. 96.

[2] P. 27, No. 14, Statistical Abstract, British India.

[3] I very much doubt whether this is not greatly overstated, but I take the figures as the Commissioners give them. And yet I find nearly the same proportion of tax to total produce is claimed in the Central Provinces. The land revenue demand 'absorbs probably not more than about 6¼ per cent. (or one anna in the rupee) of the value of a normal out-turn.' 'The poorest parts of the Province . . . where distress has been most severe, pay either no revenue at all (save an insignificant quit-rent) to Government . . . or a trifling rate (less than four annas per cultivated acre).—Para. 163, p. 115, Report on the Famine in the Central Provinces, by R. H. Cradock I.C.S., vol. i., Nagpore, Secretariat Press, 1898.

4. Loss of Excise Revenue :—[1]

		£
1877	£76,000	
1878	163,000	
1879	46,000	
		285,000

5. Loss of Customs Revenues :—[2]

1876	£13,000	
1877	74,000	
1878	118,000	
1879	114,000	
1880	88,000	
1881	72,000	
		479,000

6. Loss of Salt Revenue :—[3]

1877	£62,000	
1878	211,000	
		273,000

7. Country Silver and Silver Ornaments :—[4]

Bombay Mint returns, for years of the famine, show :—

	Country Silver. Rs.	Silver Ornaments. Rs.	Total. Rs.
1877–78	—	1,24,00,000	1,24,00,000
1878–79	67,00,000	1,16,00,000	1,83,00,000
1879–80	45,00,000	92,00,000	1,37,00,000
	Rs.1,12,00,000	Rs.3,32,00,000	Rs.4,44,00,000

Mr. Barclay said: 'The quantity which reached the mints must have been only a fraction of what was sold by the natives to the dealers.' . . . 'In the recent famine [1897–98], when the mints were closed, the silver ornaments would only realise about fifty per cent. in rupees.' Sir David Barbour testified: 'The return from the

[1] No. 14, Statistical Abstract, British India, p. 29.

[2] *Ibid.*, No. 16, p. 26.

[3] *Ibid.*, No. 16, p. 27.

[4] 'East India Currency Inquiries: Official and other figures submitted by Mr. Donald Graham, C.I.E., Appendix' [c. 7060–1] 1893, p. 304; also 'Evidence of Sir David Barbour, K.C.S.I.,' p. 305; and 'Evidence of Robert Barclay,' Ans. 11,612, Part II., 1899.

	£
Bombay Mint excludes gold; but we know that in the years of the great famine in Madras and Bombay, a large amount of gold was sent from India to England, and, I think, Sir H. Hay said he received a quantity of gold from India which was evidently composed of ornaments melted down.'[1]	
Take Mr. Barclay's 'fraction' as representing only as much more as was actually minted, and Sir David Barbour's exported gold at one million sterling, the reserves drawn upon in Madras and elsewhere (needlessly drawn if only proper means had been adopted to prevent distress) was Rs.4,44,00,000 × 2 = Rs.8,88,00,000 at 2s. per rupee = £8,880,000; gold £1,000,000...	9,880,000

The foregoing is not only of much interest, but also of great importance in the light it throws on the 'pinch' experienced by the well-to-do classes. The five millions and more who perished in the Madras Presidency, and the millions who were on relief works, or in receipt of charitable relief, would not, I estimate, contribute Rs.200,000 towards the Rs.4,44,00,000 worth of ornaments which disappeared in the melting-pot at the mint. No; all this came from the better-off people, drawn from them by the high price of food. As prices now are nearly always at what used to be considered famine prices, it may be realised how impossible it is for wealth to be accumulated by any class in India.

8. Increased Price of Food:—

The Famine Commission of 1880 estimated the value of food at £5 per ton. In Madras during the famine the Duke of Buckingham and Chandos, the Governor, stated[2] that

[1] 'Some lakhs of savings were brought out in the famine of 1876–77; the goldsmiths' melting-pots were going day and night for some months, and the mint returns alone will show what the accumulation of precious metals in the famine districts must have amounted to.'—Hon. J. B. Richey, C.S.I., Aug. 15, 1888.

[2] Speech at Famine Relief meeting held in Madras on August 4, 1877.

'two-thirds of the Presidency were suffering from the high price of food.' Two-thirds of the Presidency would be twenty millions of people. Say, they endured these high prices for six months only (an under-estimate), and that the price of food was doubled, £10 per ton, though, as a matter of fact, the price was much more than doubled.[1] The Commissioners considered eight millions of tons per annum were consumed in Madras: take half of that for six months at £5 additional cost, and the increased price of food represented 4,000,000 tons × £5 = £20,000,000: take off one-third to come into accord with the Duke's (under) statement, and the amount to be brought out is, say ... ... £ 13,000,000

9. LOSS OF CATTLE, HOUSES, AGRICULTURAL IMPLEMENTS, ETC.:—

Roughly, in normal years, there are, in the Madras Presidency:—

14,000,000 cattle.
8,000,000 sheep.
5,000,000 goats.
40,000 horses and ponies.
100,000 mules and donkeys.

Total 27,140,000[2]

Sir Richard Temple, Famine Delegate, in one of his reports, stated, 'the country was almost entirely bare of all crop or stubble, and there was no sign of fodder or grass.' Before the end of December, 1876, in the Bellary district, 'one-fourth of the cattle were said to have died, and it was thought

[1] Under normal circumstances at that time one anna would buy in Southern India nearly two lbs. of grain; in August, 1877, it would not purchase more than half a pound, or even that quantity. Rice, in ordinary seasons, sold at the rate of ten measures per rupee; in the last week of July it was quoted at three or four measures, which was as if the quartern loaf in England, instead of being sixpence, was nearly four times that amount. In merely doubling the price of grain, therefore, the estimate is a moderate one. (See 'Famine Campaign in Southern India,' 1877–79 vol. i., *passim.*)

[2] Agricultural Statistics for British India for 1888–89, p. 229.

	£
more than half would perish before June unless heavy showers fell in January';[1] but the showers did not fall: 'cattle dying for want of fodder' was a frequent item in District Reports. In Bombay careful statements were prepared, such as these:—	

Sholapur:—

Cattle before famine ...	...	224,599
Cattle in August, 1877	...	97,167
Loss	...	127,432

'Of these only 44,000 were considered fit for agricultural purposes':

Madhee and Mohul Taluk:—

Cattle before famine ...	...	16,591
Cattle in August, 1877	...	5,470
Loss	...	11,121

Indee Taluk:—

Cattle before famine ...	...	85,747
Cattle in August, 1877	...	5,644
Loss	...	80,103[2]

	£
In view of all this it will not be going too far to assume that one-fourth of the live stock in the Madras Presidency perished. One-fourth of 27,140,000 = 6,785,000; taken all round at Rs.7 each: 6,785,000 × 7 = Rs.47,495,000, or, at Rs.10 to the £[3]	4,749,500

10. Loss of Wages:—

	£
Say, 5,000,000 labourers, without work for nine months at Rs.5·5 per month[4] (the famine extended from the autumn of 1876 to September, 1877, and much longer in some parts) — 5,000,000 × Rs.5·5 = Rs.27,500,000: at Rs.10 to the £	2,750,000

---

[1] P. 56, 'Famine Campaign,' vol. i. [2] *Ibid.* pp. 364–366.

[3] It will be seen that I have not taken into consideration anything for ruined houses, loss or sale of agricultural implements, etc.; if included, they would make an appreciable difference. Their omission may be covered by any slight excess in what I have estimated.

[4] P. 310, Statistical Abstract, 1897–98.

	£
11. LOSS OF CAPITAL BY AGRICULTURISTS AND INTEREST BY MONEYLENDERS AND OTHERS :— '. . . about one-third of the land-holding classes are deeply and inextricably in debt, and at least an equal proportion in debt though not beyond the power of recovering themselves.'[1] The census of 1881[2] gives 6¾ millions of agriculturists in Madras: say two millions[3] of these indebted at least Rs.50 each = Rs.10,00,00,000; of these assume 20 per cent. lost through the famine,—Rs.2,00,00,000 at Rs.10 to the £	2,000,000
12. LOSS OF PROFIT BY MERCHANTS, TRADERS, ETC., BY DIMINUTION OF BUSINESS :— This can be no more than a guess, and, unsupported by any authority, my guess must be taken for what it is worth. Considering, however, the great contraction of business throughout the whole Presidency, Rs.10,000,000 to Rs.15,000,000 might be fairly reckoned, say the smaller sum at Rs.10 to the £	1,000,000
Total ascertained and estimated cost of the Madras Famine	**£82,736,500**
Say, *in money*	**£83,000,000**

and THE LIVES OF FIVE MILLIONS OF HUMAN BEINGS.

Who can estimate in pounds, shillings, and pence what this terrible loss in lives means to the unhappy community amongst whom it occurred!

[1] P. 181, Famine Commission Report, 1880, Part II.

[2] P. 351, Census Report, vol. i.

[3] In all India there were 29,207,150 'tenant cultivators'; as a ryotwarry (or peasant-cultivating) province, Madras would have a large proportion of these.

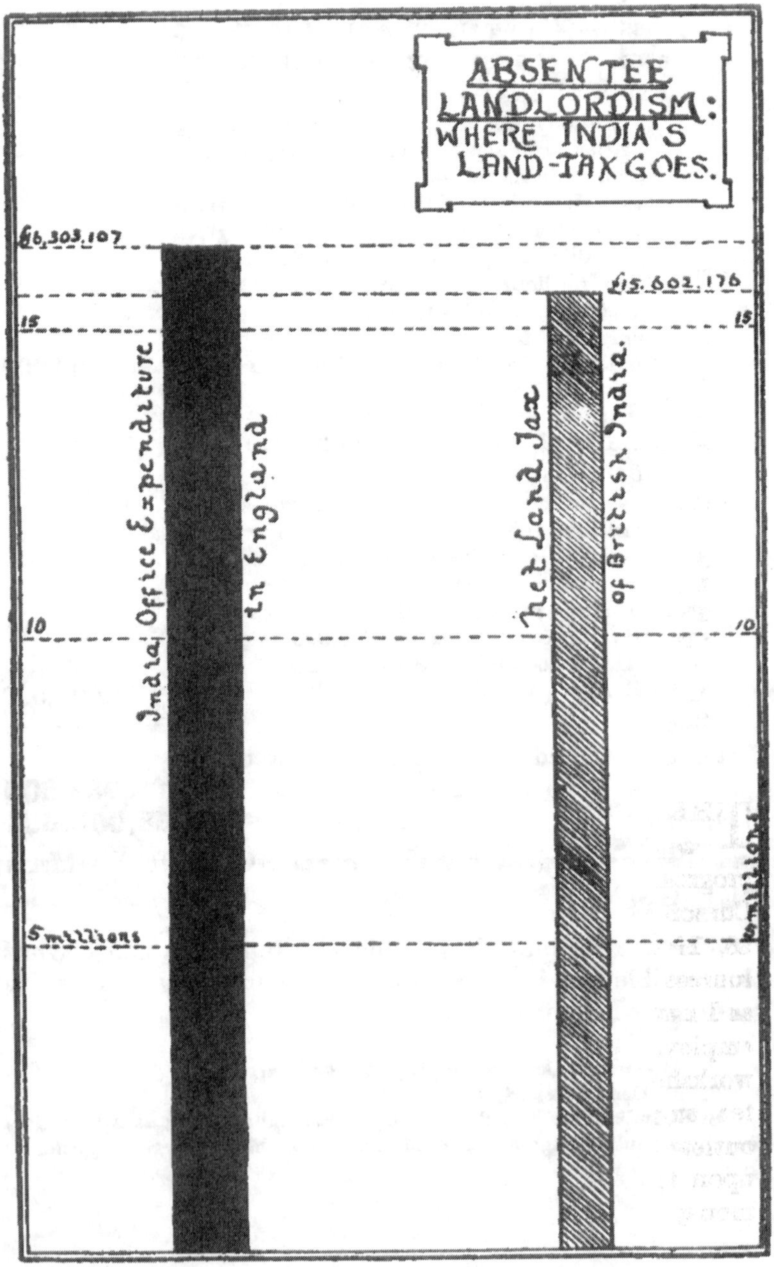
ABSENTEE LANDLORDISM:
WHERE INDIA'S LAND-TAX GOES.
£6,303,107
£15,602,176
15
15
10
10
5 millions
millions
India Office Expenditure in England
Net Land Tax of British India.

CHAPTER V

'THE EXTRAORDINARY AMOUNT OF PRECIOUS METALS THAT IS ABSORBED BY THE PEOPLE'

The *Pons Asinorum* concerning the Absorption of Gold and Silver in India.
Imports of Treasure Not Evidence of Accumulating Wealth
Statistics concerning Imports of Gold and Silver from 1835 to 1900.
Coinage of Rupees at British Indian and Feudatory State Mints.
Average 'Absorption' 8½d. per head per annum!
Mr. Dadabhai Naoroji's Illustration for Puzzled 'Economists.'
The Alleged Buried or Hoarded Wealth of India.
'The Total Absence of Anything Like Accumulated Wealth in India.'—*Sir Richard Strachey*.
Indian Wealth compared with British Wealth.
Stop the Drain and There May Be a Chance of Wealth Accumulating in India.

THE title of this chapter is the climax in a series of sentences which, like a stately march, records our progress in India. 'A prudent Government,' said Lord Curzon to his Legislative Council in Calcutta, on March 28, 1901, 'endeavours to increase its non-agricultural sources of income. It is for this reason that I welcome, as I have said to-day, the investment of capital and the employment of labour upon railways, canals, in factories, workshops, mills, coal mines, metalliferous mines, and on tea, sugar, and indigo, plantations. All these are fresh outlets for industry. They diminish *pro tanto* the strain upon the agricultural population and they are bringing money into the country and circulating it to and fro.

This is evident from the immense increase in railway traffic, both goods and passenger, in postal, telegraph, and money order, business, in imports from abroad, and in the extraordinary amount of precious metals that is absorbed by the people. These are not symptoms of decaying or impoverished populations.'

In other chapters of this work it is made abundantly clear that, apart from a small section of the population of India, and that, mainly, the foreign section, there has been no increase of prosperity among the native people of the country. Only two passages out of the Viceroy's 'baker's dozen' of disputable assertions, need be singled out for comment here. One is the remark: '. . . they are bringing money into the country and circulating it.' If it be a good thing to bring money into a country it must be a bad thing, on the balance of commercial transactions, to send money out of a country. Therefore, when Lord Curzon's eyes are opened to the 'drain' which Lord Salisbury saw (and deplored) in 1875, he cannot, consistently with his own dithyrambic speculations, fail to consider and support such means as will stop the 'drain.'

The second passage is that which records the impression that has been made upon the viceregal mind by 'the extraordinary amount of precious metals that is absorbed by the people.' This absorption of the precious metals in India is a *pons asinorum* which many people, besides a too-busy Viceroy, unable to think out the proposition he wishes to demonstrate, have failed to cross. In 1891, in reply to some strictures of my own, similar to those to which Lord Curzon was replying when he made the remark I have quoted, one of the leading journals in England used language similar to that which the Viceroy has just used. And, at the very time when Lord Curzon was being hypnotised by contemplation of 'the extraordinary amount of the precious metals that is absorbed by the people' of India, one of the chief officials of an important Chamber of Commerce in England wrote to me to ask how I could assert that India was growing poorer when it could absorb such 'an extraordinary amount of the precious metals' as the Indian people absorbed. Apparently, the issue involved in this 'absorption of precious metals' is imperfectly apprehended even by those whose business it is to know, and, in some degree, to control, the currents which, in their ebb and flow, render international traffic possible and profitable. I, therefore, ask that what follows may receive careful consideration seeing I assert that the phenomenon so vigorously described by the Viceroy of India, and so insistently brought to my attention in England by journalist and commercial expert, may exist in 'decaying or impoverished populations,' and, even, actually, become one of the signs of decay and of impoverishment.

The form in which the difficulty is generally stated is this (I quote remarks really made):—

'These imports of treasure are surely evidence of accumulating wealth. Will Mr. Digby say why this accumulation of gold and silver is going on, as it has done for centuries past, in spite of all difficulties, and why it is not good evidence of increasing wealth?'

1. I demur to the statement that India has, unremittingly, been importing treasure for centuries past. Prior to British rule, when India on her own account was carrying on a great trade with neighbouring nations in Asia, she required and received a certain quantity of gold and silver, not then producing either, needing both for commercial purposes and for ornamental and luxurious uses, and being then wealthy enough to indulge in luxuries. But, in the early years of British rule, India was depleted of its precious metals to such an extent as to 'greatly diminish in quantity . . . the current specie of the country.' (Minute of 1787, by Sir John Shore, afterwards Lord Teignmouth, Governor-General of India.) It will be admitted that some gold and silver was required to restore the equilibrium which our exploitations of those days disturbed.

2. There has been some accumulation of the precious metals in India, but, with the condition of things which exists in that country, such accumulation is not 'evidence of increasing wealth.' At the same time the amount of the treasure in question is infinitesimally small when regarded in the light of the enormous population that receives it.

3. Mr. Dadabhai Naoroji, in his 'Poverty of India' (pp. 230–272, collected works, Swan Sonnenschein and Co., Ltd.), has considered and commented upon the question very thoroughly up to 1869. In his *Contemporary Review* articles, 1887, he carried the particulars to 1884. I will now take them to a later date. Mr. Naoroji has pointed out that India does not receive its imports of the precious metals as so much profit on its exports, or to make up a deficiency of imports against exports. As Lord Salisbury so excellently put it, in the same Minute as that in which he cynically declared 'India must be bled,' 'much of the revenue of India is exported without a direct equivalent.' Even after the gold and silver has been received in India there is still a huge annual balance against that country on every year's trade; in 1889–90 the amount was Rx.23,492,000 (£15,661,334). Again, it must not be forgotten that the British introduced into India the system of the payment of revenue in cash. Our predecessors were content to take their toll in kind. It will at once be seen that this innovation alone would call for a large supply of silver with which to meet the newly-created demand.

Before specifically answering the question as to why the import of gold and silver into India is not evidence of increasing wealth, let us see what this import actually amounts to. The India Office obligingly furnishes me with statistical information, from which I find that from 1835–36 to 1899–00, both years inclusive, the imports of gold and silver have been respectively as follow :—

Imports of Precious Metals into India, 1835–36 to 1899–1900 :—

GOLD :—

Net imports in decennial periods :—

	Rx.
1835–36 to 1844–45	3,296,799
1845–46 to 1854–55	10,282,593
1856–57 to 1864–65	51,094,639
1865–66 to 1874–75	36,578,039
1875–76 to 1884–85	26,639,438
1885–86 to 1894–95	16,266,152 [1]
1895–96 to 1899–1900	25,669,487
	Rx.169,827,147

or—£113,218,085.

SILVER :—

	Rx.
1835–36 to 1844–45	20,535,269
1845–46 to 1854–55	15,327,009
1855–56 to 1864–65	100,202,614
1865–66 to 1874–75	62,460,314
1875–76 to 1884–85	65,673,631
1885–86 to 1894–95	104,285,608
1895–96 to 1899–1900	25,469,213
	Rx.393,953,658

or—£264,635,772.

In sixty-five years the combined totals amount to—

Gold	£113,218,085
Silver	261,635,772
	£374,853,857

Average per annum, £5,766,967.

The total amount imported was £374,853,857. During the period under consideration the Indian mints have coined—

Gold	£2,445,383
Silver	257,731,715
Total	£260,177,098

The details are interesting. The silver received into the mints for coinage during this period was from two

[1] In 1892–93 £2,812,683, and in 1894–95 £4,974,094, the exports exceeded the imports by these amounts.

parties, whose respective amounts are thus described and set out—

From Individuals.	*From Government.*
£219,807,917	£34,570,665

Since 1894–95 the mints have been closed to the public for coinage purposes, but silver is still minted (for Mexican dollars for circulation in the Far East), as the following particulars from (and including) the year of closing show :—

		£
1894–95	... ...	——
1895–96	... ...	487,968
1896–97	... ...	972,988
1897–98	... ...	3,681,640
1898–99	... ...	3,418,028
1899–1900	... ...	5,586,187

To the amount coined by the Indian Government must be added the coinage of the Feudatory States, whose export trade is at least—probably it is more than—one-fifth of the whole trade of India. Say one-twentieth only of the amount coined in British India has been coined by the Feudatory States, viz., about £13,000,000. This leaves out of the total of £377,853,857 imported, after Government and private coinage has been provided for, the sum of £104,676,768. This looks a formidable amount, but when closely examined its great proportions vanish.

	£
The British Indian mints have coined in sixty-five years	260,177,098
The Feudatory States have minted, say	13,000,000
	273,177,098
From this must be deducted, to replace wear and tear, estimated before a Committee of the House of Commons at £666,666 a year	43,333,290
Leaving	£229,843,808

In his calculations from 1801 to 1869, Mr. Naoroji suggested, but did not allow for, a loss of £1,000,000 a year, thus: 'Is it too much to assume in the very widespread and minute distribution, over a vast surface and vast population, of small trinkets or ornaments of silver, and their rough use, another million may be required to supply waste and loss? If only a pennyworth per head per annum be so wasted, it would make a million sterling.'

The gross total and the disposal of the treasure remaining in the country during the sixty-five years under review may be thus summarised :—

		£
Net imports		377,853,857
Less Government coinage...	34,570,665	
,, Feudatory ,, ...	13,000,000	
,, Wastage at one penny per head per annum, £1,000,000 per year 65 years	65,000,000	
,, Wear and tear of coinage Rx. 1,000,000 (£666,666) per annum	43,333,290	
		155,903,955
Leaving		£221,949,902

being coined rupees and bar silver worked into ornaments or 'hoarded' uncoined.

I assume (as I am well justified in doing by the figures of the thirty-fourth number of the 'Statistical Abstract for British India'; indeed, I might take a larger number) that the population in British India has averaged during the sixty-five years under consideration 180,000,000. The treasure over and above Government coinage received in India during these years, if divided amongst this population would amount to £1 4s. 1¼d. per head. Divide this sum by the sixty-five years during which this treasure has been imported, and it comes to the insignificant sum of 4¼d. per head per annum! But stay, it is not so much as that. The Feudatory States are greedy absorbers of the precious metals. The people in them are more prosperous than are the people in the British provinces; their share in the export trade of the Empire, as has been stated, is one-fifth of the whole at least. It is putting the matter at a low estimate to suppose they receive only one-fifth of the gold and silver imported; grant them, however, that fifth, and then in British India there remains, if all this sum could be divided, about 3¼d. per head per annum! That there is much treasure in the Feudatory States is clear from the hoards of the late Maharajah Scindia, forty million rupees after his death being invested in Government of India securities. Then, of another State it is declared, with what truth I know not, that in certain forts there were twenty years ago treasure vaults containing from 300 to 400 million rupees in gold and silver. I do not believe there is so much, but the statement, for what it is worth, may stand. British India gets no benefit from these hoards. It is certain there are not any large hoards in the British provinces. Further, Mr. Naoroji, in his reply to Sir M. E. Grant-Duff, in 1887 (the position has not materially altered since then), says:

'Next, how much goes to the native States and the frontier territories? Here are a few significant official figures as an indication. "The report of the External Land Trade and Railway-borne Trade of the Bombay Presidency for 1884–85," (page 2) says of Rajputana and Central India: "The imports from the external blocks being greater than the exports to them, the balance of trade due by the Presidency to the other Provinces amounts to Rs.12,01,05,912, as appears from the above table and the following." I take the native States from the table referred to—

Excess of Imports in Bombay Presidency.

From Rajputana and Central India ...	Rs.5,55,46,753
From Berar...	1,48,91,355
From Hyderabad	8,67,688
Total	Rs.7,13,05,796

or £7,130,579. This means that these native States have exported so much more merchandise than they have imported. Thereupon, the report remarks thus: "The greatest balance is in favour of Rajputana and Central India, caused by the import of opium from that block. Next to it is that of the Central Provinces. It is presumed that these balances are paid back *mainly in cash*." (The italics are mine.) This, then, is the way the treasure goes; and poor British India gets all the abuse —insult added to injury. Its candle burns not only at both ends, but at all parts. The excessive foreign agency eats up in India, and drains from India, a portion of its wretched income, thereby weakening and exhausting it every year drop by drop, though not very perceptibly, and lessening its productive power or capability. It has poor capital and cannot increase it much. Foreign capital does nearly all the work and carries away all the profit. Foreign capitalists from Europe and from native States make profits from the resources of British India, and take away these profits to their own countries. The share that the mass of the natives of British India have is to drudge and slave on scanty subsistence for these foreign capitalists; not as slaves in America did, on the resources of the country and land belonging to the masters themselves, but on the resources of their own country for the benefit of foreign capitalists. I may illustrate this a little. Bombay is considered a wealthy place, and has a large capital circulating in it, to carry on all its wants as a great port. Whose capital is this? Mostly that of foreigners. The capital of the European exchange banks and European merchants is mostly foreign, and most of the native capital is foreign also, *i.e.*, that of the native bankers and merchants from the native States. Nearly £6,000,000 of the capital working in Bombay belongs to native bankers from the native States. Besides a large portion of the wealthy merchants, though more or less settled in Bombay, are from native States.'

If other things were equal, if the imported treasure represented a real surplus over the balance of imports and exports, and the reasonable profits arising therefrom, British India, in course of time, would lay by something. But, it must be remembered, in addition to all that has been urged, a much larger amount of coin is required in proportion to the volume of trade in India than is the case in England. This is owing to the defective system of credit which prevails in India and to remedy which very little has been done by the Government.

In 1898–99 the Indian import and export trade (including treasure imported and exported) of £140,138,858 and the internal traffic required, on the part of the Government in India and in England was—

	£
Cash balances at the Treasuries and Agencies in India	11,177,670
Do. do. in Home Treasury	3,145,768
Coinage was added to by	3,757,642
Notes were in circulation to the value of ...	18,801,750

The foregoing particulars explain what becomes of the precious metals which are imported into India. A large portion is wanted, and is used, for the ordinary purposes of trade. Much disappears annually through inevitable wastage. But, as to the portion left in the hands of the British Indian people, and regarded as proof positive of their prosperity, it is significant that the year of greatest import of gold and silver (greater even than, except in one year, during the American war, when Indian cotton was so greatly 'boomed') was 1877–78, the years of the terrible famines in Madras, Bombay, and the North-Western Provinces. Nobody will assert that the gold and silver imported then were a proof of the prosperity of the people. Mr. Naoroji, in his 'Poverty of India,' has aptly indicated this point in an illustration which I will borrow. He says:—

'The notion that the import of silver has made India rich is a strange delusion. There is one important circumstance which is not borne in mind. The silver imported is not for making up the balance of exports and profits over imports, or for what is called balance of trade. Far from it, as I have already explained. It is imported as a simple necessity, but it, therefore, does not make India richer because so much silver is imported. If I give out £20 worth of goods to any one, and in return get £5 in other goods and £5 in silver, and yet if by so doing, though I have received only £10 worth in all for the £20 I have parted with, I am richer by £5, because I have received £5 in silver, then my richness will be very unenviable indeed. The phenomenon, in fact, has a delusive effect. Besides not giving due consideration to the above circumstances, the bewilderment of many people at what are called enormous imports of silver in India is like that of a child who, because it can itself be satisfied with a small piece of bread, wonders at a man eating a whole loaf, though the loaf may be but a very "scanty subsistence" for the big man.'

It is frequently forgotten that in dealing with British India one has to do with a huge population, with a continent as great as Europe, leaving out Russia, and with nations as varied in habits and customs as are the European nations. No doubt a few Indians have become rich, and are the better for the imported treasure—that is, have hoarded it or turned it into ornaments. They are, however, comparatively few. I doubt if they number as many as do the wealthy merchants and manufacturers of the city of Manchester. As in England the millionaire and the pauper co-exist, so in India a small number of well-to-do folk are to be found side by side with two hundred and thirty millions of struggling people, a number every year becoming more and more poor, half of whom do not receive a bare sustenance in food, to say nothing of sufficient and decent clothing, and leaving out of account everything which would give zest to life.[1] Whatever the import of treasure into India may mean, it most certainly does not fulfil the condition of 'good evidence of increasing wealth,' nor should it appear to be a gratifying phenomenon to an interested Viceroy and lull him to slumber as an evidence of increasing wealth and growing prosperity. In England the suffering and struggling poor are few; in India they are the vast majority, the well-to-do being a very small minority. The greater part of the Indian people live with hardly more pleasure than the lean and hungry cattle in their fields.

[1] 'The Economic Situation in India,' a series of articles in the *Poona Sarvajanik Sabha Journal* (the Sabha now, unhappily, quiescent, was a public body which did notable service in Western India for a time). These articles did not attract in England the attention their great merit called for, partly, perhaps, because the author thought only of an Indian audience and dealt with crores, lakhs, and percentages, with all ciphers omitted, in a way which, while easily realised by the mathematical and arithmetical mind of a trained Indian, is hard to be grasped by an English reader unfamiliar with the terminology as well as the currency involved.

Unimpeachable evidence from official records demonstrate this. I publish that evidence in great fulness later in this volume. Such an existence as they endure is incompatible with viceregal dreams of 'increasing wealth and growing prosperity.'

That there is much buried wealth in India is a favourite subject with many people who generalise not from facts, but from fancies. A few years ago, the *Pioneer* newspaper made some remarks which were freely quoted in the British Press, the following paragraph particularly proving itself a favourite with sub-editors everywhere :—

'Mr. Clarmont Daniell, if we remember rightly, gives as the result of his researches into the buried wealth of India, the sum of 270 millions sterling as a probable estimate of the amount of the treasure lying idle in the country either in the shape of hoards or ornaments. We do not know that any one has ever seriously audited the figures by which he arrives at this conclusion : and they may be indisputable. At any rate every one knows that the hoards of native families are astonishingly large in proportion to their outward circumstances; and Mr. E. S. Maclagan, who has been investigating the trade in gold and silver work for the Panjab Government, is convinced that they are much more generally undervalued than over-estimated. A competent authority, he says, guesses that "in Amritsar city alone there are jewels to the value of two million pounds sterling." As regards some other districts the figures that have been furnished are not less astonishing. The miserable waste of Montgomery is estimated to possess about fifty lakhs in ornaments. The hill-sides and valleys of Kulu are put at three lakhs and a half. In Jhelum two-fifths of the wealth of the district are said to be vested in property of this nature; and in Kohat, "probably one of the poorest districts of the province in this respect, the estimate is taken at Rs.800 for each Hindoo family, and Rs.10 for each Mussulman family, and a lakh in the aggregate for the Nawab and other Raises—making a total for the district of 75 lakhs." This estimate, Mr. Maclagan admits, is probably an exaggeration; but, he adds, "even a more exact calculation would probably surprise us in its results." Given another quarter of a century of quiet British rule and the spoil of the Panjab will be once more worth the attention of some covetous invader from the North-West. In the meantime it acts as a powerful incentive to the predatory instincts of lesser rogues—the housebreaker and the dacoit. And, in fact, such a store of wealth kept in such a manner would have been enough to

bring these professions into existence in the golden age. Stock notes have failed; Mr. Daniell's currency reforms have not had a trial; and we still seem to be as far as ever from having hit on any scheme that will induce the native population to see the disadvantages of keeping valuables in hand and the advantages that may be secured by parting with them.'

At first sight the amounts mentioned in the above paragraph may seem enormous. But when those amounts—even Mr. Daniell's guess of thirty years ago—are, as already remarked, regarded in the light of the great population of India, and it is borne in mind, as it always should be, that the greater part of such jewelry as there still is in India is inherited, that the *articles de luxe* have been heirlooms in Indian families through many generations, one marvels not at the wealth of India, but at the terrible poverty which exists, notwithstanding the two hundred and seventy millions sterling of 'hoards and ornaments.' Divided among the whole people there is

NOT FOURTEEN RUPEES (18s. 8d.) PER HEAD OF WEALTH,

including all that has been inherited! Buried 'wealth,' indeed! Miserable, naked, poverty, rather. Even the optimist General Richard Strachey, when before the House of Commons Committee on Indian Finance thirty years ago, said: 'Consider the general poverty of India. . . . Consider—

THE TOTAL ABSENCE OF ANYTHING LIKE ACCUMULATED WEALTH

in India.'

Probably if all the indebtedness of all the people be reckoned, and if all the debts were liquidated, more than Mr. Clarmont Daniell's estimate would be required to meet the legitimate demands of the moneylenders. Consequently, a return to solvency on the part of the average Indian would mean eighty per cent. of the inhabitants left without one penny's worth of inherited and acquired wealth, and the moneylenders the sole owners of that wealth. Even then those moneylenders would not be rich people. Allow one moneylender for each of India's three-quarters of a million of villages, and the wonderful amount of £270,000,000 sterling, divided equally among them, amounts to only £360 each! As to the inherited wealth amongst the population of India, its proportionate value may be judged from the following comparison :—

INDIAN WEALTH, as above estimated.	BRITISH WEALTH, estimated by Mulhall.
18s. 8d. per head.	£300 per head.

Possibly, reckoning in everything, the Indian wealth *might* be brought to £5 per head, though that is exceedingly doubtful. Even then how would it stand in comparison with the Briton's wealth?

Matters in this respect have not improved since 1872, when the *Pioneer's* inquiries were made: rather have they become very much worse. In the inquiry which, fourteen years ago, was made in the North-Western Provinces and Oudh, it was found that many households, even the households of small farmers—farmers of from five to fifteen acres—had not ten shillings' worth of 'jewels,' furniture, and utensils of every sort and kind. Again and again it was stated either there were 'no jewels' or that the 'jewels' were made of pewter. In many thousands of huts, taking the records of 1888 as the test, there is not more than one rupee's worth of 'belongings' in each. Analysed, the Daniell figures do not show much wealth per head. In Montgomery the average works out to little more than Rs.10 (13s. 4d.) per inhabitant. As for the statement, 'Given another quarter of a century of quiet British rule and the spoil of the Panjab will be once more worth the attention of some covetous invader from the North-West,' it is amusingly preposterous. It has not been shown, nor can it possibly be shown, that there has been any material addition to the wealth of the

Panjab during the fifty and more years that that province has been under British rule. No doubt in a few of the wealthier Indian and Muhammadan families all over India there are still jewels and property of considerable value. But it is mainly inherited wealth. No one would contend that all India's stored-up resources have already been drained from the country; of inherited wealth there must still be some. It is, however, lessening year by year, whilst its place is not being taken by newer creations of reserves or purchase of valuables. If students of Indian affairs would take the trouble to examine into such matters analytically and historically, first of all casting aside all preconceived notions and preserving a candid mind, even the newspaper quoted, judging by its leader of December 30, 1890, would not merely be among the prophets, but would be head and shoulders over its compeers in its exhibition of India's only too hideous poverty. That journal would then, habitually, as it did incidentally, on the date mentioned, attack the Indian authorities with vehemence and with imputations unknown to the present writer, who always assumes that every Anglo-Indian official is the personification of ability, high-mindedness, and good intentions—an Admirable Crichton among the administrators of civilised countries. Indeed, it is because such good men are the (unconscious, one hopes) producers of such ill-consequences that most occasion is found to denounce the system under which the ill grows. The evil thus becomes perpetuated. 'Indian civilians are such honourable men; some often are such good Christians—there cannot be any evil resulting from their administration.' Thus quieted, responsible British people turn over on their side and contentedly slumber.

As to some of the reserves of the well-to-do people in India being retained in the shape of jewelry, that is inevitable. While human nature is human nature some adornment of the person will always be considered essential: 'Back and body will be adorned even if the belly goes empty' is an English, not an Indian, proverb.

Further, to expect, as some English publicists appear to expect, that Indian people will sell their jewels and melt their gold and silver nose and ankle and finger rings, to enable them to find capital for industrial enterprises in which they do not believe, or to improve their land according to a foreigner's notions of improvement, is to expect from them what is looked for from no other people on the face of the earth, and what no other people does. Whence comes the capital employed in joint stock and other enterprises in the United Kingdom? Does any appreciable amount of it come from the jewelry, the paintings, the Sevres vases, the hoarded wealth of the rich people of this land? It is only as there is capital over and above what makes for the adornment of the person and the enrichment of the home that general enterprise is nourished, even in our go-ahead industrial United Kingdom. If this fact were more often borne in mind there would be less injustice done to what is called the want of energy and effort on the part of Indian so-called capitalists, while many foolish gibes as to the alleged 'hoarding' propensities of our Indian fellow-subjects would be spared.[1] Stop the drain from India, and there may be a chance of wealth accumulating; India may then be able to pay for her own industrial enterprises. While the drain continues wealth cannot accumulate, and the public works which her foreign rulers declare to be necessary must be constructed with foreign capital, and, in the process, will be brought about the further degradation, and, finally, the ruin of India.

[1] 'Much is said about the hoarding by the natives, but how little is the share for each to hoard, and what hoardings—in the shape of investments, plate, jewelry, watches, personal ornaments—there are in England! I do not suppose that any Englishman would say that the natives of India ought to have no taste and no ornaments, and must only live like animals. But, after all, how little there is for each, if every one had his share to hoard or to use. The fact is that, far from hoarding, millions who are living on "scanty subsistence" do not know what it is to have a silver piece in their possession. It cannot be otherwise. To talk of Oriental wealth now, as far as British India is concerned, is a figure of speech, a dream!'—DADABHAI NAOROJI, 'Poverty of India.'

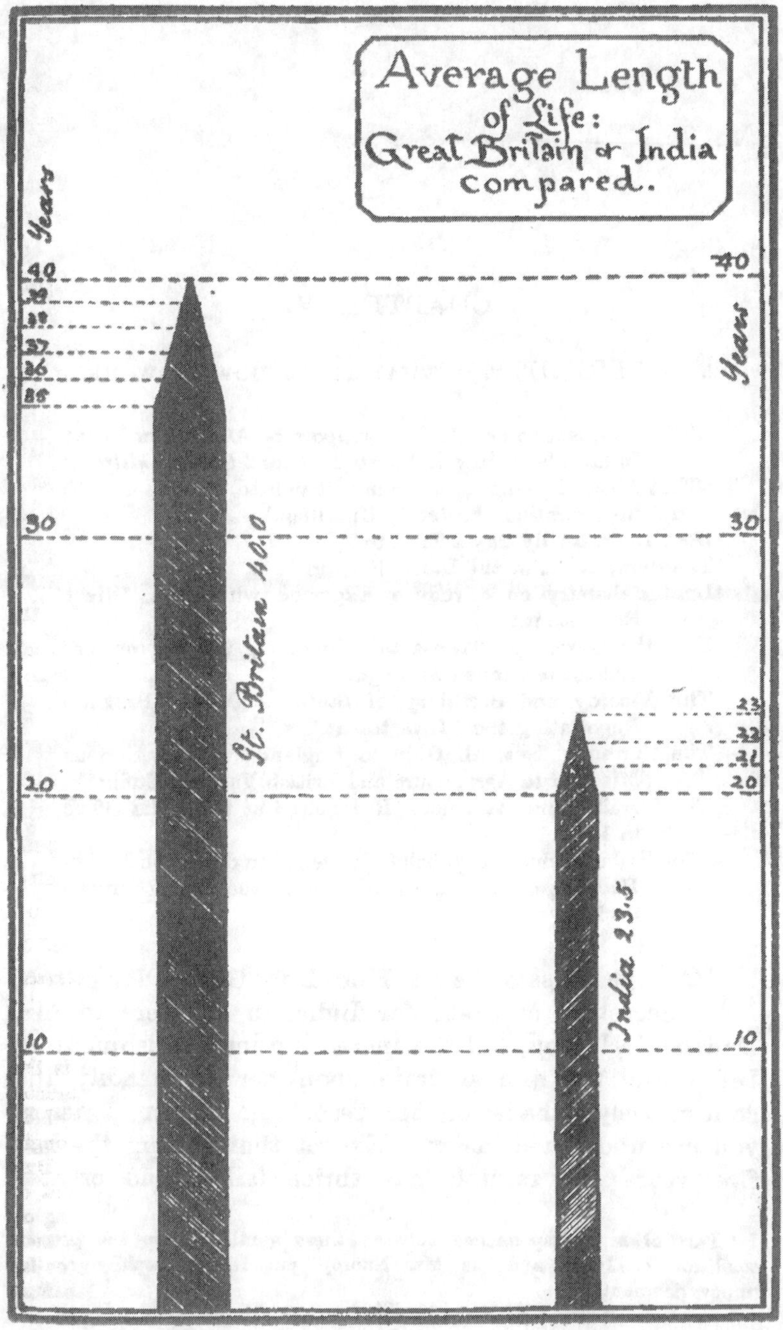
Average Length
of Life:
Great Britain & India
compared.
Years
40
37
36
30
20
10
Gt. Britain 40.0
India 23.5
40
Years
30
20
10

CHAPTER VI

THE 'TRIBUTE': WHAT IT IS, HOW IT WORKS

'. . . not a fact to be found in support of Allegations' that India is becoming Exhausted. (*Lord Geo. Hamilton.*)

'That Absurdity—about a Drain to England.'

'An Administration absolutely Unselfish.'

Does India Really Pay a Tribute?

The Symposium at the India Office in 1875.

Lord Salisbury on 'Produce Exported without a Direct Equivalent.'

How the Mercantile Transaction Involving the Payment of Tribute is Carried Through.

The Viceroy and Secretary of State, as Money Brokers, Negotiating the 'Investment.'

The 'Tribute' Not All Gain to England; it does Serious Mischief to Agriculture and British Farmers Suffer.

The 'Drain' and Its Effects Recognised at the India Office in 1875.

'The Tribute which is so balefully weighing down the Indian Exchange, . . . threatens to break the Indian camel's back.'

'YOU speak,' said the Rt. Hon. Lord George Hamilton, Secretary of State for India, in a letter[1] to Mr. Dadabhai Naoroji, 'of the increasing impoverishment of India, and the annual drain upon her as steadily and continuously exhausting her resources. Again I assert you are under a delusion. Except that, during the last five years the rainfall has thrice failed, and created

[1] Part of a correspondence between these gentlemen on the present condition of India and (as Mr. Naoroji put it) its rapidly-growing impoverishment.

droughts of immense dimensions, there is not a fact to be found in support of your allegations.'

'Does India pay tribute to England?'

'Certainly not,' the average Englishman would reply. 'We do not rule India in that way. Tribute? Oh! it is nonsense to suppose we take tribute from another country, especially a country like India. We rule India for nothing, except payment for the work we do there.'

The more than average man, the capable scholar, the high administrator, all reply with like expressions. One of the highest of ex-officials, whose service in India recently came to an end, said, in the presence of the present writer, during the present year (1901): 'Oh! that absurdity about a drain from India to England! There is no drain. If there be a drain it is all the other way.' He was highly indignant, as he thus spoke, with any one who thought otherwise.

The cynic may ask: 'Does England, indeed, then rule India for naught?' And he will get a reply in some such terms as these:—

'I have simply to repeat what I suppose is the most striking impression that India leaves on every traveller of the magnificent work that has been done, and is being done, by English Administration.' And, of course,

'All for love and nothing for reward.'[1]

'The spectacle,' continues the same writer, 'of an administration absolutely unselfish, just, scrupulous, unweariedly energetic, provident, charitable, worked by men of untiring self-sacrifice and indomitable courage from the highest to the lowest, keeping order in what would quite obviously otherwise be illimitable chaos—a Government, local as well as central, exact, firm, yet responsive to a touch, and absolutely devoted to the good

[1] Spenser's 'Faerie Queen.'

of the people, is one which makes one proud and thankful for British rule.' [1]

This is how nearly every Englishman regards the British connection with India. Yet it is wholly a fancy picture. Our 'absolutely unselfish' and 'scrupulous' rule is compatible with the existence of a drain of India's resources which is enriching an already wealthy country at the cost of insufficient food, insufficient clothing, and no comforts of any kind for enjoyment by twice as many millions of British subjects as there are people residing in the United Kingdom. Compatible, too, with one returned civilian getting as much for pension each year as the average income of thirteen hundred people. The rule has to be good, the man has to have done wonders, to justify any foreigner for 'non-equivalent services' (in Lord Salisbury's phrase) taking so much from the means of an always hungry and ill-nourished people.

The word 'Tribute' is only once mentioned in the general accounts of the Government of India. It is then employed to designate certain payments made by the Feudatory States to the suzerain Power. The total amount is £909,701 per annum. Of anything in the shape of a 'tribute' in the transactions existing between India and England nothing is said. Why? 'Because,' the reply is given to any question of the kind which may be asked, 'there is nothing in the shape of tribute from the one country to the other. Are Englishmen South American Spaniards that they should exact a tribute from the people over whom they bear rule?'

One hundred and twenty years ago there was no insuperable objection to call things by their right names. Burke [2] declared it 'must have been always evident to considerate persons that the vast extraction of wealth from a country lessening in its resources in proportion to

[1] Rev. W. H. Hutton, B.D., Tutor and Fellow of St. John's College, Oxford: 'Impressions of India,' contributed to *The Guardian*, May, 1901.

[2] Ninth Report of Select Committee on the Affairs of India, p. 57, vol. viii. J. C. Nimmo, 1899.

the increase of its burdens' was neither good in itself, nor could it be of long duration. To-day we are not wholly blind, notwithstanding the general obscurantism, which, sometimes, seems wilful obscurantism. The injury—of increasing the burdens on the land and leaving cities and towns insufficiently taxed—'is exaggerated in India,' said Lord Salisbury (April 29, 1875), 'where so much of the revenue is exported without a direct equivalent.' The Secretary of State for India, as Lord Salisbury was then, proceeded to say:—'As India must be bled the lancet should be directed to the parts where the blood is congested, or at least is sufficient, not to those which are already feeble from the want of it.' This observation makes it clear that to one British statesman out of the many who have had direct charge of Indian affairs, the fact, that India was paying tribute to England, was perfectly clear. With his great ability and luminous powers of description Lord Salisbury put the matter beyond peradventure in two striking phrases:—

> '. . . India, where so much of the revenue is exported without a direct equivalent.'
>
> 'As India must be bled, the lancet should be directed to the parts where the blood is congested, or at least sufficient, not to those which are already feeble for the want of it.'

There were others in the India Office at that time who shared these views and who did not hesitate to express them.[1] But for some reason not readily apparent, from

[1] 'More than twenty years ago the late Sir Louis Mallet (I presume with the knowledge and consent of Lord Cranbrook, then Secretary of State for India, and of my friend the late Edward Stanhope, then Under-Secretary), put at my disposal the confidential documents in the India Office, from Indian Finance Ministers and others, bearing on this question of the drain from India to England and its effects. The situation is, to my mind, so desperate that I consider I am entitled to call on Lord George Hamilton to submit the confidential memoranda on this subject, up to and after the year 1880, for the consideration of the House of Commons. I venture to assert that the public will be astonished to read the names of those who (privately) are at one with me on this matter. As to remedy, there is but one, and it is almost too late for that: the staunching of the drain and the steady substi-

that time forward no such word has been spoken, or, if spoken, has not been allowed to appear in any of the publications emanating from the Office.

The names of things concerning the fundamental facts of human nature and of administrative conditions may change: the essential conditions are unvaried. This is especially the case with India. A student of Anglo-Indian nomenclature in relation to the procedure of affairs during, say, the past thirty years, finds himself, on consulting the official records of the end of the eighteenth and the beginning of the nineteenth century, in a world of most refreshingly frank and wholly unaccustomed expressions. Yet, the burden of dispatches from the India House to 'loving friends' in India refer to much the same topics as do the dispatches which to-day pass backwards and forwards between Whitehall on the one hand and Calcutta and Simla on the other. Notably is this true of the correspondence of the finance departments. The problems to be faced now are the problems which were faced then. In the Company's days, urged by the need for dividends and by the payments to be made to His Majesty's Government for troops and in other respects, much turned upon 'the Investment.' The Investment meant so many millions of pounds sterling employed for the purchase of goods to be loaded into the Company's ships and sold in English markets to provide salaries, dividends, and interest on the fruits of 'the

tution of Native rule, under light English supervision, for our present ruinous system.'—H. M. Hyndman, *Morning Post*, July 2, 1901. In a preceding communication from the same writer names had been named to this extent: 'I may say, in conclusion, that my views on this matter have been and are shared by such men, dead and living, as Mr. Montgomery Martin, Sir George Wingate, Mr. James Geddes (Bengal Civil Service, hero of the Orissa famine of 1866), Sir Louis Mallet, Colonel Osborn, Major Evans Bell, Mr. Robert Knight, Sir William Wedderburn, Mr. Chester Macnaghten (late Principal of the Rajkumar College, Rajkote, Kattywar), Mr. William Digby, Mr. Dadabhai Naoroji, and many more; and I believe I should not be very far wrong if I added Lord Salisbury and another ex-Secretary of State for India to the list.' The name of the late Sir George Campbell, K.C.S.I., M.P., once Lieutenant-Governor of Bengal, must also be included. His remarks will be found in the succeeding chapter.

economical sin of international borrowing,' on which the directors discoursed, a sin which, notwithstanding its condemnation, was committed with impunity immediately wars with the object of conquest seemed inevitable and were taken in hand. The process was simple. If 'Commerce' had not profits for the 'Investment,' then 'Territory' provided what was needed—that is to say, the proceeds of taxation paid for the goods to fill the ships' holds and to find employment for the broker in Mincing Lane and its purlieus. The rulers of India, then, might be governing men, but, first and foremost, they were merchants. The fact was open and undisguised. Now they are rulers indeed, but no longer figure as merchants. The Viceroy does not buy wheat, and jute, and tea, and indigo, and oil seeds, and coffee, and cotton, endorse the Bills of Lading, as did Warren Hastings in his time, and consign the produce to the Secretary of the India Office in London. All the same month by month a mercantile transaction is carried through identical with that which was familiar and easily understood when done openly and above-board.

Lord George Hamilton is the head of a larger mercantile house than that over which Mr. Pierpont Morgan presides as Master of the United States Steel Trust. Mr. Clinton Dawkins, in exchanging his Finance Ministership of India for a partnership in an eminent banking firm doing business in London and New York, merely exchanged one commercial situation for another. Our whole connection with India rests upon the shop-keeping element in the relations between the two countries being strictly maintained. Let those visible signs of India's subordination to England which are manifest in the balance of exports over imports in the annual trade of the two countries be stopped by that great merchant the Secretary of State ceasing to offer Council Bills for purchase, and India would not greatly concern us as a nation, if only the inevitable liquidation provided us with twenty shillings in the £, and we received 'compensation for disturbance,' which we should certainly exact. The merchant-statesman no longer buys goods in India himself, sells them in the open market and appropriates the proceeds to pay what is due to moneylenders in England, (called, for euphony's sake, shareholders—the other name is ugly and is to be reserved for sowkars and bunniahs), annuitants, and pensioners, not to mention his own emoluments and those of his not small army of assistants. He *has* to have about sixteen millions sterling of hard cash every year to pay to the respective parties just mentioned. His Agent in Calcutta, the Head of the Civil Administration, the representative of British Majesty, has collected the money that is wanted and holds it ready for transmission. He cannot, however, very well send the rupees he has actually obtained from the taxed community. Neither would it be dignified on the part of Lord Curzon of Kedleston to buy produce and see it shipped from dock or ghat. Other people in England, merchants who have ascertained the wants of the Western people, have agents in India who buy produce and who are ready to undertake all the technicalities involved in shipping it to England. They do this, and their principals in London having received and sold the goods wish to transmit to India payment for what they have received. If Lord Curzon does not want to send over actual coin in bulk neither does the outside merchant wish to send more ingots of gold or silver or brass to India than the few well-to-do Indian people require as a metallic reserve or for conversion into ornaments—such ornaments being a kind of savings' bank whence (before the Mints were closed) the full silver value of the savings could, at any moment, be obtained (less a small commission) in current coin of the realm.

Thus, the Secretary of State wants the money which his Agent in Calcutta holds for him; the vendor merchant in London wants to pay his correspondent or Agent at an Indian port or in an inland city for the produce and goods he has received and has sold. What better course can the English merchant adopt to secure his ends than that he should pay what he has to pay to the Secretary of State in London who will instruct his Agent—the Viceroy—to pay in Calcutta or elsewhere a corresponding sum to the Exchange Bank which has come into existence as the medium for such transactions?

Because Indian produce is the only means by which these transactions can be carried through, the British farmer has nearly ceased to grow wheat. Cheap labour in India and the utter helplessness of the cultivator has helped to bring the agriculturist in the United Kingdom to the deplorable pass described by Mr. Rider Haggard in his July-October visitation through the agricultural districts of England.[1] Economic causes, as inexorable as the law of gravitation or the transmission of light from the sun and stars, from lamp and candle, have made the wealth gained by iron-master and manufacturer who send steel rails and locomotives to India paid for out of money lent by England and not provided by India, to play a large part in producing the harder struggle for life which the British agriculturist has to endure. A study of these economics would lead English landowners and farmers to hold very different political views from those they at present possess. But there is no Party in the British State with knowledge or discernment to teach them what they should know.

'The glut of Indian commodities in the English market,' says Mr. Inwood Pollard,[2] 'is the result of India's growing Home charges. For, whereas English merchants only expended 304,000,000 of tolas[3] of silver

[1] See a series of articles contributed to the *Express* newspaper, London.

[2] 'The Indian Tribute and the Loss by Exchange; an Essay on the Depreciation of Indian Commodities in England,' by Thomas Inwood Pollard. Calcutta: Thacker, Spink and Co. 1884. I have exchanged the word 'our' into 'India' to increase the perspicacity of the passage for English readers.

[3] A tola is a measure of weight. The standard tola weighs 180 troy grains, or one rupee.

in the purchase of Indian goods in the five years ending with 1884–5, they expended no less than 976,000,000 worth of substitutes for tolas of silver, during the same period, in the shape of bills drawn on the Indian Government by the Secretary of State for India—paper-money representing the Indian tribute. Whereas the average annual imports of silver into India in the five years ending with 1884–5 had *de*creased from 75,000,000 to 61,000,000 of rupees as compared with the fifteen years ending with 1874–5, the bills drawn in London and paid by the Government in India had *in*creased from 74,000,000 to 195,000,000 annually. (If we compare 1870–1 to 1873–4 with 1880–1 to 1883–4, the increase of the annual average of Indian Home charges is 82,000,000 of rupees.)'

Mr. Pollard proceeds, in a luminous passage to which I beg the reader's most careful attention, to show how the drain from India is arranged in such a way as to disguise its real purpose from every one but an expert. He says: 'How few people can be brought to realise what this means'—that is, the statement in the preceding paragraph. 'Could I demonstrate that £12,000,000 worth of Indian merchandise had been added to the English annual supply in exchange for a certain number of tons of solid metal sold to our customers at a cheap rate by Germany or the United States, not one man in ten thousand would refuse to acknowledge *that* to be the cause of the low value of Indian goods in England. Yet, when I do something more—when I demonstrate that £12,000,000 worth of these same goods have been added to the annual supply in the same market in exchange for *bits of paper*, not one in ten thousand will understand what I mean.

'I mean that, of late years (1880–1 to 1884–5) as compared with former years (1860–1 to 1874–5) 121,000,000 of rupees' worth of Indian goods had been added to the already heavy annual consignments wherewith India pays its English liabilities (other than those due on the score of commerce); that English private importers of merchandise have to compete with the ever-increasing and virtually gratuitous, consignments of the same merchandise imported by Her Majesty's Secretary of State for India; the Indian exporters send their goods to a market in which the demand for them is ever being saturated more and more by a greater and greater quantity of them having been already received by their customers as imports for which *nothing* has to be paid, for which no equivalent in merchandise or money has to be exported, which *cost* England not so much as a day's work.'

The Marquis of Salisbury, eleven years earlier, had condensed this teaching into a sentence when he drew attention to the fact that 'much of the revenue of India is exported without a direct equivalent.'[1] While such a statement remains on record it is perfectly clear that at the India Office, so long ago as 1875, 'the drain' and its effects were recognised in their true light. That not only nothing has been done during the intervening twenty-six years to staunch the open wound thus recognised while everything possible has been done to aggravate it until the wound has become an avenue to premature death and untold suffering to millions of British subjects yearly, is a condition of things for which the Secretary of State and his colleagues will have to answer at the bar of justice and of public opinion one day.

I venture to put it to Lord George Hamilton, to whom has been given the inestimable privilege of ruling India for six years continuously, of having made twelve Indian Budget speeches in the House of Commons and of having served at the India Office nearly fourteen years altogether, whether he has ever taken the trouble to realise what it is that he has done towards ruining the bodies and desolating the homes of many, many, millions of his Indian fellow-subjects, through his neglect to mark, learn, and

[1] This is one of a number of pivotal sentences which the reader will see again and again in these pages. I am less concerned with saying the same thing the second time or the third or fourth time than I am to impress the fact upon the reader's mind.

inwardly digest the facts relating to the most splendid position ever occupied by mortal man. He is responsible for the lives and happiness of three hundreds of millions of human beings, and he allows millions to starve to death every year. Why? Because to him the economic condition of India is a wholly sealed, unopened, unstudied, book. Here are passages which may give him occasion to pause, and should stimulate him to a line of reflection to which he is now a stranger. In the *Westminster Review* in 1880 Mr. W. T. Thornton penned this paragraph, which was probably the last he ever wrote on a subject on which he was an acknowledged authority. Mr. Thornton remarked:—

'Thus, it is established there is a drain from India to England. What is its nature and extent?

'Experience, as usual, deferring until too late her captious counsels, at last teaches us clearly enough how serious an oversight there has been in an important branch of the domestic policy instituted by the Government of India some twenty-five years ago, and steadily pursued ever since. Every one could see that railways, which had so marvellously developed the resources of Europe, were equally desirable for India: but neither did it occur to any practical administrator to inquire, nor did any theoretical economist volunteer to point out,[1]

[1] This is an error. The effect of the Indian tribute was pointed out, in general terms, by John Stuart Mill. He demonstrates that 'every country exports and imports the very same things and in the very same quantity' under a money system as under a barter system. In the absence of international payments of the nature of a tribute, 'under a barter system the trade gravitates to the point at which the sum of the imports exactly exchanges for the sum of the exports; in a money system it gravitates to the point at which the sum of the imports and the sum of the exports exchange for the same quantity of money. And since things which are equal to the same thing are equal to one another, the exports and imports, which are equal in money price, would, if money were not used, precisely exchange for one another.' But he shows that this equality between exports and imports is disturbed by 'the existence of international payments not originating in commerce, and for which no equivalent in either money or commodities is expected or received—such as a tribute,

how greatly the investment of English capital on Indian public works must, by necessitating the remittance to England of annual interest or profit on the investment, derange the Indian exchange, nor how grievous would be the effects of the derangement. Railways are good, irrigation is good, but neither one nor the other good enough to compensate for opening and continually widening a drain *which has tapped India's very heart-blood,*[1] and has dried up the mainsprings of her industrial energy. So grievous an error of the past having been at length, however tardily, detected, will scarcely be persevered in; and we may reasonably assume, therefore, that there will be no more guaranteeing of private British enterprise. . . . There is for India just now no other public work half so urgent as the restoration of equilibrium between income and expenditure, and all the rest should be imperatively required to wait until there shall be surplus revenue applicable to them, *unless, perchance, the requisite funds can be intermediately borrowed from local capitalists content to receive their interest on the spot.* . . . Here, then, I bring my story to a close by

or remittances of rent to absentee landlords or of *interest to foreign creditors.*

'To begin with the case of barter. The supposed annual remittances being made in commodities, and being exports for which there is to be no return, it is no longer requisite that the imports and exports should pay for one another; on the contrary, there must be an annual excess of exports over imports, equal to the value of the remittance. If, before the country became liable to the annual payment, foreign commerce was in its natural state of equilibrium, it will now be necessary, for the purpose of effecting the remittance, that foreign countries should be induced to take a greater quantity of exports than before, *which can only be done by offering those exports on cheaper terms*, or, in other words, *by paying dearer for foreign commodities.* The international values will so adjust themselves that either by greater exports or smaller imports, or both, the requisite excess will be brought about, and this excess will become the permanent state. The result is that a country which makes regular payments to foreign countries, *besides losing what it pays, loses also something more*, by the less advantageous terms on which it is forced to exchange its productions for foreign commodities.'

[1] The italics here and subsequently are not mine; they are the author's.—W. D.

drawing from it the pregnant moral that *it is India's tribute which is so balefully weighing down the Indian exchange, and that the same burden threatens, unless speedily and materially lightened, to break the Indian camel's back—miracle of endurance though the animal be.*'[1]

[1] 'The Indian Tribute' (Thos. Inwood Pollard), pp. 77–78 and 92–93.

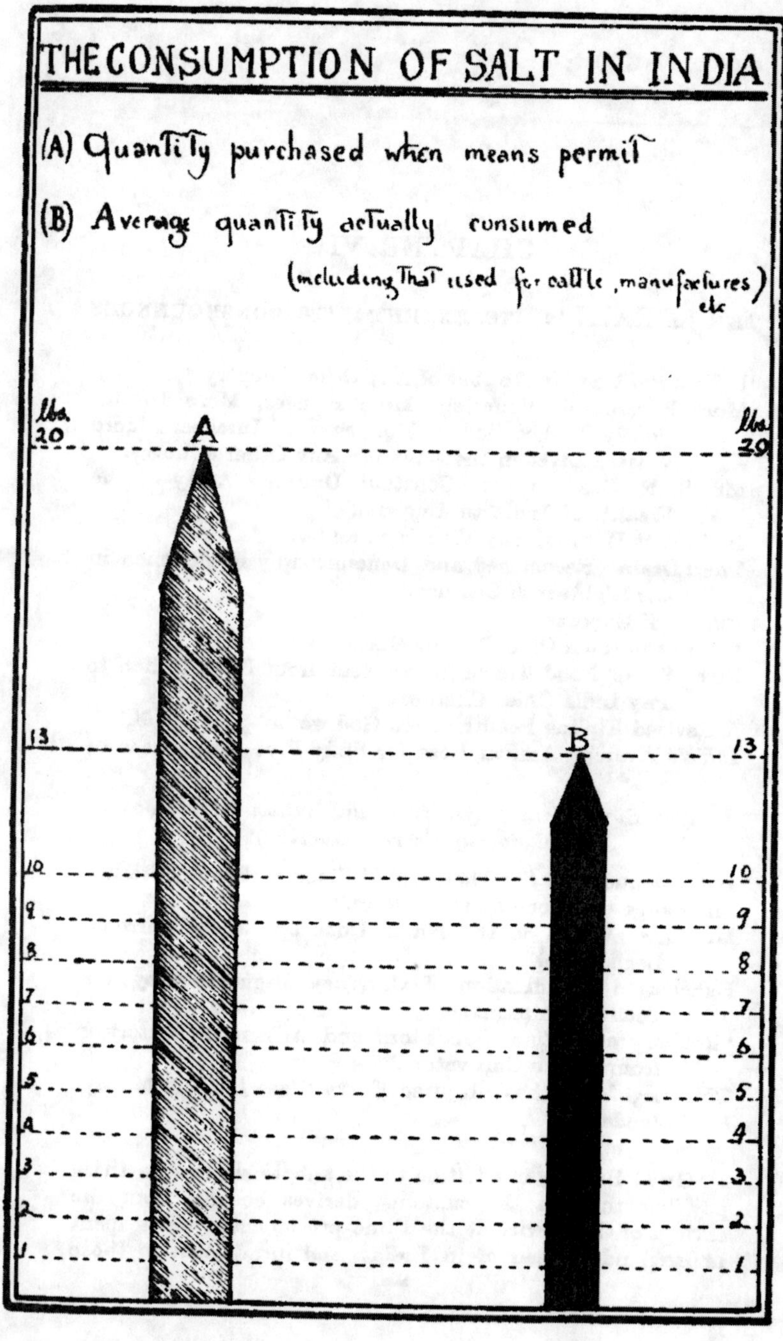
THE CONSUMPTION OF SALT IN INDIA
(A) Quantity purchased when means permit
(B) Average quantity actually consumed
(including that used for cattle, manufactures) etc
lbs. 20
A
lbs. 20
13
B
13
10
9
8
7
6
5
4
3
2
1

CHAPTER VII

THE 'DRAIN': ITS EXTENT; ITS CONSEQUENCES

India's Position Unlike that of Any Other Country.
More Preventable Suffering, More Hunger, More Insufficiently Clothed Bodies, More Stunted Intellects, More Wasted Lives in India than in Any Other Country.
Mr. R. N. Cust on the 'Constant Draining Away of the Wealth of India to England.'
India Left Without Any Working Capital.
The 'Drain' Recognised and Denounced by Englishmen in the Eighteenth Century.
Excess of Exports.
Where the India Office Money Goes
Five Weeks' Food Taken Every Year from Each Indian to Pay India Office Charges.
A Revised Kipling Poem: 'Lord God we ha' paid in full.'
India's Average Annual Loss for Sixty-Five Years, year by year

Two Significant Pages from an Indian Blue Book (photographic reproduction).

India Denuded of Six Thousand Millions of Pounds Sterling
Sir George Campbell on the 'Drain.'
Mr. J. A. Wadia on the Harm Done by Recent Currency Legislation.
Exhaustive Examination of Currency Legislation by Mr. Cecil B. Phipson.
'Robbery of Indian Depositors and Automatic Extortion from Indian Cultivators.'
This Legislation has 'Injured Every Class but the Money-lenders.'

'Great Britain, in addition to the tribute she makes India pay her through the customs, derives benefit from the savings of the service at the three presidencies being spent in England instead of in India; and in addition to these savings, which probably amount to near a million, she derives benefit from the fortunes realised by the European mercantile community, which are all remitted to England.' —Parl. Paper, 1858 (445 = II.), p. 580.

INDIA occupies a position amongst the countries of the world to which there is no parallel. She is absolutely alone in her experience. Look the globe over, there is no other land with which to make a comparison, unless it be Java, and there the circumstances are not identical. None of the other great divisions of the earth are wholly under the rule of an alien race. Elsewhere, whatever the form of government may be, the national aims, desires, aspirations, ideals, receive consideration, with here and there an exception, as in Finland. Russia, throughout its agricultural districts, may be poor, but the economic considerations and conditions which contribute to that poverty are under Russian control and are carried out with the acquiescence of the Russian people.[1] The same is true in and of China, though the situation there is tempered by foreigners holding many posts and roaming where they will throughout the land. But they are in China more or less on sufferance. Though the burden they have placed on the Chinese people is heavy, yet the final word concerning that burden is with Chinamen. South American Republics are free to do what they will, even to the extent, if they consider the weight of foreign indebtedness too great to be borne, of acting upon that ugliest and most hateful of nineteenth-century words—Repudiation. Japan has taken a foremost place among the great nations of the world within less than fifty years of awakening to her backward position; Japanese statesmen rank with the noblest and most

[1] 'Whatever course events may take, our rule in India must apparently for generations become a problem of increasing difficulty and complexity. The problem is analogous to what seems to lie before a government like that of Russia, with this difference—that the Government in Russia is a native institution, whereas in India it is that of an alien nation governing a host of subject races.'—'Essays in Finance,' 2nd ed., 1886, by Sir R. Giffen, K.C.B.

capable of European and American administrators; Japanese soldiers in the field and Japanese discipline on the march and in camp, by reason of the individual self-restraint developed, leave every Christian nation's soldiery in the rear.

And India?

There are none so poor as to do India reverence.

To adorn a spectacle and to take part in a display with the 'sons of Empire,' and even to win the admiration of a German Field Marshal by reason of their prowess in China, Indian stalwartness of bearing and high physical courage and military capacity count for much. But in other respects, what part or lot has the Indian in those world-wide dominions of Britain, which contain four hundred millions of subjects, whereof three out of four are his country-people? The Indian territory is the most compact and most easily ruled among all the Commonwealths, Dominions, and Colonies which are sisters to the Empire of India. Indians, as individuals, compel our admiration. They equal us, they often beat us, in our most fancied pursuits, whether spiritual, scientific, intellectual, or physical. Indian after Indian (even from the most poverty-stricken parts of the Empire) take the highest intellectual prizes at our Universities. In the cricket field our greatest players troop behind Kumar Shri Ranjitsinghji, and do not know which most to admire —his supreme mastery of their national game, or the sportsmanlike spirit in which he captains his county eleven, and regards his position in the 'Averages' as naught in comparison with a 'win' for his team. In the scientific world, Professor J. K. Bose, a Bengali Babu, opens the eyes of Western pundits to the vision of an undreamt-of unseen world of electrical phenomena. In the religious sphere, a saintliness of life, a fervid eloquence that captivates the heart and takes prisoner the emotions—these are conspicuously recognised in Indian teacher after teacher. In statesmanship, unhappily permitted to exist only in the Feudatory States, and not in the British Provinces, there are few in Europe, Asia, and America to surpass the achievements of Sir Salar Jung the First, Sir T. Madava Rau, Sir Dinkar Rau [1]—to refer only to the departed. In a right use of the wealth which a few Indians have acquired the noblest spirit of philanthropy has been exhibited.

And yet, in spite of all this, India and the nations of India count for nothing in the comity of nationalities—are, indeed, not a nation in any sense, but subjects of a 'righteous' raj; in the shaping of the policy most affecting themselves they are of no account. Again: in spite of all this, combined with a belief on the part of the conquering race that they are doing better for Indian kings, princes, and peoples than they could do for themselves, there is—

> more preventable suffering,
> more hunger,
> more insufficiently clothed bodies,
> more stunted intellects,
> more wasted lives,
> more disappointed men,

by a score or two of millions, in the British Provinces of India than are to be found amongst any like number of people the round world over.

Why?

Materially, because of the 'drain.'

Said one of the great host of retired Indian civilians,[2] himself on pension, drawing from India annually the income of well-nigh seventeen hundred people: 'There is a constant drawing away of the wealth of India to England, as Englishmen grow fat on accumulations made in India, while the Indian remains as lean as ever. . . . Every post of dignity and high emolument, civil and military, is held by a stranger and a foreigner; Akbar made fuller

[1] Also, while the manuscript of this chapter is with the printer, Sir K. Seshadri Aiyar, the recently resigned Prime Minister of Mysore.

[2] R. N. Cust, 'Linguistic and Oriental Essays,' Part 2, ch. 7. Trubner and Co.

use of the subject races; we make none: it is the jealousy of the middle-class Briton, the hungry Scot, that wants his salary, that shuts out all Native aspiration. . . . The consequences will be terrible.'

Morally, because of the literally besotted conceit which, in plain daylight view of innumerable facts to the contrary in recent past history and in present experience, under our own eyes, has determined that there is nothing good in Indian character, that there is nothing beneficial in present-day administration, which does not owe its being to us; and, because of our insular national pride, we are not willing to share our rule and governance with a dark-skinned people. Dark face—black heart. Dark skin—necessarily mental inferiority; dark skin—nobility of character and self-sacrifice, with other of the higher qualities of soul and mind, impossible; dark skin—business energy, commercial forethought, wholly wanting, else, it is argued, the development of India would be ensured with Indian capital. The last is a particularly cruel and stupid thrust, since we have 'drained' the country of all its spare capital.

These are among the reasons why India is poor, and, being poor, is—by the standard of the age—necessarily and irredeemably inferior.

Long prior to the time when five millions sterling represented the total amount of trade between England and India, the 'drain,' as its inevitable consequences were realised, was the subject of adverse comment. At that time 'India' meant the Lower Provinces of Bengal, several towns on the Coromandel coast, including Chinnapatnam (Madras), with much of the Hinterland, and the island of Bombay with surrounding territory and a few centres of trade such as Surat. The Bombay districts were acquired later—from the Marathas and others. When sovereignty was assumed in Eastern and Southern India the question was considered: 'In what Manner it may be most expedient to exercise it for the permanent Benefit of the governing Power.'[1] The 'Manner' would be to commit

'the internal Administration to one or more considerable Moormen; the Moormen chiefly should be employed in the Offices of Government; the cultivation of the soil should be left with the Gentoos, whose Property it is, and the Revenue fixed for ever'; '. . . the governing Power should stand paramount, and hold the Sword over the rest, watching the Administration of every subordinate Department, content with a gross but moderate Tribute proportioned to their necessary Expense, and guarding the Country from being ruined in Detail by Europeans. On these Terms the Natives should be left undisturbed in the full Enjoyment of their own Laws, Customs, Prejudices, and Religion. On these Terms they would as readily submit to our Dominion as to any other, nor could it ever be lost but by foreign Conquest.'

This was the highest wisdom of the eighteenth century concerning England's connection with India. It was very high wisdom indeed. Those dozen lines are the quintessence of a policy by which alone one country can successfully and prosperously hold rule over another, if, indeed, the achievement, at any time and in any circumstances, be even approximately possible. It is the policy which prevails in the Australian Commonwealth, the Dominion of Canada, the Colonies generally, with this exception—from none save from India is a Tribute exacted. Only as we go back to that ideal for India and realise it to the full will prosperity ever return to that country.

The easy conquest of Hindustan by the Muhammadans is accounted for by 'the Moderation of the Tribute imposed and the Simplicity of their Method of collecting it.' 'In general, they introduced no Change but in the Army and in the Name of the Sovereign. With Respect to the Collection of the Revenues, the System of the present

[1] This extract (p. 915), and subsequent extracts, are from the 'Reports from Committees of the House of Commons,' vol. v., 1781–82. Printed 1804. The capital letters and the italics are those of the Parliamentary publication.

Government is upon Principle directly the reverse of what it ought to be, and I believe, such as never was adopted by any other Government.'[1]

Then, as now, 'the eye of prophecy looked backward.' To properly forecast the future the writer glanced at what had happened before his time. 'It cannot be disputed,' he said, 'that *Bengal* was in a much more flourishing State during the last Century than it has ever been under the English Establishment.' The principle on which Akbar secured his conquest 'was to conciliate the Minds of the native Hindoos, and to unite them as much as possible to his Person and Government: some he employed in the highest Offices of the State; with others he connected himself *and his Family by Marriage*.'

When the East India Company took charge of Bengal as a governing power it was after

> 'a quick Succession of Wars and Revolutions, a Foreign Influence prevailing both in Matters of Government and Commerce, the drain of large Sums of Money carried away by Individuals, or by the Company.' In such a state of poverty and decay, 'instead of Imports of Treasure from Europe, a Tribute was actually required from hence. Large sums in specie were actually sent out.'

'The Wealth formerly enjoyed by the Natives, and diffused by an equal and constant Circulation through the Country, was engrossed by Foreigners, who either exported it directly, or, by supplying the other European Factories, made it necessary, even for them, to import Bullion, for providing their Investments.'[2] Other portions

[1] 'Instead of leaving the Management to the natural Proprietors of the Lands, and demanding from *them* a fixed Portion of the Produce, we take the Management upon ourselves, and pay them a Tribute: Government stands in the place of the Zemindar, and allows him a Pension.'

[2] Philip Francis, the author of this valuable State paper, exceeded in value by few—if any—State papers written concerning India, was not alone in the views he expressed. Many others wrote in a similar strain. Notably in a communication to the President of Council seven years before Francis wrote, it was remarked: 'It must give Pain to an Englishman to have Reason to think that, since the Accession of the Company to the Dewannee, the Condition of the People of this Country has been worse than

of this powerful *exposé* of the situation in Bengal indicate special clearsightedness. But the policy was too wise for adoption. After consideration, with one exception, other counsels were followed. That exception was the establishment of a Permanent Settlement in Bengal. This brought some measure of prosperity to these regions. In all other respects that was done which has caused lasting injury to India and has brought discredit upon English fame.

The Investment was continued. Even if Bengal, before our Accession to the Dewannee, did suffer somewhat from the diversion of a portion of its revenues to the Mogul Emperor, it appeared 'that the Company have levied higher Rents from this Country whilst [it was] labouring under the greatest disadvantages, than it ever paid to the Emperors in its most flourishing Condition, when the Principal Part of the Revenues were spent within the Provinces, and the Remainder went no farther than Delhi.' It was equally apparent 'that, under our Administration, the Desire of Increase, invariably and inflexibly pursued, is the Ruin of the Country, and, ere long, will be found the worst Œconomy.'

Ten years later, the greatest panegyrist of British rule in India—and, at the same time, himself the worst disparager of the Indian people known in British-Indian literature—Charles Grant, of the India House, was constrained to admit: 'We apply a large portion of their annual produce to the use of Great Britain.'

it was before; and yet I am afraid the Fact is undoubted; and I believe has proceeded from the following Causes: the Mode of providing the Company's Investment; the Exportation of Specie, instead of importing large sums annually; the Strictness that has been observed in the Collections; the Endeavours of all Concerned to gain Credit by an Increase of Revenue during the Time of their being in Station, without sufficiently attending to what future Consequences might be expected from such a Measure; the Errors that subsist in the Manner of making the Collections, particularly by the employment of Aumils: These appear to me the principal Causes why this fine Country, which flourished under the most despotic and arbitrary Government, is verging towards its Ruin while the English have really so great a share in the Administration.'

That there is any 'drain' from India to England is, as I have shown in preceding chapters, frequently denied to-day. It was, honestly enough, recognised when, in its earlier stages, it was a comparatively small matter (to us, but to the men of that day great). There seemed then to be no special desire to hide unpleasant truths under a guise of fair-seeming.

The material 'drain' has robbed India of the capital which hitherto had been available for the promotion and strengthening of industry. Without capital no industry, on other than the most primitive of bases, can exist. Two passages from 'Mill's Political Economy,' vol. v., will suffice for the present argument:—

'While, on the one hand, industry is limited by capital, so, on the other, every increase of capital gives, or is capable of giving, additional employment to industry, and this without assignable limit.'

'What supports and employs productive labour is the capital expended in setting it to work and not the demand of purchasers for the produce of the labour when completed. Demand for commodities is not a demand for labour.'

Indian imports and exports are, elsewhere in this work,[1] set out in detail and subjected to a more or less searching analysis. They need not be repeated here in aught but total amounts:—

	£
Exports (including Treasure) in 1898–99 ...	80,086,447
Imports " " " ...	57,531,303
Excess of Exports	£22,555,144

Or, Three Hundred Millions of Rupees—more than One Rupee per Head from All India.

That is the balance, in slightly varying amounts, of

[1] Chapter VIII. pp. 243–284.

which India is, in the matter of exports and imports, denuded year by year. But, as will be apparent to the reader on a moment's thought, it is not by any means a full representation of what India annually loses under the alien rulers who are her overlords. The amount which is shown is that which goes, chiefly to England, for expenditure in that country—no doubt 'for services rendered,' but the services could have been rendered by the Indian people themselves at a smaller cost, and maybe with equal efficiency. In 1898–99 the Secretary of State for India received £16,303,197 (Rs.244,477,650) of this vast sum. He disposed of it thus :—

	£
Interest on Debt and on other Obligations	2,805,097
Management of Debt (Payments to Bank of England and Bank of Ireland)	49,978
Charges on Account of Departments in India :—	
Post Office	57,409
Telegraphs	76,080
Political (Diplomatic Charges)	24,454
Other Charges	28,082
Railways :—	
State Railways (Interest and Annuities)	8,711,690
Guaranteed Lines (Interest)	2,162,525
Public Works (Furlough, Absentee Allowances, etc.) ...	62,089
Marine Charges	147,645
Military Charges :—	
Effective :—Payments to H.M.'s Exchequer for British Forces	764,400
Furlough Allowances	802,549
Troop Service and Passage Money	296,718
Other Charges	18,815
Non-Effective :—Payments to H.M. Exchequer for British Forces (Retired Pay, Pensions, etc.)...	527,523
Pensions to Indian Officers, etc.	1,781,693
Do. to Non-commissioned Officers and Soldiers	6,506
Do. to Widows and Families, etc.	105,957
Civil Charges :—	
Secretary of State's Establishment, including Auditor and excluding Store Department	107,934
Postages and Telegrams	6,091
Contingencies (Rent, Taxes, Coal, etc.)	12,287
Royal Indian Engineering College (including Passages)	29,883
Miscellaneous Home Charges	11,857

	£
Furloughs :—	
Covenanted Service	114,812
Military Officers in Civil Employ	78,410
Uncovenanted, Pilot, and Marine Services	66,287
Pensions and Allowances :—	
Political	11,577
East India Company's Establishments Abolished ...	17,221
Home Establishment Officers	42,836
Do. Widows and Families from Funds	17,026
Indian Officers for Distinguished Services, Judges, Uncovenanted Service, and others	350,901
Compassionate and other Allowances	14,624
Indian Service Funds (Annuities, Pensions, etc.)	1,498,474
Donations, Gratuities, and Charities...	1,835
Miscellaneous Charges	18,755
Stores :—	
Director-General's Department at Lambeth	49,823
Stationery and Printing for all Departments in India	43,658
Civil Departments	131,812
Marine Stores	57,142
Public Works (including Telegraph Stores)	95,195
Military (including Stores for Special Defence Works)	591,223
Miscellaneous Charges	4,519
Total	£16,303,197
Exchange	8,144,568
At Rs. 15 to £	Rs. 244,477,650

Before analysing these figures and showing what, in the way of dead-weight, borne by the Indian people, they indicate, it may be well to record the extent to which these Home Charges have increased since 1834–5 :—

Home Charges in 1834–5.

Dividends on East India Stock	£636,826
Permanent and Fixed Charges	833,226
,, Charges, but varying in amount...	1,205,414
Miscellaneous and Contingent Charges ...	95,458
Temporary Charges, etc.	210,198
Total	£2,981,122

At the end of sixteen years, namely, in 1850–51, the annual increase was only £436,693. A few years later the Mutiny piled up national debt, the money being borrowed from England; shortly after began the era of public works, in which railways have played the largest part; the railways have added much to the Home Charges, little to the real well-being of India. In other respects also additions have been made, especially in non-effective charges.

The payments made by the Secretary of State fall almost naturally into three classes:—

1. *Interest:*

Interest on debt incurred in the normal government of the country	2,805,097
Do. do. Railways (including Annuities)	5,874,215
Management of Debt	49,978
Total	£8,729,290

Or (Rs.15 = £1, Anna = 1d.) *d.*1,852,248,840;

i.e., EIGHTPENCE is due and payable (and is paid) from every man, woman, and child in British India per annum for interest. This, with an average income of £1 2s. 4d. per head means one-thirty-third of the year's income, or eleven days' food:

if, however, as should be done, the income is reckoned of 231,000,000 of people, less one million who are well-to-do,[1] the amount due from each person is one one-twentieth of the year's income, or, eighteen days' food.

2. *General Charges:*

All other sums (save No. 3 below) including *Pensions*, military (effective and non-effective) charges, etc., etc.	£6,464,933

Or (Rs.15 = £1, Anna = 1d.) *d.*1,397,025,606;

[1] See Chapter .

i.e., SIXPENCE per head per annum is due, or (at £1 2s. 4d., average income) eight days' food from every Indian : at 13s. per head, this charge represents fourteen days' food.

3. *Departments and Stores :* £1,108,974
Or (Rs. 15 = £1, Anna = 1d.) *d.*236,581,120 ;

i.e., ONE PENNY from every person in India, at £1 2s. 4d., one and a half days' food : at 13s. per head, over two days' food.

Summary.

	At £1 2s. 4d. Income.		At 13s. Income.	
1. Interest on Debt ...	11	days' food.	18	days' food.
2. General Charges ...	8	,,	14	,,
3. Stores, etc.	1½	,,	2⅕	,,
Totals	20½	,,	34⅕	,,

Or, about five weeks' average maintenance of each Indian outside the one million well-to-do folks is annually disbursed in this country, one of the wealthiest of lands, while the disbursing country is, omitting none, the poorest realm in all the world! Was ever such a crushing tribute exacted by any conqueror at any period of history? Is there any wonder that two millions of British-Indian subjects of the King-Emperor, Edward the Seventh, on the average, now die in each year from want of food, and that twenty times two millions are, in the Lancashire expression, continually 'clemmed'?

Rudyard Kipling, his words slightly varied, provides the Indian, of whom he has written much, but with whose actual condition seemingly he has taken few pains to acquaint himself, with a lament (altered a little from the original) which should touch even a statesman's heart or (harder still) a journalist's conscience as to whether, in his perfunctory acceptance of official statements concerning India, each is doing his duty. Sings the revised and amended Kipling :—

'We have supplied your needs for a hundred years
And you call us, still unfed,
Though there's never an hour of all our hours
But marks our Indian dead:
We have given our means to th' inex'rable call,
To the sowkar, to the raj.
If blood be the price of England's rule,
Lord God, we ha' paid in full!

'There's never a sun goes down in the West
But sees our wors'ning plight;
There's never a sun looks down on us
But sees this sorrowful sight—
But claims on the sands forlorn,
From Comorin to Panjab.
If blood be the price of England's rule,
If blood be the price of England's rule,
Lord God, we ha' paid in full!

'Must we feed your need for a thousand years,
Is that our doom, your pride,
As 'twas when first our shores ye sought
And 's continued wi' woe beside?—
Our bodies lie on the dreary waste
While our homes are bare indeed.
If blood be the price of England's rule,
If blood be the price of England's rule,
If blood be the price of England's rule,
Lord God, we ha' paid in full!'

By how much has the balance of trade, as shown in the official records, gone against India?

This branch of a great subject may seem intricate and not easily grasped by the ordinary reader, but a little consideration will be well repaid. To render my statements as non-contentious as may be, I will deal, mainly, with the figures in the official statements, though thereby I fail to indicate the full extent of the evil by not less than one-third. To the official figures I add commercial profits at ten per cent.[1]

That I may not deal with details which are not accessible to every one who may wish to check my statements I will refer only to the state of things as revealed in the accounts published in the Seventh Issue of 'Financial and Commercial Statistics of British India,' printed in Calcutta in 1900, but to be obtained of any Parliamentary bookseller in England. Both sides of the account will include Treasure.

Period.	Annual Average.		Totals.	
	Imports.	Exports.	Imports.	Exports.
	£	£	£	£
1834-35 to 1838-39	4,877,302	7,555,066	24,386,510	37,775,330
1839-40 ,, 1843-44	6,969,068	9,501,708	34,845,340	47,508,540
1844-45 ,, 1848-49	8,139,584	11,330,366	40,697,920	55,651,830
1849-50 ,, 1853-54	10,567,560	13,344,750	52,837,800	66,723,750
1854-55 ,, 1858-59	17,901,698	17,231,648	89,508,490	86,158,240
1859-60 ,, 1863-64	27,375,312	28,781,524	136,876,540	143,907,620
1864-65 ,, 1868-69	32,876,490	38,442,950	164,382,450	192,214,750
1869-70 ,, 1873-74	27,534,067	38,561,997	137,670,335	192,809,985
1874-75 ,, 1878-79	32,147,904	42,089,751	160,739,520	200,448,755
1879-80 ,, 1883-84	41,209,162	53,606,711	206,045,810	268,033,555
1884-85 ,, 1888-89	50,089,534	60,185,099	250,447,570	300,925,495
1889-90 ,, 1893-94	59,130,622	72,444,732	295,653,110	362,223,660
1894-95 ,, 1898-99	59,038,889	75,953,242	295,194,445	379,766,210
Totals ...			1,889,295,840	2,334,147,730

[1] Mr. Dadabhai Naoroji, writing in 1874, said: 'On an average, commercial profits may be taken at twenty per cent. Indian merchants generally insure by sailing vessels twenty-five per cent. more, and by steamers fifteen per cent. for profit, as by steamers the same capital may be turned over oftener.'

Exports in Sixty-Five years ...	£2,334,147,730
Imports ,, ,, ...	1,889,295,840
	444,851,690
Add 10 per cent. trade profit ...	44,485,169
	£489,336,859

The average annual loss to India on the above showing is £7,529,798. It will be remarked how enormously the totals have increased in the later years as compared with the earlier years. The percentage of increase of exports in 1898–99 over the exports of sixty-five years ago is 1,000 per cent.! And such profit as has been made on this enormous business has been made mainly by the foreigner—that foreigner who is the ruler. That ruler's one boast, daily made in the Temple of the Press, on the Platform, and in the Dispatch, is that he is in India for the good of India and of the Indian people. He leaves it to be inferred that if his presence in India were harmful to the Indian people, nothing would keep him there. To the present time, save in a solitary instance occasionally seen, he has not realised the harmfulness of his course, has not seen the evil he has done and is doing. Will his eyes ever be opened?

It is necessary to carry this matter somewhat farther. Is it possible to ascertain what this disastrous balance of trade has meant in money, which, had it been preserved to the country, and had due diligence been shown by its rulers, would have been available for that development? What has been done in Japan might have been done in India. It will be seen that the sums borrowed from England to 'develop' India are a mere bagatelle compared with what India could herself have provided, had her English rulers been as wise in India's interests as it was their bounden duty to be.

Mr. Montgomery Martin, in his survey of the condition of the people of Bengal and Behar, a survey extending over nine years, namely, from 1807 to 1816, says, in words only too familiar to students of Indian affairs:—

> 'The annual drain of £3,000,000 on British India has amounted, in thirty years, at twelve per cent. (the usual Indian rate) compound interest, to the enormous sum of £723,000,000 sterling. . . . So constant and accumulating a drain, even in England, would soon impoverish her. How severe, then, must be its effects on India, where the wage of a labourer is from twopence to threepence a day!'

At the end of the century, in the earlier part of which Mr. Martin wrote, we, whose fate it is to contemplate the work of our own hands, can tell how severe the effects of this continuous drain has been upon India. Those effects have been so severe that, outside one million wealthy and well-to-do people, the annual income of our wards in India has sunk to a halfpenny per day! Meanwhile the adverse balance of trade—dealing only with what appears in the Government records, regarding simply what the authorities themselves have put in as evidence, not understanding (not seeming to want to understand) what the story is which their records tell—has gone up to the enormous sum, in 1898–99, of Rs.302,140,050, and has been twelve per cent. higher.[1]

In estimating the loss to India in the nineteenth century the start must be made with Mr. Martin's figures:—

	£
Loss to India, prior to 1834–35, compound interest, at twelve per cent....	723,000,000
The average annual loss, taking the trade tables alone, has been shown above to be about £7,500,000. If that sum for the whole period be taken, and a charge of five per cent. compound interest be made (though the money and produce were worth vastly more than five per cent. to the	

[1] Stat. Abs., Brit. India, No. 34, p. 200.

	£
Indian banker, merchant, cultivator, artisan, and to all others in India who would have been in a position to employ capital to good account, were worth at least three times five, but I have taken only five) the result is	4,187,922,732
Total	£4,910,922,732

Thus, the adverse balance of trade against India during the last century, even at the low rate of interest I have adopted, reached the enormous total of nearly £5,000,000,000. If one could follow the money in all the ramifications through which, in India, it might have passed, its fertilising effect in every one of the five hundred and forty thousand villages, its accumulating power ('money makes money') fructifying in a land where its expenditure would have led to an increase in substance, it would, even then, be impossible to put into words the grievous wrong which (unwittingly but, all the same, culpably) has been done to India.

Now that I have reached this point in my exposition, I turn to pages 372–373 of the latest issue of 'Financial and Commercial Statistics' for another purpose, and find that, in taking £7,500,000 as a fair estimate of India's annual payments to the India Office, I have greatly underestimated the facts. I ought to have reckoned those payments at £9,500,000 for each year. The 'Amounts received in England at the India Office on Account of India' during the period 1834–35 to 1898–99 were £610,389,135

To this must be added debt in England existing at the end of 1898–99 ...	124,268,605
Total	£734,657,740

WAYS AND MEANS OF THE HOME GOVERNMENT

No. 1

DISBURSEMENTS in ENGLAND, from 1834-35 to 1[illegible]

		WAYS AND MEANS BY WHICH [illegible]					
			AMOUNTS RECEIVED [illegible]				
Year	Disbursements (excluding withdrawals against deposit accounts of Railway Companies and deducting miscellaneous receipts).*	Realisation of commercial assets.	In repayment of advances made in India and China on security of goods.	In repayment of advances made in India on account of the Imperial Government and other Public Departments.	Bills drawn on India.	Bills on London purchased in India.	[illegible]
1834-35	6,559,723	4,477,861	105,801	69,731	732,804		
1835-36	3,367,983	1,962,714	1,031,994	108,339	2,041,284		
1836-37	3,475,317	1,632,192	2,063,192	29,334	2,043,223	[illegible]	
1837-38	3,093,923	871,734	1,946,901	78,624	1,706,184		
1838-39	5,905,934	674,767	1,477,515	83,282	2,346,592		
1839-40	3,315,450	105,742	754,662	105,796	1,432,576		
1840-41	3,356,741	5,580	960,749	228,034	1,174,450		
1841-42	3,757,787	8,616	1,146,797	494,453	2,589,283		
1842-43	3,362,996	...	492,985	873,211	1,197,438	20,000	
1843-44	4,023,327	...	668,364	963,824	2,801,731	10,000	
1844-45	3,571,345	...	33,062	162,981	2,616,041		
1845-46	4,210,910	...	887,880	102,227	3,065,709		
1846-47	3,984,261	1,867	317,409	136,717	3,097,043		
1847-48	4,016,537	100	1,132,453	222,095	1,841,804		
1848-49	4,231,535	...	702,985	134,317	1,989,195		
1849-50	4,167,705	2,294	1,314,942	118,041	2,935,113		
1850-51	3,852,658	...	694,533	186,033	3,236,456		
1851-52	3,510,829	...	26	205,656	2,777,523		
1852-53	3,796,802	...	...	116,160	3,317,122		
1853-54	4,309,009	...	60	339,531	3,850,565		
1854-55	4,272,589	...	...	90,362	3,669,678		
1855-56	5,036,793	...	...	207,392	1,484,040		
1856-57	4,983,849	...	...	184,684	2,819,711		
1857-58	9,354,728	...	...	1,768,023	628,499		
1858-59	13,470,617	...	...	136,501	25,901		
1859-60	15,253,578	...	...	544,428	4,694		
1860-61	10,646,185	...	...	1,003,160	797		
1861-62	11,242,685	...	...	1,011,686	1,193,729	150,000	
1862-63	10,863,137	...	...	206,938	6,641,576		
1863-64	16,818,982	...	...	60,232	8,979,521		
1864-65	9,480,062	...	...	106,881	6,789,473		
1865-66	10,419,741	...	...	106,585	6,998,899		
1866-67 (11 months)	10,924,952	...	...	169,575	5,622,746		
1867-68	12,681,606	...	...	1,253,721	4,137,285		
1868-69	13,661,553	...	...	4,526,730	3,705,741		
1869-70	14,509,939	...	...	1,470,631	6,980,122		
1870-71	13,523,477	...	...	229,748	8,443,509		
1871-72	13,486,813	...	...	88,102	10,310,339		
1872-73	13,831,718	...	...	195,458	13,939,095	[illegible]	
1873-74	13,532,843	...	...	167,348	13,285,678		
1874-75	14,480,644	...	...	132,570	10,841,615		
1875-76	14,956,599	...	...	94,320	12,389,613		
1876-77	15,696,371	...	...	131,710	12,695,799		
1877-78	15,904,685	...	...	106,736	10,134,455		
1878-79	18,749,736	...	...	496,126	13,948,565	1,616,1[illegible]	
1879-80	27,863,324†	...	...	167,982	15,261,810		
1880-81	17,958,519	...	...	274,107	15,239,676		
1881-82	21,793,502	...	...	267,081	18,412,429		
1882-83	22,063,250	...	...	330,960	14,119,128‡		
1883-84	18,724,622	...	...	371,594	17,599,806		
1884-85	21,112,152	...	...	384,608	13,758,909		
1885-86	19,074,130	...	...	1,036,077	10,292,892		
1886-87	23,021,259	...	...	189,297	12,136,278		
1887-88	17,382,835	...	...	186,568	16,358,577		
1888-89	30,675,794	...	...	129,935	14,262,859		
1889-90	17,366,312	...	...	143,029	15,474,496		
1890-91	22,427,394	...	...	161,882	16,969,034		
1891-92	19,156,320	...	...	158,632	16,093,854		
1892-93	20,495,342	...	...	150,790	16,532,215		
1893-94	33,426,163	...	...	147,327	9,530,235		
1894-95	24,328,065	...	...	148,471	16,905,102		
1895-96	18,894,013	...	...	170,979	17,664,492		
1896-97	21,613,891	...	...	262,859	15,636,547		
1897-98	19,140,204	...	...	180,506	9,506,077		
1898-99	27,645,516	...	...	301,819	18,692,377		
TOTAL	837,108,529	9,743,467	15,758,429	24,419,955	510,301,652	2,0[illegible]	[illegible]

* For particulars of large or exceptional payments included in this column see supplementary table No. 1A.
† Includes £2,000,000, being an advance from Her Majesty's Treasury under the Indian Advance Act, 1879.
‡ Exclusive of £1,001,323 received on account of the Commission for the Reduction of Debt.

and the WAYS and MEANS by which they were met (In pounds sterling)

DISBURSEMENTS WERE MET — ON ACCOUNT OF INDIA: Remitted from India in silver	Deposits by Railway Companies in excess of withdrawals	Total remittances	Borrowed in England	Sale of stock to the public funds	Total receipts, excluding miscellaneous receipts	Cash balance at end of the year	
96,113	...	934,449	...	..	5,412,310	3,625,488	1834-35
...	...	3,186,587	...	..	5,148,301	5,405,807	1835-36
...	...	4,174,768		...	5,906,950	2,737,440	1836-37
...	...	3,731,709		..	4,6[illegible]3,443	4,246,900	1837-38
...	...	3,912,389			4,587,166	2,924,132	1838-39
...	...	2,301,863			2,467,545	2,020,227	1839-40
...	..	2,369,233		..	2,374,813	1,038,299	1840-41
...	...	4,229,533	168,900	..	4,407,049	1,887,561	1841-42
...	.	2,683,634	100,000		2,683,634	988,199	1842-43
...	.	4,442,919		..	4,442,919	1,407,791	1843-44
...	.	2,712,394	584,174	157,773	3,454,341	1,290,787	1844-45
...	...	4,055,816		212,801	4,268,617	1,348,404	1845-46
...	...	3,551,168		152,231	3,705,266	1,069,439	1846-47
...		2,896,351	502,555	275,887	3,674,793	727,755	1847-48
918,224	90,000	3,734,021	1,114,190	.	4,848,211	1,344,451	1848-49
322,365	237,491	4,927,057		.	4,930,251	2,196,977	1849-50
...	395,017	4,512,041			4,512,041	2,756,490	1850-51
...	137,113	3,120,217		.	3,120,217	2,365,848	1851-52
..	208,629	3,641,311		.	3,641,311	2,210,357	1852-53
..	378,776	4,668,932		.	4,668,932	2,410,280	1853-54
..	2,457,840	6,629,862		...	6,629,801	4,767,682	1854-55
...	2,002,130	3,700,784			3,700,784	3,431,653	1855-56
...	1,889,845	4,694,240			4,694,240	3,941,914	1856-57
...	1,638,240	4,934,762	5,688,173	941,449	10,664,384	4,351,600	1857-58
...	4,888,899	5,061,301	6,887,114	.	11,938,415	2,519,398	1858-59
...	3,273,621	3,824,743	12,805,530		16,630,273	4,196,093	1859-60
..	3,424,593	4,438,550	4,664,605		9,103,155	2,053,063	1860-61
..	7,002,651	9,327,946	4,995,387		14,323,333	5,733,711	1861-62
...	3,429,822	10,378,356			10,378,356	5,248,910	1862-63
...	4,686,593	13,725,346	2,441,000		16,166,346	4,596,274	1863-64
...	1,802,125	8,798,679			8,798,679	3,914,891	1864-65
...	1,176,508	8,440,830	882,800	..	9,323,630	2,818,780	1865-66
882,302	2,807,427	9,471,050	2,731,901	.	12,204,951	4,098,779	1866-67 (11 months)
.	4,860,423	10,251,425	1,164,497		11,415,836	2,833,909	1867-68
..	4,087,914	12,320,385	1,534,140		13,854,525	3,025,981	1868-69
.	1,886,276	10,337,029	4,039,412	..	14,376,441	2,892,483	1869-70
671,193	2,268,660	11,513,110	2,423,856	..	13,936,966	3,305,972	1870-71
	1,190,085	11,688,526	1,413,406		13,001,932	2,821,091	1871-72
	−528,622*	14,089,071			14,089,071	2,998,444	1872-73
..	57,553	13,610,579	1,037,458		14,648,037	2,013,638	1873-74
	−791,648*	10,192,537	5,070,839		15,263,376	2,756,370	1874-75
.	−1,210,174*	11,273,829	1,206,299		12,480,128	919,899	1875-76
..	−1,553,258*	11,274,271	6,216,168	...	17,490,439	2,713,967	1876-77
	−312,956*	9,928,234	4,339,141		14,267,375	1,076,667	1877-78
	−925,545*	15,054,339	3,746,600		18,791,004	1,117,925	1878-79
	−457,556*	15,459,183	13,552,781		29,016,606	2,270,107	1879-80
...	−738,572*	14,775,211	5,037,244		19,812,161	4,127,749	1880-81
	−852,529*	17,826,981	2,455,647		20,286,002	2,620,900	1881-82
	1,687,694	16,137,783	6,730,353		22,872,215	3,429,874	1882-83
...	−408,770*	17,562,029	1,841,001		19,407,969	4,113,221	1883-84
..	60,288	14,193,805	5,049,956	...	19,248,209	2,249,378	1884-85
...	5,151,537	16,480,306	5,071,031	...	21,551,337	4,726,585	1885-86
..	1,127,935	13,453,510	10,121,992		23,575,502	6,288,828	1886-87
...	2,457,659	18,002,704			18,002,704	6,280,627	1887-88
...	−724,490*	13,668,304	14,366,726	..	28,035,030	3,259,933	1888-89
...	−274,273*	15,348,252	4,161,000	.	19,609,252	6,402,873	1889-90
...	−2,106,315*	13,964,671	6,895,000	...	20,859,571	3,835,050	1890-91
...	−1,408,690*	14,843,896	4,600,000	...	19,443,896	4,122,626	1891-92
...	658,099	17,341,104	1,300,000	...	18,641,104	2,268,398	1892-93
...	−654,903*	9,022,659	13,136,000	...	22,458,659	1,303,564	1893-94
...	−522,948*	16,530,625	9,000,000	...	25,530,625	2,603,124	1894-95
...	−50,784*	17,784,887	2,000,000	...	19,784,887	2,393,795	1895-96
...	1,263,041	17,052,447	3,900,000	...	20,952,447	2,834,314	1896-97
...	−344,489*	9,342,094	9,500,000	...	18,842,094	2,634,244	1897-98
...	−533,811*	18,360,385	9,797,664	..	28,158,049	3,145,768	1898-99
2,720,197	54,053,641	510,389,135	204,[illegible]†	1,740,141	626,181,504		TOTAL

* The withdrawals exceeded the receipts to this extent.

† Against the total borrowings of £304,574,300 are to be placed £91,693,023 of debt discharged in the same period. The amount of the debt existing at the end of 1898-99 was £134,269,665.

In respect to the debt, largely for railway extension, note must be taken of the extravagant and short-sighted policy followed in connection with it. In the earlier years of railway construction, all oblivious to the signs of the times in regard to the cheapening of money and, apparently, wholly unconcerned as to the eventual liquidation of the debts incurred, a guarantee of 5 per cent. was given to shareholders, no sinking fund provided, while no means were adopted to give the borrower any portion of such appreciation in the foreign standard employed for borrowing as might take place. It surely was not beyond the art of an experienced financier to say how this might be done. But it was only India that was in those days concerned, and there was no search in the City for a Clinton Dawkins. At the time a considerable portion of the money was borrowed ten rupees represented £1 sterling. A thirty years' sinking fund, in many instances, would have procured the repayment of the capital sum at rates varying from ten to twelve rupees per £. Owing to no provision of the kind having been made, and the guarantee of the Government being regarded as absolute, £100 stock in the leading Railways rose to £150 and more in value in the London market. From that rise the nominal borrowers, the people of India, received no benefit whatsoever, nor did the lenders do aught to cause that rise. On the one part an additional burden, in the other an enormous unearned increment which the already-burdened party has to pay. Now, by means of annuities and debentures, the debt of two of the larger Companies is in course of liquidation. But £150 is being paid instead of £100 (the original sum borrowed), for the rupee has gone down considerably in value as compared with gold; therefore, instead of the debt being liquidated at an average of Rs.12 per £ sterling, or even less, it is being liquidated at Rs.22 8a., without any advantage accruing to the borrowers. On the contrary, they are being cruelly, needlessly, drained of the very means of daily existence through the short-sightedness and heedless financing of their rulers. More and more produce has to be exported year by year than need have been to meet these wholly unnecessary charges. Not one Indian at any time has been permitted to exercise any control over the unnecessary and wasteful railway extension policy adopted for his country,—unnecessary because other and cheaper means of locomotion, of which the authorities were advised, would have better suited an agricultural country such as is India.

The borrowings in India are marked by a like heedlessness of aught save the convenience of the moment. It was found, upon the death of one of them, that certain Feudatory Princes had saved considerable sums of money, —nothing like so much, it is true, as half-a-dozen commoners in England every year are found to possess on the proving of their wills. To those States, whose Princes had 'hoards,' it was intimated that the best use to which they could put at least a part of their savings was to lend them to the Government of India for railway extension. So, in 1876–77, Rs.15,000,000 (£1,000,000) were borrowed from the Maharajah Holkar for 101 years certain at four and a half per cent. From the Maharajah Scindia, Rs.10,000,000 were obtained at four per cent. as a 'Perpetual' loan. From the Nawab of Rampur, likewise a loan was secured, also at four per cent., but it is to be repaid 'after one year's notice, to be given on or after 1st of December, 1917.' A further loan which, on the 1st of October, 1900, stood in the books of the India Office at Rs.29,000,000, had been obtained from the Maharajah Scindia; it is being repaid by annual instalments of Rs.120,000. An ex-Member of the Viceroy's Legislative Council, during 1901, put it on record in London that India has been served by the most remarkable and most able financiers known to any civilised country. 'Most remarkable,' yes, seeing that the Government of India can borrow at about three per cent., to negotiate loans fixed for 101 years or to be

'Perpetual'[1] at four and four and a half per cent. respectively!

The figures indicating the drain of capital from India to England, given on page 225, must be amended.

	£
Loss to India, as already shown ...	4,910,922,732
Add, for remittances to England on official account, not shown in the trade returns, nearly £2,000,000 per annum, since (and including) 1834–5, at five per cent. per annum compound interest	1,044,980,684
Borrowings in England (net remaining after conversions, repayments, etc.)	124,268,605
	£6,080,172,021

The foregoing figures, enormously large as they are, do not represent anything like the real state of things. Even as they are presented, they are too big to be grasped by the mind: to most of us they will be like astronomical distances—mere rows of figures to which only the highly-intellectual and deeply-sympathetic can attach any real

[1] In the debate in the House of Commons on the Indian Budget on the 14th of August, 1901, Mr. W. S. Caine, M.P., made certain comments on these transactions. He pointed out that the Government of India had borrowed from the Maharajah Holkar £1,000,000 at 4½ per cent. for 101 years. 'A more ridiculous transaction was never carried out. The money could to-day be borrowed easily at 3 per cent., but here was a needless payment of £15,000 a year for at least eighty years, and before this loan is repaid the Government will have disbursed in interest, apart from the principal, £3,500,000, of which £1,500,000 represents the difference between 4½ and 3 per cent., and would have been much better sunk in irrigation than in the pockets of the wealthy Maharajah. It was impossible to understand why when the loan was raised a sinking fund was not provided to extinguish it over a number of years. Then there was another loan from Scindhia of £1,500,000 at 4 per cent. Here the position was worse than in the case of Holkar, for there was no limit of time. This loan made a present of £15,000 a year to Scindhia for ever. He had no desire to depreciate the personal loyalty and general good administration of the State of which Scindhia was the chief, but this £15,000 a year would have been a good deal better sunk in enterprises for the prevention of famine.'

meaning; nay, even by such, the utmost to which they can attain is but an approximation to the actual state of things.

As I say, this statement is only a part, a very small part, of the story. The real meaning of the 'drain,' in so far as India is concerned, is barely half adequately allowed for, even though the net borrowings are included. After very carefully considering the whole circumstances, I have determined, in this work at least, not to go farther with my investigations as to the extent of the 'drain.' Once one has got to six thousand millions sterling, the doubling or trebling of that sum tells nothing to the average British citizen who is jealous for the good name of Britain as an overlord responsible for the welfare of subject nations. If this sum fails to move him nothing will move him. It will suffice as a concluding remark on this aspect of the relations between England and India if I submit the views of the late Sir George Campbell, K.C.S.I., sometime Lieutenant-Governor of the Lower Provinces of Bengal, and, subsequently, Member of Parliament for the Kirkaldy Burghs. In his work on 'The British Empire,'[1] that eminent Anglo-Indian civilian says:—

> 'It must be remembered that we give neither our services nor our capital for nothing. Much of this is paid for by remittances to Europe. The public remittances are now £16,000,000 per annum, and it is estimated that the private remittances would be almost as much more if the flow of British capital to India were stopped, and the transactions showed only sums received in England. As it is the continual addition of fresh capital invested in India about balances. The private remittances and the balance of trade show only about the same amount as the public drawings to be depleted from India—that is, about £16,900,000 per annum. This is what is sometimes called the "tribute" paid to England. Well, it is not tribute, but it is paid for civil and military services, loans, railways, industrial investments, and all the rest; and the result is that a large part of the increased production is not retained by the Indian peasant.'

The last-preceding sentence is the merest juggling with words, and is unworthy of so notable a public servant.

[1] Cassell and Co., Limited, 1887, p. 70.

Those 'civil and military services,' were India governed with strict justice, could, all but a bare modicum, have been performed, have been well performed, at any time within the past fifty years, by the natives of the country. For, every pound sterling which has been paid to a foreigner for services which a native could have rendered is in itself an unjust charge and, in addition, is a gross injury to the country in an economic sense. Such payments and pensions constitute a tribute of the worst kind with a grievance attached.

As the result the Twentieth Century at its dawn finds India impoverished financially and morally, her people emasculated and little more than a nation of serfs, and rapidly drifting into a condition, as regards mere food for sustenance, when the vast majority of the people,

TWO HUNDRED MILLIONS OUT OF TWO HUNDRED AND THIRTY-ONE MILLIONS,

will speedily sink into an even more parlous condition than at present.

Compare—no, contrast, there is no comparison—contrast Engand against India during the past fifty years in one respect, only: the public buildings, the hospitals, the cathedrals, churches, and chapels, the free libraries, the baths and wash-houses, and the like other evidences of increasing public convenience erected in England. There is hardly a village in the land without a restored or newly-built parish church or Nonconformist chapel, or both. There is not a town of ten thousand inhabitants and upwards which does not, in its civic buildings and provision for daily wants, indicate a prosperity shared by all. But, India? Leaving out the few Presidency cities and provincial capitals, where the public buildings have been erected from public funds, throughout the length and breadth of the Empire there is nothing to be found comparable with the activity and solid advance in England. Indeed, the rupees which might have erected a temple, or built a rest-house, or planted a grove, or excavated a tank, or dug a well, or established a centre of artistic or musical culture in India, have been employed to build wash-houses and churches in England, and not even an Indian rupee can be expended twice over and in two countries.

To the mishandling of Indian affairs already recorded must be added the gratuitously serious harm done by the new currency legislation. By the closing of the Mints and giving an artificial value to the rupee the Government of India have done harm to every section of the Indian population. The mischief herein caused, if the policy be persisted in, will, in the long run, probably, do even more harm than any other evil from which India has suffered. It will run the 'drain' very closely, and complete the ruin which that has begun.[1] In this instance a moral as

[1] In the shape of communications to the press of England and of India Mr. Jamsetjee Ardaseer Wadia, of Bombay, is doing good service by putting the ill done in a popular form. In a letter to the *Times of India* in May, 1901, the position is thus described:—

'The Government have loudly proclaimed that they have obtained a surplus without any increase of taxation. But if you take from the taxpayer 1s. 4d. instead of 11½d., how can it lie in the mouth of the Finance Minister to say that he is not taking more money out of the pockets of the taxpayers?

'I will assume the price of cotton to be 4d. per lb. to-day in Liverpool. Now, if a ryot has to pay one rupee to the Exchequer, with an open mint and the rupee at 11½d., he would have to give less than 3 lbs. of cotton. But with the rupee at 1s. 4d. he will require 4 lbs. of cotton; so it is evident that with the artificial rupee he has got to part with extra produce; and yet it is said that he is paying no more in taxes. No doubt the Currency Legislation has cheapened imports. But is there any civilised country in the world which favours imports at the expense of exports which are the products of the capital and labour of the country?

'For the year 1899–1900 the import trade is given at Rs.70 crores (£47,000,000), exclusive of treasure and Government stores. Our export trade is given at Rs.108 crores (£72,000,000) for the same year, on the basis of the artificial rupee, viz., 1s. 4d. The same figures on the basis of the true value of the coin, viz., 11½d., would, if worked out, amount to about Rs.97 crores (£65,000,000) for imports, and about Rs.150 crores (£100,000,000) for exports. What is the conclusion? We would have paid with an open mint about Rs.27 crores (£16,000,000) more for our imports, and it would have come out of the pockets of the well-to-do Europeans and natives, as they are the chief consumers of imports, whilst the producers would have got about Rs.42 crores (£26,000,000) more for their exports, which would have remained in their pockets. But the producer loses over and above Rs.42 crores (£26,000,000). I will endeavour to show what that figure is.

'On the authority of his Excellency Lord Curzon, the entire annual produce of the country is valued at Rs.450 crores (£300,000,000). Deduct Rs.108 crores (£72,000,000) of produce exported; the balance is Rs.342 crores (£228,000,000) worth of produce. Ninety per cent. of the population of India live by agriculture, and they consume about Rs.308 crores (£174,000,000) worth of produce, so the remaining 10 per cent. who are non-well as a financial wrong has been committed. So far as the financial wrong goes in affecting existing 'hoards' of silver, the people had already, to a very large extent, lost those 'hoards,' but in their everyday transactions much mischief ensues. In respect to the moral wrong *that* is almost irremediable, and will be lasting. The object that the Government of India had in view in its legislation was, as a debtor to a gold-currency country, to reduce the number of depreciated rupees it had to annually provide to meet its obligations in the more valuable metal. This was its obvious duty—unless a greater duty intervened.

agriculturists consume the balance, viz., Rs.34 crores (£22,600,000). But on the same high authority, viz., that of his Excellency the Viceroy, the annual income of the ryot is given at Rs.20 (£1 6s. 8d.), whilst of the non-agriculturists is given at Rs.30 (£2) per annum, consequently the 10 per cent. of the population, instead of consuming Rs.34 crores (£22,600,000) worth of produce, consume 50 per cent. more as their purchasing power is greater to that extent. Therefore, I distribute the consumption of Rs.342 crores (£228,000,000) worth of produce as follows:—Produce consumed by the agriculturists, Rs.291 crores (£194,000,000). Produce consumed by the non-agriculturists, Rs.51 crores (£34,000,000). I maintain that the producers lose on the latter amount which they are obliged to sell on the basis of 1s. 4d. to the rupee, which loss comes to about Rs.14 crores (£11,300,000). The entire loss to the producer as far as I can make out comes to about Rs.56 crores (£37,300,000) a year. Against this loss to the country there is a saving to the Government on home charges, which saving may be computed at about Rs.10 crores (£6,600,000).

'Our attention has been drawn in the Budget statement to the development of mills and factories since 1895. The paragraph in the Budget statement runs as follows: "I may cite a few examples of industrial development. In the year 1895 there were 350 cotton factories, including spinning and weaving mills, and there were 586 such factories in 1899. The number of engineering workshops and foundries, including railway workshops, rose from 72 in 1895 to 82 in 1899, and jute mills and presses from 62 to 82. Rice mills numbered 63 in 1895 as against 84 in 1899, and sugar factories 9 in 1895 as against 14 in 1899." Our friends in England will be gratified at our progress as indicated by our Finance Minister. Let me, however, inform them that, since 1895, the market value of our capital sunk in most of the above concerns, shows to-day a shrinkage of above 50 per cent.

'The net loss to the producer as mentioned above comes to about Rs.56 crores (£39,300,000). Deduct about 10 crores (£6,600,000) saved in home charges. The balance of loss per year in my opinion comes to Rs.46 crores (£30,600,000). But this is not all. I cannot with any degree of accuracy fix the loss sustained by the country owing to the arrestation of development in the wealth-producing institutions of the country, consequent on the Currency Legislation.'

The Government forgot, or ignored—forgetfulness seems impossible—the fact that in other relations with its subjects it had duties which far transcended those of a debtor to a gold-using country. In this respect, I prefer another should tell what has been done, how it was done, and what the consequences have been and will continue to be.

Mr. Cecil Balfour Phipson, in a work recently published by Messrs. Swan Sonnenschein and Co., 'The Science of Civilisation,'[1] comments upon the 'consequences to England and India of the partial adoption by the latter of the former's money unit,' makes the following powerful and pertinent observations:—

India's yearly payments in England have risen from about £11,000,000 a year in 1870–4, to about £17,500,000 in 1895–6, an increase of just upon sixty per cent.

Now, to meet the payment of £11,000,000 a year in 1870–4, when the rate of exchange was 1s. 11d. per rupee, the Indian Government had to deduct from its revenue, roughly, Rs.115,000,000. At the same rate of exchange, therefore, it would have to have deducted for the same purpose in 1895–6, roughly, Rs.183,000,000. But as a matter of fact, it had to pay during this latter term Rs.300,000,000 a year, in place of Rs.183,000,000—an increase, that is, of 160 per cent., instead of only sixty per cent., and this because the rate of exchange between India and England had fallen from 1s. 11d. per rupee to 1s. 2d. In other words, this fall in the rate of exchange entailed upon the Indian Government as debtor an additional annual payment of Rs.117,000,000, which either had to be raised as extra taxation from the people of India or deducted from sums hitherto allocated to public works. Necessarily and rightly, therefore, the Government regarded the fall in the rate of exchange as entailing the gravest injury upon India, and imposing an all but insupportable burden upon her finances. They conceived, therefore, that it was their duty to raise this rate by whatever means were open to them;

[1] 'The Science of Civilisation; or, the Principles of Agricultural, Industrial, and Commercial Prosperity.' By Cecil Balfour Phipson. Swan Sonnenschein and Co., Ltd., 1901. I am indebted to the courtesy of author and publishers for the long extracts I am able to present to the reader. I should like to say here that, in my opinion, Mr. Phipson's remarkable study affords one means whereby India's adversity may be remedied. Of that I will speak at length when I deal with the remedies which, in my judgment, should be adopted.

not, indeed, to the original level of 1s. 11d. per rupee, but to the lower one of 1s. 4d., *and fix it there*, convinced that every rupee saved through a rise in the rate of exchange was a rupee saved to the Indian Treasury, and *therefore of necessity to the Indian people.* Accordingly, the rate has been raised from 1s. 2d. to 1s. 4d. per rupee, so that only Rs.262,500,000 are now required from India to discharge the annual debt of £175,000,000 to England, instead of Rs.300,000,000 as before. By this a saving to the Indian Treasury of Rs.37,500,000 a year has been effected, and through the means taken to raise the rate, this latter has also been permanently fixed at about 1s. 4d. The Indian Government, therefore, heartily congratulates itself on the success of its operations, and refuses to listen to any arguments, or to consider any facts which discredit them.

But sympathy is one thing and relief quite another, and this *cannot possibly be obtained through any acts of the debtor*, be he government or individual, other than those of repayment, repudiation, or bankruptcy. Relief *must come from the creditor*, either through rectification of the falsified standard, or the foregoing of such excess in his legal claim as is caused by its falsification. And that the position of defrauded debtor is that which the Indian Government occupies towards England readily appears by a reference to the only standard by which a rise or fall in the value of national money units can be measured, the quantities of each nation's chief food grain—which in India is rice, in England wheat—that must be given for them. The following Table permits of this comparison, the course of rupee values in India being expressed in wheat as well as rice to make the position clearer :—

TABLE XXXVIII.

SHOWING COURSE OF MONEY VALUES IN INDIA (BOMBAY) AND ENGLAND IN RICE AND WHEAT.

	1870-4.	1875-9.	1880-4.	1885-9.	1890-4.	1895-7.
India { Rice.........	100	89	112	100	98	89
India { Wheat......	100	98	109	107	100	97
England—Wheat ...	100	114	124	143	147	156

The above Table proves that while the value of the rupee in India, whether measured in rice or wheat, has remained practically stationary throughout the whole term of twenty-five years, 1870-94, that of the pound in England has risen over fifty per cent. during the same term.[1]

[1] Taken from the "Prices Current of Rice and Wheat" given in the "Statistical Abstracts for British India." Of course to whatever extent

What, then, are the measures by which the Indian Government conceives it has accomplished the impossible, lightening the liabilities of India to the same extent as it has reduced its own payments? And what are their real economic effects?

These measures are two: (1) It has *raised* the price of the rupee in pence, *i.e.*, the rate of exchange between India and England, from its lowest point 13 pence, to 16 pence per rupee. (2) It has *fixed* this price as a permanency, within but narrow limits of variation, and, as it conceives, has effected a yearly saving for India of Rs.37,000,000 in her payments to England, and has at the same time fixed the rate of exchange between the two countries at or about 16 pence per rupee. It remains now to ascertain the effect of these measures upon India herself, or rather upon the three great economic classes of Indian society—Depositors, Agriculturists, and Merchants.

Depositors.

Necessarily, when the Indian Government in 1893, in pursuance of its currency policy, closed its mints to the free coinage of silver, and thereby demonetised all silver in India not in the form of coins, the class affected first and most injuriously was the class of Depositors, or owners of hoards of silver money. For prior to the closing of the mints the legal money unit of India was *not the rupee*, but the 165 *grains of silver* in the rupee; just as at present the legal money unit of Great Britain is not the pound, but the 123·26 grains of gold in the pound. For any creditor in India before the above date was just as much entitled to refuse light rupees as is now any creditor in England to refuse light sovereigns. Consequently, a fixed weight of silver being the true money unit of India, and not the coined rupee, every Indian holder of rupees was as free to convert his silver rupees into bullion as the Bank of England now is to hold its gold reserves in bars. To deprive silver bullion, therefore, of its power to discharge debts in India was legally the same thing as to deprive good bullion of its similar power in England. But practically it was a much more serious thing. For while it still remains the practice of Indian depositors to themselves hoard their money deposits, this has long ceased to be the practice of British depositors, the Bank of England pretending to do for the whole of Great Britain what each Indian depositor actually does for himself. To suddenly penalise the Indian practice, therefore, by depriving silver bullion of its customary power to discharge debts and effect payments, entailed such a wanton and wholesale confiscation, or annihilation rather, of Indian monetary

---

famines reduce the normal production of food, they also conceal the effect upon food prices of currency contractions. But they conceal only, and do not neutralise them.

hoards as is scarcely to be conceived of as the act of a civilised Government, much less of a body of honourable English gentlemen.

Had imperious necessity instead of infatuated ignorance demanded such a change in the currency, the least that common honesty required is that prior to the change coming into force opportunity should have been offered during a reasonable time to all holders of bullion to convert their deposits into coined money, so that those failing to avail themselves of such offer would only have themselves to blame for subsequent loss. But such honest and open procedure would have postponed indefinitely the darling desire of the Indian Government to raise "the rate of exchange." Accordingly, it stole a march upon its confiding Depositors, and treated them as enemies to be plundered instead of as subjects to be protected. Can it be wondered at if this same class, as the nature of this trick is brought home to them, regard the Government in their turn as an enemy to be distrusted instead of a protector to be relied upon?

But members of the great class of Indian depositors are not the only or even the greatest sufferers from the currency policy of their Government. Those of two even more important classes must take precedence of them in this respect—the class of cultivators and the class of merchants.

Indian Cultivators.

The currency policy of the Indian Government, which looks to nothing but raising the rate of exchange between India and England, cannot possibly obtain effect, so far as any action in India is concerned, *save by producing a general fall in Indian prices*. Necessarily, therefore, the pursuit of this economic folly is quite inseparable from consequences which not only cut off Indian cultivators as a class from the faintest hope of prosperity, but leave them naked and defenceless against the ever-impending calamity of a deficient rainfall. As has been just pointed out, such unjust spoliation of Indian cultivators must increasingly incapacitate them from supporting the burden of bad seasons, and so force them, much sooner than would otherwise be needed, to depend upon the Government for supplying them with the bare necessities of life. Obviously, therefore, the famine expenditure of the Government must be largely increased by their currency policy, while every such increase constitutes an additional set-off against their ostensible savings on remittances.

It will now be useful to tabulate the figures so far arrived at as a debit and credit account against and in favour of the Indian people.

TABLE XL.

Profits and Losses from Currency Policy.

Dr.	PEOPLE OF INDIA.		*Cr.*
To annual loss to depositors from demonetisation of silver bullion..	Rs. 60,000,000	By annual savings on remittances to England through rise in rate of exchange from 13d. to 16d. ...	Rs. 37,500,000
To annual loss to cultivators through fall in prices of food..	Rs. 70,000,000	By annual loss to India from currency policy of the Government	Rs. 112,500,000
To annual loss to Government through extra famine expenditure... ...	Rs. 20,000,000		
	Rs. 150,000,000		Rs. 150,000,000

Indian Merchants.

But this robbery of Indian depositors and automatic extortion from Indian cultivators by no means exhausts the list of injuries inflicted upon the Indian people by the currency policy of their Government. For this class of Indian merchants, and through them all the economic interests of the country, is also made to suffer severely, as we shall now point out.

We know it to be an imperative economic duty of every civilised Government to ensure constant and increasing additions of money units to the circulation to enable their subjects to carry on freely the multiplying operations of civilised life. For money is to advanced civilisation what oil is to complex machinery, that which enables the multitudinous wheels of both to move with ease and safety. Curtail or cut off the supply of money in the one case, as of oil in the other, and immediately friction increases so rapidly as to enormously impede motion, and eventually ensure grave injury in every direction. But the Indian Government, in company with all other civilised governments, has never realised its duty in respect to the adequate supply of money units, having abandoned the regulation of such supply to external circumstances. Happily, these circumstances have been particularly favourable to India. For as its need of money units increased, there was set free for its use, through the action of Europe and the United States, vast quantities of silver, the annual importations of which proved just sufficient, so long as these were treated as money, to maintain remarkable stability in the average level of Indian prices, by keeping Indian merchants supplied with those increasing supplies of money essential to the free conduct of their operations.

But this remarkable, and from a commercial point of view, most satisfactory, state of Indian monetary affairs, which was in no way due to any intelligent attempt by the Government to do what it ought to do, viz., *ensure adequate supplies of money*, was suddenly put an end to in 1893 by its unintelligent attempt to do what it ought not to do, viz., *ensure fixity in foreign exchanges.* For by depriving silver bullion in that year of its prerogative as money, and stopping its coinage of silver rupees, it prevented, as far as it could, those essential and increasing additions to the annual circulation of India which had hitherto been so sufficiently and satisfactorily provided in complete independence of it. The growth and magnitude of these annual additions are shown in the following Table:—

(1) Periods.	(2) Quinquennial imports of silver.	(3) Equal to rupees added to circulation.	(4) Rupees coined at Government Mint.	(5) Ratio of Column (4) to (3).
	Oz.	Rs.	Rs.	
1870–4	83,334,000	250,002,000	172,850,000	69 per cent.
1875–9	136,290,000	408,810,000	371,100,000	91 ,,
1880–4	120,517,000	361,551,000	268,650,000	72 ,,
1885–9	166,766,000	500,298,000	387,650,000	77 ,,
1890–4	229,900,000	689,700,000	447,700,000	95 ,,
1895–7	82,517,000		9,605,000	
Imports for 1895–7 had Government not interfered	170,000,000	510,000,000	357,000,000	70 ,,

From this Table the following important conclusions must be drawn:—

(1) How immediately, largely and progressively the imports of silver bullion into India increased after its demonetisation in Europe and the United States.

(2) That these silver imports fulfilled all the purposes of money in India, whether remaining as bullion or coined into rupees, as over 76 per cent. of all imports were.

(3) That subsequent to 1893–4 no silver imports fulfilled any of

the purposes of money, except in so far as they were surreptitiously or illicitly coined into rupees; while the issue of rupees from the Government mints practically ceased.

(4) That but for the Government interference, the imports of silver into India during the three years 1895–7 would have reached (at the same rate of increase as before) 170,000,000 ounces, equal to an addition of over 500,000,000 rupees to the circulation; so that the action of the Government has diminished the monetary supplies of Indian merchants by the enormous sum of over Rs.500,000,000 in three years, the paralysing effect of which upon Indian trade may be better realised by merchants in Great Britain if they consider the consequences to themselves of the loanable capacities of British bankers being suddenly reduced in the same term by £500,000,000. For at least £1 is employed in Great Britain for every rupee employed in India.

We can now perceive that the Indian Government, in trying to protect itself from the unpreventable consequences (so far as it is concerned) of the value of the British money unit being falsified against it, has deliberately set itself, by the course it is pursuing, to injure every class but moneylenders of the vast community committed to its charge, to rob depositors, to oppress cultivators, intensifying the burthen of their ever-imminent scarcities, to hamper merchants, and all this for the sake of a completely fallacious saving on remittances, which one year's increased famine expenditure goes far towards consuming. While the British Government, in being a consenting party to the further extension of the British money unit to another and still poorer 250,000,000 of people, is preparing final ruin for British farmers, who, starting from wheat and returning to it in the necessary rotation of crops, will henceforth have to compete in their home markets for home money units with Indian wheat-growers, the most impoverished cultivators in the civilised world.

CHAPTER VIII

NO TRADE WITH NEARLY TWO HUNDRED MILLIONS OF THE INDIAN PEOPLE—EXCEPT IN ONE ARTICLE

A Pressing Question at Every Renewal of the Charter to the East India Company.
Sir Thomas Munro, Sir John Malcolm, and Mr. Rickards, on Indian Trade and What It Will Never Do.
What Becomes of the Imports into British India? Who Takes Them?
British and Europeanised-Indian Requirements: 171,000,000 People Almost Wholly Outside Import Influences.
Analysis of the Imports, Item by Item.
Actual Trade (apart from Cotton Cloths) of un-Europeanised India, Under One Halfpenny per Head per Annum.
The 'Prosperity' in India Not *Indian* Prosperity.
Why India Did Not Take Advantage of the Spinning-Jenny and Steam Engine when First Invented.
England's Policy towards India Dominated by Commercial Considerations.
James Mill Locking the Door against Indian Advancement in India.
India's Exports: Whose Are They? Analysis of Every Article of Export.
A Twenty-Nine Years' Comparison Yields Woful Results.
In Spite of Many Borrowed Tens of Millions Sterling to be Spent on Public Works Production Falling Off.
Consequences: Severe and Continuous Individual Suffering and Much Loss of Life.
A Famine 'Success' which shows, in Three Divisions of the North-Western Provinces, a *Minus* Population of Two and a Half Millions.

Appendix:
Condition of the Silk-Weaving Industry in Madura, Southern India.

In the days preceding each renewal of the Charter of the East India Company—notably the renewals of 1793, 1813, and 1833—no questions were asked of the witnesses, by learned Counsel representing the East India Company, more persistently, than such as related to

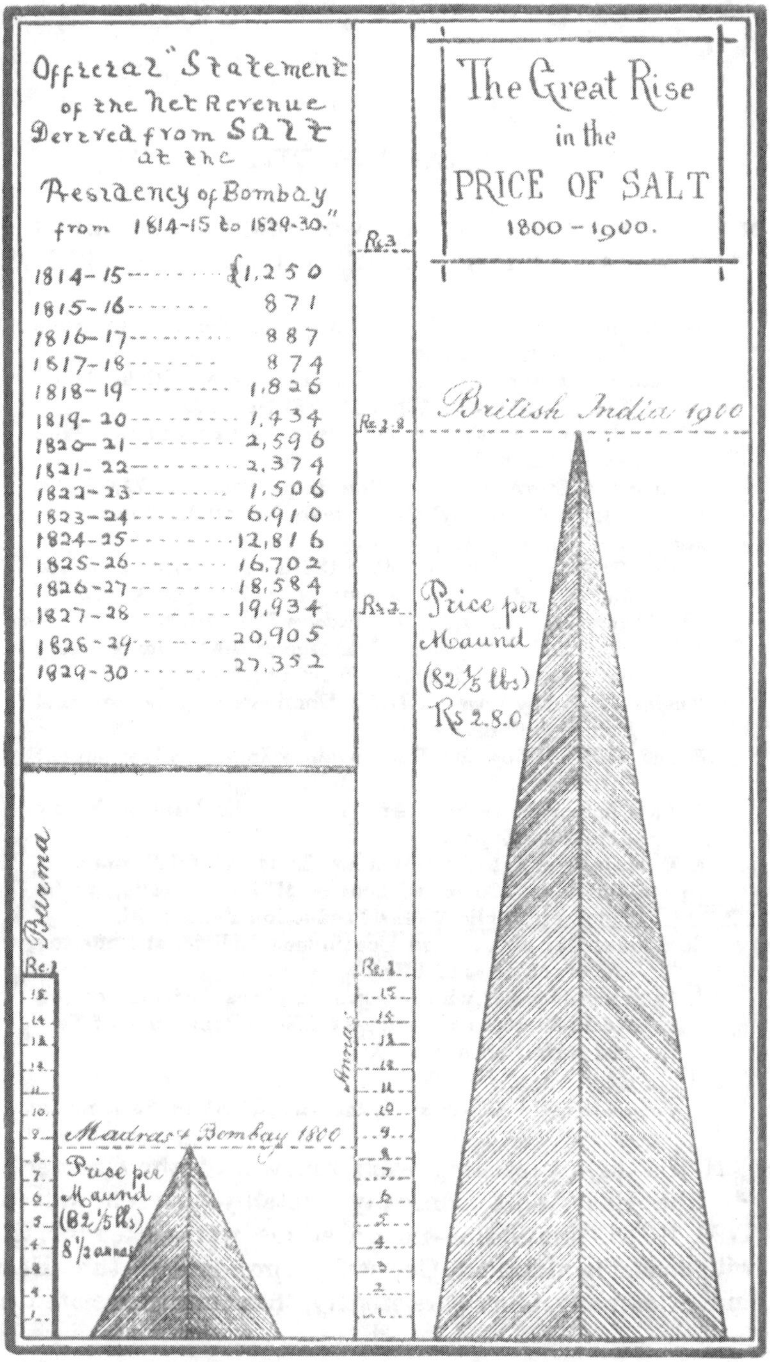

Official "Statement of the Net Revenue Derived from SALT at the Residency of Bombay from 1814-15 to 1829-30."
1814-15 £1,250
1815-16 871
1816-17 887
1817-18 874
1818-19 1,826
1819-20 1,434
1820-21 2,596
1821-22 2,374
1822-23 1,506
1823-24 6,910
1824-25 12,816
1825-26 16,702
1826-27 18,584
1827-28 19,934
1828-29 20,905
1829-30 27,352
The Great Rise in the PRICE OF SALT 1800 - 1900.
British India 1900
Price per Maund (82 1/5 lbs) Rs 2.8.0
Madras & Bombay 1800
Price per Maund (82 1/5 lbs) 8 1/2 annas
Burma
Annas
Rs.3
Rs 2.8
Rs 2
Re.1

the probability of the natives of India becoming purchasers of English manufactured goods. The prevailing opinion was that expressed by Sir (then Colonel) Thomas Munro, afterwards Governor of Madras, who, taken as a whole, was one of the very best men India has known. On the 12th of April, 1813, he was under examination.

'In the event of a free trade,' he was asked, 'are you of opinion there would be any considerable increased demand for British commodities or manufactures among the natives of Hindostan?'

'I do not think,' he said, 'there would be any considerable increase of the demand for European commodities among the natives of India.' Reasons for this opinion were given. For a cause which, shortly, will be apparent, those reasons may be stated.

'At our principal settlements,' continued Col. Munro, 'where we have been longest established, the natives have adopted none of our habits, and scarcely use any of our commodities, the very domestics of Europeans use none of them; there are a few natives at Madras, and some other places, who sometimes purchase European commodities, and fit up apartments in an European style, to receive their guests, but it is done merely, I believe, in compliment to their European friends, and what is purchased in this way by the father, is very often thrown away by the son; the consumption does not extend, but seems to remain stationary: I think there are other causes of a more permanent nature than the high price, which preclude the extension of the consumption of European articles in India; among those causes, I reckon the influence of the climate, the religious and civil habits of the natives, and more than anything else, I am afraid, the excellence of their own manufactures. In this country, people who know little of India, will naturally suppose, that as the furniture of the house and the table require so much expense, a great demand will likewise be made among the natives of India for the same purposes; but a Hindoo has no table, he eats alone upon the bare ground; the whole of what may be called his table service consists of a brass basin and an earthen plate; his house has no furniture; it is generally a low building, quadrangular, rather a shed than a house, open to the centre, with mud walls and mud floor, which is generally kept bare, and sprinkled every day with water, for coolness; his whole furniture usually consists of a mat or a small carpet, to rest upon; if he had furniture, he has no place to keep it in, it would be necessary to build a house to hold his furniture; he likes this kind of house, he finds it accommodated to the climate, it is dark and cool, and he prefers it to our large buildings; again, the food of the Indian is simple, and is entirely found in his own country; his clothing is all the manufacture of his own country, we cannot supply him, because while he can get it, not only better, but cheaper, at home, it is impossible that we can enter into competition in the market.'

Again, in regard to woollen manufactures, Colonel Munro said:—

I do not think that there is any great probability of extending the consumption of the woollen manufactures of England in India, because the natives have already coarse woollens of their own, which answer all the purposes for which they require them better than those of England do; there is hardly a native of India who has not already a large piece of woollen, as it comes from the loom, which he uses something as a Highlander does his plaid, he wraps it round him to defend him from the weather, and he sleeps upon it, and it is so much cheaper than anything which can be made in this country, that until we can very greatly reduce the price of our woollens we shall never be able to find a market in India for it. The thermometer in the greater part of India, in the interior, is for many months in the year generally as low as from forty to sixty in the morning, and the cold is as much felt as it is in this country, except during hard frost; the natives require warm clothing, but they have all their own coarse woollens, and many of the richer sort, who do not use those woollens, employ in their room quilted silk and cotton, which is both warm and light.

These descriptions reveal India as a wholly self-contained country, not needing any outside supplies.

It will at once be remarked that this prophet and Sir John Malcolm, and Mr. Rickards, and, practically, all the witnesses of that early period who spake in like manner, have been proved by events to be mistaken in their forecast. 'Look,' it will be said, 'at the continually growing imports into India, and, in them see the natives of India won over to a need of our goods and to the purchase of them.'

Be it so. The import list may, with advantage, be examined. And in its examination, and in the analysis which follows its examination, it should be distinctly borne in mind that European articles are not avoided or discarded because they would not be appreciated. The contrary is palpable to every resident in a Presidency or large provincial town in India. It was so seventy years ago. In the Inquiry of 1813 Mr. Robert Rickards was asked: 'Have the natives of Bombay, to your knowledge, evinced any antipathy to the consumption of the useful staple commodities of Great Britain, or of any other country?' He answered: 'So far from any antipathy to the use of any European commodities, those articles are very much coveted in every part of India.'

Further asked: 'To what circumstances do you mainly consider it is owing, the slight foreign and internal commerce of India in comparison with the extent and fertility of the country, and the vast population it possesses?' Mr. Rickards answered: 'I ascribe it, and always have done, to the extreme poverty of the great mass of the population, chiefly occasioned by the pressure of our fiscal institutions.'

There is no need to go to distant periods in respect of which it may be urged that the conditions compared with those existing to-day have altered: the last three decades of the nineteenth century will suffice. I submit a table showing the value of all imports in the years 1870, 1880, 1889–90, and 1898–99.[1] It is as follows:—

	1870.	1880.	1889–90.	1898–99.
	£	£	£	£
Apparel	451,280	581,081	864,268	920,824
Arms, Ammunition, and Military Stores ...	96, 52	58,860	127,727	192,675
Books, Paper, and Stationery	414,912	528,739	569,860	591,629
Coal, Coke, etc.	544,477	1,188,208	672,898	464,150
Cotton Twist, Yarn, etc.	2,715,870	2,745,806	2,821,781	1,687,097
Cotton Manufactures ...	13,555,846	16,915,511	17,594,266	16,454,057
Drugs and Medicines ...	210,167	816,075	260,155	628,610
Dyes	111,499	145,237	348,659	518,055
Fruits and Vegetables ...	845,458	90,802	145,802	75,148
Glass	808,086	829,321	431,418	441,527
Gums and Resins ...	99,817	90,761	81,757	72,918
Hardware, Cutlery, and Plated Ware		481,928	780,794	958,415
Horses	77,206	116,795	154,267	219,587
Ivory	118,022	184,727	152,161	161,137

[1] Compiled from the Statistical Abstracts of British India, Nos. 14 to 34.

	1870.	1880.	1889–90.	1898–99.
	£	£	£	£
Jewelry and Precious Stones	264,808	193,280	154,141	850,291
Liquors: Malt	314,520	254,262	308,078	319,506
Spirits ...	504,378	659,120	448,162	557,854
Wines, Liqueurs, etc.	548,329	395,908	219,521	221,427
Machinery and Mill Work	555,742	616,833	1,526,590	2,023,987
Metals: Iron	1,188,086	1,229,885	1,610,—5	1,589,018
Steel	166,377	84,547	219,160	678,699
Brass ... }	1,753,684	{ 53,848	57,777	36,447
Copper ... }		{ 1,620,155	1,481,569	744,165
Spelter	137,045	144,860	75,975	77,608
Tin	156,877	98,846	191,689	111,148
Lead	44,944	106,296	102,327	91,465
Quicksilver ...	15,510	58,893	36,162	26,659
Unenumerated..	110,426	16,985	42,299	139,233
Total... ...	3,752,899	3,413,265	3,808,991	
Oils	12,391	545,932	1,864,475	2,369,004
Paints, Colours, etc. ...	160,962	202,240	178,244	112,691
Perfumery	34,580	48,271	20,245	
Porcelain and Earthenware	93,351	122,484	149,286	124,900
Provisions	331,186	1,048,382	1,046,310	1,021,111
Railway Plant and Rolling Stock	1,217,334	1,033,049	1,214,226	1,333,210
Salt	750,095	762,582	625,678	440,806
Silk, Raw...	901,117	683,285	701,363	581,771
Silk, Manufactures of ...	466,548	337,390	1,136,401	907,363
Spices	297,381	526,328	601,567	598,703
Sugar, etc.	715,583	1,063,783	1,566,700	3,678,000
Tea	116,522	212,062	142,454	131,296
Tobacco	77,282	66,707	85,144	195,369
Umbrellas	87,174	20 ,951	204,404	162,292
Wood, and Manufactures of	59,046	50,889	106,871	110,971
Wool, Raw	54,018	87,278	71,178	60,998
Wool, Manufactures of...	596,718	927,876	972,157	1,015,821
All other Articles ...	1,390,233	2,162,918	2,248,153	2,692,598
Total value of Merchandise	32,879,648	39,742,166	44,378,414	45,596,894[1]
Treasure	13,954,807	11,655,395	11,639,667	11,984,409
Totals ...	46,834,450	51,397,561	56,018,081	57,581,303

[1] This total for the first time includes:—

Carriages and Carts ..	317,399	Grain and Pulse ..	31,264
Cotton, Raw	86,319	Instruments .. .. }	
Building and Engineering Materials	202,334	Apparatus .. .. }	341,101
		Appliances .. .. }	
Flax Manufacture ..	136,991	Matches	379,789

Reckoning in everything, including Treasure, save Government Stores, to be immediately dealt with, the totals are :—

1870	£46,834,450
1880	51,397,561
1889–90	56,013,081
1898–99	57,531,303

				%
1880 shows an increase of	£4,563,111	over	1870, or	10
1889–90 „ „	4,615,520	„	1880, „	11
1898–99 „ „	1,518,222	„	1890, „	3

Meanwhile, the population in	1870	was	185,537,859
„ „	1881	„	198,790,853
„ „	1891	„	221,172,952
„ „	1901	„	231,085,132

Population, including vast areas newly annexed—over one hundred thousand square miles in extent—and, in spite of most severe famines and plagues, is alleged[1] to

[1] 'Alleged.' In the Bengal Administration Report for 1871–72 the following significant paragraph concerning the under-estimation of population in bygone times appears :—

'Partial computations of the population, not without some value, have here and there been made by individual officers in some districts; but, on the other hand, in other districts, mistakes, clerical errors perpetuated without observation, and other causes, have rendered the estimates much more wide of the mark than those of former days; and the official statements have become more and more discrepant. As an illustration of the extreme point to which want of statistical knowledge of the people had reached in these provinces, the following figures are given, showing the difference between the population of some important districts as given in grave statistical returns by the authority of Government within the last few years, and stated in the Administration Report of 1870 "according to the latest returns," and that now ascertained by census :—

	Population according to Return of 1870.		Population according to Present Census.
'" Nuddea (perhaps the most cared-for and most fully-administered metropolitan district in Bengal)	568,712	...	1,812,795
Furrudpore	147,127	...	1,012,589
Pubna	337,679	...	1,211,594
Cuttack	215,835	...	1,449,784
Monghyr	755,389	...	1,842,986
Kamroop or Gowhatty	80,861	...	561,681

have increased by 45,547,273 since 1871. Had there been no famine, and had normal conditions of peace and prosperity prevailed, such as British peace and British administration should surely ensure, such, indeed, as was laid down by the Government of India in 1884 as a reasonable expectation, these would have been the figures of population :—

1901 :	As it should have been ...	282,179,886
,,	As it is	231,085,132
	Minus	51,094,754

To the imports given above must be added Government Stores, as follows :—

Government Stores imported in 1898–99 :—

	£
Apparel, including boots and shoes	27,984
Arms, ammunition, etc.	204,897
Books and printed matter	67,248
Building and engineering materials	17,941
Chemicals	12,788
Coal, coke, and patent fuel...	26,466
Cotton manufactures	16,889
Drugs and medicines	9,029
Instruments and apparatus	21,691
Leather manufactures	5,556
Liquors	463
Machinery and millwork	49,489
Metals and hardware, and cutlery	356,115
Paper, stationery, etc.	80,189
Railway plant and rolling stock	1,367,867
Telegraph materials	47,402

'"It will be seen that in these cases the population varied from a third to a seventh of that now ascertained."

'Similar results will always happen when popular impressions are submitted to the test of scientific processes. Whether the subject be population, or area, or agriculture, or tenures, or commerce, or other matter of importance, no Government which does not possess statistical knowledge can be said to possess the data on which alone a sound administrative system can be based. . . .'

	£
Wool manufactures	66,847
All other articles	152,594
	£2,480,791

In 1898–99—
£2,480,791
In 1889–90—
£1,758,454
In 1880—
£1,423,837
In 1873—
£1,401,536

Including Government Stores, the complete figures for the four decennial periods are :—

1873	48,235,986 [1]
1880	52,821,398
1889–90	57,771,535
1900	60,012,094

First, it must be premised that for the Feudatory States and for Asiatic countries which can only obtain their foreign imports across the British frontier, a deduction must be made. The Feudatory States, 213 in number, cover an area of 595,000 square miles, against British India 964,903 square miles; their population is over 63,000,000. Exactly how much of the imports goes into these States has not been definitely ascertained. All things considered it would not be unfair to take one-fourth, omitting Government Stores, but, for argumentative purposes, I will be content with one-sixth, say £10,000,000 sterling. The Trans-frontier trade is with the following countries :—

Lus Bela
Khelat, Zhob, and adjoining regions
Kandahar and adjoining regions
Kabul

[1] The Government Stores figures for 1873 are taken, being the earliest available.

Tirah and Bajaur	Duffla, Aka, Naga, and Mishmi Hills
Kashmir	Manipur
Ladakh	Hill Tipperah
Nepal	Western China
Sikkim	Shan States
Bhutan	Karrennee
Thibet	Zimmé
Towang	Siam

These countries take of our imports:—

	£
Cotton goods...	984,784
Cotton yarn	270,700
Salt	211,788
Provisions	150,808
Metals (mainly brass, copper, and iron)... ...	142,944
Sugar	121,384
Spices...	161,060
Tobacco	81,981
Raw cotton	77,484
Silk goods	91,226
Petroleum	53,868
Living animals	53,278
Dyeing materials	52,481
Woollen goods	42,324
	2,945,825
Treasure	432,895
	£3,378,720

Indian Cotton Goods (£267,366) and Indian Yarn (£106,454), with some minor amounts, have been omitted, though strict fairness would have included them.

The imports for 1898–99, therefore, stand thus:—

Total imports as valued...		£57,531,303
Less Feudatory States, estimated	£10,000,000	
Trans-frontier trade as valued	3,378,720	
		13,378,720
		£44,152,593

for the whole of British India, with 16,877 miles of railway needing new rails, new rolling-stock; with ever-new railway extension; with an army of 334,193 officers and men, continually requiring fresh armaments; with public works needing material from England; with articles for personal wear for 168,000 Europeans, as also furniture and food for consumption from over-sea, and with, at the outside, two millions of Europeanised Indians who live more or less after the European fashion, and who require European goods.

I make, in the analysis which follows, this broad distinction. All towns with populations of not less than five thousand are regarded as centres in which European influence is felt, and where European goods generally, including petroleum oil, sewing-machines, etc., are used. These towns number—

Twenty with populations over	...	...	100,000	
Eleven ,, from	...	...	75,000 to	100,000
Twenty-seven ,, ,,	...	...	50,000 ,,	75,000
Thirty-four ,, ,,	...	...	35,000 ,,	50,000
Eighty ,, ,,	...	...	20,000 ,,	35,000
Three hundred ,, ,,	...	...	10,000 ,,	20,000
Eight hundred ,, ,,	...	...	5,000 ,,	10,000

say 25,000,000 in all. This leaves 206,000,000 un-Europeanised and non-users (save as set out below) of European goods.

To be quite fair I should except the canal and well-irrigated parts of India from what I term the non-Europeanised population. In most cases, for example, in the districts of Godavari, Kistna, Tanjore, in Madras, certain districts in the North-Western Provinces, and others in the Panjab, with some likewise in Sind, there is prosperity, and the people may, to some small extent, purchase European goods other than those I allow for all the Indian people. If I put these at 35,000,000 I go further than I need go. However, the estimate may stand. By this elimination we are left with 171,000,000 people to whom the figures will apply.

From these 171,000,000 people this much of the revenue is obtained :—

	£		£
Total Land Revenue ...	18,806,875 ;	three-fourths of this	14,230,156
,, Salt	6,066,561 ;	,, ,,	4,549,921
,, Stamps say (on the Baring - Barbour calculations) one-twelfth	3,328,446 ;		277,370
,, Excise (the liquor shops in towns being excluded) ; say one-fiftieth, or for 171,000,000 less than one farthing's worth of liquor per head per annum	4,305,548 ;	one-fiftieth	86,111
,, Customs	3,201,442 ;		None
,, Forest	1,289,812 ;	say nearly the whole	1,000,000
,, Registration ...	294,117 ;	three-fourths of this	218,088

Total payments to Revenue by Agriculturists named £20,361,646

The above items comprise, practically, all the taxation (if the land revenue be a tax and not rent, as assuredly it is) levied for imperial purposes. The other items, with the exception of the opium revenue, which is paid by China, payments for Interest, Receipts from Post Office, Telegraph and Mint, Civil Service Departments, Railways, Buildings and Roads, and the Military Department, so far as any element of taxation enters into them, only slightly, if at all, affect the agriculturists, and they may be regarded as outside import trade influences.

It will be useful to take the items in detail :—

Apparel.—Including perhaps £20,000 for second-hand police and military coats and other woollen garments, for coolies on Tea and Coffee Estates, is for European, Eurasian, and Europeanised Indian, consumption.

Arms, Ammunition, etc.—One-tenth of the £192,675

may be for Indian sportsmen and others, apart from the Feudatory States, but they are included in the category named, *i.e.*, the Europeanised Indians.

Books, Paper, and Stationery.—Nothing of these go to the 171,000,000.

Coal, Coke, etc.—Almost entirely for Railway use, and for Cotton Mills, etc.; none for the Agriculturists.

Cotton Twist, Yarn, etc.—Less than one-tenth (£168,709) for the Feudatory States, and six per cent. (£270,700) for the Trans-frontier States.

Cotton Manufactures.—Less than one-fifth (£3,290,811) for the Feudatory States, and one-sixteenth (£984,784) for Trans-frontier States, and one-fourth of the whole (£4,113,514) for the chief towns and irrigated districts.

Drugs and Medicines.—Wholly for the Europeans, Eurasians, and Europeanised Indians.

Dyes.—Mainly employed in the colouring of Cotton and Woollen manufactures for Indian use, and as some village weaving is still done, take one-third = £419,073.

Fruits and Vegetables.—For European and Europeanised consumption.

Glass.—Wholly for ditto and for Feudatory States.

Gums and Resins.—Used mainly for the large workshops run by Europeans for the maintenance and repair of exotic enterprises—railways, mines, etc.

Hardware, Cutlery, and Plated Ware.—A small portion of the two first-mentioned gets into the districts, but not outside the towns of 5,000 inhabitants.

Horses.—None for the districts worth mentioning.

Ivory.—Used only for articles for export or manufacture in the large cities and towns, and for European and Europeanised Indian use.

Jewelry and Precious Stones.—Practically the whole of this for Europeanised residents and Feudatory Princes.

Malt Liquor.—Comparatively none consumed in the districts.

Spirits.—Ditto.

Wines, Liqueurs, etc.—Ditto.

Machinery and Mill Work.—Wholly for European and Europeanised organisations.

Metals.—Iron, steel, brass, copper, spelter, tin, lead, quicksilver, and 'unenumerated.' Of these brass and copper are required, it being a matter of pride in Indian households to obtain brass and copper vessels: the others are mainly consumed in the larger towns. If I allow twenty per cent. for the mass of the population I go beyond the necessities of the case. But take twenty per cent., say £173,931.

Oils.—The increase here is marvellous. The value of all oils imported in 1870 was £12,391. In 1898–91 the value was £2,369,004. Petroleum for heating and illuminating purposes is chiefly accountable for the increase. The requirements of wood for railway consumption, the closing of the forests against fuel collecting, and the decrease of cattle, help to account for this increase. The 25,000,000 of people referred to above, plus the 35,000,000 in the irrigated districts, consumed nine-tenths of the quantity imported, if not indeed the whole, but say nine-tenths; this leaves for all the rest of India £236,900.

Paints, Colours, etc.—Wholly used in towns.

Porcelain and Earthenware.—Ditto. With earthen chatties cheaply procured in well-nigh every village, the poorest labourer takes no European breakables, while the very few people connected with the land who do make some money, purchase copper and brass articles, as mentioned above.

Provisions.—All consumed in the large places.

Railway Plant and Rolling Stock.—Obviously the agriculturist orders none of this, and takes delivery of none.

Salt.—The imported material being of good quality, never by any chance finds its way into the hundreds of thousands of villages in which the 171,000,000 live.

Silk, Raw.—This is consumed in the seven silk mills in the towns, leaving nothing for the districts.

Silk, Manufactures of.—Nothing need be said of this

item. A blank, assuredly, is alone suitable for the man with 13s. 4d. to £1 per annum as income.

Spices.—Again, none of these go beyond the towns save to Trans-frontier States (£160,060 worth) and to the Feudatory States.

Sugar, etc.—Of this probably one-half remains in the Europeanised portions of the Empire, which would, even then, allow for them less than one shilling and sixpence worth per head per annum, £1,839,000.

Tea.—Chiefly consumed within the region of Europeanisation.

Tobacco.—Some portion of the country produce, which is replaced by this importation, may go into the villages, say one-fourth.

Umbrellas.—No appreciable number of these find their way among the agriculturalists, but allow five per cent., £8,114.

Wood, and Manufactures of.—All for European-India; none for the real unchanged India.

Wool, Raw.—None in districts.

Wool, Manufactures of.—Possibly one-tenth in the country districts, say £101,582.

All other Articles.—To be quite on the safe side one-twentieth may be taken, say £134,360.

Treasure.—In 1898–99, it must emphatically be said, no treasure went into the dry-land cultivation villages, but that a great deal from hoards—if there still be any hoards worth referring to—found a way, *viâ* the money-lender and goldsmith, into the chief towns, and thence to London, where rare Indian coins, hidden for centuries, are now (1901) said to be finding a market.[1]

[1] The following paragraph appeared in a large number of the leading provincial papers:—

'The Indian famines have afforded coin collectors many opportunities to acquire rare and old coins, which have lain buried for a great number of years. The native has always shown a very grave suspicion of banks, and has usually preferred to bury coins in what was considered a safe spot. Those hiding-places are revealed by father to son, and the accumulations sometimes go on for generations. In dire extremity the hoard has to be

Taking all these into account we have a total of £12,269,428.

The particulars thus given amount to 1s. 5d. per head. But before this calculation can be employed so as to make it at all comparable with the situation described nearly ninety years ago by Sir Thomas Munro certain deductions have to be made. Then, practically, all the cotton and woollen clothing required by the people was spun and woven by them, and the work was done in India.[1] So, likewise, were dyes, hardware and cutlery, metals, sugar, and tobacco. Take these from the total given above £12,269,428

Cotton yarns, cotton manufactures	9,312,536	
Dyes	628,610	
Hardware, cutlery, etc. ...	47,671	
Metals	173,931	
Sugar	1,839,000	
Tobacco	48,932	
		£12,050,680
The actual trade with *India* un-Europeanised and without the work it could well do for itself being done for it by another country		£218,748

trespassed upon; coins which have long since become exceedingly rare are thus brought to light, and are eagerly snapped up by collectors. Many of them are being sold in London at the present time.'

[1] At the time Sir Thomas was testifying, the beginning of the end had come. Seventeen years later (30th of May, 1829) in a Minute, the Governor-General (Lord William Bentinck) noting that one great staple manufacture had been supplanted, asked, 'Is there not reasonable ground to apprehend a failure in the means of affecting the returns without which no profitable trade can exist, *especially in a country tributary to another*, as India is to England?' The Governor-General did not realise how long a great nation takes in becoming exhausted of all its profit beyond bare sustenance and clothing. The point he indicated has now been passed, and the tribute is paid in the sufferings of many millions and in the untimely deaths of other many millions. In the same Minute His Excellency painted a graphic picture of the harm done to indigenous industries. I regret I have not space to spare for its reproduction.

Or, amongst 171,000,000 of people CONSIDERABLY UNDER ONE HALFPENNY PER HEAD PER ANNUM.

It thus appears that the 'prosperity of India,' which is annually chanted in vainglorious strains in the viceregal Council in Calcutta, and in the House of Commons in the city of Westminster, England, is NOT INDIAN PROSPERITY. Actually, that particular brand of prosperity has no existence. Practically—for the exceptions are insignificant—this trade is merely an extension of British trade with Britons who happen to be encamped in another country and with few other than Britons profiting from it. So far as the vast masses of the Indian people are concerned, and to the serious detriment of the great majority of the units in those vast masses, the enterprises which are regarded as indicating and proving the prosperity of India as a whole, have no existence.

The great fleet of superb ships which the P. and O. Company employ in the Indian trade have no relation of good to the average Indian citizen;

The even larger number of ships belonging to the British India Steam Navigation Company, which move from port to port on the immense Indian sea-board in lines like unto the glancing threads in a weaver's shuttle, concern them not one whit;

Even the now almost ubiquitous railway train is not for them, save to bring food in dire times of famine, now almost continual, somewhat within their reach if the Sirkar considers them deserving—a great gain, but, wanting railways (save as they were built out of Indian money to meet native and Indian needs) the people, properly aided by their foreign rulers, might have wanted famines; as for the one hundred and sixty million journeys taken by passengers (including season-ticket holders) in India—remember there are 294,000,000 of people—compare these journeys with those taken in the United Kingdom with but forty millions of people :—

Number of passengers (including season-ticket holders) conveyed on the several railways in the United Kingdom	475,000,000 [1]
Ditto in India	160,307,568 [2]

The prosperous Tea Gardens and Coffee Plantations, the Jute Fields and Factories, the Indigo Cultivated Area and Soaking Vats—these, none of these, belong to India proper, save in very minor respects.

Yet, it is these which require the imports, and not the people who provide the revenue.

The foregoing figures and facts are of striking, nay, of startling, significance. They demonstrate the absolute truth of the testimony of the witnesses of a long distant past, while the analysis already made shows that the import trade is only supported by the Europeans and Europeanised Indians, and by Indians who are compelled to use Lancashire piece goods, seeing these are supplied at prices lower than India itself could furnish them, and Indians have to be particular as to what they pay even to the twenty-fourth part of one penny.

It may be asked, 'Why did not India herself use Hargreaves' spinning jenny and its descendants, and turn to account James Watt's kettle o' steam?' My answer is of a threefold character—

[1] If tram and 'bus passengers were also taken, the three modes of locomotion in England, would, with less than a fifth of the Indian population, run to—

Railway	475,000,000
Tramway	812,464,404
Omnibus	480,000,000
	1,267,464,404

[2] The statistics for the tramways in Calcutta, Bombay, Madras, and Kurrachee, are not available. Were they known, the few millions they record, would not materially alter the respective proportions given above.

1. The Presidencies of Bengal and Madras, when these improvements were ready for use, had been drained of their resources, which resources had gone to England, and, therefore, their people had no money with which to profit by Hargreaves' ingenuity and Watt's genius;

2. The British Government, most lamentably, as it has proved, did not conceive the paternal duty which it had assumed towards India,—without the leave of the people being sought, though the aid of the people was relied upon to make the necessary military conquests,—called upon it to help the people in this direction. On the contrary, it deliberately strangled Indian manufactured exports and thereby gave English mercantile enterprise an opportunity to obtain a footing which, once obtained, has led to the whole country being covered with the product of English looms; and

3. The drain, begun in Bengal and openly recognised as consisting of ill-gotten gains, was, in later times, decently veiled under the guise of trade necessities and public works' improvements out of capital from a foreign country and with foreigners as controllers of such work alike in construction and management, and was continued in ever-increasing volume, until there is now no capital left in the country for investment, nor even enough for the common needs of decent folk.

These are among the reasons why the Indian people do not themselves 'develop' their own country.

Put as broadly and as graphically as I am able, the position at the beginning of the last century, as presented to the British public, was this:—

In India we have a region of vast extent and of almost unlimited resources. It has not, however, been developed to any great extent. Its people are marvellously skilful in all that makes for industrial manipulation and commercial progress, and particularly in the acquirement of languages which is so great an aid to success.[1] Indian

[1] 'One of the greatest improvements, however, of which the mind of man is susceptible has been made by natives from their own exclusive exertions.

muslins, chintzes, and cottons were so largely imported into England in the seventeenth century, that, in 1700, an Act of Parliament was passed, prohibiting their introduction. The country produces all that the people require, but, like humanity in general, their wants and desires increase according to the opportunities afforded to them to satisfy those wants and desires. But the means for satisfaction are wanting. Its taxation is declared to be as near perfection as it can be. 'Nine-tenths probably of our revenue is derived from the rent of land, never appropriated to individuals, and always considered to be the property of government; that appears to be one of the most fortunate circumstances that can occur in any country; because in consequence of this the wants of the State are supplied really and truly without taxation. As far as this source goes, the people of the country remain untaxed. The wants of government are supplied without any drain either upon the product of any man's labour, or the produce of any man's capital.' [1]

[This, in the presence of the facts of to-day, is like that political economy of Saturn with which Mr. Gladstone was once taunted, or as some topsy-turveydom from a fairy tale, so utterly out of touch is it with the things which exist. However, to continue the soliloquy :]

Mainly, India is an agricultural country. Already—I am specially referring to the Inquiry of 1831, by which date we ought as despotic rulers and paternal guardians to have come to our senses in regard to our duty to India — the era of steam machinery has established itself. In England, thanks largely to the wealth obtained from India, a great development has taken place, and Indian special manufactures, of the old handloom kind,

Their acquirement of knowledge, and particularly of the English language and English literature, of which there are many examples in Bengal, Madras, and Bombay at the present moment is quite astonishing. It may even be questioned whether so great progress in the attainment of knowledge has ever been made under like circumstances in any of the countries of Europe.'—Robert Rickards, *Qn.* 2807, *Inquiry* 1831.

[1] *Qn.* 3134, Evidence of James Mill, *Inquiry*, 1831.

known for their excellence the world over, have already been destroyed; the common goods are now threatened with destruction. To the end of the eighteenth century, and for some years in the nineteenth, India exported cotton manufactures, now, she imports large quantities of such goods.

What shall we do?

Shall we develop India from within? Shall we regard the interests of India from the point of view of the Indian people and, therefore, shut out English and other manufactures, and by so doing stop the growth of *our* British home industries? Shall we concentrate our attention upon what India can produce for her own consumption, and even for export, and so enable her to become wealthy enough to voluntarily purchase what England may produce of things which she requires? Or, shall we take care, first of all, to find a market for English goods and leave the rest to what may happen? Of course, if we adopt the last-named policy our home country will benefit and India must be content with the incidental advantages of our rule.

Such the position in which we stood. Such the questions, in effect if not in so many words, we asked ourselves.

Tho answer was given. Not, of course, in so many words. The days of Thackerayan perfect plainness of speech had passed. No wise statesmanship or liberal forethought looked ahead and decided that the good of India should be the first consideration as well as the last consideration in determining the policy of our rule of India.

The answer was given. Not by the Court of Directors in so many words; not by the Board of Control in instructions to the Court of Directors; not by the Imperial Parliament, whose word was final in all respects.

The answer was given. It was given by Commercial Considerations. 'Money talks' is an expression imported from the United States; it was true and was acted upon long before Yankee 'cuteness coined the expression. The need of a dividend for the shareholders and stock-brokers in the East India Company; of pay for the British soldiers employed in India; of a market for British manufactured goods—these factors supplied the answer, an answer was against India being considered as aught else than, primarily, a land for British exploitation. Court of Directors, Board of Control, Imperial Parliament, the British Public, took a short view of the future, saw there was money in 'carrying on as before,' and altogether avoided the long and broad view which, at a slight immediate loss of customers, would have procured greater and yet greater trade prosperity obtained in a legitimate way. More than that, we had tasted the sweets of despotic power with but few of its disadvantages. We had worked ourselves into the belief that if we did not hold the reins of power entirely in our own English hands chaos and ruin would inevitably ensue. Therefore, a few high-sounding words in an Act of Parliament to salve our consciences, and things were to go on as before. What was determined upon in 1833, that fateful year for India, was regarded as the highest wisdom. Macaulay, in the House of Commons, blessed it with eloquent words. James Mill, expert Indian Administrator and Philosopher, saw in it 'a continuance of that which had been occasion for high commendation.' 'The great concern of the people of India is,' he said in a lofty strain, which, in the light of existing facts, sounds painfully ludicrous, 'that the business of government should be well and cheaply performed, but it is of little consequence who are the people that perform it.[1] The idea generally entertained is, that you would elevate the

[1] The Earl of Ellenborough did not share the opinion that it was 'of little consequence who are the people' who administer Indian affairs. In the next (and last) of the great inquiries which preceded the re-grant of the

people of India by giving them a greater share in their own government; but I think that to encourage any people in a train of believing that the grand source of elevation is in being an *employé* of Government, is anything but desirable. The right thing in my opinion, is, to teach people' [*Indian* people only are meant] 'to look for their elevation to their own resources, their own industry and economy.' [This doctrine applied to home conditions would not have made Mr. James Mill Examiner of Correspondence to an imperial governing corporation.] 'Let the means of accumulation be afforded to our Indian subjects; let them grow rich as cultivators, merchants, manufacturers; and not accustom themselves to look for wealth and dignity to successful intriguing for places under government; the benefit from which, whatever it may be, can never extend beyond a very insignificant portion of the whole population.' Mr. John Stuart Mill, the great son of one who was himself

Charter to the East India Company, on the 23rd of June, 1853, the Earl asked Sir Charles Trevelyan, K.C.B., who was a witness—

'Do you estimate as of no value the maintenance out of the revenues of India of six thousand English gentlemen in situations of trust and great importance, and the maintenance of some fifteen hundred more in this country upon the fruits of their service in the East; should we not lose all that if India were separated from us, besides the maintenance of about forty thousand of our troops employed in that service?'

Sir Charles Trevelyan's reply is bright with a luminous exposition of policy which, had it been carried out to the full, would have made India prosperous from the interior to the boundaries of the Empire instead of, as is now the case, prosperous only in patches, and that prosperity of a dubious character. He said—

'I estimate those advantages as of considerable value; but I can conceive they are not to be compared with the immense trade which would be carried on with India if it were highly cultivated and improved, and the natives were possessed with the means of purchasing our manufactures, even in a much smaller degree than is the case in most of our colonies.'

In reply to the next question asked of him, Sir Charles Trevelyan said: 'I conceive that not only the improvement of India, but our tenure of India, depends on our doing justice to the natives, and gradually opening the advantages of their own country to them.' This answer limps, but its inner teaching is unimpeachable.

a notable person, possibly had this haughty comment in mind when he said: 'The government of a people by itself has a meaning and a reality; but such a thing as government of one people by another does not and cannot exist. One people may keep another for its own use, a place to make money in, a human cattle farm to be worked for the profit of its own inhabitants.' And on the top of all this: when the 'human cattle farm' was in full working order and some of the cattle were manifestly insufficiently nourished, the Marquis of Salisbury, then Secretary of State for India, could only utter platitudes to the effect that as India must be bled the lancet should be applied to the congested parts, and conclude with an eulogy of letting things slide, for, as he then said, 'I see no terror in a policy of drifting.'

As it was in the beginning of our connection with India—

> 'The primary object of Great Britain, let it be acknowledged, was rather to discover what could be obtained from her Asiatic subjects, than how they could be benefited,'[1]—

so it is now, and bids fair to continue so long as the present system of administration remains unchanged. Fair words, in multitude no man can number, suggest the contrary; stubborn facts, revealing the course of every-day administration, accord with the truth of the most censorious observation conceivable, and render any other statement impossible.

The decisive step which was to deny a fair field to the people of India for their abilities in their own country, and the determination to keep the land in a state of com-

[1] '*Observations* on the State of Society among *Asiatic* Subjects of Great Britain, particularly with respect to Morals; and on the means of improving it. P. 20,' written chiefly in the year 1792. East India House, August 16, 1797.

plete subjection to Britain, was taken in 1833, under the dominant but unacknowledged influence of the necessity to pay a dividend to East India proprietors, and to find England (as it was supposed) a vast market unhindered by the competition of other countries. The year before England herself had come into possession of political emancipation. One of the first things the Reformed Parliament did was to bind India in chains.

INDIA'S EXPORTS: WHOSE ARE THEY?

One side of the Indian trade statistics have been considered. So far as the imports are concerned, it has, on analysis, been found that the vast majority of the people, three-fourths of them—are, on the average, customers of England to the extent of one shilling and sixpence per head per annum. Of that one shilling and sixpence India is to the extent of more than one shilling undersold by Lancashire in the production of goods which she could herself supply had she the capital to enable her to set up in business. On the principles we, as India's rulers, have repeatedly laid down,[1] on high authority, we have taken care she shall not find the necessary capital from her own resources. These resources are to be kept down. Napoleon's 'nation of shopkeepers' does not take kindly to business rivalry on the part of a people who, they are told, in season and out of season, are much their inferiors, as morally bad as they are intellectually weak. English religious zeal will send the misguided ones missionaries, but English justice, though it be prated *ad nauseam* as the one distinguishing feature of our rule,[2] will not permit them to grow rich in their own land.

An analytical examination of imports showed those imports were taken to India for the European population and for certain millions of Indians brought into relationship with them. In a word, they were for Anglostan and not for Hindustan. For whose benefit and in whose behalf are the exports put on board ship and sent, the greater portion to England, much to European countries, some to the Commonwealth of Australia, and the remainder to Ceylon and the countries immediately east and west of India?

A statement of the exports from India and their value for the respective years of 1870 and 1898–99 is as follows:—

[1] See Mr. Thackeray's views, endorsed by Lord William Bentinck, in 1812, and Mr. James Mill's opinions, accepted by a Parliamentary Committee in 1831, pp. 38–42 and 264–266.

[2] All official speeches on India, *passim*, and particularly the speech delivered by the Secretary of State for India in the House of Commons on the 16th of August, 1901.

EXPORTS AND THEIR VALUE, 1870 AND 1898–99.

	1870.	1898-99.
	£	£
Animals, living	—	117,280
Apparel	—	194,005
Coal, Coke, etc.	—	228,520
Coffee	870,179	1,190,845
Coir, and manufactures of	151,401	225,317
Cotton, raw	19,079,138	7,460,085
" twist and yarns	122,619	4,456,871
" manufactures	1,176,188	1,096,084
Drugs and Medicines...	48,415	97,877
Dyes: Indigo...	3,178,045	1,980,319
" Other sorts	164,640	358,869
Grain: Rice	3,020,276	10,548,467
" Wheat	82,924	6,479,792
" Juwar and Bajri	—	486,804
" Wheat-flour	—	383,054
" Other sorts	168,254	248,151
Gums and Resins	210,407	82,825
Hemp, and manufactures of ...	61,872	145,467 [1]
Hides and Skins	1,691,330	4,967,089
Horns	76,654	107,529
Ivory, and manufactures of... ...	108,289	42,895
Jewelry and Precious Stones ...	87,779	88,151
Jute, raw	1,984,495	4,627,507
" manufactures of	205,928	3,865,682
Lac (of all sorts)	258,800	580,929
Manures (bones)	—	272,268
Metals	—	159,403
Oilcake...	—	102,037
Oils	825,000	544,682
Opium	11,693,330	4,750,677
Provisions	—	488,508
Rice-bran	—	162,778
Saltpetre	394,870	282,896
Seeds	2,308,942	7,901,342
Silk, raw	1,501,512	317,862
" manufactures of	142,062	110,985
Spices	174,685	426,226
Sugar	327,325	255,505
Tea	1,080,515	5,460,744
Tobacco	60,980	145,709
Wood, and manufactures of ...	156,128	726,699
Wool, raw	472,614	1,149,916
" manufactures of	255,895	169,664
All other articles	877,955	1,185,187
Indian produce or manufactures ...	50,679,545	72,900,185
Ditto (re-exports)	1,791,831	2,247,464
	52,471,376	75,147,649
Treasure	1,025,386	4,938,798
	£53,496,762	£80,086,447

[1] Raw hemp only.

The fluctuations in the comparison are of interest and significance. Ten new items appear in the later list which were not in the former:—

Animals,	Juwar and Bajri,	Metals,	Ricebran.
Apparel,	Wheat flour,	Oilcake,	
Coal and Coke,	Bones for manure,	Provisions,	

The additions are of a varied character. Coal and coke (£223,520), metals (£159,043), represent mineral wealth, though the metals are re-exports of foreign productions chiefly to Central Asian countries. Apparel, too, is a re-export, as also are provisions. The remainder come from the fields and animals of India. The living animals seem to be re-exports also, seeing India imported over £322,000 worth, while the total number exported were valued at £170,845. Breeding animals for export—horses, for example—is a business yet in its infancy, although there are localities in India unsurpassed for horse-breeding.

		£
Coffee.—An increase of 27 per cent. (£320,166) in which, at the most, Indians share to the extent of one-twentieth ...	+	16,000
Coir, and Manufactures of.—An increase of 77 per cent.; mainly, the trade is in the hands of Indian merchants on the Western Coast. All this may be credited to net Indian export; the merchants carrying it on are among the few prosperous classes in India	+	225,317
Cotton, Raw.—A decrease of £12,619,053, or 66⅓ per cent. The latest figures are fully up to the average of the preceding seven years, and may be taken partly to represent the decreased production of cotton from want of manure for the soil and other causes. Four-fifths of the cotton thus exported is from the Feudatory States.		

	£
The decrease, however, is not all due to diminished yield; a considerable portion is absorbed in India itself in the manufacture of twist and yarn. As, however, that is an increase to be immediately reckoned, the difference between 1870 and 1898–99 may be put as a loss	– 12,619,053
Cotton Twist and Yarn.—A new trade, practically, the £122,169 of 1870 being a negligible quantity. The whole of this is the product of the Bombay, and the Central and Northern India mills, the capital in them is almost entirely Indian. The advantage, therefore, is	+ 4,334,702
Cotton Manufactures.—This is an Indian loss	– 80,054
Drugs and Medicines.—In European hands chiefly.	
Indigo.—A falling off of £1,197,726, chiefly under European control, say 10 per cent. Indian, and minus	– 119,772
Other Dyes.—Increase, £188,729, or 118 per cent. Indians' share, say, one-tenth of total	+ 35,336
Grain: Rice.—Increase, 250 per cent. The gain in pounds sterling is £7,523,371, divided between Bengal and Burma—the first a fairly prosperous portion of the Empire, the latter a very prosperous province. The latter province has increased its trade during the past ten years by £3,743,527, wholly in this article, while Bengal's increase is in much smaller proportion, and is divided between a number of articles	+ 7,523,371
Grain: Wheat.—Here, again, a new article for export has revealed itself during	

	£
the past thirty years; in 1870 £33,000 worth, in 1898–99 £6,500,000. In the preceding year (1897–98) the value was only £894,101, and the year before much less. The total for 1898–99 (£6,479,792) has only once been beaten. And 1898–99 was the year after a great famine! This article of export, being grown entirely by Indians, must be credited to them, though the manner in which it is purchased by middlemen for export, and held by the sowkar, does not leave much, if any, profit to the grower	+ 6,479,792
Grain: Juwar and Bajri.—Another new item in the list. These are millets, much eaten in India, and all needed to fill British-Indian hungry bellies	+ 436,804
Grain: Wheat-flour.—Also new. First appears in 1888–89	+ 333,054
Grain: Other sorts	+ 243,151
Gums and Resins.—These have decreased by £127,582 since 1870	− 127,582
Hemp, and Manufactures of.—An increase of 140 per cent. (from £61,372 to £145,467). To be credited to European production chiefly.	
Hides and Skins.—In the totals now given dressed and tanned hides are included. This business is mostly in the hands of Indians, and the increase since 1870 shows	+ 3,275,759
Horns.—This branch of export, naturally, increases with the growth of the hide and skin trade, and is, with that trade, fostered by droughts and cattle mortality. Increase in twenty-nine years	+ 30,975
Ivory, and Manufactures of.—A decrease	

		£
meaning decay in an Indian industry of 157 per cent., and, so far, matter for regret, as the dismissed workmen, if they were to continue in existence, could only crowd the already overcrowded soil	−	65,894
Jewelry and Precious Stones.—An increase of 36 per cent.—a mainly Indian trade, say three-fourths of the gain to be credited to Indians	+	37,778
Jute, Raw.—An increase of £2,643,012, or 139 per cent. In European hands		—
Jute, Manufactures of.—A new industry which has grown at a phenomenal rate. There are now thirty-three mills in Bengal, with a capital of about £2,000,000 ; over 1870, the increase is 1,785½ per cent. This is wholly European gain, largely Scottish, and represents £3,660,889		—
Lac (of all sorts).—The growth here is, by percentage, considerable, £580,929 instead of £253,800—130 per cent. increase, meaning	+	327,129
Manures (animal bones).—A new industry, like those of hides, skins, and horns, most prosperous in famine times, wholly Indian	+	272,268
Metals.—First noted in 1888–89. Mainly re-exports of material from Europe, say two-thirds Indian	+	106,269
Oilcake.—First noted in 1891–92. Chiefly Indian	+	102,037
Oils.—An increase of 69 per cent. Probably cocoa-nut oil to a great extent. If so, the increase to be credited to Indians of South-Western Coast	+	219,682

Opium.—A portentous decrease in twenty-nine years—from £11,693,330 to

	£
£4,750,667, or 148 per cent. This is a Government monopoly. The reduction in the area cultivated has provided land for increased grain and non-food cultivation; the benefits derived by the Indians are, therefore, elsewhere accounted for ...	—
Provisions.—A new item in the list. The exports are to Ceylon, the Straits Settlements, the Western Coast of Africa, and the Persian Gulf. Probably half Indian	+ 244,254
Rice-bran.—Another new item, probably from Bengal and Burma, therefore to be credited	+ 162,778
Saltpetre.—The decrease is 70 per cent., being a reduction from £394,870 to £232,896, a minus amount of	— 161,974
Seeds.—In oil seeds, which include a number of articles, there has been a great increase—no less than 243 per cent. This expansion of export corresponds for Southern and Eastern and part of Central India to the great growth of wheat export in the North. The increase represents a value almost wholly Indian, as the cultivation is in Indian hands ...	+ 5,592,400
Silk, Raw.—A most melancholy retrospect. The production of raw silk, an eminently Indian business, is now only a fifth of what it was less than thirty years ago—401 per cent. decline. This is a serious loss in directions where variety of occupation means life,—its absence, death. The decrease since 1870 is...	— 1,243,650
Silk, Manufactures of.—A thirty per cent. decline. There are seven silk mills in all India, by whom owned I have not found	

		£
out. The old hand-weaving is dying out, in common with other Indian industries. As throwing light on Indian economic conditions, I ask the reader's perusal of the appendix to this chapter entitled 'Condition of Silk-Weaving Industry in Madras.'[1] Loss since 1870	−	31,127
Spices.—An increase of 148 per cent., from £174,635 to £426,226; difference being £251,291, probably wholly Indian growth	+	251,291
Sugar.—A decrease of 29 per cent., value from £327,325 to £255,505. Why this should be is hard to say in view of India's unrivalled means for growing sugar, especially on irrigated land, and the (occasional) large profits obtained from its cultivation. However, there is a loss of...	−	71,820
Tea.—A big jump upwards—438 per cent. increase. There are now 138 Limited Liability Tea Estate Companies with a capital of £2,141,474. All the shares in these companies are held by Europeans—with an infinitesimal exception. Of the cultivation as a whole, however, it is stated in the *Amrita Bazar Patrika,* of Calcutta, that one-twelfth of the growth is in Indian hands	+	682,509
Tobacco.—An increase is noted, which is largely due to the enterprise of a South Indian mercantile firm, whose Indian cigars are now well known throughout the United Kingdom. Probably one-half of the increase may be credited to purely		

[1] Extracted, by permission, from the Appendices to 'Progress in the Madras Presidency during the Past Forty Years,' by M. R. Ry. Srinavasa Raghava Ivengar, Dewan of Baroda. Government Press, Madras, 1893.

		£
Indian cultivation. The increase has been at the rate of 141 per cent., and the amount to be recorded is...	+	42,364
Wood, and Manufactures of.—The growth is again great, being 340 per cent. increase—£156,123 to £726,699. The 'manufactures of' scarcely count; most of the export is teak, of which six-sevenths of the whole are supplied to the United Kingdom. This business is mainly in European hands		—
Wool, Raw.—Increase, 144 per cent.—from £472,614 to £1,149,916. Mainly Indian	+	676,502
Wool, Manufactures of.—Another disquieting item, inasmuch as a decrease of 53 per cent. in manufacture of wool is shown. Yorkshire woollens evidently, like Lancashire cottons, can still beat Indian manufactures out of the field. Decrease in £ sterling	—	85,731
All other Articles.—35⅓ per cent. increase. As it is impossible to say how much of this is or is not Indian, half of the increase may be credited, say... ...	+	153,616

Treasure.—The growth here again is large—391 per cent. increase. But nothing must be put against Indian production in this regard. The gold, amounting to £1,557,764 is partly the product of British gold mines capitalised at, say, £3,000,000 to £4,000,000, and silver (not produced in India and, therefore, a re-exportation of what has been imported) £3,381,024; together £4,938,788.

Total Trade Results, as affecting purely Indian Cultivators, 1870 *to* 1898–99.

		£
Increases shown by + mark		31,805,136
Decreases " – "		14,606,657
Net increase in twenty-nine years ...		17,198,479
From the above has to be deducted:—		
Exports to Asiatic countries, on western, northern, and eastern borders, not reckoning treasure, say one-fourth goes out of India...	£774,497	
From the Feudatory States, one-fifth has to be accounted for	6,361,433	
		7,135,930
		£10,062,549

That is to say, at the end of twenty-nine years, the increased export of distinctly Indian produce, that is, produce coming from the Indian agriculturist grown from his own means, and not benefited directly by foreign capital, is £10,062,549. During this period Burma alone has increased her exports by £6,148,999 in 1898–99 as compared with 1870, leaving only £3,913,550 for all the rest of India.

This, however, is not all. No argument is more frequently employed or more strongly expressed than that the increase of public works in India would be a benefit to the Indian agriculturist in enabling him to export more and more largely. How does this dogma—it is not an assertion, it is, on Anglo-Indian lips, a dogma—square with the facts? Since 1873–74 [1]—the figures are not available in satisfactory form for an earlier date—capital has been raised—

	£
For railway expenditure	129,730,000
For irrigation works	21,680,000
	£151,410,000

[1] Statistical Abstract, British India, No. 34, p. 324.

In addition to this a large annual expenditure has been incurred on roads. Since 1873–74 over nineteen thousand miles of railways have been opened, and many millions of acres of land brought under irrigation by canals and wells.

It may be asked, 'How then is it that India presents such a satisfactory appearance of prosperity?' To which the answer is that, except to the superficial eye, or to the pen and tongue of a defender of the system whose whole life and career are involved in the success, or, what comes to the same thing, a belief in the success, of the present policy, THERE IS NO APPEARANCE OF PROSPERITY EVEN, save in certain favoured irrigated or perennially rain-fed tracts. Elsewhere there is exactly what the figures given above indicate. Let the reader turn to the description of the Deccan upland districts (pp. 349–353), and let him bear in mind that famine is now chronic in many parts of India, and that a friendly critic in the first of medical journals [1] has deduced from the Census returns the ominous and terrible fact that nineteen millions of people died from famine in the last decade of the nineteenth century. Nearly two million deaths per annum from privation and diseases induced by privation are a part only of the evidence which indicates to those who have eyes to see and ears to hear the entire absence of prosperity in 'India.' That is a broad effect, sketched by a competent hand. Let some of the details be worked into the delineation concerning a particular portion of the Indian dominions; the Lieutenant-Governor of the Provinces in question, the Upper Provinces of Bengal, prides himself on having successfully combated a famine in 1897–98.[2] For a time he could maintain the fiction.

[1] *The Lancet*, May, 1901. See preceding notes for details.

[2] I refer to the North-Western Provinces, and to that very capable civilian, Sir Antony Macdonnell. It was not judicious on the part of one civilian who had the temerity to maintain the contrary to his superior's known opinion, to assert that there had been serious mortality during this time of famine; he found, to his cost, it was not judicious. As for an official who reported that 'one thick-headed village had disappeared for want of food,' he, too, had occasion to repent his frankness and to deplore his recklessness. A legend has grown up about the North-Western Provinces famine of 1897–98 which even Indian-edited newspapers have accepted as gospel truth.

The Census returns have revealed exactly what, from the annual death returns, was apparent to all who wished to see things in a clear, unprejudiced, light; they must be very bad, and they must make viceregal and other official speeches, as to little or no famine mortality, absurd. This result was, by those who wish to see things as they are, and not as limned in an atmosphere and environment to suit preconceived ideas as to what the fruits of British rule must necessarily be, long ago anticipated. For British rule could not, intentionally, or incidentally, or accidentally, or any other 'entally,'—be any other than beneficent rule. But those who thus saw were openly contemned as enemies to the commonwealth.

Here are the figures of the population in the Allahabad, Benares, and Gorakhpur, divisions, by districts, as shown in the official table published in March, 1901:—

District.	1891.	1901.	Increase and Decrease. Per cent.
Cawnpore	1,209,695	1,259,248	+ 4·1
Fatehpur	699,157	686,411	— 1·82
Banda	705,832	631,837	—10·55
Hamirpur	513,720	458,645	—10·72
Allahabad	1,548,737	1,487,904	— 3·93
Jhansi	683,619	611,644	—10·53
Jalaun	396,361	400,619	+ 1·07
Allahabad Division	5,757,121	5,535,808	—
Benares	921,943	882,972	— 4·22
Mirzapur	1,161,508	1,082,903	— 6·77
Caunpur	1,264,949	1,202,710	— 4·93
Ghazipur	1,077,909	914,148	—15·19
Ballia	942,465	949,966	+ ·8
Benares Division	5,368,774	5,032,699	—
Gorakhpur	2,994,057	2,955,548	— 1·29
Basti	1,785,844	1,845,758	+ 3·36
Azamgarh	1,728,625	1,530,555	—11·46
Gorakhpur Division	6,508,526	6,331,856	—

Thus, while the normal increase of the population should be at least ten per cent.—and fifteen per cent. if the official ideal be reached—in the three divisions named there were increases in only four districts, and decreases in eleven, amounting in one case to over fifteen per cent. Allowing only one per cent. per annum increase, and not one and a half which the Indian authorities have laid down as the normal annual increase in a properly-governed region, in these three divisions alone, the population at the beginning of the new century as compared with ten years previously was less than it ought to have been,

In Allahabad division by	797,030	souls.
,, Benares ,, ,,	872,292	,,
,, Gorakhpur ,, ,,	828,022	,,
In the three by	2,497,344	

Decreases also occurred in the following districts (excluding Almora, where a change of boundaries with Naini Tal has occurred):—Bijnor, 1·85; Pilibhit, 3·02; Rae Bareli, 0·25; Hardoi, 1·8; Gonda, 3·9; Partabgarh, 2·17; making decreases in sixteen districts out of forty-eight. The net increase for the North-Western Provinces and Oudh is 1·68 only, although plague has had no appreciable effect, and there has only been one famine, which, as has been stated, Sir Antony Macdonnell regards as having been very successfully administered. The figures quoted tell a different tale: so would most North-Western Province civilians who were free to speak of the facts as they saw them.

For the whole of his Province, on the counting being completed, and taking the lower percentage of proper increase, Sir Antony Macdonnell had 3,899,269 fewer subjects to paternally rule than he should have had. Allowing for 'normal' increase he was short of his people by 6,244,285! And yet, since Lord Northbrook's campaign in Behar in 1873, the only really successful famine campaign known in British India, this particular fight with famine, resulting in a missing number of over six millions of people, is regarded as a triumph of administration and humanity!

APPENDIX

CONDITION OF THE SILK-WEAVING INDUSTRY IN MADURA, SOUTHERN INDIA.[1]

Number of Silk-weavers in the Town.—The silk-weavers as a class are a very prolific people. They are said to multiply more rapidly than the other classes. Fixing, therefore, the inmates of each house to be from four to five, the silk-weavers' population of the town of Madura may be roughly estimated to be between 20,000 to 25,000, including females and children. Of these about 10,000, including females, may be said to belong to the actual coolie class, who earn their living by daily wages. Next to these come the petty traders, who number from 400 to 500 families. Some of these sell threads, having purchased them in retail from the bigger merchants; some again sell lace in retail; some advance small sums of money to the holders of looms and order a small supply of cloths and sell them to the richer merchants. Some are brokers who collect cloths manufactured in the town and sell them either to the merchants in the town or to those abroad, and very few are capitalists who have any very large trading concerns. The last class may also be counted on one's fingers, and it is said they are likely to be only between ten and twenty on the whole. It is the brokers who form a comparatively large number. Some of the silk-weavers have become agriculturists, finding that the profession of weaving does not pay. Their holdings are small, and they only eke out their maintenance from the results of the agricultural labour. Some are said to keep carts and bulls, and to be employed in collecting sand from the river for building purposes.

Their Average Income.—Of the class of merchants, those who get profit of about Rs.100 and more per month, are only five or six; about twenty or thirty get from Rs.50 to Rs.100, and those who get from Rs.5 to Rs.23 are about 400 or 500. The profession of broker is not very remunerative. A broker makes a profit of one anna on every rupee, but to earn a profit of 30 or 40 rupees in a month he has to employ two agents—one to go about the town and watch the progress of the cloths entrusted to the labourers and another to keep accounts. Very often he has to borrow money to pay the weavers in advance.

The average income of a coolie family is Rs.5 a month, and it never goes higher than Rs.10 a month. Females also work; some are

---

[1] Memorandum on the Progress of Madras Presidency during the last Forty Years of British Administration, p. ccxv.

employed in preparing the threads for weaving, some in the dyeing of cloths, and others in the marking of spots, or what is called sundadis. Boys of twelve years and more also earn wages, and generally get from one rupee upwards.

Rs.500 is the highest value of a cloth which has ever been made in Madura. Merchants of their own accord do not order cloths of value of more than Rs.80 to Rs.100. The cloths made ordinarily range from Rs.6 to Rs.10 only in value.

The introduction of cotton twist from England, of lace from France, as well as of even the dyeing stuff from Bombay, has considerably affected the value of the cloths made in the town, and necessarily the wages to the coolies and profits to the merchants. Of the 14,000 cloths above mentioned as being made in a month in the town, for 7,000 to 10,000 cloths the inferior brass lace is used, and the value of these does not go over Rs.6 at the utmost. Their average price may be fixed at Rs.2½ per cloth; this gives the sum total of Rs.17,500 to Rs.25,000. The average value of an ordinary cloth with good lace may be fixed at Rs.7, and supposing that good lace is used for the remaining 4,000 cloths, their approximate value amounts to Rs.28,000. Thus the total value of cloths made in the town in a month may be fixed at Rs.50,000 to Rs.60,000.

To get an impression of how much this sum of Rs.60,000 actually benefits the townsmen and how much goes to other countries and places, what the component parts of a Madura cloth are must be examined. Let us take for illustration an ordinary white cloth which is sold in the town for Rs.10. The different items which go to make this sum of Rs.10 may be described as follows:—

	Rs.	a.	p.
Value of the thread	1	0	0
Cost of preparing the same for weaving ...	0	2	0
Profit earned by the merchant who sells the thread	0	1	0
Cost of fastening the thread to the loom ...	0	1	0
Wages for weaving thread into a cloth	1	4	0
Value of the lace	6	0	0
	8	8	0
Merchants' profit, including brokerage	1	8	0
Total	10	0	0

When the cloth is dyed the excess charge is as follows:—

	Rs.	a.	p.
For the first and rough colouring	0	12	0
For the making of spots	0	12	0
For dyeing them over again	0	12	0
Miscellaneous	0	4	0
Total	2	8	0

Thus the great portion of the value of a cloth goes for the lace which is manufactured in France. Then by the cotton twist used, it is the English merchants who are benefited. The dye is also prepared abroad and the greater portion of Rs.1 12a. spent for dyeing goes also to other hands. The portion of Rs.12 8a. which actually circulates among the townsmen may be taken at the highest to be from Rs.4 to Rs.5, or one-third of the value of the cloth. This calculated with reference to the Rs.60,000 worth of cloth yields a total amount of Rs.24,000 to Rs.30,000, and this amount may roughly be fixed to be the sum earned from the industry by coolie upwards to the richest merchant. Deducting again Rs.5,000 or so as being the profits earned by merchants, there remains Rs.25,000 to be distributed amongst 5,000 families, giving an average of Rs.5 per family, the amount mentioned above, as being the average income of a family. Generally speaking, the industry is becoming day by day less profitable to the actual working classes. The causes thereof are not far to seek. Prior to the importation of cotton twist, some fifty years ago, it would appear there were in the town of Madura 2,000 to 3,000 families employed in spinning out threads. This vocation has entirely ceased now. Again, prior to the importation of lace, there were 500 Mussulman families engaged in making lace, and in their place there are, it would appear, only ten families employed in making country lace. The preparation of colouring materials was at least done locally till a year or two ago, but this, too, has been superseded by the Bombay article. As a necessary result of the cessation of all these vocations, the labour is now directed entirely in one direction towards weaving, and it is in consequence very cheap. What used to be paid for at Rs.2 in former years is now remunerated by one rupee only.

Even as regards the merchant class, the general complaint is that the trade does not pay. It may be that a larger number of cloths are now made than before, but what merchants make as profit by reason of the cheapness of the commodity and keenness of competition seems to be considerably less than what it was in former years. A cloth which was sold for Rs.60 is now sold for only Rs.30.

As a curious illustration of how the importation of the English-made goods has affected the local weaving industry, it may be mentioned that the weavers themselves of the town of Madura do hardly use the cloths woven by them. Mulls and piece goods have taken the place of the home-made articles, and if the richer class should seek for some country cloths, it is the Conjeveram cloths that are made use of. The females likewise use the *Thombu*, and if they seek for some better country-made cloths they purchase the Koranadu cloths. Thus it happens that one or two per cent. of the town-made articles are sold in the town itself, and the rest are sent abroad.

The Habits and Manners of the Silk-weavers as a Class.—Silk-weavers as a class lead a simple life. Their food is simple and consists of cholum, cumbu, and other dry grains. Rice is used by comparatively few persons only. Their clothing is simple. The females wear a cloth of Rs.2-worth only, except on festive occasions, when they wear the Koranadu cloths. House accommodation is necessary for their profession, and each endeavours, therefore, first, to secure a house for himself. They are not also without a desire for ornaments. Even the poorest household are mentioned to have some gold jewels. A silk-weaver's property consists generally of his house and ornaments. Marriage is costly with them. About Rs. 68 must be paid to the bride even by the poorest man. To meet this item of expenditure almost every coolie before he enters on his profession begins to subscribe to some chit transaction or other, and to save out of his hard-earned wages one rupee or so to be paid monthly for a series of years extending from five to seven. Before he earns his prize in his turn, necessity, however, often compels him to borrow, mortgaging his chit and the house owned by him. It is such documents that are registered in large numbers in the town offices of Madura. There is another peculiarity about these silk-weavers. They seldom borrow from others than their caste-men. In case of loans of large sums, probably they may resort to the Nattukkottai chetti, but all ordinary loans are contracted from one of their own community.

CHAPTER IX

'IS INDIA DISTRESSED? WE SEE NO DISTRESS.' 'IF INDIA BE DISTRESSED AND NON-PROSPEROUS, WHY DO WE NOT SEE THE DISTRESS?'

Impression of Visitors that India is a Land of Great Prosperity Arises from their Never Visiting the Real India: They see Anglo-Indian Colonies on the Continent of India only.

Anglostan and Hindustan—Two Countries Included in the Indian Empire of Britain.

Eulogies of Moral and Material Welfare Blue Books apply only to Anglostan.

What is Really Going On in Hindustan? The Public Not Permitted to Know.

The Veil Partly Drawn Aside in, 1867, 1877, 1879–80, 1888, 1896, and 1897–8.

The Panjab:

Mr. Thorburn's Inquiry as to Agriculturists' Indebtedness

Fixity of Land Revenue Cause of Much Indebtedness.

Government's Duty to so Adjust its Revenue as to Obviate Unnecessary Borrowings.

Why the Sowkar is Preferred to Government when a Loan for Cattle or Seed is Required.

Results of the Indebtedness Inquiry—Widespread Ruin Revealed.

Five 'Beginnings' of Indebtedness.

Legislation and Administration Need Adaptation to Indian Requirements.

North-Western Provinces and Oudh:

Lord Dufferin's Conscience and Sir W. W. Hunter's Exposure.

'The Greater Proportion of the Population Suffer from an Insufficiency of Food.'

The Inquiry of 1887–88.

How a Summary of Evidence should Not be Prepared.

Mr. Crooke's Facts in a 'Covering Letter' and the Facts Themselves—Two Very Different Things.

Farmers, with a Well and Two Bullocks, in Good Years, Steadily Submerged.

Ninety-Nine per Cent. of Gross Produce Taken for Rent by Landlord who Pays Half to the British Government.

Farmers (If They have No Children) 'Can Afford a Blanket.'

'It is Unusual to Find a Village Woman Who Has Any Wraps at All.'
Sample Cultivators: a 'Record' in Rack-Renting.
A Village Under the Court of Wards.
Sir Antony Macdonnell on 'The Chief Causes of the Ryot's Difficulties.'
'The Common Idea as to Extravagance on Marriages Unsupported by Evidence.'
Remedies for Difficulties Frequently Propounded by Non-Officials, only to be Scorned and Passed By.
Alleged Causes of Indebtedness by Mr. Thorburn: '1. A Want of Thrift due to Heredity; 2. Climate; 3. Our System.'

The Bombay Presidency:
Chief Authority: 'J.'s' Letters to the *Times of India* Founded on Official Reports.
The Hinterland of Bombay City: a Glimpse by Vaughan Nash.
Bombay's Blunders—Comparative.
Bombay Cultivators Taxed Nearly Four Times Heavier than Bengal Cultivators.
A Non-Famine Year Comparison Between the Respective Presidencies and Provinces.
Backward Irrigational Facilities and the Decrease in Agricultural Cattle.
Incidence of Taxation in Relation to Cultivated Acreage.
Indian Official Publications Pitfalls for the Unwary—including Sir Henry Hartley Fowler, ex-Secretary of State for India
Lands with Five Fallow Years to Two Crop Years.
Ratio of Burden to Gross and Net Produce.
TEN YEARS' AGRICULTURAL EXPERIENCES IN EASTERN ENGLAND:
(*a*) The Vicissitudes of the Seasons for Ten Years
(*b*) Out-turn of Crops—a Loss of £11,724,838.
(*c*) Loss of Cattle.
(*d*) Remission only 8s. per £100 per annum, Less than Half of One per Cent.
The Prediction as to the Bankruptcy of India Fulfilled: 'India *is* Bankrupt.'
A Seven Years' old Exposure.

Appendix:
India's Greatest Peril and her Worst Enemies.

INCREDULITY, annoyance—for a moment or two anger—exhibit themselves in the average Briton when, in his presence, it is asserted that India is in a

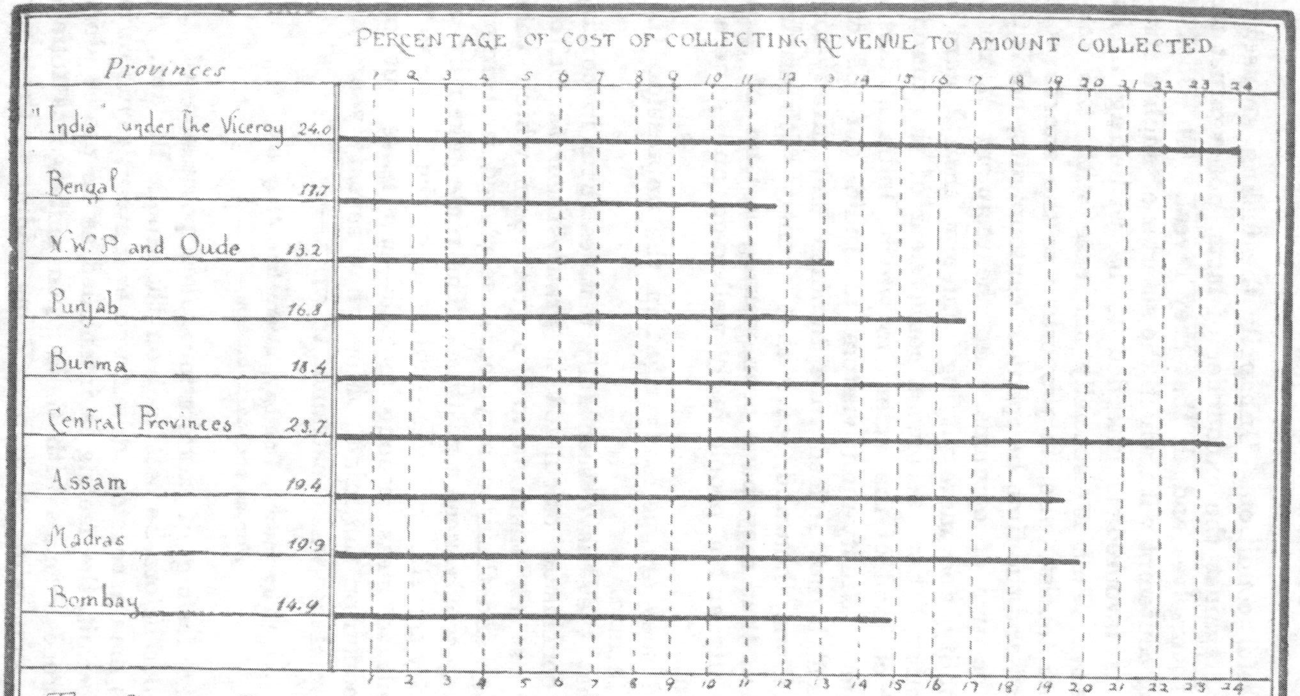

The Costly Collection of Land Revenue

distressful condition. Unhappily the feeling aroused is excited against the expounder of facts, not against the facts themselves and all that they reveal. The look of pitying contempt with which the asserter of such a statement is favoured is intended to be withering in its intensity. This is especially the case with the cold-weather tourist, who, in proportion to the shortness of his visit and the time he spent in cantonments, holds the most positive of opinions. As the recipient of much incredulity, and more pitying contempt than I care to remember, I have become a connossieur of the manner in which, and of the extent to which, India strikes a stranger. Ninety-nine visitors to India out of one hundred, if not indeed nine hundred and ninety-nine out of one thousand, leave that country with an impression that they have been visiting a land of great prosperity and a people fairly well-to-do and generally content.

And they are perfectly right in the impression they have formed.

What they have seen fully justifies them in coming to a conclusion calculated to gratify them as Britons and to satisfy them as to the great part which their country and their countrymen have played in bringing India to so advanced a position. The route taken by the ordinary traveller in India—unless he or she be the most difficult to please among mortals—can leave but one impression on the mind. More than seventy years ago Bishop Heber was constrained to write—

> 'Thy towers, Bombay, gleam fair, they say,
> Across the dark blue sea.'

A like feeling of admiration takes possession of the traveller before he sets foot on the Apollo Bunder. So far as the unaccustomed heat and ever-attentive mosquito will permit, the feeling is intensified as he passes along the broad avenues with their green umbrageous foliage partly concealing, and in so doing adding to the effect produced by, the magnificent buildings on every side. The effect is perhaps greatest when the most magnificent railway station in the world is visited—the Victoria Station, designed by the late Mr. Stevens. A journey to that part of the city occupied by the native inhabitants, with its crowded streets, its busy life, its varied animation, and its general activity brings a new phase of thought. 'All this busy scene is of our creation. This is our work, our work, our work. What *do* these people not owe to us!' No longer can it be asked as a question involving an impossibility: 'Which of you by taking thought can add one cubit to his stature?' Mentally, racially, and patriotically, practically every Englishman who goes to India through its western gate adds not one but many cubits to his stature before he really starts on his journeyings in India. An evening in a bungalow on Malabar Hill, or even an afternoon visit to the Botanical Gardens overlooking Back Bay and the many-towered city, puts the top-stone on an edifice then completely erected in the visitor's mind.

It is thus mentally equipped that the 'grand tour' through India is begun. Can there be any wonder if the frame of mind thus induced should become almost ecstatic over the many proud evidences of the great good of British rule? For pretty well all the visitor saw in Bombay *was* the creation and consequence of British rule. As I have said, everything that is seen justifies the strongest feelings of complacency which are certain to be aroused in the stranger's mind. He proceeds on his tour. Everywhere he sees similar proofs of British success. Crossing the great plains of India he may, as he gazes from the railway carriage window, wonder where the agricultural people are to be found. He has been told that India is a land of villages and that eighty-six per cent. of the inhabitants are agriculturists. Where, then, are the villages? And, where the people? It is true he sees here and there a collection of mud-huts with little or no sign of life about them, and

20

concludes that those are ruined villages of which he has read.

Allahabad, Calcutta, Darjeeling, the Northern Indian cities, with perhaps a glance at Madras, and, maybe, Rangoon, are included in the visitor's round. Soon the new impression of our greatness and success wears off. It has solidified into an article of belief, has become a part of irremovable indentation in the grey matter of the brain; an abiding addition is made to the mental equipment of the individual. So it comes about that the stoutest defenders of British rule in India are those persons who have visited that country for a short time. An example of the impression made on the average visitor comes to me whilst this chapter is in preparation.

An English gentleman, who was a Parliamentary representative for some years, who is related to the greatest Parliamentary champion India has known since the days of Burke, visited India during the winter of 1900–1901. He was in that country during the aftermath of what Lord Curzon has called 'the most terrible famine which has ever visited India.' I forwarded to him a copy of my Open Letter to the Viceroy on the Condition of India and its people. On June 24, 1901, this reply reached me :—

'I have been a long time in acknowledging the receipt of the paper you were kind enough to send me. Of course I have not the knowledge of the subject to enable me to judge of the question in dispute, but I imagine that those in power are always likely to make out the best case for themselves and the results of their rule. I went to India on a short trip last winter. I spent a few days in Bombay and Calcutta, and visited Darjeeling, Benares, Lucknow, Cawnpore, Agra, Delhi, and Jeypore. I was much interested with the people and very favourably impressed with them. I did not come across any signs of poverty or starvation, and perhaps that was not to be expected in so short a trip. In the native quarters of the cities the people seemed to be industrious and cheerful, and the children seemed plump and happy. I did not notice anything in the villages near the railway line, or in the appearance of the people who were in the fields, to lead me to think that they were in great distress, though, of course, every one could see that they are poor. I was much surprised to see the immense amount of travelling by rail which they do. Whenever I went by an ordinary train the stations were crowded with natives—

one would think that they must have some spare money to pay for this. I did not see any of the great men in India except the Chief Justice of Calcutta, whom I knew here. The military power which holds the country seemed to be very little in evidence. I should like to go again, but probably never shall.'

For an unpremeditated expression of opinion, not written with an eye to publication, the foregoing is a valuable document. Its chief value lies in its absolute accuracy. What is described is true to the life and to the letter. Personally, I should subscribe my agreement with all that is set forth.

But the evidence is valueless; the impression obtained is so misleading as to be wholly false. The writer of this letter—the ordinary visitor to the land called India, following the route described above—did not visit India. The places at which he stopped were British Colonies in India. They were not India itself. There are two Indias; the India of the Presidency and chief provincial cities, of the railway system, of the hill stations, in all of which Britain is as supreme as she is in the chief places of the United Kingdom. This is the India where the people, taken all round and allowing for the circumstances of the respective cases, are as prosperous and nearly as well content as are their brother British subjects in London, Edinburgh, Manchester, Liverpool, Birmingham, Newcastle-on-Tyne, Bristol, and Southampton—with this difference, the really rich men in all the Indian cities do not number two hundred, and that, with a trifling exception, all the big salaries earned in the administration—the biggest salaries for like work in all the world—are received by Englishmen, by foreigners. This India, at the outside, cannot affect more than fifteen per cent. of the people. Those people are not seen as Indian people, but as British Indian subjects whose daily bread comes from the political structure made in Britain according to British ideas, and is not an outgrowth of the country's needs or the people's wishes.

There are two countries situated between the mountains which constitute the roof of the world and the eighth degree north of the equator and bounded east and west by Chinese territory and the Afghan kingdom. They may be named respectively—

ANGLOSTAN, the land specially ruled by the English, in which English investments have been made, and by which a fair show and reality of prosperity are ensured;

HINDUSTAN, practically all India[1] fifty miles from each side of the railway lines, except the tea, coffee, indigo, and jute, plantations, and not including the Feudatory States.

ANGLOSTAN is the region to which the roseate statements in the Viceregal and State Secretary's speeches refer. All that is eulogistic in Indian Moral and Material Welfare Blue Books apply only to Anglostan. If only there were agreement as to this real delimitation between the two Indias, there would not be the conflict of opinion that now puzzles the outsider as he hears directly opposing statements made concerning the Indo-British Empire in the East. As a matter of fact, if the ground were but properly defined there is no real difference between the official apologists and the outside critics. The mischief in regard to the former is that while they deal with all-sufficient detail in connection with everything concerning Anglostan, of Hindustan they produce naught but glittering generalities, which dazzle but do not inform. If by any chance such evidence as will be summarised shortly—I refer to the inquiry con-

[1] Let no critic divert attention from the argument by reminding his reader that Hindustan, properly so-called, was not co-extensive with the British Dominions called India, which embrace Beluchis in the West and Shans in the East, Kashmiris, Dogras, and Afghans in the North, and Tamils in the South. It meant little more than India north of the Nerbudda. I know this, but the expression can be fairly used (with this explanation) for my purpose, and need not be regarded as in any degree misleading.

cerning the economic condition of the Indian people made in 1888—be forthcoming, it is immediately 'dressed' (with more than a shopkeeper's art for his best window), out of all recognition, even to the extent of being a misrepresentation of what it professes to summarise. The 'leading case' in my mind as I write is the covering letter of the Secretariat of the North-Western Provinces and Oudh on the inquiry which I have mentioned. That summary, which gave an inaccurate representation of the facts ascertained, was published. The evidence on which it was professedly based has, on several occasions, been refused when requests for its publication have been made in the House of Commons. Of that evidence more later; meanwhile the Parliamentary incident is narrated here as being part of a settled policy in the India Office, namely, that only such statements concerning administration as the Secretary of State and his Council think proper shall reach the hands of an interested public.

As I have said, ANGLOSTAN, with its railways, roads, and public works generally, its prosperous and prospering cities, its civil and criminal codes, its famine code, its high courts of justice, constitutes a Marvel of Governing Skill and Ability. Were these all, then, so far as mere administration goes, and, assuming it to be fitting that self-praise and egoistic eulogy at any time can be appropriate—then too much has not been said in praise of the British rule of India;—and, again, assuming also that the higher ethics of humanity will permit of even a perfect system of rule being continued—as the British Indian rule is continued—by a menace of force and without the assistance throughout and the secured consent of the governed.

Good as is British administration in the regions and to the extent described, when the price to be paid for it is the once-gradual, but now-rapid demoralisation of eighty-five per cent. of the people, and the equally rapid denudation of the country's resources to the enrichment of the foreign rulers, all this brave display becomes a mockery and a curse.

What is there behind the screen? What is really going on in HINDUSTAN?

As a rule the public are not allowed to know. We scarcely deserve the compliment paid to us in the Indian portion of the record of the tour round the world made by the Czar of Russia when he was Czarewitch ; it is there said : 'Yes, the English, to do them justice, do not hide the bitter truth from themselves that India is an unfortunate country.' It is true we use the phrase, 'India is a poor land,' as did Sir Mackenzie Wallace, and so called forth compliment to our honesty. But we never get far beyond the phraseology. We say India is a poor land, and go on ruling it as if it were a veritable mine of wealth. Glimpses behind the screen are occasionally permissible. Now and then the veil is drawn aside, and one sees what is really happening. This has occurred on the following occasions—to take recent incidents only :—

The Orissa Famine Commission, 1867 ;

The Deccan Riots Commission, 1877 ;

The Famine Commission of 1879–80 ;

The Inquiry into the Economic Condition of the Agricultural and Labouring Classes, 1888 ;

The Inquiry into Peasant Indebtedness and Land Alienation in parts of the Rawalpindi Division, Panjab, 1896 ;

The Famine Commission of 1897–8.

I will take two Provinces and one Presidency, and when these have been delineated according to the official evidence recorded, will then take India as a whole and indicate the terrible condition into which the Empire has been allowed to fall. The two Provinces are the Panjab and the North-Western Provinces and Oudh, generally considered to be the most prosperous parts of India outside the permanently-settled Lower Provinces of Bengal. The Presidency is Bombay. The language employed, as far as possible, will always be official, even if it be not contained within quotation marks.

THE PANJAB.

One man in Northern India has had the courage alike to inquire and to recommend. From his efforts has resulted the Land Alienation Act for the Panjab. That measure, which was passed in October, 1900, took from the owners of the land many of their proprietary rights. Its provisions summarised by Mr. S. S. Thorburn, retired Panjab civilian, whose report—to be immediately alluded to—produced the measure, and who is the man to whom I refer, are as follows :—

1. Prohibited the permanent alienation of agricultural land, except to defined agriculturists ;

2. Only permitted certain forms of temporary alienations to non-agriculturists up to a limit of twenty years, the land then returning unencumbered to the family of the alienor ;

3. Disabled alienors from making any further disposition during the currency of the temporary transfer ;

4. Declared the hypothecation of agricultural produce for more than one year to be illegal ;

5. Prohibited the execution-sale of agricultural lands ; and

6. Confined jurisdiction under the Bill to Revenue officers only.[1]

The genesis of this measure, as told by its author, is most interesting. It will be found at the foot of this page.[2] Having received authority, Mr. Thorburn chose four tracts, two of them 'well' circles near Lahore, a

[1] 'Agricola Redivivus,' art., *Asiatic Quarterly Review*, July 1901, page 77.

[2] *Ibid.* pp. 65–66. Mr. Thorburn says :—'I was almost despondent, when, in 1892, Sir Dennis Fitzpatrick was appointed Lieutenant-Governor of the Panjab. Though his experience had been almost wholly in the Secretariat, and his bias of mind was legal, he was known to be able, thorough, and independent. He at once read all the official literature on the subject of land-reform, and in his frank, incisive way said to me, "Half measures won't do. It is the whole hog or nothing." Soon after, per-

third one hundred miles westwards, and a fourth still farther west in the Salt Range. 'The first three were known to be depressed. The latter was supposed to be better circumstanced, though it was a densely populated rain country.' 'The four tracts or circles covered an area of about one thousand square miles, and supported an agricultural population of three hundred thousand souls scattered throughout five hundred and thirty-five villages and hamlets.' Evidence was readily available and was trustworthy.[1] The collection and sifting of facts occupied

ceiving that the statistics of land-transfers were faulty and unreliable, he initiated measures for their improvement. In the cold weather of 1894–95 he marched through my division—I was the Commissioner of Rawalpindi—and in his tour halted in the heart of a country which was sometimes a granary and sometimes a desert. As he approached his camp a great mob of excited peasants, earnest greybeards most of them, surrounded his horse, some even thrusting horny hands upon the bridle, and kept on shouting at him, "We are ruined, Lord Sahib. The Kirars (Hindu usurers) and compound interest have robbed us of our lands." He tried to get more precise information, but it was useless. The formula was taken up and repeated by an ever-enlarging circle. Recognising that they had convictions, but small powers of exposition, he rode on through them to his tents. Strolling that evening with me, he pointed out that economic problems could only be solved by evidence and reason, in which sentiment had no place, to smash a working system of old standing, except on clear proof that through it the people were being pauperised and expropriated, was impossible.

'"You have the evidence, sir," I suggested, "in all the settlement reports and the annual returns of land-transfers."

'"But the figures are worth little. For instance, they don't show redemptions; the same land may be mortgaged and redeemed half a dozen times for aught I know."

'"If you must have positive proof," I replied, "you can easily obtain it in the way proposed by me ten years ago. If you will select tracts for general statistics, and then take typical villages in them, and have each original peasant-proprietor's debt and mortgage history worked out before the whole village for the last twenty-five years or so, you will get the facts in a few months, which the superficial inquiries of the last dozen years have failed to bring out."

'Next morning His Honour told me that he had been reading "Musalmans and Moneylenders," and was willing to receive a proposal from me for carrying out an inquiry of the kind therein suggested.'

[1] 'The publicity of all proceedings protected us from the fabrication of evidence—a practice which makes the administration of justice conducted in court-rooms such groping in the dark in India. Men lie with impunity in a court-house at a distance from their homes, but not when sitting in the midst of hundreds who know the truth.'—'Agric. Red.' p. 67.

six months, after which two months more were spent in preparing a report on the whole case. Then came the Report. From a manuscript copy with which I have been favoured,[1] I make some citations which are valuable from the facts stated, and interesting because of the side-lights they throw upon the condition of the peasant farmers of the far North-West of India.

The principle of fixity of land-revenue preferred by Government to elasticity.

'Ever since, as Settlement Collector of the Bannu district (1872–79),' says Mr. Thorburn, in the sixty-seventh paragraph of his report, 'I learnt something of the actual difficulties of peasant life, I have always held that our system of fixity of land revenue is unsuitable for peasant owners, because after short harvests fixity compels many of them to borrow from lenders in order to pay their quota of the assessment. I have, consequently, whenever practicable, advocated elasticity, and I have been instrumental in introducing that principle to some, though I think very insufficient, extent in riverain tracts on the Indus, Jhelum, and Chenáb. If some degree of elasticity, which in its fullest measure is the establishment of a ratio between each harvest's out-turn converted into rupees, and the revenue demanded for that harvest, is desirable for river-flooded areas, it is often equally and sometimes more desirable for rain-dependent tracts. The reason is that, cases of avulsion and erosion excepted, the yields on river lands are on the whole more certain and more equal than on rain lands. The rainfall is so varying in quantity and time of fall, that in most rain tracts, over thirty miles south of the Himalayas, the fluctuations of out-turn from harvest to harvest are immense, ranging from *nil* plus loss of seed and absence of fodder to a hundred-fold plus practically unlimited fodder. However, as yet fixed assessments and distribution according to soils are the rule in all districts in which I have served, except in certain sub-montane strips of Dera Ismail Khan. This principle of fixity is continued on revisions of assessment, although Government loses thereby potential revenue. Loss is incurred, because the extraordinary uncertainty of the yields, coupled with the poverty of agriculturists, constrain Government to pitch the assessment considerably below the half assets standard. Whether I am right or not, the practical difficulties of extending elasticity are believed by Government—a belief not shared by myself—to be insurmountable, and the people are accustomed to fixity and prefer the ills they know of to ills unknown, so I suppose the present system will be continued.

---

[1] The Secretary of State, I believe, has consented to the publication of the Report, and it may appear before the present century ends.

'Now in this Inquiry it has been established that in widely separated tracts inhabited by widely differing tribes of peasant owners on well-lands as on rain lands, indebted owners borrow, even after good or average harvests, food grain in winter and spring and seed at sowing times, because their creditors appropriate a large part of their crops from the threshing-floor in full or part payment of debts previously incurred, or of interest due on such debts. The loss of part of the yield compels many of these owners to pay their revenue a month or so afterwards by further borrowing. If this is the case in good seasons with already indebted owners, it is also the case in bad seasons with some hitherto debt-free owners.'

Mr. Thorburn continues :—

Borrowing to pay land revenue.

'The problem then is, how can the State, without a change in its land-revenue system, reduce borrowing from money-lenders? The question of restricting unnecessary borrowing by contracting credit will be dealt with presently. Here I am considering what may loosely be called necessary borrowing. It is, of course, outside the power of Government to feed hungry peasants whenever harvests are below average or fail entirely. All that Government can do is, when drought produces famine, to find life-sustaining work near their homes for the able-bodied starving, and to gratuitously feed those physically incapable of labour. That the State is already pledged to do, and does. But with respect to borrowing to pay land revenue, to supply seed grain, and to replace plough cattle, the State can, and ought to, I think, do much more than it now does. I offer some remarks on each of these subjects, and shall first deal with borrowing to pay land revenue.

'That is a class of debt which the State, by its deliberate preference for fixity over elasticity, has to some extent driven the peasantry to incur. It is idle to say that zemindars are thriftless, quarrelsome, or extravagant, and have themselves to blame for their indebtedness. The evidence in this Inquiry brings home none of these charges, except to some small extent thriftlessness, and even if all of them were deserved, we have to deal with human nature as it is, and the obligation would still lie on the Government to so adjust its land-revenue system as to obviate all reason for unnecessary borrowing from usurers. I say "unnecessary borrowing," for do what we will the sáhúkár will always be a necessity to small farmers. He existed before annexation in the villages of the Panjab; he was found in the Kurram valley, when we recently annexed it; he was found last year in Swát, and in fact we know that he is a necessity wherever there are settled populations, and continuous farming all the world over, even throughout Afghánistán. But before our time in the Panjab the village lender was, and in the other countries named he is still, a dependant, a servant of the rural community, and never what our system is making him in the Panjab villages—that community's master. Then, as regards fixity of land revenue and borrowing to pay it in short seasons, it is idle to contend that the rules for granting suspensions and remissions of land revenue demand supply the required amount of elasticity. The answer to such an assertion is found in the revenue and agricultural histories of thousands of villages in this or in probably any other Division of the Panjab, and in the detailed debt and alienation histories of the 742 holdings specially attested in this Inquiry. Prices-current, rain statistics, and the annual Revenue Reports of districts show that fodder and grain scarcities are of frequent recurrence, and the village note-books and revenue statistics generally prove that suspensions are rare and remissions still rarer. It may be said that recent rules are more liberal, giving Collectors and Commissioners more latitude than formerly. Even so it is only here and there that an exceptionally strong, energetic, and sympathetic, Collector, helped by exceptionally good Tahsíldárs may, by comprehensive suspensions, followed by considerate remissions, save an appreciable percentage of their indebted peasants from having to borrow privately to pay the revenue. But such Collectors and Tahsíldárs are exceptional, laws and rules have to be made for and worked by average officials, and all officials have multifarious unavoidable duties which must be done. Thus from want of forethought, positive ignorance of facts, want of time, or perhaps even a disinclination to do more than the minimum obligatory, Collectors often will not or do not arrange suspensions in time, or work out remission cases with that amplitude and exactness which superior authority requires. All such work throws much additional labour on the already burdened district staff, and is naturally distasteful to average minds. Then, too, the State must have its land revenue, and is reasonably averse to suspensions and remissions, which upset budget arrangements and reduce revenue. Since I have been Commissioner of this Division, the Siálkot district, during Colonel Montgomery's *régime* (1888–94), had a Collector and several Tahsíldárs possessed of all the exceptional qualifications noted above, and yet in those years I cannot discover that any revenue was suspended or remitted. In fact, for the whole district, the revenue of which is now fifteen lakhs, I make out that in the last thirty years only Rs.6,450 have been suspended, and Rs.1,694 remitted, all on account of damage done by hail. In that period there have been several prolonged fodder famines and quite a dozen poor harvests.'

Later, in the same report, he goes on to indicate why zemindars prefer the saukars to Government when borrowing to replace cattle, and says:—

'Next as to borrowing for seed grain and to replace cattle:—Act XII. of 1884 was passed to enable agriculturists to so borrow from Government and an allotment is annually made to each district for that purpose. In few districts, I believe, is the small allotment made fully utilised, and practically, so far as my experience goes, peasants prefer to obtain money for cattle from private lenders rather than from the State. They prefer to do this in the teeth of the fact that Government takes 6¼ per cent. interest a year on such loans, counting the interest from the harvest succeeding that in which loan was made, whereas sáhúkárs take from 25 per cent. to 37·8 per cent. or more a year, either charge interest at a daily rate from date on which loan was made, or at a monthly or annual rate—broken periods being treated as full periods—and also deduct from the sum lent one anna in the rupee as discount. The explanation is that to borrow, say, Rs.50 from Government for a yoke of oxen, involves personal inconvenience, uncertainty of result of application, considerable delay, and generally the necessity of conciliating various ministerial servants of Government, first at the Tahsil, then in the village, and sometimes at District headquarters as well. Then repayment is exacted at fixed amounts and times. Further, average Collectors and Tahsíldárs do not encourage loans for cattle and seed, because each case gives much trouble, and the security is not always good—for tenants as well as owners are eligible for such loans—and none but the neediest men require them. In such circumstances the borrower naturally prefers his own sáhúkár, who lives in or near his village and lends him what he wants in one short interview, whereas did he borrow from Government he might be kept moving between home and the Tahsil or perhaps even District headquarters as well, for two or three months, and eventually be refused a loan. The same may be said of loans for seed, but as Rs.5 or Rs.10 should meet a small holder's seed requirements seed-borrowing from a sáhúkár has comparatively insignificant consequences for the debtor. The instructions and rules under the Agriculturists' Loan Act, 1884, Revenue Circular 55, paragraphs 12–14, and in Appendix III. to the Circular are fairly liberal except that unnecessary delay is caused by the obligation laid on the Tahsíldár to refer each application to the Collector for orders (Rule 8), but even were Tahsíldárs empowered to grant loans without such reference few would, without strong encouragement, take action. Whatever the reason, it is a fact that Acts and Rules are almost a dead letter. If paragraph 18 of Report and Appendix XIV. be compared it will be seen that loans for cattle by sáhúkárs aggregate Rs.68,449 for twelve villages against Rs.8,646 by Government for five hundred and thirty-five villages.'

We now come to the results of Mr. Thorburn's inquiry:—

In 474[1] villages in widely distant and differing tracts held by widely different tribes and clans are to be found the following results :—

'(*a*) Two hundred and ninety-seven villages out of four hundred and seventy-four were prosperous, or at least free from debt or alienations at time of Regular Settlement preceding late revisions.

'(*b*) Dividing the four hundred and seventy-four villages into three groups, those hopelessly, seriously, and slightly involved, moneylenders and traders held the following percentages of cultivated and of immediately alienable area (paragraphs 40 and 41 of Report) :—

Number of villages in each group, viz. A, B, and C (hopelessly, seriously, and slightly involved).		Area with Percentage.	
		Total cultivated.	Of which held by moneylenders.
A	126	64,094 100	27,765 43
B	210	143,149 100	29,672 20
C	138	94,676 100	5,456 6
Total ...	474	301,919 100	62,893 20
Add—			
(*a*) Mortgaged without possession to moneylenders.		...	2,826
(*b*) Alienated to "traders not also practising moneylending" who cultivate through tenants		...	1,759
Grand Total		301,919	67,478 22
Compare percentage on area admitted		271,518	67,478 25

'(*c*) The present indebtedness to moneylenders of these three groups of villages is approximately as follows :—

		Rs.
Group A estimated amount of unsecured debts	...	6,84,398
" B " " " "	...	10,77,105
" C " " " "	...	2,16,500
Total ...	...	Rs. 19,78,003

[1] 'Five hundred and thirty-five villages were inquired into, but here I am excluding the sixty-one referred to in para. 37 of Report.'—S. S. T.

Add—		
Debt secured on mortgages with possession	...	18,75,066
Debt secured on simple mortgages now existing	...	1,18,678
Total Indebtedness	...	39,66,762
Add purchase-money of lands sold to moneylenders	...	7,61,136
Grand Total	...	Rs. 47,27,898

'(*d*) The information given above under (*b*) and (*c*) for the Circles is as follows for the twelve involved villages attested holding by holding:—

	Total cultivated area in acres	...	18,771
Of which alienated (with percentage) to ...	Moneylenders ...	...	4,890 36
	New Agriculturists	...	585 4
	Old Agriculturists ...	...	1,804 8
	Total alienations in acres	...	7,229 58
	Total cost of acquisition	...	Rs. 2,98,097
	Unsecured debt still owed	...	1,01,229
	Total debts incurred	...	Rs. 3,99,326

'(*e*) In the above twelve villages out of 742 families 566 are now practically ruined or heavily involved — the beginnings of both conditions usually dating from after 1871 — and out of the whole number of families who were at any time indebted (650) only 13, or two per cent., have succeeded in extricating themselves—in three of these cases release was due to external causes; as regards the other ten there is no evidence.'

Mr. Thorburn's conclusions on the origins of the indebtedness are thus set forth :—

'If it be possible to generalise from the results obtained from the detailed Inquiry into seven hundred and forty-two holdings, the conclusions are that, given a holding large enough to support an average family (say, three adults and two children) in an average year the ordinary beginnings of debt are :—

'(*a*) By borrowing food grain after a short harvest and failing to repay the debt with all interest due to the next Rabi harvest, either because that crop was short or debtor careless and creditor calculatingly unexacting, or because creditor's terms were exceptionally hard.

'(*b*) By raising money to meet a misfortune, usually death of cattle, and failing to repay the debt as in case (*a*).

'(*c*) By causing Sáhúkár to pay the revenue demand, this being a subsidiary and contributory cause commonly incident to an owner already indebted, and consequent on the creditor acting as if he had a first lien on the crop.

'(*d*) Serious debt being incurred, the loss of status and pauperisation which often follow are generally due to hard terms imposed by creditors, their severity being a consequence of our present system of civil justice as administered.

'(*e*) In the case of landlord-holders or yeomen, partly self-cultivating and partly cultivating through tenants, the course of this decline and fall is much the same, the beginnings of debt arising from their practice of living up to their incomes in good or average years, and continuing to live in much the same style by borrowing in short years.'

Remedial measures—both urgent and minor—were suggested, and upon them the Act was framed. In commending these remedies, Mr. Thorburn makes a statement which is pathetic in its revelation of the difficulties encountered by a humane and earnest official if he desires to reform abuses. Our system has made no provision for such men. Systems which are regarded by their authors as all-sufficing in themselves and Holy-of-Holies in character, necessarily have no place in them for the Thorburns of the Panjab, and can only just endure the Cottons of Assam. 'In the last thirty-nine paragraphs,' says Mr. Thorburn :—

'I have in places exceeded my brief by suggesting relief measures. To do so was almost unavoidable, the disease sometimes indicating the remedy. My real reason was, however, different. With thirty-one years of service behind me, during the last twelve of which I had made ineffectual efforts to induce Government to face and decide the agrarian problem, I felt that if this attempt should fail, my Indian career itself would be a failure, and that, if so, I might regard the case as hopeless and retire disappointed. So feeling and believing that I had some claim to speak with authority—having passed all my service in constant intercourse with the people and in attempts to better their circumstances—I have ventured, in addition to answering His Honour's questions, to put forward some of the remedial or relief measures, which stand out as most urgent from amongst those suggested by the facts established or the evidence collected in this Inquiry.

'For many years now I have been representing in official papers and private publications—probably to my own disadvantage as a servant of Government—that persistence in inaction is an injustice to the people and a danger for ourselves. I have urged that the annually increasing indebtedness of "old agriculturists" and the continuous passing of their fields to moneylenders sufficed to prove *per se* that laws producing or permitting such evils are unsuitable laws for those whom they are meant to benefit, but in effect injure. Our civil legislation is in fact based on the assumption that the large majority of men are thrifty, intelligent, and business-minded—a nation of Khatris, as it were—whereas the converse is the truth. The many are improvident, stupid, and incapable of comprehending figures or the consequences or even meaning of any but the simplest contracts carrying immediate material results. The few are men of business, inheritors for generations of the commercial instinct, to whom gain is the great object of life. Naturally, then, our system operates not only in this Division, but all over British India,—wherever special laws do not exist,—exactly as this Inquiry shows that the system has been operating in this Division. That system facilitates the passing of the property of the ignorant many to the astute few, fosters usury, punishes ignorance and stupidity, and rewards business qualifications and education—now a costly thing rarely within the reach of peasants.

'I think that this Inquiry, so far as it has gone, proves that we must forthwith amend our system so far as zemindars are concerned. We must, in fact, legislate and administer *down* to their needs and capacities.

'In the four selected Circles quite half the "old agriculturists" are already ruined beyond redemption in one hundred and twenty-six villages, but the other owners can still be saved, and communities still fairly free from debt and degradation can be kept free. The same is probably the case elsewhere in the Panjab. Government cannot afford to let our peasantry sink to a condition analogous to that of the Russian mughiks—analogous, but with this great difference, that in Russia landlords, creditors, and Government are all Russians, whereas in India a handful of foreigners rule the tens of millions, and through the action of these foreigners the peasant masses are now largely dependants of moneylenders, their former servants, who are generally alien to them by caste or tribe and for nearly half the Panjab by religion as well.'

I put this record of ill-doing in the forefront of my selected examples as it is the only one I know of where remedy—if what is done should prove to be a remedy—has been applied on the initiative of a single officer, and without an insurrection. The last-quoted paragraph will show that, comparatively prompt as was the application of the remedy when the disease had been fully diagnosed, it was not in time to save many of the sufferers. 'In the four selected Circles quite half the "old agriculturists" are already ruined beyond redemption in one hundred and twenty-six villages.'

THE NORTH-WESTERN PROVINCES AND OUDH.

As Lord Dufferin's period of rule was drawing to a close, his British conscience began to trouble him concerning the condition of the people under his governance. Sir William Hunter's forty millions of starving folk, Sir Charles Elliott's statement respecting the never-ceasing hunger of half the agricultural population, and other observations of a like kind, combined with the political fervour which the National Congress was causing, made Lord Dufferin uncomfortable. Just before his last year of office began—that is, on August 17, 1887—the Viceroy issued a circular in which he said: 'The attention of the Government of India having been called to the frequency with which the assertion has been repeated that the greater proportion of the population of India suffer from a daily insufficiency of food, it is considered desirable to ascertain whether this impression is wholly untrue or partially true; and in the latter case, to attain some idea of the extent to which it is so, and how far any remedial measures can be suggested.' So far as can be ascertained at the time when the above sentence was written, nobody has said that 'the greater proportion of the population of India suffer from a daily insufficiency of food'—that is to say over one hundred millions were daily hungry and unfed the year through: now, however, this is being said, and said, too, with a good show of authority. Lord Dufferin ordered that 'an inquiry should be quietly and confidentially instituted by the Department of Land Records and Agriculture in communication with selected officials of experience and judgment, care being taken that whatever evidence is brought forward should be of a positive and trustworthy character.'

The inquiry was made. In October, 1888, fifteen months after the instructions were given, and two months before Lord Dufferin left India, a Resolution was published. While not denying there was suffering, the Resolution declared there was no occasion for undue alarm. I am not, however, concerned here with the Resolution, but with Appendix A, which professes to consist of a '*Précis* of the Reports received on the inquiry made into the condition of the lower classes of the population.' The Reports themselves have never been published. They are marked 'Confidential.' In response to a request made by the late Mr. Bradlaugh for their publication, the Secretary of State for India laid the volumes (or some of them —the Madras volume, for example, is not included) on the Table of the House of Commons, and they can, I believe, be consulted in the Library of the Legislature. On p. 80, Appendix A, the following paragraph respecting the district of Etah in the North-Western Provinces appears: 'Mr. Crooke, Collector of Etah (area 1,739 square miles; population 756,528), whose peculiar knowledge of agricultural life lends a great value to his remarks, considers the peasantry to be a robust, apparently well-fed, population, and dressed in a manner which quite comes up to their traditional ideas of comfort. In spite of the abnormally high price of food-grains, there has been no sudden increase of offences against poverty [*sic*, ? property], nor did the number of beggars seem unusually great. Mr. Crooke does not believe that anything like a large percentage of the people in Etah, or in any other district of the Provinces, is habitually under-fed. There are times, of course, when the small cultivator and field labourer do suffer privation; but this is a very different thing from habitual privation. Indebtedness is prevalent, but the fact seems to be that with the agricultural classes a normal state of indebtedness is quite consistent with the possibility of passing a life of comparative comfort.' This is what the Government of India wishes the public interested in the condition of the people to believe Mr.

Crooke, 'whose peculiar knowledge of agricultural life lends a great value to his remarks,' said, and that it is a fair summary of his views. The reader shall judge. Mr. Crooke, it is true, did use the expressions abstracted in the summary quoted, but he said a great deal more, and gave illustrations which wholly remove the impression his comments (as given) are intended to create. I quote from Mr. Crooke exactly in the order in which his remarks appear in the Report from the North-Western Provinces.

A FEW OF MR. CROOKE'S FACTS.

1. (P. 21). 'The following estimate is the result of a recent meeting of the most experienced cultivators and agents of the Raja of Awa [the estate of a great land-owner managed by the North-Western Government]. I collected them together and asked them to make an estimate of the income and expenditure of a man—owner of one pair of oxen, and a single plough, and cultivating a patch of average land irrigated from a well. The following was the result. The holding of such a tenant would be ten *pucka* bighas, or about 5½ acres. This would be cropped half in the rabi (spring), and half in the kharif (autumn). The crops grown, out-turn, and value of the produce, of such a holding would be approximately as follows:—

Income.	Rs.	a.	p.	*Expenditure.*	Rs.	a.	p.
Kharif Harvest ...	129	8	0	Rent	75	0	0
Rabi Harvest ...	84	8	0	Seed-grain	18	8	0
				Other Expenses ...	79	10	0
				Balance	45	14	0
Total ...	Rs.214	0	0	Total ...	Rs.214	0	0

Mr. Crooke then, unfairly, proceeds to suppose that a family of four only (five is the lowest average which should be taken) have to subsist on this Rs.45 14a. per annum—that is Rs.11½ each (or, in English money, seventeen shillings per head for a whole year), and adds: The family 'would consume three seers of grain per diem, which, at an average cost of 25 seers per rupee, would be Rs.43 per annum.' At the time Mr. Crooke reports, however, grain was only 17 seers per rupee! He adds: 'Clothes for the family would cost Rs.8.' The cultivator's 'expenditure thus on the absolute necessaries of life would be about Rs.51 per annum; thus resulting in

AN ANNUAL DEFICIT OF ABOUT Rs.5.'

But, in that year, the deficit was—judging from food-prices—nearly Rs.20, and, let the reader carefully remark, no provision is made for salt (at least five annas per head per annum should be expended), ghi, or condiments, or relishes of any kind with which to flavour an exclusively vegetable and tasteless diet. It is true Mr. Crooke proceeds to speak of the products which might be obtained from a buffalo, but, in his detailed estimate, he makes no allowance for the purchase or keep of a buffalo; he also alludes to the vegetables with which the food mentioned may be eked out. Nothing is here for chatties, bedding, clothes, medicine in times of sickness, well-ropes, expenses for religion, marriages, funerals. Yet were the officials (English officials) content.

The careful inquiry respecting these small landholders, each with a well and a pair of bullocks, and each cultivating five-and-a-half acres of land, shows that even in a good year they

ARE STEADILY SUBMERGED, HAVING NOT ENOUGH FOR FOOD AND WARM CLOTHING.

In a bad year, their condition must be most terrible. Yet with these facts in the very forefront of his report, Mr. Crooke is quoted as fully satisfied with the condition of the people! In such fashion are statements prepared when the parties responsible for the things described are themselves the reporters, and when there is no public opinion, or any one with power to call them to account.

2. (P. 22.) 'Comparing the periods before and after the Mutiny, there has been a rise of 45 per cent. in grain, 52 per cent. in bejhar (barley and peas), and 38 per cent. in jaur.' Of course, if all the grain, or a large portion, were grown for export, prosperity would seem to have marked out the cultivator for its own. But very, very, little is exported; the grain is grown for home consumption and to pay the heavy Government rent, or, rather, to be exact, to pay the Government rent, and *then* to go towards maintaining the lives of the cultivator and his family. The grain does not go farther in payment of rent now than it did forty years ago, owing to 'the considerable enhancements of rents which followed the current settlements in this and neighbouring districts.' That is to say, if any benefit accrued from increasing prices the Government took it.

3. (P. 23.) '. . . the assertion which is universally believed by natives, that

THE CULTIVATOR IS NOT SO WELL OFF NOWADAYS

as at the time of the Mutiny.' No doubt many causes are at work. '(1) The action of the Civil Courts; (2) the weakening of the soil by over-cropping under the stimulus of canal irrigation; (3) the excessive growth of the population under our rule of peace; and (4) the rise in rents, combined with the breaking up of inferior lands, may be all factors in the problem.' Nos. 1 and 2 are distinctly faults of administration; as to No. 3, for thirteen years prior to 1881 (latest Census figures available), there was no increase of population; the fourth reason is one which the Government might have obviated if they had paid due regard to Indian industries, and had not thrown all but an infinitesimal proportion of the people on the soil.

4. (P. 28.) As to clothes, 'the women and children are much worse off than the men.

IT IS UNUSUAL TO FIND A VILLAGE WOMAN WHO HAS ANY WRAPS AT ALL.

Most of them have to pass the night as best they can in their day clothes—a cotton petticoat, wrapper, and bodice. As a rule they and their children sleep, in the cold weather, during the warm afternoons and the early hours of the night, and

FROM MIDNIGHT TO DAWN COWER OVER A FIRE OF RUBBISH

in the yard of the dwelling-house.'

5. (P. 29.) 'It would be foolish optimism to deny that there are times and seasons when the small cultivator and field labourer suffer privation. This has been only too common recently.'

6. *Prevalence of Fever due to bad construction of canals and defective drainage and to insufficient and unsuitable food* (p. 31). 'This prevalence of fever and other diseases which originate in malaria, implies a considerable prevalence of sickness and low health, with disability to perform agricultural work. It is hardly too much to say that

A GREAT MAJORITY OF THE RURAL POPULATION PASS THROUGH AT LEAST ONE OR TWO ATTACKS OF FEVER DURING THE YEAR:

in fact in many cases the disease has a tendency to become chronic or constitutional. In many villages in the most malarious tracts the interruption to work produced by these causes is very serious. There is also evidence that

THIS PREVALENCE OF MALARIA IS OF RECENT GROWTH,

and is coincident with the development of canal irrigation followed by a rise of the water-level in the subsoil. This can only be remedied by large and costly works of drainage—a subject which is yearly becoming more pressing. It is obvious that the general question of the general health of the population is closely connected with the special question now under consideration. The prevalence of disease and ill-health may, it is true, be attributed more to defective sanitation and water-logging of the subsoil than to deficient nutrition; but it is obvious that food which, in nature and quantity, may be perfectly suitable to a man in vigorous health, may be the very reverse to a person who is exposed to periodical attacks of fever and ague, and the *malaise* and lowness of health and spirits which are the usual concomitants of disease. Thus, for instance, bread made of barley or bejhar, is, on the high authority of Dr. Parkes, "either from its laxative qualities or from the imperfect separation of the sharp husks, particularly unsuited to dysenteric cases," which is in this district one of the common sequelæ of fever.'

SAMPLE CULTIVATORS WITH THEIR RECORD OF RACK-RENTING.

7. (Pp. 31, 32.) RUP RAM, Brahmin, aged sixty years, cultivates seventeen acres.

BALANCE SHEET FOR 1887–8.

Receipts.	Rs.	a.	p.	*Expenditure.*	Rs.	a.	p.
Kharif Harvest ...	175	0	0	Rent	306	0	0
Rabi Harvest ...	146	9	0	Seed-grain	50	0	0
Sale of ghi	20	0	0				
Total ...	Rs.341	9	0	Total ...	Rs.356	0	0
Or, £20 0s. 9d.				Or, £21 0s. 0½d.			

There is thus an adverse balance of 19s. 3d. before a single mouthful of grain is provided for food! See the terrible rack-rent which the man had to pay, *and did pay.* After making allowance for bare food (without condiments) and clothing, Mr. Crooke says: 'Thus their expenditure exceeded their income by Rs.138 9a., to recoup which they have to borrow, or sell their ornaments.' Sir John Gorst, when Under-Secretary of State for India, said the Indian Government never rack-rent their tenants. What explanation has he to offer of this sweeping away of ninety-five per cent. of the yield for rent? The Government took half of what was levied. Sir James Fergusson, replying to a question in the House of Commons, thought this case was all right because the rent was paid. How the money or grain was obtained to keep the cultivator and his family alive, or whether they were kept alive, was, apparently, a matter of no concern to—

(1) The Collector of Etah,
(2) Sir Auckland Colvin, the Lieutenant-Governor of the North-Western Provinces,
(3) The Government of India,
(4) The India Office,
(5) The House of Commons.

All of them are seemingly callous and certainly heedless.

In this family, it is to be noted, there is only one little child, the household consisting of three men, two women, and one girl. In the further instances to be quoted this same feature will be observed,—small families or no families at all.

8. (Pp. 33, 34.) Bakhsha, Chamar, aged forty-five, cultivates seven acres.

Balance Sheet for 1887–88.

Income.	Rs.	a.	p.	*Expenditure.*	Rs.	a.	p.
Kharif Harvest ...	12	0	0	Diet expenses ...	50	0	0
Rabi Harvest ...	78	0	0	Rent	40	0	0
Sale of ghi	15	0	0	Seed-grain	15	0	0
Sale of cow-dung ...	2	0	0	Food for animals ...	5	0	0
				Agricultural implements	3	0	0
				Household Furniture	2	0	0
				Marriage and funeral expenses	2	0	0
				Clothing	7	0	0
Total ...	Rs.102	0	0	Total ...	Rs.124	0	0
Or, £6 7s. 6d.				Or, £8 8s. 4d.			

'Thus their expenditure exceeds their income by £1 15s. 10d. *which they have to recoup by incurring debts.*' It may be that the oxen which treadeth out the corn shall not be muzzled, but it is quite clear that the Indian cultivators shall not keep soul and body together out of the land they cultivate. If, as Regulations and Resolutions declare shall be done, the State landlord had, in this case, remitted half or two-thirds of the rent, the cultivators could, without falling into the clutches of the moneylender, have at least had food enough to eat. The family consists of one adult, one minor, two women, and one girl. The girl is of marriageable age, and, possibly, Rs.20 will be spent on her marriage.

9. (Pp. 35, 36.) Of the family of CHETA, aged thirty-five, who are cultivators and labourers, it is declared their earnings are Rs.50 per year (four in family—Rs.12¼ per head), their household furniture worth less than two shillings, and when wheat is produced in their fields they do not eat it, but 'sell it for purchasing for their food grain of lower quality, and for payment of their rent.'

10. (Pp. 36, 37.) ASA, aged fifty, a weaver, five in family, two men, two women, one girl.

Income.	Rs.	a.	p.	*Expenditure.*	Rs.	a.	p.
Average income from weaving cloth ...	48	0	0	Food	40	0	0
				Repayment of loan...	4	0	0
				Clothing	5	0	0
Total ...	Rs.48	0	0	Total ...	Rs.49	0	0
Or, £2 12s. 4d.				Or, £2 13s. 8d.			

Here, again, there is actually less than 13s. 4d. per head per annum for all purposes.

11. (Pp. 50, 51.) PARSI, Lodha, aged sixty-two, labourer, earns Rs.16 per annum, his daughter for grinding grain earns Rs.11 4a. The joint income is Rs.27 4a., which is just enough to buy two seers of grain a day, *and leaves nothing for any other purpose*. 'No children are to be married: he had one son and four daughters, who

have been all married. Through poverty in the marriage of his daughters, he had recourse to a less formal way of marriage, viz., *dola*, *i.e.*, he went to the house of the daughter's intended husband and consummated the marriage by giving only a small sum of Rs.5 or Rs.6.'

12. (Pp. 55, 56.) Of NEWAL SINGH, cultivator of twenty-four acres (for which he pays Rs.214 rent), and cart-owner, it is shown that he can save Rs.25 a year; but, somewhat inconsequentially, it is added: 'Generally, he is not able to spare grain for sowing at either of the two harvests; he has to borrow it from the mahajun, having had to pay interest of two annas per rupee for every half-year [25 per cent. per annum], and in calculating the value of grain to allow a reduction of one seer in the current price rate at the time of borrowing, and an increase of one seer at repaying.'

13. (Pp. 59, 60.) In the case of JHABNA, oilman caste, aged forty-five, cultivator and cart-owner, it is shown that he ought to make a saving of Rs.43 per annum, and it is added: 'He owes Rs.600 of debt. . . . He attributes these debts to decrease in the produce of his land and to family expenses.' He is in arrears with his rent, and 'has always to borrow grain for sowing at both harvests.' Under these circumstances it is difficult to see where his alleged savings come in.

14. (Pp. 64, 65.) HANSI, Gararia, aged sixty, earns just enough to provide food for himself and two women. 'His household furniture consists of nothing more than a cot.'

15. (Pp. 68, 69.) BIK RAM, Ahir, cultivator of four-and-a-half acres, requires Rs.116 for bare maintenance and seed for sowing, and has only Rs.38½ for the purpose! Upon this case, Mr. Crooke sapiently says: 'This cultivator, like his neighbours in this village, is hard up, *and can hardly make both ends meet.*' The dull tedium of Indian administration is relieved with a flash of humour. A minus income of Rs.77 8a. is an example of how one 'can hardly make both ends meet.'

16. (Pp. 73, 74.) Hira, Lodha, aged forty, cultivator of twenty-four acres. Here is his balance-sheet for 1887–88:—

Income.	Rs.	a.	p.	*Expenditure.*	Rs.	a.	p.
Kharif Harvest ...	51	0	0	Rent	72	8	0
Rabi Harvest ...	111	0	0	Seed-corn ...	18	0	0
				Food	120	0	0
				Clothing	24	0	0
Total ...	Rs.162	0	0	Total ...	Rs.234	8	0
Or, £10 2s. 6d.				Or, £14 13s. 2d.			

There was thus a balance of £4 10s. 8d. *on the wrong side.* 'Hira is not in arrears of rent. He, however, is in debt amounting to£15 12s. 6d.' I should think he *is* in debt. If he were not he would not be living to tell his story.

Some of Mr. Cadell's Facts about Muttra.

The Secretariat summary, which satisfied Lord Dufferin, and doubtless made him very proud of the results of his inquiry, says of the District of Muttra (population 671,690), also in the North-West Provinces:—'Mr. Cadell, Collector of Muttra, believes that the agriculturists, even after the failure of the Kharif harvest, were able to hold their own; but he admits that the condition of the labourers was worse, and that they had been severely tried by the past cold weather.' Such the head-quarters' gloss. Now, let us see exactly what is reported from Muttra:—

1. (P. 4.) 'A very noticeable feature in all the statements is

THE CESSATION OF ANY PURCHASES EXCEPT OF ABSOLUTE NECESSARIES OF LIFE.

The purchase of cloth is at once suspended in years of difficulty, and the weaver class competes with the rest of the labouring class for any work that may be going. . . . Sickness, too, added to the distress; and, when easy earthwork was opened at Brindaban, some fever-stricken people were noticed who could

HARDLY CARRY EVEN QUARTER-FILLED BASKETS.'

2. (Pp. 14–16.) KAMLE, Chamar, of Jait, thirty years old, family of six, cultivates ten acres, and, not placing his dependence upon one kind of produce only, sows seed of six different kinds—juwar, cotton, bajri, indigo, hemp, and ramas. Sometimes works for hire at 1d. and 2d. per day! 'Kamle eats twice in the day when he can, and in default once.' 'His wife has no silver ornaments, only pewter ones. He has to borrow a plough when required.' This is the balance-sheet given for him for 1887–88:—

Receipts.	Rs.	a.	p.	*Expenditure.*	Rs.	a.	p.
Crops	58	0	0	Rent	82	0	0
Ghi	22	12	0	Weeding	6	8	0
Labour	15	4	0	Food	58	12	0
				Clothing	7	8	0
Total ...	Rs.91	0	0	Total ...	Rs.104	12	0
Or, £5 18s. 9d.				Or, £6 11s. 0d.			

'The result is Kamle would have to borrow 18s. 3d. to meet his expenses.' 'He suffers from an absentee landlord.' Half of the absentee landlords live in Britain.

3. (Pp. 16–18.) ABE RAM, forty years of age, family of five, cultivates about nine acres. 'When he had grain the family ate five seers daily; at other times and now, when grain is dear, only three seers or less.' 'He ate the bajra before it was ripe.' 'He has no blanket.' And yet he is a farmer, tilling nearly nine acres! Why has he no blanket? An examination of his balance-sheet, showing how

THE LANDLORD TOOK NINETY-NINE PER CENT. OF THE GROSS PRODUCE FOR RENT,

will help to supply the needed answer. Lord Dufferin's administration had half of this sum.

'Abe Ram's yearly account stands thus':—

Income.	Rs.	a.	p.	*Expenditure.*	Rs.	a.	p.
Sale of crops ...	70	4	0	Rent	68	15	0
Sale of milk ...	18	0	0	Seed and weeding...	9	8	0
Receipts for labour	15	0	0	Food	44	0	0
				Clothing	7	8	0
Total ...	Rs.108	4	0	Total ...	Rs.129	15	0

Here there are Rs.26 11a., nearly sixty per cent. of the amount required for food, deficient.

This instance is remarkably instructive. Sir Auckland Colvin (by the hand of his Chief Secretary, Mr. J. R. Reid) thus summarises it in a letter specially addressed to the Government of India:—

'14. ABE RAM (p. 16) is a Thakur, cultivating about nine acres; his family consists of himself, his wife, and three sons, one a child; he has a male and female buffalo, and a cow, of which the milk is used; green food was also mixed during the winter with the flour. The family appears to be above want.'

In the whole history of bureaucratic obscurantism, was there ever seen such a travesty of facts as is contained in the above sentence? No notice is taken in this summary of these facts:—

(*a*) Ninety-nine per cent. of the gross produce was taken for rent;

(*b*) Rs.26 11a. was lacking of the amount needed simply to provide food and clothing;

(*c*) The moneylender would not advance Abe Ram a pie, as he already owed Rs.50 to Rs.60;

(*d*) The family were so hard-pressed for food that they 'ate the bajri before it was ripe';

(*e*) The man himself had no blanket, nor does it appear that his wife and children had any warm clothing;

(*f*) His household furniture is set down at Rs.2 (English 2s. 8d.) in value;

(*g*) Although he and his son did manual labour and earned Rs.15 4a., there was nevertheless the minus balance of Rs.26 11a.

It is of this man, and of a family so situated, that Sir Auckland Colvin (through Mr. J. R. Reid) complacently says:—'The family appears to be above want.'

4. (Pp. 18–20.) HIRA SINGH (thirty) and BHUBRA, brothers, both married, no children. Household, six in number, the two men and their wives, a cousin, and an aunt. The 'women have no ornaments.' 'Fields are irrigated from a pucka (first-class) well.' The income and expenditure account shows a debit balance of Rs.8 2a. 6p. Nevertheless, the brothers are declared to be well-to-do, 'their condition is better than either the Chamar of Jait or the Thakur of Naugam; they have more metal dishes and

CAN AFFORD A BLANKET.'

Actually, farmers in the North-Western Provinces (if they have no children) can afford a blanket!

5. (P. 6.) BHIKARI, son of Rupar, labourer, six in family; ill for four months; wife and daughter grass-sellers, son also at work; 'the son's wife, to relieve the family, returned to her parents' house.' 'During the rains [the most trying part of the year] the household had only one regular meal a day.' 'In other years they spent Rs.4 or Rs.5 on winter clothing, but none this time.'

Many similar instances might be given, such as that of TUNDA, son of Bulwant, cultivator of five acres; 'on the betrothal of his eldest daughter he received a present of Rs.12, and paid this sum to the zemindar as part of his Kharif rent,' and in the cold weather this small farmer 'slept in a thatched room alongside his bullock.'

SOME SAMPLE FACTS FROM THE ETAWAH DISTRICT.

Of the Etawah District (population 722,371), the summary says:—'Mr. Alexander, Collector of Etawah, saw a good many people in March last whose appearance showed that they had been suffering from an insufficiency of food; but, writing in May, he says that none but actual paupers are in real distress. After careful inquiry Mr. Alexander is of opinion that the bulk of the cultivators in the villages selected for investigation have not been suffering from want of food, and do not ordinarily do so; but that, owing to high prices, the labourers and a few of the smaller or exceptionally unfortunate cultivators have been pressed between December, 1887, and March, 1888.' Mark: Mr. Alexander merely says that 'the bulk'—whatever he may mean by that expression—'have not been suffering from want of food,' but a good many have been suffering. So it will appear, when we observe what his detailed report contains:—

1. '*In all ordinary years* I should say that cultivators

LIVE FOR ONE-THIRD OF THE YEAR ON ADVANCES FROM MONEYLENDERS,

and in unfavourable years they have either very largely to increase the amount of the debt to the bohra,[1] or to sell off jewelry, cattle, and anything else that can possibly be spared.'

2. When a succession of bad crops has to be faced no money is forthcoming from the moneylender, 'and then, no doubt, the average cultivator suffers severely from insufficiency of food.'

3. In the village Marhapur, 'the fifty-five

CULTIVATING HOUSEHOLDS WERE ALL IN DEBT

at the close of the year for sums varying from Rs.800 to Rs.10, and the day-labourers for sums varying from Rs.18 to Rs.2: most of the farmers were also obliged to part with jewelry or cattle.'

4. BEJAI, Gararia, holds 9½ acres, family of seven, 'the produce of his fields' was 'just sufficient to maintain his family; a marriage, a burial, and the purchase of plough

[1] Bohra, mahajun, bania, sowkar—all words signifying moneylender.

cattle necessitated the pledging of nearly all the family jewelry and an incurring of further debt to the extent of Rs.100. 'Towards the end of the year the family were in difficulties,' and in the next year, when the kharif turned out badly, '*they were reduced to absolute want.* For the greater part of January and February

THEY GOT NO REGULAR MEALS, BUT LIVED ON CARROTS AND EDIBLE WILD PLANTS.'

'There can be no doubt but that during the first six months of 1295 fasli [revenue year: A.D. 1887–88] they have lead a very miserable life, and though better off for a short period after the rabi, are likely to come to absolute want again before the kharif is cut.' Mr. Alexander does not state whether any remission of rent was recommended in this instance. The presumption is the remission was *not* recommended and certainly not granted.

General Facts.

Fyzabad Division (p. 209). Cultivator, with one plough, family three; income Rs.73; food at 40 lbs. per rupee; balance available for food, Rs.45; deficiency, Rs.9 = 17 per cent.

(Ditto.) A Hanwára; income, Rs.32; three in family; available for food, Rs.22; required, Rs.54; deficiency, Rs.32 = 60 per cent.—a truly awful result.

(Ditto.) A day-labourer; income, Rs.47; three in family; available for food, Rs.37; required, Rs.54; deficiency, Rs.17 = 31 per cent.

Out of seven instances, four show most serious deficiencies: one, a petty dealer, is Rs.14 deficient; two have just enough; and one, a moneylender, shows a surplus.

Mr. H. M. Bird, Assistant Collector of Cawnpore (p. 126), says: 'I have calculated the cost of food of a male at £1 12s. per annum; of a female, £1 7s. 4d.; and a minor, 18s. 8d.' This shows more money for food than some expert writers on India allow for every purpose to an imagined comfortably-off family!

Now let me take a whole village, one of three hundred persons, in the Allahabad Division, near the seat of Government, and see what the record is there:—

The village is Akbarpursen, Cawnpore, 'for many years under the Court of Wards,' therefore under direct British supervision and, presumably, above the average. Year, 1888.

Cultivators.	Total Produce. Rs.	Cultivation Expenses. Rs.	Balance. Rs.	*Required for food alone.* Rs.	DEFICIENCY. Rs.
36 families—70 males, 50 females, 51 minors ...	4,323	1,733	2,590	3,678	1,088 32 per cent.
17 families, labourers and others. Allow Rs.50 per family, which is an outside estimate. (In ten families there are no children) ...	850	—	850	1,405	555 39 per cent.

'The rest of the inhabitants are Gorias, who work in boats and at ghats, and are well paid. Twelve families.'

The foregoing are merely sample facts. They have not been specially selected, but have been taken page by page as I went through the book in which they are recorded. A vastly larger number remain untouched by me. I brought many of them and some other facts which will be found in my chapter dealing with the economic condition of all India, to the attention, early in 1901, of Sir Antony Macdonnell, Lieutenant-Governor of the Provinces. In his reply, dated 'Government House, Naini Tal, May 22, 1901,' after regretting that by stress of business he had been unable to reply to me earlier, and, after commenting upon the life-loss in his Provinces during the famine in 1897, putting that loss in a more favourable light than I had done, His Honor remarks :—

'Generally speaking, you seem to me to take an unduly despondent view regarding the condition of the Indian peasant. At all events your description of his state does not correspond with my own knowledge. I am far from saying that there is no room for improvement; but he is not the starving creature some people seem to imagine. I think you are much mistaken as to the effect on the ryots' condition of the Government revenue and the view which you have expressed as to the heaviness of its incidence is not in accordance with my information. The chief causes of the ryots' difficulties lie—

'in the precariousness of the climate;

'in his indebtedness owing to his recklessness in expenditure on festivals, and to the ruinous rates of interest he pays for loans;

'in the minute subdivision of holdings owing to the concentration of the people in the most fertile regions and their unwillingness to move to fresh lands only a short way off; and

'in the insufficient facilities for irrigation.

'In the recommendations of the Famine Commission,[1] now before the Government of India, I trust some mitigation for these difficulties may be found.'

[1] Of which, it may be stated, Sir Antony was President. It was as President of that Commission my two communications were addressed to him.

Of the four reasons given for 'the ryots' difficulties,' so far as the first is concerned, India, with its regular seasons of rainfall, should suffer as little as any country in the world. Certainly it does not suffer from deficient rainfall now more than it did in former centuries; privation and dire need, however, are present now as they were never present before. Further, in the fourth reason Sir Antony suggests a remedy for the first. If the remedy be effective now it would have been effective in the past, and by so much as the duty of providing this remedy has been neglected, by that much at least has culpability been incurred. If storage tanks be included in the term irrigation, then is the guilt of successive administrations very great. This remedy has been indicated times and again. None would heed. Perhaps on the present occasion, too, none will heed.

The second reason assigned is not in accordance with the facts. I take the first twenty cases exactly in the order in which they appear in the record of the Government Inquiry in which reference is made to indebtedness. They do not sustain the assertion of the Lieutenant-Governor. In only two of these twenty cases—those on pages 55 and 61—are marriage 'and family expenses' put down as the occasion of the indebtedness. In one instance the indebtedness was the trifle of Rs.10, half already repaid in monthly instalments of one rupee. That is to say, ten per cent. of borrowings only are specifically for marriage expenses; this will be found to compare not unfavourably with Mr. Thorburn's particulars from the Panjab.

'Of seven hundred and forty-two families,' remarks Mr. Thorburn, 'only in three cases was marriage extravagance the cause of their serious indebtedness.' 'This inquiry shows that the common idea about the extravagance on marriages is not supported by evidence.'

'Unnecessary marriage expenses show a tendency year by year to decrease.' These statements are susceptible of statistical proof.

		Full Indebtedness.		Marriage Expenses.		Percentage.
Circle I.	...	Rs. 142,787	...	Rs. 9,491	...	6½
,, II.	...	179,853	...	12,418	...	7
,, III.	...	88,284	...	9,687	...	11
,, IV.	...	188,145	...	15,161	...	8

Average: Less than 8 per cent.

On the general indebtedness and its real cause, Mr. Thorburn is at distinct issue with the Lieutenant-Governor of the neighbouring Province; his opinion must be accepted, based, as it is, on personal and recent inquiry, as against what 'is not in accordance with the information' generally possessed by Sir Antony Macdonnell.

These are Mr. Thorburn's conclusions:—

'There was no general indebtedness in any village before 1871.'

'Seasonal vicissitudes and the beginnings of debt' stand in direct relationship one with the other.

'Indebtedness for small or careless holders begins with grain advances for food.'

'The four direct causes of peasant indebtedness are—

(1) Fluctuation in yields; and

(2) Losses of cattle—both usually consequences of seasonal vicissitudes;

(3) The *morcellement* of holdings from the growth of the agricultural population without increase in certain production for each holder and his family; and

(4) The obligation, under the fixity principle, . . . to pay land revenue, whether there be produce or not wherefrom to pay it.

'To permit the profits of husbandry to pass to moneylenders is an intolerable revolution of an odious kind never yet known in India, and yet it is exactly, as this Report will show, what our system is bringing about.

'Out of seven hundred and forty-two peasant farmers, whose cases were investigated, only in thirteen cases did a once-involved man recover his freedom.

'. . . The aggregate of debts incurred to pay the land revenue, one of the heaviest, and in one aspect the most serious, because least avoidable of the ascertained causes of peasant indebtedness.'

Average Revenue due from each Proprietary Family.	Average borrowing per family FOR LAND REVENUE in short years. (One year in three years during the last twenty-four years.)
Rs. 14	Rs. 17
47	26
26	15
25	35
32	38
31	20
10	6
10	16
5	9
6	5
15	13
18	5

'Out of 742 proprietary families—
444 were practically ruined—
193 from bad seasons, plus small holdings,
65 ,, extravagance or bad management,
9 ,, cases in Court,
85 ,, unascertainable causes,
142 ,, from a combination of the above four;
112 were seriously involved; and
186 are prosperous.'

In Circle I.: 'The kharif of 1877 failed, and for the three following years there was no really good harvest.'

In Circle II.: 'All these villages were prosperous in 1865.'

In Circle IV.: 'The villages at first were greatly over-assessed, and did not get full relief until 1865.'

Seventy-five, forty-six, and sixty-six of the owners in three villages are 'practically ruined,' and sixteen, ten, and ten are 'seriously in debt.'

'Some of the pettiest owners'—by dint of astonishing perseverance and endurance—'have preserved their inherited three or four acres unencumbered.'

The 'incapacity' exhibited by the cultivators was due to a threefold cause:—

'A want of thrift, due to heredity;
'Climate; and
'OUR SYSTEM.'

This is the summing up of one of the most capable

servants of the Crown who have served in India; they are the result of his personal inquiries.

The Madras Presidency contributes its quota of evidence. It is of a piece with that already cited, with that to be cited. More than half of the Presidency is comprised in the districts of Kistna, Nellore, Cuddapah, Kurnool, Bellary, Anantapur, North Arcot, South Arcot, Coimbatore, and Tinnevelly. There are records of 66,396 people obtaining loans of the moneylenders in 1889, 1890, and 1891. Of these only 3,025 persons borrowed for marriage expenses, that is, 4⅗ per cent. of the total number seeking loans. The borrowings were on this scale:—

	Borrowers.
Between Rs. 1 and Rs. 100	1,425
" 100 " 500	1,528
" 501 " 1,000	62
Over 1,000	10
Total	3,025

The particulars for Southern India give no countenance to the charge against the people of extravagance on marriage expenditure, though, even in India, the English comment applies:—

'Tis a poor heart that never rejoices.'

One further piece of evidence. The Commissioners who inquired into the causes of the riots in the Deccan more than a generation ago should have made it impossible for Sir Antony Macdonnell to take such a line in discussing the unhappy economic condition of India as he did in the passages above quoted. 'The result of the Commission's inquiries show that undue prominence has been given to the expenditure on marriage and other festivals as a cause of the ryot's indebtedness. The expenditure on such occasions may undoubtedly be called extravagant when compared with the ryot's means; but the occasions occur seldom, and, probably, in a course of years the total sum spent this way by any ryot is not larger than a man in his position is justified in spending on social and domestic pleasures.'

THE BOMBAY PRESIDENCY.

Here the glimpse behind the scenes will be treated somewhat differently from that which has been given of the Panjab and of the North-Western Provinces and Oudh. In the instances mentioned, with the exception of the passage by Mr. Vaughan Nash, official evidence obtained at first-hand is tendered, and that only. In regard to Bombay I take my facts from the remarkably able communications which, in the first half of 1901, have appeared in the *Times of India* of Bombay. The writer veils his personality under the letter "J." The position in regard to Bombay is practically the same as in the foregoing instances; all "J.'s" figures are taken from official records.[1]

Over-assessment of the land and over-stringency in collection, constituting a double evil, have had this effect in Bombay: 'they have brought the ryot to the verge of economic ruin, and have made him, what we find him to be all over the Presidency, more or less the helpless victim of the inclement seasons and the predial serf of the unrelenting sowkar.'

Behind the exceedingly beautiful gateway into India which the city of Bombay constitutes lie the most heavily-burdened and distressed peasant farmers in the Empire. In all the British dominions there are none

[1] It would not be right for me to make this, my first, reference to the contributions in question without at the same time paying my humble tribute to the conspicuous ability displayed in one and all of them. Under any *régime* but ours the writer of them would have found a high official position awaiting him in which to put his teaching into practice. Under our *régime* he, and a thousand others like him throughout British India, are wholly wasted. That is one reason why India makes no real progress. Englishmen don't know, and Indians who do know are not given the opportunity to bless their country with their knowledge.

so hardly tried. The importance of the city, the great prosperity of which—barring the plague years—it is the embodiment, but serve to accentuate the sore need of its Hinterland. Yet of all the visitors to India who are impressed with Bombay, how many find their way into the country districts, as, for example, did Mr. Vaughan Nash, in the early part of the year 1900, and converse with the villagers as he did? What were the statements he heard?

'I wanted to know,' he says, 'how the cultivators were faring in the villages round Nandurbar, and the following notes of a talk I had with a group of farmers by the well at the village of Nagbode will show that the battle with famine is a hard affair, even for the men of substance.

'Maathan, a man of thirty, owned five bullocks last year. Three died from want of water, one was killed by the Bhils, and one was left. The survivor was trying to get on its feet at the moment we began our conversation, and Maathan went to help it up—by the tail. Maathan farms 60 acres, but had no produce this year. The land is mortgaged, and he is living now as a labourer. With no water and no bullocks, he can do nothing on his own land. Last year, after paying 116 rupees for land revenue (on 84 acres), 100 rupees to a moneylender, and some barley to two servants, he had 70 rupees left for himself, his son, and two daughters. His wife is dead. He has been called upon to pay his revenue this year, but has not done so.

'Murar the Patel,[1] a young man, farms 60 acres, but there has been no produce this year. The farm is mortgaged to the extent of about 3,000 rupees. He estimates last year's produce at 375 rupees, of which he paid 104 rupees to Government. He had to buy four bullocks for 100 rupees and pay 40 rupees for servants, and was therefore unable to pay anything to the moneylender. The other expenses of cultivation amounted to nearly 60 rupees. He kept the rest for himself, his wife, uncle, and two children. He has been served with notice of assessment. He had six bullocks, and has lost four.

'Laxman has 84 acres; his crops have failed; he has lost four out of eight bullocks; three are in a condition to work, and one is at the point of death. He is indebted on his personal security

---

[1] The headman of a village; his duties comprise revenue collection and police work.

for 700 rupees. He had nothing left for paying the moneylender last year after payment to the Government assessment—150 rupees—expenses of cultivation, etc.

'Nathu farms 89 acres. His crops failed, and five bullocks out of six have died. After paying the Government 60 rupees last year there remained only forty or fifty, and he had to go out to labour to keep his wife and five children. His farm is mortgaged for 700 rupees.

'Three of these men, with two others, Aunaji and Zuga, had taken the bit of garden round the well, lent to them rent free by an absentee cultivator, and were doing their best with it, but they did not see how they could hold on for more than another month. They have no grain at home, and some of the cooking-pots have been sold.

'A bullock-cart came by, and some farmers from Sarvala, a village eight miles off, seeing us talking, pulled up to see what it was all about. "Would they be willing to say how things were going with them?" I asked through the interpreter. They made no objection.

'Gutal farmed 225 acres, and had no crops. He had 100 beasts last year, bullocks, buffaloes, and two horses, and has lost 70. Last year's crops were worth from 1,000 to 1,200 rupees. He paid 500 rupees to the Government and 500 for labour, and borrowed money for maintenance.

'Dulladha owns 185 acres, and has lost fifteen cattle out of his stock of 22. After paying assessment—850 rupees—last year and the expenses of the farm, he was able to pay his way with the help of his family working on the farm. His ancestral debt is 5,000 rupees, and up to last year he has paid interest on it in money or in kind.

'The third Sarvala man was in good circumstances, and his companions discreetly moved away after explaining that his maternal uncle had left him great riches, and such was my own embarrassment that I forgot to take down his name. The prosperqus nephew owned 300 acres, but this year there was no produce, and out of 120 beasts twenty remained, the others having died for want of fodder.

'The three had been served with notices. I did not see the actual document, but the following is a literal translation of the Marathi from a copy which I have since obtained:—

NOTICE.

A. B., Inhabitant of.................
Village ....
Taluka ....
District ....

You are informed that the land marginally noted and the assessment marginally noted are in the revenue records. The assessment for instalment of year, being Rs. , was due on , and you have not paid it yet. This notice is therefore given to you that if the instalment of Rs. , and the notice fee , total , is not paid within ten days from the date of this notice, stricter measures will be taken according to the law, and the whole assessment for the current year will be recovered at once, and you will be liable to pay as fee on account of the non-payment of instalment.

Date ....

'Cold comfort this for people who are brought as low as the peasants of France before the Revolution, who have ruin and hunger as their daily portion, while plague and cholera stand over them ready to strike. To them appears the Government of the British Empire in the likeness of the broker's man. The Government may explain that what it wants is to get the money from those who can afford to pay, and especially from the bunya. To which I would reply that recovery from the bunya will in nine cases out of ten only increase the burdens of the cultivator, that it is impossible to discriminate between those who are able to pay and those who are not, and that even if the selection could be managed with a certain rough justice, the sight of Government beginning to distrain —I hear of "examples" being made as I travel about the country— will break what little is left unbroken in the hearts of the people, and lead them to suppose that their own homes and lands are going to follow.'[1]

It may be urged, 'But that was in a famine year.' True; but, more or less acutely, every year is a famine year in many parts of India, and, particularly, in parts of Bombay—as will appear.

BOMBAY'S BURDENS—COMPARATIVE.[2]

The land revenue in Bombay may be dealt with in a fourfold light:—

1. Its incidence per head of population.
2. Its incidence per acre of cultivated area.
3. Its ratio to the gross produce of the soil; and
4. Its ratio to the net produce of the soil.

1. Incidence in relation to population.

[1] 'The Great Famine,' by Vaughan Nash, pp. 66–67.

[2] 'Comparative.' Actually, they will be found set forth in later chapters.

Province.	Population in 1901.	Land Revenue in 1898–99. Rs.	Incidence per 100 Inhabitants in Rs.
Bengal	74,718,000	4,04,48,000	54
Central Provinces...	9,847,000	87,39,000	90
North - Western Provinces and Oudh	47,696,000	6,68,72,000	139
Panjab	22,449,000	2,56,41,000	114
Madras	38,208,000	5,03,82,000	132
Bombay	15,830,000	3,05,00,000	199
Totals ...	208,248,000	22,20,82,000	Average 107 nearly.

Bombay cultivators, therefore, pay nearly twice as much on the average as do cultivators throughout the whole country. This is not because of natural advantage of soil, climate, rainfall, and water supply: these all characterise Bengal, whose payment is little more than one-fourth that of Bombay. With the exception of parts of Gujarat, portions of Khandesh, which are 'good,' and the southern districts which are tolerably 'fair' the Presidency is very poor: the Deccan is especially hard-pressed, is subject to violent fluctuations of rainfall and of drought; while the Konkan, though blessed with a plentiful rainfall, is for the greater part rocky and barren.

In 1894–95, which was not an (official) famine year, the position of Bombay comparatively stood thus:—

Province.	Net Cropped Area in Millions of Acres.	Per 100 Acres of Cropped Area net.			
		Irrigated Area.	Double Cropping.	Ploughs No.	Head of Cattle.
North - Western Provinces ...	25,030,000	26	24	12	69
Oudh	8,660,000	21	32	16	88
Panjab	21,770,000	32	13	9	61
Central Provinces	16,060,000	4	10	7	43
Madras	26,420,000	24	10	11	63
Bombay ...	24,590,000	3·2	2·8	4·4	35

Of what is called 'superior cropping'—rice, wheat, oil-seeds, sugar cane, and cotton—Bombay had 3·4 per cent., against North-Western Provinces 42, Oudh 43, Panjab 45, Central Provinces 60, and Madras 37.

I do not know whether the reader grasps the deep significance of these figures in their bearing on the absolute, as well as on the relative, poverty of the people who are behind that wonderful gateway of Bombay, and who are never seen by those who are struck almost dumb at the palpable evidences of British-Indian prosperity which they see everywhere—that is, in the 'everywhere' they visit: the show-places of the Empire. Whether the tables be or be not appreciated, they will well bear translation into descriptive terms. Viewed in their mutual dependence, the figures present an altogether unfavourable picture of the condition of agriculture in the Bombay Presidency as compared with the other Provinces. It is a picture of agricultural poverty and destitution unrelieved by a single redeeming feature. 'We have on our side,' says the very capable 'J.,' whose lead I am following, 'very little irrigation—just a trifle over three per cent. of the total cultivated acreage, and very little double-cropping—not even three per cent., owing to the general poverty of the soil and the absence of irrigational facilities; we have just between four and five ploughs per one hundred acres of cultivated area, or, say, one plough for twenty to twenty-five cropped acres, and no more than thirty-five head of cattle—and all this, be it remembered, in a normal year as was 1894–95. As regards cattle, the state of things, after the dreadful havoc caused by the recent famine, is now much worse. We have now (in 1901) about 5,805,000 head of cattle in the Presidency, or about twenty-four head for every one hundred cultivated acres; the plough cattle—oxen and he-buffaloes—number only 2,400,000 (oxen 2,210,000 and he-buffaloes 190,000), scarcely a pair per twenty acres of net cropped area. As to cropping, the major part of the area is under millets and inferior grains, and the acreage under superior crops is about only one-third of the total.

The decrease in agricultural cattle—the ryot's chief wealth and stay—is general in the Presidency, excepting in the districts of Kolaba and Ratnagiri, and aggregates during the past six years no less than 2,803,000 on a total of 8,080,000, or more than one-third. In the four Gujarat districts of Ahmedabad, Kaira, Broach, and Panch Mahals, it is over sixty per cent.; in the Deccan it is over forty per cent.; in Khandesh it is over fifty per cent.; and in Nagar it is close on fifty per cent. 'This appalling loss of cattle, especially in the famine districts, is perhaps the most depressing feature of the situation. What wonder if, amidst such disheartening wreckage of famine-devastation, the ryot stands bewildered and paralysed—without heart and without hope.'

2. Incidence of taxation in relation to cultivated acreage.

On the first glance the assessment in Bombay, when compared with like conditions in Madras, appears to justify the statement of the Honourable Mr. Muir Mackenzie,[1] that it affords 'a strong presumption of the extreme moderation of our assessment as a whole.' These are the 'facts' which afford the 'strong presumption':—

	Rs.	a.	p.	
Madras ...	2	4	11	per acre on fully assessed and cultivated area.
Bombay ...	1	6	0	

The advantage in favour of Bombay appears to be considerable. In Indian statistics—so many are the ramifications in detail—it is never safe to take a statement, such as the above, and proceed to deduce conclusions from it as though the things compared were really comparable. Indian official publications, in this respect, are terrible pitfalls; many and serious have been the consequences in the case of statesmen and writers who have gone to them for needed information. Conclusions

[1] Speech in Bombay Legislative Council, Aug. 25, 1900.

drawn on the supposition that all the figures employed were of the same value are responsible for much of the loose knowledge which prevails concerning India.[1] Sir Henry Fowler, ex-Secretary of State for India, is informed that the average assessment for all India works out at eight per cent. of gross produce, and at once exclaims, 'Behold the lightness of the burden put upon the land.' There is nothing near eight per cent. payment except in Bengal, and there the incidence is about six per cent., as Sir Henry Fowler might easily have discovered if he would; investigation on his own account, however, seems never to have been undertaken by him. As for writers on India generally, the story in the footnote to this page will suffice.[2]

Here is where the difference lies which at once changes the complexion of the comparison: in Madras one acre out of every four is irrigated, bears a large crop, and pays a high assessment (Rs.5 for wet land, Rs.1 0a. 5p. for dry crops) which makes an apparently heavy charge; in Bombay only one acre out of every thirty is irrigated. The reader will find the details quoted in Sir B. H. Baden-Powell's 'Land Systems of British India' (vol. iii. p. 72); it will suffice here to state that in strictly analogous cases,

[1] There is an ex-official in England who is writing much on India for the enlightenment of the public, whose communications are vitiated from the following of this practice. He seldom or never looks behind the published statement. Consequently he is spreading the most misleading ideas concerning the condition of India.

[2] A history of India in the Nineteenth Century was written by one who claimed to have 'been writing prominently on Indian topics' for twenty-five years. He gives, as the result of low taxation on the land, an acreage under cultivation which has doubled in forty years. He specifically claims 95,587,897 acres increase. But, because the Bengal figures (owing to the permanent settlement) did not appear in the Returns until 1890-91, and the Lower Burma figures were not reckoned by the Famine Commission of 1880, he loses sight altogether of 60,000,000 acres for Bengal, 11,000,000 for Upper and Lower Burma, and 22,000,000 acres of current fallows since 1884-85—thus accounting for 92,000,000 acres out of 95,000,000—the 95,000,000 being boastfully claimed as 'an increase' of cultivation 'of over 66 per cent. in eighteen years.' In this case the authorities are not to blame, as they carefully indicate by footnotes the years when the additional areas were first included.

the Bombay ryotwari rate is about fifty per cent. higher than is the ryotwari rate in Madras, and nearly three times more than the rate in the Panjab. Taken as a whole the comparison between Bombay and Madras works out thus:—

'(1) As regards dry crops.—In Madras the range is from Rs.5 (which is the highest rate imposable for first-class soils) to annas 6, and from Rs.2 8a. to annas 4. In Bombay the scale begins with Rs.9 8a. 6p. as the maximum rate for the richest soils, and, after endless variations, drops down to Rs.1 as the lowest rate for the worst.

'(2) As to wet crops.—The Madras rates vary from Rs.12 to Rs.4, and from Rs.7 to Rs.2—as applicable to both rice and garden lands. In Bombay the *rice* rates range from Rs.18·8 to Rs.8; the *garden* rates are as high as Rs.15, Rs.14, Rs.12—the lowest rate being Rs.6.'[1]

It may be well at this point to indicate wherein the British land assessment system works so hardly upon the cultivator. For a variety of reasons our rule cannot be *paternal* as was the ancient rule; consequently payment in kind is held to be impracticable. Further, as Lord William Bentinck approved (see *ante*, pp. 38–42), when it was laid down early in the nineteenth century, a ryot must pay for all the land comprised in his holding, whether it be cultivable or not. There are some soils (the Varkas lands of the Rajapur Taluka of the Ratnagiri collectorate, for example) which lie fallow more years than they are under cultivation. 'I calculate,' says Colonel Godfrey, 'that the average proportion of fallow to cultivated Varkas is as follows:—

	Crop years.	Fallow years.
'F superior Varkas	3	3
" medium "	2	5
" inferior "	2	8
	7	16
Average	2	5

'A closer study of our present system of assessments

[1] 'J.' in *Times of India*, April 27, 1901.

and its working results will disclose yet more striking and surprising facts. For here, we find, assessments are imposed on all soils—soils of every conceivable degree of fertility and natural advantage from the richest soils of the Central Chalotar of Kaira to the poorest soils on the Satpura or Sahyadri slopes, and not a rood of land, not even a patch of grass, escapes the eye of the settlement officer, and goes unassessed, excepting, of course, the bare, bleak, barren, wastes. Good lands and bad lands alike come in for assessment—lands that pay and lands that do not and never can pay—for their cultivation. The Tisali and Kumri lands on the Sahyadri fringe—lands which cannot possibly yield any profit to any amount of labour, and are cultivated merely for subsistence, are appraised and assessed equally with the spice gardens of Kanara and the rich cotton soils of Dharwar; it is not always possible to understand the exact principle on which such assessments are imposed.'[1]

The terrible nature of the 'struggle for life' in these regions may be estimated if it be borne in mind that, in regard to from thirty to forty per cent. of the small holdings in the Presidency, each farm averaging from five to twenty-five acres is all *subsistence* farming *pur et simple;* and the ryot, who has nothing else or better to turn to, is content if he is able to scratch off his acres enough to live on for part, if not for the whole, of the year. 'Even in good seasons he does not get enough to enable him to pay his assessment and maintain himself and his family all the twelve months of the year. Usually, after the harvest is over, he goes to some neighbouring town and works as a labourer till the return of the monsoons calls him back to his acres; and it is out of these extra earnings that he pays his assessment and meets his other liabilities. When at times this extra resource fails him, he goes to the sowkar and borrows, and his debts begin. And if seasons of deficient rainfall, drought, and famine follow in such disastrous succession as during the past decade, his

[1] 'J.' in *Times of India*, April 27, 1901.

borrowings grow and accumulate, and he is hopelessly embarrassed. Even so will the Hon. Mr. Monteath come down upon him, and charge him with thriftlessness and extravagance?'[1]

3. Ratio of burden to gross and net produce of the soil.

I have before me, taken from the Bombay Revision Settlement Reports, Appendix 2, particulars concerning

Jaoli Taluk, Satara District	... ...	183	villages.
Man Taluk, Satara District	... ...	72	,,
Sangola Taluk, Sholapore District	...	70	,,
Malshuas Taluk, Sholapore District	...	87	,,
Bagewadi Taluk, Bijapur District	...	97	,,
Pamar Taluk, Nagar District	... ...	108	,,
Total	... ...	567	,,

On the revision the cropped area was extended by 1,000 acres out of 1,297,335, while the assessment was enhanced by twenty-eight per cent. It is true that the increase was only from a little less than 3½d. per acre to 4⅔d. per acre. But, as is seldom considered in India, such burdens should be regarded in relation to the production on which they are levied, and not as they appear to a race whose breed of multi-millionaires is assuming such proportions that even the masses are beginning to think in pounds sterling instead of in bronze pennies or silver shillings. The increase appears trifling; the whole amount a sum to scoff at. Worked out in detail, what does it mean to the unhappy British subject to whom it applies? It means this:—

Take a cultivator with his wife and two children in any of these talukas, having an holding of, say, twenty-five acres, which he works with his own bullocks and labour. The result of the year's working may be set forth in some such way as the following:—

[1] 'J.' in *Times of India*, April 27, 1901.

Of 25 acres, 20 cropped and 5 fallow :—

Grain yield at 160 lbs. per acre (*vide* Government Resolution No. 4515, of August 11, 1875, on Madha)		3,200 lbs.
Deduct—		
Seed at 6 lbs. per acre ...	120 lbs.	
Wastage	80 lbs.	
Expenditure in cash—		
Replacement of implements and stock Rs.10		
Labour Rs.5		1,450 lbs.
Government assessment + local cess Rs.10		
Total ... Rs.25		
At 50 lbs. per rupee ... =	1,250 lbs.	
Total ...	1,450 lbs.	
Balance of grain produce available for the ryots		1,750 lbs.
Maintenance, straw being needed for his bullocks—		
Food at 5½ lbs. per diem (2 lbs. for the ryot, 1½ lbs. for his wife, and 2 lbs. for his 2 children), 365 days		2,007 lbs.
Deficiency in respect of food supply itself ...		257 lbs.

Let alone other necessaries, *e.g.*, clothing, salt, etc.

Such is the normal state of things in these parts; the lands do not yield even enough for the cultivator's subsistence, and it will be admitted that a land revenue system which takes no account of such a position of things, but lays on thirty and forty per cent. enhancements of assessments on revision instead of giving relief from the burden already too heavy, manifestly requires justification.

Thus states the authority I am following—an authority whose statements have not been disproved, despite the commotion they have caused. His conclusions on this heading may be thus summarised:—

'1. That little or no weight is given to economic considerations in the assessment of lands.

'2. That the assessments are fixed with reference not to the actual gross or net produce of the soil, but exclusively to the productive capabilities of land ascertained by an expert Department.

'3. That the theory of State landlordism is acted up to in all its logical severity, so that not even the poorest lands are let off unassessed. And little thought is given to the consideration whether what the State claims as its share is not an undue deduction from the ryot's diminishing corn-heap.

'4. That private improvements are not always exempted from taxation as solemnly provided for in the Land Revenue Code.

'5. That enhancements of settlements on revisional settlement are levied in many cases without sufficient grounds—in some cases without any apparent reason, and generally on an imperfect view of the economic position of the local area revised.'[1]

[1] 'J.' in *Times of India*, April 27, 1901.

TEN YEARS' AGRICULTURAL EXPERIENCE IN EASTERN ENGLAND,—1890–1 TO 1900–1.

To bring home to the English reader the most grievous and sore suffering which some of the agriculturists behind the Beautiful Gate of Bombay, and out of sight of the visitors who come away from India satisfied that all is well, I propose[1] to take three upland districts of the Deccan, with an area of 16,855 square miles, a population of 2,293,793. The districts comprised are Ahmednagar, Sholapore, and Bijapur. I intend to tell the story of the seasons and of the terrible losses endured. I do not, however, intend to again mention the names of these districts. I propose instead to apply to a region comprising East Anglia (Cambridgeshire, Norfolk, Suffolk, and Essex), Lincolnshire, and a part of the East Riding of Yorkshire, the experiences of agriculturists in the part of the Bombay Presidency I have mentioned. When Mr. Rider Haggard, in his Twentieth Century Agricultural Visitation, has told the story of these counties, it will be seen that agricultural depression in this part of England, with all its drawbacks, as compared with the sufferings of the people in the three Bombay districts, is but a mosquito bite on a strong man's arm compared with ignorant 'blood-letting' which reduces a patient almost to a state of collapse. In the light of the Western India experience, let us see what the inhabitants of the English agricultural counties named had to endure during the last decade of the nineteenth century.

[1] With the aid of 'J.' in the *Times of India*, of June 1, 1901.

(a) The Vicissitudes of the Seasons.

Year.	Remarks on the Season.
1890–1.	A *moderately fair season;* rainfall below the average, and failure of grain crops in South Yorkshire, Lincolnshire, and Norfolk.
1891–2.	A *famine year* in Suffolk and Essex—a total crop failure. A *bad* year for the remaining counties, where both grain and root crops suffered.
1892–3.	A *moderately fair year.* Grain damaged in Southern Counties, and (in lesser degree) in Yorkshire and Lincolnshire.
1893–4.	A *good year* all round.
1894–5.	A *moderately fair season;* in Cambridgeshire and Norfolk grain crops suffered: in other counties yield only fair.
1895–6.	A *moderately fair season;* in Northern Counties (including Cambridgeshire and Norfolk) grain crops suffered; in Essex and Suffolk the crops were damaged by floods.
1896–7.	A *famine year*.
1897–8.	A *bad year* for all the counties, where all crops suffered. Rainfall scanty and unfavourable.
1898–9.	An *unfavourable season* for all the counties. All crops did badly.
1899–1900.	A *famine year* throughout the whole region.

(b) Out-turn of Crops.

During this period ten crops were due of each of the cereals sown. Say—Wheat, Barley, Oats, and Mustard, were cultivated to make these forty crops :—

> One-third yielded fifty per cent. and upwards to, in one instance, ninety-five per cent., but generally not much over sixty per cent.
>
> Two-thirds yielded fifty per cent. to zero.

Put these losses into money value. During the two famine years of 1896–7 and 1899–1900, two trusted officers from the Agricultural Department (the Right Hon. Henry Chaplin, M.P., then President of the Board) estimated the loss thus:—

County.	1896–7 (the Hon. Mr. Muir Matthews' estimate). *Maunds* (82 lbs.).		1899–1900 (Mr. W. P. Smith's estimate). *Maunds* (82 lbs.).
South Yorks and Lincolnshire...	11,306,000	...	12,236,000
Cambridgeshire and Norfolk ...	9,100,000	...	9,123,000
Suffolk and Essex	12,548,000	...	11,893,000
	32,954,000		33,252,000
			32,954,000
Combined totals (maunds)		...	66,206,000

This at 2s. 4d. per maund (82 lbs.) would represent £7,724,333 for the two years named.

For 1891–92, which was a famine year in Suffolk and Essex, and all but a famine year in the other counties, there should be added, say, £2,000,000, while for the crop deficiencies of the other years, notably 1897–98 and 1898–99, it would not be unfair to add £2,000,000 more. The aggregate money value of the farmers' crop losses alone in the four years is thus £11,724,333!

(c) Loss of Cattle.

So much for the crop-losses. Now for the destruction in cattle. The cultivator's losses in these counties has been heavy during the years in question, and now he has barely a pair of plough-cattle per thirty-six acres of occupied acreage as against a pair for every twenty-five ten years ago. Similarly in regard to ploughs, there is a serious deficiency, the farmer apparently not having been able to repair old and to get new ones, and there is now scarcely a plough for every eighty acres of occupied area.

PLOUGH-CATTLE AND PLOUGHS IN THESE COUNTIES.

Year.	Plough-cattle.	Ploughs.	Occupied area in Acres.	No. of acres per pair of plough cattle.	No. of acres per plough.
1889–1890 ...	696,007	158,000	8,590,000	24·7	54
1899–1900 ...	478,283	104,890	8,740,000	36·6	80

In the presence of such a state of things there is no wonder that these fair Eastern Counties of England should, at the end of ten years, have nearly six hundred thousand fewer inhabitants than, according to the Government reckoning of 1½ per cent. per annum as the normal increase, they should have. [Imagine what would be said if, in the neighbourhood of the King's favourite home at Sandringham, such a state of things really did exist. Yet these Deccani sufferers are the King-Emperor's subjects as much as his Norfolk friends and neighbours.]

THE POSITION SUMMARISED.

Meanwhile, may be noted as some of the more determining features of the Eastern England farmer's osition at the close of the decade the following:—

(1) That his crop losses alone during the period (not to mention a serious depreciation in the value of his silver surplus under the recent currency legislation) have been so heavy as not only to exhaust all his surplus of the past quarter of a century, but to leave him, further, loaded with an additional debt of over £5,000,000.

(2) That the diminution of his plough-cattle and ploughs during these ten years has been so serious that he has now not enough of either for proper cultivation.

(3) That his growing resourcelessness is painfully illustrated in the largely increased number of farmers and farmers' families on famine relief one famine year after another, thus:—

Famine Year.	Maximum No. on Relief.	
1876–1877	311,611—12 per cent. of pop.	in these counties.
1896–1897	376,575—15 ,, ,,	
1899–1900	467,521—19 ,, ,,	

And, in 1900–01, a year of only partial distress, in the month of June there were already on relief no fewer than 174,019, or over seven per cent.

It must be added that during this period of distress the rent of the farmers all round has been increased on the existing areas by nearly £7,000 per annum. It has been collected with regularity and rigour year by year. The Government landlord, for the whole ten years, has made reductions of less than four per cent., or only about 8s. per £100 per annum! And this though whole crops had, in many instances, been swept away!

	£
For the ten years in question the Government demand was ...	2,770,346
Of this there was collected	2,656,133
Total remitted in ten years ...	£114,213

'Was collected.' Collected from what? Not from the produce of the soil, save very slightly.

Collected from whom? Not from the cultivator, for he had only the barest portion wherewith to make payment.

Collected from whom? From the moneylender.[1] This feature of present-day agricultural industry in the four

[1] 'There are some people who ascribe the distress of the agriculturist to the greed of the moneylender. It cannot be denied that the agriculturist is largely indebted. The moneylender, however, is not the cause, but the consequence, of the distress. So long as the agriculturist finds that he cannot pay the Government assessment and maintain himself and his family throughout the year without borrowing, and so long as he has no reserve to fall upon during bad years, he could not do without the money-lender. The condition, however, of the person who advances loans to cultivators is not at all thriving; he finds that his risks and his difficulties in recovering his dues are growing from year to year. The better class of moneylenders are contracting their transactions, and there would be many who would be quite willing to withdraw from the business but for the fear that all their existing outstandings would thereby become irrecoverable.'—Speech by the Hon. Goculdas K. Parekh, M.L.C., at Satara, May 12, 1900.

hundred and fifty thousand villages in India has grown, and grown, and grown, until the sowkar, like a Colossus, bestrides each community: the vast majority of the villagers are his slaves. Aforetime—that is, prior to our time, as Mr. Thorburn points out in his able inquiry in the Panjab—the moneylender was the servant of the village community; now he is its master. The Indian authorities, whose creature he is, should not abuse him with the recklessness so readily adopted by Viceroy and subordinate. He has been their good friend. But for him and for his advances the whole edifice of British Administration in India would, ere this, have tottered to its fall. Mr. Hyndman is sometimes taunted with having, twenty years ago, predicted the bankruptcy of India; meanwhile, it is sneeringly urged, India goes on paying its way. Mr. Hyndman was right. India *is* bankrupt. A 'Committee of Inspection' would make such a report to the Chief Officer in Bankruptcy as would prevent, without a reconstruction, any more business being carried on by the old firm.

To return, however, to distressed Eastern England. I imagine an Indian visitor landing at Hull, and, proceeding by way of Lincoln, Spalding, Wisbech, Cambridge, and Colchester, to London, as travellers pass through the Bombay Presidency to Jubbulpore on their way to Calcutta. Because Hull is a busy, thriving, seaport, and there are signs of prosperity in its streets and on its wharves, and the other towns hurriedly passed through had not starving people on the railway platforms, of what value should we consider that visitor's views, who, in the presence of such a state of things as has just been described, should say, 'Wherever I went I saw no sign of poverty. There can be no doubt all is well in Eastern England.' The precise value of such an opinion is the precise value of the opinion of the average cold-weather visitor to India, who spends all his time in the big cities, and never by any chance visits the villages or converses with the people.

The Government of Bombay are without excuse. Years ago the agricultural condition of the Presidency was laid before them in vivid, striking, and convincing facts.[1] Then, as now (though worse now than then), an unhappy condition of indebtedness existed, and the Government was almost as much dependent upon the good-will of the moneylender as it is now. But for the moneylender the Bombay Government, notwithstanding the comparatively important industries within its borders, would have been bankrupt in fact, as it is now bankrupt in effect, but that the creditor, the much-abused moneylender, holds his hand. Let the reader observe the pregnant facts given in the passages now to be cited, and observe also that no notice whatsoever was taken of so alarming a presentment of a perilous position. Mr. Joshi wrote :—

Shortly, we may sum up the result under this first head of causes thus :—

(1) The Survey Tenure with its thirty years' settlements allows only a limited measure of property in land and proprietary security.

(2) Only thirty-five per cent. of our Survey occupants enjoy this restricted security of tenure; and

(3) The rest (sixty-five per cent.) of our cultivators are for all practical purposes a vast rack-rented cottier tenantry, without interest in their lands, holding on a precarious tenure and living in a hopeless condition of destitution.

And thus as far as the bulk of our cultivators are concerned the result may be stated in the words of Sir G.

[1] 'The Quarterly Journal of the Poona People's Association' (Sarvajanik Sabha), 'Note on Agriculture in Bombay,' written by Mr. G. V. Joshi, B.A., Headmaster, Sholapore High School, and read at an Industrial Conference held on September 14, 1894.

Wingate thus: 'The Ryot toils that another may rest and sows that another may reap'—a situation utterly devoid of all inducement to exertion or prudence. Even the upper thirty-five per cent. occupants, though still free from embarrassments, are beginning to share, through various causes, in the general insecurity of the position.

Here, then, we reach a basal fact of the utmost importance, which largely accounts for the existing situation. Condemned to work for others like a slave, the Ryot fails; and what chance has he of success? The stimulus of self-interest is wanting, and all incentives to good work are taken away from him. And yet, let it be said to his credit, no farmer in the world could stand the pressure better. No wonder if the Deccan Agriculturists' Relief Act, the most expansive measure passed in recent years, has failed to bring relief to the Deccan Ryot. Clearly, no mere change of judicial procedure could be an effective cure for an economic evil.

(2) But, again, there is yet another cause to deepen the Ryot's despair. His income—never large and ever uncertain owing to the variations of the seasons—is fast going down under the increasing double pressure of (*a*) public taxes (*b*) and debt.

(*a*) As regards public taxation. Public taxation, to which the Ryot is the chief contributor, is steadily growing with the growing needs of a progressive administration, and the weight falls upon him with peculiar pressure. The general revenues during the last twenty years show an advance from £6,366,667 to £9,133,334, or thirty-nine per cent. (the Land Revenue twenty-two per cent.), and assuming that the Ryot's share in the public burdens is seventy-five per cent., this increase of Revenue means a net increase to the State demand upon him of £1,333,334 a year. His corn-heap, however has been continually falling away, and is just now at a minimum point, barely enough for his living, and his despair can be conceived when he is called upon to pay £1,333,334 more of public taxation. Enhancement of public burdens instead of spurring him on to increased exertions, as the advocates of the Ryot's indolent-nature theories imagine, only plunges him deeper in debt and despondency.

(*b*) But the Ryot's narrowing margin of means is further, and to a more alarming extent, encroached upon from another quarter. His debts are growing and the moneylender presses him harder than ever. With his diminishing corn-heap, he can, even in average years, hardly pay his taxes and rentals and live without borrowing. His necessities in this respect are often imperative. The oscillations of the seasons, the pressure of public burdens, domestic requirements, and various other 'accidents of circumstance,' leave him no alternative but to often go to the moneylender and borrow. And borrow he must, in the absence of cheaper banking facilities, on ruinous terms. In the Deccan districts, his annual borrowings average about £353,334 a year, or ninety-three per cent. of the total assessment.

FOUR DECCAN DISTRICTS.

Population = 3,983,233. Land Revenue, £381,184.

RYOTS' ANNUAL BORROWINGS.

Year.	Mortgage Value.	Simple Bonds.	Total Value.
	£	£	£
1885	198,667	108,000	306,667
1886	197,200	75,334	272,534
1887	164,667	66,667	231,334
1888	221,336	108,000	329,336
1889	270,667	119,334	390,001
1890	290,667	106,000	396,667
1891	303,334	102,000	405,334
1892	324,000	124,667	448,667
Total for Eight Years.	1,970,538	810,002	2,780,540
Yearly Average	246,317	101,520	347,837

Borrowings... ... ... £353,000 / Assessment ... ... £381,184 = 93 per cent.

Applying these yearly averages to the Presidency:—

Land Revenue, £1,959,934, 93 per cent. = £1,822,667, the amount of the Ryot's yearly borrowing.

On the basis of the figures given above the Ryot's annual debts in the Presidency may be estimated at roughly, £1,666,667—and taking the average rate of interest on secured and unsecured debts at twelve per cent., his annual interest payment on account of annual debts comes up to £200,000. Nor is this all. The pressure of old debts is excessive. On the basis of Mr. Woodburn's figures for nine districts[1] giving on an average £1 17s. 4d. of old debt per head of the population, the total of such debt for the whole Presidency might be put at about £15,000,000, on which the annual interest charge at twelve per cent. amounts to £3,600,000. On Mr. Woodburn's data it is £3,733,334.

Nine Districts: Population = 8,950,000.	Debt per head of Population.	Total Debt on Population Basis.	Amount of interest of £6 13s. 4d. of assessment.
	£ s. d.	£	£
Khandesh ...	3 1 8	4,473,334	20
Nasik	2 10 8	2,133,334	16
Nagar	1 1 6	983,334	12
Sholapur	1 4 2	900,000	10
Poona	0 17 6	983,334	14
Satara	0 16 0	980,000	12¾
Bijapur	1 0 0	800,000	6
Ratnagiri	1 18 6	1,833,334	22½
Thana	4 18 0	3,826,667	37½
Average	£1 17 7	£16,813,337	

Interest on Current Debt	... ...	£200,000
" " Old "	... ...	3,600,000
Total yearly charge	... ...	£3,800,000

Applying these proportions to the Presidency:—

Population, 15,985,000 at £1 17s. 0d. per head.

Total old debt = £15,000,000.

Putting together both debts, annual and old, the interest charge to the Ryot at twelve per cent. seems to come to close on £4,000,000 a year. Were he only able to borrow on easier terms—say at five or six per cent., what a relief it would be to him! His pressure would be brought down by £2,000,000, and on this account of interest charge alone, and he would be placed —in seventy-five per cent. of cases—in a solvent position. However, he has no such means of relief. His personal credit is as good as ever, and his sturdy honesty of heart which leads him cheerfully to bear his load of debt and makes the very idea of going into insolvency revolting to his mind, is appreciated even by the sowkar; and he can

[1] That is to say, on the basis of the official figures.

borrow even in the worst Deccan villages small sums on personal security. Nor is there lack of capital in the country, as pointed out last year by the Hon. Mr. Justice Ranade in his paper on 'Real Credit Re-organisation.' £1,866,667 are locked up in the Savings Banks in this Presidency, and presumably, a still larger amount in Government securities, and any rate of interest, judging from the recent conversion operations, would seem to satisfy our depositors and holders of Promissory Notes. All this money, and much more, would be, and ought to be, at the service of industrial enterprise but for want of a *via media*. The divorce between capital and land and industrial enterprise is almost complete, and this divorce has been the ruin both of the Ryot and his industry. There is almost an impassable gulf—the gulf of ignorance, and want of confidence and habits of combined effort—between those who save and those who work, a bar preventing the free flow of capital to fertilise the fields of industry, and the State which alone with its limitless command of resource and organisation is in a position to bridge over the gulf and remove the bar, still declines to undertake the work, and the deadlock continues, with disastrous results to the progress of industry. So far as the Ryot is concerned, he has to pay twelve to twenty-four per cent. interest to the moneylender, while a Savings Bank depositor is content with little more than three per cent., and has thus to pay £4,000,000 nearly to his sowkar year after year, where he ought not to pay more than £1,333,333 or £2,000,000. The consequence is, that this £2,000,000 or £2,666,667, which might otherwise go to his acres, pass into other hands, and no one is any the better for it, and every one much the worse for such diversion of the Ryot's savings, not even excluding the moneylender who suffers by the general paralysis thereby caused. The State withholds the needful help; the Ryot suffers, and with him the whole nation shares the penalty in the depression of its one surviving industry.

In another respect again, the absence of cheap banking facilities is causing inconvenience. It largely tends to neutralise the effect of much of the protective legislation of the past twenty years. Taking the Deccan Agriculturists' Relief Act, we find that while, on the one hand, during the past thirteen years the Act has been in operation, the courts and conciliators have together settled in all 20,567 claims valued at £216,667 in redemption suits in respect of mortgaged lands, the Registration figures, on the other, show that the fresh mortgage debt alone (leaving out simple bond debts) contracted by the Ryot during eight years, 1885-92, amounts to over £1,666,666, nearly eight times the amount reported as settled, the annual amount increasing steadily from £193,334 in 1885 to £222,667 in 1892-3! This one striking feature of the returns is enough to show how futile it is to attempt to relieve the indebted Ryot merely by a reform in judicial procedure. The Ryot sees it, and we can understand his reluctance to seek, in too many cases, through the special courts the barren benefit of paper redemption. If thus the Deccan Agriculturists' Relief Act is a comparative failure as a means of economic relief, neither are the special relief Acts for the superior landed proprietors any more successful. On this point Mr. Baines writes in the Decennial Report (pp. 243-4): 'The most noteworthy feature in the working of these Encumbered Estates provisions is the continuous need of them. The total number of persons entitled to relief under such enactments is necessarily limited, but we find in Gujarat 108 estates under management in 1881-82, and nine more after an interval of ten years. In Sind the law has been changed on more than one occasion, so the decrease from three hundred and forty-six to thirty may be due to special and artificial causes rather than to increased providence. In the case of Jhansi, where the persons for whose benefit the special local Act was passed are of a lower social position than the talukdars of Gujarat, it was ascertained that the loan advanced by the State from public funds to keep the agricultural proprietors on their land was repaid by loans from the village moneylender, who closed in some way or other on the disembarrassed land as soon as it was out of management. In Bengal the Chutia Nagpur Encumbered Estates Act was applied in 1891-92 to fifty-nine estates, and in 1881-82 to seventy-two. The amount of debt at the close of the former year was £10,916, and £3,313 of this was ascertained during the year in question. In Oudh, again, the supply of indebted local magnates appears perennial.'

Briefly, then, under the second head of causes, we may sum up by saying:—

(i.) The Ryot's margin of means is perilously

narrowing owing to (*a*) increasing public taxation, and (*b*) his growing indebtedness.

(ii.) The net addition to his share of the public burdens has been £1,333,334 during the past twenty years. He is not permitted to enjoy even the luxury of cheap salt.

(iii.) Real credit being in a most disorganised condition and the State still withholding its aid in reorganising it, the Ryot has to pay £2,000,000 to £2,666,667, more than he ought or need, as interest to his sowkar every year.

(iv.) This double pressure increasing concurrently with his diminishing yield from the soil, makes his condition worse.

(3) Passing next to over-crowding of his field against him as another cause of his suffering, we have, according to the recent Census of the whole Presidency, a population of 10,649,811 souls—living on the soil on a cropped area of 28,300,000 of acres—or less than three acres *per capita*. Assuming with Sir James Caird that a square mile of cultivated land can give employment only to fifty persons —men, women, and children together (or 12·8 acres per head) our cropped area is not enough even for an agricultural population of three millions ; so that we have seven to eight millions of our agricultural people without adequate employment and in a condition of demoralising indolence. The loss of work and working energy to the country is, of course, enormous. But such an excessive concentration of an enormous population on the soil has the natural effect of overcrowding the field against the agricultural worker, sending up rents and bringing down the profits of husbandry and the wages of agricultural labour. Both the under-tenant and the farm labourer are heavily weighted, and equally, or even more so, is the occupancy tenant.

APPENDIX

INDIA'S GREATEST PERIL AND HER WORST ENEMIES.

India's greatest peril and her worst enemies are typified by a cultured, high-minded, able, Christian clergyman, the Rev. W. H. Hutton, Bachelor of Divinity, Tutor and Fellow of St. John's College, Oxford. He is one of our great historians of the past; concerning the present, he sees naught but the superficial, so far as India is concerned. In 1900 he was appointed a curator to the Indian Institute at

Oxford, and in the autumn he paid a visit of 'exactly seven weeks,' as he says, to India. On his return he gave the readers of the great English Church paper, the *Guardian*, a record of his impressions. Number 1 of his series concluded with two paragraphs which should cause more melancholy and sorrow to every one who is desirous of the well-being of India (India, as distinct from Anglo-India) than any other incident which could be imagined. These are the words with which Mr. Hutton sums up his forty-nine days' experience:—

'One word of conclusion I will allow myself—not to give fanciful sketches of unrest or to prophesy a coming danger, or to analyse defences; not to describe Anglo-Indian Society, even though it be a little more gently than we have been accustomed to have it described for us—for surely no man with the slightest sense of gratitude can fail to appreciate the untiring kindness that he meets with on every side; not to string together native quaintness of expression, or satirise the manners of the mild Hindu; but simply to repeat what I suppose is the most striking impression that India leaves on every traveller—a sense of the magnificent work that has been done, and is being done by the English Administration.

'It is not that the country is being Anglicised or brought to the rigid standard of a European pattern. Far from it. There seems an extraordinary liberty for every form of National idiosyncrasy or excess. But a system of Government there is of which it is doubtful if the world has ever seen the equal. I may be told that the police even (or especially) in Bombay or Calcutta are incurably corrupt. I may be told that the system of education which we have fostered with so much pride has its only result in the production of an infinite number of cleverly-trained parrots, and that our own religion is the one which has the least official countenance in the Empire. There is some truth in all these exaggerated statements. But the spectacle of an Administration absolutely unselfish, just, scrupulous, unweariedly energetic, provident, charitable, worked by men of untiring self-sacrifice and indomitable courage from the highest to the lowest, keeping order in what would quite obviously otherwise be illimitable chaos—a Government, local as well as central, exact, firm, yet responsive to a touch, and absolutely devoted to the good of the people—is one which makes one proud and thankful for the British rule.'

'What,' it may be asked, 'is there in these grand and glowing sentences which can cause you, an Englishman, anything but extreme joy?'

To which question my answer is: The statement is of such a character that, if it be true, everything is well with India, and no reform or improvement is needed or is possible. There is no man living who would rejoice more than I should rejoice if the facts were as stated. My patriotism is of an intense character. But there is something higher than patriotism, and that is humanity. Such statements as those of Mr. Hutton's constitute a fetish which we have set up concerning our rule in India, and every cultured Englishman who has worshipped at the shrine and visits India, or takes any interest in India without visiting the country, is prepared to see, and therefore does see, that and nothing else. This god of man's own making was satirised in words attributed to Sir Auckland Colvin, which he is said to have written seventeen years ago:—

'The English mind in India has been tempted to stand still, arrested by the contemplation of its fruits in former times, and by the symmetry of the shrine, the pride of its own creation, in which it lingers to offer incense to its past successful labours.'

'The worship' has reached England from India, and has taken deep root there. While English missionaries have wholly failed to turn India to Christianity, Anglo-Indians have firmly established a new faith in England, which is that perfectness only exists in Anglo-Indian Administration, that that Administration is more sacred than the Holy Grail, while to call into question any part of its immaculateness is awful profanity. The Christians now throw the critics to the lions.

What Indian reformers have to fight against to-day has practically become a religious faith. The Faithful are, at one and the same time, the God who is worshipped and the Worshippers. Against a religious faith tenaciously held naught can, at least for a time, prevail—as Islam proved.

The worst of it all is that such statements as those of Mr. Hutton's are, when dissected, found to be wholly unworthy of credence, because they have no basis of fact on which to rest. Let me dissect and comment upon that last sentence:

'. . . An administration absolutely unselfish.'

Do, then, Lord Curzon and every other non-Indian in the public service serve India for naught? Do they not only receive no pay, but, out of their own great bounty, contribute towards Indian necessities? Pass from the individual to the community: 'absolutely unselfish,' and yet India pays for the India Office establishment in England, while the Colonies, twenty times as well off, contribute nothing to the Colonial Office; 'absolutely unselfish,' and yet every man, woman, and child, in India, out of the dire poverty of two-thirds of them, have to pay from one to two shillings every year as tribute to England—a tribute no Roman or Spanish colony ever bore. 'Absolutely unselfish.'

'Just.'

And yet Lord Lytton, when Viceroy, accused the India Office of a determination to 'cheat' the Indian people out of the rights conferred upon them by the Act of 1883 and the Proclamation of 1858; 'just,' and the historian of the Mutiny had to put it on record at the end of his seven volumes that British 'bad faith' brought about that dreadful uprising.

'Scrupulous.'

And yet the relations of the Calcutta and Simla Foreign Office are marked with as many unscrupulous acts towards the Feudatory States as, in autumn, the faded leaves were thick in the brooks of Vallombrosa; 'scrupulous,' and yet we exact from the land which has *not* yielded a crop, and from the famished farmer and his family (who have no means), our full tale of that non-existent crop.

'Unwearily energetic.'

Yes, as the honest and diligent workman who feels that for the pay he receives he shall give an adequate expenditure of brawn and brains. What less than this could they be?

'Provident.'

And yet the past expenditure in India has been marked by a recklessness the like of which is not to be found anywhere else in the civilised world. As witness our wise railway capital arrangements. We borrowed money when ten rupees equalled £1, and provided no sinking fund to repay capital outlay; now we 'convert' those same railways when £1 is equal to £1 10s., owing to our 'guarantee' of dividends not always earned, and twenty-two and a half rupees are to-day required to meet what ten rupees with 'provident' management would have paid.

'Charitable.'

In famine administration, no doubt, is meant. Yes, it is quite true —charitable with the money provided by the people themselves who need charity, and with a contribution from generous people in England, supplemented, of course, by individual contributions in India.

'Worked by men of untiring self-sacrifice and indomitable courage from the highest to the lowest.'

In what is the 'untiring self-sacrifice' shown? The highest salaries are paid, and the heaviest pensions provided, for administrators, while 'leave' is granted on a most liberal scale. Where, then, is the vaunted 'self-sacrifice'? Of whom, amongst those so described, can it be said that if no salary or pension attached to the position they would continue to carry on their present work? If there be none such, whence the 'untiring self-sacrifice'?

'Keeping order in what would quite obviously otherwise be illimitable chaos."

With all my respect for this most estimable Oxford Tutor, Fellow, and Curator, I cannot refrain from saying that this is so much nonsense, neither more nor less. Was there *no* order in India before the British came into the country? Is the marvellous civilisation which extorted the admiration of Greek visitors to India, when England was occupied by a few tribes lacking in all civilisation, a figment of imagination? Was not the Empire of Vizayanagar, in all that made for good government, fully equal to its contemporaries— the England of Henry VIII. and the France of Francis I? Such a sentence as that just quoted is a sorry comment upon the powers of observance and faculties for reasoning of one of the flowers of modern culture—as an Oxford Tutor to-day surely is.

'A Government, local as well as central, exact, firm, yet responsive to a touch, and absolutely devoted to the good of the people.'

'Absolutely,' again; 'absolutely unselfish,' 'absolutely devoted to the good of the people.' What good can such extravagant and meaningless eulogy be supposed to do? Concede at once that the Indian Government, from the highest to the lowest, wish well to the Indian people. I assert that most heartily. That does not prevent them permitting famine-stricken people from 'dying like flies,' does not prevent a cholera visitation in a famine camp from producing worse horrors than a battlefield, does not improve the position of those Indian fellow-Christians of Mr. Hutton's who in Southern India (which he did not visit) are thankful if they can get food once in two days. The nonsense of this sentence is beyond all description—'responsive to a touch.' Ask Mr. H. J. S. Cotton, the Commissioner of Assam, what kind of response he found to the touch of mercy wherewith he wished to heal certain suffering Tea Estate coolies.

'Is one which makes one proud and thankful for the British rule.'

Mr. Hutton, in saying this, speaks as an Englishman, not as an Indian. What would he say if, in the England he adorns, the Russians had been supreme for one hundred and fifty years, and in all that time not a single Englishman had been allowed to enter the Cabinet, that no popular representation existed, that no Englishman, even if he were in the public service, however great his merits, could rise to the high positions for which his fellows were eligible, that the material condition of his countrymen was year by year growing worse while their intellectual manhood was denied avenues for expansion, that famines became more frequent, that in Oxfordshire in 1901 the population, through famine and other ills, was only half what it ought to be—in such case would he have agreed with a Russian University Tutor and Fellow, even if the gentleman were a Curator of the English Institute, who declared that the condition of England was 'one which makes one proud and thankful for the Russian rule?'

Why is it that the 'Mr. Huttons' of England, when visiting India, become the greatest enemies to the Indian people, and constitute the most serious peril to the regaining of the prosperity of India? This is why. Having visited India, though it be for seven weeks only, they are regarded as authorities. 'I have seen. I ought to know.' This is conceded to them by all who read their writings or who hear their observations; and while such indiscriminate eulogy is uttered, such 'absolute' perfection of rule is described, based on a visit—not to India, but, as I have said elsewhere, on a visit to British Colonies in India, millions die every year of starvation, and the tribute paid to England by the starving people grows greater year by year, the door to the highest employment is barred more and more strongly; but those who suffer are 'only Indians,' those who testify are our own priests and prophets. That settles the accuracy of the observations. If Mr. Hutton could but realise the terrible harm he has done by such inconsiderate writing founded on such shallow knowledge, if he could realise that he is making hungry people hungrier still, half-clothed people less clothed, is choking and checking the lawful and loyal ambition of the people of India to serve their own country, I cannot but think that he would be the most miserable of men, and would lose no time in looking at the other side of the shield than on that which has hypnotised him. For he does not *want* to hurt India. Yet he is wounding her with every word he has written.

As my final word to-day on this subject let me add some lines of poetry which reached me two or three days before I saw Mr. Hutton's 'impressions.' If the writer—a kinsman of my own—had seen Mr. Hutton's concluding remarks—(he had not)—he could not have more aptly answered them than he does throughout these lines :—

'From night behind to night ahead, no man but runs a weary race,
And if we bitter seem and hard, would you be milder in our place?
Would your strong spirits stand aside, and pray "God's will be done"
If each slow beat of time that passed did mark the death-cry of a son?

'A son of man who might have lived and known the joys of life,
Lies rotting in the open field, slain in a cruel strife—
A cruel strife with naked hands against the powers three:
The alien Raj, the ceaseless tax, and hopeless misery.

'Now he has fallen by the way, but when the famine lifts
And weak and wan his folk come home, loaded with precious gifts
Of bodies broken by disease, with listless step and slow,
Then will the Raj claim measure full of the tax the dead did owe.

'But you are not of our people, and when you watch them die
Your sorrow is deep, but it passes, while still the people die.
There is home and your full-fed kinsmen the half of the world away,
So you shut your eyes to the horror; you grieve a bit and you pray.

'But you draw your wage unstinted. You stand in the way of men,
You raise your arms to the heavens, and you write with a facile pen
That you are the salt of nations (but the tax on the salt is hard!),
That the gods came down from heaven to bless your perfect guard,

'That the people cannot rule themselves, that you can do it well,
That you have made fair paradise of what would else be hell.
Hell for whom? And heaven for whom? Is that your picture true?
Was the ryot worse in ages past than he is now with you?

'Is it heaven for that poor bundle there, who is too weak to walk?
Is it heaven for these vast plains of men too spiritless to talk?
Is it paradise for womenfolk to watch their children dead,
And hear no more the plaintive voice that cried in vain for bread?

'Is it heaven, O angels God-elect? Is it heaven, or is it hell?

The publication of the above led to the interchange of the following notes. The Rev. W. H. Hutton wrote :—

'I confess I think you strain my words. I do not think that payment for work necessarily (as you seem to imply) prevents a worker from being "absolutely unselfish" in his work. He is paid, in this case (is he not?) independently of the spirit in which he carries out his duties; and I confess it seemed to me that the Indian Civil servants did their work in an entirely unselfish way.

'And I am inclined to think that you would have conveyed a truer impression of my article if you had quoted the words I used as the limits of my knowledge—"*I hope that no one will think that I attach any importance to my 'impressions' or regard them as necessarily either accurate or permanent.*"

'Your letter does seem to me to suggest that I regard myself as an authority. "Sure, haven't I seen, and sure I ought to know." I am sure I should never use such an expression as is suggested—"Those who suffer are only Indians."

'But I am sure you do not mean to use my words unfairly, and I thank you for your courtesy. I confess I think the words I used, taken in their context, are justifiable.'

The response was in these terms :—

'I thank you for your note of yesterday's date, and, in reply thereto, have to state that I think it is only due to you that I should make clear the limitations which you point out with respect to the "Impressions" you record. It was farthest from my thought to strain your words in any sense, and in making use of the expression, "Sure, haven't I seen, and sure, I ought to know," I did not so much mean it to apply to you yourself as that, for example, if I were in conversation with one who had read your "Impressions" and I were to put to him a contrary view he would be justified in saying "Mr. Hutton has been to India, he states what he has seen, and I am content with his observations." It is because those observations while, in a sense correct, are also in a sense incorrect, because they leave the impression on the mind of the reader that all's well in India, whereas the now frequent famines indicate all is very far from well, and it is only as the need for the amelioration of the sad and painful condition of things is recognised that the motive power can be found to bring about that amelioration—it is only in this sense, and in no other, that I have written concerning your most interesting and, in one sense, valuable impressions in the manner you mention.

'I will make my reference this week either as though it were spontaneous or as coming from you in the way of a mild and friendly protest, as you may think best.'

Mr. Hutton's rejoinder was :—

'Thank you very much for your kind letter. I think it would be quite enough to quote the qualifying words I used about all my impressions; but you would be quite justified in adding that I should not alter what I have written, though I think your use of the words strains their meaning. I must adhere to the view that unselfish work is possible to men who receive pay.'

From London Correspondence in the *Amrita Bazar Patrika* (Calcutta) and *The Hindu* (Madras).

CHAPTER X

THE CONDITION OF THE PEOPLE OF THE NORTH-WESTERN PROVINCES AND OUDH

Wherein Lord Curzon as Viceroy Differs from his Predecessors.

His Excellency's Estimate of Crop and Cattle Loss in the 1900 Famine.

The Baring-Barbour Inquiry of 1881–82: What has been Done Since.

What the Agricultural Income was in 1900: A Series of Calculations.

An Annual Loss of, at least, £40,000,000 in the Agricultural Income, of £66,000,000 on Agricultural and Non-Agricultural Income Combined.

An Average Present Income of £1 5s. 1d. against £1 16s. in 1881.

Is there So Great a Loss? or, Was the 1881 Income Overrated?

Lord Curzon's Reply to Above:

(1) The Happiness and Prosperity of the Helpless Millions.

(2) Is India Becoming Poorer?

(3) The Poverty of the Cultivator.

(4) Concluding Words.

The Untrustworthiness of Official Figures: Numerous Instances of a Shocking Character.

Famine-stricken Bombay declared to show an Average Increase of 128 lbs. per acre Food Crops, and Madras 98 lbs.!

The Real Yield not Two-thirds of the Estimated Yield.

In Many Parts of the Empire Famine Never Absent.

The Lessons from the North-Western Provinces and Oudh.

Full Details concerning Cultivation and Yield, Cultivators and their Condition: Low Value Yields Everywhere —8s. Per Acre Being Very Common.

Seventeen Hundred and Forty Acres Which Yield their Cultivators 5s. 5½d. per Head per Annum.

In all Ordinary Years (says the Collector of Etawah) the Cultivators Live for Four Months on Advances.

THE viceroyalty of Lord Curzon of Kedleston is in marked contrast with the period of rule of many of his predecessors. To great inherent and acquired ability he adds the energy of a mentally strong man in early middle age combined with an enthusiasm for the performance of duty and a growing interest in India as a realm: these lead him to specific acts which would be full of promise in awakening opinion to the real condition of the people of India if only he were to stay in India for from fifteen to twenty years. At present, in spite of his clear desire to do India some good, he sees men as trees walking, partly owing to the defects of his high qualities and the unhappy fact that, prior to being appointed to his high office, he was for a time Parliamentary Under Secretary of State for India. There could be no worse training for a Viceroy. On the whole, however, as a Viceroy he is making possible that tearing away of the veil behind which officialism seeks to hide the real India. Should there be no faltering on his part the dawn of a better time for the great Eastern Empire of the United Kingdom has already begun. He has made some sad breaks: they were inevitable; so far they have not done irremediable harm, but they arouse serious misgivings as to his limitations, and do not inspire much hope as to the enduring mark he will leave on India, when his period of rule has come to an end.

Lord Curzon has made better use of the Viceregal Council as a means of communication with the people of India than, perhaps, has any of his predecessors. In October, 1900, the Viceroy made the following observations:—

'The annual agricultural production of India and Burma averages between 300 and 400 crores of rupees. [English sterling, Rs.15 to £1 = £200,000,000 to £266,666,666.] On a very cautious estimate the production in 1899 and 1900 must have been at least one-quarter, if not one-third, below that average. At nominal prices the loss was at least 75 crores, or fifty millions sterling. In this estimate India is treated as a whole, but in reality the loss fell on a portion only of the continent, and ranged from almost a total failure of the crop in Gujarat, Berar, Chhattisgarh, and Hissar, and in many parts of the Rajputana States to 20 and 30 per cent. in districts of the North-Western Provinces and Madras which were not reckoned as falling within the famine tract. If to this be added the value of some millions of cattle, some conception may be formed of the destruction of property which a great drought occasions.'

These observations led to much comment, and, finally, to a brief Open Letter being addressed by the present writer to the Viceroy. Among other observations addressed to Lord Curzon were these:—

An inquiry into the economic condition of India in 1882, made by Earl Cromer (then Major Evelyn Baring) and Sir (then Mr.) David Barbour, resulted in the production of a Note in which the annual income of British India was thus stated:—

	Rs.		£
Agricultural Income ...	350,00,00,000	=	233,333,333
Non-agricultural Income...	175,00,00,000		166,666,667
Total income ...	Rs.525,00,00,000		£400,000,000

Divided amongst 194,539,000 people, the then population, the average amount per head was Rs.27 (at Rs.12 to the £, the then rate of exchange, £2 5s. 0d.).

The figures for the agricultural income were arrived at thus:—

Presidency or Province.	*Value of Gross Produce.* Rs.		£
Panjab	34,15,00,000	=	22,766,667
N.-W. Provinces and Oudh	71,75,00,000		47,850,000
Bengal	103,50,00,000		69,000,000
Central Provinces	21,25,00,000		14,166,666
Bombay	39,00,00,000		26,000,000
Madras	50,00,00,000		33,333,333
	319,65,00,000		£213,116,666
Add, for India, Burma and Assam	30,35,00,000	...	20,233,334
Total ...	Rs.350,00,00,000		£233,350,000

Since that period there have been brought under cultivation—

Additional acres	16,000,000		
Capital expenditure upon irrigation has been incurred to the extent of ...	Rs.14,48,87,590	=	£9,659,173

An increased revenue from land has been secured :—

	Rs.		£
From irrigation	1,92,91,460	=	1,286,097
From additional cultivation (including Upper Burma annexed)	3,57,08,540		2,380,569
Total ...	Rs.5,50,00,000		£3,666,666

Further, it was remarked :—

The population of British India in this year of grace, calculated according to Government of India expectations, is 245,501,987.[1] Let these figures, please, be borne in mind as I proceed with my argument which is, specially, to ascertain what the income of the average Indian under Lord Curzon's rule is as compared with the average income of his father—or, it may be, of himself—in the not far-off days when Lord Ripon sat in the seat of the mighty.

The agricultural income of to-day can be easily reckoned, if it be recognised that the Government land revenue bears a definite relation to the out-turn. Some of the statistics you favour us with year by year merely require certain sums in simple arithmetic to ascertain their significance. Yet I do not know of a single official in India or in England who has ever taken the trouble to do those sums. The total produce of the cultivated land in India is to be gathered from the

[1] The Census returns for April, 1901, showed this estimate to be an over-sanguine one. Practically, all the expected increase had (in spite of the Famine Code) been swept away by famine and, in a much smaller degree, by plague, in spite of the Haffkin inoculation. I allow all the figures to stand, with bracketed corrections, where needs be, as Lord Curzon, in replying, referred to them as they then stood.

amount of the land revenue collected by your officers. So far as I am able to ascertain[1] the revenue yearly obtained bears to the gross produce of the soil a proportion of—

In Bengal	5	to	6 per cent.	
„ the North-West ...			8 „ „	
„ the Panjab			10 „ „	
„ Madras	12	„	31 „ „	say 20
„ Bombay	20	„	33 „ „	„ 25

With these figures I multiply the total revenue of the respective Presidencies and Provinces and get these results :—

Presidency or Province.	*Revenue collected.* Rs.	× by		Rs.
Bengal...	4,04,47,850	19	equals	76,85,09,150
North-Western Provinces ...	6,63,71,350	12½	„	82,96,41,875
Panjab	2,56,41,240	10	„	25,64,12,400
Central Provinces[2]	87,39,100	12½	„	10,92,38,750
Madras	5,03,84,280	5	„	25,19,21,400
Bombay	4,71,64,970	4	„	18,86,59,880
India, Assam, and Burma[3] ...	3,58,46,140	12⅔	„	45,44,51,107
	Rs.27,45,94,930			Rs.285,88,34,562

That is to say, the agricultural income of the whole of India, from North to South, from East to West, is now £190,000,000 against £233,300,000 estimated in 1882! And this falling-off has taken place, notwithstanding the expenditure on irrigation—(all good expenditure)—the increased area brought under cultivation, and the enhancement of the revenue everywhere except in Bengal! The investigation may be carried a little farther, and put, comparatively, thus, 1882 being set side by side with 1898–99 :—

[1] I take my figures from Mr. Romesh Dutt's recent work, 'Open Letters to Lord Curzon,' p. 113. They seem to have been arrived at after close investigation.

[2] I have no definite figures to go upon, and I will take the figures of the 1882 inquiry.

[3] Details not available: I take two-thirds of the best rate available, viz., that for Bengal, and, in so doing, am erring in favour of the Government.

Presidency or Province.	1882. Rs.	1898–9. Rs.	Difference + or —
Bengal	103,50,00,000	76,85,09,150	— 26,64,90,850
N.-W. Provinces and Oudh	71,75,00,000	82,96,41,875	+ 11,21,41,875
Panjab	34,15,00,000	25,64,12,400	— 8,50,87,600
Central Provinces ...	21,25,00,000	10,92,38,750	— 10,32,61,250
Madras	50,00,00,000	25,19,21,400	— 24,80,78,600
Bombay	39,00,00,000	18,86,59,880	— 20,13,40,120
'India,' Burma, and Assam (guessed at in both years) ...	30,83,00,000	45,40,63,107	+ 14,57,63,107

Summary.

Excess over 1882	+ 25,79,04,982
Minus below	— 90,42,58,420
Net deficiency as compared with 1882	— Rs.64,63,53,438

Or, £43,090,229.

I am sure there is some mistake in the two sets of figures which show increases. But I must take the official figures as I find them, although in that volume of 1888 published at the Government Press at Allahabad (refused to the public) there are examples such as this: Gross produce Rs.322, rent Rs.306; produce Rs.85, rent Rs.40; produce Rs.259, rent Rs.86; produce Rs.162, rent Rs.72½; produce Rs.183, rent Rs.93; produce Rs.70¼, rent Rs.68–15; produce Rs.67, rent Rs.40¾. In the face of all this I have reckoned the Government rent at only 10 per cent.—that rent really being one-half of the respective items mentioned. Such advantage as there is in the calculations I have made are all in favour of Indian revenue officials.

Is it possible, I then asked, that so tremendous a fall in the gross annual income of the people can have occurred in the short period of eighteen years as is shown in the above tables? Or, is there some serious error in the Baring-Barbour figures of 1882? Both Lord Cromer and Sir David Barbour, at this moment, are engaged in important work for the Empire. What they are doing—the one in Northern Africa, the other in Southern Africa

—is as naught compared with a revision of the figures they collected in 1882, the outcome of which they made an economic fact of the Empire: 'the average income of the inhabitants of India is Rs.27.'

Let me, going farther, calculate what the income per inhabitant in British India is to-day. In doing so I will follow the procedure of 1882.

	Rs.		£
Agricultural income in 1898–9 ...	285,88,34,562	=	189,588,971
Non-agricultural income—half of above	142,94,17,281	,,	94,794,486
Total	Rs.428,82,51,848	,,	£284,383,457
Estimate in 1882	525,00,00,000	,,	350,000,000
,, for 1898–9	428,82,51,848	,,	284,383,457
Decrease	Rs.96,17,48,157	,,	£65,616,548

We may now, perhaps, go a little farther with Lord Cromer and Sir David Barbour, and find out what is now the income per head in what we euphemistically call 'a *good* year'—(great God, a 'good' year!)—that is, a year in which famine camps are not established and famine is not recognised. This done we find:—

Rs.428,82,51,843 ÷ 245,501,987 people, leaves, as nearly as may be, Rs.17 8a. 5p. per head.

Not Rs.27, Your Excellency, which was poor enough, but Rs.17 8a. 5p., or £1 3s. 6½d.!

[With the population 231,085,132, instead of 245,501,987, the average works out at Rs.18 8a. 11p.=£1 5s. 1d.]

That, I say, was in a 'good' year. But last year was not a 'good' year. It was, as Your Excellency has told us, 'the most terrible year of famine India has known during the past century.' You estimated the crop-loss at from one-third to one-fourth of the gross yield. The mean of these two amounts is Rs.83,38,26,745, which is singularly near to the figure which you yourself mentioned, namely, £50,000,000 or Rs.75,00,00,000. To the deduction of this amount, add the necessary deduction on account of non-agricultural income, and the result shows that, if the income of India during 1900 had been equally divided between the two hundred and forty-five millions of Her Majesty's lieges whose 'security and material comfort' are the deserved object of solicitude to you, there would have been

for your Excellency,

for your colleagues in Council,

for all your civilian and military officers, for all the priests—Anglican bishops and Buddhist medicants, the lawyers, the merchants, the soldiers, the sailors, the farmers, the labourers, the artisans,

and

for the wives and children of such of these as have been so 'blessed' as to be family-men,

nearly Rs.12 and Annas 6 (in English money *Sixteen Shillings and Sixpence*) each!

That is to say, it has come to this in India: the average income has dropped to 16s. 6d. per head, equally divided, in the great famine year, 1900. If that be the average, and a great number of the people receive many, many, times the average, what must be the dire necessity of vast myriads? Should Your Excellency, and your honourable colleagues, have received more than Rs.12 6a. each last year, some Indian man, woman, or child, received less than this sum for all his or her necessities. Every penny you and your colleagues received over Rs.12 6a. was the proportion of one penny less for one of the millions of the miserable creatures under your rule.

To these remarks Lord Curzon made reply in the Viceregal Council, Calcutta, on March 28, 1901, upon the debate on the Indian Budget. His Excellency said:—

There are a number of other subjects which fall within my category, but of which I prefer not to speak at present, lest I might arouse false expectations. There are others again which can seldom be absent from the mind of any ruler of India, though he might speak with caution upon them. There is no need why he should not refer to the possibility of fiscal reforms leading, if circumstances permit, to the reduction of taxation. It is an object that is always in the background of his imagination. The protection of scientific propagation and agriculture for which we have instituted a separate office and an Inspector-General; the possible institution of agricultural banks; the question of assessments; the fostering of native handicrafts; the encouragement of industrial exploitation in general—these are all aspects of the larger question of the economic development of the country upon which my colleagues and myself are bestowing most assiduous attention. *Salus populi suprema lex*, and all reforms to which I have been alluding are, after all, subsidiary to the wider problem of how best to secure the happiness and prosperity of the helpless millions.

Is India becoming Poorer?

Upon this subject I should like to add a few words, which, I hope, may tend to dissipate the too pessimistic views that appear to prevail in some quarters. There exists a school that is always proclaiming to the world the increasing poverty of the Indian cultivator, and that depicts him as living upon the verge of economic ruin. If there were truth in this picture, I should not be deterred by any false pride from admitting it. I should on the contrary, set about remedying it, to the best of my power, at once. Wherever I go I endeavour to get to the bottom of this question. I certainly do not fail to accept the case of our critics from any unwillingness to study. In my famine speech at Simla last October, in making a rough-and-ready assumption as to the agricultural income of India, I based myself upon figures that were collected by the Famine Commission of 1880 that were published in 1882. The agricultural income of India was calculated at that time as 350 crores. At Simla I spoke of it as being now between 350 and 400 crores.[1] Thereupon I found my authority quoted in some quarters for a proposition that the agricultural wealth of the country had remained stationary for twenty years, while the populations had gone on increasing by leaps and bounds. Further

[1] According to the newspaper reports His Excellency said, 'Between 300 and 400 crores,' but the point need not be laboured as, in the next paragraph, it will be found he falls back upon that figure. He goes on to say that he should have put the figure at 450 crores, but he gives no *data* whatsoever for the statement. All the inquiries go to show that the true figure is considerably below the 350 crores which is the mean of his original statement—'between 300 and 400 crores.'

equally erroneous assumptions followed, that there had been no rise in the *interim* in the non-agricultural income of the community. I found myself cited as the parent of the astonishing statement that the average income of every inhabitant of India had sunk from Rs.27 in 1882 to Rs.22 in ordinary years, and to Rs.17½ in 1900, the inference, of course, being drawn that while Nero had been fiddling the town had been burning. I have since made more detailed inquiries into the matter. There are certain preliminary propositions to which I think that every one must assent in every country that is so largely dependent upon agriculture. There comes a time—it must come in India—when the average agricultural income per head ceases to expand for two reasons—first, that the population goes on increasing; and, secondly, that the area of fresh ground available for cultivation does not increase *pari passu*, but is taken up, and thereby exhausted. When this point is reached, it is no good to attack Government for its inability to fight the laws of Nature. What a prudent Government endeavours to do is to increase its non-agricultural sources of income. It is for this reason that I welcome, as I have said to-day, the investment of capital and the employment of labour upon railways, canals, in factories, workshops, mills, coal mines, metalliferous mines, and on tea, sugar, and indigo, plantations. All these are fresh outlets for industry. They diminish *pro tanto* the strain upon the agricultural population and they are bringing money into the country and circulating it to and fro. This is evident from the immense increase in railway traffic, both goods and passenger, in postal, telegraph, and money order, business, in imports from abroad, and in the extraordinary amount of precious metals that is absorbed by the people. These are not symptoms of decaying or impoverished populations.

The Poverty of the Cultivator.

Turning, however, to agriculture alone, concerning which the loudest lamentations are uttered, I have had worked out for me from figures collected for the Famine Commission of 1898 the latest estimate of the value of agricultural production in India. I find that in my desire to be on the safe side I under-rated the totalling in my Simla speech. I then said between 300 and 400 crores.[1] The total is 450 crores. The calculations of 1880 showed the average agricultural income at Rs.18 per head. If I take the figures of the recent census for the same area as was covered by the earlier computation, which amount to 223 millions, I find that the agricultural income has actually increased notwithstanding the growth in the population and an increasingly stationary tendency of that part of the national income which is derived from agriculture and that the average per head is Rs.20, or Rs.2 higher than in 1880. If I then assume—I

---

[1] See immediately preceding note.

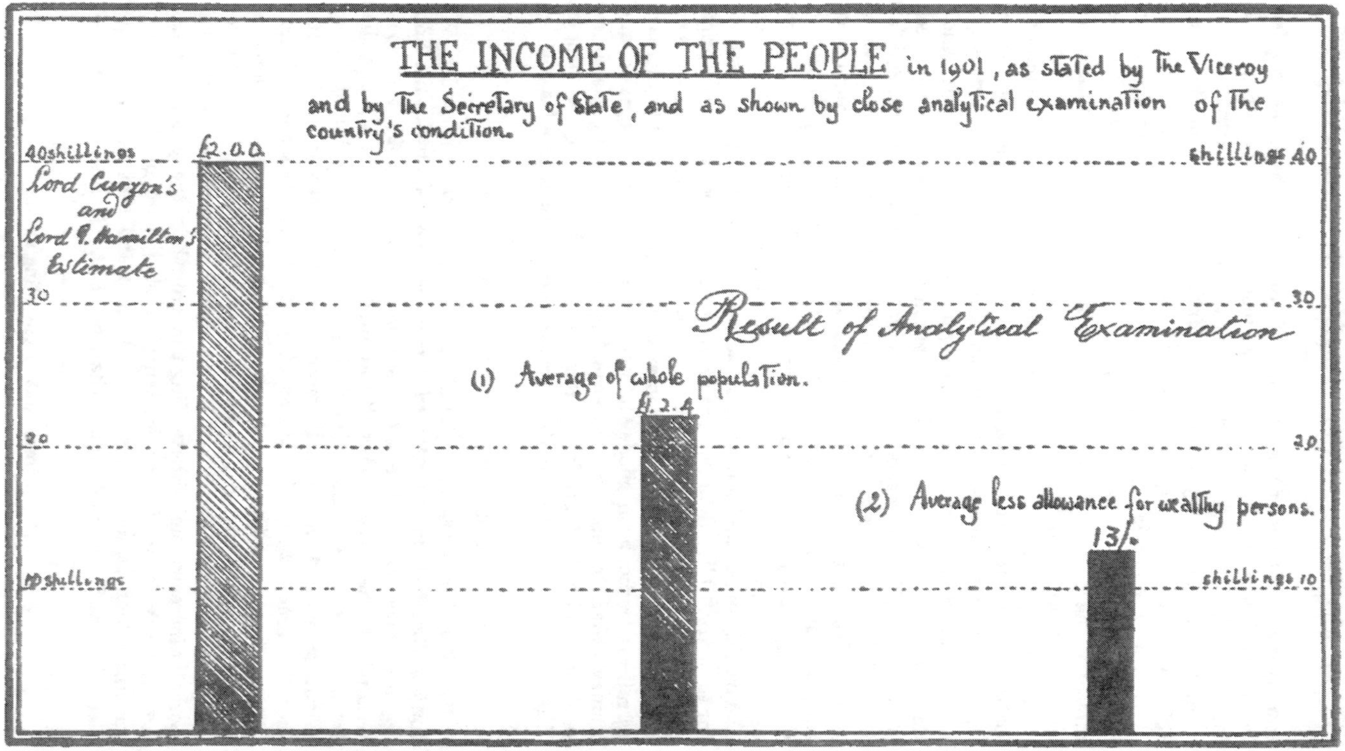
THE INCOME OF THE PEOPLE in 1901, as stated by The Viceroy and by The Secretary of State, and as shown by close analytical examination of the country's condition.
40 shillings
£2.0.0
Lord Curzon's and Lord G. Hamilton's Estimate
shillings 40
30
30
Result of Analytical Examination
(1) Average of whole population.
£1.2.4
20
20
(2) Average less allowance for wealthy persons.
13/-
10 shillings
shillings 10

know of no reason why I should not, indeed I think it under the estimate—that the non-agricultural income has increased in the same ratio, the average income will be Rs.30 per head, as against Rs.27 in 1880. I do not say that these *data* are incontrovertible. There is an element of conjecture in them, but so there was in the figures of 1880. The uncertainty in both is precisely the same. If one set of figures is to be used in argument, equally may the other. Again, I do not claim that these calculations represent any very brilliant or gratifying result. We cannot be very happy in the face of the recent census which shows an increase of population so much less than we had anticipated, the falling-off of which is no doubt due in the main to the sufferings through which India has passed and which by so much reduces the denominator in our fraction. But at least these figures show that the movement is, for the present, distinctly in a forward and not in a retrograde direction; that there is more money, not less money, in the country; that the standard of living among the poorer classes is going up, not down; above all they suggest that our critics should at least hold their judgment in suspense before they pronounce with so much warmth either upon the failure of the Indian Government or upon the deepening poverty of the people. There is one point, however, in these calculations where we are upon very firm ground. In 1880 there were only 194 millions of acres under cultivation in India. There are now 217 millions, or an increase in virtually the same ratio as the increase in the population. This alone would tend to show that there can have been no diminution of the agricultural income per head of the people. The case, for instance, results from the increased standards of yield between 1880 and 1898. Perhaps the earlier estimates were too low. That I cannot say. The fact remains that in 1880 the figures showed a yield per acre of food crops in British India of 730 lbs.; those of 1898 show a yield of 740 lbs. In some cases this will be due to improved cultivation; perhaps, more frequently, to extended irrigation. They are satisfactory so far as they go, for they show that the agricultural problem has not yet got the better of our rapidly increasing population, but they also show how dangerous it will be in the future if India, with this increase going on within, continues to rely mainly upon agriculture, and how important it is to develop our irrigational resources as the most efficient factor in the increase of agricultural production.

Concluding Words.

I have now brought to a termination this review of the present position in India and of the policy and attitude of Government. I hope I have extenuated nothing, exaggerated nothing. I am a believer in taking the public into the confidence of the Government. The more they know the more we may rely upon their support. I might have added that the policy which I have sketched has been pursued at a time when we have had to contend with a violent

recrudescence of plague, and with a terrible, desolating, famine, but these facts are known to every one in this chamber. An allowance will be made by every fair-minded person for conditions so unfavourable to advance or prosperity in the administration. Should our troubles pass away I hope that in future years I may be able to fill in with brighter colours the picture which I have delineated to-day, and to point to the realisation of many of our projects which still remain untouched or unfulfilled.

With this authoritative statement before the student of Indian affairs the whole issue can be joined, and, it may be, ere the conflict ends, some advantage may be secured to the Indian subjects of the King of Britain from the unusual, but extremely proper, action taken by the Viceroy.

I follow the course of my reply to Lord Curzon, making such interpolations and additions as further research and criticism in the newspapers call for.

THE UNTRUSTWORTHINESS OF OFFICIAL FIGURES.

At Calcutta, on March 28th, Lord Curzon said :—

'In 1880 there were only 194,000,000 acres under cultivation, there are now 217,000,000 acres under cultivation.'

This shows an increase of 21,000,000 acres. He had previously stated: 'There is one point, however, in these calculations where we are on very firm ground.' This 'firm ground,' on investigation, becomes the reverse of firm. The Director-General of Statistics, in the Fourteenth Issue of the 'Agricultural Statistics of the Empire,' page 3, gives a summary of all the agricultural statistics from 1884–85 to 1897–98. The Famine Commission Report alone furnishes the figures for 1880. They are strangely at variance with those announced :—

1880.	Acres.
Food-crop area	161,250,000
Area under non-food crops	21,500,000
Total cropped area ...	182,750,000

or eleven millions and a quarter fewer acres than was stated! The Director-General gives a total 'area sown with crops' of 194,414,057 acres, but it is in relation to 1890–91, or ten years later, not 1880. The Director-General shows, for his latest year, 'Area under crops,' not 217,000,000 acres, but 196,497,232 acres! Nearly twenty-one million acres difference, which, at the vice-regal calculation of produce, means :—

> 21,000,000 acres × 740 lbs. of produce = 15,540,000,000 lbs. of grain, or food at the rate of 547 lbs. per annum for 26,000,000 people!

The Director-General's figures are the trustworthy figures. Apparently, therefore, the Viceroy has had invented for him a full food supply for twenty-six millions of people—a supply which has no existence save in some one's imagination. In the Director-General's details can be marked an annual rise and fall, corresponding with the seasons' fluctuations, which give them the stamp of veracity. For the eight years, 1890–91 to 1897–98, the first-named being the earliest year available for this comparison, as only then were the Bengal statistics included, they are as follow :—

'Arra Sown with Crops.'

Year.	Acres.
1890–91	194,414,057
1891–92	187,752,196
1892–93	195,918,938
1893–94	197,386,536
1894–95	196,000,696
1895–96	188,922,332
1896–97	177,512,059
1897–98	196,497,232

The above statements exactly correspond with the famine of 1891–92 (which was not recognised as a famine), and shows the three fairly good years of 1893 to 1895, with a high acreage, followed by the first of the recent two famines which have caused great misery to vast multitudes.

If these figures be taken as the basis, and not the 217,000,000 acres the Viceroy mentioned, it may be well to press home their significance.

		Acres.
In 1897–98 the crop area is...	...	196,497,282
In 1880 the crop area was ...	...	182,750,000
Increase ...	Acres	13,747,282

Since 1880 the area of the Empire has been enlarged by 105,000 square miles, or 67,200,000 additional acres. From these there have been added to the crop area the considerable acreage of Upper Burma of 3,167,133, all the additional land in British India irrigated (each acre of which should yield sixfold more than a like area of unirrigated land), with an increased population as follows:—

		People.
British India, 1880[1] ...	...	191,000,000
" " 1900	...	231,085,132
Increase ...	People	40,085,132

Apparently, in British India, the increased area has not been more than ten millions of acres wherefrom to feed the additional forty millions of mouths, not counting Upper Burma, which have come in the meantime, claiming their portion. This means that the 'improved cultivation' which Lord Curzon thought 'in some cases' has been brought about, has been more than compensated for by decrease in other cases. Who, however, knows whether there really has been diminished fertility or an increased areal production? Not the Presidents of Famine Commissions or the compilers of official statistics. The moment one sets to work to endeavour to produce

[1] Famine Commission Report, Part I., 1880, p. 3.

some statement which shall be trustworthy he is met by the utmost confusion. For example, the Viceroy stated: 'The fact remains that in 1880 the figures showed a yield per acre of food crops in British India of 730 lbs.; those of 1898 show a yield of 740 lbs.'

The two Famine Commissions give results wholly at variance with this statement:—

> The figures for 1880 (par. 156, p. 150, Report of Famine Commission) show a yield per acre of 695 lbs.
>
> The figures for 1898 (par. 587, p. 357, Report of Famine Commission), show a yield per acre of 845 lbs.

If the latter were accurate Lord Curzon could have proclaimed an improved return per acre of 150 lbs. It would have been the grandest proclamation India has ever known, for it would have meant comfort and happiness brought into countless homes! If it were true an increased consumption of salt and other taxable commodities would have followed. But Sir James Lyall and his colleagues, although they publish the figures, will not permit of their acceptance. They express contempt for the particulars which the respective Local Governments have furnished to them. In para. 587, p. 357, Famine Commission's Report, it is stated:—

> 'From figures given in the table in paragraph 156 of their report, the Famine Commission, after careful inquiry, came to the conclusion that the annual food grain production in British India (excluding Burma, but including Mysore, which was then under British rule) was 51,530,000 tons; that its requirements was satisfied by 47,165,000 tons; and that a surplus of 5,165,000 tons (including a surplus of 800,000 tons in Burma) was available for export or for storage. In his "Narrative of the Famine in India" our colleague, Mr. Holderness, has carried on the calculation on the data employed by the Famine Commission, and estimates that since they wrote the population of the same area has risen by seventeen per cent., or from 181 millions to 212 millions, and the food requirements to 54,808,000 tons. During

the same period he estimates that the area under food grains has risen by only eight per cent., or from 166¼ millions of acres to 185 millions, the out-turn of which would be 56,000,000 tons. On these figures a surplus of only 1,700,000 tons would result in place of the surplus of 5,165,000 tons estimated by the Commissioners. Some of the witnesses engaged in the export trade, whom we questioned on the point, were of opinion that this result is much below the real average surplus of the present time."

The details are then given in tabular form, from which the above-mentioned yield of 845 lbs. per acre is obtained. The result is discredited by the Commissioners themselves: '. . . . The Bengal returns are particularly unreliable.' 'On the whole we are disposed to think that in the figures supplied to us by Local Governments the normal surplus in most cases is placed too high, as the exports from India and Burma by sea for a series of years, and the tendency of prices to rise, indicate the existence of a much smaller margin.' '. . . The surplus of 3,306,300 tons returned for the Province of Bengal appears to us to be greatly in excess of the reality, and the Local Government takes the same view. The average annual export from Bengal during the five years preceding the famine was only 305,000 tons, or one-tenth only of the quantity estimated from other data to be the surplus.' 'The Bombay return also appears to be far too high.' '. . . The Burma annual surplus has been pitched too high.'

As a further example concerning the alleged yield per acre, these results, deduced from the statistical tables submitted by the respective authorities, are of value:—

PANJAB.

	Food Crop Area. Acres.	*Out-turn of Food.* Lbs. per acre.
1880	18,500,000	645
1898	19,184,655	627
	Decrease ...	18

NORTH-WESTERN PROVINCES AND OUDH.

	Food Crop Area. Acres.	Out-turn of Food. Lbs. per acre.
1880	31,450,000	800
1898	35,911,650	764
	Decrease ...	36

CENTRAL PROVINCES.

1880	12,000,000	513
1898	14,000,000	480
	Decrease ...	33

BOMBAY (including SIND).

1880	21,500,000	459
1898	28,238,000	587
	Increase ...	128

MADRAS.

1880	26,000,000	782
1898[1]	21,696,000	880
	Increase ...	98

No one who knows anything of agricultural India can regard the above figures as of the slightest value on which to base accurate conclusions. Were the matter not of so much importance, did not so many serious concerns depend upon the statements, their presentation would be occasion for ridicule. They are really statements *pour rire*. For, who can believe, in view of the history of the past twenty years, that the average yield of unirrigated land in Bombay has gone up by 128 lbs. per acre? Were these statements trustworthy, there would have been no famine in the Western Presidency in 1897–98, nor, again, in 1899–1900. In fact, the Director-

[1] Madras figures refer only to ryotwari areas for which returns of cropped areas are available, and exclude zemindar and agency tracts for which no returns are available, and which comprise about a third of the area of the Presidency.—*Famine Commission.*

General of Statistics declares the Bombay returns show a decreased yield. 'The averages,' he declares in the Fourteenth Issue of Agricultural Statistics, p. xxvii, 'differ considerably from the statements prepared in 1892. For dry crops the yield is considerably below the previous estimates, but a higher rate of yield is stated for irrigated crops.' The irrigated crops in Bombay are comparatively few; the area is only 3·2 per cent. of the cultivated land. It was in face of lower averages that the Bombay Government gave the Famine Commissioners of 1898 greatly increased estimates of the productivity of the soil!

Other calculations, based on five farms of areas varying from 22 acres to 55½ acres, which Sir J. B. Peile submitted to the 1880 Famine Commissioners and declared were fair averages, may be quoted. The value of the gross receipts for each farm is given. It runs from Rs.3 per acre to Rs.14, being, respectively, Rs.14, Rs.11½, Rs.8, Rs.6, and Rs.3. I wanted to see how near these came to the yield of 730 lbs. per acre announced as typical of 1880. The average return is Rs.8½ per acre. Allow food grains sold at 60 lbs. for the rupee. a price very seldom reached during the past twenty years, the result is a yield of 500 lbs. per acre instead of 730 lbs. That is much more likely to be near the actual out-turn than the 730 lbs. the Viceroy gave, and certainly nearer than the 846 lbs. which the 1898 Commissioners' figures yield. If, however, the 740 lbs. are to be accepted, this is one of the results which follow on the Commissioners' own details: Instead of there being, as the Commissioners showed, a surplus of 9½ millions of tons of food grains for reserve, export, storage, etc., there would be less than two millions of tons. Now, the export of food grains in 1898–99 amounted to 3,071,550 tons. Consequently, on this showing, there was no surplus. Instead, one million tons had been taken from reserve for export. No wonder food prices were so high in 1899–1900, and famine-caused deaths were to be counted literally by the million!

It is often declared to be impossible to tell what the yield of Indian fields really is. Yet nowhere in the world should it be so easy to obtain such details as in India. The Supreme Government is uncontrolled landlord; the Governors, the Lieutenant-Governors, and the Chief Commissioners, are but stewards of an immense estate; obeying their orders is a large multitude of able and experienced under-stewards, whose first duty is to collect the rents and to learn the condition of that portion of the estate which is committed to their charge. As a matter of fact there is no desire to obtain the particulars most needed. It is not an uncharitable inference —or if uncharitable, it is the only inference which can be drawn—that the details are not obtained for the simple reason that they are not desired. It is felt that, in all probability, if they were obtained they would exhibit such utter distress on the part of the cultivators that the Government would be hard put to it to enforce payment of the land revenue. Enforced payment in famine years is excused because, it is alleged, famines only come occasionally. It might be found that, in many of the unirrigated parts of the Empire, famine was never absent.

The study to which this book is devoted is serious enough to even risk my wearying the friendly reader, who may examine these pages with the hope of arriving at some conclusions, by putting before him a number of facts regarding the yield of certain farms and the condition of the families who own these farms, subject to the moneylenders' lien, in the North-Western Provinces and Oudh.[1]

[1] Some few of the particulars have been quoted in other parts of this work. I make no apology for this, the Indian problem, as I present it, is a problem which will not be understood and solved by any single presentation of facts. 'Once saying will not suffice, though saying be not in vain,' and, possibly, some facts dealt with in different ways, may lead to that personal inquiry on the part of my reader, which alone can do India any good.

THE LESSONS FROM THE NORTH-WESTERN PROVINCES AND OUDH.

From 'An Inquiry into the Economic Condition of the Agricultural and Labouring Classes in the North-Western Provinces and Oudh, 1888'[1] albeit the volume is marked 'Confidential,' I propose to take out every return of crop-yield clearly enough stated to bear quotation; it will then be possible to form some idea of what the struggle of the cultivator in a fair average province in India is like. Mainly, the particulars will apply to one year only, but that is the fault of the inquirers and not of the present compiler.

Page.	Village.	No. of Acres.[2]	Character of Crop.	Rent, Yield per Acre, and Comments.
6	Mauza Hatana	15	Cotton 2½ ac. juwar and bajra 5 ac.	'The whole crop failed and the only produce was about four loads of fodder.' The tenant borrowed Rs. 50, paid Rs. 11-10-0 for rent, and spent Rs. 15 on seed for spring crop.
7	Mauza Sirthla	15	Cotton 2 ac. juwar 5 ac. guar 1½ ac. bajri 1½ ac.	Cotton Rs. 4 only. Guar failed, no bajra produce at all. Autumn rent Rs. 10 paid by produce.
8	Mauza Nabipur	3¾	Juwar and urd 2¼ ac. gram 1½ ac.	Juwar land produced nothing; floods; gram poor.
9	Mauza Kamar	10	Juwar, mung 5 ac. bajra 2 ac. cotton 1½ ac.	60 lbs. juwar 82 ,, mung 40 ,, bajra Rs. 2 cotton.

[1] Naini Tal: Government Press, North-Western Provinces and Oudh, 1888.

[2] Many of the fields are given in pucka (full) bighas or kutcha (smaller) bighas. A bigha is described as 'a measure of land varying in different places, but usually between half and three-quarters of an acre.' I reckon the bigha at little over half an acre. Where bigha only is mentioned I take the pucka bigha to be meant. Mr. Crooke, whom I follow, on p. 21, gives ten puckha bighas, as equalling 5½ acres.

Page.	Village.	No. of Acres.	Character of Crop.	Rent, Yield per acre, and Comments.
9	Mauza Gindoi	5	Cotton 8 ac. juwar 1⅓ ac. bajra ¾ ac. san ⅓ ac.	Rs. 10-4-0 cotton 3-8-0 juwar 1-4-0 bajra 2-0-0 san. 17-0-0 With this produce the family passed two and a half months and sowed for spring crops. Sought work as labourers.
10	Mauza Phalen	20	Cotton 1½ ac. juwar 4 ac. guar 2 ac. bajra 2 ac. Sublet 5 ac. same rent as paid.	Rs. 10-0-0 cotton 7-8-0 juwar 4-0-0 sub-rent guar fit only for fodder. Paid Rs. 21-8-0 to zemindar autumn rent.
11	Mauza Jamdla	15	Cotton 2 ac. juwar 5½ ac.	Crops failed, floods; grain sown for spring crop.
12	Mauza Gaubari	7	Cotton 3⅓ ac. chari ¾ ac. bajra and guar 1¾ ac. juwar 1½ ac.	Rs. 10 for cotton. Other crops almost complete failure.
13	Mauza Kharot	30	—	'Sowed 22½ acres for autumn crop; field under water for weeks and produced nothing.'
14	Do	10	Juwar, cotton, bajra, indigo, hemp, ramas urd, mung.	Rs. 16, 4, 3, 16, 13, 2, 8; total Rs.62; or Rs.6 3a. per acre. Needed to borrow Rs. 13-12-0 to get through year. Rent Rs. 32.
16	Naugaun	10¾	Juwar, urd, guar, mung, cotton, patsan, chari.	Rs. 70-4-0. Rent Rs. 44-12-0. Arrears of rent Rs. 154. Adverse balance Rs. 26-11-0, after spending Rs. 8 on entertaining guests at festival.
18	Hazara	10¾	Wheat, barley, carrots, methi, garden produce.	Whole produce Rs. 67-8-0; about Rs. 6¼ per acre. Rent Rs. 40-11-6. Adverse balance Rs. 8-2-6.

Page.	Village.	No. of Acres.	Character of Crop.	Rent, Yield per Acre, and Comments.
21	Awa State	5½	Cotton, maize, juwar, pulse, sugar cane, millet, castor oil, carrots, hemp, wheat chaff, mustard.	Autumn harvest Rs. 129-8-0; Spring ditto Rs. 84-8-0—Rs. 214. Rent Rs. 75, general expenses Rs. 93-2-0. Available for maintenance of family, four persons, Rs. 45-14-0, or Rs. 10¼ per head per annum. Note: Irrigated land, no allowance for damaged or destroyed crops.
31	Mauza Mohampur	17	Cotton, hemp, indigo, sugar cane, wheat, bejhar, mustard.	8 acres Autumn, 7 Spring; Cotton Rs. 4-4-0, sugar cane Rs. 90, indigo Rs. 18, wheat Rs. 18, bejhar Rs. 12½—average Rs. 18 p. a.; total Rs. 318. Rent Rs. 306. Expenditure exceeded income by Rs. 138-9-0; had to borrow or sell ornaments.
33	Do	7	Cotton, juwar, wheat, bejhar, mustard.	Cotton Rs. 12 p.a., wheat Rs. 15, bejhar Rs. 10: Rs. 15 p.a. all round; total Rs. 85. Juwar rotted, too much rain. Rent Rs. 40. No arrears. Adverse balance Rs. 22, must incur debts.
42	Mauza Abhaipura	11½	Cotton, bajra, maize, barley, peas, wheat, grain.	Total: Autumn and Spring crops Rs. 107-10, averaging Rs. 6 p.a. Cotton Rs. 6, bajra Rs. 5, maize Rs. 2-8, barley and peas Rs. 4-8-0, wheat and gram Rs. 47-4-0 (2¾ a.), gram Rs. 28-6-0. Two members of family, carpenters. Rent Rs. 28-8-0. Favourable balance Rs.22-13-0. This is a superior family.
48	Do.	13	Bajra, maize, wheat, gujai, gram, barley, carrots.	Rs. 183-4-0. Bajra Rs. 10, maize Rs. 12, wheat Rs. 20, gujai Rs. 6, gram Rs. 17, barley Rs. 15, carrots Rs. 10 p. a. Zemindar, grain dealer, etc. Eight in family. Favourable balance Rs. 161-13-0. Half income derived from grain-dealing, cart-hiring, etc.

Page.	Village.	No. of Acres.	Character of Crop.	Rent, Yield per Acre, and Comments.
52	Mauza Chakeri	88	Juwar, bajra, arhar, cotton, maize, oilseed, hemp, barley, peas, grain, gujai, chana.	Zemindar, cultivator, money-lender. Nominal rent Rs. 818-8-0. Autumn harvest Rs. 407, Spring Rs. 824: total Rs. 1231. Juwar Rs. 1½, cotton and arhar Rs. 20, maize Rs. 8¼, oilseed Rs. 7, wheat Rs. 18, barley and peas Rs. 12, grain Rs. 14¼, wheat and grain Rs. 11, gujai Rs. 10, chana Rs. 4 p. a. Moneylending, cart-hire, etc., produce Rs. 800 per annum.
55	Do.	24	Maize, juwar, cotton, arhar, grain, bejhar, mustard, oil-seeds, gujar, chana.	Rs. 381 from 34 acres, some cropped twice. Rent Rs. 214. Maize Rs.8, juwar and bejhar Rs. 8, cotton and arhar Rs. 16, wheat Rs. 17½, grain Rs. 6½, bejhar Rs. 10, gujar Rs. 10, chana Rs. 4 per acre. Cart-hire, ghi manufacture, etc., produce Rs. 118. Favourable balance Rs. 25.
59	Do.	18	Maize, cotton and arhar, wheat, barley grain, oilseed.	Rs. 259 both harvests. Rent Rs. 81-15-1 about 32 per cent. of produce. Maize Rs. 10, cotton and arhar Rs. 24, wheat Rs. 19, barley Rs. 12½, grain Rs. 10 per acre. Weighs grain, lets carts on hire, etc. Favourable balance Rs. 48. Owes Rs. 600, and is Rs. 25 behind with rent. Decrease in production of land and family expenses caused debt.
63	Do.	8¼	Juwar, cotton, arhar, wheat, barley.	Rent Rs. 47-11-6, nearly Rs. 6 per acre. Value of produce not stated. Annual inc. stated at Rs. 96; expenses same. Last year borrowed grain for sowing.

Page.	Village.	No. of Acres.	Character of Crop.	Rent, Yield per Acre, and Comments.
65	Mauza Chakeri	1½	Barley, peas, mustard.	Rent Rs. 10. Value produce Rs. 20. Annual expenditure for food alone Rs. 84. Rs. 30 arrears of rent, Rs. 100 debt. Apparent deficit Rs. 64 for food and Rs. 24 for clothes, Rs. 90 in all.
66	Do.	20	Juwar, cotton, arhar, maize, cotton, guar, wheat, gram, barley, peas.	Rent Rs. 107-6-0. Produce Rs. 448-6-0. Juwar Rs. 22, cotton Rs. 5½, juwar, arhar and mung Rs. 26, maize Rs. 8, cotton and arhar Rs. 6, juwar, arhar and mung, and guar Rs. 30, wheat and grain Rs. 20, barley and peas Rs. 22¾, wheat Rs. 24 per acre. These relatively large crops probably due to there being no produce from the fields during preceding two years. Rent arrears Rs. 141-10-0; debt Rs. 200. 'In very poor circumstances, and finds it hard to make both ends meet.'
67	Do.	8½	Maize, cotton, and arhar, wheat, barley and peas.	Rent Rs. 47. Produce Rs. 143. Maize Rs. 10, cotton and arhar Rs. 9, wheat Rs. 25 per acre. Annual expenses, food and clothing Rs. 96-8-0, minus Rs. 13½; rent arrears Rs. 106. Debt Rs. 40. Very little yield from fields for three years. Household furniture valued at Rs. 3-8-0.
68	Do.	5	Maize, cotton, and arhar, barley.	Rent Rs. 21-8-0. Total produce Rs. 70. Maize Rs. 9, cotton and arhar Rs. 5½, barley Rs. 18 per acre; average Rs. 14. After paying rent had only Rs. 38½ with which to meet expenditure of Rs. 116. Rent arrears Rs. 21-8-0, debt Rs. 100. Small out-turn preceding year.

Page.	Village.	No. of Acres.	Character of Crop.	Rent, Yield per Acre, and Comments.
69	Mohauli Khurd	21¼ 2½	Juwar, cotton, maize, hemp, wheat, bejhar, barley.	Rent Rs.150; 2½ a. rent free. Produce Rs.338. Juwar Rs.8, cotton Rs. 8, maize Rs. 6, hemp Rs. ½, wheat Rs. 24, bejhar Rs. 9, barley Rs. 24 per acre. Expenses Rs. 268, for which, after rent is paid, only Rs. 188 are available. Borrowed Rs. 35 towards rent, afterwards further Rs. 50. Repaid partly by sale of bullock for Rs. 25.
72	Do.	7¼	Cotton, juwar, indigo, wheat, barley.	Rent Rs. 25. Produce Rs. 141. Cotton Rs. 12, juwar Rs. 4, indigo Rs. 12, wheat Rs. 30, barley Rs. 17½ per acre. Profits from moneylending business Rs. 190. Favourable balance Rs. 74. Household furniture Rs. 5.
73	Do.	24½	Cotton, juwar, maize, rice, wheat, barley, peas.	Rent Rs. 72-8-0. Produce Rs. 162. Cotton Rs. 5¾, juwar Rs. 9, maize Rs. 8, rice Rs. 8, wheat Rs. 26, barley and peas Rs. 18 per acre. Expenses Rs. 162; available, after rent paid, Rs.72-8-0, leaving a deficiency of Rs. 89-8-0. No rent arrears. Debt Rs. 250. Outturn of land previous year very poor.
76	Mauza Jorsimi	14½	Juwar, cotton, maize, wheat, bejhar, tobacco, carrots.	Rent, 11 ac. Rs. 61-2-6; 3½ ac. Rs. 32—Rs. 93. Produce Rs. 183. Juwar Rs. 2½, cotton Rs. 20, maize Rs. 5¾, wheat Rs. 24, bejhar Rs. 7, tobacco (at the rate of) Rs. 60, carrots (do.) Rs. 45 per acre. Subletting produced Rs. 18. Income Rs. 201. Expenditure Rs. 223-14-6, minus Rs. 22-14-6. Debt Rs. 300, also grain, and a loan for payment of rent.

Page.	Village.	No. of Acres.	Character of Crop.	Rent, Yield per Acre, and Comments.
77	Mauza Jorsimi	29	Cotton, maize, indigo, wheat, gujai, dofasli.	Sublets 28¼ acres, with a net gain of Rs. 50. Produce for remainder Rs. 79. Cotton (at the rate of) Rs. 16, maize Rs. 7½, indigo Rs. 9, wheat Rs. 11, gujai Rs. 6¼ per acre. Moneylending Rs. 350 per year. Annual savings Rs. 102.
79	Do.	4½	Wheat, barley, grain.	Rent Rs. 33-1-9. Produce Rs. 42. Wheat Rs. 12½, barley Rs. 8, wheat and grain Rs. 1 per acre. Expenses not stated. After paying rent only Rs. 9 for family of six. Debt: for rent Rs. 33, sowing Rs. 7, food Rs. 90, clothing Rs. 12 = Rs. 142, and old debts of Rs. 150.
81	Barchua	33	No details.	Rent Rs. 80, land partly out of cultivation through encroachment of river. Rent, one year's arrears and other debts. 'He borrowed Rs. 25 worth of seed grain for this harvest. As long as he remembers he used to borrow his seed grain.' One debt ten years old, to pay for food and discharge rent. Happily, family dying out.
82	Nadarmai	8	Cereals, cotton, millet.	Rent Rs. 60. Reduced circumstances through river encroachment. Rent Rs. 170 in arrears; owes moneylenders Rs. 500, plus Rs. 200, plus Rs. 30—Rs. 760 in all.
83	Pinjri	5½	Bajra, arhar, cotton, wheat, barley, peas, grain, sugar cane, pulse.	Rent Rs. 17½. Total produce Rs. 128. Sugar cane yielded Rs. 20, bajra Rs. 8, wrack Rs. 4, cotton Rs. 2, pulse Rs. 4, wheat, barley, peas and grain Rs. 90. Has Rs. 30 extra income. Total Rs. 120 or Rs. 10 per month for four people. Debt trifling. Wife Rs. 15 of jewelry.

Page.	Village.	No. of Acres.	Character of Crop.	Rent, Yield per Acre, and Comments.
84	Pinjri	10	Maize, cotton, sugar cane, wheat, barley, peas.	Rent Rs. 18. Total produce Rs. 90. Six acres wheat and barley yielded Rs. 50, the average being Rs. 9 per acre. Borrowed half of second marriage expenses (whole cost Rs. 100) which he has paid.
84	Do.	5½	Pulse, rice, hemp.	Rent Rs. 28. Total produce Rs. 28, thus absorbing everything. Earns wages as water-drawer to two families, also get Rs. 8 per month for ghi from three cattle. Owes Rs. 18. Daughter married four years ago, cost Rs. 50, of which his brother found Rs. 40. Women have no blanket or quilt; they 'have to manage with their day clothes as best they can; they spend most of the cold nights cowering over a fire of rubbish in the enclosure.' Five in family.
85	Nadrala	5½	No details.	No details. 'Says he could eat twenty-five per cent. more nowadays if he got it.' Not in debt. Described as a 'broken-down small proprietor; comes of a lazy, indolent lot. The Kachchis in the village grow opium and vegetables, but this fellow is above it, and his fields are badly cultivated and unproductive.'
86	Do.	2½	Do.	Rent Rs. 9¾. Eight in family. Buys grain at 28 lbs. per rupee; 'He finds that maize makes his children's bellies swell, so he eats muth pulse in preference.' 'The women and boys have no bedding.' No debt.

Page.	Village.	No. of Acres.	Character of Crop.	Rent, Yield per Acre, and Comments.
86	Mandpura	4½	Cotton, juwar, wheat and barley, maize, sugar cane, carrots, opium.	Rent Rs. 59. Total produce Rs. 97, divided thus: cotton Rs. 15, juwar Rs. 2, maize Rs. 8, remainder estimated,—wheat and barley Rs. 20, barley Rs. 9, sugar cane Rs. 22, fœnugret Rs. 2, carrots Rs. 2, opium Rs. 5, tobacco Rs. 12. Joint family 11, one of whom earns Rs. 5 per month as gardener to Raja of Awa. Debt: Rs. 250, deficiency in rent, clothing, marriage expenses. In past ten years spent Rs. 42 in funerals. 'Every month spends 8 annas (8d.) in worship to the small goddess and the local ghost. If he did not do this he does not know what would become of his crops.' [This is the first record in the Inquiry of anything whatsoever being paid on account of religion or worship.]
88	Pahloi	15	Cotton, bajra, maize, ghaya, wheat, barley, opium, cucumber, grain.	Rent Rs. 57-2-6. Total produce Rs. 158-12-9. Franghi and home-made cotton thread receives Rs. 7 and Rs. 8. Income Rs. 168-12-9; expenditure Rs. 155-2-6; balance Rs. 18-10-8. No arrears of rent. Three in family.
92	Do.	8	Maize, cotton, bajra, juwar. barley, wheat, tobacco, assorted pulses.	Rent Rs. 8-10-6. Produce averages Rs. 11½ per acre; Autumn harvest Rs. 28, Spring do. Rs. 68-5-0. Total Rs. 91-12-0. Expenses Rs. 89-12-0, balance Rs. 2. Family, 8, no children, man aged 80. No arrears of rent; no debt.

Page.	Village.	No. of Acres.	Character of Crop.	Rent, Yield per Acre, and Comments.
95	Pahloi	7¾	Bajra, cotton, maize, barley, grain, arhar, oilseeds.	Rent Rs. 10-0-9. Produce Rs. 32-3-0, income as carpenter Rs. 60—Rs. 92-3-0. Expenses Rs. 99-8-9. Deficiency Rs. 7-5-9. Family 6. Debt Rs. 30 for daughter's marriage. During year spent 1s. 4d. for sugar, 1s. 10½d. for salt, spices 1s., ghi 2s. 8d., oil 1s. 10½d. The salt expenditure provided 8 lbs. per head; in same Provinces, when means permit, 20 lbs. each are consumed (p. 17).
97	Do.	10¼	Cotton, bajra, juwar, maura, ghaya, wheat, barley, arhar, poppy, tobacco, carrots, mustard.	Rent Rs. 29. Produce Rs. 154-11-0, other income Rs. 27—Rs. 181-11-0. Expenses Rs. 171-1-0; there appears a saving of Rs.10-10-0 per annum. No arrears. 7 children, 4 married, 3 to be married. (First instance of more than 3 or 4 children.) Marriage costs Rs. 50.
109	Mathena Zabti	10¾	Mung, dhan, wheat, grain.	Rent Rs. 19. 'Produce might be worth Rs. 103.' Income Rs. 84. 8 in family. 'No jewelry, no cart; we rarely use milk.'
109	Do.	20¾	Mung, dhan, kodon, wheat, barley, grain.	Rent Rs. 32. 'Value of crops perhaps Rs. 130.' Profit Rs.92. Eight in family. 'I have 10 maunds of grain (822 lbs.) in the house. Have Rs. 20 worth of jewels.'
110	Do.	25	Do.	Rent Rs. 46. Produce Rs. 131. Average yield Rs. 7 per acre. Owe Rs. 6. 'I have 15 maunds of grain (1231 lbs.) in the house.' Family 7. 'Rs. 20 of jewelry.'
110	Do.	12½	Mung, dhan, kodon, wheat.	Rent Rs. 25. Produce Rs. 95. Income Rs. 70. Average yield Rs. 8 per annum 410 lbs. of grain. 'Live absolutely by myself; no wife or children.'

Page.	Village.	No. of Acres.	Character of Crop.	Rent, Yield per Acre, and Comments.
110	Mathena Zabti	⅓	Gram.	Rent 10 annas. Produce Rs. 2. Hand cultivation. Day-labourer—1d. per day, £1 12s. 0d. per year. 'Live alone; no wife or child, no jewelry. . . . sometimes not enough to eat.'
110	Do.	⅓	Do.	Very much same as preceding.
110	Do.	88	Mung, dhan, wheat, kodon, sugar cane.	Rent Rs. 86. Produce Rs. 189. Average yield Rs. 8 per annum. 880 lbs of grain. No debt. Six in family. 'Rs. 10 of jewels, enough clothes, ordinary food.'
111	Do.	4⅓	Dhan, wheat.	Rent Rs. 8. Produce Rs. 19. Average yield Rs. 4 per acre. No grain in stock. Five in family. 'Am often ill with spleen disease.' 'No jewels.'
111	Do.	8⅓	Mung, dhan, wheat.	Rent Rs. 7. Produce Rs. 25. Yield Rs. 6¼ per acre. 164 lbs. grain. 'Will have to borrow seed for next harvest. Not at present in debt. Have a silver necklet worth 2s. 8d.'
111	Do.	1½	Dhan, wheat.	Rent Rs. 2-12-0. Produce Rs. 5-8-0. Yield Rs. 4¼ per acre. Have a little grain. Wife, no children; daily labourer, 1d. per day.
111	Do.	⅔	Dhan.	Rent Rs. 1-5-0. Produce Rs. 8. Surplus Rs. 1-11-0. No plough, no children; earns Rs. 24 per annum for day-labour. 'Wife has a Rs. 5 silver armlet.'
111	Do.	6½	Dhan, kodon, wheat.	Rent Rs. 4-8-0. Produce Rs. 10. Surplus Rs. 5-18-0. Three cattle, 164 lbs. grain. Not in debt. Wife and four children. Village and zemindar's servant. No jewels.

Page.	Village.	No. of Acres.	Character of Crop.	Rent, Yield per Acre, and Comments.
111	Mathena Zabti	5	Mung, dhan, wheat.	Rent Rs. 6¼. Produce Rs. 22. Average yield Rs. 4¼. Owes Rs.20. Borrows seed at 25 per cent. interest. Family 7; self, three women, three children. Rs. 24 of ornaments.
112	Do.	4	Mung, dhan, barley, grain.	Rent Rs. 5-4-0. Produce Rs. 25. Average yield Rs. 6-2-12. 164 lbs. of grain. 'Must borrow seed for next harvest.' Rs. 25 of jewelry.
112	Do.	3⅓	Mung, dhan, grain.	Rent Rs. 4-11-0. Produce Rs. 26. Average yield Rs. 8 per annum. Family: self, wife, four children. 'Not in debt. No jewels. Will have to borrow for next sowings.'
112	Do.	4⅘	Mung, dhan, wheat, grain.	Rent Rs. 6-9-6. Produce Rs. 18-8-0. Average yield Rs. 3-12-0 per acre. Borrowed 656 lbs. of grain for food, repayable with thirty-three per cent. interest.
112	Do.	1	Dhan, wheat.	Rent Rs. 1-9-0. Produce Rs. 70. In service, one penny per day wages. 'No wife nor family. Not in debt. Sufficient food and the clothes I have on.'

The above are samples of the Mathena Zabti, Paranpur. It is melancholy enough. But, take the village as a whole, as officially summarised, and the melancholy deepens, while the wonder grows as to how life can be sustained. Particulars which follow will show that fifty per cent. of the gross produce (Government take half of that fifty per cent. as revenue) was taken for rent. The yield from the soil, after rent has been paid, gives Rs.4 1a. 6p. (5s. 5½d.) per head per annum towards maintenance, clothing, etc. The cattle apparently save the people, but of these, in

1888, there were only 1,055 against 3,000 'some time ago.' A detailed consideration of the following particulars concerning this village, 'which is a typical one in this district,' will well repay the time it takes :—

MATHENA ZABTI—266 HOLDINGS.

	Rent. Rs.		Cultivated Bighas pucka (equals five-eighths of an acre).
166 Pahikasht	744	...	676
100 Resident	1,000	...	1,064
Rent			Rs. 1,744
Cultivated area...			B.p. 1,740

	B.p.			B.p.	Produce. M.k.	Rs.
Kharif ...	766 ...	Pahikasht	...	766 ...	752 ...	752
		Resident	...	400 ...	800 ...	800
				Total	... ...	1,552

	B.p.			B.p.	M.k.	Rs.
Rabi ...	964 ...	Pahikasht	...	300 ...	600 ...	600
		Resident	...	664 ...	1,328 ...	1,328
				Total	... ...	1,928

(Of this 52 biswas is do-fasli.) Total value of crops, 3,480.[1]

Census of residents :—145 men, 140 women, 71 boys, 69 girls.

CATTLE OF RESIDENTS.

Bullocks	241	Patwari states that some time ago there were as many as 3,000 cattle in the village. They have been reduced partly by disease and partly by extension of cultivation.
Buffaloes (male)	20	
Cows and calves	781	
Buffaloes (female)	52	
Pony	1	
Goats...	10	

[1] 'According to this the value of the crop is about double the rent. The estimated out-turn seems low, as it averages about two kutcha maunds the pucka bigha, or about 153 lbs. the acre.' [Lord Curzon's *average* is 740 lbs. the acre.] 'But the soil is very light. There is no irrigation, and the crops are much eaten by wild animals from the neighbouring forest. There is a great deal of waste land, which gives fairly good grazing, and most of the cultivators make something out of cattle breeding. The cattle are a poor breed, and give very little milk. They do not, however, cost anything to rear.' THE AVERAGE INCOME FROM THE LAND HERE WORKS OUT AT Rs.4 1a. 6p. (5*s.* 5½d.) PER HEAD PER ANNUM ! !

Free grazing in Government forests and in village waste. Free wood and thatching grass.[1]

Mr. E. B. Alexander, Collector of Etawah, sums up the information furnished by the Tahsildars under the directions issued by his predecessor, Mr. Whiteway. In the course of his remarks Mr. Alexander says:—

'On one point the statistics furnished do throw light, and that is the extent to which the cultivators fall in debt in anything like a bad year and the utter absence of any savings laid up in good years beyond a small amount of jewelry and occasionally a few surplus head of cattle. I am not sure that I am not leaving the point of the present inquiry when entering on this subject; but both are so closely connected that I think it is worth while going into this in some detail. The question whether the ordinary cultivator suffers from want of food may, I think, be said to depend entirely upon two factors—the general state of the loan market and his own credit, both of which are, of course, dependent in a great measure upon the seasons.

'In Muttra, for instance, the number of bad debts which money-lenders had made between 1877 and 1883 had caused the money market to be very unfavourable for borrowers; and even men who were known to be honest, and not overwhelmed with debt, had great difficulty in raising money to live on during the two months before each harvest, when nine cultivators out of ten look to their bohra to make them subsistence advances.

'In Mainpuri, on the other hand, the market was favourable, whilst I was there in 1885, and it was only men whose individual credit was bad that had any difficulty in raising such advances.

'In all ordinary years I should say that the cultivators live for at least one-third of the year on such advances, and in unfavourable years they have either to increase the amount of their debt to the bohra, or have to sell off jewelry, cattle, or anything else which can possibly be spared.

'One bad year they can generally weather by sacrifices of this kind and by a comparatively unimportant increase to the debit side of their account. But when there is a succession of unfavourable years, or even a succession of slightly below average years following a bad one, their circumstances rapidly deteriorate. They have no capital to fall back on. The bohra is averse to increasing his already heavy claim by making further advances; and then, no doubt, the average cultivator suffers severely from insufficiency of food.

'There can be no doubt but that in Muttra such deficiency drove a

---

[1] 'Econ. Inq., N.W.P.,' pp. 112–13. Since then, in all probability, the free grazing, free wood, and free thatching, have been taken away.

large number of cultivators between 1878 and 1888 A.D. to abandon their homes and remove to other parts of the country, where they could get a living by day work, or had friends to support them. Muttra, however, was exceptionally unlucky. For about eight years there were not two really good harvests running, whilst there were twice three bad ones running, and nearly all the rest were below average, or almost only average.[1]

'This district (Etawah) has, I understood, been through a rather bad time prior to the rabi just harvested (which has been a good crop); and I certainly saw a good many people when I first came here (early in March) whose appearance showed distinctly that they were suffering from insufficiency of food.

'At the present moment I do not suppose that, except absolute paupers who are dependent on alms, any class of the population here is suffering from insufficiency of food.

'I do not, however, on the other hand, think that it is at all probable that most of the persons who borrowed money during 1294 or during the first six months of 1295 have paid off their debts. They have probably paid up enough to meet the interest and to restore their credit, and in many cases have probably redeemed articles which they had pawned; but the bulk of the harvest has gone in meeting arrears of rent, the rent for the rabi, and interest on debt; and if we are to have another bad kharif there would, I am sure, be a great increase of indebtedness which, if accompanied or followed by any great rise in prices, must render it impossible for a large part of the population to obtain sufficient food during the first three months preceding the next rabi.

'The village Marhapur stands on the Jumna ravines, and did not suffer seriously from flooding. There are eighty-seven families, of whom fifty-five are cultivators, about twenty day-labourers, and the other twelve banias or artisans. The fifty-five cultivating households were all in debt at the close of the year for sums varying from Rs.800 to Rs.10, and the day-labourers for sums varying from Rs.18 to Rs.2. Most of the farmers, also, were obliged to part with jewelry or cattle.

'The largest sum actually borrowed in the year was Rs.428 by Chabnath Thakur, a man with a large household of twenty-two persons, six of whom are children under three years old, four children between three and ten, and the other twelve grown up. He cultivates twenty-three and a half acres, and keeps several cattle for use in carts and for milking. He paid his creditor Rs.388 during the year at various times; but as his debt was actually increased by

---

[1] Was Muttra so 'exceptionally unlucky'? My examination of Bombay and Madras records show that such experiences are not at all unusual. There are few unirrigated districts in India of which it can be said that there are more good years than bad.—W. D.

Rs.420 principal, and there was a considerable sum due for interest, he found himself about Rs.150 deeper in debt at the close of the year than he was at the beginning, and heads the list with liabilities amounting to Rs.800. I am afraid that the poor kharif of 1295 fasli and the high prices must have told severely on him this year; but do not think that he has reached the stage at which actual want of food begins to make itself felt. He is still one of the well-to-do class of cultivators, and it is only after a succession of bad years that men of this class come to actual want.

'Ganga Mallah, with a smaller holding of only fourteen acres, and with a much smaller household of eleven persons, of whom all but three are grown up, borrowed Rs.257 12a. 9p., and repaid Rs.172 8a. At the end of the year he was about Rs.800 in debt; but as he was obliged to incur extraordinary expenditure of about Rs.100 on account of the marriage of two granddaughters, his debt need not be considered as proof of severe pressure, and he certainly did not suffer from any want of food.

'Mani Ahir, with no family except a wife, and cultivating a little over two acres as a shikma tenant, borrowed Rs.15 and only repaid Rs.8. He was in debt, therefore, at the end of the year to the amount of Rs.17, including interest, and was also in arrears with half his rent, in consequence of which he resigned his holding. He was enabled to support life by the sale of a kaddu crop and of a bullock, but had a hard time of it, and undoubtedly towards the end of the year suffered from want of food. He must have suffered severely during the first six months of the present year, though he has been able to eke out a living by day work and the produce of two cows which he keeps.

'Ajudhya Mallah, another small tenant with a family of four persons, borrowed Rs.11, which he failed to pay back. At the end of the year he was about Rs.50 in debt, and probably in the current year has found it difficult to raise a loan, and has therefore suffered from insufficiency of food between December and the end of March.

'Generally, it may be said of this village that the day-labourers and the petty cultivators, owing to high prices and poor harvests, have suffered more or less severely during the months of January, February, and part of March, 1888 A.D.; but that they did not suffer in 1294 fasli itself, and would not have suffered this year had not a bad kharif followed on a year below the average, and had not the prices gone up to an abnormal standard.

'In the Paphund tahsil the village selected was Mahinpur. It is a small village in which there are only thirty-five houses, about half of which are occupied by cultivators, and the rest by day-labourers, one dhobi, and one hajjam.

'The tahsildar selected Balgobind Chaube and Debia Gararia for special inquiry. The former is a middle-class cultivator holding about twelve acres at a rent of Rs.68, and having a family of five, of whom one is under ten and the others adults. His kharif cultivation was very unfortunate, and in order to live from October onwards up to March he had to sell cattle worth Rs.56. The rabi was poor, though not so bad as the kharif, and in order to meet his rent he had to borrow Rs.54. At the end of the year he was about Rs.70 in debt, but had not reached the stage at which actual want begins to make itself felt.'[1]

The class immediately above the landless day-labourer supports itself partly by cultivation and partly by day-labour. The holding in such cases is generally from six to twelve kutcha bighas, or from one to two acres, and the occupant is either without any plough-animals at all, or else is possessed of only one, or at most two, miserable bullocks or buffaloes. In the former case he makes the spade do the work of a plough; in the latter case his plough often requires the loan of a neighbour's cattle. His holding grows enough, after payment of the rent and after providing for seed-grain, to keep the family in food for two or three months, and he supplements his income by working as a day-labourer whenever his own land does not require his care. He is slightly better off than the landless labourer; but it cannot be said of him that he always has enough to eat or sufficiently warm clothes. He is generally a little in debt, and he would be more in debt were the moneylender not very cautious as to the amount of his advances. Mr. Alexander continued:—

'The condition of the agricultural classes proper, by which I mean the very numerous body of rent-paying tenants whose holdings are large enough to employ and support them throughout the year, is with difficulty described in general terms. Taking the three tahsils of the district separately, the Puranpur tenant may be described as a careless agriculturist, who can obtain at any time as much land as he likes in his own or in any neighbouring village at low rates of rent, varying from Re. 1-8-0 to Re. 1-4-0 an acre, and who finds ample grazing in the tracts of waste or in the surrounding Government forest for as many head of cattle as he can collect. The soil, however, is too light and sandy to yield heavy crops, and the unhealthiness of

---

[1] 'Econ. Inq., North-Western Provinces,' pp. 101-3.

the climate and the depredations of wild animals are serious drawbacks. The Puranpur tenant on the whole enjoys, I am inclined to think, a greater degree of rude prosperity than his untidy surroundings and his unsubstantial dwelling appear to indicate. His indebtedness is not generally of a serious nature; and in a great many instances he is not only free from debt but has a little money or grain out at interest.

'The Pilibhit tenant differs from his Puranpur neighbour in depending less on cattle breeding and more on sugar cane and rice cultivation. The amount of labour employed in the former industry, from the preparation of the ground for the seed to the final stage of sugar-refining, is very great. There are few weeks in the year in which a day-labourer cannot find employment in some branch of this industry. In November cutting and crushing commence, and go on till March. In every village beheea sugar-mills are at work, and every bullock and spare hand are put on to the task of making the produce marketable. The village boiling establishments (or *bels*) create a fresh demand for labour, and after the juice has been boiled down to *rab* or *gur* all the carts in the district find remunerative occupation in carting the unrefined sugar to towns where sugar refineries are established. This goes on throughout April. In the town of Pilibhit, where there are so many sugar-refining houses, several hundreds of labourers earn from Rs.3 to Rs.4 a month in bringing in a sort of fresh-water weed called *siwar* from ponds and marshes, which is used to give whiteness to the sugar. Meanwhile the next year's crop is equally exacting of labour. Ploughing, manuring, and harrowing are incessant from January to the end of February. Planting begins with the expiry of the fires of the Holi festival; and from March till the setting in of the rains the young cane requires constant hoeings, weedings, and waterings, all of which mean employment to the landless day-labourer.'[1]

Of Shahjehanpur it is stated:—

'The landless labourer's condition must still be regarded as by no means all that could be desired. The united earnings of a man, his wife, and two children cannot be put at more than Rs.3 a month. *When prices of food grains are low or moderate, work regular, and the health of the household good, this income will enable the family to have one fairly good meal a day, to keep a thatched roof over their heads, and to buy cheap clothing, and occasionally a thin blanket.*[2]

---

[1] 'Econ. Inq., North-Western Provinces,' pp. 107–8.

[2] The italics are mine. The reader may profitably pause and spend a few moments in realising, so far as his own happy position will admit, what the italicised lines really mean.—W. D.

Cold and rain undoubtedly entail considerable suffering to such householders, as the members are insufficiently clothed and cannot afford fires. A few twigs or dried sticks constitute the height of their ambition; and these, owing to the increasing value and scarcity of wood, are more and more difficult for the poor man to obtain.'[1]

The 'Inquirer' continues:—

'I have dwelt on the cane industry because throughout two-thirds of this district it is the key to the agricultural position. If the lowest and poorest class in the towns and villages are better off, as I believe they are, than they were, if they find more constant and better paid employment, the extension of the sugar-cane cultivation has had a good deal to say to this. The economic effect, however, on the tenant agriculturist is not always good. The sure test of the prosperity of the sugar cultivator is his making *gur* himself from his sugar-cane juice, and the absence of a bania's sugar-boiling vat (*bel*) from the village. These conditions prevail throughout the greater part of the Jahanabad pargana. I have recorded the statements made by the cultivators of mauza Sudderpur, and that village is a fair type of many others in the pargana. I attribute the comparative prosperity of the cultivator partly to the canal, and partly to the practice of kind rents which here prevails. In the Pilibhit pargana the *bel* system has established itself in most of the villages, and the cultivators know to their cost that, once in the sugar-boilers' books, there is very little chance of escape. The crop is usually sold to the bania during the rains, a portion of the purchase money being paid down, and the balance doled out in subsequent months. The tenant agrees to deliver so many measures of sugar juice when the crop is ready. In order to acquire a secure footing in the village, the bania, the first year of operations, intentionally agrees to advances in excess of the value of the standing cane-crop. In April, when delivery has been taken of the cane-juice and the accounts are made up, the tenant finds himself deep in the sugar-boiler's debt for undelivered sugar. To cover this, the next year's crop has to be sold in advance. The sweating system is thus established, and the tenant becomes the bond slave of the bania. His only chance of extrication lies in his landlord, and instances are not uncommon of landlords rescuing their tenants by paying off the moneylender and recovering the advance by easy instalments from the debtor. Other motives besides generosity prompt such intervention. Sometimes the landlord fears that his bankrupt tenantry may abscond to the Tarai, and leave the village uninhabited. At other times he wishes to step into the place of the bania, and add the profits of sugar-boiling to his zemindari income.

[1] 'Econ. Inq.,' p. 107.

In the latter case he is less liberal in his advances, as he both knows the circumstances of each cultivator more intimately than the moneylender, and, unlike the latter, he is alive to the imprudence of utterly ruining the borrower. The landlord is not unfrequently the tenant's sugar merchant and banker. At other times he buys the crop in advance from the tenant in order to sell it at a higher price several months later to a sugar-boiler. The *bel* system thus takes various forms, though they are all alike in this—that they rest on the indebtedness of the agriculturist, and are designed to keep him needy and dependent. Agriculture carried on under such conditions can never be very profitable to the tenant. I find no evidence, however, that the average cultivator is generally worse off than he was eight or ten years ago, or that his debts have increased. In the Jahanabad pargana and in parts of the Pilibhit pargana the circumstances of the cultivator have probably improved. In the southern part of the Bisalpur tahsil the worst effects of the *bel* system are seen. Bad seasons and bad landlords have combined with the sugar-boiler against the cultivator. His condition in the group of villages lying between Bamrauli and the borders of Shahjehanpur district has undoubtedly deteriorated of recent years. The ploughs and the population appear to have decreased since settlement, and a good many tenants have migrated to more prosperous tracts, and in some villages the land revenue is realised with difficulty.'[1]

The detailed inquiry into the actual yield of the fields and the condition of the people may be continued over the next four pages. I abstract and collate pp. 113–117 as follows:—

[1] 'Econ. Inq.,' p. 108. Sir T. W. Holderness, K.C.S.I., then Collector of Pilibhit, now Secretary of the Revenue and Statistics Department, India Office.

Page.	Village.	No. of Acres.	Character of Crop.	Rent, Yield per Acre, and Comments.
118	Sirsa Sardar	23½	Dhan, kodon, wheat, grain, linseed, cotton, sugar cane	Headman of village. Rent Rs. 55-5-3. Produce Rs. 148. For sugar cane rent cash paid, others in kind. 'For some fields I paid one-third of the produce, for others one-fourth.' Owes Rs. 55 (twelve per cent. per annum). No fees or profits as headman. Rs. 10 jewelry. Household: self, three women, three children. Has bedsteads (charpais)[1] but no other furniture.
118	Do.	18⅓	Dhan, kodon, wheat, barley, grain, mustard, sugar cane	Rent Rs. 55-8-0. Produce Rs. 201. Sugar cane made in gur-cakes realised Rs. 45; 17½ acres realised Rs. 156, or Rs. 9 per acre. 'Owe my zemindar Rs. 60 (twelve per cent. int.). Have just repaid Rs. 6; whenever I want money get it from him at that rate. Household: self, brother, six women, four children = 12. No grain in stock. Rs.15 of jewels. No household effects save bedsteads. I save nothing; keep on borrowing and paying back.'
114	Do.	11	Sycamore, dhan, kodon, wheat, barley, alsi, urd	Rent Rs. 37. Produce (gur-cakes Rs. 60) Rs. 180. Average yield, omitting sugar, nearly Rs. 7 per acre. 'Owe Rs. 40; will repay and borrow again. Household: self, brother, four women, and seven children. Rs. 10 jewelry. Deer and pig eat crops. Forest-wood and grazing formerly free; now dues paid.'

[1] 'Charpay. (Corruption of the Hindu *charpai*, from *char*, "four," and *pai*, "a foot.") A bedstead consisting of a plain frame of wood set on four short legs; broad tapes are folded along and across the frame to form the bed' (Whitworth's Anglo-Indian Dictionary).

Page.	Village.	No. of Acres.	Character of Crop.	Rent, Yield per Acre, and Comments.
114	Sirsa Sardar	4½	Dhan, kodon	Rent Rs. 8-1-0. Produce Rs.25-12-0. 'Most of my rent paid in kind, one-third or one-fourth of produce. Owe zemindar Rs.25 (12½ per cent. interest).[1] Household: self, three brothers, one woman, three children. Brothers as labourers earn Rs. 25 per year (1d. per day). Generally have one meal a day. Have not enough clothes. Am very poor.'
114	Manderiya	24	Dhan, kodon, wheat, grain, mustard, linseed, cotton, sugar cane	Rent Rs. 55-7-0. Produce (sugar-cane juice Rs. 80) Rs. 282. Average yield, omitting sugar, Rs. 7 per acre. Owe lessee of village (a Hindu) Rs. 50 (twelve per cent. per annum); to two sugar-boilers, Rs. 80 and Rs. 40, same rate. 'As headman (mokaddam) they let me off interest in lieu of commission.' Household: self, two women, three boys, four girls = 10. 'About Rs. 17 of jewels.' 820 lbs. of grain, 'will have to go on borrowing before next harvest.'
115	Do.	5⅓	Dhan, kodon, wheat, linseed, barley, cotton, sugar cane	Rent Rs. 15-8-0. Produce (sugar-cane juice Rs. 25) Rs. 58. Average yield, omitting sugar, Rs.6⅔ per acre. Household: self, wife, two children. Earn in village 1d. per day. Borrow for next harvest. Rs. 12 jewels; bedsteads, etc., worth Rs. 2 (2s. 8d.). 'Sometimes eat once, sometimes twice a day.'

[1] 'This rate is exceptionally low: but the zemindar, who is a well-to-do and liberal Muhammadan, makes advances to his tenants at what a money-lender would regard as nominal rates. The advances are not considered moneylending, as the zemindar regards money usury as morally wrong.'

Page.	Village.	No. of Acres.	Character of Crop.	Rent, Yield per Acre, and Comments.
115	Manderiya	4½	Urd, dhan, kodon, wheat, grain, barley, linseed	Rent Rs.8. Produce Rs.11-4-0. Average yield, less than Rs. 3 per acre. Owe Rs. 25 to moneylender at twelve per cent. per annum. 86 lbs. of grain. No family. No jewels. 'I bought a buffalo with borrowed money; it died; had it lived I could have been able to plough better, and so have made more by my holding.'
115	Do.	5	Urd, dhan, barley, wheat, kodon, grain, sugar cane	Rent Rs. 13-7-0. Produce (sugar-cane juice Rs. 17½) Rs. 37-8-0. Average yield, omitting sugar, 1 a., Rs. 5. Owe Rs. 46 to village lessee. Borrow next harvest seed. Household: three men, one woman, three children. Add to income a few rupees by making and mending ploughs. No jewels.
116	Do.	6½	Sugar cane, linseed, dhan, kodon, mustard, wheat, barley	Rent Rs. 12-10-0. Produce (sugar-cane juice Rs. 2-11-0) Rs. 83-11-0. Owe Rs. 25 to sugar-boiler—over-estimated my yield. Average yield Rs. 12-6-0 per acre. Household: self, wife, 4 children. 'Have seven vessels and Re. 1 other household effects. Generally have only one meal a day.'
116	Do.	5⅓	Dhan, kodon, wheat, barley, linseed, mustard	Rent Rs. 16-14-0. Produce Rs. 40. Average yield, Rs. 8 per annum. Owe Rs. 21 (twelve per cent. interest) to sugar-boiler. Also borrowed Rs. 9 in village for food. Self, wife, two children. 'Will have to borrow for sowings.' As village shoemaker, get about Rs. 20 a year. 'Two vessels, two bedsteads worth 4d. each, no jewels, no grain in store. Generally two meals a day, but sometimes can afford only one.'

Page.	Village.	No. of Acres.	Character of Crop.	Rent, Yield per Acre, and Comments.
116	Kalianpur	80	Muth, dhan, kodon, wheat, grain, linseed, barley, urd, sugar cane	Headman. Rent Rs. 120-15-0. Nearly 8 acres under sugar cane. Contracted deliver 1,100 maunds (91,200 lbs.), but actually realised Rs. 304. Other produce worth Rs. 387 =Rs. 691. Average yield, omitting sugar cane, Rs. 5 per acre. Owe sugar-boiler Rs. 400, mostly twelve per cent. Just paid Rs. 100; debt due to delivering less than agreed of sugar-juice. Household: five men, five women, four children. Rs.25 jewelry.
117	Do.	18	Dhan, kodon, wheat, grain, urd, sugar cane	Rent 'Rs. 49, mostly in kind.' Produce (sugar cane 1 acre, Rs. 16-5-0) Rs. 88-5-0. Owe Rs.100 at eighteen per cent. Lately repaid Rs. 30. No grain in house. Borrow for harvest. Household: self, three women, three children. Rs. 4 of jewels. 'My debts cripple me.'
117	Do.	19½	Sugar cane, muth, dhan, wheat, barley, grain, linseed, mustard	Rent 'Rs. 102-13-0, most of it in kind.' Produce (sugar cane nearly 8 acres, crop failure,—as cakes Rs. 11½) Rs. 152½. Average yield, omitting sugar, under Rs. 8 per acre. Owes Rs. 250 at 24 per cent. Lately repaid nothing. 520 lbs. grain in house. Wife and two children. Rs. 20 jewels.
117	Do.	6	Sugar cane, kodon, wheat, barley, grain, linseed, urd	Rent 'Rs. 76, mostly kind rents.' Produce (sugar cane ¾ acre, Rs. 39½) Rs. 188½. Average yield, omitting sugar, Rs. 20. Owe Rs. 250 at twelve per cent. Wife, five children. 'No jewels, no other property. My debts heavy. Sugar yield bad. Last year's dhan also poor.

Result of questions to women and boys gathering fuel in Government forests. (P. 117.)

Mostly widows of low castes. 'Pay 1¼d. for permits to gather fuel. One large bundle per day. Take eight miles and sell for 3d. or 4d. We thus clear 2½d. in two days. We can just live on this. We have one meal a day in the evening; . . . we don't always get enough to eat, and sometimes we don't have a full meal in the twenty-four hours. Prices are so high now that it is hard to live.'

Result of Questions to Cultivators in Mauza Sudderpur, 'where a good deal of sugar cane is grown and canal irrigation is general' (p. 117).

'We grow sugar cane without advances from moneylenders, and turn juice into cakes.

'Our zemindars have tried to induce us to sell our sugar-cane juice in advance to a sugar-boiling bania (moneylender) as the bania would give the zemindars a commission on his profits. But we have refused, as it is more profitable to make gur (cakes) for ourselves; and if the bania should once by advances get hold of us we should never get out of his power.

'We pay "kind" rents on all crops except sugar. The general rate is one-half the out-turn of grain, but for outlying fields one-third.'

From landlord 'we borrow seed and food.'

Rate for daily labour for all who have no land is one anna (1d.) per day.

'We eat the grain produce of our fields after the landlord has taken his share; and we clothe ourselves and buy what other things we want from our sugar cane. We rarely sell our grain crops.'

Statement by cultivator within a mile of Pilibhit town:—

'I rent 2¾ acres, paying Rs.10 rent.

'I grow spring crops, on lowlying bits melons and cucumbers.

'I work entirely with a spade.

'Occasionally cut thatch grass, and earn 2½d. per day, or I do other job work.

'I have a wife and two little children. We have one meal a day, in the evening. We have just enough to eat, being careful, and enough clothes, except in the very cold weather. Then one blanket each is not enough and we cannot afford to buy wood for fires.

'I am a little in debt to the bania; I shall pay him when the spring harvest is cut and then will have to borrow again.'

Statement by cultivators in Mirpur :—

'We sold all the sugar-crop during the rains to a Bilsanda sugar merchant. We registered the instrument. In it we agree to deliver so many kutcha maunds of juice (*rab*) for the money advanced to us, and in default to pay interest on the advance. We are never out of debt. We have only one English sugar-mill. The others are the old native *kolhu*. We have not been able to afford others. We are very badly off. Have not always enough to eat, and find it difficult to pay rent. The crops have been bad for two years. Last kharif there was no rice crop at all. First it did not rain, and then it rained too much' (p. 119).

'We make our own *gur*, and do not sell it in advance. We are not now in debt to any bania. Eight or nine years ago we were very much in debt, as a bania of Pilibhit had established a *bel*, and we were all in his books. Our zemindar, who happens to be a retired Deputy Collector, freed us from the bania by paying up our debts and settling instalments for us. The tenants were beginning to run away as they were almost ruined, and he freed us to save the village. Now we are pretty well off, though the rice crop was bad last kharif' (p. 119).

Inquiry in Mauza Maurauri, a village which immediately adjoins Rupur.

'The *bel* which you see belongs to a Kurmi of Pilibhit. We wish our debts could be freed as they have been in Rupur. We have always trouble when the year's accounts are made up in April, after all the cane has been crushed. The bania gives us credit for fewer measures of *rab* than we really delivered. His karinda cheats us. He always makes out that we are in his debt. There would be no good in *our* zemindar freeing us, as *our* zemindar would oust the bania merely in order to set up a *bel* for himself, and he would make us sell him our *rab*. We should then be even worse off than we are at present, as the bania has less power to oppress us than the landlord would have' (p. 120).

Mr. A. J. Lawrence, C.I.E., then Commissioner, Allahabad Division, who retired in 1891, in forwarding two reports from subordinates, says of Banda and Hamirpur, 'I believe there is here very little between the poorer classes of the people and semi-starvation; but what is the remedy?' Mr. Lawrence himself, in spite of his (then) twenty-eight years of experience, does not attempt to propound any remedy.

Mr. White, Collector and Magistrate, writing from Banda, says :—

'The poor Oudh peasant is an industrious man; he has to work hard, and he does work hard. The true statistics of spade tilth in Oudh should certainly be ascertained. I think the Government would be astonished to find how many Oudh peasants cultivate land without any bullocks at all.'

He proceeds :—

'If I am asked "whether it be true that the greater portion of the population of India suffer from a daily insufficiency of food," I should say that the question is a vague one, and that I should first wish to know what is a sufficiency of food. No answer can be given but this, that a very large number of the lower classes of the population clearly demonstrate by the poorness of their physique that either they are habitually half-starved, or have been in early years exposed to the severities and trials of a famine. And it will be remembered that if any young creature be starved while growing, no amount of subsequent fattening of the adult will make up for the injury to growth. As to *remedial measures*, none can be suggested but those already undertaken, the *development of communications*, and the consequent prevention of oscillations in prices, and the consequent settling of a regular standard of living and work and diet and marriage among all classes.

'I subjoin some typical cases which I have collected while in camp through my sarishtadar, Munshi Amir Husain, who has managed to elicit the information without letting it be known that it was required officially. The cases have not been in any way selected, but were taken as they came.

'*Mathenjau, Kumhar, of Mau Manpur, a small village in the ravines of the Ken river, near the ruined fort of Ramgarh.*

'I live with an old mother and a married elder sister, who is visiting us. I don't cultivate. I have two swine and four little pigs: my brother-in-law gave them to me on condition that I should give him half the increase. I live by making pots for sale: sometimes sell for kind, otherwise for the rate of two *gharas* for a pice. I get three or four seers of grain every day. I eat once in twenty-four hours, rarely twice. When my pots do not sell, I get grain given to me by my clients. To-day I had gram bread and dal of arhar. I collect cow-dung and fuel for my furnace, and am charged nothing. My *pagri* is worth five annas: I bought it a year ago. My *chaddar* was given me by a zemindar when his married daughter was going away. Some relatives gave me my *dhoti*, which they bought for four annas, two or three years ago. I wear only one *dhoti* during the year. I am not in debt.'

'*Madho, Kahar, of Naseni, near the high road from Pangarra to Kartal, aged twenty-two years.*

'Ours is the only family of Kahars in the village. I have father, mother, two brothers, two sisters, grandmother, maternal uncle, and his son. I cultivate 25 bighas with two ploughs, paying rent at Rs. 2 a bigha. Have sown 12 bighas with wheat. I eat bread twice daily of barley, gram, or juwar. The family expenditure is five or six seers daily. I never eat wheat. I sell my wheat to pay my rent. I get Re. 1 a month for supplying water to certain villages. I sometimes work as a palki-bearer, getting half anna a *kos*. I also make something at weddings. I borrow seed at *sawai* rates; have not yet paid anything. I eat mung, masur, mash dals—anything that I can get. I cannot save anything. I have just enough to get on with. My clothing consist of a *pagri*, a *dhoti*, and a body-cloth. I am not a fisherman. My father is not in service: he carries the zemindar's palki as a *begari*: he gets no pay for this, but something in kind. I do not make nets. I do not sow *singhara*. My womenkind do not serve the zemindar's family. They help in agriculture, and do the house work. I have two bullocks and one cow. I have not yet paid my rent, but have set off the claim for work done in carrying the zemindar's palki. If a Kahar goes on a long trip, he is paid hal f anna a kos' (one halfpenny for 1½ miles).

Chumka, Bhat, of Barsenda Manpur, on the Ken river.

'Ours is the only Bhat family in the village. I have a mother and two brothers. I have cultivated land on Rs.60 rent. Don't know how much land. I sowed juwar, and til, but the juwar came to nothing, and I only got five *panseries* of til: I have now sown about eighteen bighas with barley. My elder brother is in service at Lahureta on Rs.18 a year, with food and clothing extra. We have three bullocks, one cow, four she-buffaloes. We do not sell milk: we make it into ghi and curds: we sell the ghi and eat the curds. This morning I have eaten gram bread with *mattha*. Wheat? Why! the *deotas* in our village don't even get wheat. In the evening I eat juwar cooked in curds. Our mother grinds the grain and cooks the dinner. We have not kept any of our own grain to eat, but buy it daily. None of us sing ballads, or keep genealogies. We get our daily food from the sale of the ghi or by borrowing from the mahajan, to whom I now owe Rs. 82.'

Guthna, Domar, of Nayagaon in the extreme south of the Banda district of Ajaigarh.

'Have a wife and one small daughter. Do not cultivate land: make bamboo baskets: make one or two daily, which I sell for six pice or one anna each. Also play the drum when there is a marriage in the village: when I am paid four annas. I cut my bamboos off the hill, for which I pay the zemindar eight annas a year. I do not clear out the house latrines: there are no such things in our village. I have three sows, but I live chiefly by basket-making. My wife helps in the work. I also keep fowls but no one in the village, wants eggs. I eat generally jau, arhar, and gram. My wife gets old clothing from the villagers. I borrowed Rs. 2 from the villagers when my daughter was born, and I gave a feast to the other Domars of the village.'

Bihari, Teli, of Nayagaon.

'Have a wife and child. Have three bighas of land, Rs.8 rent. One bullock for the oil-press, and I have another bullock during the cultivating season. I press til, sarson, mahua. Don't generally sell oil, but press it for villagers, making about three pice (three farthings) a day. My family lives on the produce of my fields, making up the deficiency from daily earnings. I borrow seed at *sawai* rates. I do not till myself, but have ploughmen at 8 annas a day in Asar and 6 annas in Kuar. I make my clothing from my own cotton. I have paid Rs.6 out of my rent. I spent about Rs.50 on my son's marriage, of which I had to borrow Rs.25. I ate arhar dal, khichri, and juwar to-day, with some oil instead of ghi. I sometimes eat once a day, and sometimes twice.'

'*Lutna, Chamar, of Lahurra, near Kalinjar.*

'There is only myself and my old mother: have been married, but *gauna* has not taken place. I work as an agricultural labourer, getting about Rs.2 a month as wages. My father died some Rs.20 in debt, and I have had to work it off. I cut grass for the zemindar's cows, and so on. Just now zemindar gives me one anna a day. I ate masur bread last night with salt. In crop time I get wheat, or gram bread: generally have to eat arhar, masur, rice, and juwar. Have been married five or six years, but cannot get my wife to live with me yet for want of money: my mother also works for the zemindar and gets wages: but she is very old and feeble. I get my clothing from my share of the cotton picking. For every five seers of cotton picked the labourer gets half a seer. Then I get the Koeri to weave it up into *dhotis*. I pay the Koeri four annas for one *dhoti*.'

'*Debi, Kurmi, of Purani, pargana Girwan.*

'Brother and self hold one and a half anna of the village (equalling one-eleventh of the area); cultivate 30 or 40 bighas sir land. I also hold 80 bighas exproprietary tenure. Am not in debt at all. Have not got any wife or children. Have a nephew and a niece living with me. Have four bullocks, two ploughs, one cart, one buffalo, and five cows. I eat kodon, kakun, juwar, gram, or wheat. I generally make my own clothes from my own cotton. I never save anything. Any surplus I have is spent in *neotas*, etc. Spent Rs.7 in the case of the marriage from which I have just returned.'

'*Jai Ram, Kalwar of Pokhri.*

'Have a father, uncle, and three brothers. I hold the liquor licence here at Godha and at Pokhri, and have four shops in native territory. Whole family engaged in distilling liquor. I pay 4 annas a day for this shop, and I sell 4 or 5 annas worth daily. Mahua is purchased at 7 panseries a rupee. From this I make 8 gharas of liquor of ten bottles each, which I sell at 1 anna a bottle. My profit is perhaps Rs.6 or 7 a month. I eat barley or gram bread, and my grandmother cooks for me. My wife is at Pokhri. Have eaten *birra* bread to-day. I do not drink myself, not even at Holi.' (P. 122–3–4.)

Mr. E. Rose, Collector of Ghazipur, in dealing with another portion of these Provinces, writes a discriminating report, in which he depreciates much of the information given by the people of their own condition. His inquiries extended to about twenty villages. 'But,' he says, 'I gained more satisfactory information in the villages which were under my superintendence in the Court of Wards than elsewhere? Food prices at this time were abnormally high owing to local harvests being destroyed by excessive and untimely rains. This, however, with insect plagues and the like, is a contingency which occurs at regular intervals of years and must be allowed for.' In paragraph eight he remarks :—

'With reference to the first of the two classes:[1] I have found, as a result of my investigation, that where the holding is of average size, and the tenant unencumbered with debt; when his rent is not excessive, and there is an average out-turn of produce; when, in fact, the conditions are favourable, the position of the agriculturist, whether as small proprietor or otherwise, is upon the whole a fairly comfortable one. He and his family are well clothed and fed; the women of his household have a little jewelry, and litigation in the courts is not an impossible luxury. When it is considered that seventy-eight per cent. of the tenants in this district are tenants who have occupancy rights (ex-proprietary, fixed rate, or otherwise) and that thirty-one per cent. of the total cultivated area is recorded as proprietary sir, it follows that unless there is some disturbing element, some variation of the conditions to which I have referred, the major portion of the agriculturist population is not in that condition to which reference is made in the Resolution of the Government of India, as one in which there is a daily insufficiency of food. But, unfortunately, these conditions do not always exist. The holding is too small for the number of persons depending upon it, the tenant is in debt, his rent is unduly high, and now and again there comes the inevitable

---

[1] (*a*) Small proprietors and cultivators of land, and (*b*) Day-labourers, servants, and artisans.

failure or partial failure of the crops, the consequence of floods, storms, or drought. As a rule, a very large proportion of the agriculturists in a village are in debt. Sometimes the debt is one which has recently been contracted for a marriage ceremony or a lawsuit, but almost always, so far as the debtor is concerned, an indeterminate quantity; he has seldom an account of it, and only knows what he paid off at the last harvest or when the last payment was made.' (P. 182.)

Mr. F. B. Mulock, officiating Collector and Magistrate of Ballia, gives particulars (pp. 139–142) of a searching character. They need not, however, be cited, as the history of this district shows that 'a scarcity in the real sense of the word, much less a famine, has never occurred in Ballia.' The district is situated between the rivers Ganges and Goghra, which render it to a great extent independent of the seasons. If the rains fail, filtration provides moisture sufficient for the growing crops; in addition the soil is exceptionally fertile, while the revenue rates are very low, and, most important of all facts, it is permanently settled.[1] Even in this prosperous district, however, 'as in the west of India, weaving, once an important industry, is dying out.' There are no industries apart from agriculture. Many of the people emigrate and enter service in other parts of India remitting from their earnings to those left behind. In 1881–82 so much as £18,200 was thus sent by money orders through the post office.

Of the Jhansi Division, the Commissioner, Mr. Ward, says:—

'It will be seen that both Mr. Hardy and Babu Sanwal Das were led by their inquiries to the conclusion that a very small proportion of the population in this Division are habitually underfed. This conclusion entirely agrees with my own observations during the last four years. But it must be remembered that they have been years of prosperity. Food has been fairly cheap and wages high, and a

[1] One reporter, Mr. D. T. Roberts, remarks: 'It is not the permanence of the settlement but the lightness of the assessment which has conferred the benefit.' As a matter of fact it is both. By the permanence of the settlement the advantages derived from a low assessment are the longer appreciated.

very large sum of money has been poured into the Division. The standard of living among the poorer classes, however, is, I think, higher than in other parts of India; it certainly is higher than in the eastern districts of the Provinces. Like everything else in India, the style of living is much governed by tradition. The people of these parts, though necessarily poor from the barren nature of the country, have always maintained a rude independence. In lieu of starving, they would rather prefer to rob than to beg; but they would not stay at home and die without a murmur. They are, indeed, too little disposed to rely on their own exertions, and in times of difficulty expect to be provided for by the State or by the bania. But there are signs that this apathy has been shaken off. In Lalitpur the agriculturists are fairly free from debt, and the zemindars are beginning to appreciate the value of their land. In Jhansi, Act XVI. of 1882 has effected a noticeable reform. But in Jalaun the burden of indebtedness is very heavy, and I cannot but think that agriculture is declining from want of capital and from too continuous cultivation of the same land for the same crops. The Betwa Canal, however, has probably rendered the whole tract of Jalaun secure from famine. It has hitherto been little used, its chief object being to supply the want of the October and December rains, and since its construction there has been a sufficiency of rain either in October or December. Jhansi and Lalitpur are, in my opinion, secured by the railway from a dearth of food; but they are by no means as yet secured from a calamity more lasting in its effects—a dearth of water. However cheap grain may be, if the people are driven from their homesteads by want of water, and if the cattle die from the same cause, all the effects of the famine are produced, and the deserted villages are not easily brought under cultivation again when the calamity is passed. I have pointed out that the most promising method of increasing the water supply would be in all probability exceedingly remunerative to Government. This method is to gradually arrest the surface drainage by a system of small dams extending from the very commencement of every ravine or water channel as far down its course as it is practicable to construct them without recourse to the professional skill of an engineer. It may be confidently predicted that by a measure of this kind, the barren rocky high lands in both districts might be gradually converted into magnificent forests, while the spring-level in the lower lands would be raised by percolation. The Government possesses in Lalitpur 92,269 acres, and in Jhansi 28,580 acres of forest land. But it is only by courtesy that the word forest can be used to denote them. They might be forests if water and soil were provided for them, and the operation would be neither difficult nor costly. It is the simplicity and cheapness of the scheme which condemns it in an age of extreme centralisation. Had a small part of the capital expended on the Betwa Canal been devoted to the humble measure of damming the ravines that feed the Betwa or its tributaries far away from the bed of the stream, the same amount of water might have been intercepted, and the Government would now probably be drawing ten per cent. instead of one per cent. on its outlay. But it is only grand and expensive works that engage the attention or deserve the skill of a big Department; and except big Departments no one now has the power of spending public money.'

Mr. Hardy gives the following interesting particulars :—

'*Sultanpur, Pargana Moth.*

'A village tenanted chiefly by a Lodh brotherhood of petty sharers. Area about 700 acres, cultivated area 450 acres, revenue Rs.724, rental Rs.1,400. An average village, with fair land a mile off the main road, with a population of 518, composed of 88 households. I should divide these households into the following classes :—

(i.) Well off from the agricultural standpoint. Four families only, comprising 88 persons, would fall under this category. They are the three lambardars and the patwaris' families.

(ii.) Persons who are comfortably off, *i.e.*, who have a sufficiency of food all the year round, and are well clad. Forty-four families, with a population of 84 men, 75 women, 71 boys 65 girls; total, 295.

Of these families 17 are sharers or ex-sharers.
" " 24 are cultivators.
" " 2 are carpenters.
" " 1 is a barber.

(iii.) Persons who, though in ordinary years are fairly well off, suffer from insufficiency of food when prices are high, abnormally high. Twenty-five families: 86 men, 84 women, 28 boys, 29 girls: total 127.

One of these families is that of a sharer.
Seventeen " " are cultivators.
Four " " are labourers.
One " " is a chaukidar.
One " " is a bania (petty).

(iv.) Persons who, except at harvest time, are habitually underfed. Ten families: 16 men, 12 women, 13 boys, 17 girls; total 58. 'Six are labourers, mostly with large families.'

Details of another village are also set forth in some detail.

Babu Sanwal Das, Deputy Collector of Kalpi, comes to the conclusion that in this district, the lower classes do not suffer from daily insufficiency of food, that, when food cannot be obtained at 32 lbs. per rupee, between five and ten per cent., 'do not have full meals'; 'the petty proprietors and agriculturists are generally more or less in debt.'

Mr. H. S. Boys, officiating Commissioner, Sitapur Division, records particulars obtained from twenty families taken at random in several villages, and shows that the returns give as near as possible

Rs.14 8a. (19s. 2d.) per annum for each adult, and
7 2a. (9s. 6d.) " " " " child.

Now our gaol returns, he says, 'show that we can keep our convicts in first-rate health and send them out in a fairer condition than when they came in on a still smaller allowance than this.' The comparison is not a very nice one, but Mr. Boys does not give particulars. Such as are before me show for the North-Western Provinces central gaol;—diet: Rs.18 1a.8¾p.; divisional gaols Rs.24 6a.10¼p.; district gaols, Rs.15 8a. 11¾p. This was in 1867–68, when an average food grain like bajri was sold at 50 lbs. to the rupee, whereas in 1882 when he wrote it was 43½ lbs. At 40 lbs. to the rupee, Rs.18 4a. are required for a man's food grain alone, not including salt and other condiments. Therefore, Mr. Boys' Rs.14 8a. would be Rs.3 12a. less than was needed, even though he dogmatically declares that this sum laid out in food is undoubtedly ample for a working-man. This loose and unsympathetic writing is especially characteristic of Mr. Boys. It was his desire to keep the Indian in a merely animal condition, which even a sufficiency of food would ensure, for he goes on to say:—'For some reasons it is not desired for the present that the standard of comfort should be very materially raised.' Mr. Boys was the Mr. Thackeray of 1807 re-incarnated.[1] He would have hailed

[1] Lieut.-Col. Pitcher, Director of Land Records and Agriculture, takes over Mr. Boys' observations and rubs them in for the benefit of an agriculturist who, in one sentence, is described as alike thrifty and thriftless. 'As Mr. Boys most truly remarks,' Col. Pitcher says, 'the absence of thrift is really at the bottom of a great deal of the present simulation of poverty by

Mr. John Stuart Mill's description of a country in the position of India as 'a human cattle farm,' as most proper.

It may be well to regard these twenty villages somewhat closely, remembering that to provide sufficient food-grain for each adult in 1882, would require Rs.18 4a., and for each child Rs.9, and then note what the average income works out at.

Village.	Tashkem.	6 persons.	Available for food, Rs.69–12–0; deficiency, Rs.13, about 18 per cent.
"	"	6 "	Rs.96; surplus of Rs. 14–4–0.
"	"	14 "	Rs. 186; deficiency Rs. 45, nearly 25 per cent.
"	"	21 "	Rs. 241–12–0; deficiency Rs. 48 or 20 per cent.
"	Barhatapur.	5 "	Rs. 62–4–0; deficiency Rs. 10.
"	"	7 "	Rs. 66–2–0; deficiency Rs. 88–4–0 or 88 per cent.
"	"	5 "	Rs. 61–12–0; deficiency Rs. 20–4–0 or 25 per cent.
"	"	7 "	Rs. 72–4–0; deficiency Rs. 72 or 28 per cent.
"	Kasrawan	6 "	Rs. 96; deficiency Rs. 4 or 4 per cent.
"	"	10 "	Rs. 195; surplus of Rs. 50; this man's crops realised the (comparatively) large sum of Rs. 330.
"	"	10 "	Rs. 91–12–0; deficiency Rs. 54–12–0 or over 38 per cent.

the people.' Simulation of poverty! Such obscurant vision in high Indian officials combined with insult to the people who provide them with princely salaries, accounts for much in Indian backwardness. The Lieut.-Colonel proceeds: 'There is, broadly speaking, no such thing as thrift, as defined in the denial to oneself of superfluous articles of food, drink, and clothing, and investment of their cost in durable articles and especially in capital which itself aids in producing. There is certainly an amount of scraping and saving carried on amongst all classes to an incredible degree; but the object in view in most cases is not that of obtaining a competency or of raising gradually the position of the family in the world. It is rather that of accumulating for the purpose of squandering the money in pilgrimages, panchayets, marriages, etc. It is notorious that the native soldier, even with ample means to command food, will starve himself to an injurious extent in order to hoard. To quote Mr. Boys again, it is for some reasons not to be desired for the present that the standard of comfort should be very materially raised. Were it to be so raised a fall in prices might cause considerable distress amongst classes where it is non-existent' (Pp. iii–iv).

Village.	Kasrawan.	8 persons.	Rs. 90-12-0; deficiency Rs. 99-4-0 or 9 per cent.
„	Behta Sidhai.	6 „	Rs.50-5-6; deficiency Rs.31-6-6 or 24 per cent.
„	„	5 „	Rs. 57-7-6; surplus of Rs. 3; wife servant in Thakur's family.
„	„	4 „	Rs. 28-8-0; deficiency Rs. 26 or nearly 50 per cent.
„	„	2 „	Rs.35-12-0; deficiency 12 annas.
„	„	10 „	Rs. 97-2-0; deficiency Rs. 48-6 or 33 per cent.
„	„	5 „	Rs. 38-14-0; deficiency Rs. 19-6-0 or about 30 per cent.
„	„	13 „	Rs. 106-5-6; deficiency Rs.84-14-10, or nearly 50 per cent. Rs. 250 in debt; contemplates flight.
„	„	13 „	Rs.119-2-0; deficiency Rs. 48-10-0 or about 24 per cent.

It is of the above record—that and none other—that the officiating Commissioner writes with such optimism as to the individual getting enough to eat, as to the amount available for food being ‘ample for a working man.’ Mr. Boys retired in 1889. Being a pensioner he is still probably living. If he be I trust he will see these lines and, in his luxurious retirement, will reconsider his expressions of nineteen years ago, and do something to repair the wrong he then did to the people out of whose necessities his retirement allowance comes. To keep him in England India has to contribute the annual incomes of considerably over one thousand Indian people. The wrong done by Mr. Boys was gross. Taking one of the cheapest grains as standard, and leaving out of account altogether very young children, though even in India little children cost something per annum to maintain, this is the result:—

Twenty households:—

Three with surplus— Rs.14 4 0, Rs.50, and Rs.3 respectively = Rs.67 4 0.

Seventeen with deficiencies— Rs.13, Rs.45, Rs.48, Rs.10, Rs.33 4 0, Rs.20 4 0, Rs.72, Rs.4, Rs.54 12 0, Rs.9 4 0, Rs.31 6 6, Rs.26, Rs.0 12 0, Rs.48 6 0, Rs.19 6 0, Rs.84 14 10, Rs.43 10 0 = Rs.564 1 0.

Deficiencies in Seventeen Families	Rs.564 1 0
Surpluses in Three Families	67 4 0
Net Deficiency ...	Rs.496 13 0

Or, £33 2s. 5d.

This would mean an average deficiency in each of the twenty households of Rs.24 (£1 12s.), and, if the seventeen households only be regarded, in each of them, a deficiency of Rs.31 6a. (£2 1s. 10d.).

The habit is inveterate with the Indian official and his prototype in the India Office: except when he wishes to show that Indian taxation, land taxation especially, is absurdly light *per capita*, he never takes the trouble to ascertain how the main facts fit in with the actual situation of the particular year with which he is dealing. From the first, all through the years since we assumed authority in India, this has been our practice. Nowhere in at least two hundred Indian Blue Books, dating from 1760 to 1901, which have been the object of my study for this book during the year in which it is written, can I, anywhere, find an honest grappling with existing statistics and their application to the condition of Ram Singh, or Hari Gour, or Cundy Pershotum, or Ahmed Khan, or Ramaswamy. There is a slight approximation to this desideratum in Sir Auckland Colvin's comments on the inquiry of 1888, but only a slight approximation; His Honor carefully avoids working out the figures according to reconsidered food prices. I forbear inquiry into or comment upon the remarkable and significant psychological fact to which the circumstance bears strange testimony.

To resume the '88 investigation in the North-Western Provinces, now, happily, the reader will probably think, nearing a close.

Mr. A. H. Harrington, Officiating Commissioner, Fyzabad Division, contributes a report which calls for quotation in full. It is addressed to the Director of Land Records and Agriculture, North-Western Provinces and Oudh, and is dated Fyzabad, April 4, 1888, and is as follows (pp. 171–2):—

SIR,—As directed in Government (Revenue Department), Scarcity $\frac{588}{1\text{–}16}$ dated 12th January, I have the honour to forward the report and opinion submitted by Colonel Noble. I have asked Major Anson to forward his reply as soon as possible; but it has not yet been received.

2. Colonel Noble's report is interesting, but I think it somewhat too optimistic. From the fact that in the months of January and February, 58 families in 17 villages, consisting of the poorest inhabitants of those villages, are found to have a sufficient food-supply, it is hardly safe to infer that in no part of the Gonda district do the poorest agriculturists or labourers suffer from a daily insufficiency of food.

3. Gonda is undoubtedly better off than many other districts. As remarked by Mr. W. C. Benett in the Gonda article ('Oudh Gazetteer,' vol. i. p. 515): 'There can be no doubt that the thinness of the population, the extent of fertile waste, and the extreme lightness of the summary settlement, have combined to give this district an almost complete freedom from the worst forms of poverty. Beggars are rare in the south, and almost unknown in the north.' But, on the same page, the same authority remarks: 'It is not till he has gone into these subjects in detail that a man can fully appreciate how terribly thin the line is which divides large masses of people from absolute nakedness and starvation.' I believe that this remark is true of every district in Oudh, the differences between them consisting in the greater or smaller extent of the always large proportion which is permanently in this depressed and dangerous condition.

4. I cite one or two facts in support of this view. Bahriach, a district of my division, like Gonda, is one of the comparatively well-to-do districts. Yet, even there, 'there are very many under-

fed and meagre creatures, no doubt; but the proportion of such is not so large as elsewhere. Perhaps high rents have not had time to produce any noxious effect' ('Oudh Gazetteer,' vol. i. p. 149). 'At present the only motive for entering into the *sewak* (contract) is *want of food, and that this is an increasing motive is shown by the increasing number of sewaks* (bond-slaves). *Every second man met with in the plains of Hissampur is a sewak.* . . . As every *sewak* is a bankrupt, and as the *sewaks* form a large proportion of the whole, it may be gathered that the agricultural classes are deeply embarrassed. That their condition is becoming worse receives support from the fact that a caste formerly exempt from this servitude is now subject to it—that of the Ahirs' (*Ibid.* pp. 147, 148). In the introduction to the 'Oudh Gazetteer,' Mr. Benett, an observer wholly free from pessimism, says of the lowest castes in Oudh that 'the lowest depths of misery and degradation is reached by the Koris and Chamars;' and he describes them as '*always on the verge of starvation.*' Now the Chamars and Koris are eleven per cent., or rather more than one-tenth, of the entire population of Oudh, [*i.e.*, nearly one and a half millions.]

Lastly, I quote the following passage from some papers contributed by me to the *Pioneer* under the head of "Oudh Affairs," in 1876. 'It has been calculated that about 60 per cent. of the entire native population[1] . . . are sunk in such abject poverty that unless the small earnings of child labour are added to the small general stock by which the family is kept alive, some members of the family would starve. With the bulk of them education would be synonymous with starvation.' And I cited the following passage from the Oudh Education Report for 1874:—

'Mr. Thompson, the Inspector of the Eastern Circle, whose thorough acquaintance with the wants and condition of the people within his own circle is well known, showed in the report for 1872–73 that a labourer in Oudh by sending his son to school would incur a loss of thirty per cent. of his income; not thirty per cent. which could otherwise be saved, but thirty per cent. of what is necessary to preserve himself, children, and aged relatives from perishing by hunger. As long as their condition remains so abjectly poor as it is, the only means on which a child could be sent to school would be that it should receive a meal a day from the Government.'

5. On the question, then, whether the impression 'that the greater proportion of the people of India suffer from a daily insufficiency of food is wholly untrue, or partially true,' I would reply that the observations already on record in Settlement reports and Gazetteers are likely to furnish much more reliable information than

[1] That is to say, nearly eight millions out of thirteen millions.

isolated inquiries here and there of a few selected, and for the most part overworked, officers. My own belief, after a good deal of study of the closely-connected question of agricultural indebtedness (*vide* my five chapters on Economic Reform in Rural India in the *Calcutta Review*, 1882–85), is that the impression is perfectly true as regards a varying, but always considerable, part of the year in the greater part of India.

6. As to the extent of the evil, this proportion, whatever it is, will be found in that one-fifth of the total population of India which comprises 'the classes most liable to famine, the labourers, weavers, beggars, and potters,' amounting in number 'to about thirteen millions of adult males, or a population of nearly forty millions, including women and children, or twenty per cent. of the total population of British India' (Famine Commission Report, part 2, section vi., paragraph II.). Of this one-fifth (20 per cent.) I do not think that it would be an over-estimate to calculate that at least one-fourth, or five per cent., of the total population suffer from a chronic insufficiency of food, and that another five per cent. just get enough food, and no more. It will be understood that I am not now referring to the quality, but only the quantity, of the food.

7. To the question how far any remedial measures can be suggested, I can only urge the vigorous adoption of that 'policy of maintaining agricultural operations at the highest attainable standard of efficiency' which, as long ago as December, 1881, the Government of India recognised as an object of paramount importance. In the extract from the Resolutions appended to the Government letter under reply, the Government of India recognised it to be 'an imperative duty to ascertain whether any legitimate means can be provided to check the degradation of agriculture which is caused by rack-renting, or any unsuitable system of collecting rent, *inability to obtain capital on reasonable terms*,' or the lack of 'irrigating machinery and agricultural implements.' And it pronounced that 'the relief or prevention of such deterioration is an object which should have prominence in the work of every provincial Agricultural Department.'

8. Up to this date this declaration of policy remains a dead letter as regards facilitating the supply of capital on reasonable terms, and the protection, repair, and extension, of wells, tanks, embankments, or other works of land improvement other than canals. It will continue to be a dead letter as long as these questions remain as at present at the unfruitful stage of fitful discussions inside the Government offices between a Secretary here and a Member of Council there, and as long as the necessary step is deferred of appointing strong Commissions to review the data and experience already gained, to make such further inquiry as may be necessary, and to map out a line of action.

Another authority on Oudh, Mr. H. C. Irwin,[1] Deputy Commissioner of Rae Bareli, presented a report which lends itself to copious citation. The information which his letter[2] gives concerning the cropping capacity of the soil and the possibilities of securing anything like decent living are of special interest. He writes (pp. 175, 179):—

I questioned each cultivator as to the out-turn of each crop sown by him. If his answers showed anything abnormal in the rate of produce I pressed him to explain the cause, and asked his neighbours or the patwari what they thought. As a rule, I have put down the final result arrived at by this exhausting, if not exhaustive, process: not with much confidence in its correctness, but deeming it at least less unworthy of record than any merely conjectural estimate of my own.

6. As regards amount of produce per acre, I found a general concensus of opinion that wheat and *rabi* crops generally nowadays do not yield such heavy returns as they did twenty or thirty years ago. I was, and to some extent still am, inclined to regard this as a sample of the *laus temporis acti* to which the unprogressive classes in every country seem prone. But Mr. Gartlan, whose experience of the Salon tahsil extends over twenty years, and who probably is more intimately acquainted with its rural life than any European official can pretend to be, assures me that it is really the fact, and is inclined to ascribe it to over-cropping and excessive irrigation. A field once irrigated must, according to him, be always irrigated; for though before it was ever watered at all it might yield a tolerable dry crop, yet, once watered, it will yield nothing without irrigation. I am not, myself, enough of an agricultural chemist to have an opinion of any value on this point, but I should think that deficiency of manure had a good deal to do with the deficiency of produce, so far as it is a fact. As cultivation has increased, grazing ground has, of course, diminished. Cattle are dearer than they were, and probably fewer in number; clearing of such jungles as there were has forced a more extensive use of cow-dung as fuel. Thus, while the area of cultivation is certainly larger, the amount of available manure is probably less than it was shortly after annexation. Of these causes a diminished out-turn per acre would not be a very surprising result.

7. The impression which I derived from this inquiry is that, speaking roughly, a first-rate crop of jarhan or transplanted rice

---

[1] Author of 'The Garden of India.' W. H. Allen and Co., London.

[2] Dated Rae Bareli, 29th March, 1898, p. 174, 'Econ. Inq. N. W. Provinces and Oudh.'

will, if the rains be abundant and well distributed, yield as much as 15 maunds or 1,230 lbs. per bigha. Anything over this would be very exceptional. Broadcast rice would, under the most favourable conditions, yield 12 maunds or 984 lbs. per bigha. For juwar and bajra, the soil of the district does not seem to be very well suited, and I believe that 656 lbs. to 820 lbs. per bigha would be regarded as a heavy crop. Wheat, barley, and spring crops generally, seldom, I should say, yield more than 820 lbs. per bigha. Average yields I should take to be for jarhan 820 lbs.; for broadcast rice 574 lbs. to 656 lbs.; for juwar and bajra 494 lbs. to 656 lbs.; for wheat and spring crops generally 574 lbs. to 656 lbs. In a year of drought or of excessive floods, or of extensive blight or hailstorms, the average out-turn would, of course, be much lower.

8. In calculating the money value of grain, I may explain that I have adopted a general average of 50 lbs. to the rupee. The market price of every kind of grain has for some time past been considerably higher than this; but it is the threshing-floor prices at harvest which have to be considered, and these were everywhere said to have been from five to six *panseries*, *i.e.*, 50 lbs. to 60 lbs. per rupee for rice, Indian corn, and other kharif staples.

9. The out-turn in column 8 is that of the past kharif and the present rabi of 1295 fasli. Questions as to the yield of the previous year would, I considered, be harder to answer. Having premised thus much, I turn to the various points brought out by the inquiry.

10. Perhaps the most salient of these is the extreme scarcity of warm clothing among the people examined. My statement (A) shows, for 178 persons, only 10 blankets, 16 razais, and 24 quilts. So that more than three-fourths of them go through the winter with no better covering than the common sheet (*galef* or *dohar*). The common country blanket, such as is made by the Gararias, and sold for from 10 to 14 annas, is not found among the more respectable families, being deemed a less creditable garment than a *dohar*. Mr. Gartlan's statement (B) shows eight blankets, two razais, and five quilts among 71 persons—a still lower proportion. Charpais seem more common. My 178 had 99 bedsteads among them, and Mr. Gartlan's 71 had 32. Sleeping on the ground is so productive of fever, that I should be glad to see charpais exempted from attachment and sale in execution of decrees.

11. None even of the working cattle get any grain, and live on grass, bhusa, and karbi. The so-called grazing grounds yield, except during the rains, practically no grass, and the so-called jungles nothing more nutritive than *dhak* leaves. To the question whether the plough and well-bullocks get no grain, the invariable answer was: 'How should *they?* *Men* can't get grain.'

12. Agricultural labour is not expensive. The best-paid form of it is reaping, which is remunerated by one-twelfth of the produce

which, with a heavy crop and a quick workman, might come to as much as 5 seers (10 lbs.) a day. Next comes watering from tanks and jhils by means of *duglas:* men thus employed get 2½ and in some part 3 seers (5 lbs. to 6 lbs.) a day, while those who water from wells get 1½ or 2 seers (3 lbs. to 4 lbs.); weeders the same; house-builders and thatchers get from 5 pice to 2 annas a day (less than one half-penny to twopence per day).

13. Indebtedness is not extensive, and heavy indebtedness is exceptional. Of my thirty examinees, eight said they were not in debt at all; and, of the others, only two could be described as heavily indebted. Most of them keep up a running account with some *mahajan*, which is balanced at the close of the year in Jeth. If the harvest has been good, the debt is generally cleared off and a fresh account started from Asarh; if bad, the unliquidated balance is carried on to the next year. The advances are usually for seed (*bisar*) or food (*khawai*), and sometimes for purchase of bullocks, and for marriage or funeral ceremonies. The common rate of interest on cash loans is twenty-five per cent. per annum; on food advances, twenty-five per cent.; on advances for seed it seems to be always fifty per cent.

14. A noteworthy point is the wide variations in the amount of food which different individuals estimate as a sufficient daily ration. The most liberal estimate is that of a well-to-do Kurmi, No. 11, who said he always ate one and a half seers (3 lbs.). The lowest is about three-quarters of a seer for an adult male (1½ lbs.). I am inclined to think that this is very much a matter of habit, resulting from a long course of easy or pinched circumstances. In well-to-do families, accustomed to eat as much as they can, I daresay a man who was at work all day would eat three pounds at two meals. In hard-up households, on the other hand, one and a half pounds would be the usual thing; and no one would think of eating more. One seer for a man, three-quarters for a woman, and half a seer for a boy of ten, would perhaps be a fair average allowance.

15. In 13 of the 30 cases in statement A, the surplus in column 15 falls short of the estimated food consumption of the year, leaving nothing for clothes and miscellaneous expenditure. This seeming anomaly is partly due, no doubt, to under-estimate of out-turn—which, as already remarked, there was a general tendency to understate. In part it is to be explained by the fact that the poorer classes don't eat a full ration of grain every day in the year. For some weeks before each harvest they bring home from their fields bundles of green corn which they roast and eat, and this they exclude from their estimate of threshing-floor totals. Again, 120 to 160 lbs. of carrots may be bought for a rupee—and these, when in season, are largely used to eke out the food supply. The same is the case with mangoes, cucumbers, and 'quashes.' Probably a quarter of the food consumed by the poorest classes consists of such beggarly elements as these.

16. To the main question—whether the poorer classes get enough to eat—a categorical answer is not easy. I believe that a great majority do, in ordinary times, satisfy their hunger at least once a day. That the poorer families eat as much as would be good for them, I very much doubt. Hunger, as already remarked, is very much a matter of habit; and people who have felt the pinch of famine—as nearly all the poorer households must have felt it—get into the way of eating less than wealthier families and less than they could assimilate with physical advantage to themselves.

17. The more one looks into the condition of the Indian cultivator and labourer, the more, it seems to me, one must be impressed by the narrowness of the margin between him and destitution. The upper class of tenant, the man with from five to ten acres of land and upwards, should, in average times, and with ordinary industry, be well above the pressure of actual want. But the small cultivators, *i.e.*, the large majority, must be always on the brink of want of food, though the services of the *mahajan* generally save them from going further than the brink.

18. Take, for instance, the case of a tenant with five bighas, with a wife and three children under ten years of age. Assume that he is paying nothing for labour, and endow him with a pair of perennial bullocks which shall never need to be replaced and never be sick or sorry, and never cost anything to feed. He sows, let us say, three bighas with rice, and gets a crop of 12 maunds a bigha, or 36 maunds. In November he again sows two bighas of this with peas and grain, and reaps 12 maunds; while the other two bighas he sows with wheat, and gets a crop of 20 maunds, or 10 maunds per bigha. Total produce, 68 maunds, worth, at 25 seers the rupee, which is a very high threshing-floor price, Rs.108. It will be admitted that he has not done badly with his harvest. Land which produces such crops as these must be of good quality, and is not likely to let under, at least, Rs.6 a bigha. His rent will thus be Rs.30. He will require about four maunds for seed, worth Rs.6 6a.; surplus for food and clothing, and all other expenditure, Rs.71 10a. Allow as daily food supply for himself one seer, three-quarter seer for his wife, and one seer for the three children. Total daily rations, two and three-quarter seers, or 25 maunds, worth Rs.40 per annum, balance available for all other purposes, Rs.31 10a. With such a surplus he would deem himself, and considering his wants and habits actually would be, very comfortable.

19. But suppose the rains to be scanty or inopportune; suppose that there are three or four nights of sharp frost in January or February, and a hailstorm early in March. Under these unfavourable, but constantly recurring, conditions, his rice will scarcely yield more than six maunds a bigha or 18 maunds; his two bighas of peas and grain will bear, perhaps, eight maunds; and his two bighas of wheat ten maunds. Total, 35 maunds, worth Rs.56. So that after paying his rent

and putting by seed, he will have left only 12¼ maunds, worth Rs.19 10a.; while, by the supposition, the food alone of his family amounts to 25 maunds, worth Rs.40. It may be said that he would earn something by field labour. A man with five bighas on his hands to cultivate, without any help but that of his wife and one or two small boys, can hardly do much else. But suppose him to work two months in the year for hire at three seers a day. This would only bring 4½ maunds, worth about Rs.7, which would not go far to make up the deficit. He would probably cut down the food consumption by a fourth, and the only other resources open to him would be either to sell his bullocks, and so disqualify himself for further cultivation, or to raise a loan at 25 per cent. Once in the mesh of the money-lender, it will go hard with him before he escapes it.

20. Calculations which I need not repeat here have led me to the conclusion that a landless labouring family of the same size as in the case above would earn about 28 maunds, worth about Rs.45, in the course of the year, supposing the man to be employed for five months in field work and for six months in building and thatching. Deducting food at the same rate, 25 maunds, worth Rs.40, there would be a balance of Rs.5 for clothing and all other expense. This small saving would, by a very moderate degree of ill-luck or ill-health, be turned into a deficit. But even assuming that the ordinary small cultivator and able-bodied labourer can always be sure of sufficient food, there remain the aged, infirm, and childless poor. The question whether these get enough to eat can only be answered by a decided negative.

21. In conclusion of this part of the subject, the nearest approach that I can furnish to a categorical answer to the question whether the agricultural population of this district are sufficiently fed, is that the mass of them in ordinary times, and the *élite* always, do get enough to eat; but that a considerable minority in bad seasons feel the pinch of hunger; and that a small minority consisting of the sickly, the weak, the old, and the childless, suffer from chronic hunger, except just about harvest time, when grain is plentiful and easily to be had. I do not understand that the indigent town populations are intended to be included in this inquiry. There can be no doubt that they suffer much more than the agricultural classes from want of food, especially the unfortunate *parda-nashin* women, and indeed men too, of good but impoverished families, who have sunk in the world, who are ashamed to beg, who live on the remnants of their property, and whom every rise in prices hits cruelly hard. For such people, dear grain means semi-starvation, while to the producer it, of course, means increased value of his produce.

22. So far actual facts. As for remedies, I must confess that I have very little to offer in the way of suggestion. The new Rent Act having been in force for little more than a year, it would, I presume, be considered out of place to point out its failure to protect the heirs

of deceased tenants from rack-renting, and to secure actual tenants from spiteful eviction; otherwise these are points on which it would be easy to dilate.

23. The gradual deterioration of the common country cattle is, I believe, mainly due to the steady diminution of grazing grounds, owing to the increased area under cultivation. Opportunity might be taken, I think, to remedy this at the next Settlement, now not very far distant. The Settlement Officer might set apart specified land, amounting to a certain proportion of the area of each village, say ten per cent., to be exempted from assessment on condition that it should be devoted exclusively to the growth of grass and other fodder, and that the village cattle should be allowed to graze on it free of charge to their owners. A portion of this reserved area might also be required to be planted with quick-growing timber for fuel, for the gratuitous use of the villagers. These measures would, it may be hoped, lead to improved agriculture by means of better and stronger bullocks, and more abundant manure, wood taking the place of cow-dung as fuel. The so-called reclamation of waste lands has, I think, been carried a great deal too far in Oudh, and should be as far as possible checked for the future. 'What is needed,' if I may be allowed to quote words which I have used elsewhere, 'is not the breaking up of fresh soils, but the better and more careful cultivation of the land already under tillage. The area available for grazing is already far too scanty in at least nine districts out of twelve. . . . The increased produce which is needed for the adequate support of the people must be derived from an increased intensity of industry, not from an extension of its area.'

24. I must plead guilty to holding the heroic heresy that the exportation of grain from Indian ports should be stopped when prices in any large portion of the country reach a certain point. It is true that the grain exported is chiefly wheat, and that wheat is not the food of the poorest classes. Still, the effect of keeping wheat down below starvation prices would be obviously to reduce the intensity of the demand for the coarser grains. This, however, is of course a remedy for exceptional scarcity only, and one which no one would advocate in normal times.

25. The only other suggestion which occurs to me is that the wide difference between threshing-floor and market prices is to a great extent the result of the necessity under which the cultivator lies of selling off a large proportion of his grain as soon as it is cleaned, to enable him to pay his rent. The *mahajan* is thus enabled for a few weeks to buy grain very cheaply, and almost monopolises the large profit arising from the increased value which the same grain possesses two months later. It may be worth consideration whether, if the revenue and rent demands were made payable in eight, instead of, as they usually are at present, in four, instalments, the tenant would not be able to hold his grain longer, and so get a better price for it.

Of course there are obvious objections which may be urged against this measure; but I am not at all sure that it would not be worth trying as an experiment in one or two districts. I am quite aware that this may be called a tinkering experiment, and that to stop exportation is an undeniable interference with free trade; but can only regret that, except perhaps the proposal contained in paragraph 23, and further alterations of the rent law, which this is not the place to discuss, I know of no other direct remedies for the condition of the poorer classes which would be less open to criticism.

In regard to the elaborate tables which follow, in which there are sixteen columns of particulars, I need only refer to the 'Remarks.'

1. *Kurmi*, cultivator and labourer. 'Weak and ill-fed in appearance. Has been ten or fifteen years in village. Has one ragged bedstead. No warm clothing of any kind. Seemed stupefied with cold. Says the family eat six lbs. of grain daily between them, which equals 2,444 lbs. per annum, or more than the surplus of grain after paying rent.'

2. *Pasi*, cultivator and chaukidar.[1] Requires for daily food for self and family 1,382 lbs. of food more than his income allows. 'No warm clothes at all.'

3. *Kalwar*, cultivator. 'Has no warm clothes. Says he is often hungry during the daytime, but satisfies his hunger at night.'

4. *Ahir*, cultivator. 'No warm clothes.' Says his fields yield less than assessment estimate. 'Owes Rs.40, incurred for funeral feast for first wife and marriage of another.'

5. *Ahir*, cultivator. 'No warm clothes. Owes Rs.14 at Rs.2 per cent. per month, which is ordinarily paid off during the year.'

6. *Kalwar*, cultivator. 'No warm clothes. Well-nourished. Owes Rs.32, incurred for a wedding which he says is generally paid within the year.'

7, 8, and 9. Much the same as 6.

10. *Kurmi*, cultivator and labourer. 'When he can, cooks twice a day; but very often has not the where-

[1] Village watchman, or any watchman.

withal. Has no clothing of any kind except a couple of shirts, and a sheet for his wife. This couple fortunately have no children; they need no charpai.'

11. *Kurmi*, cultivator. Family. 'Has been fourteen or fifteen generations in the village and never ejected. He says every labouring man will eat one and a half seer (3 lbs.) a day if he can get it.'

12. *Kurmi*, cultivator. Cattle live on stalks and straw. When asked if the cattle get no grain, says men can't get grain, how can cattle? Not in debt; eat their own grain all the year round. Make jewelry with the surplus, when they have any, but have made none for four years. Own marriage and sister's paid out of savings. This is a well-to-do little household, very much owing to the fact that they have so few mouths to feed.

13 and 14. Call for no comment.

15. *Lonia*, cultivator and labourer. 'This man is pretty well-to-do, thanks to a yearly contribution of Rs.60 from his brother, a contractor.'

16 and 17. Nothing noteworthy.

18. *Muria*, aged 60 or 65. Screams when asked if he eats his own grain all the year, and says he only does so for four months.

19. *Ahir*, cultivator and labourer. 'Says he eats grain advanced by the mahajan (moneylender) for eight months in the year.' 'Improbable,' interjects Mr. Irwin.

21. *Kurmi*, aged 60, labourer. Owes Rs.36. Paid the interest last year out of Rs.10 sent him by his son, who is employed at Dehra in a tea garden. No *razai* or blankets. Suffers a good deal from cold.

26. *Ghosi*, aged 34, cultivator and herdsman. When asked why he pays a rent of Rs.14 for land which yields only Rs.12 7a. 0p. worth of grain, explains that he only cultivates to have fodder for his cattle.

27. *Ahir*, aged 40, cultivator and labourer. 'Lives on his own produce for only two months, on wages of labour for six months, and on moneylender's grain for four months. Has no warm clothes. Cannot get as much

to eat as he would like, and thinks himself badly off. A poor, thin, but merry, creature.'

28. *Lonia*, aged 30, cultivator. 'Always borrows to pay his rent. Repays out of money he gets for opium. Family; sixty years' residence in village; never ejected. Built a well five years ago. Is well-to-do and content; said to be a first-rate cultivator. A big strong man of more than average intelligence.'

29. *Chamen*, aged 50, cultivator and labourer. 'Six generations in village; never ejected. Does not get enough to eat nowadays, only at and after harvest. For two months before each harvest victuals are short. Thin and poor-looking.'

30. *Chamen*, aged 55, cultivator. 'Three or four generations in village; never ejected. Rent enhanced three years ago. Says he means to relinquish his land this year, as it does not pay, and he has got into debt over it. Is evidently under-fed.'

Summary.

Eight out of the thirty are not in debt; twenty-two owe about Rs.794, interest on which is Rs.202—that is, Rs.36 principal, Rs.9 interest, for each, on an average.

Total income per family (average) Rs.60, or Rs.10 (13s. 4d.) per head per annum. Seventeen showed surplus, thirteen deficit.

Mr. Gartlan reports on thirteen cultivators (71 individuals) thus:—

				Rs.	a.	p.
Total income, including borrowed capital (Rs.111 for each household).				1,442	12	0
Cultivation expenditure ...	Rs.155	8	0			
Rent	258	12	0			
Interest	128	8	0			
				537	12	0
Leaving ...				905	0	0
Less borrowed capital				391	0	0
Balance ...				Rs.514	0	0

Or, on an average, of Rs.40 per family and under Rs.8 (10s. 8d.) per head per annum.

And, in that year, for cheap food like bajri there was required [1] :—

	Rs.	a.	p.
For an adult	28	8	0
For a child	14	0	0

There were eight rupees all round. That is quite clear, for extraneous sources of income are all reckoned. I find it hard to believe the food-grains prices were so high as is officially stated. During that very year Sir Auckland Colvin was Lieutenant-Governor of these Provinces: through his Chief Secretary he stated that he was fairly well satisfied with the results recorded. Those results the reader has before him. How do they strike the fresh intelligence he brings to bear on them? Neither of the functionaries named could have been content had he brought acumen and thought to bear on the figures before him. But there is so much of written matter daily coming before a Lieutenant - Governor and his Secretary that as a matter of necessity everything is 'scamped.' (I use a disagreeable word in no invidious sense, but because the secretariat and gubernatorial summary of these records can only be described by such a word.)

In the particulars collected by Mr. Gartlan [2] are one or two statements deserving of further mention. We are told that on the slightest provocation, or even on no provocation at all, the Indian cultivator will light-heartedly incur debt. Here are three citations which do not bear out this contention:—

'Prefer short allowance and inferior kinds of food to incurring debt.'

---

[1] Statistical Abstract for British India, No. 24. I think the prices on p. 294 recorded too high. But there is the authority. Current prices of food-grains Bareilly, 1880, 15·62 seers Bajri per rupee.

[2] Who, it should previously have been stated, was manager of the Palmer Waste Land Grant.

'Cannot get along without borrowing, and pay the usual rates; but owing to bad credit have difficulty in procuring supplies; and in preference to getting further into debt live on short allowance of grain, supplemented with weeds, fruit, etc. My difficulties commenced in 1877–78, the year of drought, and I have never been able to re-establish myself since. As a large cultivator in that year my losses were heavy, and my indebtedness then begun.' Mr. Gartlan adds: 'Personally the writer remembers this man before the date mentioned as a large cultivator and a person of good credit and some substance.'

'Manages to make both ends meet, but lives on short allowance in preference to getting into debt. Credit not very good, but can obtain loans when necessity forces him to do so.'

Finally Major Anson, agent of the Balrampur Estate, reports:—

Fyzabad Division (p. 209). Cultivator, with one plough, family three; income, Rs.78; food at 40 lbs. per rupee; balance available for food, Rs.45; deficiency, Rs. 9 = 17 per cent.

(Ditto). A Hanwara; income, Rs. 82; three in family; available for food, Rs. 22; required, Rs.54; deficiency, Rs.32 = 60 per cent.—a truly awful result.

(Ditto). A day labourer; income Rs.47; three in family; available for food, Rs.37; required, Rs.54; deficiency, Rs.17 = 31 per cent.

Out of seven instances, four show most serious deficiencies: one, a petty dealer, is Rs.14 deficient; two have just enough; and one, a moneylender, shows a surplus.

'To affect deep interest in things native is incorrect. A lady was asked what she had seen of the people since she came out. "Oh! nothing," she said. "Thank goodness, I know nothing at all about them, and don't wish to; really, I think, the less one sees and knows about them the better. As for Hindustani, I should never *dream* of trying to learn it."'—'*A Sportswoman in India*,' *by* Isabel Savory.

PURCHASING POWER OF ONE RUPEE.

1873–1877.			1893–1897.		
District.	Wages per Month.	Amount of Food.	District.	Wages per Month.	Amount of Food.
	Rs.			Rs.	
Patna	3–4	36 lbs. Wheat	Patna	4–5	30 lbs. Wheat
Cawnpore	Under 4	40 lbs. "	Cawnpore	4–5	29 lbs. "
Fyzabad	1·87–3·75	40 lbs. "	Fyzabad	1·87–4	27 lbs. "
		60 lbs. Millet			37 lbs. Millet
					25 lbs. Rice
Amritzar	6	29 lbs. Rice	Amritzar	7–8	19 lbs. "
Jubbulpur	4–5	35 lbs. "	Jubbulpur	3¼	25 lbs. "

MEAN PRICE OF PADDY PER GARCE (MADRAS).

1873	...	...	Rs.149·5
1874	...	...	143·3
1875	...	...	152·5
1876	...	...	245·5
1877	...	...	280·3

'Who is it we deceive?
Ourselves, or God—with all this make-believe?'

BROWNING.

'It is better to follow the real truth of things than an imaginary view of them. For many republics and princedoms have been imagined which were never seen or known to exist in reality.'—MACHIAVELLI.

'THE HORRORS OF A POPULAR REVOLUTION' OF WHICH THE STATE IS THE REAL ORIGIN.

'Historians, whose ideas have been largely coloured by those of the governing classes, have depicted in strong colours the short-lived horrors of a popular revolution, but the permanent sufferings caused by a governmental revolution have for the most part been sketched with faint touches. *And yet the latter type of revolution leads to more disastrous consequences than the former. The vital forces which in the one case are ever working towards a new social equilibrium, are in the other case not brought into play till the Government is itself overthrown. If India is to escape such a catastrophe, it can only do so by the Indian Government and the British Parliament showing more consideration than hitherto for native wants and ways.* It is not more science, but more sympathy that is demanded of us by an ancient civilisation like that of India. This is the lesson which may be read up and down the pages of British Rule in the East. All the well recognised and splendid successes of our countrymen in dealing with Orientals are due to the observance, and all their less known, but none the less ignominious, failures, are due to the breach of this principle. *Wherever we have superseded*, instead of supervising, native officials and headmen, wherever we have poisoned the social organism with English reforms, instead of purifying it by the light of the best native traditions, *there the seeds of demoralisation and disaster have been sown* broadcast. The wisest men in India are beginning to recognise this fact, but we in England are still oblivious of it, and especially in those points where commercial self-interest blinds our eyes.'—A. K. CONNELL, *Paper on Indian Pauperism, Free Trade, and Railways, March*, 1884.

CHAPTER XI

THE ALLEGED INCREASED AGRICULTURAL AND NON-AGRICULTURAL INCOME

Lord Curzon's 'Element of Conjecture' regarding the Condition of the People.

Highly Discreditable to the India Office and the Government of India that Trustworthy Facts are Wanting.

The Settlement Reports and Village Records a Gold Mine of Authentic Information.

Sir Louis Mallet on 'Absolute Disagreement as to Fundamental Facts.'

The Baring-Barbour Investigation of 1882.

Less than One Penny each Person per Day, if All Shared Alike.

The Guess (in 1882) as to Non-Agricultural Income.

Provinces Above and Below the Rs.27 Limit.

An Identification of the Parties in the Story, after the Buddhist Jatakas.

Was the Statement of 1882 Trustworthy?

The Bombay Presidency:

A Digest of the 'Report on the Economic Condition of the Masses of the Bombay Presidency, 1887–8.'

The Director, Land Records and Agriculture, declares: 'There is Much Poverty but no Pauperisation.'

***Gujarat* Division—Yield of Holdings, Strong Deficiency in Sustenance.**

Deccan	**do.**	**do.**	**do.**	**do.**
Karnatak	**do.**	**do.**	**do.**	**do.**
Konkan	**do.**	**do.**	**do.**	**do.**
Sind	**do.**	**do.**	**do.**	**do.**

The People Suffer, in Every Year, 'Without a Murmur, Most of the Hardships Incidental to a Famine.'

Receive 38 per cent., the Ryot 18 per cent., of Gross Produce.

The 'Normal Increase at 1½ per cent. per Annum' Announced in Connection with a Madras District.

During 1891 and 1901 Three Districts show Slight Increase over Normal, Nineteen exhibit Decrease.

Minus Population in 1901: 2,710,588.

THE CENTRAL PROVINCES:

In 1882 these Declared to be the Premier Prosperous Provinces, yet at Touch of Famine People Perish in Great Numbers.

Excessive Increase of Soil Production Based on the Fallacies of 1882.

Government Over-Estimate of Yield: Alleged, 600 lbs. per Acre; Actual, 372 lbs.

Agriculture the Main Dependence of the Provinces.

A Sample Poverty Case: 'Less than Half of One Farthing each Person per Day.'

Famine Mortality Results: 1,370,510 Fewer Inhabitants than Should Have Been.

ASSAM:

The Government of India Informed that the Question Raised in their Letter 'Need Cause Them No Anxiety Whatever.'

AJMERE-MERWARA:

Under Direct Control of Supreme Government.

Excess Deaths in Famine Year, 1900, Three and a Half Times Above the Average: 50,458 Deaths Against 14,609 Deaths being the Average of a Bad Decennial Period.

Details of Family Life in Various Villages.

Recourse to a Moneylender Absolutely Necessary.

'There is No Surplus in Any of these Villages.'

'The State of the Agricultural Classes is Far from Satisfactory.'

THE LOWER PROVINCES OF BENGAL:

'The Lower Classes . . . have no Resources to Fall Back Upon in Times of Scarcity.'

'There is Almost Constant Insufficiency of Food Among those who Earn their Living by Daily Labour.'

IN his speech at Calcutta, on the 28th of March, 1901, Lord Curzon, using expressions I have given in a previous chapter, said:—

'At Simla I spoke of it [the Agricultural Income] as being now between 350 and 400 crores. Thereupon I found my authority quoted in some quarters for a proposition that the agricultural wealth of the country had remained stationary for twenty years, while the population had gone on increasing by leaps and bounds. Further equally erroneous assumptions followed, that there had been no rise in the interim in the non-agricultural income of the community. I found myself cited as the parent of the astonishing statement that the average income of every inhabitant of India had sunk from Rs.27 in 1882 to Rs.22 in ordinary years, and to Rs.17½ in 1900, the inference, of course, being drawn that while Nero had been fiddling, the town had been burning. I have since made more detailed inquiries into the matter. . . . Turning, however, to agriculture alone, concerning which the loudest lamentations are uttered, I have had worked out for me from figures collected for the Famine Commission of 1898 the latest estimate of the value of agricultural production in India. I find that in my desire to be on the safe side I under-rated the totalling in my Simla speech. I then said between 300 and 400 crores. The total is 450 crores. The calculations of 1880 showed the average agricultural income at Rs.18 per head. If I take the figures of the recent census for the same area as was covered by the earlier computation, which amount to 228 millions, I find that the agricultural income has actually increased, notwithstanding the growth in the population and an increasingly stationary tendency of that part of the national income which is derived from agriculture, and that the average per head is Rs.20, or Rs.2 higher than in 1880. If I then assume—I know of no reason why I should not, indeed I think it under the estimate—that the non-agricultural income has increased in the same ratio, the average income will be Rs.30 per head, as against Rs.27 in 1880. I do not say that these *data* are incontrovertible. There is an element of conjecture in them, but so there was in the figures of 1880. The uncertainty in both is precisely the same. If one set of figures is to be used in argument, equally may the other.'

It is to the standing discredit of the Government of India and of the India Office that there should be any 'element of conjecture' in such a matter. For two hundred years, in Bombay and Madras, one hundred and thirty-two years in the larger part of India, and for over fifty years in nearly all the remainder of the country, the British raj has had full sway in India, none being able to make any effectual resistance. The rulers have carried out the detail of government so minutely that a cow cannot gender in a village but note is made of the calf that is born; so wide-sweeping is the net of taxation that on the sea-board and on the land-frontier not one maund of goods can enter or leave until the Sirkar has taken note of the same; not an acre of land is sown or the crop from it reaped without the officers under Lord Curzon's direction knowing fully all that is done. Nowhere in the world, perhaps, could more accurate statistics concerning the people of a country and their condition be more readily obtained than in India, if a real desire to possess them were only felt. The material available is ample; its completeness leaves little or nothing to be desired. In the Settlement Reports, upon which the assessment is periodically reconsidered, are to be found a detailed record better than was contained in Norman Domesday Book or the Visitations of the Judges in later centuries. The available material is not a thing of yesterday. So long ago as the 1st day of September, 1831, Mr. John Sullivan, ex-collector of the district of Coimbatore, Madras Presidency, produced before a Committee of the House of Commons a statistical statement concerning that district.[1] This statement is reproduced as an Appendix to this chapter. The information therein given differs in naught from that which has been available for every part of India (not excepting Bengal, only the information for the Lower Provinces was not in the hands of the Revenue officials) ever since India has been under our rule. With such quarries of readily verifiable facts available it is worse than idle for the Viceroy to take refuge under the phrase 'element of conjecture.' He, or the Secretary of State, could put that 'element of conjecture' beyond peradventure in less than twelve months if only one man really in earnest, with *carte blanche* to tell the truth as he found it, and with an adequate staff to assist him in sifting and arranging the facts, were turned loose upon the statistics at Calcutta and in the India Office.

Why is it, with all the information at hand, there is still 'conjecture' where there ought to be certainty?

I will not supply the answer which naturally comes to one's lips. I will merely say that if the result of the complete examination of the over-abundance of facts available would put the blessings of British rule in India beyond all doubt, why should Viceroy and Secretary of State

> '. . . do themselves the wrong,
> And others, that they are not always strong'?

Why do they not make themselves invincible in their defence of their administration by producing the facts? One is justifiably suspicious that the actual facts—in spite of all that is so grandiloquently and vaingloriously said year after year concerning the condition of India—will not bear examination; and, further, that Lord George Hamilton and all other Secretaries of State, and all other

[1] 'Statement showing the results of the Ryotwar System in Coimbatore, from 1814–15 to 1828–29, both inclusive, compiled from the detailed Accounts kept by the Kurnums, or Native Accountants, of Villages,' vol. v. p. 488. Inquiry of 1831. Evidence.

high officials of India, are not unaware that they will not bear examination. Challenge an ex-official on this point, and he will say, 'Oh; Sir Henry So-and-so and Mr. Blank Otherman know that well enough. They also know that things will last their time, and, therefore, they leave it alone.' I have had these exact words said to me on several occasions by ex-civilians; otherwise I would not venture to put such a phrase into print.

'If,' said the Permanent Under-Secretary of State [1] at the India Office in 1875, 'there is any one thing which is wanting in any investigation of Indian problems, it is an approach to trustworthy and generally accepted facts. There is hardly a subject upon which the best authorities do not absolutely disagree as to the fundamental facts. I could mention the most startling circumstances, but they must be present to the minds of all of us.[2] Now, I am compelled to say that, since I have been connected with the India Office, I have found just as strong a repugnance to the adoption of any adequate measure for the collection of a comprehensive and well-digested set of facts as to the recognition of general principles. The only occasion on which I had the misfortune of encountering the vehement opposition of some Members of Council, for whose opinions and experience I have the most unfeigned respect, was in my advocacy of Mr. Forbes Watson's proposal for an Industrial Survey.'

The condemnation conveyed in these words still hangs heavily over the India Office; the reproach is still unremoved from any one of the high officials. Probably, before we get to the end of this section, it will be recognised why those responsible shrink from an examination of the facts which they possess, or which, did they so desire, they could readily possess. For, with the India

[1] Sir Louis Mallet.

[2] 'All of us'—Lord Salisbury, Secretary of State, and some of the members of the Secretary of State's Council: Sir G. Campbell, Sir Henry Montgomery, Sir Erskine Perry, Sir Henry Maine, Sir Bartle Frere, and Sir Louis Mallet himself.

Blue Books before me, I propose to get some distance ahead of the 'element of conjecture,' even though absolute certitude is sure, from the lack of materials available to a member of the general public, to be wanting.

In 1882, Lord Cromer (then Major Evelyn Baring, Finance Minster of India) and Sir (then Mr.) David Barbour, made an estimate of the agricultural wealth in India per head of population. This they put as follows :—

Presidency or Province.	Amount per head per annum. Rs.
Bombay	22·4
Central Provinces	21·6
Madras	19·0
Panjab	18·5
North-Western Provinces and Oudh	16·4
Bengal	16·9
Burma	27·0

Making allowance for Assam and other districts the total amount reached was Rs.3,500,000,000 or (Rs.15 = £1) £233,333,333. How the amount was made up in total figures thus appears :—

Percentage of Payment compared with Gross Produce.

Presidency or Province.	Gross Produce. Rs.	Payment. Rs.	Per Cent.
Panjab	84,15,00,000	4,74,89,000	13·8
N.-W. Provs. and Oudh	71,75,00,000	11,27,60,000	15·7
Bengal	1,08,50,00,000	14,81,36,000	13·8
Central Provinces ...	21,25,00,000	1,61,40,000	7·6
Bombay	39,00,00,000	4,14,57,000	10·6
Madras	50,00,00,000	7,64,46,000	15·3

Sir David added here a corrected table of his own, in which he brought out the averages slightly different. Thus :—

	Rs.		Rs.
Panjab	14·2	Central Provinces	7·6
N.W. Provinces and Oudh...	16·0	Bombay	11·2
Bengal	18·6	Madras	13·0

'The returns on which the estimate in Table No. 3 was

based included payments made both to the Government and to the zemindars.'

I do not follow this plan. I am concerned only with what the Government takes as revenue. Whatever be left, whether it be a single profit for the ryot, or a profit divided between zemindar and cultivator, it is a profit which goes to the producers and is available for the support of them both. So long as I fairly reckon the Government impost, and nowhere overstate it, I do no injury to any one while I arrive, at one and the same time, at a fairly accurate statement of the production and the amount of the administrative burden. In the 1882 calculation, not the burden on the land, but 'total taxation per head, everything included,' is charged against the produce of the land—surely a strange proceeding, with nothing to recommend it. The non-agricultural income was assumed to be half the agricultural income (an erroneous assumption as will be seen); thus regarded the combined result was shown to be:—

	Rs.
Agricultural Income	350,00,00,000
Non-agricultural Income	175,00,00,000
Total	Rs.525,00,00,000

Or, £350,000,000.

Divided among 194,539,000 people, the average amount per head was Rs.27 (£1 13s. 9d.).

Was there a fear that some one, into whose hands the figures might fall, would analyse them and, at once, reveal the utter insecurity of the basis on which the grand edifice of British administration rests? Was this the reason why these inquiries have never been made available, their production being refused time and again? For that total sum of Rs.525,00,00,000 turned into annas—that is to say, into pennies—pence 84,000,000,000 ÷ 365 gives—

230,136,986 pennies per day to divide between 231,085,132 persons, the population in 1901, or

> *less than ONE PENNY each person per day,* assuming every one shared and shared alike.

In England the average income works out over thirty pence per head.

One penny per day in India has to provide each person with :—

House Room,	Clothing,	Salt,	Religion,
Food Grains,	Firing,	Condiments,	Medicine,
Bedding,		Pleasure,	Cooking Utensils.

that is, if no one had more than one penny per day; if any one, be he Viceroy, Governor, Lieutenant-Governor, Chief Commissioner, Maharajah, judge, civilian, barrister, or wealthy merchant, should have received more than one penny per day, some one has had to supply all the above-mentioned needs on less than one penny per day, or go without a large portion of them.

That is always supposing there are £350,000,000 per annum to divide. There is not that income in 1901. Probably there was not this income in 1882. If there were, the deterioration during the past nineteen years is as serious as it is deplorable, and should call for immediate action.

The inquiry in 1882 is the only attempt that has ever been made in India, officially, to ascertain what is the average economic condition of the people.[1] The details then ascertained and put on record, as I say, have never been published. Repeated requests, preferred by way of question in the House of Commons, have always met with an absolute refusal. One political party was as resolute in refusal as the other. Indeed, in all respects where Indian progress is concerned, there is little to choose between Liberal and Tory Secretaries of State for India. Why there should be this persistent refusal is obvious from the conclusions which have been drawn

[1] That is to say, of the people as a whole. Dr. Buchanan, in the first years of the nineteenth century, made a detailed survey of some districts of Bengal, and Mr. Montgomery Martin embodied the results in a book.

since these facts first saw light in the use I have, from time to time, made of the material in my possession; this happened in the year 1890.

There are three other tables which may be cited :—

1. *Total Taxation per head, everything included.*

Presidency or Province.	Rate per Head. As. or d.
Bengal	24·80
N.W. Provinces and Oudh	82·04
Madras	41·86
Bombay	52·80
Panjab	29·82
Burma	19·18
Central Provinces	22·48
Assam	27·45
Average	As.82·84

2. *Total Payments by Cultivators per Acre.*

Presidency or Province.	Rent. As. or d.	Stamps. As. or d.
N.W. Provinces and Oudh	49·22	1.80
Bengal	42·02	2·72
Madras	38·47	2·76
Panjab	35·47	2·53
Bombay	24·57	4·07

4. *Value of Agricultural Produce per head and of Stamp Duty per head.*

Presidency or Province.	Agricultural Produce. Rs.	Stamp Duty. Rs.
Central Provinces	20·9	1·91
Bombay	20·2	4·07
Madras	17·8	2·76
Panjab	17·1	8·53
Bengal	15·1	2·72
N.W. Provinces and Oudh	14·8	1·80

If, on the basis of Table 4, one wishes to estimate what the whole resources per head are in each Presidency and Province, it becomes necessary to add one-half (as representing the non-agricultural income), and it may be as well to omit the few annas paid for stamp duty. This produces a surprising result. Let it be borne in mind that the average income, according to the Government of India, was Rs.27 per head, and, then, observe how vast a proportion of the inhabitants of India were greatly below the average. The details are :—

Presidency or Province.	Amount per head counting all sources of income. Rs. a. p.		Above or below Gov. Estimate, plus or minus. Rs. a. p.		Per Cent. Plus or minus.
Central Provinces	30 8 0	...	+2 8 0	...	+ 8
Bombay	30 5 4	...	+2 5 0	...	+ 8
Madras	26 0 0	...	—1 0 0	...	— 4
Panjab	25 8 0	...	—1 8 0	...	— 4½
Bengal	22 8 0	...	—4 8 0	...	—20
N.W. Provinces and Oudh...	22 3 4	...	—4 12 8	...	—23

A number of obvious comments are at once suggested, as, for example, that the above figures have to be further reduced nearly thirteen per cent. (to be exact, 12·8 for India as a whole, the averages ranging from 7·6 in the Central Provinces to 15·7 in the North-Western Provinces) for rent. For the moment let them stand in the most favourable light possible. They must, however, be considered with the help of such experience as is available as to the scale of diet in India. Four examples, relating to the same period, will suffice :—

Jail diet	Rs.17·2	per head	per annum.
Sepoy's diet	31·5	"	"
Camp follower's diet	22·5	"	"
Sir J. B. Peile's agriculturist	30·0	"	"

From this comparison it will be seen that the Central Provinces and Bombay were comparatively well-to-do, while all the rest of India fell below the Government average of Rs.27. Of the population of, roughly, 200,000,000, only a small proportion—say one-fourth—were in a satisfactory condition.[1]

[1] This calculation was made in 1890, when I first published the figures, with appropriate observations, in every newspaper in India which would give space to my communications. Three out of every four with whom I communicated gave me space. I retain the statistics of that day for comparison hereafter. They make the authorities look very ridiculous, seeing that the two regions declared to be above the average of Rs.27 are precisely those

Provinces above Rs.27, with population.		*Provinces below Rs.27, with population.*	
Bombay ...	... 17,000,000	Madras ...	... 81,000,000
Central Provinces	... 10,000,000	Panjab ...	... 19,000,000
		Bengal ...	... 67,000,000
		N.W. Provinces and Oudh ...	... 44,000,000
Total	... 27,000,000	Total	... 161,000,000

Let it not be forgotten that, in the above tables, is to be found, as I have already intimated, the first and only attempt which has been made by the Indian authorities in England or in India to ascertain the economic condition of the Indian people. Unhappily, no use was made of the inquiry save to furnish Lord Cromer with a brief paragraph in his Financial Statement for 1882, and to establish a basis on which a rough estimate of an Indian's position could be made. The principles on which the estimate of an average income of Rs.27 per head per annum was ascertained were never stated; consequently, no one worked out such consequences as have already been deduced. Still, whether the consequences were worked out or not, they were there; that the eyes of the highest officials were not open to their sufferings did not diminish by one moment's ease the sufferings of many millions.

Each of the stories in 'The Jataka, or Stories of the Buddha's Former Births,' end with an identification of the parties in the story. Story 498 has, as its conclusion, these words: 'When the Master had ended this discourse, . . . he identified the Birth: "At that time, the landowner who did honour to the Law was the landowner in the story. Ananda was the king, Sariputta the chaplain, and I myself was the ascetic who lived in Himalaya."'

In like manner may I say? 'At that time the Marquis of Ripon, with a full heart to do India good, was Viceroy, Major Evelyn Baring was Finance Minister, the Duke of

regions in which the most destructive famines (of money, not of food, says Lord George Hamilton) have taken place.

Devonshire was Secretary of State for India, Mr. Gladstone was Prime Minister of England, with power over all the British realm. Yet not one of these eminent men, nor any of their successors—Lord Dufferin, Lord Lansdowne, Lord Elgin, Lord Curzon of Kedleston, as Viceroys; Sir Auckland Colvin, Sir David Barbour, Sir James Westland, Mr. Clinton Dawkins, Sir Edward Law, as Finance Ministers in India; Lord Kimberley, Lord Cross, Sir Henry Fowler, Lord George Hamilton, as Secretaries of State; the Marquis of Salisbury, as Secretary of State and Premier, in England,—has ever taken the trouble to deduce from the secretly-preserved statements of 1882, the lessons they contained. The direct outcome of this perfunctory manner of dealing with vital matters concerning India has been a vast host of deaths from starvation and an amount of daily suffering beyond the telling by mortal man or record by mortal pen. Even the Recording Angel's stylus must have needed frequent renewal. More: the forty and more eminent gentlemen who, since 1882, have led a strenuous life as Members of the Council of the Secretary of State, neither collectively nor individually have devoted any of the time they have had (and still have) in abundance, to the consideration of what Indian economic statistics really do mean in regard to the condition of the Indian people. This inference is based on the complete absence of any evidence to the contrary.'

Was the statement of 1882 trustworthy, as an indication of the actual condition of the people? Failing the production of the data on which the conclusions were founded, it is not possible to speak positively. Only on their production can a trustworthy judgment be formed. Guided, however, by what was revealed in the inquiry of 1888, either in six years the country had gravely deteriorated or too bright a picture was drawn by Lord Cromer and Sir David Barbour in 1882. The reader shall have some of the evidence of 1888 on which to base a judgment for himself and for herself. That done the agricultural produce of the past ten years accompanied by the non-agricultural development and resources for the same period, will be set out so far as published official records will permit. These will show how entirely inapplicable an average income of Rs.27 per head is to-day. The evidence in connection with the North-Western Provinces and Oudh has already been given in the immediately preceding chapter.

'On a late excursion into the Deccan I was exceedingly pleased and surprised to observe the great appearance of prosperity which the city of Poonah exhibited, and which was the more remarkable after the scenes of desolation, plunder, and famine, it had been so lately subjected to: all the principal streets and bazaars were crowded with people, whose dress and general appearance displayed symptoms of comfort and happiness, of business and industry, not to be exceeded in any of our own great commercial towns. The whole, indeed, was a smiling scene of general welfare and abundance. On noticing this to the Resident, he informed me that the Peishwa, since his return, with a view of promoting the prosperity of Poonah, had exempted it and the surrounding country from every description of tax; and, to prevent the possibility of exactions unknown to himself, had even abolished the office of cutwal. This fact is at least one proof, among various others, of the practicability of introducing what are termed the European principles of economy into Indian societies, with the same happy effects as have been experienced elsewhere.'—R. Rickards, 23rd July, 1808.

THE BOMBAY PRESIDENCY.

In the report prepared of the inquiry in 1887–8,[1] it was shown 'that the proportion of the total population, even in Sind, which live close to the margin of subsistence is not less than the rest of the Presidency, that is forty-seven per cent., of which at least one-half or two-thirds are cultivators' (p. 4). In the Konkan districts, population at that time, 3,804,344, 'there was hardly a season in which this population did not endure without a murmur the hardships of a Deccan famine' (p. 9). In spite of such statements as these, the Director of Agriculture did not consider there was much occasion for concern. He had admitted that 'the whole charge of living will amount to Rs.32, or Rs.30 to Rs.35 per adult man. Taking the average family as equivalent to a man, wife, and two children, one an infant, the man consumes two-fifths of the whole, such a family, therefore, will require Rs.75 to Rs.85 to support it. This, it will be observed, is exclusive of stimulants or narcotics. But even including a substantial charge for liquor, there are few places where a family of the working classes could not be decently supported on Rs.7 or Rs.8 per month.' The mean of this sum is Rs.90 per annum, or Rs.18 per head. That is on the basis of good crops and plenty of work, and comes to considerably less than one penny per day per annum. There is no allowance for famine, or even for poor crops, or for lack of work. This, less than one penny per head per day was considered essential.

[1] 'Report on the Economic Condition of the Masses of the Bombay Presidency, by the Director, Land Records and Agriculture, 1887–8.

The Director concluded his general summary in these words:—

'Every Indian administrator has recognised the poverty of the people of India. A man who supports life in the Bombay Presidency on two or three annas (2d. or 3d.) per day will be poor, but not so poor by half as the man who is called upon to do so in England on a shilling. The truth is summed up in Sir Richard Temple's words, quoted by Mr. Sheppard in his note on Gujarat: "There is much poverty but no pauperisation."'

The too-often casual way in which such important matters are dealt with in Indian publications is exemplified by this passage. The Indian poor man is not so badly off compared with the English poor man, it is asserted; then a fallacious illustration is employed to fasten the (alleged) fact in the mind. First, according to the Director's own showing not twopence or threepence, but less than one penny per day is the Bombay income. The Government of India showed only one penny and a fraction per head per day—if every one shared equally. Next, as to the parallel with England. That parallel is not, as Mr. Ozanne, the director, imagines, with one shilling per day as representative of an Englishman in the same position. In England the average income per head at that time was £44 per annum against, say, 23s. in India. Therefore, the true comparison is between £110 (two-and-a-half times the average as against 'two or three annas per day') and £2 18s. 6d.—that is to say, the English average income is thirty-eight times greater than the Indian; or, again, eight shillings against twopence halfpenny to threepence! So regarded, the poverty of the Indian cultivator becomes a thing to marvel at, and lifts the unhappy individuals affected by it—(say two hundred millions and more)—only a few removes above the cattle which graze on the pasturages. But what measure should be meted out to the highly-paid officials who put such false statements before the public.

In GUJARAT, 'the Garden of India' as it is called, it was found that in the

Total Population of	2,857,731
In the Lower Stratum there were 47 per cent., or	1,335,048

These ranged from 37·09 per cent. in Ahmadabad to 68·16 in the Panch Mahals. In the last-named district only 81,354 out of 255,479 were 'persons of a higher stratum,' as distinct from those 'in the lower stratum' (p. 16). The standard of living was—

	£	s.	d.
Average Minimum	1	17	2
" Maximum	2	1	6¼

'The average cost in the gaols is Rs.20 1a. (£1 6s. 9d.) per prisoner.' The *yield of holdings* shows that—

In Ahmadabad 10 per cent. of agriculturists (17,126), each representing a family, have sustenance from their fields for only ...	9 months.
In Kaira 33 per cent. to 50 per cent. (20,000 families), after paying debts, have sustenance for only	3 to 4 "
In Broach 10 per cent. (8,200 families), after paying debts, have sustenance for only	6 "
In Surat 15 per cent. (4,602 families) have sustenance for only	6 "
In Panch Mahals, percentage not stated, ditto, ditto	10 "

How, then, do they live? 'Probably . . . the moneylender keeps the poorer cultivator through the season of field operations and gets his profit by claiming the harvest' (p. 18). The people thus dragging through life are British subjects, be it borne in mind; we have abolished predial and domestic slavery in India, and yet allow farmers to live in slavery to the moneylender! 'When the field operations are over the poor cultivator has to get work. His resources in work are day labour, agricultural and non-agricultural, carting, and cutting wood and grass' (p. 20).

In the DECCAN, the 'liability of famine greatly affects the lowest stratum of the population even in normal years' (p. 27). The submerged population, the 'lower stratum,' number more than one out of five. The standard of living ranges between the average minimum, £2 0s. 6d., and the average maximum, £3 6s. 5d., which is simply a cruelly absurd statement, when the calculated average for all India was only 34s., and, probably, was actually thirty-three per cent. less than that.

'Authorities are unanimous that many cultivators fail to get a year's supply from their land. . . . The quality and natural advantages of the soil appear to be only one-fourth of those possessed by the Gujarat cultivator, though the acreage is double' (p. 29).

'Proportion of cultivators with short supply':—

	Supply.
In Khandesh, 15 to 66 per cent., say 40 per cent. (77,000 families, population 1,237,231), after paying debts, have for sustenance only	6 to 8 months.
In Nasik, 50 to 80 per cent., say 65 per cent. (91,000 families, population 701,826), after paying debts, have for sustenance only ...	6 "
In Ahmadnagar, 25 per cent. (88,000 families, population 751,228), not reckoning debt, have for sustenance only	4 to 6 "
In Poona, 38 to 50 per cent., say 45 per cent. (85,000 families, population 900,621), ditto, ditto	4 to 6 "
In Sholapore, 40 per cent. (52,400 families, population 582,487), ditto, ditto	12 "
In Satara, 37½ per cent. (say, 75,000 families, population 1,062,530), ditto, ditto	6 "

(p. 30). Satara is probably the richest of these districts, Khandesh excepted, and Sholapore the poorest, so that the particulars which give Sholapore twelve months of sustenance from the land apparently are not of much value. In spite of the facts given, and also that, according to Dr. Cornish, in the famine of 1877–78, 800,000 of the people in these regions died, and the admission that 'probably not one-half of this number' (nine per cent. of the whole population) 'habitually live below the standard in normal years, and not one-fourth (*i.e.*, 1,100,000) are compelled to live on insufficient food,' the official verdict is: 'There is no widespread distress anywhere in the Deccan' (p. 31).

The Deccannis are strange beings, with most unheard-of and condemnable practices. Note particularly this (p. 33): 'Their habit,' as Mr. Crawford says, 'is to live from hand to mouth; as the Deccanni earns more so he spends more on himself and his family—thoughtless of the future—content that the stomachs of his family and his cattle are filled' (p. 33). It is, indeed, grievous to think that, when the Deccanni cultivator really can get enough of food to satisfy himself, that he should, even within his limitations, 'eat, drink, and be merry.' Of course, every other people in the world would go on half rations when they had the means to buy full rations—especially Englishmen.

In the KARNATAK, or Southern Maratha Country, there is a population of 2,385,414. 'Despite its liability to famine it pays a higher land revenue than the Deccan or Konkan' (p. 35). The 'lower stratum' comprises 356,900 people. 'The cost of the standard diet is put as low as 18s. 4d. by Mr. Spence, but as high as £2 2s. 9½d. by Mr. Trimalrao Vyankatesh for the same district. It must be remarked that Mr. Spence's is one of the most careful and intelligent calculations made by any of the reporting officers. But it is probably rather low owing to insufficient allowance for pulse and condiments.' 'The gaol ration costs nearly Rs.20 8a. (27s. 2d.) per annum per head. The extra-mural ration costs Rs.25 4a. 6p. (33s. 8½d.) . . . more grain and animal food five times a week is given. (Certainly no agriculturist would expect the latter luxury)' (p. 36).

'On the whole the cost of living is about the same as in the Deccan, or say Rs.30 (£2) to Rs.38 (£2 10s. 8d.) per adult male and Rs.70 (£1 13s. 4d.) to Rs.80 (£2 6s. 8d.) per family of four' (p. 37).

'Seventy-five per cent. of the cultivated area is under food grains. The reporting authorities agree that there is a large number of cultivators who do not get a full year's supply from their lands.' The numbers are thus stated:—

	Supply.
In Belgaum, 40 to 68 per cent., say 50 per cent. (86,900 families, population 864,014), after paying debt, have as sustenance only ...	3 to 6 months
In Dharwar, 38 to 50 per cent., say 40 per cent. (79,458 families, population 882,907) ditto, ditto	6 to 9 „
In Bijapur, 4 per cent. (5,015 families, population 626,889) ditto, ditto	6 to 8 „

'This state of things is largely due to the amount hypothecated to the moneylender' (p. 37).

The conclusion was: '. . . with the immense possibilities of development through the new-born wheat trade and freshly-opened labour markets there is time to pause before heroic measures are initiated for the relief of any class in the Karnatak' (p. 39).

The KONKAN proper includes the districts of Thana, Kolaba, Ratnagiri, and Kanara. Out of a population of 2,209,100 there belong to the 'lower stratum' 546,700, with 336,000 out of 807,400 in Thana, and 26,500 out of 421,800 in Kanara. The standard of living is—minimum £1 17s. 5d., maximum £2 18s. 4d. Cost of living, family of four, as elsewhere, £4 13s. 9d. to £5.

'The food resources of the people in the Konkan are small. . . . Reports are unanimous that many cultivators do not get a full year's supply from their holdings.' The proportions of cultivators with short supply run—

	Supply.
In Thana, 10 to 30 per cent., say 20 per cent. (60,350 families, population 908,548), after paying debt, there remains for sustenance of family	4 to 5 months.
In Kolaba, 35 to 75 per cent., say 55 per cent. (41,969 families, population 381,649), ditto, ditto	2 to 5 „
In Ratnagiri, 50 to 85 per cent., say 66⅔ per cent. (120,947 families, population 907,090), ditto, ditto	4 to „
In Kanara—particulars not given.	

(p. 42). '. . . it is evident that the district of Ratnagiri cannot yield the food required by its population in normal years' (p. 43). 'Looking at the Ghat cultivators further south, Mr. Cumine says the greater portion cannot get enough to allay hunger in the hot weather. Mr. Rand says one-fifth cannot, and according to Mr. Candy one-fourth cannot. Mr. Crawford entirely opposes this view. He quotes, indeed, the statement he made to the Famine Commission, that on the slopes and spurs of the Sahyadris "there is not a single monsoon, however favourable, in which the people do not suffer, without a murmur, most of the hardships incidental to a famine." But he declares that the labourer of the South Konkan now rarely suffers from a deficiency of food' (p. 45). Mr. Crawford seems to think this a not unhappy position; but it does not appear that he himself ever expressed any violent desire to accommodate his own mode of living to that of the Ratnagiri 'lower stratum,' even as an experiment.

In SIND, nearly wholly an irrigated Province, the standard of living varies from £1 10s. 9d. to £3 4s. 0d. per annum. 'From nearly all quarters the district officers report with some confidence a marked improvement even in the last fifteen years.[1] *The people themselves will not admit it.*' 'On the whole, notwithstanding some drawbacks incidental to character, the Sindi has a good future before him, and, for many a year, in the absence of war or special calamity, the fear of general pauperism or acute distress will be far removed' (p. 47).

The District reports are full of interesting details. Even of Gujarat the Prosperous, it is said: 'In none of the districts do the statistics show deaths traceable to want. But the reporting officers declare them quite untrustworthy. The Collector of Broach thinks that some of the numerous deaths assigned to fever are caused by bad or insufficient clothing, food, and housing' (p. 69). In this opinion the Collector is supported by the highest medical authority in India, who, about this time, in his Health Report, declared that fever in many cases was merely a synonym for insufficient food and clothing.

[1] The reader will observe, '*Even* in the last fifteen years.'

Probably one million out of four millions of 'fever' deaths reported in so-called non-famine years are really deaths from starvation.

Mr. Kennedy says that, though better off than at the commencement of British rule, the people are less well-to-do than at the time of the last Revenue settlement' (p. 95).

I stay my hand, though the material for quotation and comment is yet abundant. That member of Parliament would do India a great service who should compel the publication of the various volumes from which, save three of the North-Western Provinces and Oudh, I have gleaned but scantily, leaving much for workers who may wish for more facts than I have recorded.

SOME MADRAS AGRICULTURAL FACTS.

Districts Settled.	Percentages of Assessments to the Value of the Gross Produce at Commutation Rates.	
	Dry Lands.	Wet Lands.
Cuddapah	20, 18, 12	22
Kistna	15, 18	21
Nellore	18	28
Kurnool	16, 18, 17	16, 17, 18, 19
Chingleput	15	20
South Arcot	15	81
Trichinopoly	18	28
Tinnevelly	...	25
Salem	12, 18	17, 21

'The Government assessment on dry lands in the settled districts varies from twelve to twenty-eight per cent. of the gross produce, and that on the wet lands from sixteen to thirty-one per cent., and not, as is often asserted, from five to ten per cent. in the one case, and from ten to 16·6 per cent. in the other. . . . Taking at random the Settlement Report of Nellore for the year 1898–99, we find that 38·22 per cent. of the lands sold had to be bought in by Government, and that in the previous year this percentage was so high as 56·28. Mr. A. Rogers, the well-known critic of the Madras Settlement System, an ex-member of the Civil Service, and the greatest living authority on land revenue settlements in India, in a letter addressed to the Secretary of State in 1898, pointed out that, of the 1,968,364 acres sold by auction between the years 1879–80 and 1889–90, so much as 1,874,148 acres had to be bought in by Government for want of bidders, that is to say, very nearly sixty per cent. of the land supposed to be fairly and equitably assessed could not find purchasers.'—*The Hindu* newspaper.

'It is not till he has gone into these subjects in detail that a man can fully appreciate how terribly thin the line is which divides large masses of people rom absolute nakedness and starvation.'—W. C. BENETT, 'Oudh Gazetteer,' vol. i. p. 515.

THE PANJAB: A LAND OF MANY RIVERS, WIDE-SPREAD IRRIGATION, YET MUCH NEED.

The Director of Land Records and Agriculture in the Panjab gave to the misleading[1] circular from the Government of India, a widespread and representative area for investigation. He had fifty-four copies which he sent to high officials at Delhi, Jullundur, Lahore, Rawalpindi, Derajat, and Peshawar.[2] Both European and Indian officials were engaged in the duty: twenty were Britons, eight were Indians (five Muhammadans, three Hindus).

At the Delhi Divisional Conference in 1888, resolutions were passed, which (1) asserted that the opinion as to the 'greater portion' of the population suffering from

[1] I use the adjective as a protest against the manner in which, in the Government circular, the question for inquiry was misdescribed. The Government instituted the inquiry to ascertain whether 'the assertion that the greater proportion of the population of India suffer from a daily insufficiency of food was wholly untrue or partially untrue.' No one, with any pretensions to knowledge had, before 1887, said that over one hundred millions of India suffered from 'a daily insufficiency of food.' That was the Government gloss. Probably it might be said now—1901—and truly said. Indeed, practically the same thing was said eight years ago.

[2] The places and names are as follows:—

Delhi.—Messrs. Machonachie, Purser, Douie, Kensington, Anderson, and M. Abdul Ghani, Extra-Assistant-Commissioner.

Jullundur.—Mr. Francis, Colonel Birch, and Maya Das, Extra-Assistant-Commissioner. Messrs. O'Brien, Harris, and M. Azim Beg, Extra-Assistant-Commissioner.

Lahore.—Messrs. Clark and Karm Chand, Extra-Assistant-Commissioner, Hutchinson, R. Dane, and Bhagwan Das, Extra-Assistant-Commissioner.

Rawalpindi.—Messrs. Wilson and Ghulam Farid, Extra-Assistant-Commissioner, Major Roberts, and Kazi Ali Ahmad, Extra-Assistant-Commissioner, Mr. Gardiner, and Ghulam Ahmad, Extra-Assistant-Commissioner.

Derajat.—Messrs. Dames, Ogilvie, Steel, and Ghulam Murtaza, Extra-Assistant-Commissioner.

Peshawar.—Messrs. Udny and Cunningham.

an insufficiency of food' was erroneous; (2) Nevertheless while that is true as regards quantity of food, 'there is little doubt that the diet is of a distinctly inferior class, even judged by the comparatively low standard of the country'; (3) 'There is no evidence to show poor feeding is on the increase'; (4) Special attention is invited 'to the great and increasing extravagance of expenditure on social ceremonies and customs among all classes' [a singularly inept observation in view of the inquiry in the Panjab by Mr. S. S. Thorburn, I.C.S., which showed, as regards recourse to the moneylender:—

'Out of 742 proprietary families—
444 were practically ruined—
193 from bad seasons, plus small holdings,
65 ,, extravagance or bad management,
9 ,, cases in Court,
35 ,, unascertainable causes,
142 ,, from a combination of the above four;
112 were seriously involved; and
186 are prosperous']; (5) 'The disease which prevents or enfeebles work is often the cause of insufficient earnings and consequent poor diet'; and (6) 'Tribal characteristics and social customs, such as the seclusion of women, also laziness of character, constitute a very large cause of the poverty where it exists.'

Mr. J. R. Machonachie, then deputy-commissioner of Gurgaon, expressed the opinion that the standard of living was nowhere lower than in Gurgaon,[1] was satisfied

[1] How did Gurgaon become the lowest in this respect of the Panjab Districts? The *Pioneer* (a pro-Government newspaper published at Allahabad), on December 30, 1890, in a long article wherein it was stated that the Financial Commissioner and the Lieutenant-Governor 'displayed a lamentable ignorance of facts or indifference to their responsibilities,' gives the reason. This was the consequence of the 'lamentable ignorance' or 'indifference':

Gurgaon, in 1877, had nearly 700,000 inhabitants;

From 1837 (Lord—then Mr.—Lawrence being Settlement Officer), the district had been steadily rack-rented;

In 1877 rents were raised. Rains failed, crops were ruined; the Govern-

that 'the average zemindar' (landowner) 'and indeed zemindars something below the average—usually get as much to eat as they want,' and then submitted the following generalisation on the situation :—

(a) In fair seasons there is no actual want of food, but the standard of living is perilously low: directly prices rise or failing health abridges labour, difficulties begin.

(b) The 'positive check to population,' disease, is painfully prevalent, showing itself, of course, most against infant or infirm life.

(c) Even short of starvation there is a stage where green crops, herbs, and even berries, are consumed in quantities larger than is good for health. I am not speaking now of that healthy supplement to grain food which is found in mustard-heads and grain-heads taken in moderate proportion, but of cases where this green and flatulent food is the only sustenance obtained for several days together at a time. This feeding must demoralise the digestion and lower the vital power, and is no doubt one of the causes why malarious fever, seizing on the debilitated frames of such poor people, works such fatal havoc among them in the autumnal months of a rainy year. Wild herbs and berries would be equally, if not more, injurious.

(d) Short food is no doubt often a cause of migration. Several of the cases show this, and interesting details will be noticed here and there which show up the under-current of life going on among the poor. They evidently in their wanderings from one tract to another take little note of district or even provincial boundaries. Such people are really too humble to be much affected by political conditions except as these bear directly on food. It is obvious that the supreme object in life for them is how to keep body and soul together, and the struggle is an arduous one.

(e) The burdensomeness of marriage expenditure is very clearly shown in some cases, and there seems real pathos in the fact that contracts loosely made, or at all events depending for their binding power on the good faith of the parties as vouched in parole agreement, are felt strong enough to last from one life to another.

(f) Special diseases generated by special employments are at least in one case suggested, and I think that more intimate acquaintance with the practical details of handicraft and mechanical labour

---

ment demand, nevertheless, was exacted; results, officially admitted: At the end of five years 80,000 people had died, 150,000 cattle had perished, 2,000,000 rupees of debt (£133,334) to pay the Government rents incurred, the people emaciated and unable to reap a good crop when it came.

might disclose other facts of the kind. The curious use of impure and inferior salt in one trade may also here be noticed.

(*g*) The immense power of the small banya is shown clearly in the enormous interest taken, and the way in which debts are paid, *e.g.*, by labour, or where loans are made for the purchase of cows of buffaloes, in ghi. Other inquiries made on this latter point lead me to think that here especially is exemplified the principle 'Væ Victis.' The poorer a man is the lower the rate he will get for his ghi—the variations in price by no means coinciding with those of the local market.

(*h*) It is at first sight extraordinary, and on reflection it can hardly fail to be suggestive, to notice, what a small portion of the life of the poorer classes comes under the direct influence of the rulers of the country. . . . The great fact of the 'Pax Britannica' is of course present, but beyond this the visible connection is of the slenderest kind. It is a fact worth remembering at times that lakhs[1] of the poorer classes never have anything directly to do with us, and that the lives of millions more impinge only once or twice on the observation of their rulers. The man who was once, and only once, called to court—the 'Kamin,' whose experience of the rulers of his district is derived from forced labour which was probably put on him by his lambardar and no one else—the episode of the young weaver growing comelier and stronger on his regular coolie labour on the canal, and the satisfactory payment of that labour—all such facts give, I think, a useful and certainly most interesting side-view of agricultural conditions which must, if duly remembered, render sober and practical any procedure we think of adopting in dealing with the masses. A higher end, however, may be obtained. A man must be either hardhearted or very ignorant if he can read such life-histories as these without experiencing greater sympathy for, and a warmer interest in, the people among whom he is called upon to work: in a word, developing qualities which it is the tendency of official routine to destroy, and which, of all rulers in the world, Englishmen can least afford to lose.

What 'daily insufficiency of food' may mean is discussed by the Deputy-Commissioner of Gurgaon, who says it may mean one or other of two things:—

'(1) It may mean such a shortness of supply of food as shall leave the man habitually hungry. Failing such an acute degree of deficiency, it may, without leaving him consciously hungry, be inadequate

[1] 'Lakhs' = hundreds of thousands.

to supply the demands of physical exertion arising from his trade or avocation. If this deficiency exists, it will in the end tell either by shortening life through depressed vitality or by causing actual disease.

'(2) There is, however, another meaning which would refer the daily supply of food to some physiological standard. An example will make this clearer. It is said that a healthy man in Europe takes into his body during the day about $\frac{1}{24}$th part of his weight in either solid or liquid food. Thus a healthy man of 12 stone weight will require 7 lbs. weight of food. Taking the weights of a thousand prisoners in the Gurgaon gaol, I find the average height 5 feet 4½ inches, and average weight 1 maund 10 seers, or, say, 108 lbs. At this reckoning the proper weight of solid and liquid food taken by a full-bodied male adult of Gurgaon should be $4\frac{7}{24}$ lbs. The ratio, however, of food taken to weight of body of consumer must depend to some extent on climate as well as on habits of life, so that these would have to be allowed for. But further, according to physiologists, there is a standard of weight according to height, and it is quite possible, referring to the average height above mentioned, that 108 lbs. is below the standard weight for the average height, 5 feet 4½ inches' ('Econ. Inq.,' 1888, Panj., p. 5).

While satisfied the allegation as to daily insufficiency of food was 'erroneous and misleading,' so far as the Panjab is concerned, this officer remarked: 'But when we go farther and inquire whether the food habitually obtained by the mass of the people is satisfactory as regards quality,' there must arise doubts.

'I remember once an epigram of the late Superintendent of Chamba, that the difference between a good and a bad year in Chamba was that, in the first, the people found half their food in roots and herbs, in a bad year three-fourths of the whole. We, of course, have nothing like this; but it is a grave fact that at certain periods of the year there is a considerable portion of the population which eke out their grain food with what they call "ság" (mainly either grain or mustard leaf), and at other times with berries or wild fruits, such as the jaman, ber, or still more frequently with pilu; at other times with melons. Coming a step above this, we reach a large class which live habitually on the poorer grains and pulses as distinguished from wheat and barley. Looking these facts fairly in the face, we cannot deny there is [an] unsatisfactory mass of low diet in the country even in normal conditions.'[1]

---

[1] 'Econ. Inq.,' 1888, Panjab, p. 5.

Certain fair-sample cases, with the life-history of the families concerned, were obtained. The light they throw on Indian village existence calls for the quotation of some of them in full. The sympathetic and diligent reader will become too much interested in these details of the daily round of certain of his fellow-subjects to resent the length to which these passages run :—

CASE I.

I. *Name, Parentage, Caste, and Residence.*

1. Ram Sukh, son of Lachman, Koli-Nai, Tahsil Firozpur, District Gurgaon.

II. *Personal and Family History up to date.*

2. I was born in village Balkhora, raj Bhartpur, one year before '90 Vicramajit (55 years now). That year '90 was one of famine. My father was also a poor man; he had four sons—Ram Baksh, older than I, Kullna and Bhura, younger. These three are settled in Satwari, Bhartpur, having left Balkhora on account of famine. We did not work till ten years old, and we used to bring wood for fuel or herbs for food. We are six of us in the household. When I became 11 or 12 I began to tend the goats of Tenti Gujar. I got only my food and clothing in return for labour. My father and elder brother used to weave. As my younger brothers got bigger they helped in weaving, or with fuel and herbs. At 14 years of age we began to work for zemindars in hoeing, etc., and got 1 anna per day; the same in sowing time. We used to borrow some grain from different zemindars for food, and work it off in labour. Two or three years matters thus went on. I became more intelligent, and took to the weaving work with father and brother. The younger ones worked still at odd jobs. Until the '8 ser' year 1917[1] we thus remained without owing anything.

3. In that famine my father and mother, under want of food, were killed off by the cold of the months December, January, but still they left us without any debt. No one indeed in that famine would give credit. As we could not get along in Balkhora we all came away to Satwari, where we hoped for easier days, as it benefits by the water of the Tikri Naddi. Our mother's sister too was there, and she helped us to settle. We lived there on herbs and on what we got by selling wood and grass, and finally fixed our abode in that

---

[1] The years mentioned are the fasli (or revenue) years, described elsewhere as having been instituted by the Emperor Akbar, and still retained in most parts of India.

village. When grain got cheaper we started a weaving business; daily labour too became remunerative. We managed not merely to make up the thread of other persons, but our own thread, bought Re.1 or Rs.2 at a time. Two seers were purchased for Re.1; from this one *thán*, 40 yards long and 1 cubit broad, was made up. This *thán* would be sold for Re.1–5 or Re.1–6. By this means we employed odd times, and became well off for food. Betrothal of all four brothers had been made in the lifetime of our parents. In 1918 my big brother married; there was no procession; he went with his sister's husband, as is usual. He married in Dabak, Bhartpur. Rs.7 were spent, given to the parents of the bride. They sent no dowry or presents. We made no feast, on account of poverty.

4. In 1920 I married the daughter of Harkishan of Nai, Musummat Phulbi. She has been a good wife to me. We don't quarrel. On my marriage Rs.8 were spent, given to my mother-in-law. No marriage feast or expenses; no marriage presents. After marriage I lived in Satwari three years. Chaina, boy, was born there; he is now 22 years old. When the woman(?) began to quarrel, and my mother-in-law having no male offspring wanted me to come to them, I came over here to my wife's family. Her father gave me then 20 seers grain and one thatched house to live in, and weaving implements, worth some Re.1–8. These implements are still in use. I have been here now about 20 years. One year after we came Sarwan, second boy, was born; now he is 19 years old. After him two boys and one girl were born; these died of small-pox. After these Ramratan (now 12 years old) was born. Five years after him Puran Mal (now 7) was born. Four sons and father and mother are our family.

5. At his birth I gave my wife 4 annas worth of 'bájra,' 4 annas 'gúr,' and 8 annas 'ghi,' ordinary food after this. Nothing was given to the 'dhái' at confinement, but she came. I gave her a little piece of 'gúr,' however. When Chaina was 3 or 4, I betrothed him in Guraksar, Rs.7 expenses—Rs.5 to the bride's parents, Rs.2 in eating. My father-in-law found this money. At 12 Chaina began learning to weave and working separately. In 1938 he married; Rs.15 were spent—rice Rs.2, sugar Re.1, ghí Re.1, cash to parents Rs.11. The food was distributed among our brotherhood and 1¼ seer to the bhisti and potter each. Nothing to anybody else, as we were poor. Five men went in the marriage procession; the bride's people, besides ordinary food, made no presents. Of this Rs.15 my brother sent me Rs.5 marriage present from Satwari. My father-in-law, when the ceremony of washing the bridegroom on the threshold was finished, gave Re.1. I spent Rs.5 of my own cash, and borrowed Rs.4 from Dhan Singh Meo of Satwari. This debt was got at 1 paisa per rupee monthly interest. It was paid off by sending Chaina himself to work as servant to Dhan Singh at Re.1 per month and food. In four months it was paid off. The four annas interest he

worked four days extra for. In 1985, when food was dear and his father-in-law wanted him to take away his wife, I borrowed some clothes from Bhontia Meo, his wife; I could not afford new clothes. No other expenses. After bringing home his wife, Chaina lived with me for three or four years, then on account of disagreement among the women he separated, but still remained here three or four years; then of his own accord he went away to his wife's people.

6. At Savan's birth I gave his mother 8 annas of ghí, 8 annas gur, borrowing the money from Jawáhir Meo. My father-in-law gave 15 seers bájri. At about nine the boy began to help in the weaving business and bring in fuel, etc.

At 13 or 14 he began to do zemindar's work, earning half or one anna at hoeing, cutting, etc. Since last year he has started the weaving business fully with me. I betrothed him when 12 or 13 in Hathin. Rs.5 expenses—Rs.3 to bride's parents, Rs.2 to guests. He was married two years ago. Rs.9 were paid to the bride's parents; no debt incurred. I got nothing from them. Three men went in the marriage procession. Bride not yet come home.

7. Ram Rattan, 12 years, has been married. No expenses were incurred. Puran Mal, seven years old, has not been yet betrothed.

III. *Daily Expenses of Food and Maintenance.*

8. No daughter. We are five persons now. Three and a half seers are wanted for our daily food. At evening 1½ seers of dalya is cooked, at noon 2 seers bajri is used (21 seers per rupee), ½ anna salt, oil, pepper. This gives three annas per day. Dalya is cooked in water; we don't get milk. We eat the 'dalya' in the evening, and what is left we eat in the early morning. The noontide meal is 'roti,' with it sometimes 'herbs,' or sometimes only salt is sprinkled over it. We don't pay anything to the bhisti, bhangi, etc. The women bring water themselves, and sweep the place, and bring fuel from the jungle, and grind flour themselves. Rs.67 8a. is the yearly expense. On Holi and Diwáli, or on the visit of any guest, a chittack, or half páo of ghi is bought, about four annas in the year, Rs.67 12a. in all.

9. We five use clothes thus: for a man, 2 chadars 5 cubits long and 3 cubits broad, and 2 dhotis 5 cubits long each, and 1 pagri of 8 cubits length. No expense in shoe-leather, as we wear none. For the woman, 1 chadar 4 cubits by 3 cubits, and 1 petticoat, 14 annas, and 1 bodice, dyed at home, are wanted in the year. The two boys only have as yet one chadar each, 2 or 2½ cubits long, in the year. They don't wear a dhoti. Expenses of this are made up by purchasing two or three seers of thread, and making up the cloth at home. Total expenses of clothes, Rs.2 6a. No clothes for the cold weather. No ornaments.

10. House vessels: only one lota and one katora of brass were bought before 1984 for Re.1, and have been used ever since. The other vessels are earthen, and are bought from the potter for a paisa or a

little grain when wanted. One iron cauldron was bought for two annas some years ago.

11. Cattle: none.

12. Living house: two houses of thatched roof and one room got from a Meo, with beams of wood put on by him. No hire. I have to thatch my houses every three or four years. Rupee 1 thatch, and 8 annas wages for putting it on. Leeping and other repairs I do myself. One chappar is badly out of repair. I have put some dried bajra stalks over half of the roof. The Meo's house fell these rains. I weave in both 'chappars.'

IV. *Earnings.*

13. Only one weaving apparatus in use at present. Fine and coarse cloth both are made. Six annas wages for weaving 40 yards. In one day 5 yards are woven, but one day is taken up in preparing the thread—five days for 6 annas. The thick cloth (dora) gives 5 annas per two seers thread made up. This takes four, or sometimes five, days to do. This work goes on for eight months; not in the rainy season. Cannot say how much I turn out in the year. I can't work now, as I am weak (looks rather more than his age), but do a little now and then.

14. In the rainy season we, father and son and sometimes wife, do work at hoeing and sowing the spring crop. One or 1¼ anna each earns and the woman as much; thus we manage to find our daily bread. At cutting of spring crops for 8 or 10 days at harvest we turn out to the field. Two or 2½ seers grain per person are earned. My wife, too, sometimes grinds flour. We have a mill. She gets half anna for grinding five seers; or she works in some zemindar's house for crushing bajra or juwar stalks, getting one or half seer as wages. The 12-years-old boy has begun this year to earn his daily food in work for some zemindar.

15. In 1928 I bought a cow-calf from Kaná, koli, for Re. 1. I brought it up for four or five years. When it grew up it got in calf, and in 1932 I sold it to Dharia, Meo proprietor, for Rs.25. He did not pay cash, but instead he mortgaged 2 bighas, 7 biswas land to me. Since then I have been in possession of the land. In the Kharif I hire a plough and sow bajra and juwar. I get only one or two maunds grain. I don't get it ploughed and sown at the right time. Last year I got only 20 seers bajra. This year hiring a plough for Rs.1. I have sown juwar, urd, and til. The crop is a good one. I pay the revenue rate of the village, which comes to Rs.2 7a.

V. *General Remarks.*

16. Expenses are about Rs.70 a year, and this is cost of hiring of five persons. Income not known exactly in detail, but though it is impossible to strike a balance, it is said by the man himself that he gets along. He is not in debt, nor does any one owe him anything.

His savings are Rs.25 mortgaged in the land. But note the very narrow margin, the extreme want of clothing, no thick clothes for the cold weather. The man's appearance is poor. He is thin. The woman is fairly nourished. Sawan is moderately so. The third boy is weak; the fourth is sturdy and well-built, but has a large stomach. Note the three deaths from small-pox; the 'disagreements among the women'; the cold after the famine killing off the old parents; the easy uprooting from one place and emigration; the apparent drawing towards the wife's family.

CASE IV.

I. *Name, Parentage, Caste, and Residence.*

1. Guta, Lohar, of Thana Khurd, Sonepat Tahsil, age 40 years, Mussalman.

II. *Personal and Family History up to date.*

2. Our family was settled four or five generations in Bhowapur, Tahsil Sonepat. My father died in 1857, when I was some 12 years old, in Bhowapur. I remained there. The second son of my father, my elder brother Kalandari, is some 10 years older. I had other brothers. One died in Bhowapur. Two are living there. My father made tools and implements for the zemindars, and also had some agriculture. The earning of the father and two brothers was some Rs.2 a day, and a very good livelihood was secured.

3. My marriage was made 19 years ago in Bhowapur. The expenses were Rs.250. The money was left by my father in the shape of ornaments, silver. My mother used to wear them. She managed my marriage. We paid Rs.250 cash to the parents of the bride, who came from Jakai, Tahsil Gohana. I have had five children by her—two girls and three boys. Three are dead—two girls and a boy. All three died under two years of age. The two boys now living are six and four years old. My wife is now some thirty years of age. She brought no ornaments with her. I was rather old in comparison to her and had to pay. It is thought a fault to marry a girl to one much older than her.

4. After our father's death we boys were young. Our uncles put us away from the shop. We began to work for the zemindars, getting one maund per plough. We used to get 20 or 22 maunds of grain in the year. We couldn't manage on this, as we were a numerous family, so 15 years ago I came over here. Some zemindars asked me to stay here, as I came round in search of employment. I came first alone, and having made arrangements and secured a hut, I called my wife. All my children were born here.

III. *Daily Expenses of Food and Maintenance.*

5. I live in a zemindar's house and pay Re.1-7 rent half-yearly. My wife works in cotton, earning 6 or 9 pies [one halfpenny to three-

farthings] per day. This she keeps, and when my employment is stopped we get our food from this.

6. No cattle, nor any land. My wife does not go out in the jungle for fear of the zemindars, lest they should insult her.

7. Have two vessels of 'kánsi,' other vessels of earth, and tools worth Rs.10. Four years ago I spent Rs.7 in repairing them. Nothing since. Four months are busy in 'takú' work. In cold season a 'takú' lasts a year. But this year there is little or no cotton, and my work is stopped. At such times I get 'sag' in the fields (channa and so on) and get food out of that. To-day I got about a seer of this, the green leaf, in the fields. The zemindars don't stop this. They help a starving man, and besides it does the channa good cutting off its head. I don't owe anything to anybody. My father left Rs.8 and Rs.7, two debts, to two men. They demand Rs.30 or Rs.40. I wanted to pay them Rs.10, but haven't got it. My elder brother here works for the zemindars, Kalandari.

8. Kalandari is married, and has two boys alive; one is 19 years, the other is some six or seven. He had a girl, who died five years old, and four other boys, who all died under two years of age.

9. On I'd (Eed = a Muhammadan festival) if I have money I spend 8 annas or Re.1 on food, some of which I give to the poor! Nothing to any priest or mullah.

IV. *Earnings.*

10. I was well here for some seven years. Since then I have been ill of spleen. I have become weak and cannot do full work as a lohár. I make big needles 'táků' for the women to use at their cotton-wheels. I make four in a day. Each needle brings 8 paisa = 8 annas. The iron costs me one anna, so I make two annas. Charcoal I get. It doesn't cost much. I also make holes (dántá) in grindstones with a tool (tánki), for which I get 2 paisa, paid in cash. At the time of harvest I work, getting 1½ or 2 annas per day. Thus I make my bread and clothes.

11. Kalandari gets along better than I do. He gets 20 or 22 maunds (maund = 82⅓ lbs.) in the year, and cultivates some two kacha bighas, paying Re.1-8 or Rs.2 per bigha. It is barani land. He has a calf about 1½ years old. He had a cow who gave him it. He sold the mother for Rs.5. The calf was some six months old. He borrows the cattle of some zemindar to plough his field, and does some blacksmith's work for him in return; doesn't pay cash.

V. *General Remarks.*

12. Guta is a decent-looking man, but his face shows marks of his disease—a much enlarged spleen. His arms are puny. Note the Rs.250 paid at marriage and Kalandari's five children all dying under five years of age.

CASE VI.

I. *Name, Parentage, Caste, and Residence.*

1. Kima, son of Maukam, weaver, of Khubru, Sonepat, 48 years of age.

II. *Personal and Family History up to date.*

2. I was born here, and my ancestors have been here three or four generations. My father died when I was 15 years old, 33 years ago, and my mother six years after him. My mother came from Khatar Daula in the Meerut district. My father died of fever when he was 60, and my mother about the same age, of 'dama' (asthma). I have no brother or sister. I had a brother older than I, who died before my recollection, 25 years of age. I was married the year before my father died, and 'gohua' four years later. My wife came from Khánpur in Rohtak. Her age is equal to mine. I have one son 24 years old and three daughters, one 28, one 25 or 26, one 7 years old. I had a daughter two years after consummation of marriage, and she died six months old from smallpox. Had no other children.

3. Marriage was made by my father. I don't know how much money was spent. My son's marriage took place seven or eight years ago, and the 'gohua' three years ago. His wife came from village Pinana in this tahsil. She has one boy six months old; no other child. In my son's marriage Rs.30 were spent—Rs.20 were given to the bride's father, Rs.10 spent in feeding the kinsmen. The bride's father gave us only Rs.7.

4. I had my eldest daughter married 20 years ago, and the second 16 years ago. I got Rs.18 on each occasion, and paid Rs.5 to the boy's parents. Rupees 12 or Rs.13 on each occasion were spent in entertaining the guests of the marriage procession, and I gave clothes to each girl worth Rs.7 or Rs.8. One girl has gone to Jowra, Rohtak, and the other to Machrauli in Pánipat Tahsil.

III. *Daily Expenses of Food and Maintenance.*

5. We are six persons—I, my wife, my son, his wife, my youngest daughter, and the son's baby. Our food is about four seers a day. We eat channa. There are two meals; half we cook in the evening and half for breakfast. Breakfast about noon, and dinner after sunset. Dinner is made of dalya. If we have sil (buttermilk) we put that in; if not, we eat it in water. Sometimes a zemindar will give us some buttermilk. We don't eat salt with the dalya, but we put 'sag' sometimes. In these days we put half grain and half channa herb tops.

It is about two seers we make up of both grain and herb. When we get a lot of herb we use less grain. There is no strength in the herb, but it helps to fill up the stomach. Our women bring in the channa herb. The zemindars don't mind when the plant is big; they do when it is little.

The 'roti' is made of channa ground and cooked by our women. If we have salt we put it in; if not, we eat it saltless (alúni). Salt is about 10 seers to the rupee. For one paisa then I get 2¼ chattacks. The banya does not give less because of the smaller quantity. Salt is certainly good for the taste.

We cannot eat wheat, as it is 15 seers the rupee; we eat channa at 22 or 23 seers the rupee.

6. We make our own clothes, buying the cotton. I have only one cloth (shows it), which does for chaddar and for sleeping blanket too. I have a vest (kamari), under it, pagri and dhoti. The 'gudri' I made this year; it cost some 8 annas for the stuff. We wear shoes if we can get them. I have a pair which belonged to a Ját who died, and I begged them from his wife.

They were too small, so I had them cut (shows them) so as to let out my feet. My women would wear shoes if they could get them, but they have none—can't afford it. My son has a pair; he bought them for 10 annas a pair last jeyt from the Chamár here.

7. I have five tools, Re.1–8 or Rs.2 value. These work for ten years. Our house is in the village Shámilat. We pay rent for the ground, Re.1–4 per six months to the lambardárs. Once a year one day has to be given in clearing out the canal channel. For this I get one 'roti.' No other service is due from me for the ground. No ornaments or metal vessels; all earthen. No cattle; never had any. No land. Just now live by weaving. We glean in harvest time (silla uthāte). This year there is nothing. We get along by my paying my father's debts, my son paying mine, his son paying his. We all live together in peace. We never have any quarrels.

IV. *Earnings.*

8. I make razai cloth (of coarse quality), and earn Re.1 for weaving 120 yards. This can be done in 15 days, including the fixing up. This is one man's work. I work with other people's thread. My share is only the making up. My son earns as much as I do, and at harvest time we each of us earn 1 or 1½ anna per day in the field work. Beside this we get 'roti' for one meal. Some pay in cash, some in grain. If they pay in grain they give one seer less in the rupee, because, as they say, if we pay in cash you have to wait a bit, ten days or so; if you take grain we will give you a little less! This goes on for 15 or 20 days each harvest. I don't work at all in sugar-cane; the zemindars all do their own work in this with the help of the chamars. When we don't get the harvest work we have to borrow from the banya, but we know this is hard for us, so we don't borrow if we can help it. The Játs made us build the school, the chaukidar beat us and made us work; but we got nothing, not even 'roti.' This was last Jeyt. Altogether twenty days' labour was given from our family and nothing paid. The Játs got the bricks and wood, and we

had to find the labour; don't know if the Government gave anything. I didn't see any official, no chaprási; no names were written.

9. I owe Rs.16 or Rs.17—Rs.10 to Nand Lal Ját. This was on account of grain, and partly on account of my son's marriage. No interest runs on this, but I have to work one or two days for him at the harvest. Khubi and Duliya, two banyas, I owe Rs.6 or Rs.7. On this there is half an anna per rupee interest per month. This was for grain last rainy season. There were great rains; I couldn't do any work. I work also as a coolie on the canal, and there earn 1¼ or 2 annas a day. This is on the new canal. I worked as a tokriwála for 1¼ annas. The chaprási stood over us and made us work well. We used to be paid daily or every third day, then once a week. The Sáhib used to pay the money himself, and no dastúri, no nothing was cut, no 'zulm' was allowed.

The women clean the cotton for weaving and fix it up too, and clean up the cloth when it is made. They work in the harvest and get one anna and one 'roti.' This is only when they are strong. My wife can't do it now. She has given it up ten years ago, since her brother died. By reason of her sorrow she doesn't do any work outside. She begs buttermilk and does very little work at home. She says, 'Why has my brother died?' He was very dear to her!

10. My father died Rs.20 in debt. This was on account of my marriage. I paid it off in the course of several years; don't remember how much interest.

V. *General Remarks.*

11. Kima is a lively man, not stupid. Rather small made, but fairly nourished. His spleen is enlarged. Hindu. His son is taller and stronger looking altogether. He explains this by saying that he has worked some years on the canal. The wife looks old and withered. The son's wife is down with fever. Her little baby is fat and well nourished, and crawls vigorously. The youngest daughter of Kima also is healthy.

Note the curious relation of cash and grain payments; the 'begar' of the school building; the fairness of payment on the canal.

Another 'case,' a glass-blower by trade, says: 'We have no ornaments save a finger-ring, silver, worth twopence, six household vessels of "kansi" and brass, value about 2s. 8d. No cattle. Our forefathers did well; used to have cattle.'

The ex-Lieutenant-Governor of the Panjab (Sir Mackworth Young), then Commissioner and Superintendent, Jullundur Division, was extremely satisfied with the condition of the people. The assertion,[1] which,

[1] 'The greater portion of the population suffer from a daily insufficiency of food.'

by the way, no one but the Government of India made, is said to be 'wholly untrue.' 'The "Ser Atá" (two pounds of flour), which in common parlance represents the daily sustenance necessary to preserve life, is, as a matter of fact, actually available to a vast majority of the population, eked out by pulse, vegetables, and condiments; and such a lot as "going hungry" from day to day falls to so few that it would be difficult to find individuals in such a condition, still more classes of people.' A comparison is drawn between the Panjabi cultivator and a Dorsetshire labourer altogether to the advantage of the former. Later, when I am dealing with the annual income of the Panjab, this illustration of the ex-chief ruler may call for examination.

Mr. Francis, settlement officer, thinks the example of rulers of Feudatory States may need to be imitated 'for maintaining the peasantry in bad years,' while Mr. Harris, officiating deputy-commissioner, considers the land is 'sufficient to support the present population,' which, he adds, 'it is to be hoped will not increase.' He concludes:

> 'As I would hold then that the starvation statement is wholly untrue, I would not seek for remedies.' But, 'if remedies were needed, I would say shortly: India is a poor country, and cannot afford a good, expensive, and scientific, Government. Our Government is already far too expensive, and gets more so every year. The departments to cut down would not, in my opinion, be far to seek. Native industries should be more protected to the exclusion, for instance, of Manchester trade.'[1]

Colonel F. M. Birch, Deputy-Commisioner, Ferozepore, forwards a report from Rai Maya Das, Extra-Assistant-Commissioner; in that report it is stated:—

> 'Although an irrigation branch of the Sirhind Canal has passed through the Fazilka Tahsil, still these unfortunate villages have not been benefited therefrom to any appreciable extent. In most places the lands are very sandy and higher than the level of the water, and many people of the thirty-three villages are reduced to poverty, so much so that many a man has to lie down hungry in the evening,

---

[1] 'Econ. Inq., Panjab,' 1888, p. 21.

and seldom get sufficient food for both the meals during the twenty four hours.'

Colonel Birch himself remarks:—

'In regard to the general question, I should myself say that in most years the state of the agricultural population of this vast continent of India is tolerable. There is sufficiency of food for all. The slightest variation, however, in season—a deficiency of rain, for instance—is immediately felt. In times of scarcity or bad crops the pinch is at once felt, and in times of the failure of the harvest starvation ensues. There is no reserve, as it were, and no poor-law or poor-houses, to which the lowest classes may resort. The operation of caste is, in this respect, beneficial. It rescues from actual starvation caste fellows, and operates to supersede the necessity of a poor-law.'

Mr. M. F. O'Dwyer, Assistant-Commissioner, Shahpur, makes some statements which conflict with the optimism so generally expressed by the higher officials—indeed, the farther the official is from the daily life of the people the greater is his optimism. Only a Secretary of State could use such language regarding India as Lord George Hamilton habitually employs. The rule holds good the other way also,—the nearer to the people the greater the pessimism. Mr. O'Dwyer says:—

'In the Thal land has little market value, and in seasons of drought very few moneylenders will advance anything on landed security. The result of this cause is that just now there is an absolute and appalling want of the necessaries of life, at least in the Thal. In most of the houses there is no grain at all, and no means of purchasing any. The people have been driven to collect the seeds of trees and shrubs found scattered over the jungle. These are pounded up and manufactured into cakes, the composition of which is similar to that of saw-dust, and eaten generally by the people. All the women of the village may be seen every morning wandering through the jungle with brooms in their hands with which they sweep up and collect the "bakra" seeds. In fact these seeds at Nurpur and other villages have obtained a marketable value, selling at two maunds (82 lbs. = one maund) per rupee.

'Out of forty-one houses of zemindars and kamins that I entered at Nurpur, Buland, Adukot, Adhisargal, etc., in only five did I find any grain at all. In all the rest bakra seed was the sole provision for

[1] 'Econ. Inq., Panjab,' 1888, p. 23.

men, women, and children, who may be considered as looking starvation in the face.

'The same description no doubt applies to the Thal tracts in Bannu and Dera Ismail Khan and Jhang, which are similarly circumstanced, and the seasons in the Thal are so uncertain that drought of the kind occurs on the average in two or three years out of every ten.'[1]

Ghulam Ahmad, Extra-Assistant-Commissioner, collected statistics and made inquiries from 'men of good experience.' 'I have obtained,' he says, 'about two hundred examples from different parts of the district, which lead me to believe that the greater proportion of the lower classes of agriculturists and persons connected with agriculture suffer from a daily insufficiency of food.'[2]

'I am very sorry that the time given me in which to make my report has been so short. In my first report I mentioned the standard which gives a sufficiency of food for man, woman, and child. I also stated how I began my inquiries into the subject.

'Since sending in my report I have continued to collect statistics, and to make inquiries from men of good experience. I have obtained about 200 examples from different parts of the district, which lead me to believe that the greater portion of the lower class of agriculturists and persons connected with agriculture suffer from a daily insufficiency of food. This assertion is at least partially true. I have been in this district for more than a year, of which time about three-quarters have been spent in camp, and I have been making inquiries into this matter for several months. The following are the causes why this insufficiency of food prevails among the class to which my inquiry was confined.

'In the Pindigheb Tahsil, and in those parts of the Fatahjang and Attock Tahsils which are dependent on rain, the cause is drought, and consequent bad harvests, but it is very strange that in those parts of the district which are irrigated by wells the same result is found in many instances. From this it appears that the principal cause of insufficiency of food is not drought, for if it were the parts irrigated by wells would not suffer.'

Another Muhammadan Extra-Assistant-Commissioner, Ghulam Farid Khan, speaking of a district with 420,771 inhabitants, of whom the Hindus number 63,000, the Muhammadans 357,742, and the Christians 29. In his

[1] 'Econ. Inq., Panjab,' 1888, p. 35. [2] *Ibid.*, p. 37.

report he throws an interesting light on the habits and practices of the people. Much of what he says will help to an understanding of Indian character. From his remarks the passages which follow are taken:—

'It cannot be denied that among the Hindus there are persons whose incomes are insufficient; and their number, though much less than that of persons of the same position among Muhammadans, is certainly not small. In this class I include the three following classes of men—(1) those who get a small quantity of juwar or bajra and chiefly subsist on vegetables; (2) those who cannot get sufficient food for two meals a day, and consequently take only one meal, and for the second either eat parched grain or nothing at all; (3) those who can get no grain at all, and subsist either upon vegetables or by begging. About ten per cent. of the total Hindu population are men who fall under one or other of the above heads. The deficiency in the quantity of daily food does not so harmfully affect them as to bring them to an early grave and make them unfit for moving about, but it causes disease, and they cannot be said to pass a happy life, but are weak and unhealthy, and sometimes even die from the same cause. This state of things seems improbable on first thoughts when we consider the case of people living in cities and towns, because the outward appearance of these people seems good, and their mode of dress and bearing in public precludes the idea of their belonging to the class of persons who cannot get sufficient food. But an acquaintance with their social state and an insight into their private affairs will give strange results. In the Panjab one considers it a degradation to give publicity to one's poverty, and it is a custom to conceal from the knowledge of equals the narrow circumstances of one's family, and to show that one is living in an easy state of life. Such persons are technically called "Sufed posh," who, though they do not go entirely without food, they can hardly get sufficient food daily. A greater number of such Hindus will be met with in villages than in towns. I mean that those men who form the ten per cent. of the total Hindu population referred to above as getting an insufficient quantity of daily food, are chiefly inhabitants of villages. Their food consists of juwar, bajra, or grain, which they are too poor to procure in sufficient quantity. But the deficiency is made up by an admixture of vegetables. Insufficiency of food evidently affects a man's health and comfort without immediate danger to life. Thus among Hindus half per cent. will be found who live at starvation point, and this is a small percentage; but a good number have an insufficient quantity of food, being ten per cent. as explained above.

'The greater part of the population of this district is composed of Muhammadans, being eighty per cent. of the whole. Their social condition is very low. They subsist chiefly on agriculture, breeding cattle, or by manual labour as weavers, washermen, shoemakers, blacksmiths, carpenters, etc. All these are now equally suffering from poverty, the reason being that the peasants (zemindars) for whom they work are themselves in a state of deep poverty. Some families of peasants (zemindars) are still in a prosperous and wealthy condition, and these may be divided into two classes—(1) those who are actually rich, and (2) those who from their appearance seem to be wealthy but are in fact heavily burdened with debt. The clean clothes and contented appearance of the latter do not bespeak their true condition, but a knowledge of their debts, and an inspection of their household furniture brings their poverty to notice. The object of this long description is to show that in outward appearance there will be found a number of persons whose seeming wealth may lead one to form a favourable opinion of the condition of a whole country or community, while their real state does not correspond to their apparent condition. The same is the case with the ordinary peasants (zemindars). In particular villages the natural fertility of the soil or well-applied labour may conduce to signs of prosperity, but the community cannot be said to be generally in a flourishing condition. Though no doubt the canals have done immense good in this district, and the people who are benefited by them are prosperous (and the same may be said of those living in the vicinity of the rivers) still the alienation of their lands and their debts are on the increase. The people of the Thal and of some parts of the Bar are poorer than the rest. They chiefly depended upon cattle breeding for their livelihood, but this has now become very difficult for them owing to the establishment of grazing reserves, scarcity of water and fodder, and owing to drought, while the expenses of the care and the keep of the animals, and the demand on account of grazing dues press heavily upon them. As a consequence they are quitting this mode of earning a livelihood.

'In the ordinary times, *i.e.*, when there is neither plenty nor scarcity, the number of Muhammadans who live at starvation point is four per cent., and the number of those who have insufficient food is very large, and in my opinion it is not an exaggeration to fix it at twenty per cent. Especially in the last two or three years the want of rain has much increased the number of such persons, and had it not been for the railway which brought down grain, wheat, and bajra from the eastern districts, a famine would have certainly occurred. But the import of grain saved the district from ruin. The number of persons at starvation point (four per cent.) is not overstated, because in the towns and villages in several parts of the district the residents are generally so poor that they cannot get food for two meals a day, and usually eat only once, and their number, viz., four per cent., if not understated is certainly not exaggerated. The twenty per cent. who get insufficient food usually get a piece of bread and eat it with turnips or sag, mixing salt with the latter, or they take along with it some bread made of bajra, juwar, or grain. The majority of the peasants (zemindars) live on such food. In this year bhakra (*Tribulus terrestris*), which is not a food grain, formed the chief food of the people in the Bar, Thal, and Mohar. Some people lived upon water-melons only, or on the dried seeds of the same mixed with a quantity of grain. In the summer the people of those parts where "pihlu" (the fruit of the wan, *Salvidora oleoides*, tree) grows, assembled in the Bar, where they lived night and day on the "pihlu," and sometimes sold their surplus gatherings of the fruit in the nearest towns or villages, and with the few pice thus earned purchased flour to eat. These were mostly Muhammadan women.

'Of all those substances which serve the purpose of maintaining life the bhakra is the worst. It causes dysentery which sometimes ends fatally. The number of persons living in this way is twenty per cent. The number of indebted peasants (zemindars) is much greater than this. They are secure against the want of the necessaries of life because they can raise money on the credit of their land produce, and the Hindus advance them funds in the hope of ultimately grasping their landed property. In this way many of them have transferred their lands to the Hindus either by sale or mortgage, and others are doing so every day. Though these people get food in the shape of juwar, grain, barley, or bajra, for the present, the day is not far distant when they will fall into the same state in which their brethren now are. Such persons are not less than fifty per cent. in number.'

Colonel Ommaney, Commissioner and Superintendent, Derajat Division, while asserting there is 'neither a regular nor partial insufficiency of daily food,' in a long and unusually interesting report, goes on to remark :—

'Their indebtedness, about which so much has been written, is a condition that landholders suffer from more or less in many other countries, and has had to be dealt with by their Governments. Much the same causes lead to similar results everywhere, *e.g.*, the Government demand in cash instead of in kind throws villages into the hands of the capitalist in Palestine (Oliphant's "Halfa"); borrowing on the security of tenure, consequent debt and interest thereon, leads to transfer of land and emigration (Froude's "Oceana"). In this Division the inelasticity of the cash revenue system has been greatly moderated by suspensions and remissions when necessary, and by the introduction into the insecure tracts of Bannu, Dera Ismail Khan, and Muzaffargarh of an assessment fluctuating with the cultivation and crops—a system that if worked efficiently is admittedly a great boon, but even under it when a man pays no revenue because he has no cultivation, he must needs—for his own maintenance, and that of his family and cattle, and for seed,—incur debt, though here again the Government are prepared to advance him money for purchase of cattle and seed, as well as for agricultural improvements. Once in debt, however, the compound interest in kind and cash rapidly swamps him; then follows the civil court, execution of decree, and if under threat of imprisonment he has not parted with his land, he may now be compelled to do so. For unthriftiness, extravagance, and dishonesty, the Government can do nothing, but where in any way our system gives an unfair advantage to one party, the creditor, over another, the debtor, who belongs to the largest and most important class of the community in this country, special measures have to be considered to protect not only the latter, but also Government interests. While large and necessary expenditure is incurred to strengthen the defences of the Empire, it is surely of equal importance to provide against the undermining of the foundations within. Slowly but surely the village banker has acquired a hold of the land such as he could not have obtained but for the conditions of the law under our rule. I am concerned only with the Mussalman districts of this Division. The people are long-suffering, but indications are not wanting of the spirit that has been aroused in the murders of exceptionally exacting creditors that occur from time to time. In Hazara, in 1879, when I was Deputy-Commissioner, the relations between the Mussalmans and moneylenders became very strained owing to the way in which the latter had run the former into court and pressed the execution of decrees. A wealthy bazar in a large village was burnt down, and the Hindus became very much alarmed and unsettled. The simple order of liberally interpreting and working the law relating to exemptions from attachment, acted like oil on water; and so also in this Division four or five years ago, suggestions to courts on similar lines brought comfort to many a home.'[1]

The final deliverance of the two Financial Commissioners—G. Gordon Young and G. R. Elmslie—is that not only does no considerable portion of the Panjab 'suffer from a daily insufficiency of food,' but 'the very reverse of this is the case, and specially with reference to the lower classes in agricultural tracts to which particular attention was directed.[2] It was added that only years of ordinary prosperity were alluded to. 'In seasons of deficient rainfall or abnormally high prices, from whatever cause, there is doubtless a large section of the people who come perilously near to starvation.'[3] 'If the statement is applicable to any section of the population at all, it is

[1] 'Econ. Inq., Panjab,' 1888, p. 44.

[2] *Ibid.*, p. 57. [3] *Ibid.*, p. 57.

rather to the poorest of the urban population than to the agricultural classes. In many cities there are classes of exceedingly poor artisans who feel the pinch of high prices acutely, and women of respectable position whose small earnings will not at the best of times do more than keep body and soul together.' [1]

The foregoing statement appears, on the whole, to be justified, as the population in 1901 is only three-quarters of a million less than, with good government, it should be. This is mainly due to 'large sums of money coming into the districts from the members of families who have taken service outside.' [2]

[1] 'Econ. Inq., Panjab,' 1888, p. 57.
[2] Col. Pitcher, Conference at Delhi, March 30, 1888.

THE ASSIGNED DISTRICTS OF BERAR.

The districts of Berar are, provisionally, administered by the Government of India. They were obtained many years ago as security for certain payments to be made by the Nizam of Hyderabad, Deccan. Some day, when the conditions are fulfilled, it may be supposed there will be a re-assignment. To 1888 the districts were amongst the most fertile and the population the most prosperous in all India. 'Famines are unknown in Berar,' said the Secretary for Berar to the Resident at Hyderabad, on April 25, 1888, 'and there is no reason to believe that any person need suffer from insufficiency of food.'

The report made by the Commissioner, Mr. Leslie S. Saunders, is so admirable an exposition of a small farmer's condition under exceptionally happy circumstances that I quote it in full:—

No. 1809, dated Amraoti, April 4, 1888.

FROM LESLIE S. SAUNDERS, ESQ., C.S., COMMISSIONER, HYDERABAD ASSIGNED DISTRICTS,

To the Secretary for Berar to the Resident at Hyderabad.

With reference to your telegram, dated the 2nd instant, calling for a reply to your confidential letter No. 2266, dated the 3rd September last, I have the honour to say that . . . although a few replies have come in and more have been promised in a few days, I do not expect to be able to submit a final communication to you on the subject before the 15th of the present month. The real facts of the case, so far as it refers to Berar, is that little or no real poverty exists in the province.

'Does the greater proportion of the population of India suffer from a daily insufficiency of food?'

This is the question on which an opinion is asked. The question, rightly understood, applies to years of average good crops only. In abnormal times of famines and droughts, the settled state of things is necessarily disturbed, and, with regard to such times, there can be only but one reply to the question, namely, that the greater proportion of the population of India must suffer from a daily insufficiency of food.

When we talk of suffering from an insufficiency of food, we must exclude from our consideration classes whose means of obtaining a livelihood are not confined to their capacity to labour only. So long as one has anything which has a saleable value in the market, or on the security of which he can get money advanced to him, starvation or insufficiency of food cannot affect him, if the year is of average crops, and the country has its usual supply of food for all. As a rule it is only when one has parted with his all, and has nothing which he can put in the market for sale, or with the Banias as a security, that he must look to his daily labour to supply him with his food; and insufficiency of food or even starvation may stare him in the face. If there are any exceptions to this rule, they are (apart from that class of misers who would even starve themselves only through a perverted nature) the cases of persons who are provident, and who, for a time only, live on scanty supplies, because they wish to get out of their temporary difficulties. The more we have of such cases the better, and the only regret is that they are so few in the agricultural population of India. This now brings me to the consideration of the normal condition of the labouring classes only. Their distinctive feature is that if labour fails them, either through their temporary incapacity to work, or from any other cause, they must first live upon less food, and finally starve.

Now, the most important and pertinent inquiries are—1st, what sort of food does an Indian labourer usually take, and what quantity of it makes it sufficient, and what is its value in money at the present prevailing prices; 2nd, what are the average earnings for the year of an Indian labourer; 3rd, what results does a comparison between the earnings and expenses point to.

To enable me to form an opinion upon these points from facts as they actually exist, I arranged two interviews—one with a few intelligent Patels, Patwaris, Deshmookhs, and Despandias in the Malkapore Taluk; and another, with the different classes of agricultural and other labourers, that I might verify the facts gathered at the first interview. Hence, I hope that the conclusions I have come to are fairly correct when applied to the limited area of the Malkapore Taluk, and not far wide of the truth when extended to the whole province of Berar generally.

The family of an Indian labourer generally consists of the husband and his wife. Generally both of them work for their livelihood. But between these two they have to support a third member who earns nothing.

This third member is either an aged, blind, helpless, parent, or a child under ten years of age, who must be fed, but who cannot contribute in the least towards his maintenance. The year's expenses of this family are for sufficient food:—

	£	s.	d.
Jowaree.—At one seer for the husband, the same for the wife, and half a seer for the child per day, 912½ seers (the year consists of 365 days). The value of this Jowaree at 20 seers a rupee is	3	0	10
Toor Dal.—For the whole family seers 91¼, at ¼ seer a day. The value of the dal at 1¼ annas a seer is ...	0	15	1
Chilli.—For the whole family 16 seers, at 3½ tolas per day. Value of this 'Mirchi' at 1½ annas a seer is	0	15	1
Salt.—For the whole family 37 seers,[1] at 8 tolas per day. Value	0	6	2
Oil for cooking purposes.—For the whole family 11½ seers, at 2½ tolas per day, at 6 annas a seer. Value	0	5	9
For petty expenses.—For the whole family, at 1½ pie a day for the year...	0	8	10
Kerosine oil for lamps.—At one anna for eight days, the value of the year's oil	0	8	10
Total	£5	10	7

Holidays.

	£	s.	d.
Dipwali	0	2	8
Akshtritia	0	1	4
Holi	0	1	4
Pitra	0	1	4
Expenses on account of guests	0	6	8
Clothing for the whole family for the year	0	16	0
Total expenses for the year	£6	19	11

Earnings.

Now the earnings of the family for the year:—

	£	s.	d.
The husband gets two annas a day and the wife one anna a day. Earnings for the year	4	11	7
Deduct for 45 days in which they have no work ...	0	11	3
Balance	£4	0	4
Excess.—Add for earnings in the harvest season for sixty days at two annas a day for the husband, and one anna a day for the wife	0	15	0
	£4	15	4

---

[1] Or 25 lbs. per head. In view of the fact that the average for all India, including cattle consumption, is a little less than one-half of this amount, the reader will not fail to note the significance of this statement in its bearing on the physical condition of the people.—W. D.

The comparison of the earnings and expenses would show that while the labouring family in question gets £4 15s. 4d. a year, its expenses on what it considers its adequate supply of food and clothing, etc., would amount to £6 19s. 11d. But I must here remark that the scale of expenditure given above is a scale which has never yet been practically reached by a merely labouring family, but is a scale which it aspires after, and beyond which its ambition does not go. In fact, labourers have freely admitted to me that they have never as yet commanded the expenditure given above, and that the scale applies actually to the class immediately above them, namely, of cultivators who follow cultivation on their own account, and not as mere agricultural labourers, but who, either from the small areas of their holdings, or from very limited means of cultivating them, or from their involved pecuniary affairs, draw only a portion of their subsistence from the land, and eke it out by offering their labour to others who have a need for it. Hence it would not be unfair to the labouring classes to deduct £2 0s. 9d. from their yearly expenditure, as given above, and say that there is an equilibrium between their earnings and their expenses.

I must note here one important fact which can never be lost sight of, that the labouring classes actually live from hand to mouth, that they have not even a day's reserve of food with them, and that if labour fails them even for a day, they must go to a kindly *koonbi* neighbour (the Marwadi would give them nothing, as they have no security; to which alone the Marwadi looks before making loans), and be indebted to him for the day's supply of Jowaree, hoping to return it only at the harvesting season.

In the scale of expenditure I have included nothing for marriages in the families of the labouring classes. But I find that these marriages are conducted with the greatest prudence and economy, and not allowed to trench upon the year's supply. A girl's marriage costs almost nothing to her parents. The bridegroom himself incurs the whole of the expenses, which again are kept quite within his means. If a boy is to be married, he is engaged by the year ('salkaroo') in the service of a farmer who undertakes to supply him with his food and clothing for the year, and makes him also an advance of abou Rs.20, the year's salary. This sum is spent on the marriage. The 'salkaroo,' in all, always earns more than one who is not a 'salkaroo.' The demand for 'salkaroo' is also in excess of the supply. But a 'salkaroo' must be always at the beck and call of his master, and has to do much harder work. The labouring classes choose to secure their comparative independence, and are content with what their minimum capacity of working brings them, and put forth their maximum capacity only temporarily, and only in such cases of necessity. This is certainly a hopeful state of things, as the labourers could be a little better off than they are now if they chose.

Incidentally, note may be taken of the fact that when a householder in Berar is in a position to purchase salt according to his requirements, he provides for 25 lbs. per head per annum, more than twice the average consumption.

The out-turn of wheat in this most fertile Province during the past nine years was lamentably low. The average for the whole region in 1896–97 was put at 754 lbs. Actually the produce was only one-fifth of that 'average'; as witness the following:—

Year.	Lbs. per acre.	Total in tons.	No. of Acres.[1]
1891–92	196	78,000	888,000
1892–93	172	76,000	985,000
1893–94	222	97,000	928,000
1894–95	206	81,882	889,826
1895–96	145	48,549	747,025
1896–97	70	11,841	881,425
1897–98	146	25,511	890,878
1898–99	112	21,892	486,862
1899–1900	81	251	17,910

Average of nine years ... ... 144¼ lbs.

What possible good can it possibly do to the Indian authorities to allow so misleading an average as that of 754 lbs. per acre to remain on record? They assert 12½ bushels should be reaped; they acknowledge but 2⅓ bushels were actually reaped. Yet the high average remains to delude the Viceroy and to mislead the public.

The very optimistic opinion of the Resident at Hyderabad is scarcely borne out by the Census returns. There ought, in 1901, if all had been as excellent as was described, a population of 3,332,114 inhabitants; there were on March 1, 1901, only 2,752,418

A deficiency of 579,696

—or one person out of eight[2] not there when the counting took place.

[1] Agric. Statistics, p. 371. [2] Stat. Abs., No. 35, p. 1.

'I have never concealed my opinion as to the extreme gravity of our financial position, and I believe that

"NOTHING BUT THE FACT THAT THE PRESENT SYSTEM [IN INDIA] IS ALMOST SECURE FROM ALL INDEPENDENT AND INTELLIGENT CRITICISM HAS ENABLED IT SO LONG TO SURVIVE."

SIR LOUIS MALLET,
Permanent Under-Secretary of State for India.

THE MADRAS PRESIDENCY.

Amongst the papers concerning the Inquiry of 1888, only the letter of the Madras Government to the Government of India and the observations of the Board of Revenue were given to me. I cannot, therefore, furnish details for the south like unto those already given for other parts of the Empire. The Madras authorities found it difficult to do all that was required of them: 'some Collectors have pointed out that the collection of such evidence is incompatible with the secrecy enjoined.'[1] As to the reports received, 'His Excellency in Council desires to express his general concurrence in the conclusion of the Board and the majority of the officers consulted that, in this Presidency, no considerable proportion of the population suffer from a daily insufficiency of food in ordinary years.' Some of the collectors were decidedly of a different opinion. Mr. Le Fanu, for example, was of opinion that 'grinding poverty is the widespread condition of the masses.' Mr. Conklin and another were of opinion that in certain sections of North Arcot many poor people go through life on insufficient food. The Madras authorities continue: 'It is, of course'—[why of course, considering there are ample statistics in every district in the Presidency?]—'very difficult to form any idea as to the real condition of the poorer classes, and still more difficult to ascertain the

[1] In respect to that 'secrecy' the Madras Government, in the covering letter to the Government of India, have this paragraph:—

'. . . the Press in Madras were aware of the institution of the inquiry forming the subject of this communication soon after the date of the first of the Circulars under reply, and they refer to a notice regarding it which appeared in the *Hindu* newspaper of the 23rd September last. This, however, was a letter from a Bengal correspondent, stating that the *Indian Mirror* had announced the institution of the inquiry. The article to which the Board make allusion, and which was published in the *Hindu* of the 23rd September, was, apparently, based upon information supplied by the Bengal Press. I am to state that every care has been taken by the authorities here to prevent the inquiry becoming in any way public.'

condition in past years so as to frame any reliable comparison; but the Government consider that it is undoubtedly true that wages have risen, that articles which formerly were luxuries are daily more and more becoming necessaries' [true, but where, and amongst what section of the population?], 'and that the old thatched hut has been and is being largely replaced by the tiled house, for ample evidence of these changes is furnished by everyday experience. At the same time the Government entertain no doubt that the native labourer generally speaking lives almost from hand to mouth, and has little reserve save a few cheap ornaments upon which he can fall back to meet bad seasons and want of work.'

It is a favourite maxim with Sir Henry Fowler, and is often repeated by him, that the portion of the produce taken by the Government amounts to eight per cent. only on the gross yield. This statement is confuted elsewhere by Government statistics—twenty-six years' old when used by me, and, therefore, available to Sir Henry Fowler, who was made Secretary of State for India on the 10th of March, 1894. It will, therefore, be well to record what cultivators of 1901 say concerning the proportion of their produce which is actually taken by the authorities.

In reply to an appeal, publicly made, for information on this point, I have received a number of communications and much information. Dewan Bahadur R. Raghunath Row, who passed from the Madras subordinate service to become Prime Minister of Indore, writes:—

'Expenses of cultivation of ordinary lands means the value of the seed and the wages paid to coolies employed by the cultivator of lands. This is generally thirty per cent. of the gross. It does not include anything for the feeding of the cultivator, much less for the proper nourishment of his family; it does not include the cost of any manure used. For other lands, viz., superior and inferior lands, expenses of cultivation are generally greater; more seed is wanted for inferior soils; more weeding for superior soils, particularly the black cotton soil.

'The word "etc." in the circular order of the 1878 Edition is a convenient loophole. It may be said that it includes the remission for bad years.

'Now the Government are said to get one half of the net produce which is never less than twenty-five per cent. of the gross. This is only in theory. Actually they receive on an average more than fifty per cent. of the gross. On paper it is shown to be between twenty-five and thirty per cent. of the gross, by over-estimating the gross produce.

'If the gross be 100, the Government professes to deduct—

'29 for cultivation expenses,
'15 for bad seasons,
'28 for Government assessment,
'28 for the ryot.

'If these would tally with the actuals the ryot would have sufficient left to him to tide over one or two bad years; but the actuals are different.

'Suppose the gross produce in reality amounts to 75 instead of 100, the result would be—

'22 cultivation expenses }
'11 for bad seasons } or 44 per cent.
'28 Government assessment, or 38 per cent.
'14 for the ryot, or 18 per cent.

or two-thirds of the net to Government and one-third of the net to the ryot.

'As the real amount of the gross produce decreases, so the share of Government would go on increasing and that of the ryot decreasing.

'A village measuring 305 acres of wet land has been assessed on the estimated gross produce of 8,557 to 9,000 colams; while it never produced more than 6,200 on an average. The yield since the years of the re-settlement,

Fasli 1303, has been colams 5,300; Fasli 1304, colams 5,275; Fasli 1305, colams 5,024; Fasli 1306, colams 5,329; Fasli 1307, colams 5,760; Fasli 1308, colams 5,108; Fasli 1309, colams 1,813. According to the theory of the letter and spirit of the Government Order, the assessment of this village should have been up to colams 1,612, or Rs.1,674. The fixed assessment is colams 2,362, which raises the percentage to thirty-seven per cent. If there is any doubt in this case, I am prepared to hand over the village to Government if I be allowed to draw from the Government Treasury annually the sum of fixed assessment perpetually.'

Other testimony of a like detailed and emphatic character will be found in Appendix II. to this chapter. The reader is begged on no account to avoid reading what is there printed.

It was in connection with the Presidency of Madras that the Government of India enunciated the dictum as to the normal increase of population under the governance of Britain. The district of Anantapur had suffered grievously from famine—(at its worst it had not suffered quite half so badly as one of the Bombay districts in 1900, in spite of all the railways in that Presidency)—and the authorities put its record forward as that which justified any expenditure and the taking of any steps so long as wasting populations were turned into increasing communities. What was the standard of growth which railways and British administration were to produce? It was this:—

> 'Population as it would have been in 1881 with normal increase at 1½ per cent. per annum.'

That is the 'normal increase' good administration in India has a right to expect, says the Government of India. Since that ideal was set up, Southern India has had some ugly scarcities, but there was not, during the period between the two censuses of 1891 and 1901, a real famine (that is, an officially-recognised famine).

How, during these (comparatively) fat years, has the Madras Presidency fared in view of the ideal set up in 1884?

Three districts show a slight increase over the 'normal';

Nineteen show, in some cases, hundreds of thousands fewer inhabitants than there ought to have been.

Yet India generally (not leaving Southern India behind the other parts of the Empire) has been covered with railways. And railways (with good administration, of course) were to ensure the 'normal.'

If the 'normal' had been reached—

Anantapur	would	have	had	25,934	additional	people.
Bellary	,,	,,	,,	88,383	,,	,,
Coimbatore	,,	,,	,,	103,251	,,	,,
Cuddapah	,,	,,	,,	150,979	,,	,,
Ganjam	,,	,,	,,	169,835	,,	,,
Godavari	,,	,,	,,	87,316	,,	,,
Kurnool	,,	,,	,,	35,760	,,	,,
Madura	,,	,,	,,	167,560	,,	,,
Madras City	,,	,,	,,	10,997	,,	,,
Malabar	,,	,,	,,	262,406	,,	,,
Nellore	,,	,,	,,	185,499	,,	,,
North Arcot	,,	,,	,,	299,168	,,	,,
South Arcot	,,	,,	,,	136,913	,,	,,
South Kanara	,,	,,	,,	79,869	,,	,,
Salem	,,	,,	,,	51,081	,,	,,
Tinnevelly	,,	,,	,,	142,715	,,	,,
Trichinopoly	,,	,,	,,	133,497	,,	,,
Tanjore	,,	,,	,,	312,969	,,	,,
Vizagapatam	,,	,,	,,	289,823	,,	,,
	Total missing			2,733,955		

In some districts the 'normal' has been exceeded:—

Chingleput	had	5,256	more	than	the	'normal.'
Kistna	,,	11,482	,,	,,	,,	,,
Nilgiri	,,	6,684	,,	,,	,,	,,
Total		23,422				

Plus: 23,422 Minus: 2,733,955

Minus over plus: 2,710,533

'In some districts, notably Fyzabad, Gonda, Kheri, and parts of Sultanpur, at a time of supposed financial pressure, the revision of the assessment was hurried on, and a greatly enhanced demand was imposed before the Settlement Officer had had time to adjust the rights and liabilities of the various sharers and under-proprietors affected by the operation. It is not difficult to understand that such a course as this necessarily entails great hardship on the persons directly responsible for the Government revenue, and results in their frequent default.'—OUDH REVENUE REPORT, 1872–3.

THE CENTRAL PROVINCES.

In the estimate in 1882 of the value of Agricultural Produce, Lord Cromer and Sir David Barbour put these Provinces at the head of the list.[1] No part of the Empire was so prosperous as these provinces. The agricultural produce per head was £1 10s. 9d. against 18s. 10d. for Bengal, and 18s. 2d. for the North-Western Provinces and Oudh. This was an utterly fallacious estimate, and ought, on the instant, to have been recognised as such. Because of it, however, on the re-assessment early in the Nineties, most excessive rents were imposed. One consequence has been seen in the dreadful experiences through which these Provinces have passed since the new assessments came into operation. To take a few districts only, the percentage of enhancement on the previous demand in various assessment groups in the various districts may be given thus :—

District.	Per Cent.	District.	Per Cent.
Bilaspur ...	102, 105	Saugor ...	68, 42, 58, 48
Seoni	95, 97, 55, 92, 50	Jubbulpur ...	95, 97, 55, 92, 50
Hoshangabad ...	69, 87, 96	Nagpore ...	20, 21, 28, 24[2]

In 1882 the value of the agricultural produce in the Provinces was put at £14,166,667. In 1898–99, on a reasonable estimate, it was found to be £7,282,574. Before proceeding to record the evidence on which so much comparative prosperity was announced, an example may be given of the manner in which the Government of India places contradictory and untrustworthy information before those who wish to follow its labours, as recorded in its own publications, with intelligent interest. In

[1] On the day on which I am preparing this chapter for the Press, the Anglo-Indian contributor of *The Outlook*, an ex-official of eminence, in spite of all the teaching of the past two famines and the fact of exorbitant increases of rent having been exacted, complacently refers to the 'low' assessment of these Provinces. The remark is made, regardless of the relative produce of the soil, and against much evidence to prove the actual highness of the land revenue.

[2] Speech by the Hon. B. K. Bose, in the Viceregal Council, March 28, 1900.

the volume of Agricultural Statistics for British India, 1900, is a section (pp. 380–413) containing a statement of the average yield for each district in the various Presidencies and Provinces. I turn to p. 410, where I find tables giving the average yield (lbs. per acre) of principal crops in each district of the Central Provinces. I take wheat, that cereal in certain districts being greatly favoured by the cultivator in this region. I abstract these particulars :—

District.	Period ending 1892	1896–97
	Lbs.	Lbs.
Saugor	640	600
Damoh	640	500
Jubbulpore	700	640
Mandla	700	600
Seoni	700	620
Narsinghpur	740	660
Hoshangabad	740	620
Nimar ... ... Irrigated...	950	900
,, ... Unirrigated...	740	640
Betal ... ... Irrigated...	—	1,000
,, ... Unirrigated...	740	620
Chhindwan ... ... Irrigated...	—	1,000
,, ... Unirrigated...	640	600
Wardhar	700	580
,, ... Irrigated...	—	1,000
Nagpur ... Unirrigated...	700	580
Chand	640	580
Bhandara	500	500
Balaghat	640	580
Raipur	700	600
Bilaspur	700	600
Sambalpur	700	600
Average for the Province :—		
Irrigated	—	925
Unirrigated	—	570
Both	—	600

That seems clear enough. It does not seem possible, with such details, to go wrong. Take the acreage, and multiply it by the number of lbs., and you have the yield. It would not be safe to do this in the present instance, for, on page 371 of the same publication, the yield in tons for the whole province for three years is given, as well as the acreage. A few columns of figures supply much food for thought:—

Year.	Yield in lbs. per acre.	Acreage.	Tons.
1891–92	437	3,904,000	760,000
1892–93	405	4,197,000	762,000
1893–94	322	3,986,000	575,000
1894–95	329	3,393,348	502,275
1895–96	307	2,714,454	368,038
1896–97	390	1,969,623	332,645
1897–98	576	2,171,714	543,095
1898–99	408	2,505,299	456,169
1899–1900	173	1,619,989	194,070

The average for the whole period was 372 lbs. per acre (6⅕ bushels) per annum. Had the tables of averages, professedly taken from selected fields, been realised, the yield would have been over-estimated on the whole period by thirty-four per cent., in some years by fifty per cent., and in one year by over seventy per cent. Such contradictory statements make an undoubted acceptance of the conclusions put forward by the Viceroy, when speaking in Council even, altogether impossible. Continual and close examination is always essential in respect to Indian statistical statements.

The story of the condition of these Provinces, as revealed in the secret economic inquiry of 1881–82, may now be considered. The region is almost wholly agricultural. Such income as is not derivable from the cultivation of the soil must be of little account. In an area as large as Italy there are only five towns with a population exceeding 30,000 each, while aggregations of people ten thousand and more in number are only sixteen.

'Agriculture affords the immediate means of support of almost the entire population, and it is on the agricultural condition of the Provinces that the well-being of the inhabitants as a whole depends.' In 1882 it was considered that the provinces were exceptionally favoured by the comparative certainty of the rainfall. 'The soil is so exceptional that it will give good return to an amount of labour which applied to most other soils would be entirely infructuous. Wheat lands seldom receive more than two ploughings before they are sown. The lightness of the Government revenue is notorious. . . . The development of railway communication has taken place subsequently to the fixation of the present revenue demand, and the State has as yet had no share in the enormous increase of agricultural profits which has accrued from the connection of the Narbada valley and the Nagpore country with the port of Bombay.'

'It is a natural inference,' the Chief Commissioner, in addressing the Government of India, says, 'that in the Central Provinces the profits from agriculture are larger, and the cultivating classes in more comfortable circumstances than is the case in many other parts of India, and that this is the fact is the opinion of all officers who have had an opportunity of contrasting the rural conditions of these Provinces with those obtaining in the more thickly-populated districts of Upper India.'

A few spots on the bright sun of these alleged comparatively wealthy Provinces are admitted by the official apologists, *e.g.*, the law courts are ruinous to the suitors, the moneylenders are extortionate rogues, and the hill tribes are too little clothed, and have too little to eat. The conclusion is this:—

'There is no doubt in these Provinces a great deal of poverty, but there is very little distress. The people are well fed, and the only section of them who can be said to be hard pressed for bare subsistence are the hill tribes, who are but little more provident than the beasts of the forests, and have to undergo similar vicissitudes in daily food. The volume of wealth is rapidly increasing, and there is no lack of employment for those who wish for it. If only more of the money which the Provinces are receiving reached the producers, and less was intercepted by moneylenders and middlemen, the condition of the people might be described as prosperous. But over them hangs the grip of the usurer, and the shadow of the civil courts.'

The indebtedness, apparently, was very great. 'Out of twenty-three whose circumstances were investigated in detail, eighteen owed money' (p. 49). 'Out of fourteen tenants, eleven were in debt—£346 in all.' 'Eleven tenants reported on were all in debt—£362' (p. 55). 'Out of 1,847 tenants, 1,588 were in debt, and the Tahsildar of Burhunpur estimates that at least nine out of ten of the tenantry of the Tahsil are in involved circumstances' (p. 60).

Then, the people can exist—if existence it can be called—on almost nothing. 'The most instructive fact brought out by inquiries into the condition of five families of the labourer class was the extraordinary cheapness of a bare subsistence. A Baiga basket-maker, whose family consisted of his wife and two small children, made, on an average, twelve baskets a week, which he sold for 2 lbs. of unhusked rice or small millet, each. His monthly earnings were thus about 100 lbs. of unhusked rice, worth rather less than a rupee. The family not only managed to live on this, supplemented with jungle fruits and roots, but saved annually about a rupee's worth of grain, wherewith they purchased the scanty clothing which sufficed for them.' This should be, as it probably is, the world's record in cheap living! The average works out thus:—

Total earnings in food per annum	...	16s.
Less, saving for clothing	... ...	1s.
Leaving for food	... ...	15s.

This was to be divided amongst four persons, and

leaves 3s. 9d. each for fifty-two weeks, or less than *half of* ONE FARTHING each person per day! That is, when unhusked rice can be obtained at 100 lbs. for 1s. 4d. But, in 1882, the year in question, common rice was selling at Jubbulpur 32 lbs., at Nagpore 33 lbs., and at Raipur at 64 lbs. per rupee. Let it be remembered this is an official statement concerning an inhabitant in what was then supposed to be the richest Province in the Empire.

Of the Raipur district it is said there could be no clearer indication of the easy conditions of life in the Chhatisgarh division than was furnished in 1886, when the rice crop was barely a quarter out-turn. The people did without relief from Government. Yet, in 1900, on the second famine within a few years occurring, that very district gained an eminence reached by no other district in India—forty per cent. of its population were, at one time, on Government relief.

These Provinces, according to the accounts freely given, and as freely (and as falsely) repeated to-day, were highly prosperous. Yet, when the shock of famine assailed them, the 'highly prosperous' people died by the hundred thousand.

FAMINE MORTALITY RESULTS OF 1897 AND 1900.

District.	Percentage of Decrease on Expected Population.	No. of Inhabitants fewer than should have been.
Jubbulpur	24	179,982
Seoni	27	99,241
Narsingpur	29	108,250
Mandla	27	92,824
Damoh	24	79,816
Saugor	35	209,111
Bagahat	30	114,126
Bilaspur	27	317,268
Hoshangabad	30	160,739
Chinkhadan State	42	15,344
Makrai ,,	45	8,309
	Total	1,370,510

Thus, in what was alleged in 1882 to be the most prosperous part of the Empire, scarcity and famine demand so terrible a total of human victims.

ASSAM.

Of this fertile region in Eastern India, Mr. Darrah concludes an examination of the condition of the Chief Commissionership, by saying:—

(*a*) The revenue is collected with ease everywhere but in Sylhet, and scarcely any arrears remain over after the close of the official year. In Sylhet, where the assessment is lightest of all, the difficulty is due to the litigious character of the people, not to their poverty. The Sylhetia has the strongest objection to paying his revenue, and exhausts all the resources of subtilty to avoid doing so. The people of Assam Proper are much simpler, and, having the money at hand, pay it with readiness.

(*b*) Every district possesses extensive areas of culturable waste, consisting largely of grass land, which could be reclaimed with comparative ease. In other words, the land available is far in excess of the population. Therefore, it is impossible that there should be the slightest difficulty as to the means of subsistence.

(*c*) Beggars are almost unknown in the Province. I have only seen one during a residence of four years and tours in every district but the Gáro and Nága Hills.

(*d*) Coolie transport is not to be obtained by Government anywhere but in the Khási Hills without impressment. It is impossible to associate the idea of poverty with a people who cannot be induced to work voluntarily for Government at even more than the ordinary rates paid by private persons.

(*e*) Regular employers of labour are compelled to import at very serious cost the labour they require. This is the difficulty which has from the beginning so prejudicially affected the tea industry of Assam. There can be no want of the means of subsistence amongst a people who by refusal to work oblige the planter to import his labour at an initial cost sometimes exceeding Rs.100 a head.[1]

The Chief Commissioner affirmed this in these emphatic terms: 'The conclusion, I am to say,' remarked Mr. Daukes, Officiating Secretary, in the letter to the Government of India, 'at which Mr. Fitzpatrick arrives, on a careful consideration of the materials before him, is that, so far as the Province under his administration is concerned, the question raised in your letter need cause the Government no anxiety whatever.'

[1] 'Note on the Condition of the People of Assam,' p. 25, 'Econ. Inq. 1888.

'Up to this date this declaration of policy [concerning agricultural improvement] remains a dead letter as regards facilitating the supply of capital on reasonable terms, and the protection, repair, and extension, of wells, tanks, and embankments, or other works of land improvement other than canals. It will continue to be a dead letter as long as these questions remain as at present at the unfruitful stage of fitful discussions inside the Government offices between a Secretary here and a Member of Council there, and as long as the necessary step is deferred of appointing strong Commissions to review the data and experience already gained, to make such further inquiry as may be necessary, and to map out a line of action.'—A. H. HARRINGTON, Officiating Commissioner, Fyzabad Division, Oudh, 1888.

AJMERE-MERWARA.

This is one of the regions under the direct control of the Government of India. In view of the censures freely meted out by 'India' to subordinate governments and especially to Feudatory States, here at least ought to be perfectness of administration. Yet, Ajmere-Merwara is selected in the report of the Famine Commission of 1901 as one of the regions in respect to which stern condemnation had to be expressed. The particulars concerning it in 1882 are of special interest. Munshi Balmakand Das, Tahsildar, Ajmere, furnished the following *exposé* and analysis of the condition of four villages:—

	Villages			
	Kerop Masuda.	Juwana Masuda.	Leeri Khurwa.	Pakaran Pisangan.
(*a*) The average number of persons in a family ...	5	5	7	5
(*b*) Total population of village and its area :—				
(1) Number of houses ...	180	135	255	125
(2) Number of people ...	880	750	1,795	625
	Big.	Big.	Big.	Big.
(4) Area cultivated ...	1,935	1,900	2,900	3,200
(5) Area uncultivated ...	565	400	2,400	9,958
Total area ...	2,500	2,300	5,300	13,158
(*c*) Approximate produce during the past 20 years	Rs. 4,20,000	Rs. 2,27,280	Rs. 6,00,000	Rs. 1,80,000
(*d*) Approximate amount of debts incurred during that period	10,000	50,000	15,000	12,500
(*e*) (1) Incidence of produce for each family (one year)	130	98	191	71

	Villages.			
	Kerop Masuda.	Juwana Masuda.	Leeri Khurwa.	Pakaran Pisangan.
(2) Quantity of produce reserved for payment of Government Revenue and debts and village menials	Rs. 41	Rs. a. p. 24 4 0	Rs. 50	Rs. 23
(3) Net available for consumption and reserve stock	89	74 12 0	141	48

(4) Quantity required by the family for consumption on account of food, clothing, and other necessaries of life, surplus or deficit; and if the latter, how it is met... ... — Generally speaking, the whole stock is consumed in feeding, clothing, etc., and no saving or surplus is kept. On the other hand, in most cases, there is a deficit, which is met by fresh loans.[1]

(5) Proceeds of occupation, besides agriculture, by members other than the head of the family:—

	Villages.			
	Kerop Masuda.	Juwana Masuda.	Leeri Khurwa.	Pakaran Pisangan.
	Rs. a. p.	Rs. a. p.	Rs. a. p.	Rs. a. p.
(a) Ordinary labour ...	69 8 0	68 0 0	70 0 0	10 0 0
(b) Sale of dry wood, thor, bush, etc. ...	*Nil.*	*Nil.*	*Nil.*	*Nil.*
(c) Sale of grass, etc. ...	"	"	"	"
(d) Sale of milk, curd, ghi, etc.	2 8 0	2 12 0	25 0 0	25 0 0
(e) Sale of cow-dung cakes, etc.	...	...	...	...
(f) Final results:—				
(1) Total earnings of a family in a year ...	161 0 0	145 8 0	236 0 0	88 0 0
(2) Total liabilities—				
(a) Old debts	38 0 0	278 0 0	40 0 0	80 0 0
(b) New debts	18 0 0	70 0 0	10 0 0	20 0 0

[1] Note by Munshi Balmakand Das, Tahsildar, Ajmere. P. 227, Inquiry of 1888.

(8) Probable forecast—
Additional profits by increased cultivation, repayments of debts, etc. ... ... } Please see below.

(g) Articles other than grain used as food { *Jawe* is not frequently used by agriculturists generally, but they use vegetables, specially onions, to the extent of about two chittaks each in addition to food.

In the case of village menials:—

	Villages.			
	Kerop Masuda.	Juwana Masuda.	Leeri Khurwa.	Pakaran Pisangan.
(1) Number of inmates in a family	4	4	5	8
(2) Receipts on account of village perquisites (average per family)	Rs. 30	Rs. 20	Rs. 40	Rs. 35
(3) Approximate income during the past 20 years ...	12,000	15,000	35,000	17,500
(4) Incidence of income on each family (one year) ...	60	50	70	25
(5) Income reserved for repayments of debts, etc. ...	10	10	20	5
(6) Net available for consumption, reserve stock, etc....	50	40	50	20

The quantity of food required is as follows:—

For an adult male ... ... 2 lbs.
Ditto female ... ... 1½ ,,
Children ... ... ½ lb.

There can be no doubt that the condition of the agriculturists generally is far from satisfactory. The average number of persons in a family is between five and seven, and the area under cultivation in the possession of each family is between nine bighas and 26 bighas. The average income of a family, calculated from an approximate income for the last 20 years, comes to Rs.88 and Rs.236 annually, or in other words, Rs.7 8a. to Rs. 24 per month. The incidence per head falls at Rs.1 8a. to Rs.3 8a. per month, which is quite insufficient considering the quantity of food required at the rate given above. For a few days after the harvest is reaped they (the agriculturists) have a sufficiency of food, provided the produce is not wholly taken away by their creditors. When they have no grain left, they either incur fresh debts or live upon *malucha* and *sanwan* (self-grown grains), which are not considered as conducive to health; on the other hand, they are said to render people weak. The case of the generality of the agriculturists is deplorable. In the first place, the share of the produce they get is hardly sufficient to keep them up for the whole year; secondly, most of them are heavily burdened with debts, and no sooner the crop is ripe, the creditors take the earliest opportunity of taking away a greater portion of what has been earned with hard labour. The agriculturists, as a rule, cannot do without a creditor. Although he may be a cause of their ruin, as soon as they get a share of their produce they would make themselves merry at all hazards, thus spending all their earnings in a short time. Then they require food and seed. They have, therefore, no other recourse but to go to their creditor, or *bohra*, as they call him. When once a debt is incurred, it is very difficult for an agriculturist to extricate himself from the clutches of his creditor. Interest upon interest is added to the capital, and eventually the poor man has to part even with his landed property. Such being the case, the agriculturists have not the means of making any considerable improvement on their land. In the Khalsa villages, they have the satisfaction of making some improvements when they like, inasmuch as they can obtain *tacavi* advances for the purpose; but the case is quite different in *istamrari* estates. Firstly, they have nothing to tempt them to make any improvements, because they cannot call any land their own. They have no proprietary right in the land, and are entirely at the mercy of the *istamrardar*, who can turn them out whenever he likes. Secondly, they have no such facility in the matter of *tacavi* advances as the cultivators in the Khalsa villages have.

As I have above stated, these agriculturists seldom use *jawe*, but they frequently use *malucha* and *sanwan*, which is rather injurious to their health. It is self-evident that, when they have not a sufficiency of food, they are generally compelled to reduce their food. Their expenses in marriages are but limited, but in *mosar* (funeral feasts) generally their expenses far exceed their means, and this is the chief reason why they incur heavy debts.[1]

Another reporter says:—

[1] Note by Balmakand Das, Tahsildar, 7th June, 1888, p. 227, 'Econ. Inq.,' 1888.

In obedience to the orders of the Government of India and the Assistant-Commissioner, I inquired into the question of the insufficiency of food grains from which the agricultural classes suffer.

I selected fifteen villages:—

5 villages, first sort.
5 villages, average sort.
5 villages, inferior sort.

From private inquiries made of these villages in regard to their food, I have been able to prepare a statement herewith submitted. From this I conclude that a villager continues to take his ordinary quantity of meal so long as he is not embarrassed, or so long as he is able to secure loans from *bohras*, and so long as he has a stock of grain. When they cannot get loans and their stocks are exhausted, they necessarily diminish their scale of diet, thus:—

Adult male	...	...	12	chittaks.
Adult female	...	...	10	,,
Minor ...	...	...	8	,,

It is this diminution of the dietary scale that eventually enfeebles the body, weakens the constitution, and breaks the health of the agriculturist.

The inquiry embraces the statistics for the whole of the population of the villages. Their receipts for the twenty years have been shown in columns 8, 28, and 29. Columns 9 and 30 show the state of loan and embarrassment of *kashtkars* and *kamins*. Columns 21 and 22 give the details of the old and new loans. Columns 10 and 31 give the details of yearly income. Columns 11, 12, 32, and 33 give the annual charges.

At this rate there is no surplus in any of these villages. Zemindars and *kamins* (village menials) are for the most part embarrassed, and their income being low, they are unable to liquidate their loans.

The incidence of receipts from agricultural and other sources, per head, comes to Rs.1 8a., Rs.1 12a., Rs.2; and only in selected villages to Rs. 28a. per month. It may therefore be safely said that the state of the agricultural classes is far from satisfactory, and specially of the villages of Ghoojra, Dhagal, Bargaon, Barla, and Palran, which are the least benefited by agriculture.

Their livelihood is mostly derived from the sale of grass, fodder, ghi, fuel, and from working on wages. It is therefore clear that the future lot of these villages will be deplorable, since they do not engage themselves in agriculture.

It is impossible under these circumstances to think that these men will liquidate any debts, or that they would get sufficient food to sustain themselves.

Although it is impossible for other villages as well to support their inhabitants on a small earning of Rs.2 or Rs.2 4a. per mensem, and at the same time to pay debts and incur marriage expenses out of that small sum, the villagers are seen to subsist on onions, plum-berries, cucumbers, and melons, the produce of the harvest for the time being; and there are others who live on game.

I am satisfied that the people do suffer from the insufficiency of food grains. On occasions of marriages and deaths, loans are taken from *bohras*, which, under the above circumstances, become a burden to them, inasmuch as they have to diminish their dietary scales, because a good deal of the produce has to be assigned to the *bohras* in payment of debts.'

Translation of Munshi Imamuddin's Report, p. 233, 'Econ. Inq.,' 1888.

THE HUNGER OF ONE HUNDRED MILLIONS NEVER FULLY SATISFIED.

'I do not hesitate to say that half our agricultural population never know from year's end to year's end what it is to have their hunger fully satisfied.

'The ordinary phrase in these parts, when a man asks for employment, is that he wants half a seer of flour; and a phrase so general must have some foundation. I believe that it has this much truth in it, that 1 lb. of flour is sufficient, though meagre, sustenance for a non-labouring man. That a labouring adult can eat 2 lbs. I do not doubt; but he rarely, if ever, gets it. But take the ordinary population in a family of five, consisting of a father, mother, and three children. The father will, I would say, eat a little less than 2 lbs., the mother a little more than 1 lb., the children about 3 lbs. between them. Altogether 7 lbs. to five people is the average which, after much inquiry, I am inclined to adhere to. I am confident that with our minutely divided properties, our immense and cramped population, and our grinding poverty, any attempt at heavier taxation would result in financial failure to the Government, in widespread distress and ruin to the people.'—Sir C. A. ELLIOTT, K.C.S.I., *when Settlement Officer, North-Western Provinces, subsequently Lieut.-Governor of Bengal, now Chairman, Finance Committee, London School Board.*

'Half our Agricultural Population' means

ONE HUNDRED MILLIONS OF PEOPLE!

What, it may be asked, since he has been living in England, after retirement from the service, has Sir Charles Elliott done to assuage this never-satisfied hunger? What is he doing now? What will he answer to the questions in verses 31–45, Matt. xxv.?

'Drought and scarcity were common enough before our time, and sometimes passed into actual famine; but the people were never so powerless before to prevent the development of scarcity into starvation. Every village in the country had its own reserve of grain stored up therein against famine. To this hour, nothing will induce the ryots in Lower Bengal or Orissa to part with their private food reserves of rice but necessity. . . . In Orissa the ryot never deems himself quite safe, we are told, with less than a full two years' store of rice in his homestead. Now the uniform result of introducing our rule into a Province seems to have been the gradual exhaustion of these stores, and at last their total disappearance.'—*India, Before our Time and Since*, by ROBERT KNIGHT (1881).

THE LOWER PROVINCES OF BENGAL.

For Bengal, as for the Madras Presidency, the particulars of the 1881–82 inquiry are a-wanting by the present writer. The following details, however, are available for Behar:—

The Settlement Officer, Mr. Collin, writing with special reference to two villages examined by him in the district, observes: 'From the foregoing description of the condition of the agricultural classes in this pergunah (Daphor), it appears that they need not at present cause any apprehension, and that in ordinary years they have sufficient means of subsistence. The picture which I have drawn does not, however, show any great prosperity and shows that the lower classes, which, including the weaving class, amounting to twenty-five per cent. of the population, have little chance of improving their position, and that they would have no resources to fall back upon in time of scarcity.'

The Collector of Monghyr remarks that he has come across many inhabitants who were thin and apparently in want of due nourishment. The Collector of Patna writes of ryots holding less than four local bighas, or two and a half acres: 'Their fare is of the very coarsest, consisting to a great extent of *khesari dâl*, and the quantity is insufficient during a considerable part of the year. They can only take one full meal instead of two. They are badly housed, and in the cold weather insufficiently clothed.' As to labourers, he adds that their condition is rather worse: 'They are almost always paid in kind, the usual allowance of a grown man being two to two and a half seers of the coarsest and cheapest grain, value about one penny farthing. Women receive about half this rate, but their employment is less regular. Ordinarily, male labourers do not find employment for more than eight months of the year. The conclusion to be drawn is that, of the agricultural population, a large proportion, say 40 per cent., are insufficiently fed, to say nothing of clothing and housing. They have enough food to support life and to enable them to work, but they have to undergo long fasts, having for a considerable part of the year to satisfy themselves with one full meal in the day.' With regard to Gaya, the Commissioner accepts a statement made by the Collector that forty per cent. of the population are insufficiently fed. Dr. Lethbridge, the Inspector-General of Gaols, writes: 'In Behar, the districts of Mozufferpore and Sarun, and parts of Durbhunga and Chumparun, are the worst, and there is almost constant insufficiency of food among those who earn their living by daily labour.'[1]

[1] Facts regarding the seven named districts of Behar, p. 252, 'Econ. Inq.,' 888.

The Bengal Government are considered to 'furnish a fair picture of the situation' in the following quotation :—

The general result of the inquiry is that, in the great part of the Lower Provinces, the industrial classes find no difficulty in supplying their primary wants, and are, as a rule, well nourished. Their prosperity is greatest in the eastern districts, and gradually diminishes as we carry our survey towards the west. It is not impaired by endemic disease, even where this has reduced the population, and left the survivors to some extent emaciated or enfeebled. On the contrary, the reports from the districts so afflicted show that the inhabitants are somewhat better off than in the neighbouring tracts. But the signs indicating prosperity cease when we reach Behar, where, though the cultivators having holdings of a size sufficient to afford full occupation to their families are well-to-do, and the middle class enjoys exceptional comfort, wages are very low, so that those who depend for their living entirely or mainly on their daily labour, earn a very scanty subsistence. The number of these labourers, including those who hold some land, is estimated at about forty per cent. of a population of over fifteen millions. The cause of the lowness of wages appears to be the multiplication of the labourers in a healthy climate and under a social system founded on early marriages, up to the point at which employment can be found on the lowest terms consistent with the continued maintenance of families. The cause is of a permanent nature, existing social and climatic conditions remaining unchanged. Its effects would not be counteracted by any conceivable development of local industry, as such development could hardly progress in geometric ratio with the increase of population. Emigration can afford a sufficient and lasting remedy, only if it be conducted on a large scale and continuously. If, after a system of emigration had been established, its operations were to be checked by the occupation of lands now waste, the existing difficulty would arise again. It is possible that popular education, which has hardly as yet touched this part of the population, might, in the course of many years, affect a permanent change for the better by altering the views and habits of the people. In the meanwhile it would greatly facilitate the application of partial and temporary remedies, such as the introduction of new industries and emigration.

The Behar Ryot.

'It is, however, a fact that the average size of the farms of the poorer classes does not exceed five bighas, and that seven persons, according to the Census, constitute a household. The average value of the crops produced in one year, taking good land with bad, on a single bigha is Rs.25, of which Rs.3 is payable in rent. Therefore, amongst the poorer classes, that is some 600,000 persons, seven persons have to subsist on Rs.102 a year, or only one rupee and four annas each month (16s. each per annum). Yet even this condition represents a state of things much more favourable than half of the poorer classes, or 300,000 persons, can obtain. Tens of thousands of them have not more than two bighas of land, and the number of those who have only two or three is equally great. There are besides the landless day-labourers, who number from ten to fifteen per cent. of the inhabitants of every village. How they contrive to subsist in years of scarcity, and particularly during such lengthened periods of dearth as the first five months of the official year under report, is a more difficult question than most people are prepared to answer.'—Mr. Toynbee, Collector of Patna, quoted by Sir H. S. Cunningham, K.C.I.E., p. 189, 'Condition of the Country and People of India,' Parl. Pap., 1881.

Comment is necessary. That comment must needs have a personal element in it, for thus only can Indian affairs become vital. It is disagreeable work, but it is necessary work. Sir Henry Cunningham, twenty years ago, quoted the above grievous description of the inhabitants of Behar. The knowledge of such a state of things imposed on the learned judge and versatile novelist a special duty. He became one who 'knew.' Did he, from '10—10—79,' the date of his memorandum, do anything for the Behari? Sir Henry, who is still living, retired from India in 1888. He has lived in England since on pension. That pension is at least £1,000 per annum, and, therefore, represents the annual income of more than twelve hundred of the poorer inhabitants of Behar. Since his retirement Sir Henry has 'eaten up' one year's living expenses of nearly thirty thousand Beharis. He has known their condition. What, in his retirement, has he done for them?

Unhappily, there are many Englishmen who have like knowledge; hardly one of them seems to think that knowledge imposes responsibility.

'India is the most wretched of countries. The way Europeans live there is absurd in its luxury; they seem so utterly effeminate and not to have an idea beyond the rupee. I nearly burst with the trammels that are put on one. I declare I think we are not far off losing it. I should say it was the worst school for young people. Every one is always grumbling, which amuses me. The united salaries of four judges were £22,000 a year. A. B. had been five years in India, and had received in that time £87,000! It cannot last. How truly glad I am to have broken with the whole lot; £100,000 a year would not have kept me there.'—*Letters of General A. G. Gordon to his sister, M. A. Gordon*, p. 208. (London: Macmillan and Co., 1888.)

I.

STATEMENT SHOWING THE RESULTS OF THE RYOTWAR SYSTEM IN COIMBATORE, FROM 1814–15 TO 1828–29, BOTH INCLUSIVE, COMPILED FROM THE DETAILED ACCOUNTS KEPT BY THE KURNUMS OR NATIVE ACCOUNTANTS OF VILLAGES.[1]

Years.	Number of Villages and Hamlets.	Population.	Black Cattle and Buffaloes.	Sheep and Goats.	Number of Persons paying Taxes.	Number of Ploughs.	Number of Wells.	Quantity of Land paying Assessments.	Amount of Assessments.	Average size of the Estate.[5]	Average payment of Proprietors.	Amount of Taxes on Arts and Professions.	Revenue from Customs.	Revenue from Licenses.	Revenue from Stamps.	Total produce of Revenue in all Branches.	Average payment per head.
[2]								Acres.	Rs.	Acres.	Rs. a. p.[6]	Rs.	Rs.	Rs.	Rs.	Rs.	Rs. a. p.
1814–15	5,791[3]	550,814	377,129	384,167	124,692	68,108	23,274	1,056,644	1,864,391	$16\frac{1}{16}$	19 10 3	109,215	113,608	19,889	12,185	1,966,389	3 9 1
1815–16	5,613	563,695	441,540	393,837	144,590	83,287	27,097	1,345,424	2,011,192		19 4 6	120,671	108,787	20,438	12,049	2,259,092	4 0 1
1816–17	5,618	585,147	417,365	372,822	145,225	83,331	26,868	1,355,436	1,931,850[5]		19 3 6	124,235	123,284	22,073	10,727	2,206,215	3 12 4
1817–18	5,748	611,823	418,586	385,306	145,664	82,762	27,366	1,373,294	2,018,407		19 4 0	123,771	153,144	23,857	15,281	2,381,509	3 14 3
1818–19	5,783	664,114	452,010	403,981	160,232	84,351	27,162	1,412,064	2,071,180		19 7 9	164,650	167,506	25,487	16,399	2,484,994	3 11 11
1819–20	5,799	637,637	457,664	398,777	160,975	83,899	28,812	1,419,746	2,086,042		19 15 10	158,716	210,734	26,167	19,199	2,550,621	4 0 0
1820–21	5,850	625,815	502,304	389,260	163,382	81,499	29,558	1,415,303	2,042,167[5]		20 5 0	174,647	193,966	32,311	22,603	2,489,165	3 15 8
1821–22	5,914	638,199	458,433	394,205	162,593	82,853	28,719	1,418,249	2,055,146		20 7 8	172,798	193,243	38,336	19,863	2,506,812	3 14 11
1822–23	5,953	677,252	485,037	394,506	168,899	81,733	29,586	1,458,459	2,142,165		20 4 5	171,537	206,291	41,169	15,716	2,611,359	3 13 8
1823–24	5,970	827,530[4]	601,881	451,102	169,422	85,639	29,889	1,464,136	2,082,190[5]		19 6 7	164,341	172,805	41,277	17,491	2,497,850	3 0 3
1824–25	5,979	842,214	606,468	465,236	172,009	85,457	30,989	1,472,844	2,218,775		19 12 5	161,319	180,390	42,084	15,890	2,636,155	3 1 10
1825–26	5,993	852,409	643,786	464,358	174,813	85,940	31,239	1,448,221	2,219,416		19 10 1	160,217	202,350	43,852	15,453	2,671,379	3 2 2
1826–27	5,993	854,050	666,357	443,847	175,418	88,159	31,592	1,444,617	2,230,030		19 9 3	159,360	203,629	44,088	14,118	2,673,999	3 2 1
1827–28	5,996	859,066	654,837	451,060	175,164	88,076	31,694	1,444,031	2,227,476[5]		19 6 11	166,231	202,743	53,661	20,986	2,680,494	3 1 11
1828–29	5,996	870,366	658,011	429,544	184,244	87,769	30,818	1,457,610	2,189,275[5]		18 10 9	179,023	214,873	54,661	21,323	2,670,760	3 0 9

[1] Parliamentary Papers, 1831, vol. v. p. 438.

[2] The province was under lease in 1814–15.

[3] Deserted villages included in these returns.

[4] Infants under five years of age are included in the last six years.

[5] A bad season.

[6] Rupees, annas pice.

II

From a number of replies in answer to an inquiry made in *The Hindu* newspaper, respecting the practice adopted by the authorities and the experience of the ryots, received by me from the Madras Presidency, I select from three districts what appear to be representative statements:—

I.—MADURA DISTRICT.

MADURA, *July* 10, 1901.

You want to know whether 'expenses of cultivation' in the Madras settlement operations include merely seed, etc., or whether any allowance is made in addition for a sufficient quantity of grain being set aside for the due and proper nourishment of the cultivator and his family.

The answer is, no such allowance is made.

Your question is directly answered in paragraph 70, page 192, edition of 1893, of Dewan Bahadur Srinivasa Raghava Iyengar's Memorandum on the 'Progress of the Madras Presidency during the last Forty Years,' where the author quotes Mr. Pedder, Revenue Secretary in the India Office, from the Statement of Moral and Material Progress and Condition of India for 1882–83, Part I., page 115, as follows: 'The only way of finding the average cost of cultivation is to ascertain what it would cost to cultivate a given holding by hired labour, and, as this labour would be needed for only a certain number of weeks or months, it is obvious that *nothing would be allowed as wage for the subsistence of the cultivator and his family during the rest of the year*.'

Here, of course, is the direct official answer to your question. As to what the 'expenses of cultivation' mean, I append two extracts, one from the 'Manual of Standing Information for the Madras Presidency,' published by the Superintendent, Government Press, Madras, 1893, and sold for Rs.1 8a.; the other from the 'Manual of the Administration of the Madras Presidency,' in 3 vols., Government Press, Madras, 1885. Both books, I believe, are by Dr. Maclean, of Salem fame, and I think Sir M. E. Grant Duff prided himself on the completion of the Manual of Administration during his *régime*. You will see from the extracts I append that the expenses of cultivation include only (1) ploughing cattle, (2) agricultural implements, (3) seed, (4) manure, (5) labour required for ploughing, sowing, reaping, etc.

The only doubt that can possibly arise as to the above is, as to the 'labour required for ploughing,' etc. You also want actual instances. I can give you two instances at present, also from official sources. The first is from the letter of Mr. G. P. Clerk, Deputy-Commissioner of Revenue Settlement, dated September 30, 1890, No. 288B to the

Board of Revenue, embodied in Madras Government Order dated July 31, 1893, No. 697, passing orders on the Tanjore Settlement Scheme. In para. 89 of his letter (page 26 of the G.O.), Mr. Clerk says in regard to *wet* cultivation expenses :—

'In the following statement the cost of cultivating an acre of the best soil is given in detail. The amounts noted against each item are the averages of all the statements taken from the Mirasdars. The average of the estimates received from the Tahsildars is also shown. [*See next page.*]

This list shows conclusively that the cultivation expenses does not include any subsistence for the cultivator's family. It must be borne in mind that Rs.14 is, in Mr. Clerk's words, 'the maximum cost of cultivating an acre of the best soil.' For inferior soils he takes the cost of cultivation to be less, instead of more, as he ought to do. I append an extract from the same letter of Mr. Clerk's giving the out-turn for each class of land and the deductions made and the tax proposed, from which it will be seen that the cost of cultivation is taken as low as Rs.2 12a. for the most inferior land. Certainly Rs.2 12a. cannot include anything for the subsistence of the family. I may add that the Board of Revenue was itself struck at the allowance of Rs.2 12a. per acre for cultivation expenses, and said that Mr. Clerk's 'lowest figure hardly allows for anything beyond the cost of seed.' The Board reduced Mr. Clerk's scale for the higher classes of lands in some cases and adopted Rs.4 8a. as the lowest figure. (Para. 50 of Board's resolution, printed at page 157 of the same G.O.) So much for wet lands. With regard to dry lands, the cultivation expenses are thus estimated by Mr. Clerk (para. 101 of his letter, page 29 of the G.O.).

	Rs.	a.	p.
1. Cost of Bullocks...	1	0	4
2. ,, Plough	0	7	8
3. ,, Ploughing	1	6	0
4. ,, Manure	1	4	0
5. ,, Seed	0	7	0
6. ,, Weeding...	1	0	0
7. ,, Watchman and Vettigan ...	0	2	1
8. ,, Harvesting	0	13	9
Total ...	Rs.6	8	10

This again is 'the cost of cultivating an acre of the *best ordinary dry land*,' and he has a sliding scale from Rs.6 8a. 10p. to Rs.3 0a. 10p. for cultivation expenses.

My next quotations will be from Mr. Clerk's letter to the Board of Revenue (containing proposals for the re-settlement of Godavari) dated November 9, 1895, No. 571A, printed in Board's Proceedings

No.	Items.	Average Cost as per Settlement Inquiries.	Average Cost as per Statements of Nine Tahsildars.	Total.	Average.	Maximum Cost Proposed for Tanjore.
1	2	3	4	5	6	7
		Rs. a. p.	Rs. a. p.	Rs. a. p.	Rs. a. p.	Rs. a. p.
1	Cost of a pair of Bullocks	1 5 6	...	...	...	1 5 6
2	" Plough	1 7 8	...	...	...	1 7 6
3	" Ploughing	1 10 5	...	...	...	1 10 8
4	" Manuring	2 12 1	...	...	...	2 12 0
5	" Lowering the level of fields (Kuli Vettu) ...	0 10 6	...	...	...	0 10 8
6	" Repairing Channels	0 3 5	...	...	...	0 8 0
7	" Seed	2 3 4	...	...	...	2 8 0
8	" Removing Seedlings	0 9 8	...	...	...	0 9 0
9	" Transplanting	0 11 1	...	...	...	0 11 0
10	" Weeding	0 11 3	...	...	...	0 11 0
11	" Wages of Nirkatti	0 2 10	...	...	...	0 2 8
12	" Kanal or Watchman	0 5 2	...	...	...	0 5 0
13	" Coolies for reaping...	1 6 6	...	...	...	1 6 0
	Total	14 8 0	14 5 8	28 8 8	14 4 1	14 0 0

(Rev. Sett. L. Rds. and Agri.) March 12, 1896, No. 48. In para. 41 (page 81 of the B.P.), Mr. Clerk gives the details of the 'expenses' of cultivation for the BEST *wet* land as follows:—

	Rs.	a.	p.
1. Cost of Bullocks and Ploughing ...	8	8	0
2. " Implements	0	8	0
3. " Seed	0	12	0
4. " Manure	2	12	0
5. " Labour	6	8	0
Total ...	Rs.14	0	0

In para. 42 (page 82 of the B.P.), Mr. Clerk gives 'the cost of cultivating black paddy on an acre of *dry* land'—paddy-growing dry land is, of course, the best dry land—as follows:—

	Rs.	a.	p.
1. Bullocks and ploughing	3	0	0
2. Implements	0	8	0
3. Seed	0	8	0
4. Labour	4	0	0
Total ...	Rs.8	0	0

Mr. Clerk's sliding scale for 'wet cultivation expenses' varies from Rs.14 to Rs.6, and that for 'dry cultivation expenses' from Rs.8 to Rs.2 6a.

Your question is, I think, answered sufficiently by the quotations and extracts I have given. With regard to the Madras Settlement operations generally, I would refer you to paras. 69 to 79 in Mr. Srinivasa Raghar Iyengar's 'Forty Years' Progress' from which I have already quoted, under the heading 'Periodical Revisions of Land Settlement.' It is a great mistake to suppose that the Government proceeds upon its theory of a scientific settlement from actual facts. What it does is first to make up its mind to raise the revenue demand of a particular district by so much, and then to prepare tables of out-turns, cultivation expenses, etc., leading up to the theoretical '*half-net*' to be found in the Standing Order. It is not that the conclusions are based on actual facts bearing upon each item of calculation in the theoretical process; but the facts are adjusted to suit the increase of revenue previously fixed upon. Upon this point, I may quote to you again from the 'Forty Years' Progress,' para. 70, page 192, where Mr. Srinivasa Raghar Iyengar quotes from Pedder: 'The first step in a Madras settlement practically is to determine, on general considerations (such as those described under Bombay), whether the tract coming under settlement requires a decrease or will bear an enhancement of its land revenue and to what extent.

The total amount of assessment to be imposed having thus been decided on, the results of the process above described are adjusted so as to yield it.'

Vide also Hon. K. Kalyana Sundaram Aiyar's speech in the Congress of 1894 on the Land Settlement question. *Vide* also Sir Auckland Colvin's remarks on the Madras Settlement printed in appendix to the same book at page ccxxxvii, *et seq.*

You will find that Sir Auckland quotes (page ccxxxix) Mr. Bensen, one of our Settlement Directors, as remarking that 'the system of calculating the working expenses of the ryot by which these decrease in proportion to the assessed value of the land is radically wrong,' and that 'in fact, within certain limits the expenses for the production of the standard crop of jowra vary rather inversely to the quality of the land dealt with.'

As to what is the actual cultivation expenses, in our practical experience as against the theoretically adjusted figures of the Government officers, I would refer you to a memorial signed among others by Sir V. Bhasbyam Iyengar—a gentleman who will never put his signature to any memorial to Government unless the facts were absolutely true, who has been often consulted by Government, and is in its confidence, who was the first native to officiate as Advocate-General, and who has now been made judge of the High Court. The memorial is about the Pisgar assessment. You will find that he estimates the cost of cultivation to be Rs.36 8a. per acre (not including anything for the subsistence of the cultivator and his family), whereas the Government estimate is Rs.11 11a. 5p. and Rs.10 10a. 5p. In fact, the maximum allowance for cultivation expenses of the Government officers that I know of is Rs.14 per acre that I have mentioned above.

You may ask, how it is that the ryots keep up their lands instead of relinquishing them when cultivation expenses are taken so low and the tax is very high. My candid opinion on this matter is that though the Government has estimated the out-turn very high and the cultivation expenses very low, still the ryots are able to bear the assessment because the prices have continually increased since the Seventies, and the ruling prices are much higher than the prices taken at the Settlements. This rise in prices has acted as a providential set-off to the iniquitous figures of the Settlement Department. Otherwise many people would have been forced to relinquish their lands. Now that a sort of gold standard has been established in India, if the prices should fall hereafter the ryots would suffer indescribable woe and misery on account of the Settlements.

Extract from DR. MACLEAN'S '*Manual of the Administration of the Madras Presidency,*' vol. i. p. 109, par. 111.

The third step is to get what is technically known as 'net produce.' The money-value of the net produce is found by deducting from the money-value of the total produce arrived at as just described the expenses of cultivation. *These are made up of the cost of cattle, implements, manure, seed, and sowing, transplanting (in wet), and the wages of servants, permanent and temporary.* The expenditure on all these items except the first and second must be freshly incurred every year; but cattle and implements will last for several years, and their cost is distributed equally over all. The cost of cattle, implements, seed, the wages of permanent servants, and the cost of transplanting are taken as constant whatever the soil. It is obvious that the ryot will employ the same cattle and implements on any land he may have without reference to its soil; the quantity of seed sown is much the same on all kinds of soil; the wages of permanent farm servants do not depend upon the soil of the farm they are employed on; the cost of transplanting is a question not of soil, but of area; and the cost of sowing is properly included in the hire of the permanent farm servants. The only items of the cost of cultivation that may be regarded as varying therefrom are manure and harvest labour. The soils having been valued at so much per acre, it is necessary to determine the cost of cultivation by the same standard. This is done by ascertaining the size of an average holding in wet and in dry and by distributing the various items which make up the total cost of its cultivation rateably over its acreage. The difference between the value of the produce adjusted and commuted in the manner indicated above and the cost of cultivation is the value of the net produce, half of which is the land assessment.

Extract from the 'Manual of Standing Information for the Madras Presidency.' Government Press, Madras, 1893.

Against the average value of the produce thus determined has to be set off the 'cost of cultivation,' the estimation of which used to be one of the most difficult and the most conjectural of the various steps in connection with a Settlement. The items of cost usually included in the estimate were—(1) Ploughing cattle; (2) Agricultural implements; (3) Seed; (4) Manure; (5) Labour required for ploughing, sowing, reaping, etc. The method of calculation varied according to the description of crops grown, and of culture, as well as according to the practice of making the various payments in each district. In some, these are made in grain, in others in money, and in some in both grain and money. The payments made in grain were converted into money at the commutation price adopted for the Settlement. The cost of bullocks and of the implements of husbandry was distributed over the number of years during which they were estimated to be serviceable, and the other items were calculated for each year. Calculations were made for the area which could be cultivated with one plough and one pair of bullocks, and then reduced to terms of an acre. The usual practice was to work out the expenses for the best soil, and then to proportionately diminish this standard as the quality of soil descends. This method is open to objection on the ground that the cost of cultivating poor soils is greater than for superior soils. But it is to be borne in mind that the cultivator is content with a much smaller relative out-turn from inferior soils and omits many processes, such as repeated ploughings, manuring, weeding, and hoeing, which are resorted to on the higher class lands. Now the cultivation expenses are taken to be the same as has already been determined in neighbouring settled districts. These expenses being deducted from the gross assets, *i.e.*, the value of the total out-turn, the result is the approximate net produce of the land under examination, and half of this is taken as the Government demand.

[*For additional extract see Table on opposite page.*]

II.—THE NELLORE DISTRICT.

NELLORE,
July 10, 1901.

SIR,—Referring to your communication published in the issue of the *Hindu* of July 8, 1901, I beg to communicate to you the following information as regards 'cultivation expenses.' The information refers to the Nellore district.

The Board's Standing Orders in force now say:—

'The assessment is to be fixed so as not to exceed half the net produce after deducting the expenses of cultivation.'

Your question is what items are included in the expression, 'expenses of cultivation, etc.'

The following items are included in the above term:—

1. Cost of Bullocks.
2. Cost of Implements.
3. Cost of Manure.
4. Wages of Labourers (yearly and daily).
5. Cost of Seed.

I append a statement showing how the 'net produce' has been worked up.

Theoretically, the method of calculation adopted seems to be excellent, and none but the ryot knows where the shoe pinches. Read the above to the ryot; he will at once point out the fallacies. To begin with, he will take exception to the gross out-turn adopted per acre. He will say that for the kind of soil which his land is composed of, the estimated out-turn is too high.[1] He is apt to com-

[1] The estimated out-turns given in the statement are for soils most common. Higher out-turns are estimated for richer soils, which are not common.

Extract from Mr. Clerk's Letter, *showing how he arrived at the Net Produce for Tanjore District.*

Irrigation.	Taram.	Grain Produce Madras Measures.	Value at Rs. 128 per garce.	Deduction. 15 per cent. for Vicissitudes of Seasons.	Deduction. *Cultivation Expenses.*	Deduction. Total.	Net Value.	Half-net.	Proposed Rates.
			Rs. a. p.	Rs. a. p.	Rs. a. p.	Rs. a. p.	Rs. a. p.	Rs. a. p.	Rs. a. p.
First Group	1	1,125	45 0 0	6 12 0	14 0 0	20 12 0	24 4 0	12 2 0	12 0 0
	2	1,000	40 0 0	6 0 0	13 8 0	19 8 0	20 8 0	10 4 0	10 0 0
	3	900	36 0 0	5 6 5	12 4 0	17 10 5	18 5 7	9 2 9	9 0 0
	4	800	32 0 0	4 12 10	11 0 0	15 12 10	16 3 2	8 1 7	8 0 0
	5	700	28 0 0	4 3 2	9 12 0	13 5 2	14 0 10	7 0 5	7 0 0
	6	600	24 0 0	3 9 7	8 8 0	12 1 7	11 14 5	5 15 3	6 0 0
	7	500	20 0 0	3 0 0	7 4 0	10 4 0	9 12 0	4 14 0	5 0 0
	8	450	18 0 0	2 11 2	6 0 0	8 11 2	9 4 10	4 10 5	4 8 0
	9	400	16 0 0	2 6 5	5 4 0	7 10 5	8 5 7	4 2 9	4 0 0
Second Group	2	1,000	40 0 0	6 0 0	13 8 0	19 8 0	20 8 0	10 4 0	10 0 0
	3	900	36 0 0	5 6 5	12 4 0	17 10 5	18 5 7	9 2 9	9 0 0
	4	800	32 0 0	4 12 10	11 0 0	15 12 10	16 3 2	8 1 7	8 0 0
	5	700	28 0 0	4 3 2	9 12 0	13 15 2	14 0 10	7 0 5	7 0 0
	6	600	24 0 0	3 9 7	8 8 0	12 1 7	11 14 5	5 15 3	6 0 0
	7	500	20 0 0	3 0 0	7 4 0	10 4 0	9 12 0	4 14 0	5 0 0
	8	450	18 0 0	2 11 2	6 0 0	8 11 2	9 4 10	4 10 5	4 8 0
	9	400	16 0 0	2 6 5	5 4 0	7 10 5	8 5 7	4 2 9	4 0 0
	10	350	14 0 0	2 1 7	5 0 0	7 1 7	6 14 5	3 7 2	3 8 0
Third Group	3	900	36 0 0	5 6 5	12 4 0	17 10 5	18 5 7	9 2 9	9 0 0
	4	800	32 0 0	4 12 10	11 0 0	15 12 10	16 3 2	8 1 7	8 0 0
	5	700	28 0 0	4 3 2	9 12 0	13 15 2	14 0 10	7 0 5	7 0 0
	6	600	24 0 0	3 9 7	8 8 0	12 1 7	11 14 5	5 15 3	6 0 0
	7	500	20 0 0	3 0 0	7 4 0	10 4 0	9 12 0	4 14 0	5 0 0
	8	450	18 0 0	2 11 2	6 0 0	8 11 2	9 4 10	4 10 5	4 8 0
	9	400	16 0 0	2 6 5	5 4 0	7 10 5	8 5 7	4 2 9	4 0 0
	10	350	14 0 0	2 1 7	5 0 0	7 1 7	6 14 5	3 7 2	3 8 0
	11	300	12 0 0	1 12 10	4 4 0	6 0 10	5 15 2	2 15 7	3 0 0
Fourth Group	4	800	32 0 0	4 12 10	11 0 0	15 12 10	16 3 2	8 1 7	8 0 0
	5	700	28 0 0	4 3 2	9 12 0	13 15 2	14 0 11	7 0 5	7 0 0
	6	600	24 0 0	3 9 7	8 8 0	12 1 7	11 14 5	5 15 3	6 0 0
	7	500	20 0 0	3 0 0	7 4 0	10 4 0	9 12 0	4 14 0	5 0 0
	8	450	18 0 0	2 11 2	6 0 0	8 11 2	9 4 10	4 10 5	4 8 0
	9	400	16 0 0	2 6 5	5 4 0	7 10 5	8 5 7	4 2 9	4 0 0
	10	350	14 0 0	2 1 7	5 0 0	7 1 7	6 14 5	3 7 2	3 8 0
	11	300	12 0 0	1 12 10	4 4 0	6 0 10	5 15 2	2 15 7	3 0 0
	12	250	10 0 0	1 8 0	3 8 0	5 0 0	5 0 0	2 8 0	2 8 0
Fifth Group	5	700	28 0 0	4 3 2	9 12 0	13 15 2	14 0 10	7 0 5	7 0 0
	6	600	24 0 0	3 9 7	8 8 0	12 1 7	11 14 5	5 15 3	6 0 0
	7	500	20 0 0	3 0 0	7 4 0	10 4 0	9 12 0	4 14 0	5 0 0
	8	450	18 0 0	2 11 2	6 0 0	8 11 2	9 4 10	4 10 5	4 8 0
	9	400	16 0 0	2 6 5	5 4 0	7 10 5	8 5 7	4 2 9	4 0 0
	10	350	14 0 0	2 1 7	5 0 0	7 1 7	6 14 5	3 7 2	3 8 0
	11	300	12 0 0	1 12 10	4 4 0	6 0 10	5 15 2	2 15 7	3 0 0
	12	250	10 0 0	1 8 0	3 8 0	5 0 0	5 0 0	2 8 0	2 8 0
	13	200	8 0 0	1 3 2	2 12 0	3 15 2	4 0 10	2 0 5	2 0 0

plain under this head that there is failure of successive seasons; that, all the same, the land-tax has been screwed from him with relentless vigour, on the ground that a few grains have been found scattered in the fields, which was evidence of out-turn. Remember, also, the Madras rules on remissions, under which no remission is granted if the inspecting officer is satisfied that the land has produced one-thirty-second of a normal crop. Ten or twelve years before, the rule was to grant remission if the estimated out-turn fell below one-eighth. In other words, if the normal out-turn was estimated at 32 bushels per acre, and if in a year of short rainfall it produced only, say, four bushels, the ryot can have no remission. Supposing another bad year follows, and in this year an acre of the land produced two bushels, no remission can be granted under the rules. Now, remember the fact that the ryot had spent on the land in both the years much labour and money for ploughing, seeds, weeding, etc., and the out-turn in both the years is found to be far short of the expenses incurred. As if this is insufficient, Government comes with its demand for land-tax to complete the ryot's ruin. I am not drawing on my imagination, for the above are stern facts. We *are* having a succession of bad seasons; and even in the best of years the estimated normal out-turn cannot be got.

Expenses of Cultivation.

1. *Cost of Bullocks.*

Then, coming to the first item of expenses of cultivation, *i.e.*, cost of bullocks, I am unable to find out how the amount has been worked out. It was estimated that four pairs of bullocks, costing Rs.250 in the aggregate, are required to till twenty acres of land. A sum of Rs.17 6a. is deducted under this head for ten acres (*vide* statement attached), and this is what I don't understand. Of course new bullocks are not required each year. A set purchased in one year may, if all goes well with the ryot, last for a maximum period of five years. But in these days of famine and pestilence and forest reservation, the cattle mortality from diseases alone is terrible, not to speak of mortality from want of fodder, so that in the case of unlucky ryots—and the majority are unlucky—a set will not last for more than three years. Even supposing that his cattle serve him out the full term, the average cost of bullocks for a year is Rs.25 for ten acres.

In calculating the cost of bullocks, it is not sufficient that the average cost of bullocks for each year is deducted from the gross produce, but provision must be made for meeting the interest on the capital raised in purchasing the bullocks. I shall make the point clearer. Say I own twenty acres of land. I want four pairs of bullocks, which cost Rs.250. (I take this figure, being more easy of calculation.) I borrow this amount from a moneylender. I have to pay a yearly interest of Rs.30 at 12 per cent. per annum—a very moderate rate indeed for a ryot. If I lay aside Rs.50 a year from my gross produce, I shall recoup the original capital raised in five years. But how am I to meet the interest due on the amount? No doubt I may pay to my creditor my yearly saving under this head, and thus lessen the burden of interest; but even then, how am I to pay the interest? This must, I fancy, be met from my net produce! At the end of the fifth year, my cattle, even if they are alive so long, are of no use to me, and I have to purchase new ones; and I have to raise a loan again, so that the sum of Rs.250 I originally borrowed is a permanent debt, and the interest thereon should, in the ordinary course, be deducted from the gross produce as part of the cost of bullocks. According to my contention, the cost of bullocks for ten acres comes to Rs.34 per annum.

	Rs.
Cost of bullocks for ten acres	125
Total interest on capital for five years at 12 per cent. per annum, a sum of Rs.25 being supposed to be paid towards capital every year	45
Total for five years	Rs.170
Total for one year	Rs.34

As I have already stated, I shall have to raise again a loan of Rs.125 at the beginning of the sixth year to purchase new cattle, and the same process as stated above continues.

It will be observed that the Government has allowed only Rs.17 6a. under this head, or only half of what might fairly be claimed by the ryot, without taking into consideration other vicissitudes, such as premature mortality among his cattle from diseases so prevalent, into consideration.

2. *Cost of Implements.*

Under this head a sum of Rs.5 4a. is allowed. When this is mentioned to the ryot, he heaves a long sigh, and recounts with tears in eyes how little by little his privileges in getting certain agricultural implements *gratis* from his village forests have been ruthlessly cut off by the all-absorbing Forest Department, and how he has now to pay for every stick which he wants. Times have greatly changed now, and the allowance under this head, which may have been fair at one time, is now found inadequate.

3. *Manure.*

One curious inconsistency occurs under this head, displaying the ignorance of the Settlement officer. His Code probably teaches him that the richer the constitution of the soil, the greater the manure it requires, and the poorer the soil, the less the manure. But we all understand that the poorer the soil, the more the manure required to make it productive. This inconsistency apart, the ryot in most places is denied the benefit of the manure which his cattle give him by the enforcement of the so-called sanitary laws. He cannot store up the manure in his back-yard because the sanitary officer condemns it. In municipalities and unions he has to purchase the ashes of his own household and the dung of his own cattle at extraordinarily high prices from those bodies. It thus happens that the provision under this head also is not sufficient.

4. *Wages of Labourers.*

This communication will be unusually lengthy if I begin to demonstrate the utter inadequacy of the provision under this head. Suffice it to say that the expense is much underestimated. If, however, it is desired that this must be thoroughly sifted, I should be very glad to give the results of my experiences.

5. *Cost of Seed—Sufficient.*

It is unnecessary for me to say that any allowance is made and deducted from the gross out-turn for the due and proper nourishment of the cultivator and the members of his family. The ryot manages to keep his body and soul together, by himself, and all his family members, toiling in the field, taking the place of daily labourers, for whom some provision is made in the expenses of cultivation.

A RYOT.

[*See Table opposite.*]

III.—SOUTH ARCOT DISTRICT.

Dear Sir,—In response to your letter dated 17th June, 1901, published in the *Hindu* of yesterday, I beg to inform you that, according to the former practice of the Madras Land Revenue Settlement Department, the expenses of cultivation included the following items:—

1. Cost of Ploughing Cattle.
2. Cost of Agricultural Implements.
3. Seed.
4. Manure.
5. Price of labour required for sowing, transplanting in wet, reaping, threshing, etc.

The expenses of cultivation do not allow for any quantity of grain being set aside for the nourishment of the cultivator and his family.

The cost of feeding cattle is not provided for in the estimate of cultivation expenses, as the straw is taken as a set-off against this item. If, however, in any district or tract the feeding charges are known to be specially higher, owing to grain being given to ploughing cattle, this is taken into account.

Supposing that the cultivation expenses were calculated at Rs.11 for the best land, they would run something as under, viz., wet:—

PARTICULARS REFERRED TO IN THE LETTER OF A RYOT.

	Gross estimated outturn per acre.	Expenses of Cultivation for Ten Acres.							Average for one Acre.	Net produce per Acre.	Half net produce.	Assessment fixed.	Assessment which ought to be fixed.	Remarks.
		Bullocks.	Implements.	Manure.	Yearly Labourers.	Daily Labourers.	Seed.	Total.						
						As Estimated by Settlement Officers.								
	Rs.	Rs.	Rs.	Rs.	Rs.	Rs.	Rs.	Rs.	Rs.	Rs.	Rs.	Rs. a. p.	Rs. a. p.	
1	25	17	5	7	45	22	9	105	$10\frac{1}{2}$	$14\frac{1}{2}$	$7\frac{1}{4}$	7 0 1	3 8 0	This is for three classes of soils which predominate.
2	20	17	5	7	45	20	9	103	$10\frac{3}{10}$	$9\frac{7}{10}$	$4\frac{3}{4}$	4 8 0	2 12 0	
3	16	13	5	4	45	16	9	92	$9\frac{1}{5}$	$6\frac{4}{5}$	$3\frac{2}{5}$	3 4 0	1 12 0	
						As Estimated by Ryot.								
1	20	34	6	8	45	30	9	132	13	7	3 8 0		3 8 0	
2	18	30	6	9	45	25	9	124	$12\frac{2}{5}$	$5\frac{3}{5}$	2 12 0		2 12 0	
3	14	25	6	10	45	20	9	115	$11\frac{1}{2}$	$3\frac{1}{2}$	1 12 0		1 12 0	

Items.	Cost per acre. R. a. p.
Ploughing Cattle	1 12 9
Agricultural Implements	1 0 1
Seed	1 2 5
Manure	1 10 8
Wages	5 6 1
Total	Rs.11 0 0
Dry, one-half	5 8 0

The way in which the expenses were arrived at was to ascertain, separately, what extent of wet land and what of dry could be, under the ordinary conditions of the district, cultivated by one plough and one pair of bullocks.

The method of calculation varied according to the description of crops grown and of culture, as well as according to the practice of making the various payments in the district. In some these are made in grain, in others in money, and in some in both grain and money. The payments made in grain were converted into money at the commutation price adapted for the settlement.

The cost of bullocks and of the implements of husbandry was distributed over the number of years during which they were estimated to be serviceable, and the other items were calculated for each year.

Suppose the commuted money value of the gross produce per acre of land was Rs.27 9a.

A sixth of this (=Rs.4 9a. 6p.) was deducted to compensate for vicissitudes of the season;

leaving Rs.22 15a. 6p.;

from which again was deducted Rs.11 for cultivation expenses;

leaving the net value of Rs.11 15a. 6p.;

of which half (=Rs.5 15a. 9p.), or say Rs.6, was taken as the Government share.

The present practice of the Settlement Department is not to work out separately the cultivation expenses for each district dealt with, but to adopt those arrived at for the neighbouring districts.

July 9, 1901.

If any reader has omitted to peruse the foregoing most valuable documents, and this paragraph should catch his attention, I beg him to turn back the pages and read them. Their intrinsic interest is so great, they throw so clear and vivid a light upon the Indian Governments as practical land stewards, as well as exhibit the actual position of the cultivator, that no one, wishing to really understand the ryot's position, may pass these 'human documents' by unread and unpondered.

DIAGRAM ILLUSTRATING THE NATURE AND DISTRIBUTION OF A NATIONS INCOME

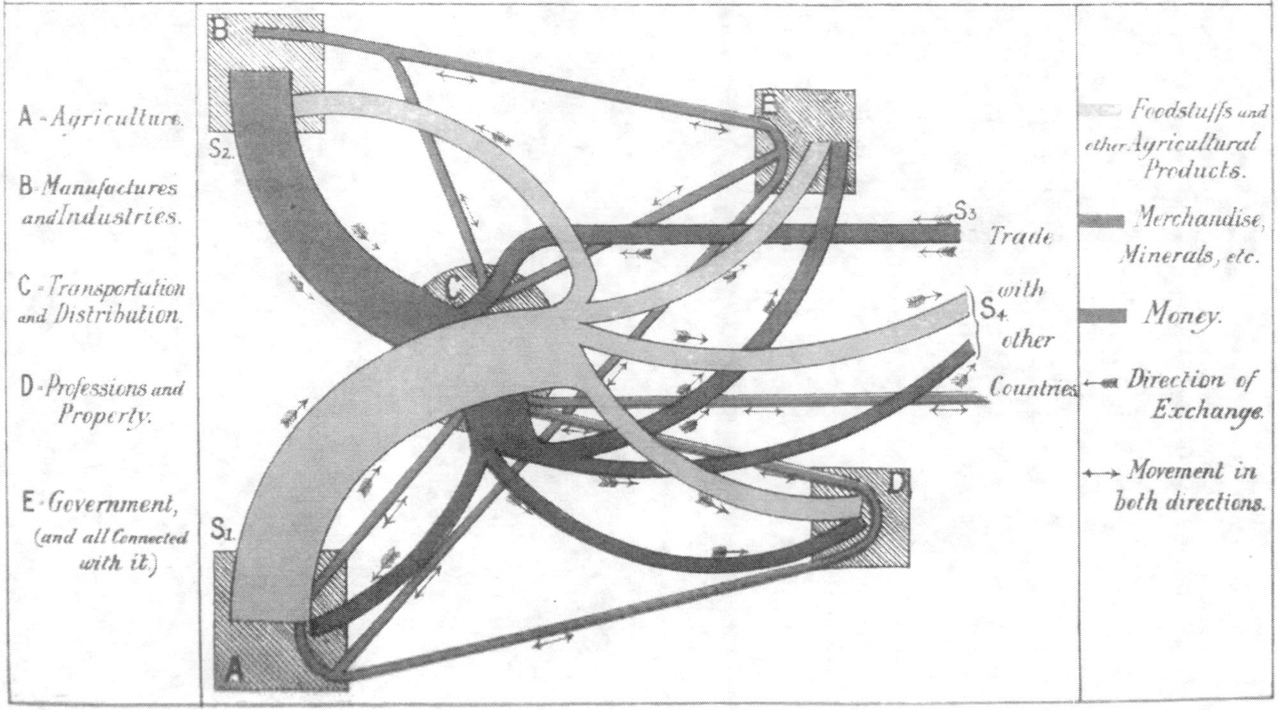

AN EXPLANATORY STATEMENT

Producing and Consuming Classes:

Agriculturists, Manufacturers, Miners, Artisans, etc., Carriers and Middlemen,	**Professional and Property-Holding Classes, Government and all Parties Connected With It.**

Total Income of Country: $S_1 + S_2 + S_3 - S_4$.
Money Value of Crops not Accurately Obtainable in India.
Therefore Government Revenue (its Ratio Ascertained) Made the Basis of Calculation.
Reply to a (possible) Rigorous Critic as to How so Many People Still Continue to Survive, the Average Visible Income being Below Maintenance Line.

The chapter which follows, the longest in this work, consists mainly of an estimate of the whole income of India in an ordinary year. From the estimate thus made the average income of every Indian is obtained, and, as the Government of India professed to take a like course twenty years ago, a comparison between the results of to-day and of 1882 is made. A pending discussion, in certain English reviews, on a cognate subject affecting the detailed income of the United Kingdom, which is proceeding whilst these pages are passing through the press, indicates the desirability of my stating explicitly the principle upon which my calculations are made. It appears that there are in use two or three mutually exclusive methods of reckoning a nation's income. The great point of difference seems to be this: Ought income derived from stocks and shares earning dividends in the same country, and from professional and clerical services, to be added to the total value obtained from the products of the soil—surface-planting or growth and mining—and from the value imparted to those products by agricultural and industrial labour? In the opinion of the present writer the answer is in the negative. Those incomes ought not to be included, seeing that they are paid from the respective products described. To include them would be to reckon a portion of the total income twice over, and thus vitiate the result.

The diagram and explanation which face this page are

given to make more clear than any words of mere description could do, my basis of calculation. They should, it seems to me, make my position discernible at a glance.

In the calculations which follow I have given the income in money value. It is necessary, then, to state how I have obtained this value, and to examine generally the factors involved in the problem. The diagram shows the respective classes of a country segregated into five broad natural divisions:—

Agriculturists,	Professional and Property-holding Classes.
Manufacturers, Miners, Artisans, etc.	Government, and all parties connected with it.
Carriers and Middlemen.	

The Economic Wealth produced by or brought into the country is represented by the broad streams of yellow and blue—foodstuffs and merchandise; the red streams indicate the flow of money between the various classes.

Now, in estimating the *total* income of a country or people it is evident that the only wealth produced by or coming into the country is represented *in quantity* by the various streams—S_1, S_2, S_3, and the outward stream S_4. The only action within the country is the distribution and consumption of this wealth, and also, maybe, certain rearrangements of the accumulations of wealth [if such a phrase can be used in connection with India after Sir Richard Strachey's observation, 'Consider the total absence of anything like accumulated wealth in India']. But this distribution, this consumption, and this rearrangement, do in nowise add to the income of the country, for they are but a transfer of the country's wealth amongst the various classes, the producers giving to the consumers of their produce as taxpayers, as tenants, as employers of carriers, middlemen, and professional parties.

Also, in such an estimate, the currents of currency within the country need not be allowed for. So far as they are concerned, the arrows in the diagram point both ways, to indicate that the total backward and forward flow are approximately equal during the year.

Therefore, as regards the quantity of the substances forming the income, the position may be stated shortly, thus,—

Total Income of Country—

$$S_1 + S_2 + S_3 - S_4.$$[1]

But, in the chapter following, I have given the income in money value. It is necessary, therefore, to state how I have obtained this value, and to examine the validity of comparing such value for one year with that for another year.

The money value for the streams S_1 and S_2, to ensure accuracy, should be obtained by reckoning it at the current price in the market for such portions of S_1 and S_2 as may be the subject of buying and selling. Of course, in a country like India a large part of the foodstuffs is consumed by the actual producers without becoming the subject of barter. (Not, however, without a pricing —of a sort : most of the crops are hypothecated to the moneylender who puts a value upon them which to the producer is never excessive.) Still, it would be approximately correct, in a comparison of year with year, to apply the average market value to the whole quantity of the streams S_1 and S_2. This mode of calculation has been denied to me. There is an entire absence of trustworthy data, showing the market or money value of the total production of the country so far as the yellow stream is concerned. I have, consequently, had to adopt another mode. The Government revenue is intended to bear a definite ratio to the assumed (or ascertained) produce of the soil reckoned over a number of years. That ratio differs in the respective Presidencies and

[1] It is scarcely necessary to state that if the red currency stream with other countries is greater one way or another the excess value must be added to or abstracted from this total.

Provinces. It is approximately ascertainable, and I have ascertained it as nearly as may be. Possessing it, to arrive at the money value, I have multiplied the land revenue the necessary number of times, and have thus reached the result I announce.

> [I am not aware whether this course was adopted in 1882, as the particulars on which the Baring-Barbour estimate was based have not been published. Nevertheless I make the comparison as though the methods were identical, partly with the hope that my doing so will induce the Government of India to furnish the full details. My acquaintance with the Note of 1882 is but fragmentary; certain lines followed then are indicated, and those I have adopted. In the absence of actual investigation, the principles in each case must be so nearly alike as, I contend, to make the respective estimates comparable.]

In other respects the requisite data are available, and exact figures are given; where an estimate only has been possible I have indicated the fact.

The money value of streams S_3 and S_4 is obtained from the Blue Books.

The average income per head is, then, the total value of these streams divided by the number of the population,—

Or

$$\text{Average income per head} = \frac{S_1 + S_2 + S_3 - S_4}{\text{population,}}$$

S_1, S_2, S_3, S_4 now standing for the value of the four streams.

One last observation by way of explanation to a rigorous critic. The average income of an individual Indian, worked out on this basis, gives the appalling total of £1 2s. 4d. per annum, or, allowance being made for the well-to-do people, of 13s. per head for two hundred and thirty millions of British Indians. This will suffice to give him food, at 50 lbs. of grain to the rupee (which is *sometimes*, but not often, the rate nowadays) for less than eight months in the year, leaving nothing for clothing and other purposes. But, as has been stated, the larger proportion of the food consumed is obtained without the intervention of a middleman, save the ubiquitous moneylender, and *he* has become ubiquitous and can fix what price he likes: fortunately, it is to his interest to keep his debtor alive. The food of some cultivators may, therefore, in such circumstances, come to them at a cheaper rate than the market price would indicate. But the difference thus allowed for could not amount to more than one or two months' supply of food, and if such a cultivator and his family should have enough to eat the year through it can only be at the price of his becoming more and more deeply the bond-slave of the moneylender. The point is merely mentioned to show to a possible objector that it has not been overlooked.

ADMISSION BY THE RT. HON. LORD GEORGE HAMILTON, M.P., SECRETARY OF STATE FOR INDIA, IN THE HOUSE OF COMMONS, AUGUST 16, 1901:

'I admit at once that if it could be shown that India has retrograded in material prosperity under our rule we stand self-condemned, and we ought no longer to be trusted with the control of that country.'

[An analysis shows that during his period of service at the India Office the present Secretary of State for India has drawn as salary a sum which represents one year's average income of ninety-thousand Indian people !]

The DIMINISHING INCOME of The Indian People

NON-OFFICIAL ESTIMATED INCOME IN **1850**:

2D. per head per day.

OFFICIALLY ESTIMATED INCOME IN **1882**:

1½D. per head per day.

ANALYTICAL EXAMINATION OF ALL SOURCES OF INCOME IN **1900**, LESS THAN

¾D. per head per day.

CHAPTER XII

THE PRESENT ECONOMIC CONDITION OF INDIA: THE REAL INCOME OF THE PEOPLE

The Diminishing Income—A Typographical Sketch.

Presidencies and Provinces to be Separately Considered as to Agricultural and Non-Agricultural Income.

First: a Non-Agricultural Estimate for India as a Whole.

Government Greatly to be Condemned for Leaving such a Task to Outsiders.

Decreased Income in 1899 (Treated as 'a Good Year') Compared with 1881–2, nearly £60,000,000.

Statement and Analysis of the Whole Non-Agricultural Income of India—Seventy-two Items and a Total of £85,000,000.

Presidency and Provincial Estimates:

BENGAL:

Diagram Showing Average Income—Guessed and Ascertained.

Area under Cultivation during Five Years.

Land Revenue in 1898–1899, £15,000,000 Less than in 1882.

Government Estimates of Rice-Yield Averages: 126 lbs. Per Acre Too High; of Wheat 208 lbs. Per Acre Too High.

Statement and Analysis of Non-Agricultural Income.

Total Income £1 0s. 3d. Per Head Per Annum.

Mr. Grierson on the District of Gaya: the *Pioneer's* Review and Conclusion that 'Nearly One Hundred Millions in British India are Living in Extreme Poverty.'

THE MADRAS PRESIDENCY:

Diagram Showing Average Income—Guessed and Ascertained.

Casual Character of '82 Estimate: the Contradiction between Board of Revenue Statements and the Baring-Barbour Figures.

Government Collection 15, 20, and 31 per Cent. of Gross

Produce respectively; Famine Commission State per Cent. Only All Round.

Proportions of Wet and Dry Cultivation with Statement as to Yield.

Estimate of Famine Commission of 1880 Too High by £12,189,868.

'Choppings and Changings' in Money Nomenclature (first £, then Rs., then Rx., and finally £ Sterling again) render Statements for Different Years Difficult of Calculation.

Statement and Analysis of Non-Agricultural Income.

Average Income: 18s. 10d. Per Head Per Annum.

First-Hand Facts Proving General Accuracy of Foregoing Estimate.

'If We Can Eat Food Once in Two Days, We Will Not Ask For More.'

THE BOMBAY PRESIDENCY:

Diagram Showing Average Income—Guessed and Ascertained.

Wide Difference between Condition of People prior to 1876 and in 1882.

A Poona Middling Maratha's Requirements Day by Day: Requires £2 7s. 1d. per annum; if Agriculturist has only £1 6s. 2d.

Sir James Peile on Out-turn and (Indirect) Testimony to Greater Prosperity in Feudatory States.

Lord Curzon's Yield Estimate—740 lbs. Per Acre; Actual (Wheat), 588 lbs.

Mr. Wingate's Examples of Juwar:

1873–4 .... 408½ lbs.

1875–6 .... 842¼ lbs.

The Over-Estimation of Wheat-Yield in Sind 331 lbs. Per Acre.

Indebtedness of Ryots in Four Deccan Districts—Annually New Debts are Incurred to 93 per Cent. of Land Revenue: the Moneylender Provides the Revenue

Land Revenue Bill of 1901: Non-Official Members' Emphatic Protest.

Minus Difference between Value of Yield in 1882 and 1898–99: £9,788,652.

Nevertheless the Viceroy in Council Declares an Increase of £3,602,655 Per Annum over 1882!

Statement and Analysis of Non-Agricultural Income; Latter Comparatively Large; owing to Manufactories at Bombay and Ahmedabad.

Average Income: £1 18s. 8d. per Head per Annum.

THE NORTH-WESTERN PROVINCES AND OUDH:

Diagram Showing Average Income—Guessed and Ascertained.

The Legend as to the Great Prosperity and Easy Land Revenue of these Provinces.

Individual Rack-Renting Higher Here than in Any Other Part of India.

Another Over-Estimate of Out-turn: 104 lbs. per Acre Excess.

Difficulty in Ascertaining Proportion Revenue bears to Yield.

Even Here, where there is Much Irrigation, Figures for Out-turn £8,585,770 Below the Guess of 1882.

Statement and Analysis of Non-Agricultural Income.

Agricultural Reduction since 1882—7s. 6d. Per Head Per Annum.

Average Income: £1 8s. 8½d. per Head per Annum, 16s. 3¾d. Lower than Viceroy's Estimate of March, 1901.

THE PANJAB:

Diagram Showing Average Income—Guessed and Ascertained.

Fifty per Cent. Cultivated Areas under Irrigation, Nevertheless Famine is Frequent.

What Over-Assessment and Rigidity of Our System Have Done to Reduce the People to Destitution.

A Significant Blue Book Entry:

'Property.'

'Rs.200 in Debt. No Grain or Property.'

Illustrative Incidents—All Painful.

Share of Gross Produce Claimed by Government.

Jullundur Wit—According to 'The Little Friend of All the World' and Mr. Rudyard Kipling.

Yet One More Over-Estimate of Yield—This Time 100 lbs. per Acre.

Statement and Analysis of Non-Agricultural Income

Lord Curzon's Additional 2s. 8d. per Head, Agriculturally, Represented by a Fifty per Cent. Reduction on Old Alleged Income.

Average Income per Head per Annum: 17s., as Against the Viceregal Estimate of £2.

THE CENTRAL PROVINCES:

Diagram Showing Average Income—Guessed and Ascertained.

The Most Prosperous of the Provinces Nineteen Years Ago Collapsed under Stress of Scarcity.

Terrible Suffering and Unmerited Poverty the Consequence of Exaggerated Estimate in 1882.

In Face of the Foregoing, What is England's Duty?
The Destruction of the Propertied Class and the Nearly-Complete Realisation of the Bentinck-Thackeray Ideal of Ninety Years Ago.
The Lamentation of a Bengali Publicist.
Professional and Mercantile Classes in Utter Despair as to the Future.
The Great and Touching Faith of the Indian People as to Coming Political and Material Redemption through Britain.

God Save India!

Appendices:

I. The Incidence of Land Revenue in Bombay, by the Hon. Goculdas K. Parekh, M.L.C.
II. The Inquisition Inseparable from the Ryotwar System.
III. The Prosperity of India in Olden Days.
IV. 'The Slow, Systematic, Starvation of India.'

HAVING seen what the condition of the people of India was six years subsequent to the first estimate of the average income, and, being thoroughly assured, after the two recent disastrous famines, each with a money loss to the people of India of at least £120,000,000, or, together, nearly a whole year's income from every part of India, that it cannot now be better, it may be as well to take the Presidencies and Provinces separately, note what is the agricultural and what the non-agricultural income, setting forth the grounds on which the respective statements are based.

But, before doing this, it is necessary to indicate in detail what appears to be the present non-agricultural income for the whole of India. Since 1882, when it was put at Rs.9 per head of the whole population, 15,000 miles of new railways have been opened for traffic, 16,000,000 additional acres have been brought under cultivation, while upon irrigation has been expended the capital sum of £9,659,172. Thousands of miles of new roads have been made. Industries of all kinds have sprung into existence, not, it is true, counting for very much when the extent of India is considered, but additions—for what they are worth. Yet, a most generous calculation in respect to every conceivable item that can be called non-agricultural, shows that, even in 1900, the proportion of annual income which was estimated eighteen years previously, does not exist. The present writer, after diligent study and untiring examination, collation, and analysis, of the figures, cannot find that income. The authorities may have been right in 1882 in the estimate they then made, but they afford no means whereby their statement could be tested. For so humble a student of Indian affairs as is the writer of these lines it may seem to savour of presumption that he should endeavour to set forth so stupendous a matter as is involved in testing the agricultural income of the whole of India, and to trace out and set forth the non-agricultural production of a whole continent of diverse countries. Somebody, however, must begin. If the Governmental authorities in India and in England (especially in England) resolutely refrain from doing that which they could, if they would, do thoroughly, seeing the supreme necessity for its being done, the humblest student and critic is justified in attempting the task, and in presenting what he has discerned to those who are interested. This is my apology for undertaking what others, with ample resources, sufficient time, and receiving large salaries, refrain from doing.

That first step which, the French say, is the step that costs, that first lesson which, as the Germans put it, is so hard to learn, but there would be no following learning were it not mastered—that step has to be taken, that lesson has to be learned, by some one. I do not profess to have arrived at absolute accuracy in my statements, but, at least, I have taken extreme pains to be correct. At the worst, my effort to ascertain the real condition of India may be the means of causing others to fully investigate the facts and so achieve the success at which I aim. The facts I have collected would seem to indicate that an over-estimation to the extent of more than one-third, compared with results of 1882, and, probably, of one-half compared with the facts of that day, marked the 'guess' of the statesmen of 1882. The 'guess' for that year was :—

Non - Agricultural Income of India : Rs.175,00,00,000 = at Rs.12 to the £	£145,833,333
Investigation for the year 1899 shows Rs.136,00,00,000 = at Rs.15 to the £	85,000,000
Decrease 1899 compared with 1882	£60,833,333

Avoiding the unsatisfactory practice of the Finance Minister and his Secretary in 1882, who have furnished no details of their calculation, and whose successors persistently refuse to furnish them, the items which make £84,751,905 will be given. They are as follows :—

No.	Source of Income.	Value in £ Sterling.
1.	Opium	3,166,887
2.	Salt	6,066,661
3.	Country-made Liquor, say	20,000,000
4.	Fisheries (300,000 fishermen together obtain and sell fish to the value of) ...	1,930,140
5.	Clothing: Allow 2s. 4d. per head per annum to the 231,000,000 inhabitants, the total requirements would be of the value of £28,950,000. Of this amount English looms supply £15,432,082 worth, Cotton mills in India (173) £9,469,490 worth (of which £1,636,294 worth are exported), leaving for village looms in all the 450,000 villages and the two or three hundred populous towns, £3,784,722; or, say, £8 worth for each village,[1] carry	

[1] 'Weaving is practised on a small scale by men and women in their own homes or in small workshops.'—'Fin. and Com. Stat. of Brit. India.' As there cannot be less than forty millions of homes throughout British India, the aggregate of home production must be very considerable.

No.	Source of Income.	Value in £ Sterling.
	out the proceeds of Indian mills and village looms	13,517,918
6.	Forests (total receipts)	1,239,932
	Manufactures, etc.	
7.	Jute and Hemp Goods (less Raw Material, included in Agricultural Income) ...	1,937,841
8.	Iron and Brass Foundries	585,079
9.	Paper Mills (8)	416,060
10.	Breweries (28)	371,354
11.	Oil Mills	946,159
12.	Living Animals	117,230
13.	Cement Works	13,600
14.	Chemical Works	33,722
15.	Coir, and Manufactures of	225,317
16.	Cutch Factories	1,946
17.	Dairy Farms	16,951
18.	Dye Works...	47,329
19.	Drugs and Medicines	95,374
20.	Flour Mills...	1,424,917
21.	Gas Works...	122,184
22.	Glass Factories	3,864
23.	Gums and Resins	80,492
24.	Hemp Presses	2,480
25.	Hides and Skins	4,967,089
26.	Horns	107,530
27.	Ice Factories	52,313
28.	Ivory, and Manufactures of	42,362
29.	Jewelry and Precious Stones	88,151
30.	Lac (of all sorts). The Lac Factories account for £330,484 only; I carry forward the Export statement ...	580,930
31.	Manures, chiefly Animal Bones. (Again a minus discrepancy in the details: £71,298). Export statement ...	272,268
32.	Mineral and Aerated Waters	69,956

No.	Source of Income.	Value in £ Sterling.
33.	Potteries (not including village pottery work)	43,167
34.	Potteries, Village: earthen chatties and cheap goods for all uses	375,000
35.	Rope Works	178,295
36.	Printing Presses (this is wholly an estimate of my own: Government records show a blank)	750,000
37.	Saltpetre (the export value is given, but the details, Presidency and Province, amount to only £107,350)	232,896
38.	Silk, Raw	317,872
39.	,, Manufactures of	116,602
40.	Soap Factories	34,126
41.	Sugar ,, ...	290,999
42.	Tanneries	420,424
43.	Tile Factories	63,035
44.	Tobacco Farms and Factories	88,560
45.	Wool, Raw...	1,150,898
46.	,, Manufactured	170,530
47.	,, ,, (not produced in classed mills)	18,307
48.	Wood, and Manufactures of	1,090,048
49.	Miscellaneous: Carpets, Benares ware, Silver ware, etc.	88,560
	Mineral Products.	
50.	Coal...	1,034,398
51.	Iron Ore [1]	12,507

[1] The production of iron is yet quite in its infancy, the ore being worked for the most part only in the Raniganj district of Bengal, where it occurs in close proximity to the coal fields. According to the figures, which, however, are of doubtful accuracy, the production for all India in 1898 amounted to only 50,000 tons, of which nearly 42,000 tons were produced in Raniganj. Whether or not it will be possible hereafter to utilise the iron deposits of other parts of India—in the Central Provinces, Madras, and elsewhere—is a question which cannot yet be answered. ('F. and C. Stat. of British India, p. lx.) While these pages are passing through the press the Directors of the Bengal and Nagpore Railway are said to be arranging to develop large fields of manganese ore in Chota Nagpore.

No.	Source of Income.	Value in £ Sterling.
52.	Gold. (It may be explained that, practically, all the gold mined in India comes from the State of Mysore)[1]	10,993
53.	Alum	4,200
54.	Gypsum	450
55.	Manganese Ore	32,240
56.	Mica	15,004
57.	Soaps, fine	533
58.	Tin Ore	2,553
59.	Clay—for building material	55,157
60.	Granite „ „	60,000
61.	Gravel and Rubble	3,835
62.	Laterite[2]	766,991
63.	Limestone	141,479
64.	Sandstone	108,838
65.	Slate	4,029
66.	Petroleum Oil	80,000

Other Objects.

No.	Source of Income.	Value in £ Sterling.
67.	Ploughs: Not many new ploughs are made in each year, possibly under 100,000; in a portion of the Deccan it is stated that no new plough has been made since the disastrous year of 1877	66,666
68.	Carts: Making new ones and repairing old	189,500

[1] No account is taken of the gold produced in parts of Northern India from the washings of river sands because there are no means of stating the quantity statistically, but it is well known that it is entirely insignificant. Until the beginning of 1900 the gold produced in the mines was shipped from Bombay to London, there to be refined and coined; but, since then, most of the mining companies have been sending the gold to the Bombay Mint.—'F. and C. Stat. of British India,' p. lx.

[2] This may be over-estimated. No value is placed in the Records against the 5,495,047 tons produced in Madras. I have put the value of this at about 2s. 8d. (Rs.2) per ton.

No.	Source of Income.	Value in £ Sterling.
69.	Boats on Rivers and at Ports: New Boats and Repairs	1,000,000
70.	Indian Ships: Total tonnage, 66,728; some are wrecked, others are withdrawn, every year fewer—a great industry at Calcutta and Bombay has been allowed to die; say, for repairs, etc.[1]	100,000

Cattle.

71. Following the precedent of the Baring-Barbour inquiry I include existing cattle produce in the Agricultural production, with a set-off. That is to say, like the two gentlemen named, in my calculation, too, profit for milk, ghi, etc., balances deductions which might be made on account of cultivation. All increase of cattle is counted as an addition to income in the year when the increase occurred. The period taken is prior to the last great famine and, in so far as the terrible loss of cattle is concerned, my calculation is defective, if taken as representative of the present condition of things. That condition is very much worse than these figures indicate.

Increase of Cattle in 1898–99 *compared with* 1897–98.

	Number.
Bulls and Bullocks ...	1,579,915
Cows	758,560
Buffaloes	931,429

[1] See *ante*, page 88, where particulars will be found of shipbuilding in Calcutta and Bombay one hundred years ago.

36

No.	Source of Income.		Value in £ Sterling.
		Number.	
	Young Stock	5,433,486 [1]	
	Sheep	1,229,377	
	Goats	3,269,014 [1]	
	Horses and Ponies ...	195,730	
	Mules and Donkeys ...	96,518	
	Camels	61,196 [1]	
	Total ...	13,555,225	
	If a value of Rs.10 be put upon these animals all round, the calf one day old with the mature beast, it will represent a fair average. Take Rs.135,452,250 at Rs.15 to the £		9,030,150
72.	Sundries, for sources of income which may have escaped consideration, say about fifteen per cent....		13,601,399
	Total		£84,751,905

In the sundries is included £300,000, approximately the contribution of Catholic and Protestant Missionary Societies towards the support of Mission Agents throughout India, and expended in India.

Thus the total for the whole of India. I will now deal in like manner, but in more detail, with each of the Presidencies, Provinces, and Chief Commissionerships of the whole Empire.

[1] There is something surprising in the figures from which these details are taken. For four years the young stock stood at 17,000,000 odd; in the last year of the series there is a jump of five and a half millions! Again, with the goats; after being in the 15,000,000 rank for four years there is, all at once, an addition of 3,269,014; yet, again, camels show a like susceptibility to mysterious influences—the mystery of which, perhaps, has to do with inaccurate statistics rather than with natural causes.

BENGAL.

In 1882 the total agricultural income of this Province was estimated at Rs.103,50,00,000 or (Rs.12 to the £) £86,250,000. Other parts of India will enable comparisons to be made as to area under cultivation, if not in 1882 at least within three or four years of that date. Bengal statistics, however, are not available until 1890–91. Considering the settled condition of the Lower Provinces, it is not likely there has been much increase of cultivation during the past eighteen years. The figures for the past five years show slight variations only :—

YEARS.	NET AREA CROPPED. ACRES.
1894–95	54,716,300
1895–96	53,441,200
1896–97	51,823,200
1897–98	55,128,700
1898–99	55,398,000

The changes in this period are few and the total, probably, has not varied one-tenth, or even one-twentieth, since 1882. However, the only course to be taken in this instance—in the absence of statistics for comparison—is to ascertain what was the land revenue in Bengal for the last year in the series. Knowing the proportion which the actual amount paid to the Government of Bengal under the Permanent Settlement bears to the total produce, it should not be difficult to arrive at a figure which not only is likely to be near the truth, but which may be generally accepted. A consensus of opinion, founded on close investigation, gives between five and six per cent. of gross produce as represented by that payment. Take the lower amount, as tending to show a higher yield, this result follows :—

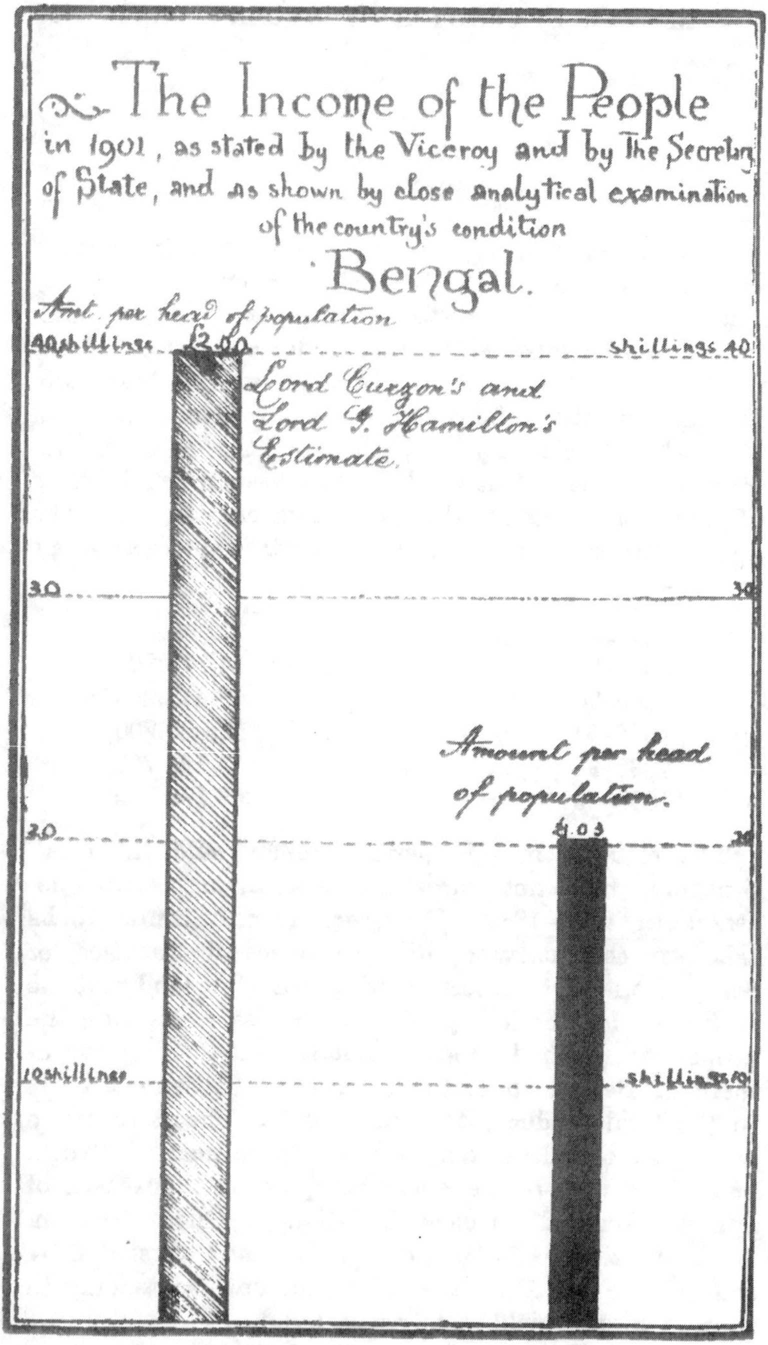

The Income of the People
in 1901, as stated by the Viceroy and by The Secretary of State, and as shown by close analytical examination of the country's condition
Bengal.
Amt. per head of population
40 shillings
£2.0.0
shillings 40
Lord Curzon's and Lord G. Hamilton's Estimate
30
30
Amount per head of population.
20
20
10 shillings
shillings 10

Land Revenue collected in 1898–99: £2,696,524 × 20 = £53,930,480, gross produce.

This is £15,069,520 less than the estimate of 1882. In the absence of details justifying the larger figures I must ask credence and acceptance for my own; or, failing their acceptance, that satisfactory reasons may be given why my statement should not be accepted.

It is altogether impossible, in any calculation as to crop-yields and crop-values, to accept the figures of the Bengal Government. When the Famine Commission of 1897 wanted a statement from Bengal showing the probable annual yield of food grains so that it might see what surplus would be available after the people had been fed, the Bengal authorities put their food crop area at 50,596,000 acres and the out-turn of food at 24,407,000 tons, or nearly half a ton per acre,—actually, 1,072 lbs. How does this compare with the facts? About four-fifths of the area is under rice. These are the yield statistics for nine years as published by Government; although they are termed 'estimates' there are many reasons for considering that they are fairly accurate statements of fact:—

YEAR.	YIELD IN LBS. PER ACRE.	ACREAGE.
1891–92	813	39,552,008
1892–93	1,011	37,324,907
1893–94	1,100	37,856,500
1894–95	1,191	38,639,500
1895–96	880	37,447,600
1896–97	587	36,177,400
1897–98	1,115	39,549,500
1898–99	1,111	39,605,400
1899–1900	1,069	39,069,700

The average is 986 lbs., or 126 lbs. per acre below the estimate made by the Government of the Lower Provinces. On 40,000,000 acres this means 2,751,800 tons, or two lbs. of rice per day for eight millions five hundred thousand full-grown men for one year. With such care are Indian statistics officially put forward!

Again, take wheat. In 1898–99 there were 1,600,000 acres under cultivation with this cereal in Bengal. The selected averages are for 1892, and range as follows:—

	Lbs.		Lbs.
Nadia	861	Darbhanga	984
Murshidabad ...	861	Muzaffarpur	984
Dinajpur	861	Saran	984
Rajshahi	861	Champarun	984
Pabna	861	Monghyr	984
Patna: Irrigated ...	895	Bhagalpur	984
,, Unirrigated...	984[1]	Purnea	984
Gaya: Irrigated ...	895	Malda	984
,, Unirrigated...	994[1]	Ranchi	451
Shahabad: Irrigated	895		
,, Unirrigated...	984[1]		

No average for the whole Province is given, but, from the above figures, 950 lbs. would not be an unfair estimate. The year in which the estimate was made was, apparently, not a very good year. Famine prevailed in many parts of the Empire, Bengal included, although none of the Provinces were scheduled as famine-stricken. An analysis of statements giving 'estimated' actual yields reveals these unsatisfactory results:—

Year.	Yield in lbs. per acre.	Acreage.	Yield in tons.
1891–92	431	1,300,000	250,000
1892–93	670	1,559,000	466,000
1893–94	704	1,461,000	459,000
1894–95	1,088	1,413,000	686,300
1895–96	542	1,427,400	345,600
1896–97	646	1,341,700	386,900
1897–98	846	1,569,500	592,600
1898–99	929	1,582,500	656,400
1899–1900	823	1,555,800	572,600

[1] This is indeed a marvel; unirrigated land giving a larger yield than irrigated!

The average works out at 742 lbs. per annum, or 370 lbs. per acre less than is alleged by the Bengal Government as applicable everywhere, enough to give to 750,000 full-grown Bengalis food for one year at 2 lbs. per head per day. Why, it may be asked, did not the Famine Commission expose these fallacious statements in some such detail as is being here attempted instead of merely describing the Bengal returns as being particularly unreliable? The measure of the unreliability ought to have been stated as a guide to the student of Indian affairs. The principle on which such obvious deductions are avoided by all Indian officials, in every conceivable circumstance, is past finding out, unless one imputes a motive for such reticence. At the best it is singular.

The non-agricultural income was assumed to be fifty per cent. of the agricultural produce; so far as is known, that was purely an assumption. It amounted, in 1882, for Bengal, if the estimate then made be correct, to the large sum of £34,500,000. That amount cannot be found, even now, after much additional expenditure, mostly with borrowed money, has been employed to 'develop' the country.

I put in everything that can legitimately be claimed for the Lower Provinces, and yet cannot get anywhere near, even for 1900, the amount alleged to have been received in 1882. Until the contrary be proved, I say once more, the following must be taken to represent the non-agricultural income of Bengal:—

No.	Sources of Income.	Value in £ Sterling.
1.	Cotton Mills, with one-tenth of the spindles and a like percentage of the production, say	500,000
2.	One-fourth of the total village production of cloths, say	1,200,000
3.	Jute and Hemp Mills	1,937,841
4.	One-fourth of the Liquor Production ...	5,000,000
5.	Paper Mills	416,000

No.	Source of Income.	Value in £ Sterling.
6.	Breweries	6,000
7.	General Factories (one-fourth), say ...	6,000,000
8.	Coal Mines	700,000
9.	Saltpetre	92,869
10.	Iron Ore	7,000
11.	Various Minerals	41,626
12.	Boat Building and Ship Repairing (half)	500,000
13.	Forests	64,841
14.	Potteries	75,000
15.	Cattle Increase: one-fourth	2,250,000
16.	Opium (one-third)...	1,000,000
17.	Ploughs and Carts	60,000
18.	Printing Presses and other concerns in proportion	200,000
19.	One-fourth for Sundries (including fisheries)	1,650,000
	Total	£21,685,177

The busy shores of the Hughli, the mercantile houses in the streets of Calcutta, the great importance of the capital city of the Empire, the thronging millions on all the broad alluvial plains from Mirzapore to Chittagong, from Orissa to the borders of Assam and the fever-ridden Terai, might have been expected to show better returns than these. If there be omission on my part, of material sources of income, it is because I do not know, after most diligent search, where to find them; certainly the Government records contain no others than those I have set out, and by no means all of them. Many I have had to 'work out' for myself. Taken together the gross annual income of the Province would seem to work out thus:—

Agricultural Income ...	...	£53,930,480
Non-Agricultural Income	...	21,701,177
		£75,631,657

The whole amount, divided among 74,713,020 of population, yields :—

Twenty Shillings and Three Pence per head per annum (£1 0s. 3d. ; or Rs.15 3a.).

And this Lieutenant-Governorship is generally described as the richest Province in the Empire !

There is much evidence to support the view as to the condition of the Bengali people which such a deduction as this pre-supposes. I had hoped to cite the facts narrated in 1893 by Mr. G. A. Grierson, C.I.E., of the Indian Civil Service, in his 'Notes on the District of Gaya.' My inquiries, however, both in England and in India, have failed to obtain for me a copy of the work. I, therefore, take a review of the book (which is also a synopsis of its contents) from the *Pioneer* newspaper of May, 1893. The information seen through the medium which this paper provides, acquires additional value as evidence. In the course of the review it is stated :—

Mr. Grierson's 'Notes on the District of Gaya' is an admirably faithful and complete picture, not only of the physical features, but of the economic and social conditions of the district. In this latter respect the little volume is a wonderfully complete exhibition of the real India—not the India as it appears to the casual visitor in his swallow-flights across the continent, but the India of the millions. The picture has its bright side and its dark. There is little evidence of the strife and antagonism of class against class, which in these days unhappily bulk so largely in the life of the Western world. The divisions of society are clearly cut ; but as the position of everybody is plainly defined in the social scale, so also are his duties. No doubt there are ways in which the individual endeavours at times to get more than communal custom allots him. The reaper will try to make the sheaf in which he takes his payment at harvest-time bigger than the rest: or the goldsmith may not put all the silver or gold he ought into the ornament. But, on the whole, the conflict of interests is not obtrusive, and the broad impression, personal feuds apart, left by the economic microcosm, is one of harmony.

But there are features in the district life upon which it is less pleasant to dwell. In Gaya one-half the population live by cultivation of the soil; but Mr. Grierson tells us that one of the most remarkable facts about cultivation in the district is that it does not, as a rule, pay for its expenses. It is found that when the holding s less than 12½ acres in extent, even in the most fertile portion of the district, it will not suffice for the support of an average family, which, in the case of a ryot, usually runs to six persons. In that case the ryot and his family must either eat less than two full meals a day, or have supplemental sources of income, and perhaps even then he may not have enough food or clothing. Mr. Grierson proves this by a careful examination of the income derivable from holdings of various sizes; but he also instituted an interesting experimental test in the case of four villages, with a population of 163 families and 1,210 cultivators. A native gentleman, in whom the cultivators had entire confidence, was deputed to find out from each ryot his actual income and expenditure. The 1,210 ryots cultivated in all about 1,428 acres, and the net income realised was Rs.9,248. From other sources there was an income of Rs.5,810, so that the total net income of the 1,210 cultivators was Rs.15,108, or an average of Rs.12·4 a head. But to let a person live in comfort with two full meals a day and sufficient clothing you require Rs.15 a year, so that in the case of these four villages there was a deficit of Rs.2·6 a head. This, too, without reckoning expenditure on social ceremonies, which are compulsory and are never pretermitted. In the case of the four villages in question this item came to over one rupee a head, which brings the deficit up to Rs.3·4 (4s. 4d.) a head.

Coming to the labourers of the district, who form about one-fourth of the population, the poverty is still more general. There are two classes of labourers, the free labourer or *mazdur*, and the serf or *kamiya*. It sounds strange to speak of subjects of the British Crown as serfs: but though the *kamiya* has been prohibited by law from selling himself and his heirs for ever, as he once did, he achieves virtually the same result by 'hiring himself, in consideration of a stated advance or loan, to serve for a hundred years or until the money is repaid, which comes to very much the same thing.' The *mazdur* is a free labourer: but one year with another he gets much the same income as the *kamiya*. He has higher wages, and of course greater independence, but his work is less regular. The *kamiya*, too, has the first right of gleaning, and often receives presents, such as money for drinking toddy and gifts of old clothes. Supposing that a labourer and his wife are fully employed, Mr. Grierson calculates that their total annual income comes to about Rs.41·12 per annum; but as the family usually consists of four persons, this gives Rs.4·9 short of the Rs.15 which is necessary for a comfortable existence. 'Part of this,' writes Mr. Grierson, 'may be made up by odds and ends, supplemental sources of income, such as cutting fuel in the *jangal* and the like, but the greater part must be met by insufficient clothing or food. This calculation is borne out by practical experience. It is universally stated that a labourer has frequently to content himself with one meal a day in order to avoid curtailment of the food of the children, and that even when two meals are taken they are rarely of the full amount.' Lastly, there is the artisan class who, like the labourers, form about a fourth of the total population. For the most part the various handicrafts are flourishing: but there are two exceptions. In these latter days the mills of Manchester and Bombay have run the weaver (*jolaha*) so hard that he is disappearing from the district. 'If,' says Mr. Grierson, 'all the members of the *jolaha* caste had to depend on the produce of their looms, they would have died out long ago.' Most of them now earn their living by agriculture, and a good many also by service and trade. Along with the weaver the dyer also (*rangrez*) is suffering from the competition of the West. 'Cheap European dyes can be bought for a pice in the bazaar, and people dye their own clothes. The profession of dyer is fast disappearing, and with it the beautiful old permanent Indian dyes.' Thus even of the artisan class, who are naturally the best to do, two entire groups are becoming merged in the labourers, of whom there are already too many in the district, and who, as we have seen, all live on the wrong side of the margin of comfortable subsistence.

If we sum up the facts Mr. Grierson thus puts before us regarding the various sections of the district population, the conclusion we arrive at is certainly not encouraging. Briefly, it is that all the persons of the labouring classes, and ten per cent. of the cultivating and artisan classes, or forty-five per cent. of the total population, are insufficiently clothed, or insufficiently fed, or both. In Gaya district this would give about a million persons without sufficient means of support. If we assume that the circumstances of Gaya are not exceptional—and there is no reason for thinking otherwise—it follows that nearly one hundred millions of people in British India are living in extreme poverty. No doubt extreme poverty means something far less repulsive and appalling in the East than in the West. Mr. Grierson is careful to point out that his inquiries do not warrant the suggestion, that 'this large number of human beings (he is speaking of course only of Gaya) is, as a rule, in actual want of food, or has never more than one meal a day. In the majority of cases two meals a day form the rule, but they have often to curtail the number of their meals for a few days at a time, to enable them to tide over difficulties.' Equally unwarrantable is it to suppose, though doubtless Mr. Naoroji will turn Mr. Grierson to his own uses, that British rule is in any way responsible for the poverty of so large a proportion of the Indian people. Less is taken from each individual, and they have vastly more to distribute in the aggregate than they ever had under Hindu Raja or Muhammadan Emperor.[1] If the excess is swallowed up by the increase in numbers, that is no sin of the Government. Nevertheless the fact of the poverty is there, and a most unpleasant fact it is. The remedy is less obvious: is indeed remote to the point of obscurity. It is no doubt a beautiful trait of native life, that the meals which the elders of the family deny themselves, go to the children. As one of Mr. Grierson's informants puts it, 'The children always get their two meals: we cannot see them die.' Nevertheless, to reduce the problem to the simplest terms, it were better if the children were less numerous. The difficulty is much as Bill, the crossing sweeper, stated it to an enterprising interviewer bent on discovering the causes of the squalor in the East End of London: 'There's too many on us, and that's the fact.'

[1] The remarks in this and the preceding sentence are highly provocative, but, in view of the facts recorded in these pages, the reader will not find it difficult to make allowance for such 'special pleading,' the statements in which have not the merit even of being true.

THE MADRAS PRESIDENCY.

If an example were wanted of the casual character of the estimate of 1882 and a justification were admissible for the hesitation exhibited to make the whole Note public, they might be found in the haphazard character of the particulars supplied to the Famine Commission of 1878–80 for Madras in regard to the agricultural income of that Presidency. The line in the Note of 1882 by Earl Cromer and Sir David Barbour concerning Madras reads thus :—

	Produce.	Payment.	Per Cent.
Madras	R.50,00,00,000	Rs.7,64,46,000	15·3

The Famine Commissioners of 1878–80 presented (para. 156, Report : Part I.) an approximate and rough estimate in which they put the yield of food-grains from 26,000,000 acres in Madras at 8,500,000 tons, valued at £5 per ton, and amounting to £42,500,000; the 2,500,000 acres under non-food crops were apparently valued at £3 per acre, or £7,500,000—together the Rs.50,00,00,000 in the Note. But six millions of acres were wrongly included; these are in Zemindary tracts, and, in the estimate of the Famine Commissioners of 1897 are (rightly) omitted. This leaves 20,000,000 acres alleged as under cultivation, whereas the actual area in 1880–81 was 15,059,000 acres, plus the districts of South Kanara and Malabar (omitted)—say, 1,800,000 acres, or 16,859,000 acres in all. The settlement in vogue was that ranging from 1860 to 1890, and was for thirty years from the respective dates of the conclusion of the inquiry in the respective districts. Elaborate tables show that

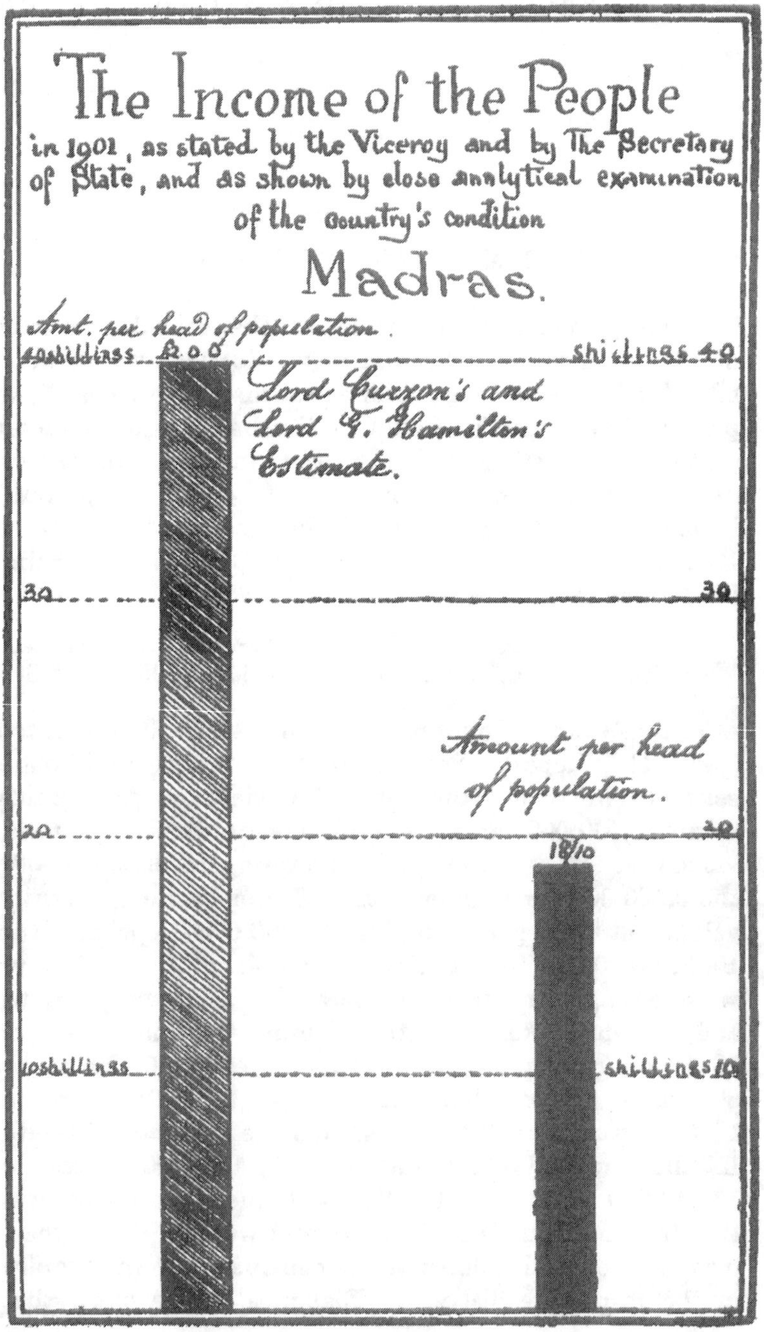

The Income of the People
in 1901, as stated by the Viceroy and by The Secretary of State, and as shown by close analytical examination of the country's condition
Madras.
Amt. per head of population.
40 shillings
£2.0.0
shillings 40
Lord Curzon's and Lord G. Hamilton's Estimate.
30
30
Amount per head of population.
20
20
18/10
10 shillings
shillings 10

the proportion taken of the net value of crops by the Government ranges from thirty-one per cent. on wet land in South Arcot to twelve per cent. on dry land in North Salem, taking the maximum in such instance. The particulars from South Arcot may be cited as a sample :—

	Value of Gross Produce.	Deduction for Season Changes.	Cultivation Exs.	Value Net Produce.	Government Revenue.	Percentage.[1]
	Rs. a. p.	Rs. a. p.	Rs. a. p.	Rs. a. p.	Rs. a. p.	
Dry	11 15 10	2 15 11	4 4 6	4 11 5	1 13 5	15
Wet	17 9 9	3 8 4	7 4 2	6 13 3	5 8 7	31

The average for the eleven districts is given thus :—

	Value of Gross Produce.	Deduction for Season Changes.	Cultivation Exs.	Value Net Produce.	Government Revenue.	Percentage.
Dry	8 2 4	1 11 6	3 3 7	3 3 3	1 3 7	15
Wet	26 5 9	4 11 1	9 13 2	11 13 6	5 5 1	20

These figures enable us to judge what the Government estimated value of the whole crops really is: The proportions are four acres of dry to one acre of wet cultivation.

Land Revenue for 1882–83	£4,506,459[2]
Add for Irrigation (one-fourth of total credited to Land Revenue from Irrigation)	35,000
Total	£4,541,459

This is divisible not into fifths, but, practically, into halves, the superior yield on one-fifth of irrigated lands bringing up its value to that of the product of the remaining four-fifths.[3]

[1] In face of these percentages Sir Henry Fowler should cease to proclaim that the Indian authorities take only a slight percentage of produce as revenue.

[2] 'Stat. Abs. Brit. India,' No. 18, p. 64.

[3] Many of the foregoing particulars are deduced from 'Replies to Chap. i. of the Circular of Questions circulated by the Famine Commission (1879) compiled in the office of the Board of Revenue, Madras.'

Dry Lands: £2,270,729 × 6⅔ =	... ...	£15,138,192
Wet Lands: £2,270,729 × 5 =	... ...	11,353,645
Total	... ...	£26,491,837

To carry the comparison further the £ sterling must be turned into rupees at the rate for the year—12 to the £1: £26,491,837 × 12 = Rs.31,79,02,044.

Estimated by the Famine Commission	Rs.50,00,00,000
Board of Revenue Actual Results ...	31,79,02,044
Over-statement ...	Rs.18,20,97,956

Or, £12,139,863.

Reference may now be made to the yield in Madras during 1898–99: the increase in irrigated area disturbs the proportions of wet and dry cultivation only slightly, as pressure on the soil by dispossessed industrials and increased population have brought more dry land under the plough. The dry-land area cultivated has increased one-third; the irrigated area has doubled; wet produce, therefore, must be reckoned as 7 and dry as 5, or in other words 7–12ths of the revenue must be multiplied by 5 (twenty per cent. for wet lands) and 5–12ths by 6⅔ (fifteen per cent. for dry land).

Gross land revenue in 1898–99: £3,358,832.

Divided, as in the previous instance:—

Dry Lands: £1,399,902 × 6⅔ =	... ...	£9,332,680
Wet Lands: £1,959,902 × 5 =	... ...	9,799,510
Totals ...	...	£19,132,190

Explanation again is necessary. From the figures it would appear as if the gross land revenue of Madras in 1898–99 were £1,200,000 less than sixteen years before. It is not. The confusion arises from the 'choppings and changings' made in the official accounts and the seeming carelessness on the part of responsible officials to make statements square with one another. In No. 18 of the Statistical Abstracts the Madras revenue is put at £4,506,459; in No. 27 the same revenue is put at Rx.4,506,459. The average rate of exchange in 1882–83, to which both these statements refer, was 1s. 7½d. per rupee. Rs.12½ = £1 sterling; consequently the sum was neither £4,506,459, as first stated, nor Rs.4,50,64,590, but £3,610,944! The pre-requisite to any thorough administrative reform in India is the reduction of all Indian figures since 1850 to one denomination, and their publication in that denomination. Otherwise comparison becomes misleading to a dangerous degree and the task of the Indian student is made almost impossible of accomplishment. It only needs that a start should be made on the right lines; this done it will be as easy to give the right figures as it now is to give the wrong.

Tested by the figures of 1882–83 the returns for 1889–90 appear to show a reduction of £252,112; the difference is accounted for by the difference in the sterling value of the rupee—as a Government coin, that is to say, as a token, not as a piece of silver representing the intrinsic value of the precious metal.

The non-agricultural income of the Presidency may be thus set forth:—

No.	Source of Income.	Value in £ Sterling.
1.	Salt	97,010
2.	Saltpetre	11,515
3.	Country-made Liquor (one-sixth) ...	3,333,333
4.	Fisheries (one-third)	600,000
5.	Clothing (village production one-sixth) ...	750,000
6.	Forests (total income)	154,234
7.	Coir, and manufactures of	225,317
8.	Hides and Skins (one-fourth)	1,975,660
9.	Cotton—piece goods (exported)	540,543
10.	„ Twist and Yarn (exported) ...	117,562
11.	„ Village production (one-sixth) ...	2,000,000
12.	Timber and Wood	107,355

No.	Source of Income.		Value in £ Sterling.
13.	Live Animals (exported)		112,374
14.	Oils		613,163
15.	Flour Mills (one-twentieth)		71,245
16.	Breweries		22,545
17.	Wool, Raw (nearly one-half)		475,000
18.	Minerals : Quarry Stones	Rs.55,000	
	Granite ...	80,000	
	Laterite ...	1,110,000	
	Limestone ...	140,000	
	Sandstone ...	90,000	
	Slate	1,750	
	Manganese ...	48,360	
	Gold	16,490	
			711,067
19.	Pottery of all kinds (one-sixth)		70,000
20.	Various Manufactories, etc.		100,000
21.	Tobacco Farms and Factories (say three-fourths of whole of India)		70,000
22.	Ploughs—repairs, etc. (one-sixth) ...		10,600
23.	Carts—new, repairs, etc. (one-sixth) ...		32,000
24.	Boats on Rivers and at Ports (one-fourth)		250,000
25.	Cattle—increase in year (over one-fourth)		2,400,000
26.	Sundries, to cover omissions		800,000
	Total		£15,650,523

The combined totals of income from both sources show :—

Agricultural Income	£19,132,190
Add Coffee (value at port of shipment) ...	1,190,448
Non-agricultural Income	15,650,523
	£35,973,161

Divide this sum, £35,973,161, by population, 38,208,000, the result is :—

Eighteen Shillings and Tenpence per head per annum; or Rs.14 2a.—Five-Eighths of One Penny per day per person.

With such an average income available, if the whole sum be equally divided between thirty-five millions of people, the awful significance of such a narrative as that which follows becomes palpable to the most indifferent reader. 'Leaving out other questions,' writes the Rev. J. Knowles,[1] a missionary of long experience in Southern India, 'cannot we save millions from starvation? Now I do not think one out of a thousand of your readers has any idea how poor the poor in India really are. Let us look first at the question of food. Do these poor people, even under ordinary circumstances, get enough to eat? Here are two extracts from letters from missionaries I know, given in this month's *Chronicle of the London Missionary Society*:—

'"I think the most trying experience I ever had," writes the Rev. J. I. Macnair, of Cuddapah (January 13), "was a three weeks' tour in September of last year, in a part of the country where our people are specially poor, and where they have had no proper crops for several years. My tent was surrounded day and night, and one sentence dinned in my ears perpetually—'We are dying for lack of food.' We do not expect that the present year (1901) will be any improvement on the last. The famine will be only local, we hope, but it will be a time of terrible hardship."

So one missionary. Now for another and older missionary, the Rev. G. H. Macfarlane, who writes:—

'"The grain which each householder is usually able to lay in store has this year been very meagre. It can serve only for a few weeks at most. After that comes the period of no work and gradual starvation. It is the tiding over this period—till June or July, when rain may

[1] Letter to the *Manchester Guardian*, March, 1901.

begin again—that is the difficulty. We cannot present harrowing tales of starvation and death as yet. But

PEOPLE ARE LIVING ON ONE MEAL EVERY TWO OR THREE DAYS;

the poorer classes in India are always prepared for this. As one of our Christians said, 'If we can eat food once in two days, we will not ask for more.'"

'In my own missionary experience I once carefully investigated the earnings of a congregation of three hundred, and found the average amounted to

LESS THAN A FARTHING A HEAD PER DAY.

They did not live; they eked out an existence. I have been in huts where the people were living on carrion. I have taken photographs of famine groups which are enough for most people; *yet in all these cases there was no recognised famine*. Further, the salt tax alone amounts to between two and a half and five per cent. of the income of a labouring-class family; and the poorer the people are the worse is their food, and the more they crave for salt. Now, for nearly all these poor people the food is only a little rice or food grain, the bulk is less nourishing food. So it comes to pass that, living as they do, and that from hand to mouth, if they fail for a few days to work they have to face starvation, and when famine really comes it is ready to claim its millions as victims unless prompt and timely help is given.'

THE BOMBAY PRESIDENCY.

In the Note of 1882 the Bombay Presidency was described as having:—

Agricultural Produce valued at	...	£33,800,000;
or (Rs.12½ to the £)	... ...	Rs.39,00,00,000.

Scarcely anything more startles the student of Indian Blue Books than the wide difference in the reports written concerning the condition of the people generally in 1876, the year before the great famine of 1877, and those written in 1881 and 1882 in obedience to Lord Dufferin's behest. In no instance is this more marked than in relation to the Bombay Presidency and the Panjab. The Bombay officials describe a state of things which would indicate that the good cotton times of ten years before the '77 famine still left the general cultivator in a position to do some justice to the soil, and, therefore, to reap good crops. One must suppose the crops described by the highest officials in the Presidency as being grown, in some considerable measure at least, were really reaped. If they were, then the decadence in the districts of this Presidency has, during the past thirty years, proceeded at a most terrific rate. The officials of that day, with food prices—

Rice	16 lbs. per rupee	Bajra	36 lbs. per rupee[1]
Jowari	32 " " "	Nachni	32 " " "

state that a Poona middling Maratha cultivator would require, and presumably would, in the way of daily food, have:—

[1] 'Condition of the Country and People of India,' Parliamentary Paper, p. 306. 'Articles required each month to make up the ordinary meals of a field cultivator and labourer in the Deccan and of a Kunbi in the Konkan.'

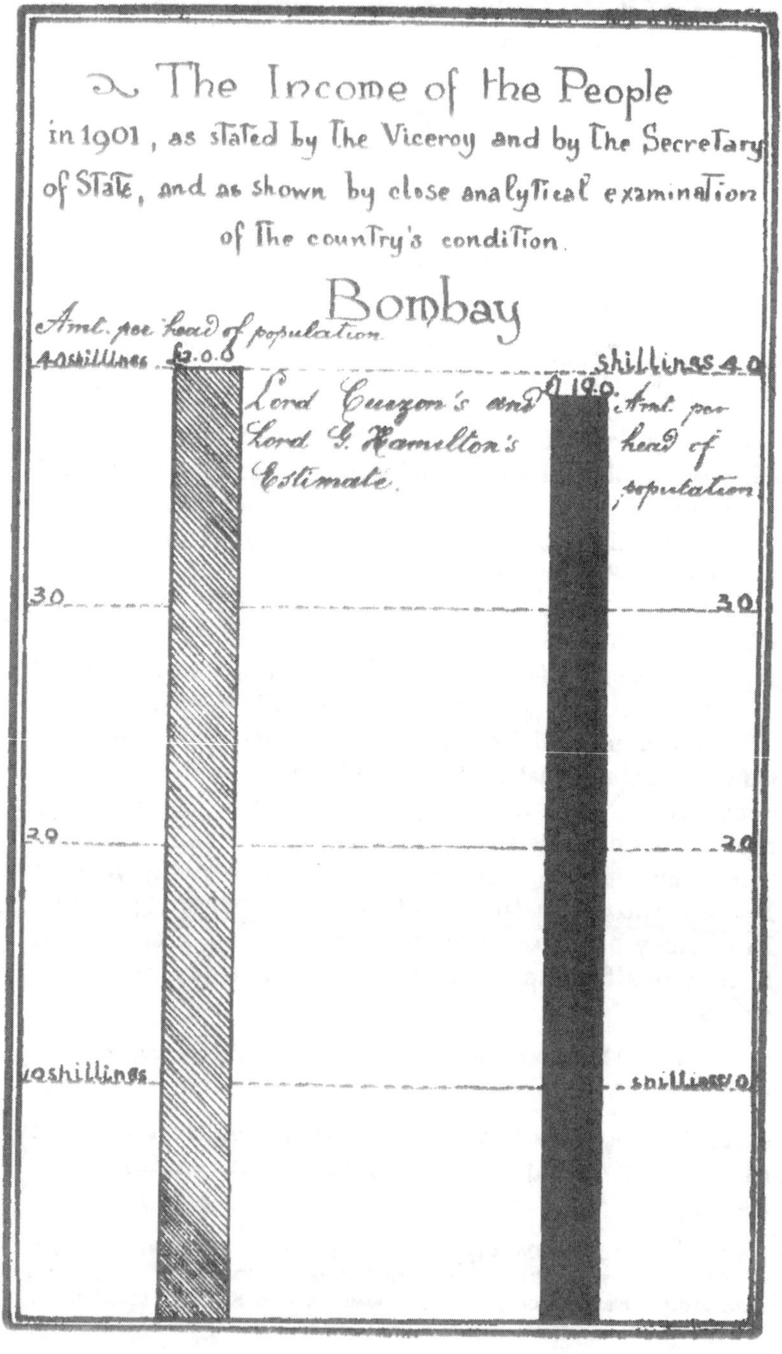
The Income of the People
in 1901, as stated by the Viceroy and by the Secretary of State, and as shown by close analytical examination of the country's condition.
Bombay
Amt. per head of population
40 shillings
£2.0.0
shillings 40
Lord Curzon's and Lord G. Hamilton's Estimate.
0.19.0
Amt. per head of population
30
30
20
20
10 shillings
shillings 10

No.	Name of Articles.	Grown up and Working Male and Female.		Boy of Ten Years.	
		Weight.	Value.	Weight.	Value.
			a. p.		a. p.
1.	Rice, second sort ...	½ lb.	0 6	1 lb.	0 6
2.	Jowari	1½ lb.	0 9		
3.	Bajri	—	—	—	—
4.	Wheat	—	—	—	—
5.	Grain	—	—	—	—
6.	Ragi or Nachni ...	—	—	—	—
7.	Ghi	—	—	—	—
8.	Oil	180 gr.	0 1	90 gr.	0 0½
9.	Salt	400 gr.	0 1	180 gr.	0 0½
10.	Vegetables or Pulse	about 4 ozs.	0 8	—	0 1
11.	Milk	—	—	—	—
12.	Kokamb				
13.	Cocoanut Kernel ...				
14.	Chilly Powder ...				
15.	Turmeric				
16.	Coriander				
17.	Jira	1⅔ ozs.	0 4	—	0 2
18.	Assafoetida ...				
19.	Onions				
20.	Garlic				
21.	Salt Fish				
22.	Jagri	—	—	—	—
23.	Fuel	8 lbs.	0 8	—	—

Total per day	2 3	0 1 0
Days per month	30	30
	Rs.4 3 6	Rs.1 9 0

That is to say, to sustain life, with some variety in food, and without reckoning clothes and other necessaries, there is needed for a family of four :—

	Rs.	a.	p.	£	s.	d.
Father	50	10	0	3	17	6
Mother	50	10	0	3	17	6
Boy of ten years	18	12	0	1	5	0
Young child	6	4	0		8	4
Total ...	Rs.126	4	0	£9	8	4

or, say, Rs.31½ (£2 7s. 1d.) each. It will be seen later what the agricultural produce to-day in Bombay provides. Suffice it to say here that it provides nothing like Rs.31½ (£2 7s. 1d.) per head, nay, nor half that sum. Lord Curzon says the Bombay cultivator should be Rs.2 (2s. 8d.) per head better off in 1901 than he was in 1882, that is, his income should be Rs.33½ (£2 9s. 9d.), always assuming he could live as well now as it is described above he lived then.

For a Poona kunbi similar tables are given, as also for a kunbi of Kolhapur and for a kunbi of Ratnagiri. The totals in each case (same number of members of family) are :—

	Rs.	a.	p.		£	s.	d.
Poona: Kunbi ...	108	4	0	or	5	17	6
Kunbi of Kolhapur ...	108	4	0	,,	5	17	6
Kunbi of Ratnagiri ...	131	18	0	,,	6	12	1

The official responsible for the tables whence the above facts are gathered is Sir James Braithwaite Peile, K.C.S.I., now a member of the Council of India. In the course of the paper accompanying the tables Sir James Peile says: 'The incidence of the Government assessment on land has been ascertained by careful experiments to be less than one-sixth of the gross return on very ordinary cultivation. The new cash rents of the Bhaunagar State are about one-third of the gross produce, in some districts more, and yet the State is very flourishing. The zemindars of Ahmedabad, after a few deductions, divide the entire gross produce with the tenants in equal shares, yet they have no difficulty in keeping their tenants. Of course the produce rent varies with the season, but if Rs.12, Rs.6, and 0 are taken as the produce in a good, a middling, and a bad, season of an acre assessed at Rs.1, the produce rent on the three years will be Rs.8, while Government assessment will be Rs.3—that is to say, the Government collection' ('assessment' means collection) 'is in the circumstances described more than one-third of the average gross produce and not one-sixth.'

Further passages in Sir James Peile's report show that the Bombay cultivator must have enjoyed halcyon days prior to the famine of 1877, though, as one remembers the total collapse of the Western Indian agriculturist during the famine and, in many cases, his inability even to the time of succeeding famines to right himself, one wonders whence all this prosperity departed ere the time of distress came.

The condition of the Bombay cultivator, according to the particulars garnered in 1888, has already been recorded in these pages. They show, indubitably, that, from one month to eight months in various districts, the land does not produce enough to maintain those who cultivate it. The reader, if he be following these illustrations and arguments with the interest incumbent upon him, may not unprofitably turn to pp. 451–458 before proceeding farther, and reperuse what is there set forth.

It may now be well to inquire what is the probable agricultural income of the Presidency at the present time. Towards the end of the decennial period, 1880–89, times were not good. Yet there had been a long series of more than average years of prosperity. Since then twelve years have passed; nine of them have been bad years, involving, in some instances, the total loss of crops and of everything that could be turned into value, however trifling. Not only in the arid Deccan districts, but also in the rich Gujarat division, calamity upon calamity has fallen upon the people. How great the decline in production has become may be judged from a statement as to yield of wheat in the Presidency generally and in Sind. The particulars are available for wheat only among good grains, but what applies to this cereal, *quantum valeat*, will apply to other products of the Bombay fields; anyhow the responsible Government which gives one aspect which is detrimental, when understood, to itself, does not give the other aspects which, it may be supposed, would be favourable.

The estimated average yield per acre of wheat in

Bombay in 1896–97 was *575 lbs.* The actual out-turn in tons, and from them reduced to lbs,[1] was :—

YEAR.		LBS.	YEAR.		LBS.
1891–92...	...	433	1896–97...	...	464
1892–93...	...	524	1897–98...	...	756
1893–94...	...	681	1898–99...	...	703
1894–95...	...	618	1899–1900	...	174
1895–96...	...	440			

AVERAGE : 532 5/9 lbs.

How near these figures are to the actual facts and how utterly visionary is the Viceroy's complacent (but, in view of the consequences, wholly cruel) talk of an average yield of 740 lbs. of food grains to the acre, is proved by Sir James Peile. In his Note on Crop Experiments in the Bombay Presidency,[2] he says :—

'11. Mr. Wingate says of the produce of Juwar, "The favourable season of 1872–73 gives about 1,000 lbs. to the acre, but next year the failure is almost complete, and 1874–75 is, if anything worse." And, he infers, the failure was such as to drive the ryot to borrow money to pay his assessment.

'Turning to his table, I see the rates of production quoted are :—

1873–74 ... 676, 212, 370, 376, lbs. per acre.

AVERAGE : 408½ lbs.

1874–75 ... 200, 133, 757, 640, 112, 240, 240, 420, lbs. per acre.

AVERAGE : 342¼ lbs.'

Sir James Peile goes on to make some remarks which must be quoted here because of their pertinency to the point involved, and which the reader is begged to bear in mind when the Central Provinces yields come before him. 'I see,' says Sir James, 'the average produce assumed for

[1] 'Agricultural Statistics of British India,' fifteenth issue, p. 371.

[2] 'Condition of the Country and People of India,' Famine Blue Book 1881, p. 69.

Juwar in the Central Provinces is in various districts, 300, 302, 322, 364, 400, 406, 435, 467, 480, 500, 582, 716, lbs. per acre. So that these 408 lbs. or 432 lbs. would be called an average rather than a complete failure. No doubt, however, the 1,000 lbs. rate is exceptional for the Deccan, and an average above 500 lbs. would not be safe.'

In Sind the average yield was put at 944 lbs. The actual out-turn in tons is here again reduced to lbs. :—

Year.	Lbs.	Year.	Lbs.
1891–92...	... 536	1896–97...	... 644
1892–93...	... 765	1897–98...	... 664
1893–94...	... 763	1898–99...	... 484
1894–95...	... 719	1899–1900	... 435
1895–96...	... 508		

ACTUAL AVERAGE : 613⅓ lbs.

It will be noted that in no single year was the officially-stated average reached by 179 lbs., and on the whole period the average decrease was 331⅓ lbs. per acre. The average area under the cereal was about 500,000 acres each year. Consequently the diminished produce annually during this period in Sind amounted to 165,500,000 lbs., enough to support every able-bodied man in the Province fully three months on rations at 2 lbs. per day. And in Sind the cultivation was almost wholly on irrigated fields. Whence, then, the falling off in estimated yield of thirty-three per cent?

Further evidence, and this of a most startling character, must be pondered by the reader before we come to actual figures concerning the present agricultural income of Bombay.

First, the indebtedness of the ryots in the four Deccan districts with a population of nearly four millions. The average land revenue of the years 1885 to 1892 was Rs.57,17,000 (Rs.12 to the £ = £476,417). During that period the average annual borrowing was Rs.53,70,000 (£447,500)! Thus:—

Land Revenue.	Borrowings.	Percentage of Borrowing to Revenue.
Average for 16 years ... £ 476,417	Average for 16 years ... £ 447,500	93

On the basis of these figures, says a most able author[1] of a 'Note on Agriculture in Bombay' in the *Quarterly Journal of the Poona Sarvajanik Sabha*, October, 1894, 'the ryots' annual debts in the Presidency may be estimated at Rs.2,50,00,000 (£1,666,667), and taking the average ratio of interest on secured debts at twelve per cent., their annual interest payment on account of annual debts come to Rs.30,00,000 (£200,000). Nor is this all. The pressure of old debts is excessive. On the basis of Mr. Woodburn's figures of nine districts, giving, on an average, Rs.28 (£2 6s. 8d.) per head of the population, the total of such debt for the whole Presidency might be put at about Rs.45,00,00,000 (£30,000,000), on which the annual interest charge at twelve per cent. amounts to Rs.5,40,00,000 (£4,500,000). On Mr. Woodburn's data it is Rs.5,60,00,000 (£4,666,666).'

It is in the presence of such a calamitous state of things nine years ago, with two severe famines in the interim, that the Bombay Government think to restore prosperity to the people by reducing the security which can be given by a landowner to the moneylender for his accommodation in times of disaster. To stroke a hill-side in Assam for the purpose of soothing the land during an earthquake is on a par with the production of such a remedy for such an evil.[2]

[1] The editor of the journal says: 'This note, written by Mr. G. V. Joshi, B.A., Headmaster, Sholapore High School, and read at the Industrial Conference on the 14th of September, 1894, has been kindly placed at our disposal.' The remarks which immediately follow will be found in their appropriate place in a citation which appears on pp. 347–353.

[2] When the Bill referred to passed its most critical stage seven out of the nine *quasi*-elected Indian members of the Bombay Legislative Council withdrew from the assembly—wisely as I hold—as a protest against the Government's refusal to agree to eight months' adjournment to allow of full consideration of its proposals.

At the end of this section I quote some passages from the Presidential address at the Bombay Provincial Conference held at Satara on the 12th and 13th of May, 1900. It would repay the careful reader at once to turn to the Appendix and read the Hon. Mr. Goculdas Parekh's remarks before proceeding farther.

With the above facts in evidence it would not be safe to reckon for the present day an average gross yield of more than the Rs.9 (12s.) per acre which Sir James Peile stated long ago had been accepted as a fair average, though he discards it for a higher sum. Thus regarded :—

> The agricultural income of the Bombay Presidency for 1898–99 amounted to 27,018,913 acres × Rs.9 = Rs.24,31,70,217, or, in £ sterling, £16,211,348.

This is not two-thirds of the amount reckoned in 1888. The statistics for the respective years come out thus :—

Produce (alleged) in 1882	...Rs.39,00,00,000
,, computed for 1898–99 ...	24,31,70,217
DIFFERENCE, being	Rs.14,68,29,783

Or, £9,788,652.

And yet the Viceroy, comparing the two years, declares from his place in Council at Calcutta there was a gain of Rs.2 (2s. 8d.) per head by the agricultural population! In favour of the general accuracy of the present calculation is the circumstance that the Rs.4,71,64,970 which the Bombay Government have collected, bears a smaller proportion to the whole produce, namely, one-fifth, than the less than one-third which Sir James Peile allowed on the produce rental.

The agricultural income thus failing to support the assertions that Indian well-being is not lapsing, Bombay occupying a special position in this respect, the non-agricultural income will probably help to redress the balance. We will see.

An examination of the sources of the non-agricultural income reveals the following :—

No.	Source of Income.		Value in £ Sterling.
1.	Salt		69,074
2.	Forests		20,605
3.	Mines and Quarries		—
4.	Cotton Twist and Yarn, and manufactured goods, say: Cotton Mills (127)	£	
	Twist and Yarn	4,170,762	
	Manufactures, 300,647,593 yards at 4 as. (4d.) per yard	5,004,792	
	Village manufacture, say one-tenth of £4,636,294 ...	463,629	
			9,639,183
5.	Fisheries—one-third of £1,930,140, say ...		650,000
6.	Country-made liquor, one-fifth of total, say		4,000,000
7.	Apparel		54,486
8.	Cabinet-ware and Furniture		16,579
9.	Coir: manufactures		5,612
10.	Tobacco		33,607
11.	Dyeing and Tanning Materials		301,074
12.	Hides and Skins		691,367
13.	Horns		64,166
14.	Jewelry and Plate (half of export) ...		8,617
15.	Animal Bone Manure		194,043
16.	Oils		44,630
17.	Silk (manufactured)		12,107
18.	Wood (teak and sandal)		26,433
19.	Wool: raw	£482,956	
	,, manufactures	75,072	
			558,028
20.	Articles (not specified) exported by post, one-fourth		40,306
21.	,, (not enumerated), one-fourth ...		141,269
22.	Potteries (village manufactures and others), one-seventh		53,571

No.	Source of Income.	Value in £ Sterling.
23.	Shipping and Boat Repairs (one-third) ...	333,333
24.	Printing Presses (including newspapers)	62,500
25.	Paper Mills	2,616
26.	Breweries	23,534
27.	Flour Mills, 24 out of 103 (say one-fourth)	1,068,690
28.	Iron and Brass Foundries (,, ,,)	120,000
29.	Mineral and Aerated Waters	11,000
30.	Oil mills	26,000
31.	Ploughs—repairs, etc.	38,000
32.	Carts: making new ones and repairing old	31,550
33.	Yearly increase of cattle (the records show decrease in 1898–99, but for normal year, reckon one-eighth of general increase, probably an over-estimate) ...	1,128,892
34.	Sundries, to cover small sources of income and overlooked sources	625,000
	Total ...	£20,065,872

The totals of agricultural and non-agricultural are:—

Agricultural Income	£16,211,348
Non-agricultural Income	20,065,872
Combined Totals ...	£36,277,220

Here the non-agricultural exceeds the agricultural income by about twenty-five per cent.; probably £1,000,000 or £2,000,000 are too generously credited to Bombay, the produce being merely Bombay's as Bombay is one of the two great gates of India. Besides, I have reckoned the full value of Mill productions, when strictness should have led me to credit only the value given by manipulation to raw material. The big Mill industry, not only in the chief city, but in many other parts of the Presidency, accounts for the comparatively large figures. Further, much of the income thus shown belongs to wealthy bankers and others whose homes are in the Feudatory States. So good a result is shown in spite of the badness of trade throughout the whole region governed from Bombay Castle.[1]

[1] How bad the trade was may be judged from the following remarks which appear in the latest Administrative Report of the Presidency:—

'The chief industries other than agriculture in the Bombay Presidency, namely, the cotton mill industry, the manufacture of salt and the distillation of liquor, are dealt with elsewhere. The remaining industries are of local importance only, and the majority of them declined considerably in the unfavourable circumstances of the year. The cream and butter industry in Ahmedabad and Kaira suffered severely owing to the great mortality among cattle in consequence of the fodder famine. From the latter place the output of cream was less than half that of the previous year. The iron and brass foundry at Nadiád was closed throughout the year. Broach cotton is reported to be losing its reputation by adulteration with inferior local products, and the Surat cotton industry declined owing to the closure of the South African market. Surat is, however, noted for the manufactures of gold and silver thread work and of shoes, of which the latter is one of the very few industries in the Presidency that advanced in the year of report. A factory for the preparation of agave fibre commenced work in the Thána District, but the business is still in its infancy. The Thána silk industry has finally succumbed to the machine-made goods of Bombay. The brewery, paper mill, and silk mill at Poona continued to do a large business, but the sugar refinery was not so successful and only worked spasmodically during the year. The evacuation of the town of Sholapore owing to plague, together with the influence of famine, reduced the weavers of that place to such a condition that relief was administered by Government in the form of work suitable to their craft. Similar assistance was granted also to weavers in Khándesh. Beyond the industrial schools under the charge of missionaries which continued to turn out good work, the industries of Ahmednagar are of little account. The silver-ware industry is languishing and exists principally by occasional European patronage. The hand-weaving industry of Bijápur, which suffered in the outbreak of plague in the previous year, made no recovery during the year of report. In Belgaum the Gokák water mills were stopped for want of water. Dhárwár had a bone mill, a distillery, and two oil mills working during the year, but the carpet industry showed a further decline. The cloth embroidery done by the desert women of Thár and Párkar, which is becoming known to Europeans, commands a ready sale and is beginning to be exported. Elsewhere in Sind the manufactures were confined to cloths, carpets, and the ordinary metal and earthen ware. A considerable business in the adulteration of ghi and the manufacture of imitation ghi is reported from Shikárpur, the ingredients used being kopra oil, turmeric and lime. Efforts are, however, being made by the introduction of the Adulteration Act and the co-operation of local bodies to put down the industry which had been stimulated by the high prices of the year.'—*Bombay Administrative Report*, 1899–1900, pp. 91–92.

Compared with the statement made in 1882 the figures work out thus :—

1882.	1899–1900.
£37,333,333	£35,978,220

An apparent decrease of £1,355,113.

The average amount per head per annum is :—
£1 18s. 8d. or Rs.29 1a.

Here the Rs.27 of 1882 are passed, owing to the exceptional character of the non-agricultural income and the comparatively small number of inhabitants. But the prosperity is wholly in spots, and affects only a comparatively small number of people. As to the agriculturist, in spite of the perennial water supply in Sind, instead of being Rs.2 better off in 1901 than he was in 1882, *qua* agriculturist, he was Rs.5 14a. worse off. This is precisely what the caustic analysis of the position of the Bombay agriculturist by "J." in the *Times of India* would lead one to expect. Side by side with industrial progress in Bombay and Ahmedabad the agriculturist is sinking lower and lower in the economic and social scale.

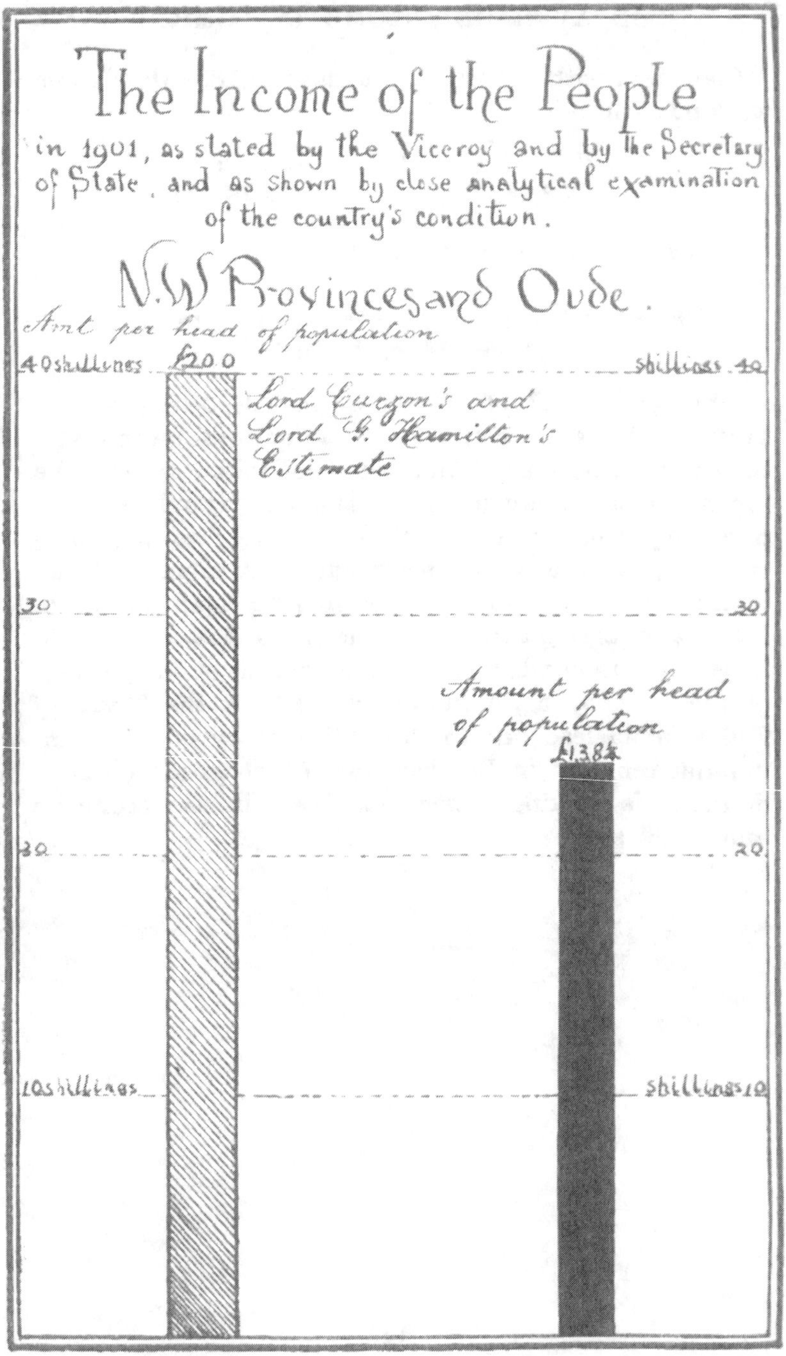
The Income of the People
in 1901, as stated by the Viceroy and by the Secretary of State, and as shown by close analytical examination of the country's condition.
N.W. Provinces and Oude.
Amt per head of population
£2 0 0
Lord Curzon's and Lord G. Hamilton's Estimate
Amount per head of population
£1 3 8½
40 shillings
shillings 40
30
30
20
20
10 shillings
shillings 10

THE NORTH-WESTERN PROVINCES AND OUDH.

A legend has gained currency, and has taken deep root in the minds of some critics of British administration, that the Upper Provinces of Bengal (as they were once styled) and the ex-Kingdom of Oudh rank higher in prosperity than any other part of India. There are, on the face of things, reasons for such a belief. The whole region is fairly well watered, while the Ganges Canal renders a vast area independent of the seasons. As a part of the legend the excellence of the land assessment finds strenuous support, even amongst those who assail the land assessment throughout India generally. It is true that the support is based on (alleged) comparative betterness—the least bad among great communities where the assessments are all beyond the ability of the cultivator to bear, save as a crushing burden. The Provinces are comparatively, and not positively, prosperous;—that is all. I am bound to confess my own researches do not lead me to a community of views with the apologists for these Provinces. I attentively examine the evidence procured and subsequently produced by the officials who were instructed to inquire into the truth or otherwise of certain alleged statements concerning the condition of the Indian people. It may not be supposed that these officers deliberately selected the worst districts and the most hardly-tried cultivators as the objects of their inquiry. Rather must it be supposed that they acted with full candour, impartially took what came, and honestly told all the facts. What are those facts? For full details the reader is referred to the analysis contained in pp. 382–432 in Chapter X. Here I will simply remark that, again and again in the case of individual cultivators, a rent is taken here, as in other parts of the Empire, which approximates almost to the entire proceeds of the land cultivated. Of this rent one-half goes to the Government, the other half to the landowner. Time after time the return for the land under cultivation comes to only Rs.3 to Rs.4 per acre, or as in the case of one cultivator who himself farmed fifteen acres (out of twenty he held and sublet five acres at the same rental he was paying), and for his fifteen acres received less than one rupee and a quarter (1s. 8d.) in produce for each acre. An examination of the evidence will show the interested reader that such cases are neither few nor far between. In the case of the villages dealt with as a whole, while the general returns are a great deal better than the instance just mentioned, enough of produce is not raised (after the double rent has been paid) to more than half or two-thirds feed the cultivators. Even where from five and a half acres the Autumn harvest yielded Rs.129 8a. (£8 12s.), and the Spring harvest Rs.84 5a. (£5 13s.), after rent was paid and cultivation expenses were met, only Rs.10½ (14s.) per head were left for food and clothing and all other needs for a whole year. This, too, was irrigated land. In the very next example given in the book the produce of seventeen acres are stated to reach Rs.318 (£21 4s.), while the rent amounted to Rs.306 (£20 8s.), and the Reporter says the rent is paid every year. With such examples, if the system in the North-Western Provinces be—next to Bengal 'Permanency'—the best in India, how bad must be the remainder!

However, the particulars given above are thirteen years old. Has there, in the meantime, been any improvement in the yield of the land in these regions? A nine years' average in the only cereal concerning which particulars are afforded to the Indian student may help us to a judgment. The average yield of wheat in these Upper Provinces and the ex-Kingdom ranges from 1,440 lbs. per acre on irrigated land in Dehra Dun to 440 lbs. on unirrigated land in Fatehpur. About twenty-seven per cent. of the whole cultivated area is irrigated, and the average yield is recorded :—

For irrigated land	... ...	980 lbs.
,, unirrigated land...	...	803 ,,
,, both	... ...	890 ,,

As has just been stated, more than one-fourth of the whole cultivated area is under wheat. That cereal, therefore, furnishes an excellent test of the yield generally. The Government estimate of wheat, year in and year out (for all deductions on account of bad seasons, insect plagues, and troubles of all sorts, are supposed to have been taken into consideration), is that 890 lbs. per acre will be produced; 3,483,287 acres are irrigated, and, therefore, are beyond mischance. Once more, as in every preceding instance, the estimate and the out-turn differ, the estimate being considerably higher than the out-turn.

ACTUAL OUT-TURN.

Year.		Lbs.	Year.		Lbs.
1891–92	...	762	1896–97	...	860
1892–93	...	877	1897–98	...	881
1893–94	...	677	1898–99	...	840
1894–95	...	555	1899–1900	...	910
1895–96	...	712			

Average ...	786 lbs.
Estimate ...	890 lbs.
Minus ...	104 lbs. per acre.

Only in two years did the area under consideration fall below an average of 4,600,000 acres. The difference between the expectation and the realisation, at 2 lbs. per day, represented full rations for nine millions of able-bodied men for nearly eight weeks. Only in one year out of the nine was the average exceeded. Working on the basis of the Bombay and Sind yields—if Rs.9 were considered a fair average value per acre, largely in view of the recent famines which have been most destructive in Bombay; considering, further, the evidence available as to actual yield in 1881–82, as officially reported, and the additional fact that the soil cannot in the meanwhile have increased its yield—it will not be unfair to these Provinces and the ex-Kingdom to put the yield all round at Rs.10 per acre. With the evidence of actual out-turn before me I dare not give a higher figure. In the days when famines were few in the land—that is within the memory of men little past middle age—and eagerness was exhibited to discern what it all meant, that there should be famine in the land, as ants are eager when their nest is partly destroyed, much official literature was produced. Among other matters put forward Sir James Peile, in his 'Note on the Economic Condition of the Agricultural Population of India,' submitted sample transactions of ordinary agriculturists. Two of these were from the North-Western Provinces. They showed average receipts per acre of Rs.6 (8s.) and Rs.13½ (18s.) respectively. The three other farms selected gave Rs.8 (10s. 8d.), Rs.3 (4s.), and Rs.11 (14s. 8d.) each. [It is interesting to note that the details show the value of the produce to be in direct proportion to the amount spent on cultivation.] Taking, therefore, Rs.10 (13s. 4d.) per acre to represent the value of the produce—

The agricultural income would be Rs.6,63,71,350 × 10 = Rs.66,37,13,500 (or in sterling) £44,247,567.

These results are the nearest approach to the agricultural figures of 1882 that the investigations have yet yielded. Even then the deduction is by so much as Rs.5,37,86,500 (£3,585,770), a decrease of one-twelfth, and nearly the whole rental acknowledged as received by Government. Clearly it is not in these old-time Provinces of Britain in India, and in the ancient Kingdom tacked on to them for administrative purposes, that Lord

Curzon will get any help towards the additional Rs.2 (2s. 8d. extra) which each agriculturist is said to now receive. If not here, where irrigation plays so large a part, nor in Bengal, the land of abundant rainfall, where is alleged increase to be found?

Possibly the non-agricultural income may serve to redress the balance. Lord Cromer and Sir David Barbour estimated this at £23,916,667 (Rs.35,87,50,000).

No.	Source of Income.	Value in £ Sterling.
1.	Forest Receipts	106,221
2.	Mines and Quarries	4,782
3.	Hides and Skins	1,008,146
4.	Shellac	314,824
5.	Ghi	640,114
6.	Saltpetre	137,373
7.	Animals (net export, 31,545 at Rs.50 each)	104,817
8.	Salt (under 'Northern' India the Panjab mines, and Mandi, Kohat, Nuh, and Sultanpur works are all lumped together); including 49,74,889 maunds from Rajputana States, the whole is 7,916,980 maunds; after deducting the Rajputana amount, two-thirds of the remainder are credited to the North-Western Provinces, and one-third to the Panjab	255,962
9.	Fisheries (River), say one-tenth	193,014
10.	Country-made liquor (population, one-fifth, no manufactures, say one-sixth of £20,000,000)	3,333,333
11.	Cotton manufactured in villages, one-fifth of total	927,258
12.	Cotton ditto in Cotton Mills, say	315,403
13.	Woollen Mills	80,473
14.	Paper Mills	33,520
15.	Breweries (6)	816,996
16.	Limestone	15,467

No.	Source of Income.	Value in £ Sterling.
17.	Sandstone	417,529
18.	Flour Mills	203,581
19.	Lac (44 Factories)	193,643
20.	Mineral and Aerated Waters	10,000
21.	Minor Manufactories	50,000
22.	Ploughs—repairs, renewals, etc. (one-fifth)	11,000
23.	Carts, do. (one-sixth)	32,000
24.	Cattle, yearly increase of	2,250,000
25.	Pottery (in villages)	70,000
26.	Sundries, to cover small and overlooked sources of income	750,000
	Total ...	£12,275,456

The totals from Agricultural and non-Agricultural income are:—

Agricultural Income	£44,247,567
Non-Agricultural Income ...	12,275,456
Total ...	£56,523,023

Here the non-agricultural income, instead of being one-half of the agricultural, is only one-fourth. On the basis of the figures of 1882, these Provinces and the ex-Kingdom have fallen off greatly:—

Estimate in 1882 (both sources) ...	£71,750,009
Actuals in 1899–1900 ,, ...	56,523,023
Diminution ...	£15,226,986

Whether this sum represents a falling-off since the earlier year, or an exaggerated estimate then, this much is apparent that, instead of there being Rs.2 additional for the agriculturist, and Rs.1 to the non-agriculturist, as Lord Curzon, on the information given to him, declared there was, there is a considerable reduction in both instances. The reduction is so much as Rs.5 10a. (7s. 6d.) per head. Reckoning sustenance at one penny per person per diem, the minus sum represents food for forty-seven millions of people (the whole population of this part of India) for nearly twelve weeks. Even with the progress he believed he was in a position to report the Viceroy deprecated the 'advance' as giving little occasion for congratulation; it was nothing at all to boast of; he said he regarded it as little enough at the best. His Excellency was speaking more truly than he knew. What is to be said should it be found, as I am confident it will, that my statements are as near to accuracy as the available information permits?

The total income works out:—

£1 3s. 8½d. per head per annum, or Rs.18 0a. 3p.

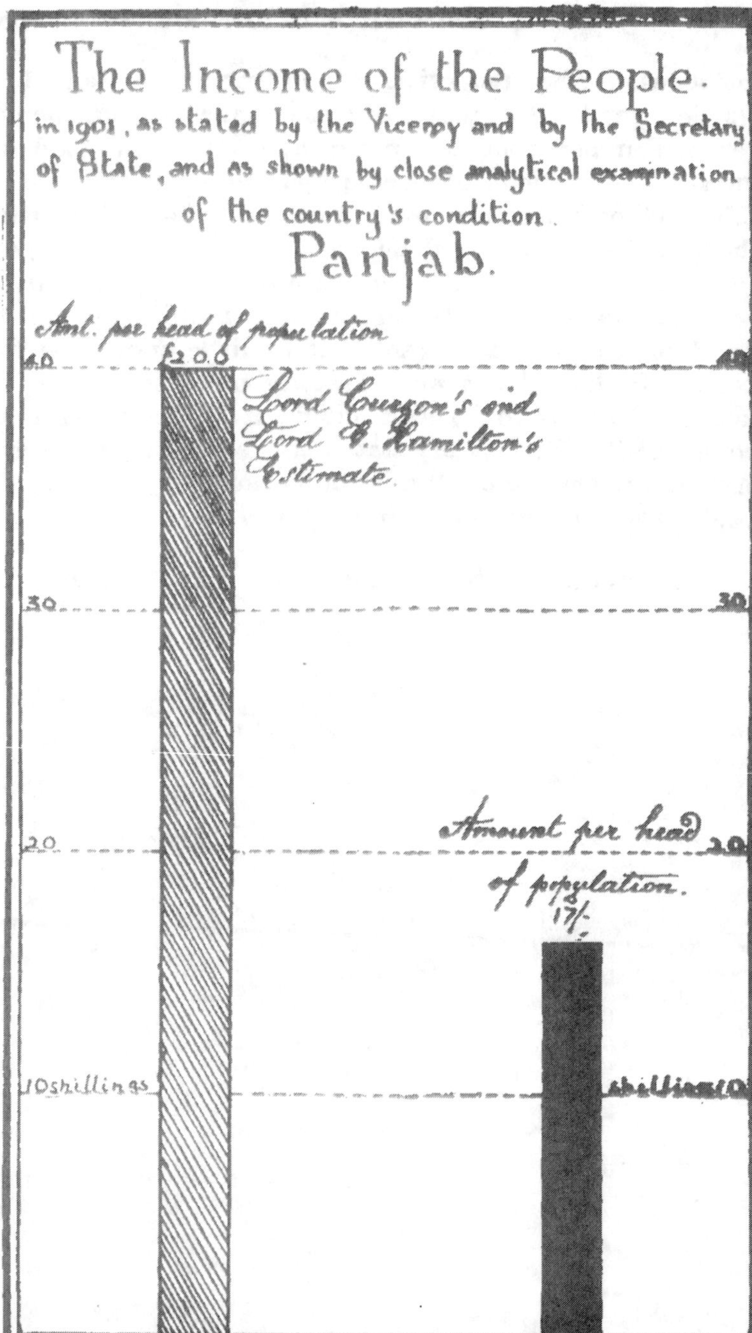
The Income of the People.
in 1901, as stated by the Viceroy and by the Secretary of State, and as shown by close analytical examination of the country's condition.
Panjab.
Amt. per head of population
40
£2.0.0
Lord Curzon's and Lord G. Hamilton's Estimate
30
20
Amount per head of population.
17/-
10 shillings

THE PANJAB.

With such a plenitude of water as the name indicates (" the Five Rivers "), and the fact that fifty per cent. of the cultivated area is under irrigation,[1] combined with the peace and security of British rule, marked prosperity should be the chief feature of this Lieutenant-Governorship if of any part of the Empire. Before, however, prosperity could come to the people, we had, within twenty years of our assuming possession of Ranjit Singh's dominions, to undo much ill that we had wrought. Everywhere we too highly assessed the territories over which we assumed sovereignty, and so laid a burden upon the shoulders of the people which was too great to be borne. One of our achievements in this region was, if not the actual introduction of the moneylender to, certainly his becoming the dominant factor in, village life. There was no general indebtedness in any village before 1871, says a high authority on this subject. The same gentleman has remarked: 'The indebtedness of a large proportion of the Marwats is due, I think,' wrote Mr. S. S. Thorburn,[2] of the Indian Civil Service in 1878, 'chiefly to over-assessment and the rigidity of our revenue system, but there is also no doubt that, without any assessment at all, in bad years or famine cycles, debts would be incurred, and some old peasant proprietors would have to sell or mortgage their holdings. In this settlement the over-assessed villages have received substantial reduction, but Government still owes them reparation for the great injury of having for the twenty-two preceding years rack-rented them, so to say; and, as the rigid revenue system remains, the district officer is under

[1] 'Admin. Report, 1899–1900,' p. 131.
[2] 'Condition of the Country and People of India,' p. 246.

an obligation to work the rules sanctioned for suspension and remissions with a wise liberality.'

Of a village in the Muzaffargarh district, it is said: 'In this village there are 164 cultivators; of these only one (Daulat) is not in debt; all the others are involved more or less.'[1] In the next village discussed 'there are 110 cultivators; only seven are free from debt.' Of one (comparatively) large farmer's operations it is remarked: 'There has been no surplus for the last ten years.'[2] Again, 'Rent rates are so high that, with one or two exceptions, all the tenants are largely in debt.'[3] Of another, after recording the yield of a good year, and reckoning the earnings of 'two men of the family who work as labourers for others,' it is stated: 'Deficiency of Rs.15, hence debt.' In the tabulated particulars of the same family is this significantly grim statement:—

'Property.
'Rs.200 in debt. No grain or property.'[4]

In another instance, after deducting the rent, 'which is one-third of the produce in Jatpura,' the cultivator's expenses were Rs.139 8a., or Rs.27 10a. above his income. This amount he borrowed without any deed being written 'at twenty-four per cent.'[5] Of a farmer of forty-six acres it is said: 'The women's jewels are not valued at more than Rs.10' (13s. 4d.); 'there is no store of grain. After paying the interest on the debts the family have no surplus income.'[6] One more instance and this page may be closed. Family: man, wife, four sons. Cultivator. 'The house consists of one thatched room. All the household property—it was only a charpai and brass dish—has been sold; there remains a hookah and some earthen pots. Has two bullocks and a she-goat. The wife has no ornaments. The children have no clothes. They have no store of grain.'[7] In winter time the climate is inclement: the

[1] 'Condition of Country and People of India,' p. 249.
[2] *Ibid.*, p. 250. [3] *Ibid.*, p. 254. [4] *Ibid.*, p. 254–55.
[5] *Ibid.*, p. 259. [6] *Ibid.*, p. 260. [7] *Ibid.*, p. 262.

body needs the sustenance of a sufficiency of good food and the protection of warm clothing. These people had neither. As to wasting money on 'tamashas,' it is said of a cultivator of seven acres, 'the only festival he can remember of late years was the birth of his first-born, when he spent thirty shillings in making merry.'

The details elsewhere given [1] indicate with much clearness that the condition of the Panjab agriculturist has not improved in the interval since the Great and Secret Inquisition met in 1887–88. The recent passing of a law for this region, interfering with the rights of property, is proof, if further proof were needed, of this fact.

The condition of the cultivators to-day may be judged by the report of Mr. Thorburn on Indebtedness of the Landed Classes, which has already been freely used by me.

The two incomes of the Province may now be dealt with. In 1882 it was alleged that the

Agricultural income was Rs.34,15,00,000,
or (Rs.12½ to the £1) was £29,822,485.[2]

It is asserted that the rental is but ten per cent. of the total produce. But with instances given in foregoing pages of thirty-three per cent. it is idle to deal with a mere tithe in ascertaining the true proportions of the impost. If I regarded twenty per cent. all round, I should probably be near the mark; I will, however, content myself with fifteen per cent.

Confirmation of the percentage I have selected with which to multiply the produce, namely, fifteen per cent., is to be found in particulars given in 1878 concerning the last preceding statement. These particulars are as follow :—

[1] See pp. 295–305, *ante*.

[2] At Rs.15 per £, the present standard, the value would be £26,700,000.

Division.	District.	Share of the gross produce which the Assessment, when made, was intended to cover so far as can be stated.[1]
Delhi	Delhi	One-sixth
	Gurgaon... ...	,,
	Karnal	Not stated
Hissar ...	Hissar	,,
	Rohtak	One-sixth
	Sirsa	Not stated
Umballa ...	Umballa... ...	,,
	Ludhiana ...	,,
	Simla	
Jullundur ...	Jullundur ...	One-fourth
	Hoshiapur ...	,,
	Kangra	Not stated
Amritsar ...	Amritsar ...	One-sixth
	Sialkot	,,
	Gurdaspur ...	,,
Lahore ...	Lahore	,,
	Ferozepore ...	Not stated
	Gujranwala ...	One-sixth
Rawalpindi ...	Rawalpindi ...	Not stated—perhaps one-sixth
	Jhelum	Not stated
	Gujrat	One-sixth
	Shahpur... ...	Not stated
Mooltan ...	Mooltan... ...	One-eighth
	Jhang	One-tenth
	Montgomery ...	One-sixth (?)
	Muzaffargarh ...	One-seventh
Derajat ...	Dera Ismail Khan	Varies generally from one-sixth to one-tenth
	Dera Ghazi Khan	One-eighth
	Bannu	One-twelfth
Peshawar ...	Peshawar ...	Irrigated land—one-sixth Unirrigated land — one-twelfth
	Kohat	Irrigated land—one-fourth Unirrigated land — one-eighth
	Hazara	Less than one-sixth

[1] 'Condition of the Country and People of India,' p. 336.

If the 'share of Gross Produce' under the assessment 'was intended to cover' rates from twenty-five per cent. to eight and one-third per cent., this at least is certain: The revenue collected represents the respective percentages. In this one thing the revenue official does not fail the Sirkar which appoints him. When the 'guess' of 1882 was made the above facts were in existence: how came they to be wanting when material upon which to express a judgment was obtained? The mischief which has been done to country and to people by the inflated statements which were then made, which are added to and confidently repeated, who shall tell?

Before applying this percentage it may be well to show here, as in the other Provinces, that over-estimation of the yield is a prevalent vice of the authorities. In 1896–97 the estimated production of wheat for most of the districts is carefully set out: the averages range from 1,280 lbs. (irrigated) in Jullundur,[1] to 560 lbs. (unirrigated) in Sialkot. Half the acreage in Jullundur is 'well' irrigated. The averages for the whole Province were:—

Irrigated	917 lbs.
Unirrigated	576 „
Both	728 „

After the crops were grown these were estimated as results:—

Year.		Yield per Acre.		Acres.
1891–92	...	526 lbs.	...	6,224,000
1892–93	...	708 „	...	7,020,000
1893–94	...	717 „	...	8,265,000
1894–95	...	670 „	...	8,051,800

[1] That Jullundur is one of the most fertile of the districts, indeed reckons itself *primus in Indis*, is amusingly shown in Mr. Kipling's novel, 'Kim':—

'"They are all alike, these jats," said Kim softly. The jat stood on his dunghill and the king's elephants went by. "O driver," says he, "what will you sell those little donkeys for?"

'The jat burst into a roar of laughter, stifled in apologies to the lama. "It is the saying of my own country—the very talk of it."'

Year.		Yield per Acre.		Acres.
1895–96	...	545½ ,,	...	6,893,400
1896–97	...	599 ,,	...	6,584,300
1897–98	...	660½ ,,	...	8,013,800
1898–99	...	546 ,,	...	7,729,200
1899–1900	...	680 ,,	...	6,366,500

Average: 628 lbs. per acre per annum.

The difference between anticipation and realisation in regard to wheat in the Panjab is on the same lines as in the other Provinces considered; here the shortage is 100 lbs. per acre. The average annual acreage under cultivation was 7,000,000 acres. The deficiency, then, is 700,000,000 lbs., enough at 2 lbs. per head to maintain 6,000,000 of able-bodied men for four months.

The land revenue collected in 1898–99 was Rs.25,641,240, or £1,710,416: multiplied by 7 = £11,972,912.

As compared with the statement of 1882 there is a minus difference of £5,121,248, the rupee taken at the present standard. If, however, the rupee be taken at Rs.12½, the value in 1882 is increased by £1,995,486, so that the minus difference is £3,125,762 only.

What is the non-agricultural income of the Panjab?

It should be £8,500,000 according to Lord Cromer and Sir David Barbour; it should be £6,000,000 to-day, if the fifty per cent. proportion works out accurately. We will take the details:—

No.	Source of Income.	Value in £ Sterling
1.	Forest Receipts	96,403
2.	Coal Mines	48,220
3.	Silk Manufactured	26,667
4.	Carpets and Rugs (say)	50,000
5.	Stone and Lime	20,000
6.	Breweries	133,334
7.	Leather (manufactured)	
8.	Hides and Skins	500,000
9.	Dressed Sheep-skins	

No.	Source of Income.	Value in £ Sterling.
10.	Cotton: manufactured in mills ... £596,059 ,, in villages £463,269	1,059,328
11.	Salt (see particulars N.W. Provinces)	127,981
12.	Fisheries, River (say one-tenth)	193,014
13.	Country-made Liquor (one-twelfth)	1,666,666
14.	Woollen Mills	41,779
15.	Other Industries: Flour Mills, Mineral and Aerated Waters, Factories and Brass Foundries, Potteries, public and private, etc. (say)	250,000
16.	Ploughs—repairs, renewals, etc. (one-seventh)	10,000
17.	Carts — repairs, renewals (one-twelfth)	16,000
18.	Boats ,, ,, say:—	10,000
19.	Cattle (including horses for remounts, one-fourth of total of all India)	2,250,000
20.	Sundries, to cover small, and overlooked, sources of income	400,000
		6,899,392

Taken together, the two incomes exhibit a great difference compared with those of 1882. Instead of thirty-four crores' (£22,666,667) worth of agricultural produce, I can only find eighteen crores' worth (£12,000,000); and against seventeen crores (£11,333,333) of non-agricultural produce, I can discern but eleven crores (6,889,392). Lord Curzon's two rupees per head additional for agriculture is replaced by an income only one-half of what he declared it to be.

If these figures be correct the combined totals run thus :—

Agricultural Income	... ...	£11,972,912
Non-agricultural Income	... ...	6,899,392
Total	... ...	£18,872,304

Divided amongst 22,449,484 people the combined income comes to (say) Seventeen Shillings per head per annum; or Rs.12 10a.,

which is less than that in Madras where the climate is warmer and less clothing and even less food are needed than in the North. No doubt there is some serious mistake somewhere, but the Government records lead to the above figures and to none other.

THE CENTRAL PROVINCES.

It is in one sense singular, in another significant, that the Provinces and the Presidency which stood at the head of all the divisions of India nineteen years ago should have proved the hollowness of the agricultural 'prosperity' then attributed to them, by suffering more keenly under the stress of famine than any part of India has suffered at any time respecting which there is trustworthy information. The Central Provinces were at the head of the list in 1882 with Rs.20 4a. (£1 7s.) of agricultural income, and Rs.10 2a. (13s. 6d.) of non-agricultural income per inhabitant. Yet, at the first touch of distress, practically the whole population were affected, and, in one district, as time went on four out of every ten of the people were on Government relief. Nothing could better demonstrate the essential untrustworthiness of the inflated estimate of 1882. Unhappily every one believed the beautiful story which it told, because every one knew Britain's disinterestedness deserved such a record. The responsible authorities, never daring to sift their own statements, believe it still, and embroider it with fancy observations and with an increased income, which has no existence save as an expression of what they sincerely wish for the people they rule. The belief of 1882 bore fruit when, in the early Nineties, a revision of the settlements in the Central Provinces was imminent. The authorities determined they would reap some of the rich harvest of wealth which the estimate of the Finance Minister and his Assistant had, it was considered, proved to exist. Among other things there were to be no more thirty-year settlements. Wealth in this wheat-growing

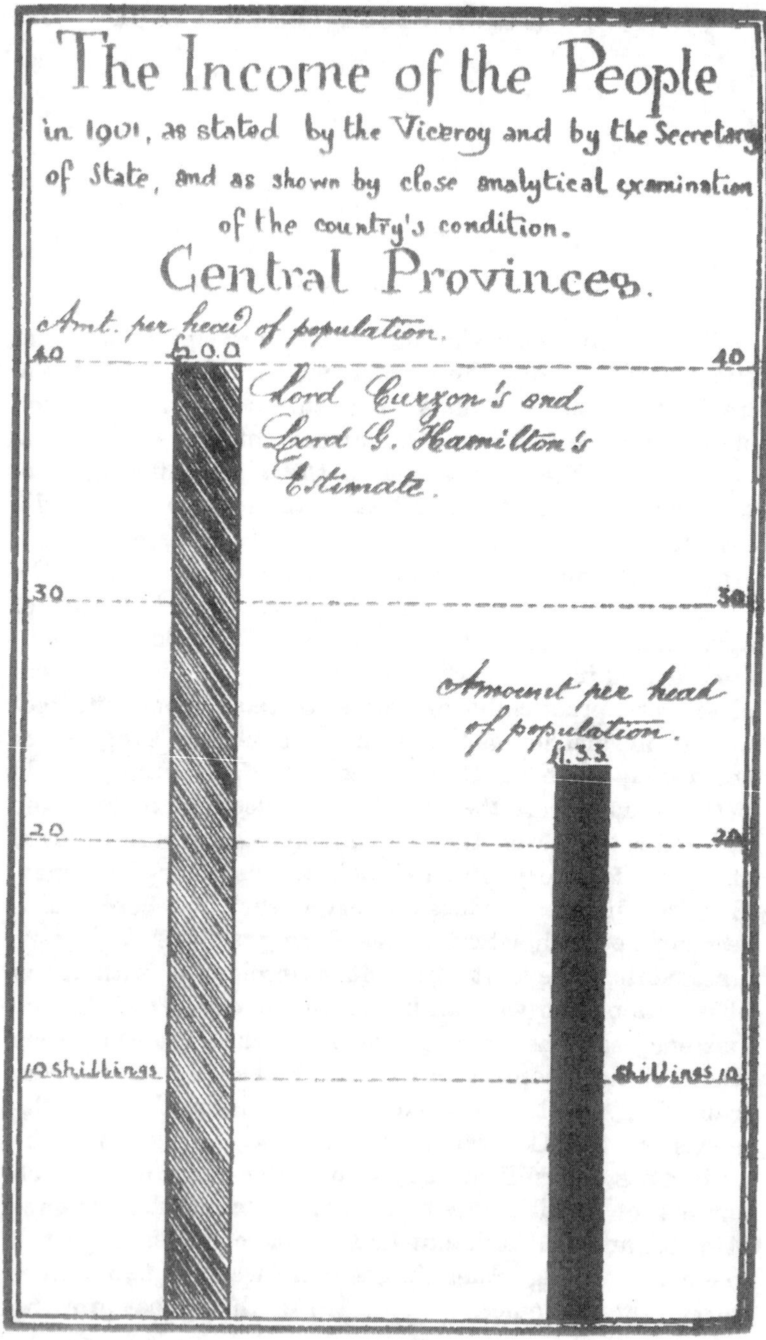
The Income of the People
in 1901, as stated by the Viceroy and by the Secretary of State, and as shown by close analytical examination of the country's condition.
Central Provinces.
Amt. per head of population.
40
40
Lord Curzon's and Lord G. Hamilton's Estimate.
30
30
Amount per head of population.
£1.3.3
20
20
10 shillings
shillings 10

region, a region which tipped many of the late Robert Knight's arrows of adverse criticism with indignation and sarcasm—'wheat rotting by thousands of tons in Chhattisgarh because you are too supine to make railways by which it can find a market,'—wealth was produced so rapidly in these favoured regions that the authorities must have the opportunity of sharing in it at more frequent periods than were customary, otherwise nobody knows how wealthy these Central Provincials might become. Therefore, instead of thirty-year settlements a twelve-year period must be substituted, while the rates of assessment were to be run up to hitherto unheard-of figures. Faith had to be broken with the people, but that did not deter us, and, if it were broken, 'as well be hanged for a sheep as a lamb.'

What was practically a confiscation of the property of the cultivators was carried through without any one in England save a dozen to twenty people knowing anything about it. The present writer happened to be one of this small number. He tried, ineffectually, to get Parliamentary attention concentrated upon the facts, so that the wrong might be stopped. Unhappily the late Mr. Bradlaugh had recently died, and no member of the then House of Commons apparently understood that anything was wrong, or felt that he ought to inquire if anything was really wrong. At least a dozen of them had all the facts placed before them. Now that the predicted consequences have followed, the reader must suffer some detail to make him acquainted with facts which it was his duty to know years ago. His representatives in the House of Commons, I must repeat, did not concern themselves. Will you, courteous reader, to-day, act as they did then? What was the prediction? Already, says a writer in the *Nyaya Sudha*,[1] 'public revenue is, we have been told by many respectable people possessing local knowledge, being

[1] Published, I think, in 1890 or 1891; the paper named is referred to in a pamphlet which, like so many documents one meets with, contains neither date nor year by which to definitely fix the period of its issue.

paid either by encroachment upon the capital of the people or by aid of borrowed money. It must be so. The people have been accustomed since years past to regulate their expenditure on a certain scale. All of a sudden they are called upon to pay in the shape of tax on land double, treble, four times, and five times, the sum they were paying before. Before they can so adjust their domestic relations as to be able to live the life of paupers, some time must necessarily elapse, and in the meantime they will for ever alienate from themselves all their other property to make good the inexorable State demand. But this cannot last long. As soon as the capital created during the currency of the last settlement is exhausted, the people are bound to verge to the lowest ebb of pauperism. The evil may be staved off for some time. But come it will, though Mr. Fuller and his able lieutenant the Rai Bahadur may not be then present to witness the effect of their handiwork. Though the *personnel* of the Government may change, the Government itself will be there face to face with the tremendous responsibility of providing for an utterly impoverished population.'

I do not know who the writer of these passages may have been, but it is almost needless to say that what he uttered as prophecy ten or twelve years ago is now accurate history. Whoever it be, he sent me a number of copies of his pamphlet, which I distributed without comments among certain parliamentary representatives. 'We are all Members for India,' said a right hon. member vaingloriously one day in Parliament about that time, and himself, though he became Secretary of State for India, carefully avoided doing India any service. Nobody, however, took any notice of the pamphlet. The copy I am using, I daresay, is the only one in existence out of the many then circulated.

Is it possible that British administrators can have reduced the period of settlement by less than half and increased rents four or five times beyond the normal? Here is the answer:—

Name of Village.	Land Revenue under the Old Settlement.	Land Revenue under the New Settlement.
Pendri	Rs.78	Rs.280
Tehka	70	285
Katmi	20	145
Akattora	80	885
Lawai	90	260
Akoli	50	140
Gotni	100	840
Lamti	80	145
Madra	25	150
Singarpur	120	855
Buchipar	40	150
Dawanpali	125	450
Majgaon	100	250
Baresi	20	110
Goodi	150	430
Sonbarsa	80	200
Ortura	100	460
Tikoli	80	240
Hathni	85	250
Dourabhuta	50	160
Gadadi	80	100
Khokli	60	200
Umdipar	25	110
Khupradi	40	180
Patkar	80	180
Ourdi	50	160
Sarajpura	80	165
Surkhi	20	820
Bijrahdi	50	190
Kahmathi	40	150
Bedri	15	150
Madhobun	40	185
Magarwar	20	115
Dhudwadi	80	200
Odia	80	260
Amlihdi	50	150
Tobatar	200	600
Topa	60	220
Kokdu	40	190
Oomri	25	160
Hasda	40	820
Chairu	80	260
Mirgi	100	840
Muldi	100	450
Torma	60	285
Jathani	25	175
Dewarani	25	280
Tikari	50	265
Matia	80	180
Chamari	60	290
Dabedihi	80	106

Name of Village.	Land Revenue under the Old Settlement.	Land Revenue under the New Settlement.
Benakar	Rs.80	Rs.170
Ladwadihi	15	186
Koni	50	285
Baghudwa	40	180
Melwa	70	820
Kosumda	50	865
Mopka	150	800
Khairi	40	190
Borsi	25	400
Gudhalia	80	820
Chichpole	60	400
Lachchanpur	80	800
Patan	100	895
Dhanoli	200	600
Chamargudi	40	180
Bikuli	80	250
Pasid	180	890
Rumpur	80	260
Lalpur	80	140
Butachand	60	185
Karahi	120	850
Guchpur	40	275
Kesla	100	760
Bijepur	120	800
Belpana	140	800
Dhunrao	80	250
Nagchuwa	50	260
Mooh	125	550
Amner	100	800
Daree	20	90
Butchora	50	454
Kukurde	50	187¼
Amgaon	80	198⅛
Manock-chowra	60	442¾
Chewaha	65	200
Sarsenee	50	240
Chedi Paia	100	895
Solenee	50	248
Bahunee	15	70
Dhunwa	28	128
Kanada	80	220
Bhamree	100	822½
Lagru	100	892
Zulan	60	215¾
Bohage	28	108
Koramey	86	175
Charhashoo-hanpur	40	95
Pole	200	400
Pendridoh	21½	150

'This list could be very much enlarged if we descended to cases where the enhancement has been one hundred per cent. or thereabouts.'

Some English people recently were shocked to see an address on Famines in India announced with this title: 'Are Famines in India God-sent or Man-made?' What was suggested was blasphemous, they said, so far as the Almighty was concerned, and, as for man, he could not make a famine. Man not make a famine! Not of one man merely is it true—'He made a solitude and called it peace,' nor has a like thing happened but

'once or twice in our rough island story.'

Though not meaning to do so, we of British blood have made famines, and at this moment are more busily manufacturing fresh famines than we are even adding to our annual military expenditure the Empire over. Probably, it would not be difficult to procure pretty general assent to the proposition quoted above, that, in the failure of the inhabitants of the Central Provinces to withstand the recent scarcities which have affected the region in which they live, the hand of man is plainly discernible, while the influence of a God of Mercy is distinctly wanting.

The extravagant—'iniquitous' it has been termed—settlement still remains, and is taking from the cultivators that which the Government by no measure of right or reason ought to take.

The same extravagance of estimate marks the estimated yield of produce per acre here which the Government announce, as elsewhere. For wheat that yield is put at 600 lbs. per acre. Actually, on the area cultivated the *production was but* 372 *lbs., or* 228 *lbs. per acre below expectation!* [1]

[1] Previously to this one Hon. Member had asked a question in the House of Commons about the settlement of Bilaspur. The pamphleteer thus remarks on the incident:—

'The recent question in Parliament, which, strange as it may appear,

What is not the least astonishing feature is that, although the returns for 1891–92 to 1895–96 were in the hands of the authorities, with these ascertained yields :—

has become widely known in Bilaspur, and the public utterances of the present Chief Commissioner breathing a spirit of sympathy with the people, have raised a vague and indefinite hope of redress from an almost intolerable state of things which is eating into their vitals and sucking out their life-blood. If the Government is desirous of knowing the real feelings of the people about the new settlement, we make bold to say that such a knowledge it is impossible to acquire from the usual official reports. We would take the liberty to suggest the deputation of a Special Officer in whose justice the people have faith and whose sympathy for them and theirs is well known, to make a thorough inquiry into the whole matter, and then will a tale be unfolded which will perhaps astonish the Administration and give a rude shock to the comforting assurance which has been so sedulously pressed upon it as to the satisfaction of the people with the new assessment and their appreciation of the fairness of the settlement proceedings. But whether there is such an investigation or not, facts are facts, and they speak with a power and effect which scarcely leave anything to be added to by way of comment.

'To add to the misery of the people, they have been informed that the present settlement will inure only for a period of twelve years. Now, referring to the Administration Report of 1862–63 by Sir Richard Temple, we find that he distinctly gave the people to understand the settlement then in progress was "to extend to thirty years for all districts alike." "This has been sanctioned by Government," it was said. Further, hopes were held out of a permanent settlement in the following words: "It has also been recommended that the boon of a permanent settlement, that is the limitation of the Government demand in perpetuity, should be conceded to those landholders who might have brought their estates to a high state of cultivation. The Government have decided that, after a lapse of ten years from the commencement of the new settlement, and therefore even within the period of that settlement, those landholders who may be thought worthy of the concession and who may desire a perpetual limitation of the Government demand, may have their assessment revised with a view to such limitation in perpetuity being declared." What a melancholy interest these promises possess in the face of what is transpiring now! From a thirty years' settlement, with a promise of a permanent limitation of the State demand, to a twelve years' settlement with the certainty of fresh increments at every revision of settlement, what a falling off is here! Suppose a Malguzar, having strictly complied with the condition laid down in the above-quoted public declaration of Government, were to come forward and ask it to fulfil the promise it embodies, with what grace could the Government refuse to give it effect, and what answer could it give to such a prayer, except that it must decline to be bound by the ordinary rule of natural justice and equity, which, in the case of private individuals, it enforces through the agency of its Courts of Justice.'

YEAR.		LBS.	YEAR.		LBS.
1891–92	...	437	1894–95	...	329
1892–93	...	405	1895–96	...	307
1893–94	...	322			

the average yield for 1896–97 (to stand for the succeeding four or five years; it still stands in the 1900–1 Blue Book) was put at 600 lbs. for both irrigated and unirrigated lands, and at 925 lbs. for the former, and 570 lbs. for the latter! An explanation will, probably, never be forthcoming; because nobody (in Parliament, for example) who could compel an answer, will take the trouble to do so. Nevertheless, it is needed.

In estimating the produce in the Central Provinces, at the present time it may be noted that in 1867–68, Mr. W. G. Pedder, of the Bombay Civil Service, estimated the value of the yield per acre in the Nagpore District at Rs. 8 (10s. 8d.). Twelve years later Sir James Peile gave particulars of a farm of 44 acres in the same region which averaged Rs.8 (10s. 8d.), and of another which showed Rs.7 2a. (9s. 6d.) per acre. Since that time, save in the enforced fallows which the successive famines have compelled, the land has received nothing which can have put it into better heart or have enabled it to grow more produce. What gain there may have been prior to 1890 has been removed by the heavy assessment since made.

The area actually cropped in 1898–99 was 15,808,881 acres, which, at Rs.8 per acre, gave a total of:

AGRICULTURAL INCOME of Rs.12,64,71,048; or, in Sterling £8,464,736.

But the estimate for 1882 gave Rs.21,25,00,000 as the value of the produce, or at Rs.12½, £18,558,333. Again: so far from the Viceroy finding Rs.2 (2s. 8d.) additional income per head from agriculture, there is a diminution of Rs.8,60,28,952.

In this instance, it was ridiculous to add half the estimated agricultural income for non-agricultural income, as these Provinces are, practically, wholly agricultural.

It is true there are minerals—besides the coal at Warda—to be mined, but too much encouragement is not given to pioneers in this direction; indeed positive discouragement has been the rule. Mr. Jamsetjee N. Tata, of Bombay, however, has lighted the candle of manufacturing industry at Nagpore, and is doing no little good.

NON-AGRICULTURAL INCOME.

No.	Source of Income.		Value in £ Sterling.
1.	Forest Receipts		66,340
2.	Cotton Manufactures ...	£650,000	
	" " Villages	185,452	
			835,452
3.	Breweries		13,845
4.	Coal		56,742
5.	Iron		395
6.	General Manufactures		15,000
7.	Hides and Skins		200,000
8.	Country-made Liquor		850,000
9.	Pottery: Village manufacture		15,000
10.	Ploughs and Carts—renewals and repairs		20,000
11.	Cattle (one-twelfth)...		750,000
12.	Sundries, to cover small and overlooked sources of income		180,000
			£3,002,774

Agricultural Income ...	...	£8,464,736
Non-Agricultural Income	...	3,002,774
	Total	£11,467,510

Divided among the population of 10,784,794, the result is £1 3s. 3d., or Rs.16 12a. per head.

Alleged Income in 1882	...	Rs.30	8	0
Estimated " 1900	...	17	7	0
Apparent Decrease		Rs.13	1	0

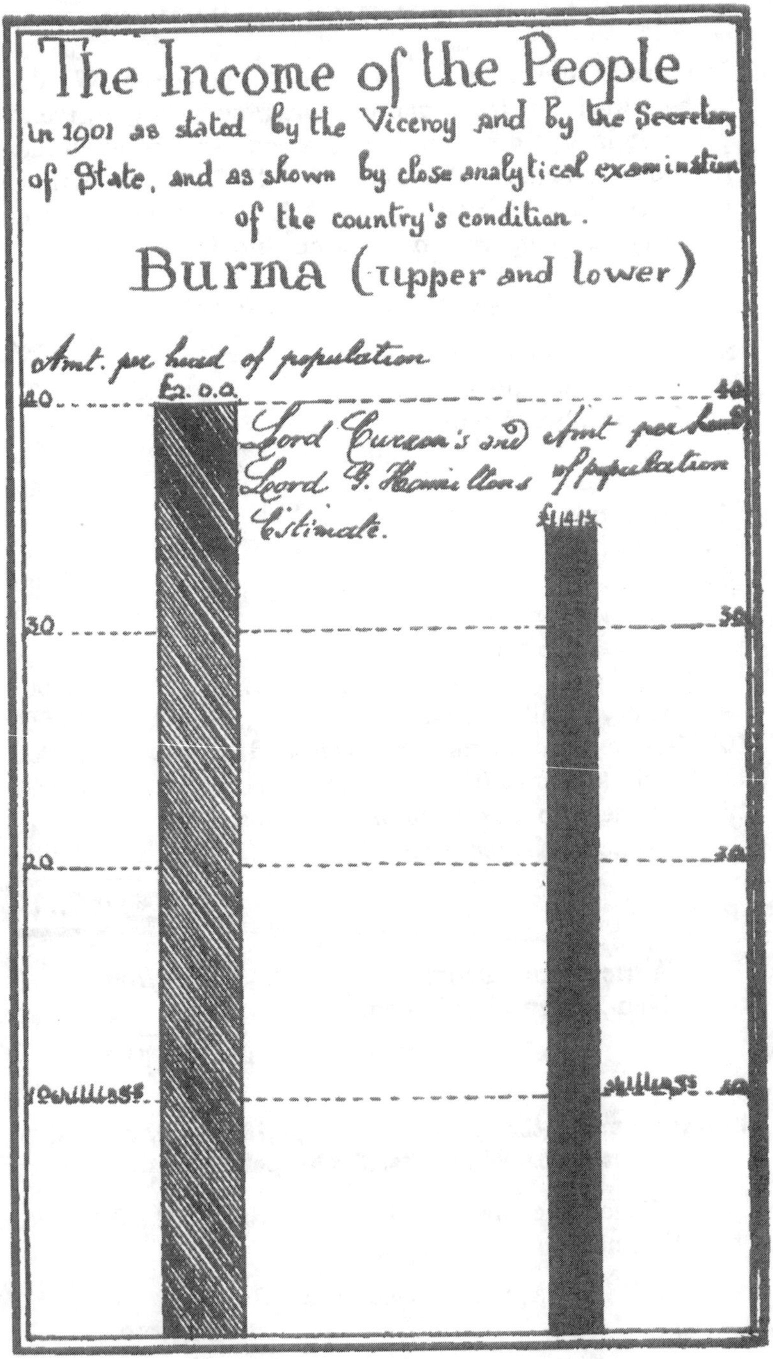
The Income of the People
in 1901 as stated by the Viceroy and by the Secretary of State, and as shown by close analytical examination of the country's condition.
Burma (upper and lower)
Amt. per head of population
£2. 0. 0.
Lord Curzon's and Lord G. Hamilton's Estimate.
Amt. per head of population
40
30
20
10 shillings
40
30
20
10

UPPER AND LOWER BURMA.

There is no comparison here with 1882 or with any other year, Lower Burma being lumped with 'India' in the year of the earlier inquiry.

Area actually cropped in 1898–99 :—

Lower Burma...	...	6,665,056	acres.
Upper ,, ...	...	3,167,133	,,
Total	...	9,832,189	,,

In the exceptional circumstances of Burma, with its enormous rice production, and in the absence of details, the out-turn may be put at Rs.17½ per acre (£1 3s. 4d.). The rate is high, but seems justified by the appearance and condition of things.

9,832,189 acres × Rs.17½ = Rs.17,20,63,308, or, in Sterling £11,470,887.

This would give, as agricultural income, £1 9s. 7d. per head. Probably the value from the Burmese fields is over-estimated to the extent of several shillings.

Of non-agricultural income the Burmas show :—

No.	Source of Income.	Value in £ Sterling.
1.	Forest Receipts	556,726
2.	Cotton Manufactures—Villages	500,000
3.	Country-made Liquor	1,000,000
4.	Cattle	250,000

No.	Source of Income.	Value in £ Sterling.
5.	Petroleum	250,000
6.	Pottery	553,334
7.	General: including Rubies, Jade, etc. ...	750,000
8.	Boats—repairs, renewals, etc.	200,000
9.	Sundries—to cover all omissions	200,000
		£4,260,060

Agricultural Income	£11,470,887
Non-agricultural Income ...	4,260,060
Total ...	£15,730,947

Average income per head, £1 1s. 1½d., or Rs.22 12a.

ASSAM.

Of no portion of India in 1888 are more detailed particulars given in the course of the Dufferin Inquiry than in connection with the Chief Commissionership of Assam. There is no need to quote here any of the voluminous particulars given, especially as some citations have elsewhere been made; it suffices if it be stated that, while they reveal poverty in some parts, they differ from the records of the other Provinces in that they show there is as yet no serious pressure of want. The references to jewelry possessed are even more frequent than, in earlier records, were quoted concerning other parts of the Empire whence, long ere 1900, these reserves have almost entirely disappeared. One reference may be made, namely, to the changes which have occurred in prices in the district of Nowgong during the memory of Rai Bahadur Gunabhiram Sarna Barna, Extra-Assistant-Commissioner, who entered the subordinate executive service in 1859. There were obtainable :—

	Per Rupee.			Per Rupee.
In 1857-58	276 lbs.	of Paddy	In 1887-88	82 lbs.
,,	92 ,,	Common Rice	,,	36 ,,
,,	82 ,,	White Rice	,,	28 ,,
,,	92 ,,	Kasari	,,	26 ,,
,,	70 ,,	Mustard Seed	,,	24 ,,
,,	4 ,,	Oil (mustard)	,,	5¼ ,,
,,	4 ,,	Ghi	,,	2 ,,
,,	40 ,,	Molasses	,,	16 ,,
,, 67	82 ,,	Milk	,,	18 ,,
,,	64 ,,	Fish	,,	10¾ ,,

A comparison between Assam in 1885 and in 1900 is

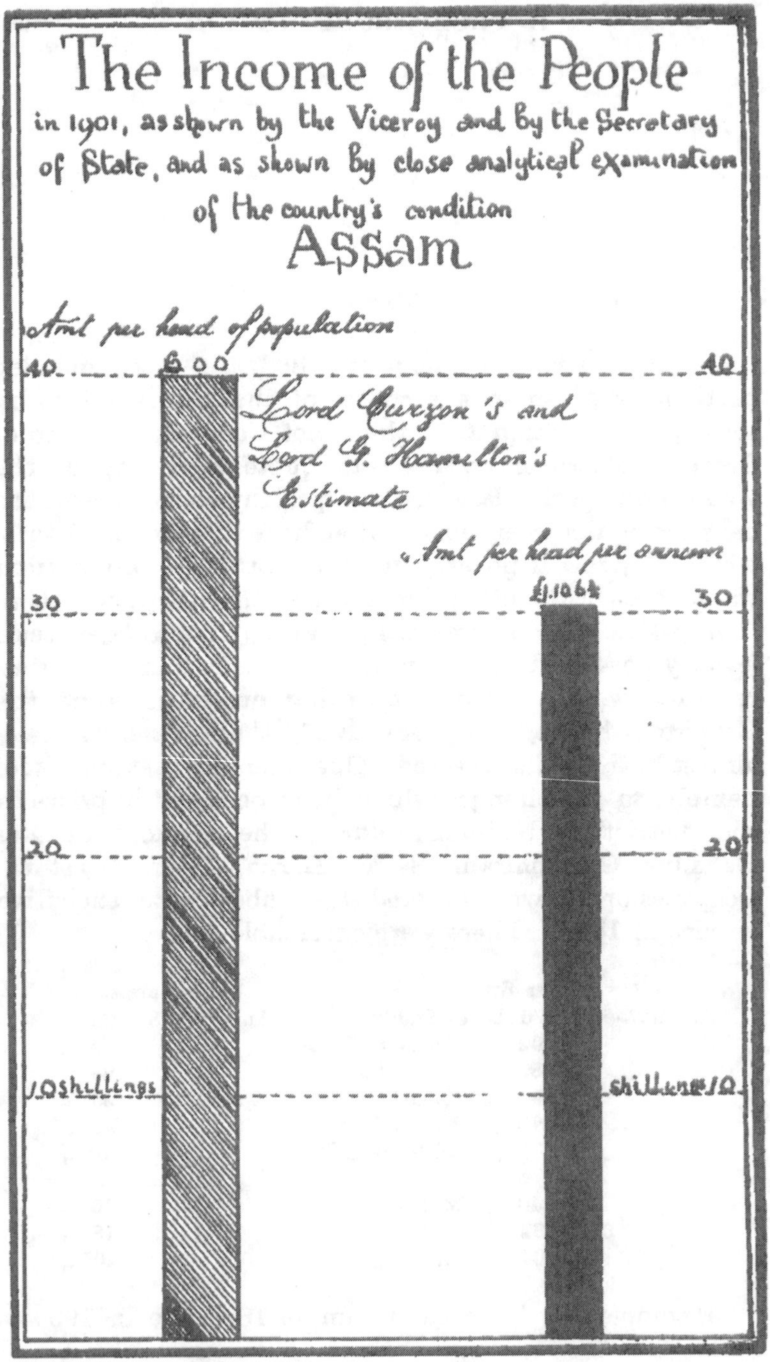
The Income of the People
in 1901, as shown by the Viceroy and by the Secretary of State, and as shown by close analytical examination of the country's condition
ASSAM
Amt per head of population
40
£ 0 0
40
Lord Curzon's and
Lord G. Hamilton's
Estimate
Amt per head per annum
£1.10 6
30
30
20
20
10 shillings
shillings 10

not possible. This Commissionership was included under 'India.' Nor is there anything to show what is the proportion of produce which the authorities claim as rent or revenue. If, therefore, I take the revenue at ten per cent. I shall, probably, not be far out.

The land revenue in 1887 amounted to Rs.4,306,420 or, in sterling, £287,095. Multiplied by ten the

Total Agricultural Produce then would have been £2,870,950.

In 1898–99 the revenue was Rs.6,284,110, or in sterling, £419,041. Multiplied by ten the

Total Agricultural Produce now would be £4,190,410.

I assume that this increase is largely due to the extension of tea cultivation.

		Acres.
Area under Tea in India in 1898–99	...	481,959
,, ,, 1886–87	... ...	203,963
Increase	...	Acres 277,996

Nearly the whole of this increase is in Assam. It seems clear where the increase noted comes from, and tea is included in agricultural produce. But, so that no injustice may be done to the position, and to make up for anything I may elsewhere have missed, I will include tea, which, in 1898–99, was valued at Rs.81,911,150, of which Rs.70,000,000 should be credited to Assam.

Produce in 1898–99, as above	...	£4,190,410
Add Tea, valued at port of shipment		4,006,667
Total	... ...	£8,197,077

As to the non-agricultural income, the customary procedure in this analysis may be followed:—

No.	Source of Income.		Value in £ Sterling.
1.	Forest Receipts		37,863
2.	Mines and Minerals:—		
	Lime Quarries, say ...	£35,000	
	Coal, say	100,000	
			135,000
3.	Petroleum		16,000
4.	Saw Mills (for Tea boxes)		30,000
5.	Railway Workshops		10,000
6.	Various Manufactures		5,000
7.	Country-made Liquor		400,000
8.	Pottery—Village manufacture		10,000
9.	Cattle—(one thirty-fourth of increase throughout India)		265,000
10.	Sundries—to cover small and overlooked sources of income, including River Fisheries		150,000
	Total		£1,058,863

Agricultural Income	£8,197,077
Non-agricultural Income	1,058,863
Total	£9,255,940

Divided among the population of 5,433,668 (of whom probably more than one thousand are tea planters with fair incomes) the result is—

£1 14s. 0¾d., or Rs.25 8a. 9p. per head per annum.

Not even in favoured Assam, and counting all the Tea cultivation, are there, in 1900, even the Rs.27 which was declared to be the average throughout India nineteen years before, and which has been the stand-by for the British Indian apologist throughout that period.

[*The diagram on p. 608 needs amendment: the ascertained income is £1 14s. 0¾d.*]

PROVINCE.	INCOME.	£	£	Rs.	a.	p.	£	s.	d.
Bengal	Agricultural Income ...	53,930,480							
	Non- " " ...	21,701,177	75,631,657	15	3	0	1	0	3
Madras	Agricultural " ...	20,322,638							
	Non- " " ...	15,650,523	35,973,161	14	2	0	0	18	10
Bombay	Agricultural " ...	16,211,348							
	Non- " " ...	20,065,872	36,277,220	29	1	0	1	18	8
North-Western Provinces and Oudh	Agricultural " ...	44,247,567							
	Non- " " ...	12,275,456	56,523,023	18	1	6	1	4	0½
Panjab	Agricultural " ...	11,972,912							
	Non- " " ...	6,899,392	18,872,304	12	10	0	0	17	0
Central Provinces ...	Agricultural " ...	8,464,736							
	Non- " " ...	3,002,774	11,467,510	16	12	0	1	3	3
Burma, Upper and Lower	Agricultural " ...	11,470,887							
	Non- " " ...	4,260,060	15,730,947	22	12	0	1	14	1½
Assam	Agricultural " ...	8,197,077							
	Non- " " ...	1,058,863	9,255,940	25	8	9	1	14	0¾
		Total	259,731,762						

Ajmere-Merwara, and other Minor States under the direct Government of the Indian Foreign Office, are omitted in the above Summary, the details not being available. They, however, if included, would not appreciably affect the results arrived at.

The above estimates, if they err in aught but details, err—I believe—on the side of optimism. They also refer to a good year. Singularly enough, they work out almost exactly to the rough estimate I made in addressing Lord Curzon in April, 1901.[1] Take such a year as 1900–1901, when the Empire was visited by the most terrible and most calamitous famine India has known, and make the

[1] 'Once more, my Lord, I have to ask whether it is possible you can be right in declaring that the average Indian has now Rs.30 (that is, forty shillings) per annum of income. This question is forced from me when I examine the general statement of revenue and expenditure with which Sir Edward Law concluded his Financial Statement less than a month ago. It is therein stated that the net land revenue for 1899–1900 was £17,205,056. With this sum before us it should not be impossible to ascertain the exact agricultural income. There is no little disputation between Government officers, outside critics, and the man who has to pay, as to the amount of the gross produce the authorities take as land revenue. For reasons set forth in the Postscript to my Open Letter addressed to your Lordship, I am of opinion these percentages are not very far from the fact:—

In Bengal	5 to 6 per cent.	
In the North-West	5 „ 8 „	
In the Panjab	5 „ 10 „	
In Madras	12 „ 31 „	say 20
In Bombay	20 „ 33 „	say 25

A rough calculation shows me that if I take the Panjab rate of 10 per cent. and apply it generally I shall not be far from the real state of the case. I will so apply it—

£17,205,056 × 10 = £172,050,560; or in Rupees, 15 to the £ = Rs.258,07,58,400.

That is to say, 258 crores instead of 450 crores! We must not stop here. Although I have given what I conceive to be good reasons why you should not claim the non-agricultural income to be equal to half the agricultural income, I will allow that rate in a calculation which must follow. Let us now see what the average income of the Indian people is:—

Agricultural Income	Rs.258,07,58,400
Non-Agricultural Income	129,03,79,200
	Rs.387,11,37,600

Rs.387,11,37,600 divided by 228,000,000 = Rs.17 5a.!

Almost to an anna the sum you scorned when it was deduced by me from your first statement—the statement made at Simla.'

necessary deductions, the result is, as Lord Curzon described the famine to be,—'terrible.' So that as close a connection as possible may be maintained with Lord Curzon's statements and reasonings, the figures at which we have arrived must be pursued farther.

Seeing, as I have said, a sharp line cannot be drawn between the agricultural and non-agricultural population, many persons being both agriculturist and artisan, a further analysis is made. In it the population is divided into agricultural and non-agricultural communities and the respective incomes have been divided per head accordingly. The proportions are :—

Two-thirds agricultural :	and one-third non-agricultural :
Bengal.	Bombay.
Madras.	Panjab.

Three-fourths agricultural :	one-fourth non-agricultural :
North-Western Provinces and 'India.'	Central Provinces.
Burma.	Assam.

The agricultural income is :—

PROVINCE.	POPULATION.	AGRICULTURAL INCOME. £	AVERAGE. £	s.	d.
Bengal	49,808,647	53,930,480	1	1	8
Madras	25,472,160	20,322,638	0	15	5
Bombay	12,389,664	16,211,348	1	6	2
North-Western Provinces and Oudh	31,797,551	44,247,567	1	7	10
Panjab	14,566,589	11,972,912	0	16	5
Central Provinces...	7,383,989	8,464,736	1	3	0
Burma	6,915,851	11,470,887	1	13	2
Assam	4,591,651	8,197,077	1	15	8
	152,926,102	174,817,645	1	2	2
			or Rs.17		

The estimate in 1882 was £250,000,000, which indicates a decrease of £75,886,869.

As to the non-agricultural income, it works out, among the respective populations, as follows:—

PROVINCE.	POPULATION.	NON-AGRICULTURAL INCOME.	AVERAGE.		
		£	£	s.	d.
Bengal	24,904,373	21,701,177	0	17	1
Madras	12,736,229	15,650,523	1	4	1
Bombay	6,194,832	20,065,872	3	3	10
N.W. Provinces and Oudh	15,898,773	12,275,456	0	14	7
Panjab	7,483,295	6,899,392	0	18	5
Central Provinces...	2,461,329	3,002,774	1	4	0
Burma	2,305,290	4,260,060	0	9	$4\frac{3}{4}$
Assam	1,530,550	1,058,863	0	12	1
	73,514,671	97,535,004	1	12	11
			or Rs.24 11a.		

This is £35,491,237 less than was reckoned in 1882. The division I have made between agricultural and non-agricultural income is largely speculative, inasmuch as considerable income which is called non-agricultural is earned by the agriculturist to eke out the insufficiency of his land and to counteract the minus food income which the land produces. Again, it is most difficult to apportion the income with accuracy, as a considerable number of people get much more than the average. The employés of Government, for example, in India and in England take for four and a half millions of people who are engaged in 'Administration by State or by local bodies' and are occupied in military and naval defence, £37,000,000. Deduct this from the £264,000,000 representing total income, there remains £227,000,000 to be divided amongst 226,500,000 people; or

just over £1 per head per annum—20s. 1½d. to be precise.

This condition of poverty, be it never forgotten, represents income in an ordinary year; in a famine year things become worse.

Even now, however, low as we have got, we may not stop in our investigation as to what really is left to the ordinary agriculturist and artisan, when the official, the merchant, and the well-to-do person generally, has had his portion. An attempt was made in 1884 by Mr. J. Seymour Keay, M.P. for the Elgin Burghs, to ascertain the number of wealthy and well-to-do upper-class and middle-class people in the whole of India—British Provinces and Feudatory States together. His estimate will serve for the early years of the twentieth century, except that it indicates more wealth than appears to exist, owing to causes already described.

The combined populations of British Provinces and Feudatory States number 294,266,701. Among these there are, say:—

10,000 Reigning Princes, titled Maharajas and Rajahs, Zemindars, and other landowners, possessing, on an average, incomes of £5,000 each per annum ...	£50,000,000
75,000 Bankers, Merchants, Professional men, and others with incomes averaging £1,000 each	75,000,000
750,000 Traders, Shopkeepers, etc., with £100 a year each	75,000,000
These absorb	£200,000,000

Reckoning the Feudatory States in respect to annual production with the corresponding British Provinces, and assuming for them Lord Curzon's estimate of Rs.30 per annum per head, we have this combined income :—

Total Income in British India	£266,000,000
Estimated Total Income in Feudatory States	126,363,138
Combined Total ...	£392,363,138
Less Income of 835,000 Princes and others as estimated above	200,000,000
Resultant Total ...	£192,363,138

This amount divided among 294,266,701 people, less the 835,000 provided for, leaves—

THIRTEEN SHILLINGS and ELEVENPENCE HALFPENNY, as the Outside Visible Income per Head per Annum;

or

LESS THAN ONE HALFPENNY PER HEAD PER DAY per British, and British-Protected, Subject in India.

That, once more be it remembered, is in 'a good year,' and assumes that full average crops have been sown and garnered, notwithstanding the ravages of drought, locusts, and other plagues, and all mischances.

The Viceroy, in 1900, reckoned the loss of crops through the Famine at... ...	£50,000,000
Including loss of cattle and losses in other respects there must be added an additional	70,000,000
Total ...	£120,000,000

Subtract that sum from the £264,000,000 coming to the British Indian people, and leaving out of calculation what the rich men get, in fact, reckoning them with the others, to share and share alike, there remain £144,000,000 to divide among 230,000,000 people: or about

Twelve Shillings and Sixpence Farthing per head for the whole of India.

The more closely Indian facts are examined the more likely does this statement seem to bring us very near to certitude. And, in whatever of several ways one works the figures down to bed rock, not more than One Half-penny per day per head seems available for the vast majority of the people.

For the moment, however, leave Famine out of consideration (though Famine has the Empire now in its relentless grasp—Famine and Moneylending, and do not seem ready or able to let go their hold), and, still dealing with the British Provinces, take £1 2s. 4d. per head as a tolerable sure quantity. That does not come to One Penny per head per day. There is not a decent living in it, even if it were equally divided: There is not the living of the cattle on a respectable farmstead in a Western country, to say nothing of the stimulant to the higher life which even British subjects in a country ruled on the principles on which British India is supposed to be ruled, might expect to share. What are those principles? Let the recently departed and much-loved Empress say:—

'We hold ourselves bound to the Natives of our Indian territories by the same obligations of duty which bind us to all our other subjects, and those obligations, by the blessing of Almighty God, we shall faithfully and conscientiously fulfil.

'And it is our further will that, so far as may be, our subjects, of whatever race or creed, be freely and impartially admitted to offices in our service, the duties of which they may be qualified, by their education, ability, and integrity, duly to discharge.

'In their prosperity will be our strength, in their contentment our security, and in their gratitude our best reward. And may the God of all Power grant to us, and to those in authority under us, strength to carry out these our wishes for the good of our people.'

In the framing of the foregoing noble passages Her Majesty had more than a conventional part. The first draft of the Proclamation failed to please her. She laid certain suggestions before the late Earl of Derby (then Lord Stanley, M.P., Secretary of State for India), and asked him to put them into shape. One of the noblest Proclamations in the English language, or in any other language, was the result. Her Majesty died in the belief that her good wishes for India were finding expression in adequate and appropriate deeds.

Unless the most thorough means are taken to improve the condition of India ere many years have elapsed, the general average will, in the presence of higher and higher prices, and a continually-increasing drain, have fallen to One Farthing per day for all the necessities of human existence. In some parts it is actually that to-day.

What, in face of this, is England's duty?

The state of things prevailing is especially harmful in respect to the limited extent to which a well-to-do upper and higher middle class in India may hope to continue in being. Distressfully indeed has our system worked amongst the intellectual and professional classes in India. Competent observers in Bengal predict that in less than fifty years the higher and middle classes in that great Province will have entirely ceased to exist. The Brahman caste has become a memory and little more. There will be two classes,—the wealthy rulers at the top, few in number but all-mighty, a degraded multitude, as vast in numbers as a diminishing food-supply will maintain in bare existence, at the base. Fifty years ago the

British Authorities were specifically warned of this. In 1852, when the Charter of the East India Company for the last time was under consideration, one of the witnesses [1] before a House of Commons Committee, said:—

But no consequence perhaps of the introduction of our system has been more prejudicial than the utter extinction it has occasioned of the upper classes of society among the natives. Not a single individual can now be found among them answering to our description of a gentleman. Every avenue to creditable employment is closed against them, and whether in civil or military service, they are equally excluded from distinction. No native of India can attain to a civil office of sufficient rank to admit of his sitting down without permission in the presence of the youngest writer that has arrived from England; and in the army he must enlist as a private soldier, and can never rise to a rank that will place him above being commanded by an English sergeant. The distance between us and our Indian subjects has been said to be 'immeasurable.' Why has that distance always been so great? Why are we still so ignorant of their real views and opinions? Why have we acquired so little of the very information which it most imports us to possess? Not for want of a knowledge of their language, not for want of diligence or curiosity, but partly from the reserve of our national character, and still more from the prevalence of a system which precludes the possibility of confidential intercourse, and rigidly severs those whom it ought to be its object to draw together. We hold no other relation with them than that of master and servant. Other European people have kept themselves much less apart from the natives of India; the French, in particular, live on more friendly terms and treat them with more familiarity than we do; they are consequently more popular, and wherever they have been known, are still considered with more kindness than the English. The common people of Hyderabad think that they do honour to an European by addressing him as 'Monsieur Bussy,' though it is upwards of seventy years since Monsieur Bussy left the place; and the tomb of M. Raymond is still illuminated by a contribution from the corps which he commanded, though it is between thirty and forty years since any Frenchman was attached to it.

It may now be difficult for us to retrace our steps, but I am satisfied that it will be wise in us to do so. We should simplify our system, and make it cheaper, more expeditious, and more summary. As we cannot make the people conform to institutions, we should make our institutions conform to the people. We can accustom

---

[1] Mr. H. Russell, p. 445; vol. vi.

ourselves to the Indian laws and customs more easily than we can reconcile the Indian people to those of England. Laws are meant for the people they are to govern, not for those by whom they are to be administered. We should take care not to admit, under the plausible semblance of improvement, changes that might by degrees impair the efficacy of a system that it ought to be our object to maintain. It is from the very desire to improve that most of our errors have arisen. Above all, we ought to find respectable employment for the natives, to acquire some hold upon their interests if we have none upon their affections. Native agents would be infinitely cheaper than European, and there is hardly a branch of the government in which they might not be extensively employed with advantage to us as well as to themselves. In the collection of the revenue, if their own method be adopted, as it ought to be, they must be more at home than we are; the details of commerce they understand, and conduct quite as well as ourselves; as diplomatists they are eminently skilful; and in the administration of justice their superior knowledge of the language and manners of one another gives them a decided advantage over us. We often complain of the difficulty of eliciting the truth from the testimony of native witnesses. The reason is, not that the natives will not tell the truth, but that they tell it in their own way, in a conventional manner, which they themselves understand, but we do not. We certainly should not find among the natives now the same integrity that we consider essential among ourselves; but if bad example and bad habits have degraded, good example and good habits might by degrees restore them; at all events, we should hold out some inducement to them to behave well, and if we desire them to become deserving of confidence, should show that we are willing to place confidence in them. Our native army is the most important branch of our government; it is at once that to which we must look for the support of our power, and from which I fear we have most to apprehend the subversion of it. Yet even there I cannot but think that we might employ the natives in higher ranks and with more authority than we do now. Indeed, if we raise them in some branches of the service, we must raise them in others also. We should endeavour to give them, if possible, an interest in the maintenance of our whole system, and although there will be greater risk in confiding military than civil authority, a time must come when it will be a question, not whether it will be safe to trust, but whether it will be possible to exclude them.

Not longer ago than the 13th of August, 1901, a leading publicist in Bengal, writing to me concerning the present work, which he knew I had in hand, uttered the following despairing remarks:—

'I am glad that your book will soon be published, and

I doubt not that it will be appreciated by the Indian public. But, as for expecting any practical good from your writing, or our writing, or anybody's writing—that is, of course, out of the question. Sir Antony Macdonnell has the reputation of being a liberal-hearted official. Yet see the heartless manner in which he has sought to dispose of your Letter.[1] The vast majority of the English people are becoming more and more deadened to high and noble sentiments, and thus India has, practically, no future. Our race is simply quietly waiting for the time when its members will, like other great nations of the past, be swept off the face of the earth. It is a pity that such an intellectual and so deeply spiritual a people as the Bengalis should perish under the rule of Great Britain. . . . The middle classes here, in very rare exceptions, live from hand to mouth. Then, the failure of the Congress movement, especially on the English side, has dealt a death-blow to all political movements. The fall of the Liberal Party in England has destroyed all the hopes the people cherished for the political regeneration of the country, while a rapid succession of repressive measures, every one deadly in its effects, which has marked the past few years, has completed our degradation and left us hopeless. It is Despair All Along the Line,

[1] 'Generally speaking,' said Sir Antony, in writing to me, 'you seem to me to take an unduly despondent view regarding the condition of the Indian peasant. At all events, your description of his state does not correspond with my own knowledge. I am far from saying that there is no room for improvement, but he is not the starving creature that some people seem to imagine. I think you are much mistaken as to the effect on the ryot's condition of the Government Revenue; and the view which you have expressed as to the heaviness of its incidence is not in accordance with my information. The chief causes of the ryot's difficulties lie in the precariousness of the climate, in his indebtedness owing to his reckless expenditure on festivals, and to the usurious rates of interest he pays for loans; in the minute subdivision of holdings owing to the concentration of the people in the most fertile regions, and their unwillingness to move to fresh lands even a short way off; and in the insufficient facilities for irrigation. In the recommendations of the Famine Commission, now before the Government of India, I trust some mitigation for these difficulties may be found.'

and scarcely any one has any hope for his country. So, let your efforts be never so energetic, and complete, and disinterested, we have been brought so low by our British rulers that it is not in us even to second such efforts as you and others who love India are making.'

The professional and mercantile classes in India are lying prone under a feeling which is akin to utter despair. As is not indicated above, but as is the fact, unhappily, a sense of complete resignation to the Divine powers who are supposed to control the lives of men is induced in the Indian mind. If they cannot live on this earth they can, they argue, pass to a better state of existence. Acquiescence in what seems to be inevitable is the dominant feature in the minds of many pious men who have in them the making of splendid citizens. With any other people in the world than the easily-ruled people of India (and, therefore, being so easily ruled, the more deserving of sympathy and encouragement) the couplet with which John Bright once moved the House of Commons in one of his great Reform speeches—

> 'For men will burst, in their sublime despair,
> The bonds they can no longer bear'—

would, long ere this, have become applicable to what has happened in India. With the Indian people there is little or no fear of a tumult or an attempt to overthrow the Dominant Power. In one sense such an attitude of mind is to be regretted. The Indian people still cherish confidence and trust in British rule. How great and touching their faith! Instead of its manifestation leading us to make the position of the faithful better and better, we are induced to treat them with more and more of contempt. Because the people of India will bear, they shall bear. That is true the world over. In a large family the child with amiable qualities and kindly disposition too often becomes the victim of more ruthless and determined brothers and sisters. In the 'struggle for existence' in a whole world of children of larger growth the higher qualities of mind and disposition lead to political and social and national degradation. Supremacy is to the more brutal qualities. Thus has it conspicuously been in India. With what result? Look around. Look deeply. And, steel your heart for that which you shall see and hear, for you will gaze upon a sum of human misery, and will contemplate a mental and political degradation the like of which, among civilised and progressive countries, is nowhere else at this moment to be seen and, probably, was at no time, during recorded history, anywhere to be seen.

GOD SAVE INDIA.

APPENDICES

I

THE INCIDENCE OF LAND REVENUE IN BOMBAY.

(From the Presidential Address at the Bombay Provincial Conference, May, 1900,—the Hon. Goculdas K. Parekh, M.L.C., President.)

Heavy incidence of Land Revenue cause of distress.

19. It appears to me that the heavy incidence of the Land Revenue is the main cause of agriculturist distress. The incidence of taxation per acre in ryotwari villages of Ahmedabad, Kaira, and Broach is Rs.2 11 1, Rs.5 0 7 and Rs.5 1 6 respectively and the incidence of taxation per head of population of the fully assessed area is Rs.2 7 8, Rs.8 12 6 and Rs.8 1 2 respectively. This incidence is very heavy.

Crop experiments reports showing lands highly assessed.

20. The crop experiments reports also show that the incidence of taxation in these districts must be very heavy. In the report for 1897–98 we notice that out of nine experiments made in the Kaira District one in which the local estimate was ten annas showed 72 per cent. and another of the same local estimate nearly 67 per cent. as the incidence of assessment on the gross value of the produce. In Broach thirty-one experiments are reported in that year, one of them shows the incidence at 42 per cent., and in six it was over 30 per cent. In one of these six cases the crop was locally estimated at 12 annas, in another at 11 or 12 annas, and in a third at 9 or 10 annas. In the report of 1896–97 we find nine experiments of Kaira; one of these gives the incidence at 96 per cent., one at 78 per cent., one at 63 per cent., and one at 50 per cent.; in Broach out of four experiments we find one in which the local estimate was 18 annas giving an incidence of over 35 per cent. The report of 1895–96 gives four experiments for the Kaira district, and in one case where the crop was locally estimated at 10 annas it showed an incidence of 68 per cent. on the gross produce. There are eight experiments mentioned in Broach in that report, one of these in which the local estimate of the crop was 4 annas gives an incidence of 180 per cent., and another in which the local estimate of the crop was 8 annas an incidence of 40 per cent. The report of 1894–95 mentions six experiments in the Ahmedabad District. One of these in which the crop was locally estimated at 12 annas gives an incidence of 66 per cent., another in which the crop was

locally estimated at 11 annas 47 per cent., and the third in which the crop was estimated at 12 annas 87 per cent. of the gross produce. The same report gives six experiments in Broach, one of them in which the crop was estimated at 10 annas gave the incidence 88 per cent., and another in which the estimate was 12 annas at 81 per cent. of the gross produce. The report of 1893–94 gives ten experiments in the Ahmedabad District, two of which give an incidence of 81 per cent. It gives four experiments in Kaira District, one of them in which the estimate of the crop was 8 annas giving an incidence of 65 per cent. and one incidence of 41 per cent. It gives six experiments in Broach, one of them in which the estimate of the crop was 13 annas, gives an incidence of 192 per cent., another in which the estimate was 16 annas 91 per cent., a third in which the estimate of the crop was also 16 annas 49 per cent., and a fourth in which the local estimate was 14 annas 82 per cent. of the gross produce. In these reports in each year the highest percentage of incidence is always found in one of the Districts in Gujarat, and taking the average of the percentages of each District those of these three Districts would be found much higher than that of any other part of the Presidency.

Holdings small and their economic effect.

21. In these Districts again there is much larger proportion of small holdings than elsewhere. In the District of Ahmedabad out of 40,917 holdings of Government lands 15,857 are under five acres, in the District of Kaira out of 57,965 of such lands 31,788 are under five acres, and in the district of Broach out of 29,146 holdings of Government lands 9,800 are under five acres. On making calculations of the yield of these holdings and deducting the cost of seeds and the Government dues, it is to be found that even in an average year barely enough is left for the maintenance of the occupant and his family. As the maintenance of the family is to be provided for from this produce the occupants of small holdings find the burden of assessment pressing more heavily on them than occupants of bigger holdings, and the first succumb to the effect of bad years.

Consequences of heavy assessment.

22. The consequences of this heavy incidence of taxation have become apparent in various forms. The occupants have felt themselves unable to meet even the Government demands without considerable difficulty. In one of these Districts during the last five or six years the amounts of the unrecovered Government dues have been growing from year to year.

The numbers of notices of demand have considerably increased, and so have the cases of distraints and sales of movable property for the realisation of these dues. The number of distraint cases in Ahmedabad was 25 in 1892–93, this rose to 248 in 1898–99. The number of distraint cases in Broach was 16 in 1892–93; it rose to 599 in 1898–99. The number of cases in which Government had to forfeit holdings for default of payment has also largely increased.

Another circumstance that shows the inability of people to bear the assessment, is that large quantities of lands are being relinquished in all these Districts of Gujarat. In 1896-97 the relinquishments in the Ahmedabad, Kaira and Broach Districts were 25,676, 6,549, and 435 acres respectively. In 1897-98 they were of 13,935, 4,716, and 454 acres respectively, and in 1898-99 they were of 10,099, 4,597, and 974 acres respectively. These Districts, which are so thickly peopled and where there is so much competition for the acquisition of lands, such large relinquishments continuously for more than three years furnish a very strong evidence of their being over-assessed.

23. Having tried to show that the incidence of assessments is very high in these Districts I shall proceed to show in what way it came to be so highly pitched.

Causes of our assessments.

In the greater part of these Districts the first settlement of assessment took place when Gujarat was in an abnormal condition of prosperity in consequence of a long sequence of good harvests, the high prices of agricultural produce in consequence of the war in America and the large demand of labour, and the high wages by reason of the construction of the railways. The high price of land, the result of these causes, was the chief element which governed the fixing of the assessment in these Districts.

Inequality of skill to industry between different classes of cultivators not considered.

24. In fixing the rates the circumstances of the inequality in skill, intelligence and power of sustained work between the different classes of the agriculturists was never taken into account. In every Talooka there are cultivators of different castes and classes, some very industrious and skilful, and others whose skill and industry are far inferior. Assessment which may be borne with tolerable ease by the former would fall with great weight on the latter.

25. Though within a short time the price of produce fell, and though under altered circumstances reduction of assessment was required at each revision, survey assessments were raised considerably, and that on grounds which would have no bearing whatever on the question whether the Ryot's powers of bearing the burden of taxation with ease had improved in the interval.

The grounds for increase not proper.

26. Among the grounds urged for the increase of assessment are mainly the increase of population, of tiled houses, carts and cattle, the passing of roads and railways, rise in the price of lands, increase of exports, subsoil water, position, class advantages, etc. Now increase of population, as in this country, where all people marry and celibacy is very exceptional, can be no indication of any increase in prosperity. In thickly-peopled districts where additional lands are not available for the increased population, the increase of population would lead rather to distress than otherwise. The average quantity of land available to a family for cultivation would diminish, and therefore

their means of sustenance would also decrease. The increase in the number of tiled houses is also a deceptive test. In most cases the tiled houses were the consequence of the prosperity near the period of the first settlement, houses built twenty or thirty years ago would be no indication of existing prosperity, the revision survey officers never try to inquire during which period of the lease the majority of the houses were constructed. The increase of carts and cattle would very often be the result of the increased population or the result of prosperity of classes other than the agriculturists. The passing of roads and railways through a Taluka do not cause much appreciable pecuniary gain to the cultivator. And he does not sell his produce more advantageously by reason of them. On the other hand, it often happens that he suffers by the construction of the railway, by the reduction of his business in carrying goods and passengers. The rise in the price of lands is also a very deceptive test; it may be the result of increased prosperity in a neighbouring town or city, by means which have no connection with agriculture, or from the scarcity of lands to meet the agricultural wants of the increasing population. Increase of exports is also deceptive, as it often happens that the commodities exported come from another Taluka; and so far as the increased exports are not the consequence of increased produce, but the result of other accidents, they furnish no good ground for raising the assessments. With reference to the question of the propriety of the increase of assessment on account of the advantage of subsoil water, it rests upon an assumption that the occupant is in a condition to take the benefit of the advantage; but when the majority of the occupants have not the means to profit from this advantage, and when they get no practicable benefit from it, this increase cannot but press harshly on the agriculturist. The ground of position class often enables survey officers to tax on improvements, the result of the labour and expenditure of the agriculturist, and this term includes miscellaneous grounds which may have no possible effect in increasing the gain of the agriculturist. Frequently the increases are made by alteration in the number of groups and the transfer of villages from one group to another, which is often based on merely arbitrary reasons.

Spirit of rules for not taxing improvements a far limiting increase of assessment disregarded.

27. The spirit of the rules made for the purpose of protecting improvements made by occupants from taxation and limiting the extent of increase at revision surveys is practically disregarded. The tenants are never asked whether they have made any improvements or not. They are never given any notice requiring them to give evidence in the matter, and evidence of expenditure which ordinarily they are not likely to possess is expected of them. Occupants are given no benefit of improvements made at considerable cost of labour.

The people of the village are informed only of the increase of assessment on the whole village, they are not informed of the increase or decrease of the amounts of assessments of individual fields. They are not informed of the grounds on which assessments are sought to be raised, and without being furnished with the necessary information they are called upon to state their objections within a certain time; and the sanctions of Government and the Secretary of State are obtained before the people know anything of the grounds of increase and have an opportunity to meet them.

Rules protecting the taxing of improvements and restricting increases beyond particular limits disregarded.

28. The consequences of these high assessments are:—

Result of over assessment.

(a) that the agriculturist is obliged to borrow.

(b) that he is unable to manure the land properly.

(c) that he is prevented from keeping his lands fallow, or to have a proper rotation of crops, and is obliged to utilise all his lands for the crop that pays him best quite irrespective of its effect in impoverishing the land. There is a general complaint that the productive power of the soil is far under what it was twenty or thirty years back.

29. From the combined operation of these causes the agriculturist gets more and more impoverished every year, while he has no reserve left him to fall upon during years of difficulty.

This results in impoverishment of cultivators.

II

THE INQUISITION INSEPARABLE FROM THE RYOTWAR SYSTEM

THE ryotwar system, which obtains in Madras and Bombay, is one in which the Government is directly landlord. The Governor's position is that of a great landlord. This system necessarily involves a close inquisition, an inquisition 'which has converted the most cherished and immemorial *rights* of the ryot to timber and even to fuel into mere grudging *concessions* and *privileges* strictly regulated, which carefully studies his resources and his cultivation in order to store data for the eventful revision of settlement, the inquisition which subjects his field to so many inspections every season—inspections at which he has to attend and which oblige him to court the favour of the village officer and his myrmidons.'

A Bombay writer, veiling himself under the pseudonym of 'Raniji Bin Rowji,' in a pamphlet written in September, 1901, says, that a 'district officer, if he has time to master all the laws and all the rules and all the statistics, may well say to the ryots:

'My good tenants, I know all your ins and outs. I know what numbers each of you cultivates. I know what the waste attached to your village realises. I know what crops you raise, and indeed even the proportion of two or more crops raised by you in a single field. I know what encroachments you have made, and know who is liable to me for not repairing his boundary-marks.

'I know what family each of you has and what cattle. I know the number of your ploughs and carts, the number of your wells, tanks, dams, water-lifts, and even of your kacha wells and springs. I know how much of each commodity you have produced, consumed, and exported. Nay, I even know what your fruit-trees have realised. The Government I serve does not disdain to derive what revenue it can from fruit, grass, timber, and even sand, kankar and muram.[1]

'If, for example, you don't choose to farm the grass in your village, I have no alternative but to farm it to an outsider. The highest bidder must carry the day, whether he is one of you or not.

'You must, also, remember that, your assessment being very low, we cannot grant you any remissions, as a matter of course, when your crops suffer, for the Government have ruled, as early as 1841, that one of the great objects of Survey "is to diminish the necessity of remissions," and, in 1847, they directed that individual losses occasioned by alleged failure of crops should never be inquired into, and that when a group of villages suffers from "an exceptionally bad season," an average reduction of assessment all round might be made "if necessary." These old orders are still binding on us. I cannot, therefore, I am sorry to say, behave as your *Ma Bâp* ("Father and Mother"), and forego the full survey assessment due from you. You may have a better season next year, and I shan't then ask you for an increased assessment. This proves the justice of my demand, though I know that you are all deep in the Sowkar's books. But we have now passed a white-washing Act, under which, if you make default in paying the assessment, your creditor loses his security, and you get back the land as a Government tenant. If, however, you wish to retain your land as a full survey occupant, you must prove you have been a *bonâ fide* agriculturist, and have paid a *reasonable* proportion of your assessment, in the last two years, before I can suspend the demand; and remember that I can only suspend the demand for a time—and that, too,

---

[1] See Hope's Forms for all these details.—R. B. R.

after some correspondence. Indeed, I can't be sure of anything, and I can give no pledges.

'I can see from the Village Forms, that almost every one of you has cultivated much less than in the last year, but that, according to our rules, is no reason for a reduction. Our assessments are "hard and fast," if you please. They are not so elastic as your old system of paying the land-tax, I should say land-rent, in kind. And you must at least admit that our accounts are neatly kept. Under the old system you could see yourselves whether the Government was taking more than its due. Under the present system we see to this ourselves on your behalf. We give you a written receipt book, and examine it carefully. If there is any the least over-collection, we pay it back to you. We have never asked you to pay any perquisite to the Talati or any small cess per every rupee of your rent. We have never asked you to pay our Karkuns or to come out with *Rasad*, whenever an official comes to your village. We have never asked you to pay 14 or 15 per cent. (when you get Takavi) in the shape of presents to Peons and Patels and Kulkarnis and Karkuns. We have never asked you to incur debts in order to save yourselves from being prosecuted for one or other of the numerous offences we have created under our special and local laws, and by our Land Revenue Rules. If you choose to make fools of yourselves, you are welcome. But don't say that our system forces you to corrupt our officials.

'Haven't we provided for appeals of all sorts? Is not our Penal Code perfection itself? Why, then, are you afraid of complaining? You say that if your complaint is not heeded, or proved according to the requirements of our law, the officials complained against would make it too hot for you to live in the village, where generations of your ancestors have been duly cremated. But it is not possible at all that a true complaint cannot be proved in our Courts. Does not our law say that no particular number of witnesses is necessary to prove a fact? Remember, faint hearts never win the fair queen of litigation. Woo her boldly and briskly, and she will certainly yield. You say, pleaders will bully you and browbeat you, and that you are unused to the Courts. But recollect, you can't take the good we provide for you without its evil. We have given you perfect laws. You never possessed any such. We have given you perfect Courts, though they have generally to employ interpreters, and are often bamboozled by the bosh and the bombastic legal "rot" of those limbs of the law, of whom you are so afraid. I admit your own old village tribunals were good in their way, but then you must keep pace with the whirling cycle of progress in which it is your pleasant lot to live, and to live, too, at peace even with your worst creditor and oppressor.

'We have thousands of bayonets and tons of shot and powder at our back—you cannot revolt as you sometimes used to in the good or bad old days before—you must pay your dues with the best grace you can, and as you have to pay them you had better pay punctually, at least before any process is issued against you. For remember, if you force us to issue processes, you may deprive us of the flattering unction which we every year lay to our souls that you are all well-to-do and able to pay your way, but you will have to pay the cost of the processes as fixed by the rules.

'You say our bureaucratic administration weighs like an incubus upon you, but, have we not given you roads and railways, and post and telegraph offices, and schools and colleges? You ought to be thankful. Indians are a grateful race, and you should not belie your ancestry. It is true the roads and the schools are paid for by you. It is true that you are too homely and too home-loving to care much for railways and postal and telegraph facilities and distant colleges.

'But, supposing all these to be no gain to you at all, what harm have we done? We merely threaten you with imprisonment for a month or a fine of Rs.500 at the most, if, without due authority, you "dig or remove or attempt to dig or remove any earth, stone, kankar, sand, or muram, or any other material, from land belonging to Government," or if, without such authority, you "remove or attempt to remove the grass or any other produce of land belonging to Government," or if, without such authority, you "cut down or remove, or attempt to cut down or remove any jungle or trees belonging to Government or the right to which has not been conceded by Government," or if, without such authority, you "take or attempt to take any produce of any tree belonging to Government." These are most equitable provisions—for is not the Government the sole landlord, while all of you are mere occupants?

'Do not, pray, think that your landlord does not know your tricks and your ways. Extreme watchfulness is enjoined on us all. You are such loons that it is just likely you will "destroy or materially injure for cultivation" the land that has been given to you. In that case, you know, you can be fined 500 rupees after a magisterial trial. We allow you to excavate your land in order to lay the foundation of farm-buildings (any other buildings we can't permit you to erect), without exacting a heavy fine, or to sink wells or to make grain-pits. But no other excavation are you at liberty to make, without the written permission of his Honour the Collector. No, your Patel's or your Talati's or your Mamlatdar's permission won't do. The matter is too serious.

'What other restraints do we impose upon you? We don't allow you to let your field overgrow with prickly-pear or rank grass, so as to be dangerous to the health or safety of the neighbourhood. But this is for the public good. So it is evidently for the public good, that you should maintain your boundary-marks. We have, it is true, forbidden you to dig earth within a space of two cubits of any earthen boundary, on pain of a fine. But this is not an unreasonable precaution.

'The truth is we cannot let you alone. We are the lords paramount of the soil, and must see that the soil fares well in your hands. Our railways and our armies and our hosts of underlings enable us to see every detail of our duty, and you must submit. After all you have no cause to complain. Under the old tax system, you were mainly your own master, until the tyrant, personally, or by deputy, swooped down upon you. Now you enjoy security because we are strong. That very strength enables us to impose our laws, altogether repugnant to your traditions, but nevertheless most salutary, upon you. Our assessment is on the whole moderate, but excepting the occupancy of your land, everything else is ours, including the ditches and the nullas—the stones and the sand, and all standing and flowing water and the land under it.'[1]

'Formerly, if your rulers increased your tax, you used to fall back upon virgin soil, and bring as much of it under your cultivation as you could. But now no soil, not in your occupation, is yours for the asking. You must pay us before you have its *occupancy*, for, as a rule, we do not sell our property in land. You had several ways of evading the demands of former kings, but those evasions will not do with us. You should learn our laws and understand their beneficent spirit. Our intentions are never bad. We wish you well. We want to show you how to thrive. We want to make you prudent. Can't you admire our own prudence in first of all telling you plainly that we won't increase your assessment if you sink any wells in your land, and then keeping our word, after you had sunk several wells, by taxing merely the advantage of subsoil water brought to light by your wells. The law permitted us to revise the assessment "with reference to the value of any natural advantage, when the improvement effected from private capital and resources consists only in having created the means of utilising such advantage." Yet we generously gave a general assurance in 1881, that this would not be applied to wells. You can perfectly understand that this did not mean that we won't apply it to subsoil water. To make the matter clearer, we have, in 1886, passed a law that in revising assessments regard shall be had "to the profits of agriculture," but that no such profits, *increased* by *improvements* in land effected by or at the cost of the holder thereof, shall be taken into account. Of course, it is for us to determine whether anything done by you is an improvement, and if so, whether it has increased your profits or the value of your land. But you may depend upon it, we shall give you due credit for any reforms that you carry out.

'We are really sorry to see you so apathetic. The "magic of occupancy," it is true, is not like the "magic of property," and somehow we have now no faith in either, but still considering that we have amended our Land Revenue Code at least twice, and

[1] See Sec. 37 of Bom. Act. V. of 1879.—R. B. R.

passed Acts for loans to agriculturists and regarding agricultural improvements, it *is* surprising that you do not avail yourselves of your opportunities at all. It is not only surprising, but disgusting. However, these be the ways of orientals, and there is no help.'

This is a long yarn. But it shows how unattractive is the system which has become an article of faith with some officials. As we said before, the Joint Report made it barely tolerable. The new law of 1901 has made matters a thousand times worse.

III

THE PROSPERITY OF INDIA IN OLDEN DAYS

The continual tendency of events since the British occupation of the country has been to turn the people more and more towards agriculture, and less and less towards manufactures. This subject has been well discussed by Lieutenant-Colonel R. D. Osborn than whom no truer friend of India ever came to this country. In the first place, the invention of steam engines and the development of machinery enormously cheapened the cost of production in England. The English manufacturers were soon in a position to undersell the Indian artisan. At the same time, the operation of a strict monopoly of heavy transit duties in India, amounting to 44 lakhs of rupees per annum, and of heavy and ruinous import duties in England, amounting to no less than 75 per cent., combined to repress all the exertions of local industry. The introduction of Manchester goods was accompanied by the collapse of indigenous industries.

And yet

THE MANUFACTURES OF INDIA WERE ONCE IN A HIGHLY FLOURISHING CONDITION.

The various Native Courts encouraged large towns and urban enterprise. European traders were first attracted not by the raw products, but by the manufactured wares of this country. The fame of the fine muslins of Bengal, her rich silks and brocades, her harmonious cotton prints had spread far and wide in Asia as well as Europe. 'The Bengal silk cloths, etc.,' writes Mr. Verelst, one of our earliest Governors, 'were dispersed to a vast amount, to the west and north inland as far as Gujarat, Lahore, and even Ispahan.'

The Indian cities were populous and magnificent. When Clive entered Murshidabad, the old capital of Bengal, in 1757, he wrote of it: 'This city is as extensive, populous, and rich as the City of London, with this difference that there are individuals in the first possessing infinitely greater property than in the last city.'

ALL THE ARTS THEN FLOURISHED, AND WITH THEM URBAN LIFE.

Now out of a population of 250,000,000 only five and a half millions of people live in towns of over 50,000 inhabitants; nine-tenths of the people live in rural villages, and the colonies of workmen who were settled in the large towns are broken up. I will cite as an example the city of Dacca. It was during the time of the Mogul Government that this city (Calcutta) reached the highest degree of its prosperity. But even less than 100 years ago, the whole commerce of Dacca was estimated at one crore of rupees, and its population at 200,000 souls. In 1787 the exports of Dacca muslin to England amounted to 30 lakhs of rupees; in 1817 they had ceased altogether. The arts of spinning and weaving, which for ages afforded employment to a numerous and industrious population, have now become extinct. Families which were formerly in a state of affluence have been reduced to penury; the majority of the people have been driven to desert the town and betake themselves to the villages for a livelihood. The present population of the town of Dacca is only 79,000.

This decadence has occurred not in Dacca only, but in all districts. Not a year passes in which the Commissioners and District Officers do not bring to the notice of Government that

THE MANUFACTURING CLASSES IN ALL PARTS OF THE COUNTRY ARE BECOMING IMPOVERISHED.

On the other hand, agriculture is everywhere expanding at the expense of manufacturing industry. Every exertion is being made to increase the area under cultivation with staple crops. The area under cultivation is increasing by leaps and bounds, and the increase in the amount of agricultural produce exported from the country is pointed to as an irrefragable evidence of increased national prosperity. This is a vain delusion. The Indian foreign trade has, indeed, been developed, but while the soil of the country has been impoverished by overcropping, foreign competition has filled the Indian markets with the produce of foreign manufactures. The most profitable Indian industries have been destroyed, and the most valuable Indian arts have greatly deteriorated or died out. 'With the weavers,' writes Mr. James Cotton in his treatise on 'India' in the English Citizen Series, 'with the weavers have gone the numerous caste of dyers. In the same way, many other handicrafts have suffered either from the abolition of the Native Courts or from English rivalry. Carpet-making, fine embroidery, jewelry, metal-work, the damascening of arms, saddlery, carving, paper-making, even architecture and sculpture, have all alike decayed.' Mr. Samuel Smith recently declared his belief, in the House of Commons, that if the figures could be ascertained, it would be found that handicrafts by which ten million or fifteen million people gained their living had been destroyed by the substitution of foreign for home manufactures.

'There is no class,' exclaims Sir James Caird, 'which our rule has pressed harder upon than the native weaver and artisan.' Sir George Birdwood's excellent treatise on the 'Industrial Arts of India,' shows conclusively how India has suffered from the destruction of its ancient manufactures. I doubt whether the public at large is possessed of any adequate conception of the deplorably small proportion of persons in this country who are engaged in art or mechanical production or in working and dealing with mineral products. The census statistics show that in England out of the total male population of all ages, the number of persons so engaged is 19·6 per cent.; in Scotland the number is 19·8; in Ireland, that unfortunate annex of the British dominions, the number is only 8·4; in Bengal, the number falls to the incredibly small proportion of only 1·7. On the other hand, the proportion of the total male population of the country of all ages engaged on agricultural pursuits is in England 12·4; in Scotland it is 11·6; in poverty-stricken Ireland it is 88; and in Bengal it is 37·9.[1] The ratio of these figures affords an index of the relative prosperity of these countries. It is perfectly true that in some minor trades and industrial professions there has been increase in India in recent years. There are more shoemakers now in existence, more carpenters, more tailors, more blacksmiths. The demand for shoes, furniture, clothes, iron ware, and the like has increased with the increase of Western civilisation and the greater appreciation of comfort which accompanies it. Wealth and treasure have undoubtedly poured into India in exchange for her exports. The immense cheapening of cotton piece-goods and of other articles imported from Europe cannot be without its corresponding advantage to the people. I am far from thinking that the material prosperity of the agricultural classes has not improved. This may not be the case in all provinces, but it certainly is true of the Province of Bengal proper, with which I am personally acquainted. New wants have arisen, and increased facilities have been afforded for their gratification. Yet who will be disposed to gainsay the truth of the late Viceroy's statement at the opening of the Exhibition of Industrial Arts in Calcutta, when he said: 'No one who considers the economic condition of India can doubt that one of its greatest evils is to be found in the fact that the great mass of the people of the country are dependent almost exclusively upon the cultivation of the soil. This circumstance tends at one and the same time to depress the position of the cultivators, to aggravate the evils of famine, and also to lower wages generally. It tends also to maintain the population in the depth of ignorance in which it is now sunk. It will always be found in all countries of the world that the artisans are more highly educated than the peasantry.'

The development of petty industries, the establishment of the jute

---

[1] These are the statistics for all ages; it has been estimated that about 34 per cent. of males are not specified as of any occupation, as they are not of an age to be gainfully employed.

and cotton mills to which I have already alluded, even the accumulation of gold and silver, the increased use of ornaments, brass pots, cotton cloths, and umbrellas among the people afford but a poor compensation for the variety of social life once spread through the country. The resources of India will vie almost with those of America itself. The dimensions of Indian trade are already enormous, and yet

NO COUNTRY IS MORE POOR THAN THIS.

The expansion of trade is at the expense of manufacturing industry. The economic conditions upon which material prosperity depends are lacking.

An India supplying England with its raw products and in its turn dependent upon England for all its more important manufactures, is not a spectacle which is likely to reconcile an Indian patriot to the loss of the subtle and refined Oriental arts, the very secret of which has passed away, to the loss of innumerable weavers who have perished from starvation, or have sunk for ever to the lot of agricultural labourers, or to the loss of that constructive genuis and mechanical ability which designed the canal system of Upper India and the Taj at Agra.—H. J. S. COTTON, *in "New India," published before* 1890.

IV

'THE SLOW, SYSTEMATIC, STARVATION OF INDIA'

11th January, 1901.

'Your brief Open Letter to Lord Curzon is very sad reading. The slow, systematic starvation of India revealed by your figures is, to my thinking, far more terrible than the worst horrors denounced by Burke one hundred and twenty years ago. But nobody listens to anything now.'

The writer of the above is one of the most distinguished of living Englishmen. Owing to the official position he occupies, he may not, in his own name 'take a side': otherwise his courage in public life is such that he would not hesitate to permit his name to be printed with his remarks. My great correspondent is right: the condition of things in India is far more terrible to-day—more terrible in itself and in what it is leading to—than it was under Warren Hastings' masterful and unscrupulous handling. Let me indicate, in slight measure, how this has come about, and in what its worseness consists, if haply somebody may be moved to intervene ere it be too late.

1. WHAT LED TO THE IMPEACHMENT OF WARREN HASTINGS?

It is difficult to put into a few sentences the substance of what fills several volumes in the collected works of Edmund Burke. But, *imprimis*, there is one great difference between the incidents of that period and of this. Then, a large part of the indictment of Hastings consisted in charges of deliberately false conduct on his part towards individuals, involving gross personal wrong and injustice. Now, generally, we are not particularly unjust towards individuals; we confine ourselves to 'cheating' (Lord Lytton's word) whole communities, and to withholding rights and privileges we might safely grant, or to withdrawing them after years of satisfactory working and after the people had depended upon them. Hastings' crimes, assuming that everything that Burke and his fellow-managers of the Impeachment asserted, to be true, affected at the outside fifty millions of people, who resided in a portion of Eastern and Southern India, while the wrongs extended over a short period of years only. Although, according to Lord Cornwallis, certain Bengal cultivators suffered greatly because of the exactions of the tax-gatherers, hard put to it to meet Hastings' demand, the wrongs done by the Governor-General were mainly directed to the spoliation of Princes, Ministers, and very wealthy merchants and bankers. Vast sums of money were obtained illegitimately in that time, and were shipped to England in the shape of bullion and of jewels.

The Impeachment failed. Was, then, the whole effort useless? Mr. John Morley says: 'No.' 'Though the offender was, in form, acquitted,' says Mr. Morley, 'yet Burke succeeded in these fourteen years of laborious effort in laying the foundations once for all of a moral, just, philanthropic, and responsible, public opinion in England with reference to India.' Alas! the historian is too sanguine. The facts do not fit his description. 'Nobody listens to anything now.' Certainly, Mr. Morley himself does not contribute aught to that public opinion which he so warmly eulogised. It is true he tells the present writer the needs of India are never out of his mind, but he never listens to Indian grievances, or does anything to remove them, and so, in his own most powerful person, disproves his own statement.

2. WOULD IMPEACHMENT TO-DAY BE JUSTIFIED?

If what Hastings did, and the consequences thereof be of any value, the answer is: Undoubtedly, many times over. As to whom the articles of Impeachment should specifically include, I am not concerned to set forth. If absolute *mala fides* were to be a basis of indictment, I do not know that any one could be indicted. For it is certain that neither in that Palace of Lassitude, the India Office, nor in high places in India, is there any overt intention to do injustice. This, regarded in the highest interests of humanity, is a pity. If only half-a-dozen wickedly malignant men could be pointed to as personally responsible for the awful condition of things in India, and could be brought to the bar of public opinion, there would be some hope for Indian sufferers, some chance of remedies being found. So inadequately is human sympathy developed by our civilisation and system of education, that only as a struggle centres round an individual, can any widespread interest in a people's cause be aroused. This is why the Indian cause is so almost hopeless. Only when some Viceroy of commanding power is subjected to a conversion as sudden as was that of the Persecutor Paul when on his way to Damascus, and his mind illuminated with divine light as that would-be persecutor of Christian worshippers declared his mind had been penetrated with an effulgence seldom seen on sea or land, and this Converted Viceroy testifies, even to martyrdom, to the new faith born in him, will India ever be lifted out of the pit in which she now lies helpless. A united people, very much in earnest, might do even more, and much more speedily, than the Converted Viceroy. But that is past praying for. There is, unhappily, alike in England and in India, among reformers, not unity of purpose, but cross currents and miserable jealousies.

What is the condition of things which the distinguished Englishman, whose letter I have quoted, declares is worse than that which led to the impeachment of Warren Hastings?

It is the alien rule of India—in its present form: it is the economic drain of India's resources; it is the subordination of the interests of the sons of the soil to the interests of the foreigners; it is the consideration always of England before India; it is the blindness which has been brought about by the too-admiring and continuous contemplation on our part of the administrative and industrial edifice which we have reared.

The last of these causes is the worst. How dense the blindness is may be judged when even so acute an observer as is the present Viceroy cannot see things as they actually are: no, although they be put as plain, politically, as A B C, by a popular body like the Mahajana Sabha of Madras. The British mind is made up as to India! British work there has been all-beneficent; Indians, as Tennyson's Northern Farmer said of the poor—taken as a whole, are bad. And even Lord Curzon, after all he has seen in India, acts as though he, too, held the narrow, insular, view. *He* cannot be so blind.

If any man wishes to maintain the thesis of the 'terrible' (Lord Curzon's word regarding the last famine) condition of India now as compared with more than a hundred years ago, nay, worse than that, its 'terrible' condition as compared with twenty years ago, the material lies ready, in ample volume, to his hand. Here are two out of hundreds of economic facts available.

INCREASED COST OF FOOD, PER RUPEE.

Year.		Common Rice.		Wheat.		Barley.
1790	...	150 lbs.	...	170 lbs.	...	284 lbs.
1871	...	88 ,,	...	40 ,,	...	54 ,,
1892	...	25 ,,	...	25 ,,	...	38 ,,

The more recent famine years in the above comparison have been avoided.

GROWING DESTITUTION OF CULTIVATORS.

In 1892 such a village-to-village economic inquiry as Sir William Wedderburn has, in vain, tried to secure was privately made in the Bombay Presidency. Five villages were investigated. This is the investigator's report :—

'The population of the five villages whose census I took came to 236 persons. The land farmed by these villagers amounted to 1,400 acres. We have, from the village books, what the whole gross crop amounted to, viz., £193 sterling. The fact came out that through sheer poverty not a vestige of manure had been placed upon these 1,400 acres within the last ten years. Now, if you allow starvation support at Rs.14 a year only to each of these 236 persons and allow Rs.11 a year for each of the 58 pair of agricultural bullocks necessarily kept for the tillage of these 1,400 acres of land, you have the fact that the whole net produce, after deducting Rs.14 a year for the support of each person of each of those five villages, amounted only to £5 sterling in the year. And what had these poor people paid to the revenue? They had paid in land tax in that year no less than £78, although there was only £5 of real net produce coming from their fields. The village books show that the assessment was paid by borrowing from usurers at twenty-four per cent. per annum. The persons in the five villages for these loans owe the usurers now Rs. 12,000, or ten years of the whole assessment. I say it with pain, but I say it with confidence, that this is not an unusual, but a usual, condition of the cultivators in the Deccan at this moment. Some little money was made, moreover, by the women and children who got employment in the adjacent town of Sholapore.'

These facts were stated in the House of Commons some years ago. They have never been disproved. They form a very good reason why the Secretary of State should object to a village inquiry. I wish I could feel that I did Lord George Hamilton an injustice in saying this, for then it might be possible to get an inquiry. But, no other reason than fear as to what would be revealed, *can* account for the persistent refusal of the present Secretary of State to grant what was asked for.

How has all this come about? Because, among other things, we have destroyed native industries, and, besides, have taken from India since 1834–5 (according to a calculation made by that sane and moderate journal, the *Economist*, two years ago)

MORE THAN TEN THOUSAND MILLIONS OF RUPEES.

Against this England has *lent* to India for public works and other purposes, perhaps, a quarter of that amount, an advance, on which she always gets interest, and has, besides, a morgage on all Indian property.

India, on the other hand, has entirely lost her much more than ten thousand millions; this, with interest, and if circulated in the ordinary way among her people, at five per cent. interest value only, would, by this time, have been of the value at least of

FIFTY THOUSAND MILLIONS OF RUPEES.

Further the money lent to India, save in respect to irrigation works, has only partly gone to that country: most of it has been spent in England,—England being thus doubly enriched, while India's poverty was thereby doubly deepened.—LONDON CORRESPONDENCE of the *Amrita Bazar Patrika* (Calcutta) and *The Hindu* (Madras), March, 1901.

THE REMEDY

Statement of Remedies Postponed until Some Agreement be Arrived At as to Whether Any Need for Remedy Exists . . . . . .

The Statement of the Evil, for the Moment, is Enough .

It may be asked, 'Assuming your conclusions are indisputable, what is the remedy? Having said so much, you must say more. It is of little use to diagnose the disease unless you can indicate means of cure.' Such a question in ordinary circumstances would receive but one answer. 'Certainly. Though it is not always the duty of the critic to be prepared with a remedy for that which he criticises, unless indeed the "case" be put in his hands, I will state what, in my opinion, should be done to remedy these evils. The steps to be taken are as follows':—

On the present occasion, however, I do not propose to submit any remedies. Not, however, because I have none to submit. Quite the contrary. In respect to every department of effort in India where reform is needed, I have something to say; and, more particularly, have I special proposals to submit and urge concerning the increased productivity of the soil, a reform which the late Sir James Caird strongly urged twenty years ago, and towards the realisation of which practically nothing has been done.

Remedies are of value for discussion only when there

is agreement between the parties interested that a condition of things exists for which remedies are needed. We are far from such a desirable situation in India. In words already quoted in these pages, Lord George Hamilton finds nothing whatever in the vast continent he rules to call for remedy. 'You speak,' he says, 'of the increasing impoverishment of India, and the annual drain upon her, as steadily and continuously exhausting her resources. I assert that you are under a delusion. Except that during the last five years the rainfalls have thrice failed, and created droughts of immense dimensions, there is not a fact to be found in support of your allegations.' With such views propounded by the Secretary of State, it is out of the question to talk of remedies. If there be no wrong, no suffering, no complications, save those caused by the Great Cloud-Compeller of the Universe, there can, assuredly, be no remedy required.

Further: with the abnormal and unsatisfactory condition of things now obtaining in India, men who believe in the remedies they suggest, who are fully satisfied that they will remove existing ills, who, because they have thought out thoroughly the difficulties to be overcome, are ready with amendment and adaptation to ensure the success of what they recommend, are refused opportunity of association in the application of the remedies they advise. The inception of the reform ideas comes from one set of brains. The realisation of that inception is entrusted to others who do not believe in its realisation, do not consider anything requires to be reformed. Consequence: Failure of the remedy which, in hands that understood, and worked by minds which believed in it, would prove successful.

Here, at present, there is no need to discuss a remedy. Lord George Hamilton's remark dismisses, with a contempt which commands admiration for its magnificent audacity, the very idea of anything being wrong. The admiration ordinarily due to heroism must, however, be withheld. Every moment that the noble lord's heroic attitude is maintained there is needless suffering in hut and home, there is continued nakedness for man and woman, there is denial of the comforts of life, there is a continued barring of the door against high official employment of capable people in their own land. With the Secretary of State on his high horse of absolute satisfaction with things as they are in India, six times as many people as live in the United Kingdom remain doomed to a subjection which is physically and morally destructive. Strange are the destinies of men, marvellous is civilised rule, when one weak hand can thus hold in subjection so many millions of one's fellow-subjects!

If this work should be so far successful as to win attention, and some measure of public opinion in England and in India be aroused by the story which has been told in the preceding pages, then the Remedies which the present writer has carefully considered, will be published.

Till then, such feeling as may be called forth by these studies had better be turned to a thorough realisation of the extent to which the deplorable state of things in India has spread. One thing at a time. The statement of the evil for the moment is enough.

OBITER DICTA FROM THE *SPECTATOR*, LONDON

Taxation in India is, no doubt, lighter now than it was under Moghal rule; but we get the money and the Moghals did not, and the system prevents the rise of an agricultural middle class.

. . . . .

There are districts in India where a man with Rs1,000 (£66 13s. 4d.) is a millionaire.

. . . . .

The average European almost denies ordinary mental capacity to every coloured man.

. . . . .

Five people cannot live, and pay a direct tax in money and the interest of old debts at sixteen per cent., upon five acres of overcropped soil, without danger, in bad years, of a catastrophe. That is the position of whole districts in India, and the comparative wealth of other districts is nothing to the purpose.

. . . . .

Let the statesmen say what will meet the economic danger, or face the consequences, which in India will be either recurrent famines or a bewildering, passive, insurrection of men whom the Government cannot blame or shoot down.

INDEX

D.

E

F

I

N

T

U